The Internet Resource Directory for K–12 Teachers and Librarians

2000/2001 Edition

The Internet Resource Directory for K–12 Teachers and Librarians

2000/2001 Edition

Elizabeth B. Miller

College of Library and Information Science
University of South Carolina

LIBRARIES UNLIMITED, INC.
P.O. Box 6633
Englewood, CO 80155-6633
1-800-237-6124
www.lu.com

Suggested Cataloging:

Miller, Elizabeth B.
    The Internet resouce directory for K–12 teachers and librarians/
    Elizabeth B. Miller. --2000/2001 ed.
        p. cm.
    Includes indexes.
    ISBN 1-56308-839-8
    1. Internet (Computer network)--Directories. 2. Databases--
United States--Directories. 3. Education, Elementary--United
States--Information services--Directories. 4. Education,
Secondary--United States--Information services--
Directories. I. Title.
TK5105.875.157M55 2000
371.3'34574--dc20

Contents

Contents

Contents

Contents

Social Studies and Geography (*cont.*)

Acknowledgments

Many thanks to my family for all their love and support. This seventh edition would not have been possible without them, especially my husband Henry. My older daughter, Lisa, started working toward her master's degree in library and information science and hopes to graduate with certification in school library media in August 2001. She still has her paint-it-yourself pottery studio, Flying Saucers, in downtown Spartanburg, South Carolina, at the end of West Main Street near the Clock Tower. My younger daughter, Susan, completed her junior year at Duke University and had her one-act play produced by the Duke Players during "Theater 2000: New Works for the Stage," a festival of new plays and works of theater by students, faculty, and guest pro-fessionals. After exploring engineering and economics as potential majors, she's cho-sen art history. She's active in her sorority, Alpha Phi, and working part-time in the housing and admissions offices of Duke University.

I would like to thank faculty friends and colleagues at the College of Library and Information Science at the University of South Carolina for their enthusiastic support. My dean, Fred Roper, has been wonderfully supportive and caring.

A special thank-you goes to Claire Clemens, who provided invaluable profes-sional assistance in selecting and updating the chapter on foreign languages.

Finally, I'd like to thank Libraries Unlimited and all the members of the LU team for making the commitment to publish *The Internet Resource Directory for K–12 Teachers and Librarians* on an annual basis, making the book a top priority so that it is published in record time while ensuring the book's quality and accuracy from manu-script to print. Libraries Unlimited is a very special publisher: small enough to care about employees, authors, customers, and quality publishing, yet large enough to be on the forefront in their outlook and technology. Providing a Web page for corrections and changes to the directory is just one example. Be sure to look for the free, monthly up-dates to the 2000/2001 directory on the Web (http://www.lu.com/lu/irdupdates.html). Please feel free to e-mail me at (emiller@vnet.net) with any suggestions, questions, or alerts to changes.

Introduction

The 2000/2001 edition of *The Internet Resource Directory for K–12 Teachers and Librarians* is the seventh in a series of annual publications. The directory presents a broad sampling of some of the best Internet resources for educators, school library media specialists, students, and parents. With 1,515 entries, this edition has 1,078 more entries than the original edition published in 1994. All entries continue to remain selective and evaluative, rather than comprehensive. Resources are evaluated and selected according to criteria. (*See* "Selection Criteria" below.) Internet resources are organized by curriculum areas. Annotated entries help users determine the more useful resources for their specific information needs and suggest ways to integrate resources into the curriculum.

Libraries Unlimited will continue a free Web page providing monthly updates to all entries listed in the 2000–2001 edition of *The Internet Resource Directory for K–12 Teachers and Librarians*. Look for monthly corrections and changes of URL (uniform resource locator) addresses on the directory's own Web page (http://www.lu.com/lu/irdupdates.html). This is a new URL for the updates. Bookmark this page, and plan to check it frequently. Be sure to use the Reload or Refresh button on your browser each time you visit. Each month, all URL addresses in the directory will be checked; any changes will be noted and new URL addresses with accompanying HTML links will be provided. *The Internet Resource Directory for K–12 Teachers and Librarians* Web page will help to guarantee the accuracy of the entry addresses during the 12-month interval between publications. Checking more than 1,500 entries each month is a monumental task. However, it demonstrates the level of commitment of the author and the publisher to ensure that *The Internet Resource Directory for K–12 Teachers and Librarians* is a reliable and meaningful tool for finding and integrating quality Internet resources into the curriculum throughout the year following publication.

The Internet Resource Directory for K–12 Teachers and Librarians continues to be used as a textbook in college courses, in professional development courses, and in workshops focusing on integration of the Internet into the curriculum. It is used for ready reference in public libraries and school media centers. This directory is designed to help educators plan lessons that are enriched with up-to-date and accurate online information that complements and enhances traditional information resources. However, the directory has also found its way into homes for use by parents and students. Students can learn from experts, tap into major library collections and scientific databases, and communicate with other students around the world. They can virtually visit the world's greatest museums and view art treasures; explore the human heart, comparing the sounds of a healthy heartbeat to one with a murmur; see the images from the Hubble telescope and the Galileo mission; and travel with scientists to Antarctica or the rain forests of the Amazon basin.

The Internet Resource Directory for K–12 Teachers and Librarians aids educators in planning learning experiences that incorporate collaboration, teamwork, problem solving, and global awareness. This directory is also offered as a starting point for teachers and school library media specialists to use in designing their own directories of Internet resources to meet the unique curriculum needs of their schools.

What's New in This Edition

New and Updated Entries

This edition of *The Internet Resource Directory for K–12 Teachers and Librarians* has 440 new and updated entries. All entries retained from the previous edition were reevaluated and carefully checked. Corrections were then made to URL addresses and entry annotations when discrepancies or changes were noted. All entries were double-checked, to ensure their accuracy, just before publication.

National and State Standards

National and state standards provide benchmarks for learning for students, teachers, and parents. Whenever possible, online resources for national and state standards are listed at the beginning of each chapter. For example, Linking Art Standards to Internet Resources (entry 107), National Standards for Arts Education (entry 108), and National Standards for Theatre Education (entry 109) are the first three entries in the second chapter, "The Arts: Visual Art, Dance, Music, and Theater."

Expanded Chapters

The chapter, "Resources for Educators," has more entries for lesson plans across the curriculum and resources for teachers. These lesson plan databases focus more on integrating technology and meeting national standards. The foreign languages chapter has been expanded, completely updated, and renamed to show an emphasis on multicultural appreciation. In addition to language studies, the chapter "Foreign Language Studies and Cultural Appreciation" has sections on the history and culture of China, France and French-speaking peoples, Germany and German-speaking peoples, India, Italy, Japan, Russia and the countries of the former Soviet Union, Mexico, and Spain and Spanish-speaking peoples. The applied arts chapter has been expanded to include "Family Life Education," which covers clothing and textiles, early childhood education, meal planning, and nutrition. Using various online calculators, students in consumer education can calculate payments on car loans, mortgages, and insurance.

The computer science chapter has been expanded to include tools, tips, and templates for teachers to use in creating interactive Web pages for use with students as worksheets, hotlists, and WebQuests. Tools such as Quia! (entry 293) provide templates for teachers to produce their own interactive online quizzes and online games, including flash cards, matching games, concentration (memory) games, and word search puzzles. The science chapter has more information on DNA, plate tectonics, deep-sea ecology, submarine geology, and the relatively unexplored areas along the Earth's midocean ridges. The social studies chapter contains more resources with primary documents for student use, such as those from the National Archives and Records Administration, Web sites focused on Library of Congress collections, and others. Look for information about famous trials, famous criminals, disasters such as the Chicago Fire and the San Francisco Earthquake and Fire, orphan trains, the Gilded Age, the Roaring

Twenties, and the Harlem Renaissance. World history students can do research on ancient Greece using the Perseus Project database, take a virtual walk through the Roman Forum, and attend a Renaissance Fair.

The chapter, "The School Library: The School Information Resource Center," includes more Web pages created by and for media specialists, as well as entries to help with in-service and staff development workshops on technology competencies and skills.

Features of the Directory

Site and Subject Indexes

The site index is an alphabetical listing of all the entries in the book. The subject index is helpful for finding all the sites in the directory related to a specific topic. For example, all African American studies and Black history sites are listed under "African American." The two indexes and a detailed table of contents make this directory extremely user-friendly and make it easy to locate specific information.

Cross-References

Cross-references have been added, making it simple to locate various resources on a single topic or theme. For example, a cross-reference links Robert Louis Stevenson's *Treasure Island* (entry 483) in the language arts chapter and the PIRATES! home page (entry 1274) in the social studies chapter. The "History and Culture of Japan" section has cross references to the Origami Page (entry 125), Haiku for People (entry 570), The Tokugawa Art Museum (entry 137), and Kabuki Theatre for Everyone (entry 197).

Multicultural Resources

More multicultural resources are available on the Internet. There are general sites as well as sites specific to Asian American, Native American, Jewish, Latino, and African American cultures. The Multicultural Pavilion at the University of Virginia provides resources on multicultural issues and activities. Negro Baseball League, African American Heritage in the American West, and *Kids Zone* are outstanding resources, as is the Golden Legacy Curriculum, which focuses on Chinese culture and history. Native American resources highlight both general information and individual tribes, such as the Seminole, Cherokee, Hopi, Pueblo, and Cheyenne.

Gender Equity

Numerous sites are devoted to gender equity, including science lesson plans and sites featuring women in the sciences, math, and architecture. Women of NASA (entry 726) provides interview information about top NASA women scientists and includes information on career planning and what a typical day is like for these NASA scientists. Other sites focused on women in math and science include Biographies of Women Mathematicians (entry 594), Contributions of 20th Century Women to Physics (entry 894), and The Ada Project: Tapping Internet Resources for Women in Computer Science (entry 273).

School-to-Work and Life After High School

Look for careers in aeronautics, the armed forces, environmental science, construction, the hospitality industry, oceanography, marine science and marine biology, the newspaper industry, science and math, and sports.

The Internet

The World Wide Web

An estimated number of Internet users worldwide at the end of 1998 was 147,800,00; of those, 76,856,000 users live in the United States. The number of users in the United States is expected to be more than 100,000,000 by 2001. The World Wide Web is growing exponentially. Thousands of new Web sites are created and added each day. Some estimates state that 1.5 million Web pages are added daily. According to Hobbes Internet Timeline, as of February 1999, there were 4,301,512 Web sites. Commercial domains and K–12 make up two of the largest blocks of Web sites. According to the most recent report from the National Center for Education Statistics, 95 percent of the K–12 schools in the United States are connected to the Internet; 65 percent of teachers use the Internet in their teaching; and most schools have their own Web pages. Specific information is included in this directory on how to create a K–12 Web presence and register your school's Web site with an international registry, Web66. See "Resources for Educators" for lists of outstanding school sites, and see the Web Page Design and Development section in "Computer Science" for detailed information on how to create a Web page. Because so many resources for K–12 are available on the World Wide Web, very few Internet resources listed in this directory are not Web resources.

Gopher

A significant number of Gopher sites have been discontinued or have migrated to the Web. Notices on many Gopher servers warn users that the servers are not being updated or maintained or will be discontinued soon. Some organizations, such as the Library of Congress, continue to offer both Gopher access and Web access to certain information, but warn that the Gopher has been discontinued as a way of providing information except for a handful of documents in ASCII format. It should be noted that most information available on Gophers is older information, usually no longer updated.

Multimedia Access

The Web is graphics-rich and getting richer. The Web requires more from your computer than standard desktop applications do. You will need an up-to-date version of a graphical browser, a fast processing speed (MHz), a VGA color monitor, a sound card, speakers, double the amount of RAM (random access memory) that you think you need, and fast connectivity to the Internet. It is well worth the expense of quality multimedia hardware and software to bring into the classroom some of the world's most famous art treasures, which are presented in multimedia format, and other technological innovations available via the Web. (*See* Software and Software Collections and Archives [entries 243–249].)

Newer versions of graphical interface browsers, such as Internet Explorer and Netscape, come with the built-in ability not only to view graphics (pictures), but also to hear sound. Macintosh computers come with sound cards and built-in speakers. PC users may have to add sound cards and speakers. You may need to upgrade your browser to accommodate the newest programming language for the Internet, Java, and Java applets (applications), and install additional plug-ins to enhance your browser's capabilities to display different types of audio or video messages. For example, to see a Shockwave or multimedia object, you need the Shockwave plug-in, a program that integrates seamlessly with your Web browser to support audio, animation, and video. Many multimedia sites require RealPlayer, RealAudio, and Flash. Some documents need Adobe Acrobat Reader for downloading. Virtual reality sites can't be viewed without software such as QuickTime VR. It's important to keep up with all the plug-ins to take advantage of the multimedia aspects of the Web environment.

Online Discussion Groups

Many discussion groups for educators are listed in this directory. Join some of these discussion groups to connect with other educators who have similar interests. To find out which discussion groups are most beneficial, try subscribing to several. Monitor these discussions for a few months, then quit the groups that do not meet your information needs. To find an online discussion group not mentioned specifically in any of the chapters, see "Finding Tools for Discussion Groups and Newsgroups" (entries 1370–1371).

Selection Criteria

The resources in this book were selected according to the following guidelines:

1. The resource supports and enriches the K–12 curriculum, including science, math, social studies, language arts, foreign-language studies, art, drama, music, physical education, home economics, business education, and technical and vocational preparation.

2. The resource supplements school library media core collections because of its uniqueness or searchable features.

3. The resource is free and either noncommercial or minimally commercial.

4. The resource is current and updated regularly.

5. The resource is specifically designed to help educators develop professionally, collaborate with peers, and share information and ideas.

6. The resource aids students in preparing for school-to-work, college, and careers.

7. The resource helps students develop online search skills.

8. The resource promotes a global awareness and appreciation of other cultures.

9. The resource promotes collaborative learning, problem solving, authentic tasks, and enthusiasm for learning.

10. The resource helps to promote lifelong learning.

Accuracy and Caveat

Resources on the Internet are constantly changing. New information files are added, and menus and directories undergo constant reorganization. In some cases, when information is moved from one location to another, a pointer to the new location is given, but this is not always the case. Each URL, FTP address, Gopher path, and telnet login was checked thoroughly prior to publication. If you experience difficulty in following a path to a resource, it is probably due to the changing nature of the Internet. Please e-mail the author at (emiller@vnet.net) to let her know about any changes you find. Changes and updates to the 2000/2001 directory will be posted monthly at *The Internet Resource Directory for K–12 Teachers and Librarians* World Wide Web site (http://www.lu.com/lu/irdupdates.html). Bookmark this site and check back frequently.

How This Book Is Organized

This directory is divided into 11 chapters, each addressing a different area of the K–12 curriculum. Two chapters, "Resources for Educators" and "The School Library: The School Information Resource Center," contain professional information as well as lesson plans and general information specific to education, K–12 schools, and the school library media center. The "Reference" chapter focuses on resources that can be used across the curriculum.

Clear directions for access are given for each resource. There is an entry name for each resource; notes on how it is accessed (that is, by WWW or other means); and the URL, address, path, login, or other instructions. When available, the name of a contact person associated with the resource is given. Following the basic citation is a descriptive annotation, which includes an overview of the resource and, in some cases, a brief list of some of the contents. Some resources are not annotated because they are self-explanatory.

Within each section of the book, entries are listed alphabetically by entry name, with one exception. If standards are available, the standard is listed first with alphabetical entries following.

Conventions Used in This Book

Uniform resource locators (URLs) and e-mail addresses in the text appear in parentheses. Do not include the parentheses when typing these URLs or addresses. For example, the author's e-mail address is (emiller@vnet.net). When typing in the address type: **emiller@vnet.net**

Throughout the directory, names of resources appear in normal type, and keystrokes for the user appear in **bold type**. When there is an option (for example, when you are to type in your name), the option appears in brackets. Do not type the brackets themselves. To see how this works, consider the following example:

To subscribe to A Word a Day vocabulary mailing list, send a message to (wsmith@wordsmith.org).

On the first line of the body of the message type:

subscribe [your first name and last name]

In this example, you type the words in **bold type**, but you do not type the brackets.

Some resources may be accessed in more than one way. For example, information might be accessed through Gopher, WWW, telnet, or file transfer protocol (FTP). When this is the case, instructions for each way of accessing the resource precede the annotation.

Finally, when resources are mentioned in chapter introductions and *See* or *See also* references, the entry number(s), in parentheses, follow the name of the resource. For example, Educational Standards (entry 1) is the first entry in this book.

Resources for Educators

Many resources on the Internet are specifically for educators. These resources allow teachers and school library media specialists to access information; share ideas and lesson plans; ask for help or specific information; discuss problems; and obtain free software, graphics, and text files. Most of the resources in this chapter are of interest to all teachers, educators, and school librarians, regardless of grade level or subject area. Look for specific sites related to early childhood, gifted and talented, and special education. Resources are also available for K-12 counselors. In addition to general information such as Internet Resources for School Counselors (entry 55), there are career and guidance resources, including aids for college planning. Look for Peterson's Education Center (entry 86), college rankings from *U.S. News & World Report* (entry 85), and information on financial aid (entry 87).

Of particular note are AskERIC (entry 8) and AskERIC's Virtual Reference Desk (entry 6). These are wonderful general resources for all educators. ERIC is the Educational Resources Information Center, a federally funded national information system that provides access to an extensive body of education-related literature. ERIC provides a variety of services and products at all education levels.

Some of the award-winning school Web sites provide good examples of Web page design and integration of student work, as well as resources for finding creative and innovative educational curriculum lessons.

Hundreds of quality lesson plans are available on the Internet. "Lesson Plans Across the Curriculum" (entries 33–44) highlights some of the most comprehensive sites. Lesson plans encompass all subject areas and all grades. Most lesson plans have been written by classroom teachers, and many of these address the subject-area content standards. Others demonstrate how to integrate the use of technology into the school curriculum. This extremely popular concept of teachers sharing information online has created online resource centers specifically for teachers, such as Dr. Scott Mandel's Teachers Helping Teachers (entry 48).

National and State Standards

1.

Educational Standards
http://putwest.boces.org/Standards.html

Putnam Valley Central Schools (New York) has compiled an annotated list of Internet sites with K-12 educational standards and curriculum frameworks documents. These sites have categories for national standards, standards by state, and standards by subject area. Links are provided to state education departments, centers, clearinghouses, labs, state-focused groups, and foreign countries. This repository of information located on the Internet about educational standards and curriculum frameworks is maintained by Charles Hill (chill@putwest.boces.org), assistant superintendent in Putnam Valley Schools, New York.

2.   **Standards from McREL**

http://www.mcrel.org/standards/

The McREL (Mid-continent Regional Educational Laboratory) site provides links to documents written on the topic of standards-based education. What are standards? What eight questions should be asked before implementing standards at the local level? What is the status of state standards? Much of this literature addresses identifying standards and benchmarks in subject areas. In one document, standards have been linked to an extensive index of online education resources. Also online is *Content Knowledge: A Compendium of Standards and Benchmarks for K-12 Education* by John S. Kendall and Robert J. Marzano (http://www.mcrel.org/standards-benchmarks).

Other educator resources, projects, and programs from McREL can be found as links from the home page (http://www.mcrel.org).

3.   **StateStandards.com**

http://www.statestandards.com

Provides the state standards for each of the United States, with links to lesson plans and resources. Information is easily accessible through a clickable map or by choosing the name of a state from a pop-up menu. Teachers can search for lesson plans from state standards. Lessons that support the standards are linked to the Microsoft Lesson Connection database. At the time of publishing, standards for more than 40 states were available. This fantastic Web site is provided as a free service for educators by EdVISION.com Corporation.

Professional Associations

4.   **AECT (Association for Educational Communications and Technology)**

http://www.aect.org

Information is available on membership; publications; professional development; and AECT affiliates, divisions, and chapters. The Placement Center offers job listings. Find out more about AECT/ECT awards and how to participate in the AECT listserv.

5.   **ISTE (International Society of Technology in Education) Home Page**

http://www.iste.org

The International Society of Technology in Education promotes appropriate uses of technology to support and improve teaching and learning. On this page educators can find information about membership, conferences, training, and publications. ISTE publishes *Learning and Leading with Technology* and the *Journal of Research on Computing in Education*, as well as eight special-interest periodicals and educator-developed books and courseware. A list of selected resources for educators is provided with links. ISTE is the professional education organization responsible for recommending guidelines for accreditation to NCATE (the National Council for Accreditation of Teacher Education) for programs in educational computing and technology teacher preparation. The National Standards for Technology in Teacher Preparation are outlined with links to both curriculum guidelines and unit guidelines.

General Interest

6. AskERIC's Virtual Reference Desk and ERIC

http://ericir.syr.edu

The AskERIC library, virtual reference desk, and archives are extensive. Archives include postings to educational listservs, including LM_Net. AskERIC organizes lesson plans by subject area and grade level. Educational materials for both the *Discovery Channel School* and *Newton's Apple,* as well as other television series companion materials are available. The extensive ERIC database can be searched from the Web site.

7. U.S. Department of Education

http://www.ed.gov

The U.S. Department of Education Web page provides information about the National Education Goals, as well as a teacher's guide and a researcher's guide to the department's resources. Pointers lead users to programs, initiatives, newsletters, press releases, funding opportunities, selected speeches, and publications. A list of frequently requested materials includes financial aid information for students, an encyclopedia of education statistics, disabilities education (IDEA), and the America Reads program.

Question-and-Answer Services

See also KidsConnect (entry 1438).

8. AskERIC

E-mail: **askERIC@ericir.syr.edu**

AskERIC is a question-answering service for teachers, library media specialists, and administrators. Anyone involved with K-12 education can send an e-mail message to AskERIC. Drawing on the extensive resources of the ERIC system, AskERIC staff will respond with an answer within 48 working hours. If you have questions about K-12 education, learning, teaching, information technology, or educational administration, contact AskERIC. Relevant resources will be compiled and sent from the ERIC system and from other Internet resources. Although AskERIC is for adults, a similar question-answering service, KidsConnect (entry 1438), is available for K-12 students.

Networks

National and International Networks

9. Canada's SchoolNet

http://www.schoolnet.ca

SchoolNet is designed to help Canada's public libraries and schools connect to the Internet and to promote the effective use of information technology. Learning resources are organized by curriculum areas, including entrepreneurship studies, library resources, and Canadian resources. A list of programs and initiatives is available. Links are provided to the 12 provincial educational networks. The Web site is bilingual (French and English).

10.   **The Global Schoolhouse**

http://www.gsn.org

The Global Schoolhouse is a nonprofit, public service organization that focuses on using communications technologies to support learning. The Global Schoolhouse is part of the Global SchoolNet Foundation (GSN), formerly called FrEdMail (Free Educational Mail). The Global Schoolhouse sponsors an Internet Projects Registry, a central clearinghouse for collaborative classroom projects for all grade levels, as well as GeoGame, CyberFair, and a travel buddy named Woodsy Woodchuck. Global School maintains an archive for the K12opps mailing list, a list of announcements of interest to educators and parents about free software, contests, conferences, training opportunities, and educational Web sites.

State and Regional Networks

11.   **Florida Information Resource Network**

http://www.firn.edu/index.html

The Florida Information Resource Network (FIRN) is an extensive statewide network linking all of Florida's public education entities; it also allows access to various computing resources. Links are provided to the Florida Department of Education, Florida Public Schools, Instructional Resources, and Florida and U.S. government information.

12.   **North Carolina Department of Public Instruction**

http://www.dpi.state.nc.us

The North Carolina Department of Public Instruction has an excellent Web site for educators and parents. Parents can link to A Parents' Guide to the Internet. The Educators' Resource Center addresses issues and current topics of interest such as copyright in an electronic environment, and provides links to instructional resources. An interactive state map links schools by county.

13.   **Ohio Public Library Information Network (OPLIN)**

http://www.oplin.lib.oh.us

The Ohio Public Library Information Network provides a centralized network of information for residents of Ohio, but nonresidents will also find much of value here. Information is available from categories such as Current Events, Libraries, Electronic Resources, OH! Kids, and Discover Ohio. OH! Kids is a collection of selected Internet resources for kids: WebTots (3–5), WebKids (6–9), WebKidsToo (10–13), and WebTeens (14–17). Discover Ohio has lots of state-related information, including a tree identification page for identifying unknown trees indigenous to Ohio. Students can identify trees by name, leaf, or fruit. What's the Point provides assistance in identifying flint artifacts as well as historical information and a timeline of Ohio's prehistoric Indian cultures. The Webmaster's address is (webmaster@oplin.lib.oh.us).

14.   **Texas Education Network**

http://www.tenet.edu

The Texas Education Network (TENET) provides information for educators in and outside Texas. Categories of information include Curriculum Resources, Professional Resources, Resources for

Texas Educators, K-12 Schools, announcements of what's new, and information about TENET. Be sure to look in Curriculum Resources for the TENET Halls of Academia (http://www.tenet.edu/academia/main.html). Here, Internet resources are available for many curriculum areas, including early childhood, career and technology, home economics, geography, multiculturalism, special populations, and sports and physical fitness.

Special School Days

See also lesson plans for Earth Day (entry 679) and Education Calendar and WWW Sites (entry 1427).

15.   The 100th Day of School Web Site

http://users.aol.com/a100thday/

Created by Joan Holub, illustrator of the book *The 100th Day of School*, by Angela Medearis (Scholastic), this Web site celebrates the 100th day of the school year. Look for 100 Questions from students and answers by Joan Holub on illustrating children's books; 100 Ideas shared by classroom teachers for activities on the 100th day; and a bibliography of 100 Day Books. Links are provided to other Internet sites related to 100th Day Activities. See also the 100th Day of School Celebration from Loogootee Elementary (http://www.siec.k12.in.us/~west/proj/100th/index.html).

Schools and School Districts on the World Wide Web

Directories of K–12 Schools and School Districts

16.   Web66

http://web66.coled.umn.edu

Since the advent of graphical browsers, Web66 has been on the forefront, leading the way for K-12 schools with a vision of global connectivity. The site is based on the idea that the World Wide Web is a catalyst that will integrate the Internet into K-12 school curricula just as U.S. Highway Route 66 was a catalyst for Americana. Web66's goals are to help K-12 educators learn how to set up their own Internet servers, link K-12 school communities via their Web servers, and help K-12 educators find and use K-12 appropriate resources on the Web. Web66 maintains the Internet's oldest and most complete list of K-12 Web servers in its International Registry of K-12 Schools on the Web. The Web66 Classroom Internet Server Cookbook gives recipes with step-by-step instructions for setting up a WWW, Mail, and FTP server on a Macintosh, Windows 95, or Windows NT computer. The cookbook includes hypertext links to every needed ingredient. Hillside Elementary School (entry 18) is the pilot school for the Web66 project. Mustang: A Web Cruising Vehicle for Teachers gives detailed information for effective and successful integration of Internet resources into the K-12 curriculum. Web66 was created and is maintained by Stephen E. Collins (sec@umn.edu), professor at the College of Education and Human Development at the University of Minnesota.

School Web Sites

Elementary Schools

17. **Groveland Elementary School (Wayzata, MN)**

http://www.minnetonka.k12.mn.us/grv/

Groveland Elementary School's home page has a parent handbook and a parent volunteer handbook. The lunch menu is listed. The media center provides links to authors and other reference information for research, including a list of Web resources organized by the Dewey Decimal system. Student work is highlighted, and there is information about each class and links to what they are learning.

18. **Hillside Elementary School (Cottage Grove, MN)**

http://www.sowashco.k12.mn.us/he/

Hillside Elementary School works in partnership with the University of Minnesota College of Education and Human Development to incorporate Internet resources into the elementary curriculum and to have students participate in creating resources and making them available on the Internet. Students and teachers use the Internet to publish student work, to obtain information and conduct research, to communicate and share ideas, and to collaborate. Students have been involved with a variety of projects, including the Invention Unit, in which they explored the four roles of the creative process based on *A Kick in the Seat of the Pants* by Roger van Oech. Projects are listed by grade level and include work from previous years, beginning with 1993–1994. This is an excellent site to "mine" for creative teaching ideas and lessons integrating Internet resources. Students are always enthusiastic about publishing their work online.

19. **Honea Path Elementary (Honea Path, SC)**

http://www.anderson1234.k12.sc.us/hpe/

The home of the Stingers has lots of information to share. Each one of the classroom Web sites for grades K-4 is filled with the adventures of learning, including Web sites for the co-curricular specialists in music, resource, physical education, art, guidance, and speech therapy. The library resource page provides links to children's book awards, 100 Days Celebration, family reading literacy, and reference. Other online information includes Web sites of the month, faculty and staff e-mail addresses, and events and news of school interest. This Web site was created and is maintained by Dr. Julia Ashley (ashleyj@anderson2.k12.sc.us), school library media specialist.

20. **Loogootee Elementary West (Loogootee, IN)**

http://www.siec.k12.in.us/~west/

Loogootee Elementary West is home to kindergarten through third-graders. This exemplary Web site demonstrates a wonderful integration of Internet resources into the curriculum. Something Fishy (http://www.siec.k12.in.us/~west/proj/owl) integrates *The Owl and the Pussycat* (written by Edward Lear and illustrated by Jan Brett) into a unit on oceans. At the time of publication of this book, the second-graders had an Emu Page. The first-graders had created a class book, *Months of the Year!*, in conjunction with Houghton Mifflin's Invitation to Literacy. The third-graders had theme pages devoted to pigs, wolves, sharks, the desert, and Hawaii.

Two programs have been designed to help teach children how to safely use the Internet as a research tool. Surfing for ABC's is for grades K-1, and Safely Surfing on the Internet (using Yahooligan's search engine) is for grades 2–3.

Note: Loogootee East (http://www.siec.k12.in.us/east/) is home to fourth- through sixth-graders, and Loogootee Junior/Senior High School (http://www.loogootee.k12.in.us/ high/homepage.htm) is where you'll find the seventh- through twelfth-graders.

Loogootee Elementary West's Web site was created and is maintained by first-grade teacher Tammy Payton (tpayton@dmrtc.net).

21. Marshall Elementary School (Lewisburg, TN)

http://www.marshall-es.marshall.k12.tn.us/index.html

Marshall Elementary, a K-2 school, is a leader in academic and technological excellence. Visitors can take an online tour of the school, and information is easily available about Internet projects and other student work. Vice-principal and Web editor Hazel Job is one of the Franklin Institute Online Fellows pioneering the use of the Internet. She has authored cross-curriculum units using Internet resources. Be sure to see Hazel's page (http://www.marshall-es.marshall. k12.tn.us/jobe/index.html).

High Schools

22. Berea High School (Greenville, SC)

http://www.greenville.k12.sc.us/bereah/index.htm

The home of the Bulldogs provides a comprehensive look at school-wide student activity at Berea High School. Some of the links on the home page lead to a current school calendar, alumni pages, school history, athletics and athletic schedules, departments, guidance, the media center, and a SAT question of the day. The media center has links to a WWW catalog, a collection of Web resources listed alphabetically by subject headings; links to online magazines and news resources; bibliographies by departmental interest of videos in the library's collection; and a list of books nominated for the state young adult reading award, with student reviews. The Webmaster is Boris Bauer (rhodies@earthlink.net), media specialist.

Home Schools

23. The Teel Family Web Site

http://www.teelfamily.com

The Teel family lives in Chugiak, Alaska, and the five Teel children are homeschooled. The Education page and Activity page have lots of lessons for sharing. Look at some of the projects on themes of snow, polar bears, trees, the night sky, and the aurora (aurora borealis). There are seasonal activities, and lessons and activities change often. Bookmark this site so you can return often.

24. **WindyCreek Homeschool Site**

http://www.windycreek.com

Join the Lande family at WindyCreek Homeschool. Read their goals for homeschooling, share some of their educational activities, and be a "fly on the wall" as they homeschool. This site changes, so visit often. Nancy Lande has written and published a new book, *Homeschooling: A Patchwork of Days*.

Science and Math Schools

25. **The Mississippi School for Mathematics and Science**

http://www.msms.doe.k12.ms.us

The Mississippi School for Mathematics and Science is a public, state-supported high school for intellectually gifted 11th- and 12th-graders. The school is located in Columbus, Mississippi, on the campus of the Mississippi University for Women.

Students and faculty have their own home pages. Student home pages are organized by year of graduation, beginning with the class of 1990. Students have posted their pictures, artwork, music archives, interdisciplinary papers, friends' pictures, and links to favorite Internet resources. These student home pages are great yearbook pages. Each is creative and unique, with unexpected information and insights.

26. **The North Carolina School of Science and Mathematics**

http://www.ncssm.edu

The North Carolina School of Science and Mathematics, which is affiliated with the University of North Carolina, is the nation's first state-supported, residential school for students with talent for and interest in science and mathematics. It opened in 1980 for students in the 11th and 12th grades. Pointers are provided to campus life, admissions, and summer programs. Links are provided to other schools that are a part of the National Consortium for Specialized Secondary Schools of Mathematics, Science, and Technology, as well as to faculty and student home pages.

School Districts

27. **Bellingham Public Schools (WA)**

http://www.bham.wednet.edu

Bellingham School District provides a unique collection of information for staff development, technology integration, and collaborative teaching strategies. A variety of lesson plans are available for teaching adults about new technologies and integrating the use of technologies into the curriculum. The Tech Plan and Library Documents area has a copy of the district's Technology Plan and the Library Media Program Frameworks. Student artwork and writing are showcased, along with a district thematic unit on Explorers of the World. Curriculum pages and teaching resource indexes highlight links to Internet resources of interest to classroom teachers. Additional links to virtual field trips and virtual museums provide interesting alternatives for learning through the magic of multimedia.

Interactive Learning and Telecommunications Across the Curriculum

See also "Key Pals" (entries 425–430); "Interactive Math" (entries 602–609).

28. Annenberg/CPB Exhibits

http://www.learner.org/exhibits/

Provides a collection of quality interactive exhibits on topics such as the weather, amusement park physics, the making of Hollywood films, why civilizations collapse, what makes individual personalities, the Renaissance, and math in everyday life. Some of the other topics explore garbage and recycling, the Middle Ages, South Africa, volcanoes, and medical ethics. This site is sponsored by the Annenberg School of Communication and the Corporation for Public Broadcasting.

29. BBC Education Web Guide

http://www.bbc.co.uk/plsql/education/webguide/pkg_main.p_home

The British Broadcasting Corporation (BBC) maintains a searchable directory of more than 3,000 of the best Web sites for learning. Each Web site has been selected and reviewed by subject specialists. The directory is also browseable by subject. In addition to academic curriculum subjects, topics include careers advice, design and technology, hobbies and interests, media studies, religion, and special needs.

30. The Digital Education Network (DEN)

http://www.actden.com

Recognizing that education is rapidly changing from traditional curricula to innovative and increasingly interactive learning that includes the Internet experience, ACT Laboratory currently provides six DENs. Each DEN offers up-to-date information and interactive features that encourage students to learn, think, and participate in the online community. MathDEN presents challenging math problems; WritingDEN teaches students how to write effectively; NewsDEN presents current events in exciting new ways; GraphicsDEN shows students how to create cool digital art; SkyDEN offers a visually stunning introduction to basic astronomy; and InternetDEN presents an introduction to using the Internet. ChineseDEN and TOEFLDEN will soon be added. Log on as **guest** and use **guest** as the password.

31. Eduscapes: A Site for Life-Long Learners

http://eduscapes.com

New topics are posted each week in the 42eXplore section, and the archive of past topics is available for browsing. Each topic has four Web resources to explore for further information. Each topic also includes activities, WebQuests, definitions, links to Web pages created by students and teachers, and other resources. A few of the topics located in the archives are bridge building, Buffalo Soldiers, ancient Africa, careers, the Great Depression, and the underground railroad. Internet Expeditions explains how to create WebQuests and provides examples of WebQuests. There are also free online workshops and lists of Web resources. Created by Annette Lamb (alamb@eduscapes.com) and Larry Johnson (ljohnson@mail.escapees.com).

32. **The WebQuest Page**

http://edweb.sdsu.edu/webquest/webquest.html

WebQuests are inquiry-oriented activities in which most or all of the information is gleaned from various Web sites. For those wishing to create WebQuests, there are models and examples. For those wishing to find a WebQuest to use in the classroom, this site offers more than 200 to choose from, categorized by grade level: K-3, 4-5, Middle School, High School, and College/Adult. This page is maintained by Bernie Dodge (bdodge@mail.sdsu.edu), professor of Educational Technology at San Diego State University. *See also* Building Blocks of a WebQuest and "Web Page Design and Development" (entries 258-272) for information about how to create your own WebQuest pages.

Lesson Plans Across the Curriculum

See also "Lesson Plans" sections in each chapter, as well as these sites: Classifying Galaxies: An Interactive Lesson (entry 691), Good News Bears Stock Market Project (entry 1093); Ocean Planet Home Page (entry 660), Weather Here and There (entry 850), and Whales: A Thematic Unit (entry 770).

33. **Apple Learning Interchange**

http://henson.austin.apple.com/edres/curric.shtml

Apple Education (Apple Computer, Inc.) provides collections of lesson plans to help integrate technology into the curriculum. The Apple Learning Interchange Resources Section is searchable by subject and grade level. The Curriculum Center houses curricular themes such as The Weather, Nutrition, The Civil War, Geology, The 50 States, Insects, and The Environment. The Lesson Plan Library contains lesson plans across the curriculum, selected from many different online resources. All the curriculum resources listed on this site are searchable by subject and keyword.

34. **AskERIC Lesson Plans**

http://ericir.syr.edu/Virtual/Lessons/

AskERIC's collection of K-12 lesson plans, written and submitted by educators, continues to grow. Lessons are organized by subject area. Other sources of lesson plans are also listed. These include links to educational materials for the science television program *Newton's Apple;* lesson plans from the print journal, *School Library Media Activities Monthly;* and the Apple Computer K-12 Lesson Plan Library.

35. **Busy Teacher's Web Site**

http://www.ceismc.gatech.edu/busyt/

Information is organized by K-12 subjects and interests. Teachers will find resource materials, lesson plans, and classroom activities. Each site is briefly annotated, and links are provided to related subjects. Created and maintained by Carolyn Cole (carolyn.cole@ceismc.gatech.edu), a research faculty member at the Georgia Institute of Technology in the Center for Education: Integrating Science, Mathematics and Technology.

36. Encarta Online Lesson Plans

http://encarta.msn.com/schoolhouse/

Microsoft's Encarta Online has a collection of lesson plans written and field-tested by teachers. Lesson plans are categorized by subject area. Each lesson plan has an overview and suggested grade level. For each lesson, the purpose, objectives, resources, and materials are given. Activities, procedures, and culminating activities are clearly stated and easy to follow.

37. Gareth Pitchford's Primary Resources

http://www.primaryresources.co.uk/

Provides hundreds of worksheets, activities, and resources for teachers of students ages 5 to 11 (primary school in the United Kingdom). Curriculum subjects cover language arts, math, science, art, and much more. Some of the resources have been submitted by practicing teachers, and contributions to the database are continuously being solicited from this area. Web site created and maintained by Gareth Pitchford (gareth@primaryresources.co.uk).

38. Microsoft Lesson Connection

http://www.k12.msn.com/LessonConnection/Teacher.asp

Allows searches for ready-to-use lesson plans that match your school's learning objectives. Search by keyword(s) or subject and topic—such as The Arts and Theater Arts—and by grade level, choosing from the following grade level categories: K–2, 3–5, 6–8, and 9–12. Searching examples and tips are given.

39. The Mid-continent Regional Educational Laboratory (McREL) Lesson Plans

http://www.mcrel.org/resources/links/

McREL has one of the largest collections of links to individual lesson plans, lesson plan collections, and topical and thematic units. Categorized into subject areas, links to lesson plans are also available in areas of Technology and Connections+, a special area of lesson plans, activities, and curriculum resources identified with corresponding subject-area content standards from *Content Knowledge: A Compendium of Standards and Benchmarks for K-12 Education* (http://www.mcrel.org/standards-benchmarks).

40. New York Times Teacher Connections, Grades 6-12

http://www.nytimes.com/learning/teachers/index.html

Each school day, teachers can access a lesson plan based on the day's news and print it out for classroom use if they choose. The archive of lessons is browseable by curriculum subject, such as language arts, mathematics, social studies, health, journalism, civics, media studies, and geography. Lessons are linked to *New York Times* articles, copies of worksheets, Web resources, and academic content standards. Lesson format is thorough, including overview, objectives, materials and resources needed, activities (including a warm-up and a wrap-up), further questions, evaluation, vocabulary, extension activities, interdisciplinary connections, and additional related articles and Web resources. There is a printer-friendly version of each lesson. New lessons are continuously being added.

Also provides news of interest to educators, and offers ways for educators to communicate with one another and submit lesson plans to share.

41. **Smithsonian Education**
   http://educate.si.edu/educate.html

   Smithsonian Education is an area within the Smithsonian Institution's Web site designed just for educators. Lesson plans are provided in the curriculum areas of the arts, language arts, science, and social studies. Reflecting the many areas of the Smithsonian collections, lesson plans focus on broad topics ranging from the art of the United States, Asia, and Africa to plant life, space sciences, political and social history, animal life, and zoology. Some lesson plans may be downloaded in Adobe Acrobat format, and all include step-by-step lessons and activity pages. Recommended resources and links to Web resources are part of each lesson plan. Some of the lesson plans include: "Plants and Animals: Partners in Pollination"; "Japan: Images of a People"; "Decoding the Past: The Work of Archaeologists"; "Teaching from Objects and Stories: Learning About the Bering Sea Eskimo People"; and "Contrasts in Blue: Life on the Caribbean Coral Reef and the Rocky Coast of Maine."

42. **Teacher Features**
   http://www.teacherfeatures.com

   Teacher Features offers a wide array of information for elementary educators. Databases of units and lesson plans are growing as teachers submit and share their favorites. Each month there is a theme for various activities and lessons, as well as a featured school Web site. Each week a different Web site is highlighted. Elementary school teachers will also find articles of interest and suggested book titles. Created and maintained by Kristan Williams (Kwilliams@teacherfeatures.com). See also Online Education's Weekly Online Lesson (http://www.learnersonline.com/lessons/lessonindex.htm) for thematic lessons for grades 4–8.

43. **Teaching Ideas for Primary Teachers**
   http://www.teachingideas.co.uk/index.shtml

   Looking for teaching ideas for geography, music, information and communication technology, design and technology, time fillers, math, language arts, science, art, or physical education? This is the place to come. Primary teachers in the United Kingdom have contributed their teaching ideas for sharing. Created and maintained by Mark Warner (mark@teachingideas.co.uk).

44. **Webquests and Resources for Teachers**
   http://www.davison.k12.mi.us/academic/hewitt14.htm

   Provides a collection of links to WebQuests and lesson plans organized by such curriculum areas as history, social studies, science, math, language arts, and miscellaneous. WebQuests are appropriate for upper elementary, middle, and high school students. When this site was reviewed, some examples of WebQuests available included: Exploring the Ancient World (grade 8); Dear King George III, a WebQuest on the American Revolution (grade 5); and The Impact of Jim Crow Laws (grade 10). Part of a ring of Web-based leassons, this site also has links to large indexes of lesson plans as well as links to Web sites designed to help teachers create their own WebQuests. Maintained by Paul Hewitt (phewitt@tir.com) at Davison High Shool in Davison, Michigan.

Resource Centers for Teachers and Educational Web Site Archives

45. Awesome Library

http://www.awesomelibrary.com

More than 12,000 selected Web sites are organized by topics for teachers, parents, and students. A small percentage of the sites in this database are further recognized with a star, indicating an outstanding site. During browsing, suggestions of other topics to try is a useful feature. The Awesome Library is both searchable and browseable. Project director is Dr. R. Jerry Adams (adamsj@neat-schoolhouse.org), Executive Director for the Evaluation and Development Institute (EDI). The Northwest Regional Educational Laboratory (NWREL) houses the same database of educational Web resources under the name Library-in-the-Sky, located at (http://www.nwrel.org/sky).

46. Education Index

http://www.educationindex.com

Education Index is an annotated guide to more than 3,000 education-related Web sites covering a variety of subjects and lifestages. Subjects include traditional curricula as well as agriculture resources, conservation, construction trade resources, engineering resources, military technologies, public administration, theology, and women's studies. Entries are also sorted by lifestages, including prenatal and infant, parenting, preschool, primary education, secondary education, distance learning, college education, careers, and continuing education. The Webmaster's address is (webmaster@educationindex.com).

47. Gateway to Educational Materials (GEM)

http://www.thegateway.org

The United States Department of Education has made it easy for teachers, students, and parents to access lessons and educational materials on any topic at one of more than 140 Web sites. Gateway to Educational Materials (GEM) provides one-stop access to high-quality lesson plans, curriculum units, and other education resources on the Internet, which users can access by browsing through lists organized by subject and/or keywords, or by searching using fields for subjects, keywords, titles, and grade levels, preK-12.

48. Teachers Helping Teachers

http://www.pacificnet.net/~mandel/

Teachers Helping Teachers is a home page by teachers for teachers that provides basic teaching tips to inexperienced teachers and ideas that can be immediately implemented in the classroom; offers new ideas in teaching methodologies for all teachers; and provides a forum for experienced teachers to share their expertise and tips with colleagues around the world. This site offers advice on stress management, classroom management, teaching strategies, and curriculum lesson plans. Teachers will want to bookmark this Web site for frequent visits.

Updated weekly during the school year. Created and maintained by Dr. Scott Mandel (mandel@pacificnet.net), Pacoima Middle School Television, Theatre and Fine Arts Magnet, Pacoima, California.

49. Teacher's Resource Center

http://mountmike.creighton.edu/classrooms/teachers_resource_center.html

The Teacher's Resource Center contains links to professional development resources, lesson plans, and other resources of interest to teachers. Teachers may also want to access some of the K-12 newsgroups listed.

50. The *World Book* Encyclopedia

http://www.worldbook.com

World Book does not provide a free online version of its encyclopedia; however, this site is valuable for its learning resources and suggestions for teachers, parents, and students. Teachers can explore the Teacher Resource Center for ideas and resources for enriching K-12 lesson plans across the curriculum. Selected curriculum topics include excerpts and graphics from *World Book*, a list of materials available in *World Book*, classroom activities, discussion ideas, a suggested reading list, and topic-related Web sites. Parent Resources include Hands-on Help, with suggested educational activities for parents to use when working with their children on specific K-6 learning topics. These activities are designed for complementary use with *World Book*, and the assumption is that parents would have access to the print version and/or a multimedia version of the *World Book* encyclopedia. (Product ordering information is available.) In the Fun and Learning section, *World Book* presents facts about each month of the year in Through the Year; and interesting information about cities, regions, and countries, complete with maps, in Around the World. CyberCamp appeals to students with many online activities and suggestions, including craft ideas, easy recipes, riddles, and a virtual nature walk through a forest or wetland to learn about plants and animals. Behind the Headlines provides students with additional information for understanding the complex events in world news. Special Reports is a collection of reports, special focus stories, and in-depth articles.

Scholastic Competitions

See also MATHCOUNTS Home Page (entry 617), the Annual Robotics Competitions for High School Students (entry 902), and Bridge Building Contest (entry 884).

51. 2000-2001 High School Debate Topic Online: Privacy

http://www.ukans.edu/cwis/units/kulib/docs/debate2000.html

The University of Kansas Government Documents Library presents an excellent and information-packed Web site to assist debaters with the 2000–2001 High School Debate Topic. "Resolved: That the United States federal government should significantly increase protection of privacy in one or more of the following areas: employment, medical records, consumer information, search and seizure." Links are well organized, and include online articles, government sources, legal sources, state-by-state information, other debate sites, and additional sources of information.

52. National Science Olympiad Homepage

http://www.scioly.org

Science Olympiad is a national science competition with four division levels within K-12 grades. Teams of students compete at three levels: regional, state, and national. There are 22 events covering all aspects of science. The majority of events test how well students apply the scientific method using creativity and ingenuity. Most of the events involve a team of students taking a test, doing a lab project, testing a construction, or operating a model. Students can join the Science Olympiad online discussion list, access event pages, and locate a list of teams that qualified for nationals. Links are provided to study sites and schools with competing teams.

53. ThinkQuest

http://www.thinkquest.org

ThinkQuest is an annual competition that challenges students, ages 12 to 19, to use the Internet as a collaborative, interactive teaching and learning tool. Students in grades 4–6 may participate in ThinkQuest Junior competitions. Students participate in teams with coaches. A list of ThinkQuest winners, with links to their award-winning Web sites, is available beginning with the first year, 1996. Awards are given in several categories: Arts and Literature, Interdisciplinary, Math and Science, Social Sciences, and Sports and Health.

Guidance Counseling

General Information for Guidance Counselors

See also "Addiction: Alcohol, Drugs, and Tobacco" (entries 973–974).

54. Center for Adolescent Studies Home Page

http://education.indiana.edu/cas/cashmpg.html

The Center for Adolescent Studies is based at the School of Education at Indiana University in Bloomington, Indiana. Some of the information includes a study of the indicators of a caring middle school culture and of caring behaviors in teens; a computer-based decision aid to help schools select the drug prevention program most likely to meet their needs; and a workshop that teaches skills to deal with teen risk and crisis intervention. Teacher Talk provides a place for teachers and counselors to exchange practical advice, strategies, and lesson plans for use in secondary schools.

55. Internet Resources for School Counselors

http://www.indep.k12.mo.us/WC/wmccane.html

The Internet Resources for School Counselors site is organized by topics for easy access to information about colleges, SAT testing, and financial aid; careers; mental health; substance abuse; testing; violence and abuse; and youth suicide prevention. The Web editor is Bill McCane (bmccane@indep.k12.mo.us).

56.   **Learning Disabilities Online**

http://www.ldonline.org

LD Online is an interactive guide to Learning Disabilities (LD) and Attention Deficit Disorder (ADD) for parents, teachers, and children. Understanding learning disabilities can make teaching and learning a more meaningful and positive experience. This great resource includes background information, news updates, current research, relevant articles, and conference information. An explanation of LD tests and measurements is helpful. Personal essays written by teachers, parents, and students offer insights into what it is like to have a learning disability or to work or live with someone who has a learning disability.

57.   **School Psychology Resources Online**

http://www.bcpl.lib.md.us/~sandyste/school_psych.html

School Psychology Resources Online provides a vast number of resources on topics of interest to parents, educators, and the school psychology community. A table of contents is helpful in locating specific information. Some of the many topics addressed are behavior disorders, disabilities, substance abuse, and suicide. Links lead to assessment and evaluation information, brochures, pamphlets, ERIC documents, journals, e-zines, and related Internet sites. A What's New section helps users keep up-to-date. Maintained by Sandra Steingart (sandyste@ umd5.umd.edu), Ph.D., Office of Psychological Services, Baltimore County Public Schools, Towson, Maryland.

58.   **Warning Signs of Teen Violence**

http://helping.apa.org/warningsigns/index.html

Warning Signs is a violence prevention guide for youth from MTV and the American Psychological Association (APA), available both online and as a printed brochure that will be mailed free of charge if you call (800) 268-0078. Violence is one of the major issues facing young people today, especially those between the ages of 12 and 24 who are at the highest risk for becoming victims of violence. The guide covers such topics as the reasons for violence, how to deal with anger, and how teens can control their own risk for violent behavior. By helping youth identify warning signs of violent behavior and giving information on how to get help if they recognize these signs in themselves or their peers, MTV and APA are hoping to proactively address the problem of teen violence. "Violence is a learned behavior, and like any learned behavior, it can be changed," says Russ Newman, Ph.D., J.D., executive director for professional practice, American Psychological Association. "In order to do that, though, it is important to recognize the warning signs of violence and to get help before violence occurs. The more young people understand about violent behavior and its warning signs, the better prepared they'll be to help prevent it."

Warning Signs is part of APA's public education campaign, "Talk to Someone Who Can Help," about the importance of good mental health and the role of psychological services. See the APA's online Help Center (http://helping.apa.org/index.html) for more information on how to cope with life's problems, such as stress, depression, and serious illnesses. See also Early Warning, Timely Response: A Guide to Safe Schools with research-based practices designed to assist school communities identify warning signs early and develop prevention, intervention, and crisis response plans (http://www.ed.gov/offices/OSERS/OSEP/earlywrn.html).

Career and College Guidance

See also Contributions of 20th Century Women to Physics (entry 894); Women of NASA (entry 726); and "The Future Is Yours!," part of Science Bytes (entry 653).

Career Information

59.   **2000-2001** *Occupational Outlook Handbook*

http://stats.bls.gov/ocohome.htm

The first *Occupational Outlook Handbook* was issued in 1946 to make available to World War II veterans information concerning the need for general education and for trained personnel in the various trades, crafts, and professions. Recognized nationally as a source of career information, the handbook is published biennially in even-numbered years. Today, global competition, changing technologies and business practices, and shifts in the demand for goods and services continue to reshape America's job market. The *Occupational Outlook Handbook* from the Department of Labor, Bureau of Labor Statistics, provides comprehensive, up-to-date, and reliable career information and describes employment in approximately 250 occupations, accounting for seven out of every eight jobs in the economy. Helpful information is given to job seekers, including how to write a resume, tips for job interviews, and how to look at the want ads. The chapter on Tomorrow's Jobs discusses trends and factors that will affect the U.S. job market for the next 10 to 15 years. The handbook is keyword-searchable and browseable using a table of contents with in-text links.

60.   **America's Job Bank**

http://www.ajb.dni.us

America's Job Bank provides information for employers and job seekers, as well as job market trends and projections. There are job seekers' FAQs and tips on how to search. The Job Bank is searchable by using a menu of occupations, keywords, or various occupational codes. Links are sometimes provided to employers' Web sites, private placement agencies' sites, or public employment services in specific states.

61.   *CAREERMagazine*

http://www.careermag.com

CAREERMagazine is published on the Web. It provides a listing of job openings, a resume bank, and articles to inform and educate job seekers. The magazine has regular, full-text feature articles and columns on various career topics. To stay current, you may want to subscribe to a free e-mail update service.

62.   **CareerMosaic**

http://www.careermosaic.com

CareerMosaic allows you to use the J.O.B.S. Database to search among thousands of available jobs to find your next career opportunity. A section on employers gives profiles of hundreds of world-class employers. In ResumeCM, you can post or update your resume for free. International Gateway lists job opportunities around the world, and HealthOpps lists job openings and career information for professionals in the health care industry. Online Job Fairs provides links to recruiting events in cyberspace. Students can learn some useful tips by reading How College Students Connect with Employers.

63. *FutureScan*

http://www.futurescan.com

FutureScan is an online career guide magazine for teenagers. Look for a collection of selected Web sites for teens and their parents to learn more about careers. In addition to these general sites, the section on FutureScanners explores individual careers, such as veterinary science, architecture, law, and the environment. I Want to Be a Veterinarian discusses the differences among companion animal veterinarians, large animal veterinarians, and veterinarians who work in research and public health. I Want to Be an Architect covers careers in architecture, interior design, construction management, and landscape architecture. I Want to Be an Attorney makes a distinction between business law and environmental law. I Want to Work in the Environment contains information on environmental careers. Students can also read a series of articles on how to get real-world experience during high school and why this type of experience is important.

64. Kids and Careers Web Site

http://www.bcit.tec.nj.us/childcareer/

Kids and Careers Web Site is designed for grades K-4, in accordance with the Goals 2000 Act, as a means to provide children with an opportunity to learn more about careers available for consideration as they get ready to enter their middle and high school years. Teachers will appreciate a very informative online manual, *Teaching Elementary School Children About the World of Work*. Online activities include matching pictures to occupations, coloring pages showing different careers, and renaming job titles such as *meter maid*, *anchorman*, *postman*, and *paperboy*. Be sure to check out the list of links to other career Web sites. Created by Jason B. Tucker (admin@getnuked.com).

65. Quintessential Career and Job-Hunting Resources Guide

http://www.quintcareers.com

Everything a job seeker needs to know is listed on this Web site. Look for information about how to write great resumes and cover letters, and how to interview effectively. There is an online marketability test. One section is devoted to teens and teen employment. Created and maintained by Dr. Randall S. Hansen, Department of Marketing, Stetson University.

66. State Occupational Employment Projections for 1995-2006

http://www.dws.state.ut.us/bls/

Projections of occupational employment growth are developed for all states and the nation as a whole. One of the most important uses of the projections is to help individuals make informed career decisions. Information on this site allows you to compare employment growth in specific occupations among states. It also allows you to compare among occupations within one state. There are two ways to search the database. You can search on an occupation in which you have an interest to identify states that have the fastest employment growth for that occupation. You can also search the data to find occupations with rapid employment growth or large numerical growth in a specific state in which you have an interest.

67.   **Summer Jobs**

http://www.summerjobs.com

Summer Jobs is a database of summer jobs searchable by keyword and geographical location. Links are provided to other jobs and employment sites, such as the Overseas Jobs Express and *The Wall Street Journal*'s Top 10 Job Links.

Careers in the Armed Forces

Air Force

68.   **United States Air Force Air Base**

http://www.airforce.com

Visitors may pick up a pass at the main gate to find out what life is like on an Air Force base. The career center provides information on a variety of jobs in the United States Air Force (USAF), including technical, administrative, medical, and civil. The base hospital lists career opportunities in medical, dental, and health service-related fields, and the education center gives information on technical training opportunities, college degree programs, and officer training programs. Be sure to look at the Hottest Jobs section, which describes some of the higher-demand positions, such as linguist, computer programmer, and navigator. Other areas to visit on this "base" include the hangar, which has information on all the current USAF aircraft; Life On The Base, to find out what it's really like to work on an air base; and the Info Center, for a brief history of the Air Force, a virtual visit to the Wright Patterson Air Force museum, and a link to the official Air Force Web site. See also Air Force Link (http://www.af.mil).

69.   **U.S. Air Force Academy Admissions**

http://www.usafa.af.mil/rr/

The Academy Catalog is downloadable. Admission criteria are listed, as is admissions information. Students can fill out a form and request an Air Force Academy application via e-mail. The Air Force Academy Home Page is located at (http://www.usafa.af.mil).

Army

70.   **Army Recruitment Page**

http://www.goarmy.com

Army opportunities are explained. Students can find out more about the Army Band, Special Forces, and the Golden Knights. Benefits of enlistment are explained, as are the Army Reserves. See also Army Link: The U.S. Army Home Page (http://www2.army.mil).

71.   **U.S. Military Academy**

http://www.usma.edu

The United States Military Academy (USMA) in West Point, New York, provides online information about admissions and visiting, including driving directions and current weather and road conditions. Find out more about USMA athletics, the band, and Academy news and upcoming events from the public affairs office.

Coast Guard

72. U.S. Coast Guard Academy

http://www.uscg.mil

Find out more about the U.S. Coast Guard Academy, its military program, cadet life, academic program, and athletic program. Links are also provided to admissions information, a calendar of events, Academy history, and the Coast Guard band.

Marines

73. U.S. Marine Corps

http://www.Marines.com

The Few. The Proud. The Marines! To find out what it takes to become one of the few, students enter the processing center where they will be asked their gender and current education level. The Web site drill instructor then takes students on an interactive tour of what it's like to be a member of the U.S. Marine Corps, including career and educational opportunities. By selecting their gender and education level, students can individualize the online recruitment tour. Expectations are outlined for recruit training and life as a member of the U.S. Marine Corps. See also Marine Corps (http://www.usmc.mil).

Navy

74. U.S. Naval Academy

http://www.nadn.navy.mil

Established in 1845, the Naval Academy is the undergraduate college that prepares young men and women to become professional officers in the Navy and Marine Corps. The Web site provides information about the academy.

75. U.S. Navy Opportunities

http://www.navy.com

The Navy is looking for people to join the fleet to take advantage of all the job opportunities the Navy has to offer. This recruitment Web site details information on job opportunities for high school and college graduates, including career opportunities for health care professionals. Find out how the Navy can help finance a college degree and the benefits of joining the Naval Reserve. See also Navy Online (http://www.ncts.navy.mil).

Careers in Construction

76. Construction Trades Resources

http://www.educationindex.com/construct/

A collection of annotated Internet resources is available for students desiring to know more about the construction industry. Links lead to information about heating and air conditioning, masonry, concrete, and building. Find out construction statistics from the U.S. Census Bureau as well as answers to frequently asked questions.

Careers in Environmental Sciences

77.   **Futures: Environmental Sciences**

http://www.futures-careers.org

The field of environmental science addresses some of the greatest challenges that humankind will face in the coming century. Professionals in this field will be using their math and science skills to save endangered animals, solve the problems of global warming, explore the oceans, and ensure a sustainable quality of life for Earth's population. Find out what five professionals in each of these areas of science have to say about their varied careers: meteorology, ocean exploration, renewable energy, and environmental science and technology. Requires RealPlayer for video and sound clips. Support for this site is provided by the National School to Work Office, a joint initiative of the U.S. Departments of Education and Labor.

Careers in the Hospitality Industry

78.   **Hospitality Net**

http://www.hospitalitynet.org

The global hospitality industry sponsors Hospitality Net, where students can discover the trends and facts about the hospitality industry. There is a virtual job exchange, which lists job opportunities, and a calendar of global hospitality events and conferences. Links are provided to the International Hotel Association and other hospitality-related information sources.

Careers in the Newspaper Industry

79.   **Careers in the Newspaper Industry**

http://www.nie.northcliffe.co.uk/careers/index.html

Students can learn about 18 different jobs in the newspaper industry, from advertising creation to promotions and transportation. Although this site reflects a job market in the United Kingdom, all students will benefit from reading the job descriptions and accompanying skills. For example, those contemplating a career as a newspaper photographer are advised to prepare a portfolio of work to present at an interview, and to understand that newspaper photographers must be flexible and prepared to work irregular hours—because news can happen any time, day or night.

Careers in Oceanography, Marine Science, and Marine Biology

80.   **Careers in Oceanography, Marine Science & Marine Biology**

http://scilib.ucsd.edu/sio/guide/career.html

Provides a career directory for those interested in careers in oceanography and marine science as well as marine biology, marine mammals, zoos, and aquariums.

Careers in Science and Math

81. Do Your Math

http://www.futures-careers.org/wantthisjob/index.html

Through video clips and slide shows, 12 people explain their diverse and interesting careers that use math and science. In these online interviews, listen to a recycling planner, veterinarian, solar engineer, skateboard designer, architect, wildlife biologist, musician, inventor, astronaut, and marketing specialist. Requires RealPlayer. Those connecting via modem can view a different version using slide shows. Support provided by the National School to Work Office, a joint initiative of the U.S. Departments of Education and Labor.

Careers in Sports

82. Online Sports Career Center

http://www.onlinesports.com/pages/CareerCenter.html

The Online Sports Career Center is a resource for sports-related career opportunities and a resume bank for potential employers. Current job openings, listed with descriptions and salaries, include gymnastics instructors, publications staff, sales and advertising for sports products, golf course positions, football camp counselors, and high school basketball coaches.

Lesson Plan

83. Women in Careers

http://quest.arc.nasa.gov/women/POW.html

Women in Careers is a Women's Issues and Career Research Unit written for social science or women's studies classes, grades 7–12. Students explore careers via the Internet and e-mail dialogs with working women. Students also use the Internet to explore current women's issues. This unit, developed by Jenny Otter, takes four to six weeks to complete. It meets the goals of the Women of NASA project (entry 726). One of these goals is to provide as role models women who have succeeded and thrive in a high-tech environment.

College Guidance

84. The College Guide

http://www.mycollegeguide.org/index.html

From the high school online magazine *FishNet*, this Web site contains pointers to college information, articles on the college admissions process, and a way to ask questions of an admissions expert. Information on finding money for college is given. Students can download either a Macintosh or a Windows version of the Common Application from the National Association of Secondary School Principals, the creators of the "Common App." Links are provided to colleges and universities so that you can order information directly. Colleges and universities are divided by region and alphabetically. Not all colleges and universities are represented.

85. Current College Rankings from *U.S. News & World Report*

http://www.usnews.com/usnews/edu/college/corank.htm

College rankings are taken from the current edition of America's Best Colleges, published annually by *U.S. News & World Report*. Ranking categories include national universities and national liberal arts colleges; regional colleges and universities and regional liberal arts colleges; and special undergraduate programs in engineering, business, and the performing and visual arts. Ranking methodology is given along with a list of "Best Value" institutions. Selected full-text articles about dealing with the high cost of higher education, finding quality honors programs, career planning, and advice from experts on the college search are available.

86. Peterson's Education Center

http://www.petersons.com

Peterson's Education Center provides one-stop access to educational resources and opportunities at every level. The home page has pointers to K-12 public schools, K-12 private schools, undergraduate colleges, graduate schools, testing, careers and jobs, summer programs for kids and teenagers, vocational-technical schools, and learning for fun and enrichment.

Financial Aid

87. FinAid!

http://www.finaid.org

There is no need to pay money to a scholarship search service when students and parents can search some of the best scholarship and fellowship databases for free on the World Wide Web. Fin-Aid: The Financial Aid Information Page provides a free, comprehensive, independent, and objective guide to student financial aid. Sponsored by the National Association of Student Financial Aid Administrators and maintained by Mark Kantrowitz (mkant@finaid.org), author of *The Prentice Hall Guide to Scholarships and Fellowships for Math and Science Students* (Prentice Hall, 1993).

Special Education

Adaptive Technologies

88. Adaptive Technologies

E-mail: **listserv@listserv.american.edu**
Instructions: On the first line of the body of the message, type:
subscribe ADAPT-L [your first name and last name]

89. EASI's K to 12 Education Technology Centre

http://www.rit.edu/~easi/ak12/k12.html

EASI's K to 12 Education Technology Centre is dedicated to providing information to educators, parents, and students about increasing access to science, technology, and math resources for K-12 students with disabilities. EASI (Equal Access to Software and Information) is a nonprofit organization affiliated with the American Association for Higher Education. Its mission is to help make information technologies more accessible to users with disabilities. A glossary of adaptive technology and special education terminology and two online handbooks of hardware and software products are available as guides toward understanding what is available for disabled students. Teachers will find information to assist them in using the computer as a tool for inclusion of students with disabilities. Links are provided to advocacy issues, government legislation and policy, journal articles, and other Internet resources related to special education and adaptive technology. The Webmaster's address is (rbanks2@discover-net.net). EASI's home page is located at (http://www.rit.edu/~easi).

Blindness and Deafness

90. Adaptive Technologies for the Blind

E-mail: **listserv@uafsysb.uark.edu**
Instructions: On the first line of the body of the message, type:
subscribe BLIND-L [your first name and last name]

91. Deaf-Blind Discussion List

E-mail: **listserv@tr.wou.edu**
Instructions: On the first line of the body of the message, type:
subscribe DEAFBLND [your first name and last name]

92. Deaf Education

E-mail: **listserv@lsv.uky.edu**
Instructions: On the first line of the body of the message, type:
subscribe EDUDEAF [your first name and last name]

Deaf Education is a practical discussion list for educators of deaf students.

93. DEAF-L

E-mail: **listserv@siu.edu**
Instructions: On the first line of the body of the message, type:
subscribe DEAF-L [your first name and last name]

How to Access the DEAF-L FAQs:
http://www.zak.co.il/deaf-info/old/index-abbrev.html

Talented and Gifted

94. Hoagies' Gifted Education Page

http://www.hoagiesgifted.org

Hoagies' Gifted Education Page is a comprehensive resource guide for education of gifted children. Information is divided into categories to help parents and teachers with resources for identifying and testing gifted children. Online articles and research studies address topics such as academic acceleration, home schooling, and young gifted children. Links are provided to reading lists, software products, books, journals, and magazines. Links are also provided to lesson plans and Internet resources of interest to kids and teens. The Web editor's address is (webmaster@hoagiesgifted.org).

95.   Talented and Gifted Discussion List

E-mail: **listserv@listserv.nodak.edu**
Instructions: On the first line of the body of the message, type:
subscribe TAG-L [your first name and last name]

Education Journals and Magazines

See also "Computer Science Journals and Magazines" (entries 275–282), "Electronic Periodicals for Students" (entries 574–579), "Magazines" (entries 1408–1413), and "Staying Current" (entries 1494–1508).

96.   *Creative Classroom Online*

http://www.creativeclassroom.org

Creative Classroom Online is a complement to *Creative Classroom* magazine in print format, and contains information of interest to K-8 teachers. Look for feature articles, technology articles, strategies for tough-to-teach topics, activities for integrated classroom projects, and book reviews. The Web site is updated bimonthly and includes information from past and present editions of *Creative Classroom*.

97.   *Education Week* on the Web

http://www.edweek.org

Provides a weekly electronic journal for persons interested in education reform, schools, and the policies that guide them. Information is comprehensive and informative. Each issue is browseable and searchable. Archives of past issues are searchable from 1981.

98.   *From Now On: The Educational Technology Journal*

http://www.fno.org

From Now On is a monthly technology newsletter published by Jamie McKenzie (mckenzie@fromnowon.org), Director of Libraries, Media, and Technology for the Bellingham Public Schools. Regularly covered topics include copyright, curriculum, grants, Internet use policies, libraries of the future, technology planning, staff development, Web site development, and networks and connectivity. An archive of articles from past issues is browseable by subject and is keyword-searchable.

99.   *Instructor*

http://teacher.scholastic.com/products/instructor.htm

Instructor magazine is aimed at elementary (K-6) teachers. The print format has been published for 100 years. The online version provides information about professional development opportunities, assessment tips, strategies for integrating the curriculum, ways to meet students' needs, and more. Full-text articles and a searchable database are available.

100. *Teacher Magazine*

http://www.teachermagazine.org

Teacher Magazine is a monthly online magazine featuring current events related to education and the classroom, regular columns, features, research, and books aimed at K-12 teachers. Each issue is browseable and searchable. An archive of past issues, including both *Teacher Magazine* and *Education Week* (entry 97), is keyword-searchable.

101. *Teachnet.Com*

http://www.teachnet.com

Teachnet.Com is more than a weekly newsletter. It is a K-12 teachers' Web site that publishes teacher contributions and maintains a mailing list. It provides information about a number of topics, from key pals and classroom management to classroom decor and humor. Of interest are the many lesson plans across the curriculum. Published by Lee Shiney Design in Wichita, Kansas. Contact Lee Shiney (staff@teachnet.com), editor, and Lajean Shiney at Lawrence Elementary School.

102. *The Times Educational Supplement*

http://www.tes.co.uk

For more than 80 years the *Times Educational Supplement* has been at the forefront of education journalism. Its news, reviews, and analysis of education in Britain and abroad are now available in this online edition. Registration is required, but access is free.

Education Discussion Groups

103.   Educators Network (Ednet)

E-mail: **listserv@lists.umass.edu**
Instructions: On the first line of the body of the message, type:
subscribe Ednet [your first name and last name]

Ednet is an independent, unmoderated discussion group that explores the educational potential of the Internet. The purposes of Ednet are to link educators with similar or overlapping interests; introduce students to current concerns and actual work in a number of fields; introduce students to local or nonlocal Internet sources of information; informally criticize or suggest ideas for projects, proposals, and articles; and provide a community in which ideas or questions are taken seriously in friendly opposition or eager collaboration.

104.   Independent School Educators Discussion List (ISED-L)

E-mail: **listserv@listserv.syr.edu**
Instructions: On the first line of the body of the message, type:
subscribe ISED-L [your first name and last name]

ISED-L provides an online forum for discussion of the needs and interests of the independent school community. ISED-L allows independent school faculty, staff, and administrators to share ideas, seek advice, establish new friendships, locate collaborators for online and offline projects, and post conference and other announcements. The ISED-L listserv archive can be accessed from January 1995 to the present.

How to Access the ISED-L Archive:
http://www.askeric.org/Virtual/Listserv_Archives/ISED-L.html

105. K-12 Administrators

E-mail: **listserv@listserv.syr.edu**
Instructions: On the first line of the body of the message, type:
subscribe K12ADMIN [your first name and last name]

K12ADMIN is an online discussion forum for K-12 educators interested in educational administration. The K12ADMIN listserv archive can be accessed from January 1995 to the present.

How to Access the K12ADMIN Archive:
http://www.askeric.org/Virtual/Listserv_Archives/K12ADMIN-List.html

106. Middle School Teachers Discussion List

E-mail: **listserv@vmd.cso.uiuc.edu**
Instructions: On the first line of the body of the message, type:
subscribe MIDDLE-L [your first name and last name]

Middle-L is an online discussion group for educators interested in middle school education and early adolescence (ages 10 to 14). It provides a place for sharing ideas, problems and solutions, and issues related to middle-level education. The Middle-L listserv archive can be accessed from January 1996 to the present.

How to Access the Middle-L Archive:
http://www.askeric.org/Virtual/Listserv_Archives/MIDDLE-L.html

The Arts: Visual Art, Dance, Music, and Theater

Students can virtually visit museums around the world, studying paintings, sculpture, and other artwork at close range. Sound files help with the study of music and musical compositions, particularly those connected to theater and movie soundtracks. Theater productions come alive in the multimedia environment on the World Wide Web.

More arts education resources are available on the Web now than in years past. The Metropolitan Museum of Art (entry 132) has focused on interactive activities and games to help students understand how art is created. The National Gallery of Art (entry 134) provides online teachers' guides to help with the study of some of the Gallery's online exhibitions. The Smithsonian Institution's National Museum of American Art (entry 136) provides online learning materials packets with links to graphical images of some of the museum's collection, to help teachers create exciting and innovative lessons. Why Is the Mona Lisa Smiling? (entry 128) uses art and the Internet to explore the mystery behind the Mona Lisa's smile and learn more about the artist Leonardo da Vinci.

The WWW Dance Library (entry 150) contains an extensive list of links to dance resources on the Internet. ARTSEDGE at the Kennedy Center provides lesson plans involving movement and dance for grades K-6 (entry 113).

Music educators have created a number of Web sites to share music education resources and teaching tips online, such as Music Teacher Resources (entry 163), K-12 Resources for Music Educators (entry 160), and Music Education Launch Site (entry 161). Of special note is A Guide to Copyright for Music Librarians (entry 172), which addresses copyright law and fair use in K-12 schools. Students can also learn more about classical composers, such as Johann Sebastian Bach (entry 167) and Wolfgang Amadeus Mozart (entry 169).

Drama teachers will want to refer to the Web page for the International Thespian Society (entry 183) and locate other schools with drama programs by looking at High School Theatre Programs (entry 200). For musical theater enthusiasts, two notable composer/playwrights now have home pages: Stephen Sondheim (entry 193) and Andrew Lloyd Webber (entry 192). Many musicals have their own home pages, such as Les Misérables (entry 194) and Miss Saigon (entry 195). Don't miss the puppets' activity page (entry 198) and an in-depth look at Kabuki, a traditional form of Japanese theater (entry 197).

National Standards

107.   Linking Art Standards to Internet Resources

http://www.mcrel.org/standards-benchmarks/standardslib/art.html

The Mid-continent Regional Educational Laboratory (McREL) Web site lists the National Art Standards and provides Internet links appropriate for use in implementing each content standard. Teachers can also link to McREL's collections of lesson plans and Connections+ lesson plans, activities, and curriculum resources, which are also specifically designated for use with the corresponding subject-area content standards for visual art, music, theater, and dance.

108.   National Standards for Arts Education

http://artsedge.kennedy-center.org/cs/design/standards/intro.html

What Every Young American Should Know and Be Able to Do in the Arts was written in 1994, to describe the benefits of an arts education for K-12 students and to outline what students should be able to do at various grade levels: K-4, 5–8, and 9–12. Standards address dance, music, theater, and visual arts.

109.   National Standards for Theatre Education

http://www.byu.edu/tma/arts-ed/

The content standards for theater education in grades K-4, 5–8, and 9–12 (at both the proficient level and advanced level) can be found at this site. Also given are suggestions for lessons in improvisation; suggestions for lesson plans; games and activities; a bibliography of teaching resources and professional reading; and a state-by-state list of requirements for theater teaching certification.

Professional Associations

110.   Association for the Advancement of Arts Education

http://www.aaae.org

The Association for the Advancement of Arts Education (AAAE) works in the Cincinnati, Ohio, area to ensure that the arts are an integral and equal element in the general education of all students in grades K-12, and fosters collaborative efforts between schools and professional arts organizations. Information on this Web site is of interest and relevance to all K-12 teachers of the arts. How do the arts contribute to education? A commissioned study reports its findings. Tap into the Lesson Plan Exchange for lesson plans on architecture, dance, drama, music, and the visual arts. The Theatre Education Literature Review section contains a list of 60 annotated literature sources on theater education (preK-12) and arts education in general. Links are provided to other arts and education sites on the Web. The Webmaster is Jim Ashton (info@aaae.org).

Visual Arts

See also the ArtLex dictionary (entry 1389) and Shakespeare Illustrated (entry 478).

General Interest

111. **@rt room doorway**

http://www.arts.ufl.edu/art/rt_room/@rtroom_home.html

Like art rooms in schools everywhere, this virtual art room offers opportunities to create, to discover, to imagine, to invent, to learn, and to make thoughts become things. After entering the @rt room doorway, students and teachers can choose from seven activity centers. @rt sparkers provides ideas for art projects; @rtrageous thinking introduces what it means to "think like an artist"; @rt gallery is an online exhibition area for student-produced artwork; @rt demos gives instructions on how to do and make things; @rttifacts contains historical facts and trivia about the world of art; @rt library has a bibliography of books written for kids about art and artists; and @rt links is a selected list of links to other art-related sites on the Internet. Created and maintained by Craig Roland (rolandc@grove.ufl.edu), professor, Department of Art, University of Florida (Gainesville, Florida).

112. **The Art Teacher Connection©**

http://www.inficad.com/~arted

The Art Teacher Connection© encourages innovation in art education through the use of technologies. Look for links to art resources on the Internet on how to use the World Wide Web, computer software, and other technology in the classroom, as well as links to lesson plans, Internet projects, and thematic units. Many of the lessons have student objectives that address the national standards. Teachers are encouraged to submit lesson plans for further sharing. Created and maintained by Bettie Lake (arted@primenet.com), an art teacher at Herrera Magnet School of the Arts in Phoenix, Arizona.

113. **ARTSEDGE**

From the Kennedy Center
http://artsedge.kennedy-center.org

Using technology to link the arts and education, ARTSEDGE helps artists, teachers, and students gain access to and share information, resources, and ideas that support the arts as a core subject area in the K-12 curriculum. This site includes links to NewsBreak, an online newsletter for arts education, and Web Spotlight, an annotated catalog of arts-related World Wide Web sites. Curriculum Studio contains innovative arts-based curriculum materials, programs, and strategies that support national education goals. Of special interest are the Student Research Pages, thematic units incorporating Internet resources. Some topics include Arts of Native Americans; Arts of Colonial America; Arts of the 1920s: The Jazz Age; Arts of Africa; Arts of China; and Arts of Japan. The Community Center maintains a catalog of listservs on the arts and education, and includes listservs sponsored by ARTSEDGE, K12ARTSED, and MUSIC-ED. ARTSEDGE was established and continues its development under a cooperative agreement between the Kennedy Center and the National Endowment for the Arts, with additional support from the U.S. Department of Education.

114.   ArtsEdNet

http://www.artsednet.getty.edu

ArtsEdNet provides support for K-12 art educators by facilitating the exchange of ideas and information and the sharing of lesson plans and ideas. Classroom Resources contains a variety of teaching and learning materials, including lesson plans appropriate for elementary, middle, and high school. Mona Lisa: What's Behind Her Smile? is designed to guide high school students on a study of contemporary art interpretation. Looking to the Sky for Color is written for elementary students studying color as revealed in the many skies painted by Vincent van Gogh. The Browsing Room contains a bibliography of full-text articles, essays, and book extracts that address approaches to arts education and the issue of arts education advocacy. Image Finder allows access to ArtsEdNet's virtual exhibition sorted by artist, title, and date. Copyright permission is granted to teachers and students for personal use. ArtsEdNet is sponsored by the J. Paul Getty Education Institute for the Arts.

115.   ArtSites on the Internet

http://artsnet.heinz.cmu.edu

The Carnegie Mellon Center for Arts Management and Technology provides a central access point to cultural resources on the Internet. Extensive listings of Web sites cover the visual, performing, media, and literary arts, as well as interdisciplinary arts.

116.   The Incredible Art Department

http://www.artswire.org/kenroar

Teachers looking for art lesson plans will probably skip directly to the Favorite Lessons section, where lesson plans have been posted and sorted into categories: early childhood, elementary, middle, and high school. An additional list of art lessons and games includes: The Alphabet of Art (learning about the elements of art); Art Q and A (art definitions and recipes for art media); Warner Bros. Animation Page; and Crafts for Little Hands. Art Jobs explores some of the careers available in art-related fields, such as Web design, illustration, animation, cartooning, and desktop publishing. Look for art in the news, especially crazy art news as reported in *News of the Weird*. Links are provided to art department home pages at elementary and secondary schools and colleges and universities. Created and maintained by former art teacher and principal at Paragon Elementary School (Paragon, Indiana), Ken Rohrer (kenroar@scican.net).

117.   World Wide Arts Resources

http://wwar.com

World Wide Arts Resources (WWAR) offers a comprehensive registry of visual arts information organized into 500 arts categories. Some categories are art museums, galleries and exhibitions, academic resources, and publications. Excellent organization provides easy access, and there is a searchable database.

118.   Ask Joan of Art

http://www.nmaa.si.edu/referencedesk/

Art information specialists at the National Museum of American Art use print and electronic reference resources to help answer questions about American visual art and artists. An online form is provided for users to fill out and submit electronically. Answers are sent by e-mail, usually within 14 days. A list of FAQs is provided.

Art and History

119.   Artistas Españoles

http://www.uncg.edu/rom/courses/klrauch/civ/art.htm

Provides a timeline of Spanish artists from the early Gothic period in the 13th century to the surrealism of the 20th century. More than 125 Spanish artists' biographies are available, with information about their artworks. Find out more about El Greco, Goya, Picasso, and Miró.

120.   World Art Treasures

http://sgwww.epfl.ch/BERGER/index.html

Take your students on visual and multimedia journeys into the past. With color slides from the Jacques-Edouard Berger Foundation, this site helps students better understand civilizations through art. In the program Pilgrimage to Abydos, students follow the pilgrimage undertaken 3,300 years ago by Seti I and his people to the temple of Abydos. Other programs include: Roman Portraits from Egypt, Sandro Botticelli, and The Enchanted Gardens of the Renaissance. Taken from Berger's lectures, the Botticelli program includes information such as Botticelli's biography and images of his more famous works, as well as a unique section that relates what was happening in 1470s Italy to events in France, England, Spain, the Ottoman Empire, China, and Japan. The Botticelli program is a great resource for art students and for students studying European history.

Clip Art

Check for copyright restrictions at each site. *See also* "Copyright Laws and Issues" (entries 1467–1470).

121.   Barry's Clip Art Server

http://www.barrysclipart.com

Barry's Clip Art Server provides an extensive collection of clip art gathered from all over the Internet.

122.   Clip Art Searcher/Gallery of Graphics

http://www.webplaces.com/search/

Search the Web for graphics and images using this clip art database and search engine.

Other Sources of Clip Art

Animated GIFs, Clip Art, and Backgrounds
http://www.desktopPublishing.com/cliplist.html

Billy Bear's Clip Art
http://www.billybear4kids.com/clipart/clipart.htm

Clip Art Center.com
http://www.clip-art-center.com

The Clip Art Connection
http://www.clipartconnection.com

Clip-Art.com
http://www.clip-art.com

Jim's Cool Icons
http://snaught.com/JimsCoolIcons/

Kid's Domain Icon Mania
http://www.kidsdomain.com/icon/index.html

The Mouse Pad
http://www.vikimouse.com

The Road Kill Cafe's Graphics
http://www.calweb.com/~vbooth/graphics.html

ASCII Art

123.   **ASCII Art Discussion**

Newsgroup: **rec.arts.ascii**

ASCII Art Discussion (rec.arts.ascii) is a moderated newsgroup devoted to the discussion and exchange of ASCII art. ASCII stands for American Standard Code for Information Interchange; it is the universal standard of communicating letters, numbers, and symbols on computer keyboards among computers. Before computers could display graphics, people used ASCII characters to create pictures and diagrams. The original, unmoderated version of the newsgroup is available at (alt.ascii-art).

124.   **Christopher Johnson's ASCII Art Collection**

http://www.chris.com/ascii_art_menu.html

ASCII art is organized in several categories, such as holidays, Star Trek graphics, unicorns, *The Lion King*, *The Little Mermaid*, *Winnie the Pooh*, bats, frogs, and signatures.

Other ASCII Art Collections

Allen Mullen's ASCII Home Page
http://users.inetw.net/~mullen/index.html

Joan Stark's ASCII Art Gallery
http://www.geocities.com/SoHo/7373/

StrawberryJAMM's ASCII Artwork Collection
http://www.jamm.com/asciiart/ascii.html

Paper Art

125. Origami Page

http://www.origami.vancouver.bc.ca

The Origami Page provides complete directions on how to fold paper to make various figures. Look for diagrams, step-by-step instructions, and pictures of completed origami figures. Directions are given for simple as well as more complex figures. *Origami* is a Japanese word that means "to fold paper." Directions are available for many origami creations, such as a jumping frog, crane, toad, seal, praying mantis (100 folds), butterfly, and a simple two-fold angelfish. To print some of the patterns, you will need a PostScript printer or PostScript decoding program. Created and maintained by Joseph Wu (josephwu@ultranet.ca).

Lesson Plans

See also "Lesson Plans Across the Curriculum" (entries 33–44).

126. Arts and Visual Arts Instructional Resources

http://artsedge.kennedy-center.org/db/cr/icr/visual.html

The Kennedy Center provides a collection of lesson plans, labeled as appropriate for elementary, middle, and high school grades. Lessons cover different media and techniques, including clay and ceramics, mask making, collage, architecture, tinwork, sculpture, drawing, and painting. Some lessons incorporate math, social studies, and science. Others are designed to promote literacy; study individual artists and their artwork; explore careers in art; or view artwork as unique creations of various peoples from different times, places, and cultures.

127. Eyes on Art

http://www.kn.pacbell.com/wired/art2/index.html

Eyes on Art makes educational use of the resources on the Internet by providing teachers and students with five progressive activities based on the national standards and research from art education literature. You Choose! is for beginning students of art. As students become more visually aware and involved, they learn to apply a visual arts vocabulary to specific works of art, in ArtSpeak 101. A more advanced activity is Double Visions, in which students use critical thinking skills to compare and contrast pairs of artworks. No Fear o' Eras allows students to critically look at three sample works from a major era in art history to discovery stylistic evolutions. Eras include Byzantine, Renaissance, Dutch School, Rococo, Impressionism, Cubism, and Abstract Expressionism. Your True View is a culminating activity that asks students to interpret and critique a contemporary artwork with little or no supporting information. The Eyes on Art Expert's Quiz should be taken when art students have completed all five art activities. A Teacher's Guide is provided. Developed by Tom March (tom@ozline.com).

128.   Why Is the Mona Lisa Smiling?

http://library.advanced.org/13681/data/davin2.shtml

Using art and the Internet, students are able to explore the mystery behind the Mona Lisa's smile and learn more about the artist Leonardo da Vinci. This project was created collaboratively by students at John F. Kennedy High School in Bronx, New York, and students in Borlange, Sweden; it was a semifinalist in the 1997 ThinkQuest competition (entry 53). Why Is the Mona Lisa Smiling? has been added to the Microsoft Encarta Online collection of lesson plans (entry 1344). By looking at a morphing online computer image of Mona Lisa, students are asked to critically think about a theory proposing that the image of Mona Lisa is actually that of da Vinci. Students can listen to original music composed by da Vinci while learning more about the man and his work. An interactive quiz and digital postcards promote student involvement. Links are provided to other related Internet resources. E-mail should be addressed to ThinkQuest Competition Head Coach and Computer Graphics Instructor, Steve Feld (sjfeld@erols.com). *See also* Exploring Leonardo (entry 878).

Museums and Exhibits

Museums

129.   Art Museums on the World Wide Web

http://www.comlab.ox.ac.uk/archive/other/museums.html

An excellent jumping-off point for explorations in art, this page provides links to both U.S. and world museums. The latter are listed alphabetically by country. Webmaster is Jonathan Bowen (Jonathan.Bowen@comlab.ox.ac.uk).

130.   The Egyptian Museum

http://www.tourism.egnet.net/attractions_detail.asp?code=6

The Egyptian Museum in Cairo, Egypt, houses a vast collection of artifacts and mummies from ancient tombs and palaces. Look for artifacts from the tomb of Tutankhamen, the mummy of King Ramses II, Book of the Dead of Maiherperi, a collar necklace worn by Neferoptah, and the canopic jars of Inpuhotep. Color thumbnail images can be enlarged for more detailed study.

131.   The Institute of Egyptian Art and Archaeology

http://www.memst.edu/egypt/main.html

The University of Memphis (Tennessee) Institute of Egyptian Art and Archaeology's Web site invites online visitors to find out more about the institute, view an exhibit of Egyptian artifacts, take a short tour of Egypt, and link to other selected Egypt sites on the Internet. There are more than 150 objects in the university's collection, spanning the centuries from 3,500 B.C. to A.D. 700. There are graphics of mummies, religious and funerary items, jewelry, and objects from everyday life. To date, only a few examples are online. These few are displayed via color graphics with descriptions and a brief history. Students can find information about a 4,000-year-old triangular loaf of bread and the mummy of Iret-iruw, with mask, pectoral, and coffin, from the Ptolemaic Period (323–30 B.C.).

The virtual tour of Egypt includes color pictures of modern Egypt and some of the pyramids. Each color graphic is accompanied by explanatory text. Maintained by Annette Webb Lane (awebb@cc.memphis.edu).

132. The Metropolitan Museum of Art, New York City

http://www.metmuseum.org

The Metropolitan Museum of Art's Web site provides online visitors with an overview of the collections on display in the museum's galleries. Students can use the Indexes area to browse the online collection either by timeline or by country. The Exhibition area summarizes both current and upcoming exhibitions. The Museum's Explore & Learn section (http://www.metmuseum.org/explore/index.asp) is excellent, offering a variety of educational experiences, information, and activities for teachers, students, visitors, and families. At the time of publication, the Explore a Work of Art section offered several interactive activities to help students look more closely at how art is created. Students can examine *Washington Crossing the Delaware* by Emanuel Gottlieb Leutze to look at the elements of perspective, light, color, form, motion, and proportion. In A Closer Look, students explore portraits by Ingres. Artists' lives and works are highlighted in Learn About an Artist. The Try an Activity area offers art games, museum hunts, and family guides to art. Exhibits, games, interactive activities, and family guides related to art in the Metropolitan Museum of Art's collections change often, so be sure to bookmark this site for frequent visits.

133. Museum of Modern Art, New York City

http://www.moma.org

Visit this site to find out more about the Museum of Modern Art (MoMA) in New York City. MoMA owns exceptional groups of work by van Gogh, Cézanne, Matisse, Picasso, Miró, Mondrian, Brancusi, and Pollock, to name just a few. Students can view Cézanne's *Bather* and van Gogh's *Starry Night*. The Education Resources area contains an Art Safari that visits four paintings, asking students to describe what is happening in each of the artworks. What's On Now highlights current exhibitions.

134. The National Gallery of Art, Washington, D.C.

http://www.nga.gov

The National Gallery of Art houses an impressive collection of paintings, sculpture, and graphic arts from the Middle Ages to the present. The collection can be searched by specific artist, title, or a combination of criteria. Online tours by either medium or artistic school are available, such as a tour of selected Mary Cassatt color prints. In-depth studies focus on artists and works of art, such as Edouard Manet's "The Railway" and John Singleton Copley's "Watson and the Shark." Online teachers' guides are available for some of the exhibitions. For example, the guide for *Picasso: The Early Years, 1892-1903* includes background information, discussion questions, suggested activities, and helpful in-text links to additional information.

The National Gallery of Art's Education Resource Program loans color slide programs, teaching packets, films, videocassettes, and videodisks to schools, libraries, community organizations, and individuals in the United States. (There is no charge for this service.) Programs are designed to meet national standards in visual arts. A catalog describing more than 150 teaching resources is available online, as is an order form to print out. Orders must be sent by U.S. mail, and it is recommended that orders be placed at least one month in advance.

135. Pushkin Museum of Fine Arts

http://www.global-one.ru/english/culture/pushkin/

The Pushkin Museum of Fine Arts, one of the major art collections in Russia, exhibits non-Russian works of art from ancient times to the present. Different areas of the collection are highlighted using thumbnail sketches; these graphics can be enlarged for closer study and appreciation.

136. The Smithsonian Institution's National Museum of American Art

http://www.nmaa.si.edu

More than 4,000 images are available for online viewing, and are accessible by subject browsing or searching by artist's name. The museum also contains images from Helios, an online photography center; and Renwick Gallery, a center for American crafts. Students can tour 16 online versions of exhibitions past and present; Elihu Vedder's original illustrations for *The Rubáiyát of Omar Khayyám*; Lost and Found: Edmonia Lewis's Cleopatra; Metropolitan Lives: The Ashcan Artists and Their New York; and American Photographs: The First Century. The Office of Educational Programs at the National Museum of American Art (NMAA) develops teacher guides, student activity packets, and other materials that complement the NMAA exhibitions. Learning materials currently available, with links to NMAA collection images, are "Art and Life of William H. Johnson: A Guide for Teachers"; "Mythology and the Art of Paul Manship"; and "Pueblo Indian Watercolors: Learning by Looking."

137. The Tokugawa Art Museum

http://www.cjn.or.jp/tokugawa/index.html

Located in Nagoya, Japan, the Tokugawa Art Museum houses art and heirloom objects from the Owari branch of the Tokugawa family, including objects from the first shogun, Ieyasu, and most of the extant sections of the 12th-century *Illustrated Tale of Genji*. The library preserves more than 3,000 written materials from the Edo period. Explanatory text accompanies color photographs of selected art objects in six exhibition rooms.

138. WebMuseum, Paris

http://metalab.unc.edu/wm/

The WebMuseum is an excellent site for learning more about art history and viewing hundreds of images of world-famous artworks. This Web site houses three major exhibitions of artwork: Paul Cézanne, Medieval Art, and the Famous Paintings Collection. The Paul Cézanne exhibition contains a biography of Cézanne, more than 100 images of his works, and information on Impressionism and Cubism. The Famous Paintings exhibition is divided into periods such as the Italian Renaissance (1420–1600) and the Baroque (1600–1790), and also into themes focusing on Pop Art, the Art of the Fantastic, and the Age of Machinery. Almost 200 artists are listed alphabetically in the Artist Index, and the list is growing as more information is added to this site. A glossary of painting styles is particularly helpful to art students who are studying Baroque art, Classicism, Impressionism, the Renaissance, Expressionism, Realism, Surrealism, or other major painting styles. The Medieval Art exhibition focuses on *Les Très Riches Heures*, the classic example of a medieval book of hours. Pictures in this exhibition are from the calendar section of one of France's great art treasures. Painted sometime between 1412 and 1416, these pages illustrate the beautiful art of illuminated manuscripts.

The WebMuseum was begun as one Web site in 1994 by Nicholas Piochas, a computer science teacher at the École Polytechnique, École Nationale Supérieure des Télécommunications, Paris, who was concerned that profit-seeking companies might gain monopolistic control over some of the world's most treasured artworks. This year, more than 30 Web servers in 21-plus countries mirror the information on the WebMuseum site.

Exhibits

See also prehistoric art at the Chauvet Cave, France (entry 1241).

139. **Age of Enlightenment in the Paintings of France's National Museums**

http://mistral.culture.fr/files/imaginary_exhibition.html

The Age of Enlightenment art exhibit includes the works of 100 selected artists for a panorama of 18th-century French painting.

140. **Treasures of the Czars Museum Tour**

http://www2.sptimes.com/Treasures/

The Treasures of the Czars exhibit first appeared at the Florida International Museum in St. Petersburg, Florida. This site gives online visitors a taste of that exhibit, which included more than 250 artifacts from 300 years of Russian history. A timeline begins with the Romanov Dynasty in 1613 and ends with the Bolshevik Revolution in 1917.

Photography

141. **California Museum of Photography**

http://www.cmp.ucr.edu

The California Museum of Photography, founded in 1973, houses the world's largest body of stereoscopic prints and negatives. It also includes fine art prints and collections of historical photographs as well as cameras and camera equipment. Online exhibitions include a sampler of California photographs, ca. 1865–1950, that reflect California history; Nancy Buchanan's interactive artwork, "Development"; and a collection on Theodore Roosevelt, the "First Media President." Exhibitions are grouped by theme, with emphasis on the usefulness of the images for class projects in K-12 schools. In addition, information about current exhibits at the museum is given. The museum is sponsored by the College of Humanities and Social Sciences at the University of California, Riverside.

142. **Masters of Photography**

http://www.masters-of-photography.com/index.html

This growing database of photographers and their works has more than 40 names to choose from. There is a summary for each photographer, articles, samples of photographs, and a bibliography of online and print resources for further study. The Webmaster's address is (mastersofphotography@webgalleries.com).

143. **Wilson A. Bentley, Photographer of Snow Crystals**
http://www.snowflakebentley.com

"Snowflake" Bentley (1865–1931) was a farmer in Jericho, Vermont, who took pictures (photomicrographs) of snow crystals for most of his adult life. On view are 12 of the more than 5,000 images Bentley produced. Also available is a short bibliography of journal articles, most with links to full text, for further study and information. Sponsored by the Jericho Historical Society (info@snowflakebentley.com).

Artists

Edouard Manet (1832–1883)

144. **The Railway by Edouard Manet**
http://www.nga.gov/collection/railwel.htm

This Web feature is an in-depth study, from the National Gallery of Art, of Edouard Manet's painting, *The Railway* (1872–1873). Information is provided about the artist, who depicted life in Paris during the late 19th century, as well as the context of the painting in relation to the city of Paris, which was changing and rapidly growing during this period. It discusses Manet's influence on other artists and writers of the era and the artistic strategies of Impressionism and the French Impressionist artists. Best viewed with 4.05 or higher browsers with JavaScript.

Pablo Picasso (1882–1973)

145. **On-Line Picasso Project**
http://www.tamu.edu/mocl/picasso/

Here students can learn about Picasso the man, through biographical references to events in his lifetime. The digital archive contains scanned images of Picasso's work suitable for teaching and research. Links are provided to critical analyses of Picasso's work, museums holding copies of his works, and a comprehensive bibliography of Picasso on the Web. Officially recognized by the Pablo Ruiz Picasso Foundation, the Web curator is Dr. Enrique Mallen (emallen@aca.tamu.edu) at Texas A&M University.

Discussion Groups

146. **Discussion of Art Education Issues**
E-mail: **listserv@listserv.arizona.edu**
Instructions: On the first line of the body of the message, type:
subscribe UAARTED [your first name and last name]

147. **Discussion of K-12 Art Curriculum**
Newsgroup: **k12.ed.art**

Art teachers use this newsgroup to discuss K-12 art curricula.

148. **Pottery and Ceramic Arts Discussion Group**

E-mail: **listserv@lsv.uky.edu**

Instructions: On the first line of the body of the message, type:
subscribe CLAYART [your first name and last name]

Dance

General Interest

149. **Dance Directory**

http://www.SapphireSwan.com/dance/

The Sapphire Swan Dance Directory is a guide to dance resources available on the Web. It lists almost 50 types of dance styles, including ballet, jazz, modern dance, clogging, Greek, Irish, Latin, and country western. For each dance style, there is a pointer to a collection of Internet resources related to that dance style. Ballet leads to a collection of more than 25 links to resources on the history of ballet, ballet terms, the Bolshoi Theatre, the New York City Ballet, and dancewear and dance products. The Webmaster's address is (webmaster@SapphireSwan.com).

150. **WWW Dance Library**

http://www.artswire.org/dance/dance.html

The WWW Dance Library provides a comprehensive collection of dance-related information available on the Internet. Find out the different types of dance, including ballet, ballroom, folk, tap, Scottish, swing, tango, and Western square dancing. This meta-list of resources provides alphabetized lists of dance pages, dance resources, and dance schools, including college and university dance programs.

Ballet

151. **Ballet and Dance Home Page**

http://balletdance.about.com/arts/balletdance/

About.com's site for ballet and dance provides collections of annotated Internet resources in two main categories: NetLinks (topics) and In The Spotlight (current-interest feature articles and news). Look for biographies about dancers, such as Mikhail Baryshnikov, Isadora Duncan, and Rudolf Nureyev. Students will be able to locate information on dance companies, books, periodicals, costumes, shows, summer programs, and music. Maintained by Cheryl Cowan (balletdance.guide@about.com), a dance professional and teacher living in Switzerland.

152. **Ballet Behind the Scenes**

http://www.national.ballet.ca/scenes.html

The National Ballet of Canada provides background information on the topic of ballet, including ballet terms and what ballet is. The first ballet that told a story through dance was *Le Ballet Comique de la Reine*, which was presented at the French court in 1581. Look for this fact and others in the History of Ballet section. Those interested in ballet as a career can find out more about training for ballet. Topics for further study include ballerinas, male dancers, dance footwear, stage scenery, costuming, and music. This site provides a good look behind the scenes at ballet as an art as well as ballet as a career.

153.   **Online Ballet Dictionary**

http://www.abt.org/dictionary/index.html

What is an *arabesque*, a *pas de deux*, or a *pas jeté*? The American Ballet Theatre's new Online Ballet Dictionary provides definitions and QuickTime video clips to explain 170 terms from the *Technical Manual and Dictionary of Classical Ballet* by Gail Grant (Dover, 1982). Dancers from the American Ballet demonstrate how different ballet movements are performed. Note: QuickTime plug-in is required to view the video clips. The Webmaster's address is (comments@abt.org).

Country-and-Western

154.   **Let's Dance!**

http://www.interlog.com/~rfielder/CWLinks.html

R step, L step, R touch front, get those hips moving! These are some of the instructions for the steps to After Midnight, a country line dance choreographed by Judy MacDonald in Ontario, Canada. This site provides step instructions to Country-and-Western dances, as well as a wide variety of information of interest to country music and dance fans. There are links to Country-and-Western sites, the Billboard Top Country Chart, Country-and-Western clip art sites, and mailing lists for dance or music enthusiasts. So what are you waiting for? Let's Dance! Created and maintained by Robert Fielder (rfielder@interlog.com).

155.   **Western Square Dancing**

http://www.dosado.com

Square dancing in the United States traces its roots back to the New England colonies, where it evolved from European folk dances. As the population spread westward, so did the dancers. Early pioneers held dances as a way to socialize with neighbors. All that was needed was a wooden floor, some music, and a caller. Today, Western square dancing is still popular as a way to socialize (and exercise). If you don't know the difference between an "allemande left" and a "right and left grand," refer to the Western Square Dancing caller lists and dance terminology pages. Additionally, look for information about Western square dancing clubs, schools, software, history, clothing, and, of course, dance steps. Information about regional contacts and international mailing lists is also provided so that you can find others in your area with whom you can DoSaDo. This site is maintained by Robert French (rfrench@dosado.com).

Jazz

156.   **Jazz Dance Homepage**

http://www.jazzart.org

Learn more about the history of American jazz dance and jazz dancers such as Jack Cole and Matt Mattox. The history of jazz dance is explored in an online version of *Image of Perfection: The Freestyle Dance of Matt Mattox*, by Robert Boross (New York University, 1994). Discover that the beginnings of American jazz can be traced to early American plantation dancing and African dances imported to America via the slave trade. The influence of American jazz is illustrated in musicals like *Damn Yankees* (1955) and *The Pajama Game* (1954), both choreographed by Bob Fosse; and *West Side Story* (1957), choreographed by Jerome Robbins, who is credited with being one of the first to combine movements from jazz dance with concepts from ballet. Links are provided to jazz companies and jazz schools. Also available are collections of "Jazz Dance" columns from June 1996 to July 1998, originally published in *Dancer*, a monthly newspaper. Created and maintained by Bob Boross (bob@jazzart.org), artist in residence, Department of Theatre and Dance, Western Kentucky University (Bowling Green, Kentucky).

Tap

157. The Tap Dance Page

http://www.tapdance.org

What is tap dancing? Imagine the floor as a drum and a dancer's feet as the drumsticks. To make this image more vivid, click on the audio files in the Sights and Sounds of Tap to listen to Ira Berstein, a well-known tap dancer who refers to his art as "Ten Toe Percussion." To find out more about tap dancing, visit The Tap Dance Page's reference section, which contains lists of films and videos that include tap dancing, books and other sources about the history of tap dancing, and information about Who's Who in Tap. An online glossary of tap terminology explains brushes, steps with weight changes, taps without weight changes, and combination moves. Look for links to information about the International Tap Dance Association (ITA); dates and locations of current and forthcoming jazz tours, festivals, and jams; places to tap dance; and how to join Tap-Jazz, an online discussion group. The Tap Dance Page provides a wide variety of information for both amateur and professional dancers, as well as individuals interested in learning more about the art and history of tap dancing. Created and maintained by Paul Corr; questions or comments can be sent to (http://www.tapdance.org/tap/ita/author.htm#FEEDBK).

Lesson Plans and Activities

158. Arts and Dance Curriculum Resources

http://artsedge.kennedy-center.org/db/cr/icr/dance.html

ARTSEDGE provides a collection of online curricula for teachers. Integrated Dance Curriculum is a collection of lesson plans appropriate for K-6. Each lesson integrates dance with at least one other curricular area, including language arts, math, music, science, and social studies. Other lessons include integrating movement with the study of the human anatomy and developing an understanding of dance within the context of the story of Hansel and Gretel. One lesson demonstrates how high school students can explore the structures of atoms, molecules, and chemical reactions through movement and exercise involving the kinesphere. Mirroring is described as a calming activity, helping students "refocus the classroom energy." Teachers are asked to submit their own examples of dance curriculum to add to this online collection. The Web editor can be reached at (editor@artsedge.kennedy-center.org).

Music

See also Sounds Like Science lesson plans in Gender Equity Science Lesson Plans (entry 677).

Professional Associations

159.   Music Educator National Conference (MENC)

http://www.menc.org

The Music Educator National Conference (MENC) is a national professional association of music educators dedicated to providing a balanced and sequential music education for K-12 students. This site provides information about membership, music careers, job openings, classroom resources, and publications. Teacher guides and programs are available, such as "In Harmony with Education," an interdisciplinary curriculum for music, science, and math at the middle level.

General Interest

160.   K-12 Resources for Music Educators

http://www.isd77.k12.mn.us/resources/staffpages/shirk/k12.music.html

Categories include compositions by students; sites for band teachers, orchestra teachers, vocal and choral teachers, and classroom music teachers; and general sites of interest to all music educators. Links lead to a broad range of resources, from biographies and works of great composers to lyrics to music of the Beatles. Created and regularly updated by Cynthia Shirk (cshirk1@dakota.isd77.k12.mn.us), Independent School District Number 77, Mankato, Minnesota.

161.   Music Education Launch Site

http://www.talentz.com/MusicEducation/index.mv

Music educators looking for lesson plans will find a gold mine at this site. Don't miss Mr. Note, an animated lesson unit on musical notation. Links are provided to Allegro, a music education search site. This database of music-related resources is keyword-searchable and browseable. Links lead to a comprehensive collection of other Internet resources of interest to music educators. The creator and Webmaster is Jeff Brenan (talents@snoopy.bunt.com).

162.   Music on the Internet

http://toltec.lib.utk.edu/~music/net.html

Music on the Internet is a guide to finding music information online, created and maintained by the Music Library at the University of Tennessee at Knoxville, Tennessee. This comprehensive collection of online resources is easily accessible through topics such as Classical Music (including history, theory, research, and performers); Popular Genres and Jazz; Downloadable Software, Scores, and Pictures; and Performing (including instruments, ensembles, vocal, and conducting). The Web site is maintained by Michelle H. Branne (musiclib@utk.edu).

163. Music Teacher Resources

http://home.earthlink.net/~bluesman1/teacher.html

A music educator shares lessons and techniques from a 20-year career. Some of the categories are: music games; Kodaly Method; Lorna Zemke; instruments; dance and movement; Tom Chapin interview; jazz greats; Mozart; and the blues.

164. MuSICA

http://www.musica.uci.edu/index.html

MuSICA is a comprehensive compilation of citations and abstracts of scientific and related publications on music, including education, child development, psychology, brain, clinical medicine, and therapy. Includes links to the current and previous issues of *MuSICA Research Notes*, a newsletter that provides reports and critical analysis of research on music and behavior, including education, child development, psychology, cognitive sciences, neuroscience, clinical medicine, music therapy, and allied fields. Dr. Norman M. Weinberger (nmweinbe@uci.edu) of the University of California, Irvine, California, is the director of MuSICA. E-mail should be addressed to (mbic@mila.ps.uci.edu).

165. MusicNet: The Online Guide to Music Education

http://library.thinkquest.org/3306/

MusicNet was the winner of the first-place award in the Arts and Literature category of the 1996 ThinkQuest Internet competition. It features an interactive encyclopedia, tips from inside the music profession, and contests and games. MusicNet was created by three high school students—Ben Concepcion, Don Fitz-Roy, and Dana Seibel—who believe that music education plays an important role in school systems throughout the United States and around the world.

166. The New York Philharmonic Kidzone!

http://www.nyphilkids.org

Students can explore the musicians' lounge, composers' gallery, instrument storage room, instrument laboratory, conductor/soloist dressing rooms, newsstand, and composer's workshop of this New York Philharmonic Orchestra Web site especially for kids. In the composers' gallery, images and brief biographies of composers can be accessed alphabetically, by nationality, by musical style, or by time period. A sample of each composer's work can be played using a baton mouse pointer. Instruments for the orchestra are stored in the storage room and grouped by musical families, such as woodwinds, strings, brass, and percussion. Storage lockers can be opened to find out more about specific instruments and hear their sounds. In the dressing rooms, brief biographies are given for famous conductors and soloists, and many creative hands-on musical activities are suggested in the instrument laboratory. The Composer's Workshop is a place to explore different ways to create and play with music.

Composers

Classical Composers

Johann Sebastian Bach (1685–1750)

167.   **J. S. Bach**

http://www.jsbach.org

Students can learn more about Johann Sebastian Bach's life and musical works by reading a well-researched biography accompanied by many photographs, listening to his music, and studying a biographical timeline. Bach's complete works can be accessed online by category, key, title, or year. Links are provided to the Bach online discussion group and other Internet resources, such as a classical MIDI archive containing all of Bach's major instrumental works. This site was created and is maintained by Jan Hanford (jan@tile.net) and Jan Koster (koster@let.rug.nl).

Ludwig van Beethoven (1770–1827)

168.   **Ludwig van Beethoven**

http://www.enteract.com/~rjackson/LVBMainPage.htm

A chronology of Beethoven's life is provided, along with a complete listing of his works, images of portraits, a list of his contemporaries, and samples of his handwriting. Sound files of selected symphonies, piano concertos, violin sonatas, string quartets, and masses are available and require RealAudio. Created by Randy Jackson (ixlandia@email.com).

Wolfgang Amadeus Mozart (1756–1791)

169.   **The Mozart Experience**

http://www.geocities.com/Vienna/Strasse/2914/

Learn more about Mozart by reading his biography with in-text links to additional information. Students will enjoy looking at images in the Picture Gallery and linking to information about *Amadeus*, the movie. An organized collection of Mozart's music is available online in QuickTime MIDI files. Additional notes are provided for some works such as the *Requiem* and the *Mass in C minor*. Links are also provided to other composers, including Beethoven, Chopin, Schubert, and Tchaikovsky. Created and maintained by John Moreno (wolfiemozart@geocities.com).

Modern Composers

George Gershwin (1898–1937)

170.   **Celebrate 100 Years of Gershwin!**

http://welcome.to/penumbra1

"The melody lingers on" with this tribute to 100 years of George Gershwin's music. Biographical information includes photographs, anecdotes, and quotes. A complete chronology of Gershwin's works is available, along with MIDI sound files of his music.

Cole Porter (1891–1964)

171. Cole Wide Web: The Cole Porter Resource Site

http://www.coleporter.org

Adam's Rib (1949), *Anything Goes* (1936), *Don't Fence Me In* (1945); *The Gay Divorcee* (1934), *Kiss Me Kate* (1953), *Eye for an Eye* (1996), *Indiana Jones and the Temple of Doom* (1984), and *Jumanji* (1995): What do all these movies have in common? They all include Cole Porter songs. Porter is known for his wit and playful style in lyrics and music that bursts with energy, style, and an appreciation for subtlety. This site has biographical information and photographs, a bibliography of books, and information on movies, lyrics, sheet music, stage performances, and current CDs. Created and maintained by J. Christopher Bell (cole@coleporter.org).

Copyright

See also "Copyright Laws and Issues" (entries 1467–1470).

172. A Guide to Copyright for Music Librarians

http://www.musiclibraryassoc.org/Copyright/copyhome.htm

Sponsored by the Legislation Committee of the Music Library Association, this site provides information about current issues in copyright that affect students, educators, and musicians. Links are provided to copyright guidelines adopted by professional organizations; one important set of guidelines is the Music Library Association's Statement on the Copyright Law and Fair Use in Music. A general FAQ section and a FAQ on preservation are especially helpful. Webmaster is David Gilbert (dgilbert@wellesley.edu).

Folk Music

173. Contemplations from the Marianas Trench: Music and Deep Thoughts

http://www.contemplator.com

Provides lyrics and MIDI files for folk music of England, Scotland, Ireland, Wales, and America. Look for popular songs in American history, such as *Blow, Ye Winds, Blow; Greensleeves;* and *Yankee Doodle*, with lyrics, music, and background information. From Songs of the Sea, students can listen to *Blow the Man Down* and find out more about sailing ships in the early 1800s. Gives information about Turlough O'Carolan (1670–1738), an Irish harper who was a gifted composer and poet. There is a folk music microencyclopedia for the Web site and a link to *A Folkie's Dictionary*. This Web site is searchable. Created and maintained by Lesley Nelson (lesley@contemplator.com).

174. Digital Tradition Folk Song Database

http://www.mudcat.org/threads.cfm

Look for the DigiTrad Lyrics Search boxes. Browse this list of more than 6,500 songs by title or tune, or search using keywords. (A list of keywords is provided.) You can also search by browsing through an alphabetized listing of tune titles. The lyrics for each tune are available, and the music may be downloaded. This author is amazed at the clarity of the digitized sound; she downloaded *Bill Bailey* and is still humming. Music is in MIDI (musical instrument digital interface) file format (.mid), and additional software is needed on some browsers to download the music.

Jazz Music

See also The Great Gatsby (entry 1177), Jazz Dance Homepage (entry 156), F. Scott Fitzgerald Centenary Home Page (entry 446), and Poetry and Prose of the Harlem Renaissance (entry 556).

175. Duke Ellington: A Celebration

http://www.dellington.org/scrapbk/scrap00.html

Click on the scrapbook to begin turning the pages on a lifetime of memories of one of the greatest jazz musicians and composers: Duke Ellington (1899–1974). Follow Ellington's career as a professional musician through a collection of photographs and text. This Web site is part of *Duke Ellington: Celebrating 100 Years of the Man and His Music*, published by the National Museum of American History, the Music Educators National Conference, and the Kennedy Center's ARTSEDGE.

176. The Red Hot Jazz Archive

http://www.redhotjazz.com

Find out more about red-hot musicians such as Louis Armstrong, Duke Ellington, Jelly Roll Morton, and Fats Waller, and the music they played—jazz. Created around 1895 in New Orleans, jazz combined elements of ragtime, blues, and marching-band music with a new variation, improvisation. This Web site provides a history of jazz before 1930, with information about musicians and bands (including sound files of their music). Links are available to some of the jazz films produced in the late 1920s and early 1930s. (To view these movie clips, the VivoActive Player plug-in is required.)

Lesson Plans and Activities

177. Arts and Music Instructional Resources

http://artsedge.kennedy-center.org/db/cr/icr/music.html

The Kennedy Center provides a collection of music lesson plans and activities. Lessons are marked as appropriate for various grades. Some lessons cover topics such as medieval music, the history of jazz, music in American culture, the study of composers, and the relationship between music and mathematics.

178. The Charlie Horse Music Pizza

http://www.menc.org/guides/charguid/charopen.html

Provides teaching activities for younger children to accompany the Shari Lewis PBS television show, *The Charlie Horse Music Pizza*. Gives links to activities such as exploring instruments, learning more about singing, and improvising. A teacher's guide is available, as is an online matching game, Name the Instrument!

Musical Instruments

179. The Piano Education Page
http://www.unm.edu/~loritaf/pnoedmn.html

A must for anyone interested in piano music, the Piano Education Page offers more than 250 pages of information for teachers, students, parents of students, and fans of the piano all, of it updated biweekly. The site is bilingual (English and Spanish). Some of the categories of information are Learning to Play the Piano (what to expect from a piano teacher, student etiquette during piano lessons, and how to purchase a piano); Just for Kids; Music and Sounds; a competition calendar; and an interview each month with a different artist/educator. Created and maintained by the West Mesa Music Teachers Association, a nonprofit professional association of teachers, parents, and students in Albuquerque, New Mexico.

Rock and Roll Music

180. Rock and Roll Hall of Fame and Museum
http://www.rockhall.com

Eddie the Elevator Man will take you on a virtual tour of the Rock and Roll Hall of Fame and Museum (actually located in Cleveland, Ohio). While you are there, check out a list of 500 songs thought to have shaped and defined rock and roll over the years. The list is alphabetically sorted by artist. Selected links provide additional biographical information about rock and roll songwriters, artists, and performers; most include sound files (wave, .au, or Real Audio). Today in Rock and Roll History features top hit(s), awards, and birthdays of rock and roll artists for the day's date. There are interesting Curator FAQs, and the Multimedia room in The House That Rock Built features sound, video, and pictures.

Discussion Groups

181. Discussion of All Forms and Aspects of Music
E-mail: listserv@listserv.american.edu
Instructions: On the first line of the body of the message, type:
subscribe ALLMUSIC [your first name and last name]

182. Discussion of Music and Performing Arts
Newsgroup: k12.ed.music

Teachers discuss music and performing arts curricula in K-12 education.

Theater

See also Shakespeare and the Globe Theatre, London (entry 477).

Professional Associations

183.   **Educational Theatre Association/International Thespian Society**
http://www.etassoc.org

The Educational Theatre Association, a nonprofit service organization founded in 1929, promotes and strengthens theater arts programs (including film, television, and other related electronic media) in education. The International Thespian Society, a "wing" of the association, is a student honor society organized into troupes at middle and high schools around the world. International Thespian Society troupes are each headed by an adult educator who must be a member of the Educational Theatre Association. This site offers information about membership, conventions, publications, and the yearly International Thespian Festival at the University of Nebraska in Lincoln, Nebraska.

General Interest

See also The History of Costume (entry 935).

184.   **The Costume Page**
http://members.aol.com/nebula5/costume.html

The Costume Page provides a complete wardrobe of costuming resources for those interested in costumes (theatrical, historical, ethnic, and folk), fashion, textile art, and costume history. Trick-or-treaters, theater professionals, and costume makers will all find interesting and rich information on a broad range of topics, from ideas on how to make a truly creative Halloween costume to hundreds of online images from costume exhibits and museums from around the world (including a picture of a pair of bear-fur shoes worn by a Japanese samurai). With more than 2,000 links to both primary and secondary sources, including references to both print and nonprint materials, The Costume Page is an extremely comprehensive site covering the history, materials, and techniques involved in the creation of a wide range of clothing and costume designs. This site was created and is maintained by Julie Zetterberg, a nationally known, award-winning costumer.

185.   **Theatre and Drama Resources from the WWW Virtual Library**
http://vl-theatre.com

A broad range of resources for professional, academic, and recreational use can be located at this site. Full-text plays appear in English, French, German, Greek, Italian, and Spanish; all are searchable by author and title. Maintained by Barry Russell (barry@sol.brookes.ac.uk).

186.   **Women in Theatre**
http://www.geocities.com/Broadway/Alley/5379/

Featuring playwrights, actresses, directors, managers, and producers from both the past and the present, this site is dedicated to women who have devoted their lives to theater. Find out more about Hallie Flanagan, who founded the Vassar College Experimental Theatre in 1925, and who headed the Federal Theatre Project in the 1930s; or investigate Megan Terry, an internationally renowned playwright and author of more than 60 published plays and musicals, who has been called the "Mother of American Feminist Drama." This site also includes valuable links to women's theater groups and an excellent bibliography of print resources for further research on the topic of Women in Theatre. The Webmaster's address is (sayruh@wwisp.com).

Awards

187.   Tony Awards Online

http://www.on-broadway.com/tony.asp

More than a listing of the Tony Award winners, this site features news, interviews, and a gallery of pictures and information about Tony winners from 1947 (the first year that Tonys were awarded) to the present. What's Playing provides information on productions currently playing on Broadway and across the United States. Look for many feature articles on all aspects of drama, from stagecraft to personalities, the current season, and Broadway life.

Theater and Musical Theater

188.   On Broadway WWW Information Page

http://www.on-broadway.com

These pages provide information on Broadway plays and musicals, both past and present. Find out about off-Broadway and off-off-Broadway productions as well. Summaries of the seasons provide links to reviews, awards, recordings (sound files), and other Web pages related to specific Broadway productions. There is also a list of theater-related Web sites. Maintained by Joe Geigel (jogle1@rpa.net).

189.   *Playbill On-Line*

http://www1.playbill.com/playbill/

Playbill provides information about Broadway, off-Broadway, and London theater, as well as jobs, books, news, recordings, and features. Links are provided to amateur, scholastic, and professional groups; services; and resources. Follow the link to Theatre Central to find information about specific theater-related pages.

London Theater

190.   A Guide to London Theatre

http://www.londontheatre.co.uk

This site provides information about various London theaters, including their seating plans and addresses. A news section contains the "latest news and rumours." Current plays are reviewed, and there is a small archive of reviews of past plays. Schedules of West End shows are given, as is a list of what's playing at other London theaters, including the Royal National Theatre and the Barbican. This frequently updated site is maintained by Darren Dalglish (dalglish@londontheatre.co.uk).

191. **The World of London Theatre, 1160-1800**

http://web.nwe.ufl.edu/~craddock/lonthe1.html

Covering almost 700 years of London and British theater, this site contains a chronology with year-by-year information about theatrical developments; a map of London indicating important sites; an annotated bibliography; a collection of pictures; and brief biographies of the people connected with British theater during the time period covered. This site is a work in progress, produced collaboratively by students in Patricia Craddock's LIT 3041 course at the University of Florida.

Playwrights and Productions

Playwrights

192. **Andrew Lloyd Webber Online**

http://www.westegg.com/unmaintained/alw/

Use this site to find a list of Webber's works online, as well as lists of actors, actresses, and lyricists involved in Webber productions. Find out where Webber's shows are playing and other miscellaneous information. Links lead to biographical information and other resources about Webber. Maintained by Steven Morgan Friedman (morgan@english.upenn.edu), a 1998 graduate of the University of Pennsylvania. See also the official site at (http://www.reallyuseful.com/home/index.html).

193. **Stephen Sondheim Stage**

http://www.sondheim.com

Stephen Sondheim Stage features an expanding database of titles, synopses, essays, musical references, libretti, and other information related to award-winning composer/playwright Stephen Sondheim. Students, educators, theater professionals, writers, and others can conduct in-depth research on biographical data, musical themes, and individual works. Created and maintained by Mark Bakalor of hijinks design (mark@sondheim.com), who aims to make this site the premiere online source of information about the man and his work.

Productions

194. ***Les Misérables* Home Page**

http://lesmis.pegasusnet.com

Providing more than stage production information about the musical, this comprehensive site hosts multimedia information. Information is available on the novel and its author, Victor Hugo (1802–1885), including a chronology of his life and times. A Study Guide invites students to look at the universal themes in *Les Misérables* as compared to other works such as *Hamlet, The Red Badge of Courage,* and *The Scarlet Letter,* and to current events. Through suggested activities and research questions, students are asked to investigate issues of poverty, crime and punishment, prejudice, civil rights, and the political and historical climate in France and other countries from the time of the French Revolution (1789–1799) until the student insurrection in 1832, described in *Les Misérables.* The Web site manager is Nicole Hudson (nhudson@wasserworld.com).

195. **_Miss Saigon_ Home Page**

http://www.clark.net/pub/rsjdfg/

This colorful and well-designed site is excellent for locating extensive information about the musical _Miss Saigon_, including performers, lyrics, various productions, and ticket information. The Musical in Pictures offers many online images of the stage production, while video and audio clips make this a multimedia experience. Links lead to other Web pages related to _Miss Saigon_ and to other musicals. Maintained by Ron San Juan (rsjdfg@clark.net).

196. **_Phantom of the Opera_ Home Page**

http://www.thephantomoftheopera.com

The official Web site for _The Phantom of the Opera_ features information about the musical, including a story summary and history. The Sights and Sounds section contains photographs organized by actor, character, scene, and location; video clips (RealVideo); and short musical selections (RealAudio). There is also a section on the Paris Opera House. Find out more about Gaston Leroux, author of the novel _The Phantom of the Opera_. A helpful study Guide is included.

Kabuki Theater

197. **Kabuki Theatre for Everyone**

http://www.fix.co.jp/kabuki/kabuki.html

Kabuki is a traditional form of Japanese theater founded early in the 17th century. All characters, both male and female, are played by male actors. Videos of recent productions and the sounds of the instruments used in Kabuki are available. A video demonstrates how an _onnagata_, a male actor specializing in female roles, transforms himself into a beautiful woman. A history of Kabuki is given, along with links to other traditional Japanese theater Web sites. This site can be accessed in either English or Japanese. The Webmaster is Matthew Johnson (matthew@gemini.bekkoame.or.jp).

Puppet Theater

198. **Stage Hand Puppets' Activity Page**

http://www3.ns.sympatico.ca/onstage/puppets/

This activity page has patterns for puppets, instructions for making scrap puppets, and tips for ventriloquism. It also offers puppet play scripts ready to produce. Students are encouraged to submit their own plays.

Theater Education

199. **Creative Drama and Theatre Education Resource Site**

http://www.creativedrama.com

"Let's pretend" is a good introduction for creative drama, acting without the goal of a performance. Creative drama (for ages four through nine) can include dramatic play, story enactment, imagination journeys, theater games, music, and dance. This site provides classroom ideas, resources, and theater games, as well as an annotated bibliography of books about theater education, theory, and practice; acting techniques and methods; improvisation; technical theater; and sets, costumes, and props. Look for a sample lesson plan using the book, *Wacky Wednesday* by Theodore Lesieg (Random House, 1974). A list of plays appropriate for young people to perform is also available. Created and maintained by Janine Moyer-Buesgen (janine100@aol.com).

200. High School Theatre Programs

http://www.fn.net/~east22/HSprograms.html

The High School Theatre Programs Web site provides a collection of links to school theater sites and to general theater sites on the Web. A clickable map and postal zip code locator will help you find high school theater programs in the United States; links to junior/middle school theater programs are listed. To add your school's theater department, club, or troupe's Web page to this list, send an e-mail request to (east22@feist.com), and be sure to include the Web page address. The site is maintained by the Theatre Arts Department at Wichita High School East, Wichita, Kansas.

Discussion Groups

201. Discussion of Musicals

E-mail: **listproc@lists.efn.org**
Instructions: On the first line of the body of the message, type:
subscribe MUSICALS [your first name and last name]
or
Newsgroup: **rec.arts.theatre.musicals.newsgroup**

The FAQs for rec.arts.theatre.musicals can be found at this address: (http://www.juglans.demon.co.uk/Tim/Theatre/TheatreLinks.htm).

202. Theatre History

E-mail: **listserv@postoffice.cso.uiuc.edu**
Instructions: On the first line of the body of the message, type:
subscribe ASTR-L [your first name and last name]
Theatre History is the official discussion list for the American Society for Theatre Research.

Computer Science

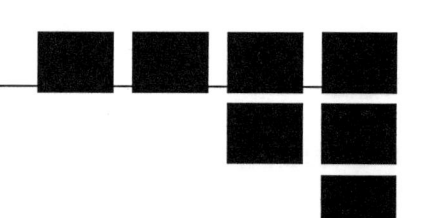

All URL addresses in this chapter are checked and updated monthly. If a link does not work, please refer to the Directory Update Web page located at (http://www.lu.com/lu/irdupdates.html).

Students studying the history of computer science will have a number of sites to choose from: Michelle A. Hoyle's History of Computers (entry 225), The History of Computing (entry 226) from the Department of Computer Science at Virginia Polytechnic Institute and State University, and the Virtual Computer History Museum (entry 229). The Ada Project (entry 273) promotes women's involvement in high-technology computer science and addresses gender equity in computer classrooms.

A number of lesson plans and resources are available for computer science educators. Look at the Apple Education Web site (entry 213) and The Computer Teacher's Resource Page (entry 236). Online tutorials make it easy to create Web pages and teach Microsoft software, including PowerPoint. See entries 239–242 in this chapter and the Staff Development tutorials (entries 1478–1490).

As more and more teachers develop their own Web pages, there are lots of sites to assist. Look for clip art sites (entries 121–122) and the RGB Color Chart (entry 264); entries 258–272 offer tips, tools, and templates for Web Page design and development and creation of Web page activities and WebQuests.

Software archives allow teachers to download and use software from the Internet. Most software is either freeware or shareware. Be sure to check out sites such as TUCOWS (entry 248) for quick location and retrieval of specific software. Because it is more important than ever to protect computers from viruses, the section on antivirus software (entries 250–251) should be particularly useful.

Copyright is a concern for most educators. Specific copyright information pertaining to computer software is available (entry 210), whereas more general copyright laws and issues are discussed in "The School Library: The School Information Resource Center" (entries 1467–1470).

This section contains tutorials on desktop publishing, Microsoft Windows, Adobe PhotoShop, and Adobe Acrobat Reader. You will need Adobe Acrobat Reader to download PDF (portable document format) documents from the Internet.

General Interest

203. Computer Reviews

http://compreviews.about.com/compute/compreviews/mbody.htm

Thinking about buying a new computer? Check out all the reviews listed on this site. Computers are listed in alphabetical order and cover all the major brands. Spotlight feature articles focus on comparisons, review the latest items on the market, and describe how to purchase a home computer. Johnny Newberry (compreviews.guide@about.com), a Data Center Operations Manager for STAR Systems, Inc. maintains this site.

204. Focus on Mac Hardware

http://machardware.about.com/compute/machardware/mbody.htm

An alphabetized list of topics makes for easy access to a wide variety of information about Macintosh computers, covering iBooks, G3 upgrades, G4 Power Macs, Powerbooks, and Previous Macs. Feature articles focus on timely events and news and helpful tips. This is the place to find reviews about Macintosh computers and information to help with troubleshooting. Maintained by Ryan J. Faas (machardware.guide@about.com), a computer consultant and trainer who specializes in Macintosh computers.

205. MacInTouch

http://www.macintouch.com

Find out all the current news and information about Mac computing at MacInTouch, a comprehensive Macintosh Web site. Special Reports includes topics such as viruses, rebates, and the gray market. Links are provided to Macintosh software archives, other Mac sites, and online Apple support, such as Ted Landau's MacFixIt Web site and a basic troubleshooting guide. Reports from readers are solicited and available for online reading. The creator and Webmaster is Ric Ford (ricfordw@macintouch.com).

206. The PC Guide

http://www.pcguide.com

The PC Guide is intended for newcomers to the world of computers; however, seasoned users will also find this to be a handy reference tool. The Guide describes computers in general terms, detailing how they work and what they do. It also provides an overview of the different parts of a PC and how they work. The PC Guide is well-organized and clearly written, but does not include illustrations or graphics. Charles Kozierok is the Webmaster.

207. Yahoo! Computers

http://shopping.yahoo.com/computers

Yahoo! Computers provides up-to-date and in-depth information and news on computers, software, and the Internet. Topics include product reviews, product comparisons, top sellers, shopping tips, technology news, ZDNet columns and features, shareware information, and message boards. Access this site to stay current, communicate with others, and become informed before purchasing software or hardware.

Computer Programming

208. Java: Cafe Au Lait

http://metalab.unc.edu/javafaq/

Java: Cafe Au Lait offers extensive links to resources about Java. There is a Java FAQ section; a tutorial (Brewing Java); Java Course Notes; a list of books about Java; mailing lists for Java developers; and links to Java users groups around the world, to name a few of the resources. Cafe Au Lait is updated almost daily by Elliotte Rusty Harold (elharo@sunsite.unc.edu). Harold wrote *Java Developer's Resource* (Prentice-Hall, 1997), *Java Network Programming* (O'Reilly & Associates, 1997), and *Java Secrets* (IDG, 1997).

209. PERL Archive from The University of Florida

http://www.cise.ufl.edu/perl/

The programming language PERL (Practical Extraction and Reporting Language), written by Larry Wall (lwall@netlabs.com), is a good language for almost any kind of shell scripting or processing text. It is similar to the C language, but includes some UNIX facilities, and is used for developing Common Gateway Interface (CGI) programs. According to Wall, PERL "is an interpreted scripting language optimized for scanning arbitrary text files, extracting information from those text files, and printing reports based on that information." The Webmaster for this site can be reached at (japh@cis.ufl.edu). For a simple and straightforward tutorial on PERL, see also Take 10 Minutes to Learn PERL (http://www.geocities.com/SiliconValley/7331/ten_perl.html) by Barry B. Floyd (floydb@city-of-troy.com). The PERL Language Page edited by Tom Christiansen is located at (http://www.perl.com/pub).

Copyright

See also "Copyright Laws and Issues" (entries 1467–1470).

210. University of Florida's Software Copyright Information Home Page

http://www.ifas.ufl.edu/WWW/PIRATE/index.html

With links to the Software Publishers Association, this site covers software piracy as a form of copyright infringement. It provides a thorough explanation of copyright infringement, discussion of court cases, steps toward prevention, and methods of enforcement pertaining to the software industry. Training materials for inservice are available for nonprofit use.

Corporate Sites

211. Apple Computer Home Page

http://www.apple.com

The Apple Computer Web site provides product information, customer support, information on technology and research, links to special communities of users, and outside resources.

212.   **Apple Computer's Disability Resources Online**

http://www.apple.com/education/k12/disability/

Children and adults with disabilities will benefit from this online information from Apple Computer. Information is given about alternative input devices, creative solutions for customers with visual impairments, and links to other resources of interest to those with special needs.

213.   **Apple Education**

http://www.apple.com/education/

From this page, you can choose K-12 Education or Higher Education. The K-12 Education area offers parents, students, and K-12 educators a wealth of resources and information, including education news and events, lesson plans, international education projects, education products and promotions, and links to education sites. Find out about the Apple Educator Advantage Home Computer Purchase Program, including eligibility requirements. Information is available on all Apple hardware and technologies. Also available is information on Apple Research and Apple Education news and events. Of interest to educators writing technology plans and grants are Apple's Effectiveness Reports, which are two-page summaries consisting of a description of the role that technology plays in addressing a particular grade level and subject area, a list of the major research findings, full citations for the findings, additional useful readings, and places to call or visit.

214.   **IBM Corporation**

http://www.ibm.com

Updated daily, this site provides headline news about new products and IBM activities. Learn more about sales, support, employment opportunities, research and development, and IBM's presence in countries around the world.

215.   **Intel In Education Home Page**

http://www.intel.com/education/index.htm

Intel provides online resources to enrich classroom learning. Look for topics such as How Transistors Work, How Microprocessors Work, Jobs at Intel, and the Intel Web Page Wizard to help create classroom Web pages. Links are provided to lesson plans, resources by subject, virtual libraries, and print resources. What's New highlights news about grants, scholarships, and information related to K-12 schools. Be sure to check out suggestions for how to use technology in education.

216.   **Microsoft**

http://www.microsoft.com

Information is available on new products, training and support, news and events, academic pricing, and press releases. Download Microsoft Internet Explorer for free, and subscribe to a free Microsoft Newsletter. Be sure to visit the Microsoft in Education page (http://www.microsoft.com/education/) and the Microsoft K-12 page (http://www.microsoft.com/education/schools/default.asp).

217. Netscape

http://www.netscape.com

Use this site to check out industry news, the new beta versions of the Netscape browser, or various plug-ins. Locate documentation on Netscape products and technologies. The General Store is where you can buy Netscape products that are no longer free. Destinations is a launch pad to some of the best sites on the Web.

218. Sun Microsystems

http://www.sun.com

Sun Microsystems pioneered Java technology, and this site helps to keep you current on the latest news and breakthroughs from this innovative company. Links are provided to *SunWorld*, a monthly publication from International Data Group (IDG) Communications.

Dictionaries and Glossaries

219. *Computer Currents* High-Tech Dictionary

http://www.currents.net/resources/dictionary/dictionary.phtml

This searchable database contains more than 7,000 computer terms. Provides an exact match and similar matches. A search for Java produces six similar matches such as hotJava, Java applet, and JavaScript. Quick link buttons reveal emoticons, file types, HTML tags, and Y2K terms.

220. Webopedia

http://www.pcwebopaedia.com

Webopedia is an online computer dictionary for Internet terms and technical support. The more than 2,000 terms in its database are searchable by keyword and subject. Explanations of terms have in-text links to further information. A related terms list is available in a sidebar for each search result. Links are also provided to top news stories that include the search term.

221. Whatis.com

http://www.whatis.com

Whatis.com defines computer-related terms clearly and concisely. An alphabetical listing of terms, such as *cable modem* and *Ethernet*, are presented as links to explanations. What is the difference in speed between ISDN and T-1? An in-text linked chart explains the speeds of various connections. Also, look for an explanation of how the Internet works, who runs it, and information about the U.S. backbone.

History of Computer Science

222. Charles Babbage (1791–1871)

http://www-groups.dcs.st-and.ac.uk/~history/Mathematicians/Babbage.html

Charles Babbage is known as the father of the present day computer. By the time Babbage became Lucasian Professor of Mathematics at Cambridge in 1827, he was already engrossed in the development of mechanical computers. Provides biographical information, a poster with a picture of Babbage, some of his quotations, a picture of Babbage's difference engine, and an image of the cover of Babbage's *Economy of Manufacturers and Machinery* (1832). Links are available to related information for further study.

223. Bill Gates (1955–)

http://www.microsoft.com/BillGates/

The official biography Web site for Bill Gates, Chairman of Microsoft, includes biographical information, essays and columns, transcripts of speeches, voice recordings, and information about causes that he is supporting around the globe. The latest news articles are available, as are a Microsoft timeline and photographs. The Web site is searchable.

224. Grace Murray Hopper (1906–1992)

http://www.agnesscott.edu/lriddle/women/hopper.htm

If Charles Babbage is the father of modern-day computers, then Grace Hopper is the mother. She worked as a programmer of the Mark I, the world's first large-scale, automatically sequenced digital computer and its successors, the Mark II and Mark III. She later worked on the BINAC (Binary Automatic Computer) that paved the way for the first commercial computers, UNIVAC I and II. Hopper helped to create the standard manuals and tools for COBOL, a software programming language. Her assistance with the development of computer software was so critical that she was recalled from retirement and eventually promoted to Rear Admiral—the first woman to be elevated to this rank. Hopper is credited with coining the term "computer bug." Be sure to click on the links in the Reference section for additional information about Grace Hopper and a photograph of the first computer bug. Written by Rebecca Norman, Class of 2000, Agnes Scott College.

225. History of Computers

http://www.eingang.org/Lecture

"History of Computers: From the Past to the Present" by Michelle A. Hoyle is easy to understand and covers important people and dates, from Stonehenge through Pascal, Babbage, Hollerith, Turing, and Gates. If you are using a graphical browser, be sure to click on the graphics icons for pictures and definitions of such things as an abacus, Pascal's gear system, a binary representation, the Turing machine, transistors and integrated circuits, and computer chips. Links are provided to information about the Web and HTML. Created and maintained by Michelle A. Hoyle (eingang@cogs.susx.ac.uk).

226.   **The History of Computing**

http://ei.cs.vt.edu/~history/

The History of Computing is an in-depth collection of materials related to the history of computing. These resources were collected and written by J. A. N. Lee (janlee@cs.vt.edu), past
editor-in-chief of the IEEE *Annals of the History of Computing*, past chair of the IEEE Computer
Society History of Computing Committee, and current chair of the IFIP Working Group. An index organizes information by topic, such as people and pioneers, machines, programming languages, calculators, publications, and networks. This in-depth collection of materials is
provided courtesy of the Department of Computer Science at Virginia Tech (Virginia Polytechnic Institute and State University, Blacksburg, Virginia), and is sponsored in part by a grant
from the National Science Foundation. See also ENIAC 50th Anniversary Celebration
(http://www.seas.upenn.edu/~museum/).

227.   **Smithsonian Computer History**

http://www.si.edu/resource/tours/comphist/computer.htm

The Smithsonian Computer History site provides links for exploration of six different areas. Of
special note are the Information Age; Oral/Video History; the Archives area; and the National
Science Foundation's Directorate for Computer and Information Sciences and Engineering
(CISE), which contains a comprehensive discussion of computer sciences and links to computer sites around the world. The Information Age Tour provides a slide tour of Information
Age: People, Information & Technology, a current exhibition opened in May 1990 at the National Museum of American History. Oral/Video History is a growing area of oral and video his-
tories of people who have played significant roles in the development of modern
communications and computers, such as Marc Andreessen, chief technical officer of Netscape,
Inc.; Steve Jobs, chief executive officer of NEXT; and Bill Gates, chief executive officer of Microsoft. The Archives houses historical documents, such as the original press release for the
ENIAC computer (February 16, 1946). These documents can be downloaded as Adobe Acrobat
(PDF) files.

228.   *Triumph of the Nerds*

http://www.pbs.org/nerds/

Triumph of the Nerds is a companion Web site to the PBS special of the same name. Its contents feature some of the computer industry's most recognizable characters, including Microsoft's Bill Gates and Paul Allen and Apple founder Steven Jobs. A timeline includes a color
world map showing Internet connectivity. Though most have Internet, Bitnet, or e-mail connectivity, a few countries still do not have any connectivity. Links are provided to more in-
depth coverage of the history of the Internet on a companion Web site featuring the PBS series Life on the Internet (http://www.pbs.org/internet).

229.   **Virtual Computer History Museum**

http://video.dlib.vt.edu/~history/

Students can view the historical exhibits by taking either a text-only or an illustrated look at
the past, browsing extensive galleries of images, taking a tour, or searching by keyword.
Events in computer history are organized by time segments, such as the 1600s, the 1800s, and

pre-World War II 1900s. Beginning with the 1950s, each decade is divided into two-year segments. The exhibit ends with a quick look at the 1990s. Links point to other related museums. Created and maintained by Virginia Polytechnic Institute (Blacksburg, Virginia).

Internetworking

230. Internetworking Basics

http://www.cisco.com/cpress/cc/td/cpress/fund/ith/ith01gb.htm

Cisco Systems, Inc., a company that produces routers and other networking equipment, offers a sample chapter from *Internetworking Technologies Handbook* (2d ed., Cisco Press Publications, 1998), written by the Cisco staff and Kevin Downes. The book is a survey of technologies and protocols; the chapter on "Internetworking Basics" explains everything about Internetworking, with helpful illustrations. Topics include flow control, error checking, and multiplexing, but mainly focus on mapping the Open Systems Interconnect (OSI) model to networking/Internetworking functions and summarizing addressing schemes within the context of the OSI model. For more information about Cisco Systems, Inc., go to its home page (http://www.cisco.com).

Lesson Plans and Teacher Resources

See also "Lesson Plans Across the Curriculum" (entries 33–44).

231. Anguilla Library Computer Club

http://www.web.ai/club/

The objective of the Anguilla Library Computer Club is to promote computer literacy in all Anguillans, especially children. Anguilla is an island in the northeastern part of the Caribbean, near St. Martin. Click on the link to Lessons to find some of the instructions used to teach basic Windows skills. Some files are available as zipped files (.zip). For more information on how to donate used computers and used computer parts to the Anguilla Library Club's Anguilla Computes! Program, see (http://www.web.ai/club/donors.html).

232. Build Your Own PC

http://www.verinet.com/pc/

Provides step-by-step instructions for building a personal computer. Identifies component pieces of hardware and provides photographs of motherboards, hard drives, RAM, video cards, floppy drives, CD-ROMs, and more. Even if you don't use this site to build your own PC, you'll want to use it as part of a lesson on how computers work. Web page creator and webmaster is Jeff Moe (jeffpc@verinet.com).

233. Computer Applications Lesson Plans

http://www.fred.net/nhhs/lessons/ca.htm

Lesson plans for computer and technology teachers are posted on this site at North Hagerstown High School (Hagerstown, MD). Topics for some of the lessons include: The Computer in Society, Computers Today, Basics of Using Windows, What It Means to Be a Professional

Webmaster, and Using the World Wide Web. Some lesson plans contain a number of activities, comprising a mini-unit, and some also contain quizzes and answers. Created and maintained by George Cassutto (nhhs@fred.net), teacher of social studies and computer applications.

234. Computer Science Online

http://www.crews.org/media_tech/compsci/

Computer science and business education syllabi, course outlines, lesson plans, assignments, and student-produced work are all online for sharing. This site is a gold mine for computer science teachers, particularly those who teach keyboarding, word processing, spreadsheets, Web page design, LOGO, desktop publishing, and business education. All students at Alton C. Crews Middle School (Lawrenceville, Georgia) are expected to learn computer basics. Students learn how to save, print, create, and edit simple word-processing documents; basic online Internet skills; how to create spreadsheet documents; and the correct techniques for keyboarding. See the work of seventh-grade students who program Web games using MicroWorlds. The Crews Stock Market Simulation Game is for eighth-grade students. For more information, be sure to see the Handbook (http://www.crews.org/media_tech/compsci/8thgrade/stkmkt/index.htm). More than 200 student-produced Web projects are available in archives, accessible by grades 6–8 and date beginning with 1997. Each project is accompanied by a brief description. Find out about the Crews Web Club, and read online articles on topics such as computer ethics, viruses, and the future of technology. Don't miss the special collection of Internet links for business and computer science educators. Created and maintained by Rod Hames (rod_hames@ gwinnett.k12.ga.us), a computer science and business education teacher at Crews Middle School.

235. Computer Skills Lesson Plans

http://www.dpi.state.nc.us/Curriculum/Computer.skills/lssnplns/CompCurr.LP.html

The North Carolina Department of Public Instruction has posted lesson plans that meet state standards in grades K-8 in areas of keyboarding, word processing, telecomputing, and creating databases and spreadsheets. In addition to computer skills, lessons also address other curriculum objectives in art, mathematics, English language arts, science, social studies, and information skills.

236. The Computer Teacher's Resource Page

http://nimbus.temple.edu/~jallis00/

The Computer Teacher's Resource Page is designed for the elementary (K-8) computer teacher, who may be called upon to teach a computer class, maintain a computer lab, or provide guidance to other teachers. This collection of Internet links can be used as a launching pad for creating classroom projects for every subject in the elementary curriculum, including social studies, science, music, art, math, and language arts. A list of links is also provided to educational research sites, Web page development tools, and software resources. This Web site was created and is maintained by Jane Allison (allison@netreach.net), computer technology teacher.

237. ***The Hand-Me-Down PC***

http://www.daileyint.com/hmdpc/handtoc.htm

Although a newer version of *The Hand-Me-Down PC* is available in print format, the original version is online. Many older computers are given away to schools—but these free computers may not be bargains, because PCs evolve so rapidly (more than nine major generations in just a few short years). Frequently, it takes more money to upgrade an older PC than to purchase a new PC, and the more expensive refurbished computer still might not have the capabilities of a newer, less expensive computer. Using this online book may help in determining whether it makes financial sense to invest money in hand-me-down technology that may already be obsolete. Additionally, the book can be used as a teaching guide to the parts of a computer and how a computer works. Content covers four areas: hardware parts and technical jargon; software and operating systems; buying refurbished computers versus do-it-yourself upgrades; and a hardware troubleshooting guide. *The Hand-Me-Down PC: Upgrading and Repairing Personal Computers* (1997) is written by Morris Rosenthal.

238. **Microsoft in Education: Productivity in the Classroom**

http://www.microsoft.com/education/lesson/productivity/default.asp

Microsoft provides across-the-curriculum lesson plans that incorporate various computer software programs. Look for lesson plans aimed at intermediate, middle school, and high school abilities and curricular interests using Microsoft Word, PowerPoint, Access, Excel, Publisher, and the Internet. Some of the lessons cover learning about zoological classification, developing an investment portfolio, evaluating the real cost of car ownership, creating dictionary pages, designing Web pages, and creating a newspaper reflecting life in ancient Egypt or Mexico. See also a collection of more than 2,000 lesson plans developed by teachers to integrate the use of computers into their curricula (http://www.eduniverse.com/edu/lessonp.asp). Top-ranked lesson plans for the Intel ACE project are listed, and the entire database is searchable.

Online Tutorials

See also the Digital Education Network home page (entry 30) for links to other tutorials and "Staff Development and Online Tutorials" (entries 1478–1490).

239. **Front Page 98 in the Classroom**

http://www.actden.com/fp/

Introduces Microsoft's Front Page as an HTML editor to create Web pages. Provides step-by-step instructions on how to create a Web page, add graphics, create links, build tables, and add forms. Suggestions are given for producing dynamic content and managing a Web site after it has been created.

240. **Outlook Express in the Classroom**

http://www.actden.com/oe/index.htm

Provides a tutorial for K-12 students on how to use Microsoft Outlook Express for e-mail. Covers five basic steps, including sending and receiving e-mail, fancy e-mail, and organizing e-mail. Goes over how to set up an address book and customize the Outlook window.

241. **PowerPoint 98 in the Classroom**

http://www.actden.com/pp/

Shows how to make and create PowerPoint presentations. Also provides a step-by-step guide to teach K-12 students how to create multimedia presentations using PowerPoint. Eight steps walk students through the basics of making simple slides, and then adding images, charts, motion, and sound. The last two steps in this lesson concentrate on timing, rehearsing, and ways to make a PowerPoint presentation portable and useable elsewhere.

242. **Webmonkey for Kids**

http://hotwired.lycos.com/webmonkey/kids/

Webmonkey promises to make learning how to build your own home page fun and entertaining. Provides basic lessons, suggests projects, and gives a list of essential tools, with links for downloading if needed. The Playground area shows students examples of what they can do with their Web pages for fun. A planning guide for parents and teachers includes tips and advice on how to use Webmonkey with children. Child safety and rules for using the Internet safely are discussed. Produced by Wired Digital, owned by Lycos, Inc., and part of the Lycos network of sites.

Policies

See "Acceptable Use Governing Internet Access" (entries 1465–1466).

Software

Software and Software Collections and Archives

243. **Kids' Shareware for PC and Mac**

http://www.kidsdomain.com/down/index.html

Kids are advised to check with their parents before downloading software from this page. Shareware and freeware for the Mac and PC are available and sorted by age level. Demos, icons, and graphics are also available. This page is part of the Kids Domain Web site (http://www.kidsdomain.com/kids.html). The Webmaster's address is (tigger@kidsdomain.com).

244. **Macintosh Info-Mac HyperArchive Search Engine (MIT)**

http://hyperarchive.lcs.mit.edu/HyperArchive.html

The Info-Mac archive has the largest collection of software for the Macintosh on the Internet. The archive includes shareware, freeware, demos of commercial applications, tools, resources, and information. The search engine allows searching for a specific program name, author, and even for words found in the abstract of the program. The Boolean operator AND is assumed. A keyword search for NCSA telnet returned the most current downloadable version. This easy-to-use site is an excellent source for Macintosh software.

245. **Mosaic WWW Browsers**

     http://www.ncsa.uiuc.edu/SDG/Software/Mosaic/

     Mosaic is available for three platforms: Macintosh, Windows, and X Window System. Documentation is provided and is searchable. Find out what's new and check out the FAQs.

     ### Other Sites for Mosaic

     Mosaic for Macintosh
     http://www.ncsa.uiuc.edu/SDG/Software/MacMosaic/MacMosaicHome.html

     Mosaic for Windows
     http://www.ncsa.uiuc.edu/SDG/Software/WinMosaic/HomePage.html

246. **Netscape's Free Software**

     http://home.netscape.com/computing/download/index.html

     Netscape offers free browser software and plug-ins. Check this site for the most up-to-date freeware. Educators and students can download, without charge, the latest versions of Netscape (Navigator and Communicator), as well as plug-ins and extras to extend and enhance the browser experience.

     To access older versions of Netscape Navigator software, including Netscape Gold, go to: (ftp://archive:oldies@archive.netscape.com/archive/index.html).

247. **Stroud's Consummate Internet Apps List**

     http://cws.internet.com

     Stroud's list is an excellent source of freeware and shareware for PCs. The CWSApps (Consummate Winsock Applications) List is a one-stop shopping site for the latest and greatest software on the Internet. The index lists hundreds of Windows-based utilities and Internet tools; it is searchable and is updated often. Software applications are accessible by categories, such as network tools, online applications, Web development, and Internet applications. Each entry includes the version number, file size, required operating system, and price. Reviews are provided, and links are to the actual software. You can check out what's cool, what's new, and what's most popular, including the top 25 downloads of the past week or past month.

248. **TUCOWS**

     http://www.tucows.com

     TUCOWS provides an extensive list of Winsock-compliant freeware and shareware for Windows 3.1 and Windows 95, as well as software for Macintosh users. TUCOWS provides a one- to five-cow rating for each software listing. You can browse by application type or by product name. Each entry has a brief description and is tagged with file size and location, version number and revision date, and price. TUCOWS provides a mailing list for anyone who wants to know about updates.

249. **Windows Archive at WinSite**

http://www.winsite.com

Self-proclaimed as the planet's largest archive of Windows freeware and shareware, this archive has a Windows 3.x collection; Windows 95 files; Windows NT files; and starter files, such as compress/zip/zoo. Software is appropriate for education, business, and home use. Archives are browseable and searchable.

Antivirus Software

250. **AntiVirus Software Page**

http://antivirus.about.com

Visit this site weekly for updates on new viruses and relevant antivirus information. You can expect quality information about viruses, guidelines for protection, reviews of viruses, sites, software, and solutions that work. Ken Dunham (antivirus.guide@about.com), regional training director for CenterPoint Technologies and middle school computer/journalism electives teacher, created this site so that both PC and Macintosh users could find the latest information about viruses and antivirus software. Users can download freeware and shareware as well as 30-day limited-use commercial programs. Make sure your computer is protected.

251. **Dr. Solomon's Computer Virus Information and More**

http://www.drsolomon.com

Find out more about computer viruses and Dr. Solomon's antivirus software. This site offers virus information and assistance, including virus alerts, a searchable virus encyclopedia, a full tutorial, advice, a technical paper, the virus gallery, and help with virus infections. Links are provided to other antivirus companies, research centers, and IT security sites. Dr. Solomon's Anti-Virus Toolkit is sold commercially, but you can download free a time-limited version of the *Find Virus for DOS* antivirus software and scanner.

Software Product Reviews

252. **Benchin' Software Review**

http://www.benchin.com

More than 100,000 commercial software products are reviewed. The database is searchable by keyword, type of software, product, or company. You can also browse through topical lists with headings like Business, Personal and Home, Professional, Industry Specific, System and Utilities, and Internet. Each software product is rated using a star system. Information is provided on platform compatibility, as well as system and other hardware requirements. Check out Benchin' Hits to discover the hottest downloads. Children's software, including curriculum-based software, is located in Personal and Home.

253. **Discussion of Children's Software**

Newsgroup: **misc.kids.computer**

The focus of this discussion group is anything relevant to children's software and hardware.

254. The GSLIS Multimedia Product Reviews

http://www.gslis.utexas.edu/~kidnet/reviews/index.html

Reviews of children's software products prepared by graduate students at the Graduate School of Library and Information Science (GSLIS) at the University of Texas at Austin are available online. Criteria for evaluation are listed. Reviewed software is accessible by alphabetical listing, by publisher, and by subject area. Reviewed products are also searchable. Each review has the bibliographic information, a summary of the contents, recommended audience, system requirements, overall recommendation, and links to other online reviews. This project is supervised by Dr. Barbara F. Immroth (immroth@tnet.edu), professor.

255. Kid's Domain Review

http://www.kidsdomain.com/review/index.html

More than 800 reviews for children's commercial software products are available. Guidelines are given for how software is reviewed, and volunteers are asked to submit additional reviews.

Because this Web site combined with two other sites, there is also a Kids Home with games, icons, holiday fun, and links to fun Internet resources. This site is updated weekly. The Web editor is Anise Hollingshead (anise@kidsdomain.com).

256. School House Software Review

http://www.worldvillage.com/wv/school/html/scholrev.htm

Software titles are presented in alphabetical order. Each review gives an overall score and breakdown scores in areas such as ease of use, learning value, entertainment value, graphics, and sound. Each reviewer's name and e-mail address are given. Reviews are well written and detailed.

257. SuperKids Educational Software Review

http://www.superkids.com

SuperKids provides a guide to unbiased educational software reviews for parents and teachers. For each software title, there is a separate rating by parents, teachers, and kids. For ease of use there is a category index: math, reading, interactive books, early learning, CD encyclopedia, science, social studies, and the like. There is also an alphabetical name index.

Web Page Design and Development

See also "Clip Art" (entries 121–122) and Webmonkey for Kids (entry 242).

Tools, Tips, and Templates

See also Quia! (entry 293).

258. Building Blocks of a WebQuest

http://edweb.sdsu.edu/people/bdodge/webquest/buildingblocks.html

WebQuests are online curriculum modules that engage students in learning about an authentic topic or problem. WebQuests provide inquiry-oriented activities and are more complex than

Web-based activity or worksheet pages. Because the resources of a WebQuest are usually found on the Internet, a highly unstructured environment, the underlying structure of a WebQuest allows students to successfully investigate an authentic topic in a collaborative manner. Learners can focus on using information for thinking at levels of analysis, synthesis, and evaluation rather than on searching for information. Explains the six essential ingredients for creating a WebQuest: introduction, task, process, resources, evaluation, and conclusion. See also how to assess your own WebQuest and how to evaluate others (http://www.ozline. com/webquests/rubric.html). For more about the WebQuest model, as well as examples of WebQuests, *see* (entry 32).

259. Classroom Internet Server Cookbook

http://web66.coled.umn.edu/Cookbook/

If your district, school, or classroom is interested in creating a WWW server, this is the place to come. If you have access to a Macintosh or a PC running Windows 95 or Windows NT, this page has the essential links you need to download to create your own Internet server. Information from the Eight Minute HTML Primer explains how to make picture thumbnails and interlaced and transparent GIF pictures.

260. Design a Web Page

http://www.siec.k12.in.us/~west/online/design.htm

Follow six easy steps to create your own Web pages. Information available on this site helps you determine the type of Web page you want to create for your classroom or school, such as home pages, treasure hunts, collaborative activities, hot lists, and Web-based activities. Discusses design tips, covers some copyright issues, and furnishes rubrics for assessing Web pages—yours and others. Provides excellent examples of Web pages designed for Loogootee West Elementary School by teacher and Web editor, Tammy Payton (tammy.payton@mciworldcom.net).

261. Filamentality

http://www.kn.pacbell.com/wired/fil/

If you don't know any HTML and you want to put together a fast Web page, Filamentality allows you to create different Web page formats, such as Hotlists, Scrapbooks, Treasure Hunts, Samplers, and WebQuests, from fill-in-the-blank templates. All templates support Web-based learning activities, and can be used by teachers, students, librarians, trainers, and anyone else. Immediately after you complete a Web page, it can be posted from this site with a unique Web page address so that others can visit your page. Those who want to do more to customize their Web pages should be sure to see the section called Beyond the Son of Filamentality. Created by Pacific Bell Fellows and supported by Pacific Bell as part of its Knowledge Network.

262. Getting Started in HTML!

http://www.iainc.net/~rapunzel/web.html

Rapunzel's page, Getting Started in HTML, lists all the ingredients for writing a Web page, including tutorials, browsers, editors, conversion tools, and links to pages with archives of backgrounds, icons, and images. There is also an advanced HTML page for Webmasters. Created and maintained by E. Seifert, aka Rapunzel (rapunzel@iainc.net).

263. An Idiot's Guide to Creating a Home Page

http://www.voyager.co.nz/~bsimpson/html.htm

Anyone can create a Web page following these illustrated, step-by-step directions. The tutorial is divided into five parts that cover the basics, including graphics, fonts, colors, backgrounds, links, and tables. Bruce Simpson (bruce@faxmail.co.nz) created this Web site.

264. RGB Color Chart

http://home.flash.net/~drj2142/

The RGB Hex Triplet Color Chart contains the corresponding letters and numbers for colors and shades of colors on a color chart. These identifying codes can be used to indicate color in HTML documents. Color can be used in the background, text, and links. Created by Doug Jacobson (drj2142@flash.net).

265. Teachers.net Homepage Maker

http://www.teachers.net/sampler/

Provides a simple fill-in-the blank form for teachers to use to create their own home pages. Once created, these pages are sent to you via e-mail. You can then upload them to a server at your school or elsewhere. With this template, you don't need to know HTML, and you can have your own home page finished in just a few minutes! Part of Teacher's Net Web Services.

266. Ten Tips for Webmasters

http://www.cyberbee.com/master.html

Keep it simple, small, and short is the advice of Linda C. Joseph (ljoseph@iwaynet.net), library media specialist with the Columbus, Ohio, Public Schools and Webmaster of the Adventures of CyberBee Web site (http://www.cyberbee.com). See also Eighteen Tenets for Good Web Page Design by Jamie McKenzie (http://www.bham.wednet.edu/homeswee.htm).

267. Web Design

http://webdesign.about.com/compute/webdesign/mbody.htm

Provides one-stop shopping for all your Web page design needs. An alphabetical list of Web links makes finding information easy. Topics include such diverse range as Flash tutorials, clip art, graphics tips, HTML editors, and CGI. Look for a tip of the day and a site of the day along with feature articles on the top of Web page design. Web site maintained by Jean Kaiser (webdesign. guide@about.com), a Web developer.

268. The Webmaster's Reference Library

http://www.webreference.com

Webreference provides the latest information on Web design and development for novices and experts. Information is updated frequently. A free weekly newsletter, *The Webreference Update*, alerts subscribers to updates on Webreference.com and news from the Web of interest to Webmasters.

E-mail: **listserv@listserv.internet.com**
Instructions: On the first line of the body of the message, type:
subscribe webreference-update [your first name and last name]

HTML Guides and Tutorials

HTML Guides

269.   Barebones Guide to HTML

http://werbach.com/barebones/index.html

The Barebones Guide to HTML lists all of the HTML tags commonly used to create Web pages. The HTML FAQ section answers some of the most common questions about Web page design, and the WWW Help Page provides links to resources on developing frames, Java graphics, GIF animation, sound, CGI, style, and colors. This excellent site was created and is maintained by Kevin Werbach (barebones@werbach.com).

270.   Beginner's Guide to HTML

http://www.ncsa.uiuc.edu/General/Internet/WWW/HTMLPrimer.html

The Beginner's Guide to HTML is a primer designed to help novices produce documents in HTML. Links are provided to additional information. It includes Terms to Know and a good explanation of tags.

HTML Tutorials

271.   HTML Tutorial

http://www.ncsa.uiuc.edu/Edu/Tutorials/TutorialHome.html

Learn more about HTML so you can create your own Web pages. Several very basic tutorials created by NCSA's Education Group appear on this page. Versions are in HTML, and a downloadable copy is in Microsoft Word. These tutorials may be used for professional development and with students as long as they are not sold or used for profit.

272.   Writing HTML: A Tutorial for Creating WWW Pages

http://www.mcli.dist.maricopa.edu/tut/

Writing HTML was developed to help teachers create learning resources that access information on the Internet. By following the tutorial on how to create a lesson on volcanoes, teachers learn to create curriculum resource Web pages. This is a must for teachers who want to learn how to integrate Internet resources into their curricula. Lessons 1 through 14 cover the basics, and lessons 15 through 23 go on to a more advanced level. The Webmaster for this site is Alan Levine (levine@maricopa.edu), Maricopa Center for Learning and Instruction, Maricopa Community Colleges (Arizona).

Women in Computer Science

273. The Ada Project: Tapping Internet Resources for Women in Computer Science

http://www.cs.yale.edu/~tap/tap.html

The Ada Project Web site promotes women's involvement in high-technology computer science, inspiring young girls and celebrating women (past and present) who have made careers in fields where women are currently underrepresented. The Ada Project (TAP) serves as a clearinghouse for information and resources relating to women in computing. TAP provides information about conferences, projects, discussion groups and organizations, fellowships and grants, and notable women in computer science. TAP also maintains a substantive bibliography, including, for example, "Silicon Valley Girls: Educated, Experienced, Well Capitalized," *Forbes* (December 30, 1996). Links are provided to two articles from *The Wall Street Journal:* "History of Software Begins with the Work of Some Brainy Women" and "Female Pioneers Fostered Practicality in Computer Industry" (both November 1996).

274. The Backyard Project

http://www.backyard.org

The Backyard Project seeks to build young women's awareness of careers in the computer industry. Provides information about careers through online interviews with women who use computers in their careers; includes discussions of educational requirements and salary ranges. Gives a brief history of the computer industry, definitions of basic terms, and some exercises to do while seated at a computer. Information is also available on a summer computer camp. Slide shows give an overview of previous summer camps at Stanford University.

Computer Science Journals and Magazines

See also "Education Journals and Magazines" (entries 96–102) and "Staying Current" (entries 1494–1508).

275. *Computerworld*

http://www.computerworld.com

For information technology leaders, *Computerworld* provides current news on the computer industry and new developments. The Resource Center contains articles, features, and reviews of publications, as well as information on conferences. IT (information technology) Careers features articles on career opportunities and training developments. Past issues are archived and can be searched.

276. *HotWired*

http://hotwired.lycos.com/

HotWired provides information from the digital front, including Wired News, commentary, Webmonkey for Kids, examples of animations, an RGB gallery, and Webmonkey Guides to help find specific information on the Web. Links are available to *Wired* magazine and selected full-text articles. The *HotWired* archives contain selections of articles published from 1994 to the present.

277.   *JavaWorld*

http://www.javaworld.com

Published by IDG Communications, *JavaWorld* is a magazine for the Java community. In Nuts & Bolts, beginners and experts can find tutorials, tips, and tricks. In News & Views, you can find opinions, trends, and real-world applications of Java. Links are provided to Java resources. Each issue is searchable and there is an archive. Subscribe to the free news service to receive alerts on new articles.

278.   *Macworld Online*

http://macworld.zdnet.com

Macworld Online is a monthly publication that can be accessed from this site along with *MacWeek*, a weekly newsletter. *Macworld Online* focuses on providing all the information Mac users need. From top stories and product news to new software products, *Macworld Online* offers news and articles about all aspects of Macs. Students can browse the archives of previous issues by year and month, or use the convenient search engine to locate specific information.

279.   Online Magazines from ZDNet-Ziff-Davis Publishing

http://www3.zdnet.com/findit/mags.html

Available online are *Computer Gaming World, Family PC, MacUser, MacWeek, PC Computing, PC Week*, and *PC Magazine*, to name a few of the online publications available from ZDNet-Ziff-Davis Publishing. See ZDNet's home page at (http://www3.zdnet.com).

280.   *PC Magazine Online*

http://www.zdnet.com/pcmag

PC Magazine Online provides articles and regular features on technical developments and opinions of interest to computer and Internet users. New product reviews and comparisons are especially helpful. Trends Online looks at trends in industry, hardware, software, and the Internet. There is an archive of the complete contents of previous issues.

281.   *SunWorld*

http://www.sunworld.com

SunWorld is published by IDG Communications for the Unix professional. *SunWorld* includes news articles and regular columns, features, letters to the editor, reviews, and advertisements. *SunWorld* is a monthly magazine with insightful articles and lots of useful information. Subscribe to the free news service to receive announcements of new articles by e-mail.

282.   *TidBITS*

http://www.tidbits.com

TidBITS is a free, weekly e-mail and Web publication that covers news and views related to the Macintosh and the Internet. *TidBITS* has been published weekly since April 1990, making it one of the longest-running Internet publications. Past issues are archived, and issues are searchable. *TidBITS* is available in English, German, French, Japanese, or Dutch. Maintained by Adam C. Engst, author of the *Internet Starter Kit for Macintosh*.

Discussion Groups

Computer Technology in Education

283.   **EDTECH (Discussion of Educational Technology)**

E-mail: **listserv@H-NET.MSU.EDU**
Instructions: On the first line of the body of the message, type:
subscribe EDTECH [your first name and last name]

Newsgroup: **bit.litserv.edtech**

EDTECH WWW Archive Site
http://h-net2.msu.edu/~edweb/
or
http://www.h-net.msu.edu/~edweb/

More than 3,500 subscribers from 50 countries subscribe directly to the online discussion group, and about 8,000 readers participate through the newsgroup Web site. EDTECH is a forum for discussion among students, faculty, and anyone else interested in educational technology. This discussion group is an excellent resource for getting answers to questions or finding out how other schools are using technology. Some topics of discussion include problems in using educational technology and how to solve them; articles and books that are stimulating or worthwhile; conferences; continuing education courses; current research projects; and notable hardware and software projects. This list generates heavy incoming mail on a daily basis, but it is extremely valuable for staying up-to-date in the field of educational technology.

The archives of the mailing list are searchable and browseable by month. Archived messages can be sorted by author, date, subject, and thread. If you have access to a newsreader, you can access and participate in EDTECH discussions without subscribing to the list.

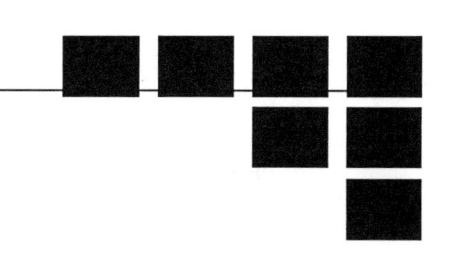

Foreign Language Studies
and Cultural Appreciation

All URL addresses in this chapter are checked and updated monthly. If a link does not work, please refer to the Directory Update Web page located at (http://www.lu.com/lu/irdupdates.html).

The resources in this chapter enhance foreign-language lessons for teachers and students. Using e-mail, students can communicate with other students who are studying the same language or who speak it as their first language. Because foreign-language teachers usually make up a small group at any one school, e-mail communication with other foreign-language teachers helps to overcome any feelings of isolation.

Foreign-language resources on the Internet, such as daily news sources from foreign countries, are valuable, up-to-date resources absent from most school library media centers or classrooms. French Newspapers Online (entry 323); *This Week in Germany* (entry 345); *La Jornada*, a daily Spanish newspaper (entry 411); and *Mundo Latino*, a Spanish magazine (entry 406) are excellent resources. Students can read newspapers in a foreign language online if their language skills are good enough, or teachers may want to point out specific articles for discussion of country-specific news, cultural events, or grammatical idioms. Listening to sound files containing the correct pronunciation of words and phrases is also particularly useful. Sites like Fast and Friendly French for Fun (entry 309) provide interactive learning through self-paced, online tutorials.

Some sites provide useful classroom teaching aids: interactive color maps, artwork by indigenous artists, country flags, virtual museum tours, and color images of rare treasures, such as fragments of papyrus sheets used to write the text of Homer's *Iliad* (entry 372), circa 30 BC.

Although some cultural resources have been included in this chapter, to help students gain broader cultural experience from their foreign-language studies, educators and students will want to check both the indexes and the tables of contents to find related resources in other chapters. For example, Spanish teachers will want to refer to the indexes to find information on South American rain forests. Japanese teachers will want to look at the Arts chapter for information on origami and Kabuki theater. Don't miss some of the resources in the Reference chapter. The CIA *World Factbook* (entry 1424) contains concise country information, and the World Atlas (entry 1423) and Flags of the World (entry 1425) sites provide additional information to enrich foreign-language teaching and learning.

Newsgroups also provide ways for foreign-language students to find out more about the countries and cultures they are studying and to practice their language skills. Foreign-language teachers can use newsgroups to communicate with one another and native speakers. *Note:* Newsgroups are open to the general public, and are therefore susceptible to occasional "graffiti" postings that might be offensive.

Newsgroup: soc.culture.china Chinese culture and society
Newsgroup: k12.lang.francais French conversation
Newsgroup: soc.culture.french French culture and history

Newsgroup: k12.lang.deutsche-eng German conversation
Newsgroup: soc.culture.german German culture and history
Newsgroup: k12.lang.japanese Japanese conversation
Newsgroup: soc.culture.japan Japanese culture and society
Newsgroup: k12.lang.russian Russian conversation
Newsgroup: soc.culture.russian Russian culture and society
Newsgroup: k12.lang.esp-eng Spanish conversation
Newsgroup: soc.culture.spain Spanish culture and society on the Iberian Peninsula
Newsgroup: soc.culture.latin-america Latin American culture and society
Newsgroup: soc.culture.mexico Mexican culture and society

National Standards

284. National Standards in Foreign Language Education
http://www.actfl.org/public/articles/details.cfm?id=33

Language Learning: Preparing for the 21st Century was first published in 1996, and the latest version of the standards, *Standards for Foreign Language Learning in the 21st Century*, which includes information applying the standards to specific languages, was released in 1999. An eight-page Executive Summary of the 1999 version in .pdf format (requires Adobe Acrobat Reader) is available from the American Council on the Teaching of Foreign Languages (ACTFL) Web site (http://www.actfl.org); copies of the full-text standards may be ordered at a cost. The new standards identify five goal areas: Communication, Cultures, Connections, Comparison, and Communities, and 11 standards. A summary of the 1996 version of the foreign language standards is available online from the Mid-continent Research for Education and Learning (McREL) Web site as Chapter 14 of *Content Knowledge: A Compendium of Standards and Benchmarks for K-12 Education* by John S. Kendall and Robert Marzano (http://www.mcrel.org/standards-benchmarks/standardslib/forlang.html).

Teaching Foreign Languages

See also Intercultural E-Mail Classroom Connections (entry 427).

Professional Associations

See also ACTFL: American Council on the Teaching of Foreign Languages

(http://www.actfl.org/) and NNEL: National Network for Early Language Learning (http://www.educ.iastate.edu/nnell/)

285. FLTeach: Foreign Language Teaching Forum
http://www.cortland.edu/flteach/

The main topics of discussion for Foreign Language Teaching Forum (FLTEACH) include foreign-language teaching methods in K-12 schools and colleges, training of student teachers, classroom activities, curriculum, and syllabus design. Students, teachers, administrators, and other professionals interested in any aspect of foreign-language teaching are invited to participate in online discussions, although this active list seems to be dominated by teachers sharing and communicating with one another. In addition to information about FLTeach, the Web page has information about accessing archived messages and member biographies. Archives are keyword-searchable. Don't miss the FLTEACH FAQs, dealing with topics such as classroom discipline, oral participation, student teaching, advice to new teachers, and accent marks. Look for WWW Resources for Language Teachers. Annotated links are grouped into General Resources and Collections as well as language-specific sites for Chinese, German, French, Italian, Japanese, Latin, Portuguese, Russian, Spanish, and Turkish. Co-moderators for FLTEACH are Jean LeLoup (LeLoupJ@cortland.edu) and Bob Ponterio (PonterioR@cortland.edu).

E-mail: **listserv@listserv.acsu.buffalo.edu**
Instructions: On the first line of the body of the message, type:
subscribe FLTEACH [your first name and last name]

General Interest

286. AltaVista Translations

http://babelfish.altavista.digital.com/cgi-bin/translate?/

Don't let Web pages or text written in foreign languages become stumbling blocks to finding information. AltaVista Translations allows you to translate text from German, Italian, Portuguese, Spanish, or French to English, and from English to any of these languages. If you type in a URL address, AltaVista Translations will translate the entire Web page. This is an excellent foreign-language translation tool.

287. BBC Languages Online

http://www.bbc.co.uk/education/languages/

The British Broadcasting Corporation (BBC) offers information about four languages (Spanish, French, German, and Italian) and four countries (Spain, France, Germany, and Italy). For each language and country, information is provided for the student, the traveler, or the person who needs to communicate for business. The online resources for business provide interactive practice with immediate feedback and tips on social etiquette and customs. Bitesize reviews for Spanish, French, and German provide interactive drills for students who are studying to take the GCSE exams. For each country, there are maps, short histories, places of interest to visit, and information about culture, food, and drink.

288. Foreign Languages for Travelers and Travlang

http://www.travlang.com/languages/

Travelers and armchair travelers can learn a few essential phrases in more than 70 different foreign languages. Sound files accompany a list of common words and phrases translated into the language you choose. A link is provided to Travlang, an ancillary Web site. Travlang contains links to travel-related services and language-related services. Travel-related services include maps, European train schedules, online currency converters, international traffic signs and road rules, and international calendars. Language-related services focus on translating software, multilingual dictionaries, online translating dictionaries, a Travlang word of the day, and language schools and student exchange programs. Foreign Languages for Travelers and Travlang were created and are maintained by Dr. Michael C. Martin (president@travlang. com), a physicist currently doing research at the Advanced Light Source Synchrotron at Lawrence Berkeley National Laboratory (Berkeley, California).

289.   **Kickapoo High School Foreign Language Page**

http://sps.k12.mo.us/khs/khshome.htm

Students at Kickapoo High School in Springfield, Missouri, have created five language pages to help students with their studies of German, Japanese, Latin, French, and Spanish.

French resources are organized into categories such as French Literature, Sports, Travel, French Canada, Culture, and Film and TV.

Links on the German page lead to personal home pages, school and university pages, teacher resources, film and television, newspapers and magazines, sports, and German cars. The Culture category offers links to Munich and *Oktoberfest*. The Literature category provides a link to Labyrinth's medieval German page, and the Travel category has links to the subway systems in Frankfurt, Berlin, and Munich, as well as German train schedules and general travel information.

Selected Spanish Internet resources include a verb conjugator, links to newspapers and magazines, Spanish comics, and travel and culture information.

The Japanese Page has useful links to Japanese-related resources, divided into categories such as school and university pages, newspapers and magazines, food, language resources, travel, and culture. Some links lead to Japanese myths and legends, *ikebana* and traditional arts, Tokyo food, and how to roll your own sushi. The *Japan Times Online* (http://www.japantimes.co.jp) provides selected full-text articles in English about news in Japan. Check back often, as this site continues to grow. Maintained by Brian Zahn (bzahn01@mail.orion.org).

290.   **Language and Instructional Media Center**

http://www.artsci.wustl.edu/limc/

Washington University in St. Louis maintains collections of extremely useful foreign-language sites. The Department of Asian and Near Eastern Languages provides resources for Chinese, Japanese, Hebrew, Persian, Arabic, and Turkish. Germanic language resources include German, Dutch, and Swedish. The Department of Romance Languages and Literatures provides resources for French, Italian, Spanish, Portuguese, and Galician. The Russian Department and the Department of Classics also have their own resources. Information is available about foreign-language courses and programs at Washington University and abroad. Foreign-language teachers will find a plethora of information to integrate into their curricular programs.

Dictionaries

291.   **LOGOS Dictionary**

http://www.logos.it/dictionary/owa/sp?lg=EN

LOGOS provides an all-in-one dictionary for 31 languages. The dictionary translates more than 8 million terms among all these languages, including French, Russian, Japanese, Italian, and Spanish. In addition to providing definitions to words in multiple languages, LOGOS also provides a crossword dictionary for partially completed words (such as _a_n) and an anagram maker.

Using the Internet to Teach Foreign Languages

292. Internet Activities for Foreign Language Classes

http://members.aol.com/maestro12/web/wadir.html

California foreign-language teachers have written a collection of lesson plans integrating the Internet into foreign-language teaching. Most of the lessons are for Spanish, Italian, French, or German. New lessons are added each year. This page is maintained by Lewis Johnson (lewis_johnson@eee.org).

293. Quia!

http://www.quia.com/index.html

Quia (pronounced *key-uh*) is short for Quintessential Instructional Archive. Quia provides a variety of educational services, including a directory of thousands of online games and quizzes in more than 40 subject areas. There are hundreds of activities in French, German, Chinese, Latin, Spanish, Chinese, Russian, Italian, and English. Using templates, teachers can produce their own interactive online quizzes and online games, including flash cards, matching games, concentration (memory) games, and word search puzzles. Once completed, these are stored on the Web site and assigned a specific Web address. Registration is free and is required to create learning activities and quizzes. No registration is required to play the games or participate in the educational activities.

294. Teaching with the Web

http://polyglot.lss.wisc.edu/lss/lang/teach.html

Teaching with the Web suggests ways to use the World Wide Web as a language teaching tool. There are general activities and language-specific activities for African languages, Asian languages, ESL/EFL, French, German, Italian, Latin, and Russian. Links are provided to teaching resources and sites with pedagogical information. Created and maintained by Lauren Rosen (lrosen@facstaff.wisc.edu).

American Sign Language

295. A Basic Dictionary of ASL Terms

http://www.masterstech-home.com/ASLDict.html

This dictionary has both animated and text definitions of terms. It also includes the basic alphabet and numbers 1–10. The sign images are seen from the perspective of the viewer, not the signer. Signers are reminded that facial expressions and body language are integral parts of communicating, giving meaning to what is being signed, much like vocal tones and inflections for spoken words. Apple's QuickTime plug-in is required to view the animated sign definitions. Created and maintained by the Master's Tech (masterstech@masterstech-home.com).

Chinese

Language Studies

296. A Is For Love

http://www.chinapage.com/love.html

Provides a set of flash cards for learning Chinese, A–Z. Click on the word; the flash card turns over and the meaning is given. For most cards, there is also an accompanying sound file for pronunciation. This is part of a Web site titled China the Beautiful, by Dr. Ming L. Pei (entry 302).

297. Chinese Dialect Exercise

http://www.askasia.org/frclasrm/lessplan/l000007.htm

Demonstrates the obstacles to communication created by the presence of dialects and stresses the need for a common writing system. Provides a lesson and worksheet to help students understand that many Chinese people cannot communicate orally with one another, because of the vast number of dialects spoken in China as well as the physical distances between the areas in which these dialects are spoken. This exercise is reprinted online with permission from the Stanford Program on International and Cross-Cultural Education and was originally printed in *Focus on Asian Studies: Asian Languages, New Series* vol.1, no. 3.

298. On-Line Chinese Tools

http://www.mandarintools.com

Created for both novice and more advanced Chinese-language students, this page uses Web technologies to provide tools to help learn and use the Chinese language. Look for character flashcards, a Chinese namer to convert an English name to a Chinese name, Chinese/English dictionary, a Western/Chinese calendar converter, and a Chinese text annotator. Tools are available for Chinese-language programmers. To access the information on this page, Netscape Communicator is recommended or Internet Explorer 3 or higher. Created and maintained by Erik E. Peterson (erik@mandarintools.com), a Chinese linguist and computer programmer.

History and Culture of China

See also WebQuest: Searching for China (http://www.kn.pacbell.com/wired/China/ChinaQuest.html).

299. Art of China

http://pasture.ecn.purdue.edu/~agenhtml/agenmc/china/china.html

Students studying Chinese culture will find online graphics depicting examples of pottery, paintings, miniature crafts, paper-cut art and photographs of famous scenery such as the Forbidden City, the Great Wall, the Imperial Gardens, and the Yellow Mountain. Recipes translated into English provide a taste of China, sound files let students access Chinese music and survival skills, such as how to say "Hi" in Chinese, order food, travel around, and shop. Links are provided to other related sites. Web information provided by Purdue University international students.

300. China
http://www.fi.edu/fellows/fellow1/apr99/

Third-graders at Loogootee Elementary West studied China and demonstrated their computer skills by sharing some of their interactive, student-created information. Online activities include writing numbers from 1–12, making paper, discovering facts about China from A to Z, and finding out personality characteristics from a Chinese calendar. A quiz is included.

301. China: Dim Sum: A Connection to Chinese-American Culture
http://www.newton.mec.edu/Angier/DimSum/chinadimsumaconnection.html

Dim sum is a Cantonese term meaning "a little bit of heart," and this cross-curricular unit gives dim sum to elementary lessons in math, language arts, science, social studies, and the arts by enhancing awareness and understanding of Chinese-American culture while building basic academic skills. Developed for the Angier School (Newton, MA); the Webmaster can be contacted at (janet_panaggio@newton.mec.edu).

302. China the Beautiful
http://www.chinapage.com/china.html

Focuses on classical Chinese art, calligraphy, poetry, history, literature, painting, and philosophy to present a part of 5,000 years of Chinese cultural heritage. Visitors may enter two main rooms. The China Room does not require any special software or a knowledge of the Chinese language. The Chinese Reading Room requires special Chinese fonts to read materials in Chinese. Created and maintained by Dr. Ming L. Pei (pei@chinapage.org), professor emeritus.

303. Chinese Wedding Traditions
http://www.chcp.org./Vwedding.html

Chinese wedding traditions reflect more than 2,400 years of history. This site, created by the Chinese Historical and Cultural Project (San Jose, California), describes ancient Chinese marriage customs and compares them to contemporary wedding customs in China and the West. A bibliography is provided, and in-text links are helpful in providing further information. Students will find all the details about the proposal, betrothal, wedding preparations, and wedding day.

304. Golden Legacy Curriculum
http://www.chcp.org/Pgolden.html

The Golden Legacy curriculum was developed by the Chinese Historical and Cultural Project and the San Jose (California) Historical Museum, to complement the California State Social Studies Framework. It contains more than 30 lesson plans, a vocabulary section, an annotated bibliography, and an index. Color graphics by Ng Shing Gung supplement the curriculum. Text-only versions of all 30 lesson plans are available at this Web site.

Three sample lesson plans with illustrations from Golden Legacy are available at the AskERIC Virtual Library (http://ericir.syr.edu/Projects/CHCP): Bound Feet, Abacus, and Lunar Calendar. For more information about the Chinese Historical and Cultural Project and other CHCP projects, see the home page (http://www.chcp.org).

305. **People's Republic of China**

http://www.edu.cn/china/

Find out more about the history and culture of the People's Republic of China, including arts, festivals, and food. Links are provided to information about China's 31 provinces, which are numbered on an accompanying map for easy identification. The section on Chinese Art discusses traditional and contemporary painting, watercolor, and papercuts.

English As a Second Language

306. **EFLWEB**

http://www.eflweb.com

EFLWEB is a clearinghouse for information about teaching and learning English as a foreign language. Students can find resources to help them practice their English skills and find guides to language schools. Teachers of English can post their résumés and read about teaching experiences written by other teachers of English as a foreign language. Look for a FAQs and links to other useful information.

Two online discussion groups focus on teaching English as a foreign language.

K-12 Teachers of English as a Second Language or Foreign Language

E-mail: **listserv@cunyvm.cuny.edu**
Instructions: On the first line of the body of the message, type:
subscribe TESLK-12 [your first name and last name]

and

Teaching English as a Second Language

E-mail: **listserv@cunyvm.cuny.edu**
Instructions: On the first line of the body of the message, type:
subscribe TESL-L [your first name and last name]

307. **The ESL Quiz Center**

http://www.pacificnet.net/~sperling/quiz/

A growing collection includes interactive quizzes in current news, geography, grammar, history, idioms, slang, words, people, reading comprehension, science, vocabulary, world culture, and writing. The software automatically checks answers in seconds and provides feedback so students can learn the correct answers as well as their individual scores. This site is maintained by Dave Sperling (sperling@pacificnet.net).

French

French is officially spoken in France, Andorra, Belgium, Benin, Burkina Faso, Burundi, Cameroon, Canada, Central African Republic, Chad, Comoros, Congo, Côte d'Ivoire, Djibouti, French Polynesia, Gabon, Guadeloupe, Guinea, Haiti, Luxembourg, Madagascar, Martinique, Mauritania, Mayotte, Monaco, New Caledonia, Niger, Reunion, Rwanda, Senegal, Seychelles, St. Pierre and

Miquelon, Switzerland, Togo, United Kingdom (Channel Islands), Vanuatu, Wallis and Futuna, and Zaire.

See also the CIA *World Factbook* entry for France, (http://www.odci.gov/cia/publications/factbook/).

Professional Associations

308. American Association of Teachers of French (AATF)

http://aatf.utsa.edu

As a professional association of French teachers, AATF promotes and encourages the study of French as a foreign language. This bilingual Web site provides access to information such as summaries of the National Standards in Foreign Language Education and "The Importance of the French Language," a document that compiles many facts to demonstrate the importance of the French language in the modern world. Be sure to check out the FAQs devoted to Teaching French with the Internet (http://aatf.utsa.edu/twiafaq.htm) for links to examples of Internet activities for French classes.

Discover French Culture on the World Wide Web is a page of links to bilingual and French Internet resources originally published in the *American Association of Teachers of French National Bulletin*, and is updated regularly. Students can find out what's happening on the Paris entertainment and cultural scenes by reading the weekly online edition of *Pariscope;* take a guided tour of Nîmes to see Roman ruins; explore Brittany, where prehistoric ruins still hold the secrets of people who lived there 6,000 years ago; and browse through La Redoute's mail-order catalog for the latest in French fashions, home decorations, children's toys, and recreational sports accessories. A link to the Web site Camembert: A Village, A Cheese offers an interesting tour of Camembert, a village in Normandy, noted for its cheese, which is packaged in small, round, wooden containers.

Language Studies

309. Fast and Friendly French for Fun

http://library.advanced.org/12447/

An excellent online resource for beginning French students, this site contains grammar lessons, interactive games in French, and information about France's geography, people, and food. Navigation buttons at the bottom of each page allow easy access to all information. Each lesson is followed by an interactive quiz so that students can test their knowledge. Sound files in three different formats (RealAudio, Wave, and SunNeXT) allow students to hear French words and phrases spoken by a French teacher. Links are provided to other French-related sites on the Internet. Created by high school students Amy Deal (Amydeal@aol.com), Gregory Smith (tocard@geocities.com), and Jaclyn Streich (streich@osf1.gmu.edu), as a ThinkQuest project.

310. Really Useful French Teaching Site

http://www.btinternet.com/~s.glover/S.Glover/languagesite/Default.htm

Provides links to many interactive exercises on the Web for learning French culture and language. Includes teacher-created interactive lessons about the cinema, links to other interactive exercises, and links to software to help create interactive lessons. A seasonal page contains a collection of links to information appropriate to particular seasons, events, and holidays. Listening exercises incorporate RealAudio. Created and maintained by Steve Glover (S.Glover@ BTInternet.com), Habergham High School, Burnley, Lancashire, England.

History and Culture of France and French-Speaking Peoples

See also prehistoric art at the Chauvet Cave, France (entry 1241) and Age of Enlightenment in the Paintings of France's National Museums (entry 139).

311.   Christmas Traditions in France and Canada

http://www.culture.fr/culture/noel/angl/noel.htm

How do French families celebrate Christmas? This site explores some of the Christmas traditions in France and Canada. Students can learn more about the origins of Christmas in France, communal festivities, religious ceremonies, and the history of Christmas as a cultural tradition in France from the Middle Ages to today. The French version of this same information is available at (http://www.culture.fr/culture/noel/franc/noel.htm).

312.   The Embassy of France (Washington, DC)

http://www.info-france-usa.org

Ambassade de France provides excellent information written in English about France. Topics include Culture, Travel, and Education; News and Statements; France & America; Trade & Science; France on the Internet; and Profile of France. Middle and high school students will find current information to support their research. Elementary school students will want to explore Just 4 Kids, an informative and interactive site that encourages a lot of fun learning. Students will discover maps; color pictures; games, such as Hangman and the Slide Puzzle, using words found in both French and English; reasons to learn the French language; French facts; national heritage sites; and more about France's history, economy, and art culture. Using helpful in-text links, students can read monthly articles from *Les Clés de l'Actualité Junior*, a French magazine for children. See (http://www.lescles.com/main.html) for more information as well as information on other magazines written in French for children and teenagers, including *Les Clés de l'Actualité* for teens.

313.   French Culture Home Page in French

http://www.culture.fr

Written in French from the office of the Ministre de la Culture et de la Communication (Paris, France), this page offers information on topics that include architecture, art, libraries, movies and theater, cuisine and recipes, special events, language, literature, magazines, museums, music, sports, politics, science, and humanities. Some texts are available in English from the English-version page (http://www.culture.fr/cgi-bin/cookie-test-en).

314.   French Page: La page française

http://www.acs.appstate.edu/dept/fll/french.html

Long lists of sites provide links to information about French culture, language, history, art, and literature. Though aimed at older students studying French, many links could be enjoyed by younger students; these include a satellite image of France, images of famous French art-works, *World Fact Book* information, and recipes. This page was developed for use by B.A. and M.A. students studying French at Appalachian State University in North Carolina. Information about the department's Study Abroad program in Angiers, France, is provided.

315. French Studies Web

http://www.nyu.edu/pages/wessfrench/index.html

The French Studies Web provides access to scholarly resources in French studies. The geographical coverage includes France and the francophone regions of Belgium and Switzerland. In addition to links to library catalogs, online reference materials, and professional information, the subject resources are excellent. Links lead to archaeology, architecture, art, business and economics, education, history, literature and culture, politics and government, theater, women's studies, and information and computing technology. The collection of French primary historical documents is impressive; it includes transcriptions, translations, and facsimile copies of originals. Some of the most impressive pieces in this collection are photo facsimiles of French Revolution-era pamphlets. The section on French theater includes an archive of primary sources on the Parisian fairground theaters during the 17th and 18th centuries. The entire educational process, from preschool through higher education, is outlined with accompanying graphics in the Education in France section (http://cri.ensmp.fr/mesr/), allowing educators to compare schooling in France to schooling in the United States.

316. Le Cordon Bleu, Paris

http://metalab.unc.edu/expo/restaurant/restaurant.html

Le Cordon Bleu held its first cooking class in the Palais Royal on January 14, 1896. Learn more about the school's history and examine seven full menus, one for each day of the week. Recipes are given for each menu, with the warning that some may be too difficult for amateur cooks. However, delicious-looking color images of *Éstouffade de Boeuf Provençale* (Provençal Braised Beef Casserole) and *Feuilletés de Saumon aux Asperges* (Puff Pastry Cases with Salmon and Asparagus and a Lemon Butter Sauce) may prompt culinary activity despite the caution. These and other recipes can be found in *Le Cordon Bleu at Home*, published by Ebury Press (1992).

317. Le Tour de France

http://www.letour.fr

Le Société du Tour de France provides information about the Tour de France, an annual, grueling three-week bicycle race through France, undertaken by top cyclists from around the world who try to conquer long distances over mountains, hills, and flatlands in record times. Questions about the history of the Tour de France are answered in a FAQs section. Information about each of the race years can be found in Tour Chronicles, a database of races that is searchable by year, rider, and country. Legendary Tours highlights race years with notable events. Gives information about the routes of future races, including maps. Provides a French/English glossary for cycling jargon. Information on this Web site is available in French, English, German, and Spanish.

318. The Museums of Paris

http://www.paris.org/Musees/

The Museums of Paris is an index to all the museums in Paris. Information is available in both English and French, and museums are indexed alphabetically by name. Museums can also be accessed by categories such as tapestries, scale models, jewelry, paintings, and sculpture. The Must See Museums are the Musée du Louvre, the Musée d'Orsay, and Cité des Sciences et d'Industrie. These museums are treated to more in-depth coverage and are linked to images as visual examples from their respective collections. An interesting feature is an interactive map of Paris that allows students to locate major monuments and museums. A picture and a bit of history are given for most monuments. For example, students will discover that the Arc de Triomphe was commissioned in 1806 by Napoleon, shortly after his victory at Austerlitz, but it was not finished until 1836.

319. The Paris Metro

http://metro.ratp.fr:10001/

The Subway Navigator allows you to find a route using the Paris subway network. French or English can be used for this geographic exercise. In addition to Paris, the Subway Navigator allows you to find routes in subway systems in many cities around the world, for example, Montreal, Quebec; Toronto, Ontario; Lille, France; Lyon, France; Frankfurt; Hong Kong; Boston; and Washington, D.C.

320. Paris Zoom

http://paris-anglo.com/zoom/

Take an interactive photographic journey to Paris. Fifty-one photographs are currently available, with three levels of graphics—close, closer, and closest. Experience some of the details of Parisian daily life, including images of street workers, traffic, croissants, children, dogs, a butcher shop, and so on. Links are provided to Paris-Anglo.com for more information about Paris, visiting Paris, studying in Paris, and everyday life in Paris.

321. Regional French Cooking

http://www.beyond.fr/food/index.html

Entitled Gastronomy Beyond the French Riviera, this site offers recipes for many typical provincial French dishes. There is an excellent metric conversion link to help convert quantities for ingredients. Preparing French dishes, such as *salade niçoise, bouillabaisse,* and *pâtes au pistou,* is easy when you know that 30 grams equals 2 tablespoons and that the French word for garlic is *ail*!

Other French recipes can be found at chef Paul Bocuse's home page (http://www.ec-lyon.fr/tourisme/Rhone-Alpes/Cuisine/index.html.en) and the Campanile Hotel Web site (http://www.campanile.fr/english/rctsom.htm).

322. **Yahoo! France**

http://fr.yahoo.com

French-language students can test their language proficiency by searching on the Internet in French. Yahoo! provides a French version with Web pages written in French. Look for *Catégorie Yahoo! équivalente en anglais* to help translate categories into English or change to the English version of this Web site directory. This is a great way for French students to find resources written in French on the Internet.

Periodicals

323. **French Newspapers Online**

http://www.nyu.edu/pages/wessfrench/news.htm

Provided by the Western European Specialists Section of the Association of College and Research Libraries, this is part of the French Studies Web, offering links to French newspapers and other news sources. News is divided into daily news, full-text newspapers, and a union list of selected West European newspapers and news magazines in New York metropolitan libraries. Daily news is provided from Radio France Internationale, *France-Press* online, *Edicom Presse*, and a daily weather bulletin from Météo-France. Full-text news sources include *Le Monde* (http://www.lemonde.fr), *Le Monde Diplomatique*, and *Revue de Presse Quotidienne de RFI* (Radio France Internationale).

German

German is officially spoken in Germany, Austria, eastern Belgium, Liechtenstein, Alsace-Lorraine (France), several Swiss cantons, and South Tyrol (Italy). There are also German-speaking minorities in Romania and southern Denmark. A dialect of German is spoken in Luxembourg.

Professional Associations

324. **AATG Home Page**

http://www.aatg.org

The American Association of Teachers of German home page provides valuable information for German teachers. Teaching tips are one of the highlights shared online, along with conference news and employment opportunities. Resources are available to enrich the teaching curriculum, such as learning scenarios, resources and sample lessons from AATG Summer Technology Workshops, and an annotated bibliography of German-language learning software (http://ucaswww.mcm.uc.edu/german/bib.htm). To join the AATG online discussion group:

E-mail: **listserv@listserv.iupui.edu**
Instructions: On the first line of the body of the message, type:
subscribe AATG [your first name and last name]

Note: Although AATG is the online discussion group for members of the American Association of Teachers of German, teachers of German who are nonmembers are also welcome to join.

Language Studies

325.   Deutsch im Netz: German on the Web

http://nosferatu.cas.usf.edu/german/frames/DimNetz/

Provides creative, interactive grammar exercises based on current pedagogical practices and using authentic materials and supplementary Web resources for studying the German language, people, and culture. Gives interesting annotated links to everything German for younger students and high school students. Look for German comics, German music, German games, a German-language song index, fairy tales, songs and rhymes, and children's e-zines. There are also links to German folk songs; sound files with different German dialects; and information about Germany, including travel, leisure, and food. Created and maintained by Lizz Caplan-Carbin (lcaplan@chuma1.cas.usf.edu).

326.   German Language Home Page

http://german.about.com/education/german/

Information on the home page can be accessed from two areas: In the Spotlight and NetLinks. The NetLinks area includes links to German-language-related topics such as bookstores, culture, dictionaries, teachers, grammar, language, music, pen pals, reading, and translation. In the Spotlight showcases Web sites and feature articles to assist those who are learning or teaching the German language. Past articles have focused on bilingual parenting, how to make a PC keyboard bilingual, and different grammar tips. Maintained by Hyde Flippo (german. guide@about.com), the About.com guide to German language.

327.   German Studies Trails on the Web

http://www.uncg.edu/~lixlpurc/german.html

Interdisciplinary German resources include links to online museums, literature, teaching tools and software, children's pages, and theory. Be sure to check out links to German studies exercises on the Web. Links are also provided to topical studies, such as language and civilization, art and culture, science and technology, and German-language instruction and research. Created and maintained by German Professor Andreas Lixl-Purcell (lixlpurc@hamlet.uncg.edu) at the University of North Carolina in Greensboro.

328.   The German Way: For Teachers and Students of German

http://www.german-way.com/german/teach.html

Part of a companion Web site (http://www.german-way.com) for *The German Way: Aspects of Behavior, Attitudes, and Customs in the German-Speaking World* by Hyde Flippo (NTC Publishing Group, 1996), this Web page offers suggestions for classroom projects and ideas that incorporate Internet resources. Photos and information pages are available for Austria, Germany, and Switzerland. Biographies, German cinema, and German language and cultural Web links provide great information for the classroom. Other sites are specifically for German-language teachers. Created and maintained by Hyde Flippo (hflippo@powernet.net), who also maintains the About.com's German Language Home Page (entry 326).

329. **Goethe-Institut (New York City, New York)**

http://www.goethe.de/uk/ney/enindex.htm

The Goethe-Institut is a nonprofit organization with 135 institutes in 70 countries. Its mission is to foster appreciation for the German language and culture and to enhance international cultural cooperation and understanding. The head office is located in Munich, Germany. The New York office is a regional office for both the United States and Canada, coordinating the efforts of 13 institutes within the region. The Goethe-Institut frequently offers courses, workshops, and seminars for German teachers, and also provides invaluable teaching materials and resources for classroom use.

330. **Really Useful German Site**

http://atschool.eduweb.co.uk/haberg/reallyusefulge/default.htm

Provides interactive lessons for German grammar and vocabulary; information about software; and links to *Juma*, a downloadable German-language magazine requiring Adobe Acrobat. Images of food and transportation are available to download to use in PowerPoint presentations or worksheets. An exercise about *Weihnachten* in Deutschland requires RealAudio. Be sure to check out the link to BBC's Deutsch Plus Online at (http://www.bbc.co.uk/education/languages/german/index.shtml); it has Bitesize reviews for students studying for the GCSE exams, as well as travel information and essential conversation skills and etiquette necessary for conducting business in Germany. Created and maintained by Steve Glover (S.Glover@BTInternet.com), Habergham High School, Burnley, Lancashire, England.

History and Culture of Germany and German-Speaking Peoples

331. **19th-Century German Stories**

http://www.vcu.edu/hasweb/for/menu.html

A collection of short narrative works in German from the late 18th to the early 20th centuries is mostly accompanied by English translations. Look for children's stories such as *Max and Moritz*, by Wilhelm Busch; *Struwwelpeter*, by Heinrich Hoffmann; *A Fairy Tale*, by Johann Wolfgang von Goethe; and some of the stories from *Fairy Tales for Home and Nursery* by the Grimm Brothers. Ten Grimm fairy tales are presented in a choice of two formats: side-by-side dual English/German texts and German text side-by-side with an online German/English dictionary. There is a quiz in German for each Grimm fairy tale. Similar side-by-side formats are used to present stories from *Struwwelpeter* and *Max and Moritz*. This excellent site was created and is maintained by Robert Godwin-Jones (rgjones@vcu.edu), a German professor at Virginia Commonwealth University. See Professor Godwin-Jones's Web Office for more information on Web authoring for language teachers (http://www.fln.vcu.edu/gj.html).

332. **Christmas in German Europe**

http://www.german-way.com/german/christmas.html

Written in Austria in German, "Stille Nacht" ("Silent Night") is the world's most famous Christmas song. The Christmas tree (*Tannenbaum*) custom also came from Germany. Discover more about German customs and traditions at Christmas. Learn how to make gingerbread (*Lebkuchen*), *Stollen* (fruit bread), and *Marzipan*, made with almonds and sugar. Links are provided to pictures, markets, holiday graphics, music and German carols, German Christmas postcards to send to friends, and lots more information. See also Weihnachten or Christmas in Germany (http://www.serve.com/shea/germusa/xmasmain.htm), one of Robert J. Shea's Web pages from (http://www.serve.com/shea/germusa/customs.htm). *See also* entry 339.

333.   Deutsche Internetquellen

http://www.tcd.ie/CLCS/deutsch/deutschhome.html

Covering a broad range of topics and well organized, this Web site offers links to German media sources, including RealAudio broadcasts from German radio and newspapers, magazines, and other print resources. Other links provide tourist information, glimpses into the culture of German-speaking countries, and information on science, art, history, and literature. Information is available in both German and English. Created and maintained by Klaus Schwienhorst (kschwien@tcd.ie), at the University of Dublin, Trinity College.

334.   The German Embassy (Washington, DC)

http://www.germany-info.org

The German Embassy Web site is an information center for the Federal Republic of Germany, and an ideal starting point for student research. The Embassy shares this Web site with the German Information Center (GIC), which provides materials on political, economic, and cultural aspects of German society. Look for quick facts as well as more in-depth facts about health care and social welfare, the environment, religious issues, and education. Also available are comparative economic data, highlighting German trade with the United States. Find out more about German holidays and festivals. Each month a different recipe is featured, and the Recipe Archive is browseable by month and year beginning with February 1996. Some other topics of interest on this information-packed Web site include German history, student study opportunities in Germany, sports news, and travel and weather information.

335.   German Folk Songs

http://ingeb.org/Volksong.html

Fill your classroom with the sound of music. Thousands of German folk songs are listed alphabetically in this database of folk songs from around the world. Many song titles are accompanied by the lyrics written in German, digitized sound files (.midi), and musical notations. Students can practice their German by singing traditional German folk songs. Created and maintained by Frank Petersohn (frank@dccnet.com). See also the German Music Database (http://www.cory.de/music/gmd.html) for a list of artists and lyrics, including the Beatles, other popular European artists, and Christmas carols. Don't miss the link from this page to Other Music Sites.

336.   The German National Tourist Board

http://www.deutschland-tourismus.de/e/ [English version]

http://www.deutschland-tourismus.de/d/ [German version]

Travel the regions and cities of Germany via the Web. Find out why Berlin is called the City of the Dancing Bear. The searchable city database was not working when this site was reviewed, but the alphabetical listing of cities provides an easy way to city-hop around Germany. Color maps of Germany in Europe and Germany's roads, *autobahns*, and railway network are available.

Good travel tips cover topics such as accommodations, transportation, weather, money, and public telephones, as well as general information about time, weights and measurement, value-added tax (VAT), shop and restaurant hours, traveling etiquette, and gratuities. Major events are highlighted, and there is a searchable database of events that can be personalized by areas of interest and periods of time. Information on this Web site is available in either English or German.

337. Movieline

http://www.movieline.de

Written in German, this site provides information about movies and films. Newly released movies are listed, and students can read advertisements for movies in German and then compare to those written in English. A searchable database of movies allows searching by film title, actor, director, film company, or film category. The News section provides news articles written in German about various films and film reviews. To access a site written in English about Hollywood films with a German connection, see The German-Hollywood Connection (http://www.german-way.com/cinema/).

338. Project Gutenberg DE: The Digital Library

http://www.gutenberg.aol.de

Project Gutenberg DE contains texts written in German of more than 250 classical authors. With more than 120,000 book pages, this represents one of the largest German Internet sites. Look for novels, fairy tales, fables, legends, and poems. Works include those by Daniel Defoe, Charles Dickens, Johann Wolfgang von Goethe, Jacob and William Grimm, Edgar Allan Poe, and Mark Twain, to mention just a few. Look for a picture and brief biographical notes for each author. This is the place to come for Grimm fairy tales written in German. To search for books in print and currently available from publishers, go to the German version of Amazon.com (http://www.amazon.de/).

339. Robert J. Shea's German Resources

http://www.serve.com/shea/germany.htm

Robert Shea has several Web sites from which to choose. German Americana (http://www.serve.com/shea/germusa/germusa.htm) covers mostly German-American resources on the Internet. German Customs and Holidays (http://www.serve.com/shea/germusa/customs.htm) organizes holidays around a 12-month calendar, with links to further information. The German 1848 Revolution (http://www.serve.com/shea/germusa/1848.htm) provides an in-depth look at the revolution and a German-American perspective. The German Resources Web site provides a well-organized listing of resources on the Internet for topics such as news and media, computer applications, German-language education, German sports, and German music. Created and maintained by Robert J. Shea (nihan@stlnet.com), German instructor at Rockwood School District, Eureka, Missouri.

340. Yahoo! Deutschland

http://www.yahoo.de

Familiarity with the English version of Yahoo! will make it relatively easy for both beginning and more advanced students of German to use the German version of Yahoo! for searching and accessing Web pages written in German. For example, categories include Computers, Education, Reference, Health, Art and Culture, Sports, and Cities and Countries. Students can check *das Wetter* for many German cities to find out the current weather forecast. Will there be *Schnee* or *Regen, teils wolkig*, or *sonnig*? Students might need to consult the WWW Temperature Converter (entry 1436) to find out if a high of 10 and a low of 6 means a coat or sweater should be worn outside.

Periodicals

341. *The German American Corner*

http://www.germancorner.com

Home of the *German American Corner*, the first German-American Internet magazine, published by Davitt Publications in Marina, California. This Web site offers much more than online articles written in both English and German on topics of interest to German-Americans. The Cook's Pantry contains recipes and conversion charts. German-American travel information covers Austria and Germany as well as places in the United States with German heritage. The German-American History and Heritage page (http://www.GermanHeritage.com) contains biographies of more than 200 German-Americans, excellent teaching resources for the classroom, and links to German-American online books.

342. *German Life*

http://www.germanlife.com

German Life is a bimonthly magazine, written in English, for people interested in the diversity of German culture, past and present, and in the various ways that North America has been shaped by its German population. The table of contents and selected articles from current and back issues (since June/July 1995) are available. The archive of back issues is searchable.

343. **K–12 German Teacher Resources**

http://www.ahshornets.org/k12-german/Welcome/welcome.html

Provides a semi-monthly newsletter by e-mail and on the Web, with suggested Web resources to use in teaching German in K–12 classes. A new Web site, started in January 2000, with support from the South Carolina State Department of Education and the Milken Family Foundations, hopes to promote sharing of resources and activities with German K-12 classes around the world.

344. *Munich Found Online*

http://www.munichfound.com

Munich Found Online is Bavaria's leading English-language, monthly magazine. It is dedicated to providing its international audience with a discerning mix of culture, history, commentary, art, and politics. The restaurant guide offers choices from low budget to exclusive gourmet dining. Find out the current four-day weather forecast for Munich and the surrounding area.

345. ***This Week in Germany***

http://www.germany-info.org/nf_gic/index_news_publications.html

The German Information Center provides a free weekly newsletter, *This Week in Germany* (English) or *Deutschland Nachrichten* (German), that summarizes current events in Germany. News articles focus on German politics and the economy as well as top news stories and general-interest items. Archives of back issues are available online in both English and German from February 1996. Archives are browseable by month and year.

To receive free subscriptions to *This Week in Germany* by e-mail:

E-mail: **listserv@dartmouth.edu**
Instructions: On the first line of the body of the message, type:
sub gic-e [your first name and last name]

To receive free subscriptions to *Deutschland Nachrichten* by e-mail:

E-mail: **listserv@dartmouth.edu**
Instructions: On the first line of the body of the message, type:
sub gic-d [your first name and last name]

Hindi

Along with English, Hindi is the official language of India. In addition, it is the state language of Bihar, Haryana, Himachal Pradesh, Madhya Pradesh, Uttar Pradesh, and Rajasthan. Hindi is spoken in the South Asian countries of India, Pakistan, and Nepal as well as Mauritius, Trinidad, Fiji, Surinam, Guyana, and South Africa.

Language Studies

346. **Hindi/Urdu Conversation Lessons on the Web at Syracuse University**

http://syllabus.syr.edu/hin/jshankar/hin101/hindi.html

Ranked as one of the five most widely spoken languages of the world, approximately 600 million people speak Hindi as either a first or second language. Online lessons include topics such as letters of the alphabet, numbers, colors, and identifying things. Three lessons on conversation include sound files. Jishnu Shankar, Associate Director, South Asia Center, is the instructor for first- and second-year Hindi language courses at Syracuse University, and can be reached at (jshankar@syr.edu).

History and Culture of India

347. **Cooking for the Gods**

http://www.arth.upenn.edu/nalin/nalin.html

Cooking for the Gods: The Art of Home Ritual in Bengal was an exhibition presented at the Newark Museum in 1995–1996. It is now an online exhibition, featuring 80 eclectic small objects from eastern India. Objects pictured include color images of deities, lamps, incense holders, dishes, bells, and votive offerings; the images are accompanied by brief explanations. Maintained by Michael W. Meister (mmeister@sas.upenn.edu), History of Art Department, University of Pennsylvania.

348. Discover India
http://www.indiagov.org

Discover India is sponsored by the Ministry of External Affairs, Government of India, and includes everything you want to know about India, past and present. Links are provided to information about sports, tourism, foreign relations, India perspectives, social issues, culture, history, and more. Be sure to see Mahatma Gandhi: A Retrospective (http://www.indiagov.org/Gandhi/intro.htm). The information on this Web site is searchable, and there is a What's New feature. The Webmaster's address is (webmaster@meadev.gov.in).

349. Festivals & Religious Occasions of India
http://india.indiagov.org/culture/festival/festival.htm

India is known for its festivals and holidays. More than 30 festivals and religious occasions are listed here, with links to additional information. There is also a calendar of Indian festivals. Find out more about Shivaratri, New Year's Day, Diwali, and the Ladakh Festival.

350. The *Ramayana*
http://www.maxwell.syr.edu/maxpages/special/ramayana/

The *Ramayana* is a great Indian epic that tells about life in India around 1,000 B.C.E. and presents models in *dharma* through the characters of Rama, Bharata, and Sita. The hero of the story, Rama, lived his whole life by the rules of *dharma*. He was the perfect son as a young boy; later in his life he was an ideal husband to his faithful wife, Sita, and a responsible ruler of Aydohya. For 2,000 years, young Indians have been taught to "Be as Rama" and to "Be as Sita." Be sure to see the list of children's books on the topic of India under Links and Resources; also look for the excellent list of links to lesson plans and Web sites on the culture of India. A comic-book version of this beautiful story is available in nine parts at (http://www.askasia.org/adult_free_zone/virtual_gallery/exhibitions/index.htm).

Italian

Italian is officially spoken in Italy, San Marino, Somalia, and Switzerland.

Language Studies

351. Italica
http://www.italica.org

The Radio Televisione Italiana (RAI) sponsors this Web site, which is dedicated to promoting Italian language and culture. Provides information about computer connections to radio programs on RAI International via satellite and RealAudio available 24 hours a day. The language section contains 15 grammar and language lessons developed by the University of Nôtre Dame. The Arts section contains information about Italian fine arts and music. This Web site is written in Italian.

History and Culture of Italy

352. In Italy Online

http://www.initaly.com

Students, travelers, and those interested in their Italian ancestry will appreciate the broad range of interesting information available at In Italy Online. A clickable map of Italy allows students to visit any of the regions to find out more about that area's history and culture. Links lead to virtual tours and graphical images of interesting attractions and beautiful countryside. Find out how Christmas is celebrated in Italy, where each church has a tradition of creating its own individualized *presepio* (nativity scene), and Babbo Natale (Father Christmas) comes with presents on *epifania* (Epiphany, January 6). Use the recipe given for *biscotti alle mandorle* to make Italian Christmas cookies. The Italy at Your House section features a listing of videos highlighting Rome, Lombardy, and Campania, as well as information on Italian food and wine, with recipes for special Italian dishes such as *frittelle di riso,* an Easter specialty.

Italy on the Web provides many links to other Web sites about Italy, and an opportunity to try out your knowledge of Italian in a chat room. Kristin Jarratt (initaly@initaly.com) is the editor.

353. Italia Online

http://www.iol.it/

Italia Online is a searchable directory of Italian Internet sites written in Italian. Look also for categories to browse, such as arts and culture, entertainment, travel, government, education, sports, politics, health and medicine, weather, and shopping.

354. Italian Embassy (Washington, D.C.)

http://www.italyemb.org

The Embassy of Italy in the United States provides this Web site, which is written in English and has lots of information related to Italian government and country studies as well as information about the people and culture. Some of the links lead to news sources, museums, music, movies, literature, history, cuisine, travel, and study. Provides information about Italian activities in the United States and economic and trade statistics.

355. Italian Literature

http://www.crs4.it/HTML/Literature.html

Various literary works written in Italian, including narrative and poetry from *La Divina Commedia* to contemporary literature, are available on this site. Riccardo Scateni (riccardo@crs4.it) is the Webmaster.

Japanese

Professional Associations

356. The Association of Teachers of Japanese
http://www.Colorado.EDU/ealld/atj/

Look for the Standards for Japanese Language Learning for Preschool to College, an index of links to Japan-related topics, and information about scholarships, study programs, and job openings for teachers of Japanese. Association news is published in an online newsletter, and announcements for meetings, seminars, fellowships, and grants are posted. The Association of Teachers of Japanese (ATJ) provides comprehensive information about its Bridging Project for Study Abroad and encourages students to consider study in Japan as a unique opportunity to develop or improve language skills, discover a fascinating culture, and grow personally. Online you will find interviews from students who have participated in past exchange programs, as well as FAQs and scholarship information. *Note:* For information on Japanese language software, see (http://www.jsnet.org/jls.html).

Language Studies

357. Calligraphy of Japan
http://www.japan-guide.com/e/e2095.html

Learn what components are necessary in a Japanese calligraphy kit and see the difference in styles: *Kaisho* (square style), *Gyosho* (semicursive style), and *Sosho* (cursive style). Links point to other calligraphy sites. An introduction to Japanese calligraphy written by Graham Hawker (http://metrotel.co.uk/ohmori/intro1.html) explains calligraphy as an art form and what distinguishes good calligraphy from bad; it also gives a brief history and a bibliography.

358. Japanese Language
http://www.japan-guide.com/e/e621.html

Three writing systems can make learning how to write in Japanese very complicated. *Kanji* is made up of Chinese characters; *hiragana* and *katakana* are two different syllable-based alphabets. Students learn that women speak a different Japanese than men do, and that special words are used when speaking to an elderly person, child, or family member. This site provides information on some of the difficulties of studying Japanese and offers links to related Japanese-language resources, including pages devoted to dialects, online English/Japanese dictionaries, and what is needed to display Japanese characters on your computer.

History and Culture of Japan

See also the Origami Page (entry 125), Haiku for People (entry 570), The Tokugawa Art Museum (entry 137), and Kabuki Theatre for Everyone (entry 197).

359. Bonsai Information and Inspiration
http://www.stonelantern.com

Stone Lantern Publishing provides information about *bonsai* care and training, as well as photographs and photoessays. Information is also available on how to order *bonsai* books, videos, and subscriptions to *Bonsai Today*. Links are provided to other excellent *bonsai* Web sites.

360. Japan Information Network

http://jin.jcic.or.jp
or
http://www.jinjapan.org (U.S. Mirror site)

Make this a first point of entry for accessing information about Japan, because this site provides a comprehensive look at Japan—its people, language, and culture. This site is comprised of links to excellent resources, including Japan Access, Japan Atlas with clickable map, The Virtual Museum of Traditional Japanese Arts, Japan Insight, Trends in Japan, Kids Web Japan, Statistics, Japan Directory, Region & Cities, Japan Web Navigator, *Nipponia*, The Japan of Today, Puzzle Japan, and JIN Plaza. This site is keyword searchable.

Kids Web Japan and Puzzle Japan provide information for younger students. Japan Access provides facts sheets on various topics related to Japanese life and culture, each with colorful photographs and several pages of explanatory text written in English. More than 20 fact sheets are currently online, including Annual Events, Architecture, Art, Bunraku, Energy and Resources, Fashion, Flora and Fauna, Gardens, Geography and Climate, Ikebana, Japanese Language, Kabuki, Literature, Martial Arts, Music, Noh and Kyogen, Regions of Japan, Religion, Sumo, Tea Ceremony, and Winter Sports.

The Virtual Museum of Traditional Japanese Arts offers online images of works of art that have been designated national treasures. Regions & Cities provides a virtual tour of Japan, with information and photographs of Japan's prefectures and major cities. *Nipponia* is a quarterly magazine introducing contemporary Japanese culture and society. Previous editions are archived online beginning with the first edition, published in 1997. Special features in past editions include such topics as martial arts, getting married in Japan, Japanese vegetables, Japanese gardening, and the many dances of Japan.

361. Japan Links

http://www.lafayette.edu/~stocktoj/home/japanl.html

Provides a mega-index to links about Japan in English. In addition to Web sites about government, politics, business, and economy, look for lists of links to food, history, religion, sports, popular culture, music, visual arts, literature, and architecture. The travel section includes links to an atlas, maps, and information about different prefectures. Links are also available to the current time in Japan and the current news. Created and maintained by J. Larry Stockton (stocktoj@lafayette.edu), chairman of the department of music at Lafayette College (Easton, PA).

362. The Japan Window Home Page

http://www.jwindow.net

The Japan Window provides information about technology, business, government, living, and travel. It also includes a special section for kids. Each week, the Top 10 Japan Web sites are featured, along with other links to sites in Japan. This Web site was originally developed through a joint research project by Stanford University and Nippon Telegraph and Telephone Corporation (NTT), as a United States-Japan collaboration for Internet-based information on Japan; it is now operated by NTT (http://www.ntt.co.jp/index_e.html). The Webmaster's address is (jw@jwindow.net).

363. Kids Web Japan

http://jin.jcic.or.jp/kidsweb/

or

http://www.jinjapan.org/kidsweb [U.S. Mirror Site]

Find out more about Japanese schoolchildren—their likes, interests, culture, and language. This Web site introduces Japan and the Japanese people to students in elementary and middle school, through explanatory text, photographs, and graphics. Look for interactive activities and information about Japanese culture, holidays, folk legends, cooking, and games. Provides a virtual visit to a Japanese high school and middle school. The language lab has many activities to help learn the Japanese language. Each month, top news stories of interest to Japanese children are listed. The Kids Web Plaza has a FAQs section and a form to submit questions. Maintained by the Japan Center for Intercultural Communications.

364. Kid's Window to Japan

http://www.jwindow.net/KIDS/kids_home.html

The Kid's Window to Japan allows students to practice and learn the Japanese language in a multimedia format. Students are invited to travel to a Japanese village to experience Japanese culture and life. In the Library, students find a Japanese folktale written in both English and Japanese. A multimedia picture dictionary lets children hear and see words in Japanese. In the language classroom of the School, students are introduced to *hiragana*, *katakana*, and *kanji*. In the Restaurant, children can click on a menu item and hear its pronunciation. This is an excellent resource for use in a multicultural unit or Japanese-language studies for almost any grade.

365. MixPizza

http://www.mixpizza.omron.co.jp/mp/svc/html.index_c

MixPizza provides a directory of information about life in Japan written in English. Contents cover a broad range of topics, including everyday life in Japan, business information, news, and directory listings with more than 75,000 maps to businesses. Find out about cultural events, travel, and restaurants. There are also sections focused on working, living, and shopping in Japan. VOX POP is a section where Japan's international community can communicate and share information about living and working in Japan. The Web site's database is keyword searchable. The Webmaster's address is (webmaster@mixpizza.omron.co.jp).

366. Schauwecker's Guide to Japan

http://www.japan-guide.com

With more than 200 pages, and just as many color images, this site covers all aspects of traditional Japan and modern Japan, including information of interest to tourists. The food section offers instructions for eating with chopsticks, important rules for table manners, recipes with illustrations, and a description of Japanese teas.

367. Tokyo Food Page

http://www.bento.com/tokyofood.html

Find out what foods are enjoyed in Japan, including regional and specialty dishes. Learn sushi vocabulary such as *ama-ebi* (raw shrimp), *kani* (crab), and *tako* (octopus). The Recipe Collection includes recipes for *tonkatsu* (pork cutlet), *niku-jaga* (beef and potato stew), and *oyako-donburi* (chicken and egg over rice). Links are provided to other resources for Japanese food, the Shin-Yokohama Ramen (Chinese noodle) Museum in Yokohama, and photographs of the Ohmicho Market (a 300-year old open-air fish market in Kanazawa), department store specialty vendors with fresh octopus tentacles, and various varieties of Japanese apples. New articles and updates are added to the Eating and Drinking in Tokyo section the middle of each month. See also Tokyo Meltdown (http://www.bento.com/tleisure.html) for information on architecture, music, entertainment, transportation, and shopping in Tokyo. Maintained by Robb Satterwhite (webmaster@bento.com).

368. Tomoe Soroban Co., Ltd., Abacus Makers

http://www.soroban.com/index2.html

The Tomoe Soroban Company has been making *sorobans* (abacuses) since 1921. A virtual museum displays various sorobans with colorful graphics and brief explanations. A few articles extol the merits of teaching students how to calculate math using an abacus. Information is available in English and Japanese. *See also* The Abacus: The Art of Calculating with Beads (entry 595).

Periodicals

369. *Aichi Voice*

http://www.pref.aichi.jp/aia/voice/

Aichi Voice is a colorful English-language publication issued twice a year (in the spring and fall) by the Aichi International Association, a nonprofit organization established by the Aichi Prefectural government. The Web site contains the magazine's contents in electronic form to introduce Aichi, its people, and its traditions to a worldwide audience. The first World Exposition of the 21st century will be held in Aichi in 2005. Past issues are archived online, beginning with fall 1997.

370. *Hanabi*

http://www.asij.ac.jp/journalism/hanabi.html

Hanabi is the school newspaper for the American School in Japan (ASIJ) located in the western suburbs of Tokyo. *Hanabi* is published five or six times a year, and articles from students' writings reflect Japanese news and a student's point of view from living in Japan. Look for featured articles, recent articles, past articles, and links to the home page for the American School in Japan. The Webmaster's address is (hanabieditor@hotmail.com).

371.   ***The Japan Times* Online**

http://www.japantimes.co.jp

Find out the daily news from Japan. In addition to daily news and a daily editorial, the top news stories are collected in the Weekly News Roundup. The Technotimes section includes information about computers, the Internet, and music URLs. Look for a festival report by geographic section. Landmark chronicles includes historical news. This is also the place to follow news about the sport of *Sumo*.

Latin and Greek

See also Forum Romanum (entry 1253), *Bulfinch's Mythology The Age of Fable or Stories of Gods and Heroes* (entry 547), Perseus Project (entry 1252), and Encyclopedia Mythica (entry 1340).

372.   **Homer's *Iliad* from the Duke Papyrus Archive**

http://scriptorium.lib.duke.edu/papyrus/

The Duke University Papyrus Archive WWW site provides electronic access to texts about and images of 1,373 papyri from ancient Egypt. As an example, to find papyrus fragments with text from the *Iliad*, click on Search the Duke Papyrus Archive and type in the keyword *Iliad*. This will bring up 37 matches in 10 files. Each file includes a color thumbnail graphic of a papyrus fragment and a written description. Each graphic can be enlarged for close-up study.

373.   **The Internet Classic Archive**

http://classics.mit.edu

Provides 441 full-text works of translated classical literature by 59 different authors, including Julius Caesar, Plato, Sophocles, Herodotus, Tacitus, and Homer. Most of these works are Greco-Roman in English translation. Reader commentary is available for most works, and readers can add commentary and recommend Web sites appropriate to the work. The database is browseable and searchable by work, author, or keyword. To search authors and their works in the *Encyclopedia Britannica*, use the public access address (http://search.eb.com).

374.   **The Latin Page**

http://www.geocities.com/Athens/Acropolis/3773/

Paginam Latinam is designed for Latin students in grades 7–12, and provides links to information of interest to teachers and students of Latin. Links are available to software for computer-assisted Latin, lesson plans, maps, food recipes, dictionaries, and a Pig Latin converter for Web sites. The Webmaster is Joe Kelly (jrkelly@unlserve.unl.edu), University of Nebraska, Lincoln, Nebraska.

Russian

Language Studies

375. Russian Alphabet with Sound

http://www.friends-partners.org/oldfriends/language/russian-alphabet.html

The Russian alphabet consists of 33 letters, composed of 21 consonants, 10 vowels, and 2 letters without sound (soft and hard signs). Students can see the Cyrillic alphabet, look at a pronunciation guide, and hear the pronunciation.

Another great page to help with learning the Russian alphabet is (http://www.geocities.com/Colosseum/Track/7635/alphabet.html). This page offers links to information to help students learn how to count, say hello and goodbye, understand nicknames, and gymnastic terms, common phrases, and Western signs in Russian. Maintained by Vladimir Gurov (gurovv@sncac.snc.edu).

376. RussNet—Your Russian Internet Resource

http://www.russnet.org

RussNet provides a centralized location for resources related to teaching and learning Russian. Step-by-step instructions are given for downloading special computer fonts. Teaching modules are based on learning Russian for business, conversation, and cultural purposes. Gives a list of teaching materials, including printed materials, textbooks, and online resources. Information is available to benefit current and prospective students of Russian, such as PowerPoint presentations, crossword puzzles, and interactive online Russian grammar references. Also included on this site are resources listing professional associations, study and work opportunities, and ways for Russian teachers and students to communicate with one another. A proficiency assessment quiz is available.

History and Culture of Russia and Former Soviet Union Countries

See also the Pushkin Museum of Fine Arts (entry 135), Treasures of the Czars Museum Tour (entry 140), and the CIA World Factbook entries for Russia and former Soviet Union countries where Russian is spoken (http://www.odci.gov/cia/publications/factbook/).

377. The Alexander Palace Time Machine

http://www.alexanderpalace.org/palace/

The Time Machine provides a virtual tour of the Alexander Palace, home of the last tsar of Russia and his family. There are maps of four areas of the palace that you can tour. Palace treasures are on display, including Fabergé works in the Mauve Room. In addition to visits to various rooms, there are 30 thumbnail images of characters in the story of the Alexander Palace, with links to brief biographies. There is also a brief history of the palace. Bob Atchison (batchison@flifo.com) is the creator and Webmaster. He is working to restore the Alexander Palace and to reopen it to the public as a museum, focusing on life both upstairs and downstairs during the reign of Nikolas and Aleksandra.

378. **Bucknell University's Russian Studies**

http://www.departments.bucknell.edu/russian/index.html

Filled with rich information on the history and cultural heritage of Russia and the Russian language, this comprehensive site also has online research materials and links to information about every aspect of Russian life and society, including politics, news, art, music, literature, and business. Look for a chronology of Russian history, the family trees of the House of Rurik and House of Romanov, and links to Russian literature available online in both Russian and English. Learn about Russian holidays, folklore, cuisine, and humor. Interested students will want to investigate Bucknell University's Russian Studies program and some of the careers available to Russian Studies majors. For more information, contact Robert Beard (rbeard@ bucknell.edu), professor at Bucknell University, Lewisburg, Pennsylvania.

379. **From Republics to Independent States**

http://www.geocities.com/Colosseum/Track/7635/history.html

In 1991, the 15 republics of the United Soviet Socialist Republic (USSR) split up, forming 15 newly independent states. This page shows the transition from republic to federation by providing the name of each former republic and a graphic of its flag, along with its new, independent state name and image of its current flag. Created and maintained by Vladimir Gurov (gurovv@sncac.snc.edu).

380. **Moscow Kremlin**

http://www.online.ru/sp/cominf/kremlin/english/

Visit Moscow on a virtual tour. Take a look around the Kremlin, and then visit some of the famous cathedrals, churches, palaces, buildings, monuments, towers, and squares. Provides thumbnail pictures to enlarge for greater detail and brief explanatory text. Access is easy, through a sidebar with names of sites categorized by the above topics or through a clickable map. Supported by Russia-On-Line (http://www.online.ru/english/index.html), an online daily news Web site accessible in both Russian and English.

381. **Radio Free Europe: Radio Liberty**

http://www.rferl.org/newsline/index.html

Daily news broadcasts and reports of developments in Eastern Europe, Russia, the Caucasus, and Central Asia are posted on this Web site.

382. **Russia: How Has Change Affected the Former U.S.S.R.?**

http://www.learner.org/exhibits/russia/

This site is one of the online exhibits in the Annenberg/CPB (Corporation for Public Broadcasting) Projects Exhibits Collection. This exhibit provides an online interactive learning experience for students studying the Russian Federation and the changes that have occurred since the dissolution of the Union of Soviet Socialist Republics (U.S.S.R.) on December 26, 1991. For other online exhibits in the Annenberg/CPB collection, see (http://www.learner.org/exhibits).

383. **Russian and East European Studies**

http://www.ucis.pitt.edu/reesweb/

Russian and East European Studies (REESWeb) is a comprehensive index of electronic resources on the Balkans, the Baltic states, the Caucasus, Central Asia, Central Europe, the CIS (Commonwealth of Independent States), Eastern Europe, the NIS (New Independent States of the former Soviet Union), the Russian Federation, and the former Soviet Union. Resources for Russia and East Europe can be located by discipline (history, business, science, government, and the arts) or by type (document repositories, interactive databases, software, lists, academic programs, and multimedia). Created and maintained by Karen Rondestvedt (rondest+@pitt.edu), a Slavic bibliographer at the University of Pittsburgh Library System.

384. **St. Petersburg, Russia**

http://www.spb.su

Links are provided to news, cultural information, travel information, and business information. Be sure to check out the gallery of pictures of St. Petersburg and the collection of cartoons by Victor Bogorand.

385. **Welcome to the New Russia**

http://www.interknowledge.com/russia/

The official site of the Russian National Tourist Office welcomes online visitors to the New Russia. Look for information about Russian history, art, and architecture; tips for tourists; and a guide to modes of transportation. Find out more about travel on Russia's waterways and the Trans-Siberian Railway, the longest continuous rail lines on Earth, which cover almost 6,000 miles. Explore the theaters, historical sites, and cathedrals of Russian cities such as St. Petersburg and Moscow. Through pictures and text, students will learn more about the new country of Russia, a part of the former Union of Soviet Socialist Republics.

Periodicals

386. *The Moscow Times*

http://www.moscowtimes.ru

The Moscow Times, published daily except for Sundays and Mondays by Independent Press since 1992, contains top stories, news articles, feature articles, business and financial news, and opinions, all with a Russian focus. See also *The St. Petersburg Times* (http://www.sptimes.ru), the English-language newspaper of St. Petersburg, Russia, published twice weekly on Tuesdays and Fridays since May 1993 by Independent Press.

387. **Russia Today: Daily News**

http://www.russiatoday.com

Russia Today is an online news service from the European Information Network, updated daily Monday through Friday. News from Russia is divided into regular sections, such as Election News, Today in TV, Today in Moscow, and The Weekly Roundup. There are other main sections, such as Russia at a Glance. This is an excellent current-news resource.

Spanish

Spanish is officially spoken in Spain, Argentina, Bolivia, Chile, Colombia, Costa Rica, Cuba, Dominican Republic, Ecuador, El Salvador, Equatorial Guinea, Guatemala, Honduras, Mexico, Nicaragua, Panama, Paraguay, Peru, Puerto Rico, Uruguay, and Venezuela.

See also Aztec Calendar (entry 1426); Latino and Hispanic Images in Picture Books (entry 497); and Artistas Españoles (entry 119).

Language Studies

388. **Elementary Spanish Curriculum Development**

http://www.veen.com/Veen/Leslie/Curriculum/

General goals and instructional objectives are given, as are guidelines for teachers, in this guide to writing and developing a Spanish curriculum for grades K-8. Cultural awareness, listening comprehension, speaking skills, and writing skills are all addressed. Expectations are listed for each grade level. Expectations are also listed for students who complete eight years of Spanish study. Prepared by Leslie Veen (leslie@veen.com).

389. **¡EspañOlé!**

http://members.yourlink.net/kappa/espanole/principal.html

Teachers and students will cry "¡Olé!" when they see the contents of this Spanish Web site—it contains everything needed for the study, teaching, and appreciation of the Spanish language, including Spanish literature, arts, music, people, history, foods, countries, and AP exams. Created by Susan Seraphine-Kimel (kapa@yourlink.net), a teacher at Astronaut High School, Titusville, FL.

390. **Interactive Spanish Grammar**

http://www.travlang.com/languages/index.html

Choose the Español/Spanish flag to reveal seven interactive Spanish grammar lessons. To hear words and phrases pronounced, click on links to accompanying sound files. At the end of each lesson, students can take an interactive quiz to see how much they have learned. Lessons include basic words, numbers, shopping and dining, travel, directions, places, telling time, and dates. There is also a searchable Spanish/English, English/Spanish dictionary.

391. **Learn Spanish**

http://www.lingolex.com/spanish.htm

Provides lists of Spanish words and phrases, such as words associated with soccer, things in a house, clothes, the human body, jobs and professions, shops and public places, church, and food. Information about Spanish/English cultural exchanges by e-mail and online chat is available. Links are provided to other information to help learn Spanish. Created and maintained by Sarah and John of Lingolex (john@lingolex.com), professional Spanish translators.

392.   Learn Spanish

http://www.studyspanish.com

Provides free online tutorials, including written exercises, oral exercises, and written tests. Lots of verb drills and vocabulary practice are available using oral exercises and interactive games. Cultural Notes is a collection of paragraphs on topics of cultural interest, written in Spanish with accompanying photographs. These reading selections have comprehension questions, an English translation, and a RealAudio reading of the paragraph in Spanish. Look for a top 10 list of idioms that do not translate well and a random idiom generator. Other information on this site includes a list of Spanish schools, information for teachers, and a FAQs section. Provided by Spanish Learning Resources (webmaster@studyspanish.com).

393.   Spanish Language Exercises

http://mld.ursinus.edu/~jarana/Ejercicios/

Examples of language exercises and drills are available to facilitate the learning and teaching of Spanish in an Internet environment. Self-check online interactive exercises in Spanish grammar allow students to test themselves. Requires Netscape Navigator 4.0 or later. Juan Ramón de Arana, Spanish professor at Ursinus College (Collegeville, Pennsylvania), is the creator and Webmaster (jarana@ acad.ursinus.edu).

History and Culture of Mexico

394.   Amigo! Mexican Web Center

http://www.mexonline.com

Amigo! Mexican Web Center contains a comprehensive list of information about Mexico. Information is organized by topic, similar to a Yellow Pages directory. Geography resources include links to the environment, maps, nature, and the weather. History is divided into pre- and post-Columbian periods. If you need information about Mexico, you'll find it at this site.

395.   The Azteca Web Page

http://www.azteca.net/aztec/

Focusing on contemporary descendants of the indigenous peoples of Mexico, this site provides a taxonomy to explain and define the terms *Chicano, Hispano, Mexican American, Mexican, Latino, Hispanic,* and *Spanish*. The site also provides cultural heritage awareness for everyone. Find out more about the indigenous peoples of Mexico and the Nahuatl language. This page was created and is maintained by Mario Araujo (mario@azteca.net).

396.   Culture and Society of México

http://www.public.iastate.edu/~rjsalvad/scmfaq/faqindex.html

Culture and Society of México provides access to frequently asked questions (FAQs) about Mexico, with answers as well as links to Mexican Internet resources. Check the Daily Almanac for Mexican dates and events. Read this document before posting questions to the (soc.culture. mexican) newsgroup. Some of the questions include: What is the origin of the term *gringo*? What is the meaning of the word *Mexico*? What is the Indian population of Mexico? What can I read to learn more about Aztec history and the Spanish conquest? Are there any Mexican newspaper services online? What are the lyrics to the Mexican national anthem? Are there online databases of Mexican cooking or famous Mexican artists?

397. Mexican Poetry of the Twentieth Century

http://www.columbia.edu/~gmo9/poetry/index.html

This Web site presents a personal collection of Mexican poetry by 20 different 20th-century poets, including José Juan Tablada (1871–1945), considered the first modern poet in Mexico. Poetry can be read online in the original Spanish, with accompanying English and sometimes French translations. Poetry is not included for Mexican poets born after 1940. For Mexican poetry by younger poets, students will want to go to the Web site Horizontes de Poesía Mexicana (http://www.arts-history.mx/horizonte/home.html). Links are provided to other Mexican and Latin American poetry resources on the Internet. Created and maintained by Gustavo Ortiz Millán (gmo9@columbia.edu).

398. Mexico for Kids

http://explora.presidencia.gob.mx/index_kids.html

Kids can follow Balero to discover interesting facts about Mexico's history, geography, and government. A timeline helps students understand Mexico's history from the first civilization until modern times. Find out more about Ernesto Zedillo Ponce de León, the Constitutional President of the United Mexican States. Hands-on activities include learning how to make a maraca and designing stationery. Sponsored by the Presidency of the Republic of Mexico, this site is available in English, Spanish, and French.

History and Culture of Spain

See also Artistas Españoles (entry 119).

399. Discover Spain

http://www.okspain.org

The Tourist Office of Spain maintains this page in English (as well as Korean, Japanese, and Chinese). This site provides general information about Spain, its social customs, national parks, transportation and communication, and world heritage sites. Also available is information on bullfighting, the Flamenco, and Spanish cuisine. Links are provided to museums. To get travel information, select the cities, islands, regions, or coastal areas you wish to visit.

400. Golden Age Spanish Sonnets

http://ingber.spanish.sbc.edu/SonnetTexts/

Provides a searchable database of 16th- and 17th-century sonnets by Spanish poets. The database includes more than 101 sonnets written by 18 poets. Each sonnet is available in both Spanish and English translation. Created and maintained by Alix Ingber (ingber@sbc.edu), professor of Spanish, Sweet Briar College (Roanoke, Virginia).

401. Sí, Spain

http://www.DocuWeb.ca/SiSpain/

Sí, Spain has links to Spanish history and culture, current foreign affairs, geography, education, and Spanish courses online. Information is available for those planning to travel to Spain. Links are also provided to Spanish newspapers on the Internet, such as *EL PAÍS*. This site is maintained by Professor José Félix Barrio (barrio@DocuWeb.ca).

History and Culture of Spanish-Speaking Peoples

See also Latino and Hispanic Images in Picture Books (entry 497).

402. ¡Bienvenidos Amigos!

http://www.sbcc.cc.ca.us/academic/span/

The home page of the Spanish department of Santa Barbara City College provides comprehensive lists of links to useful Spanish-language resources on the Web. Links are provided to Spanish-language magazines and sports, travel, and cultural information. Spanish-speaking countries are listed by geographical area, such as Central America, South America, or the Caribbean, as well as the countries of Spain and Mexico. Information for each country includes a color graphic of the country's flag and country-specific information. For example, one of Ecuador's links is to the endangered Galapagos giant tortoise; a link from Peru leads to a virtual trip on an Inca trail; Venezuela provides a link to Venezuelan recipes; there is a travelogue from Guatemala; and Argentina has music files.

403. Bilingual Spanish Page

http://mainst.monterey.k12.ca.us/edlinks/bilingua.htm

The Soledad Unified School District, Soledad, California, offers this site with links to bilingual Spanish pages. Categories include language arts, science and health, history and culture, newspapers, and general resources. Here you will find lots of bilingual sites, including interactive virtual frog dissection sites in English, Español (Spanish), Deutsch (German), Nederlands (Dutch), Français (French), Cêská (Czech), Italiano, and Portuguese.

404. Indigenous Peoples of Latin America and South America

http://www.lanic.utexas.edu/la/region/indigenous/

Find out more about the customs, culture, and people of Brazil, Ecuador, Mexico, Chile, Bolivia, and other countries. Links are organized and divided by topic and country. Information is also organized into ethnic groups. Links are provided to the Center for World Indigenous Studies and other international resources.

405. LatinoWeb

http://www.latinoweb.com/index.html

LatinoWeb is an information center for Latinos and those wanting to know more about Latino history and culture. The directory contains links to Latin and Chicano sites. One category in the directory contains a listing of newspapers and magazines. In this section links can be found to the *America Latina Magazine*; the *El Boricua Newsletter* from El Paso, Texas; Chico comics; and more. Some other directory categories include education and history, business, jobs, and art and music.

406. *Mundo Latino*

http://www.mundolatino.org

The culture section of this Spanish directory offers information about the arts, music (tango, folklore, caribe, rock, and brasil), and literature.

407. **Mythology: A Study of Puerto Rican Myths, Legends and Folktales**

http://www.yale.edu/ynhti/curriculum/units/1982/5/82.05.09.x.html

Part of the curriculum resources collection at the Yale-New Haven Teachers Institute, an educational partnership between Yale University and the New Haven Public Schools, this well-written teaching unit developed by John C. Warner is designed to supplement the curriculum for beginning and intermediate-level Spanish courses. Because the unit provides an introduction to the study of Puerto Rican mythology with examples and exercises in English, it is accessible to most students. Students will learn different vocabulary as they are exposed to Spanish as it is spoken in Puerto Rico rather than traditional Castilian Spanish. The folklore also opens a window to the family customs, traditions, and religious values of Puerto Ricans. Includes detailed lesson plans and an annotated bibliography. See also Mary Jo Ramos's lesson plans on pre-Columbian myths and legends (http://artsedge.kennedy-center.org/db/cr/cx/myth.html).

408. **Spanish Language and Culture Home Page**

http://www-as.phy.ohiou.edu/Departments/Mod_Lang/spanish/index.html

The Spanish Language and Culture Web site is comprehensive, providing links to many Spanish resources: museums, art, music, culture, literature, history, journals, newspapers, and teacher resources.

409. **Yahoo! en Español**

http://espanol.yahoo.com

Spanish-language students can test their language proficiency by searching on the Internet in Spanish. Yahoo! provides a Spanish version with Web pages written in Spanish. For some categories, but not all, Yahoo! provides a little help with English translations. Look for *Categoría Yahoo! equivalente en inglés*. This is a great way for Spanish students to find resources written in Spanish on the Internet.

Periodicals

410. *¡del Corazón!*

http://nmaa-ryder.si.edu/webzine/index.html

¡del Corazón! is an interactive, educational Webzine for teachers and students, featuring the National Museum of American Art's collection of art by Latino artists. Information in each issue is organized into four topic areas: artists, activities, themes, and comments. The museum,

working collaboratively with Texas Education Network, publishes online issues that contain curricular lesson plan activities for the K–12 learning community; these activities are based on a constructivist educational model featuring primary source materials, such as reproductions of collection objects and videos of artists.

411. *La Jornada*

http://unam.netgate.net/jornada/
or
http://serpiente.dgsca.unam.mx/jornada/index.html

La Jornada is a daily Mexican newspaper written in Spanish. This version has selected full-text stories, articles, and editorials with some graphics. Thumbnail graphics of the front page can be enlarged for projection and group reading. Archives of past issues are available from March 1995 to the present.

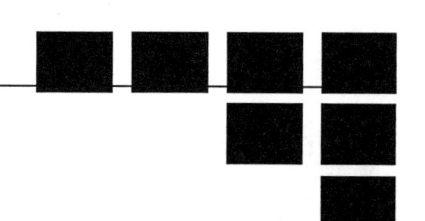

Language Arts

All URL addresses in this chapter are checked and updated monthly. If a link does not work, please refer to the Directory Update Web page located at (http://www.lu.com/lu/irdupdates.html).

The Internet's language arts resources are becoming more encompassing and diverse, offering many choices for curriculum inclusion. Writers' reference tools; electronic books (e-texts or e-books) and online journals and periodicals (e-zines); and resources related to all forms of literature, including poetry, myths and legends, specific authors, and children's literature, are growing in numbers and availability.

Look for poetry resources representing diverse times, cultures, and philosophies. Students can experience Japanese haiku (entry 570), Persian Sufi poetry (entry 571), and collections of favorite children's poetry (entry 569), as well as 19th-century poets like Emily Dickinson (entry 558), the 1920s Harlem Renaissance poets (entry 556), the Beat poets (entry 554), and contemporary poets, such as Maya Angelou (entry 557).

Children's literature resources continue to expand. The Children's Literature Web Guide (entry 489) is a good starting place. More and more multicultural children's literature resources are available, to be used individually or in conjunction with the multicultural resources in the chapter on social studies. Teachers and children alike will delight in the new home pages of author/illustrators Jan Brett (entry 504) and Eric Carle (entry 505) and authors Susan Cooper (entry 507), Virginia Hamilton (entry 509), and Laura Ingalls Wilder (entry 521).

Project Gutenberg (entry 535) continues to convert literary classics and reference works into electronic format for free dissemination on the Internet. As copyrights expire, more and more works are appearing online from other sources as well. Aesop's fables are part of Project Gutenberg, and many of these can be found in the section on "Folklore: Fables, Folktales, and Fairy Tales" (entries 536–541).

Look for lesson plans to accompany classroom reading projects from Language Arts SCORE (entry 415) and comprehensive directories for author studies, such as Charles Dickens: A CyberGuide Author Study (entry 467) and Mark Twain Resources on the WWW (entry 459). Sites such as The Macbeth Home Page (entry 475) demonstrate how English teachers are making available their methods for engaging students in the study of Shakespeare. Interactive sites, such as Shakespearean Insults (entry 480) and the Shakespeare Sonnet Quiz (entry 479), should be helpful in gaining the interest of even the most indifferent students.

Student work is increasingly being published on the Internet, and student online magazines and newspapers have proliferated. Check out *MidLink Magazine* (entry 576), *CyberKids* (entry 574), and *Kids Zone* (entry 575). Students can even try their hand at creating their own online newspapers through an interactive program at a site called CRAYON: CReAte Your Own Newspaper (entry 431).

National Standards

412.   *Standards for the English Language Arts*

http://www.ncte.org/standards/

The National Council of Teachers of English and the International Reading Association worked together to write the national *Standards for the English Language Arts,* designed to prepare all K-12 students for the increasing literacy demands of the twenty-first century. What should English-language arts students know and be able to do? These standards address six interrelated English-language arts: reading, writing, speaking, listening, viewing, and visually representing.

Professional Associations

413.   **National Council of Teachers of English**

http://www.ncte.org

In addition to membership and conference information, the National Council of Teachers of English (NCTE) Web site offers teaching ideas; lists of publications; and access to position papers, professional development, grants, awards, and job announcements. English teachers can find out how to subscribe to the NCTE-talk online discussion list. Links are provided to research, news, and NCTE affiliates. The Web site is searchable.

General Interest

414.   **Collection of Classics**

http://library.thinkquest.org/27864/data/index2.html

Explores the meaning of classics and looks at more than 25 authors who have written classics, including Louisa May Alcott, Jane Austen, F. Scott Fitzgerald, Harper Lee, C.S. Lewis, George Orwell, Edgar Allan Poe, J.D. Salinger, and Jules Verne. Discusses the writing process and provides interactive quizzes. Explains the parts of a story and analyzes poetry and drama in addition to fiction. Also highlights authors of children's books, such as Natalie Babbit, L. Frank Baum, and Frances Hodgson Burnett.

415.   **Language Arts SCORE**

http://www.sdcoe.k12.ca.us/score/cla.html

Hosted by the San Diego Country Office of Education (California), Language Arts SCORE (Schools of California Online Resources for Educators) has links to CyberGuides; frameworks and standards; reading initiatives; lesson plans; literature; bilingual resources; homework aids; and sites highlighting student work. All links are to resources specifically selected to help language arts teachers enrich and enhance their classroom curricula. General comments should be addressed to Don Mayfield (donmayfi@sdcoe.k12.ca.us) and Linda Taggart-Fregoso (ltaggart@mail.sandi.net), directors of the SCORE Language Arts Project.

416.   **Novel Analysis**

http://www.novelguide.com/novelanalysis.html

NovelGuide.com provides literary analyses for a selection of classic and contemporary literature. More than 30 titles are available, including *Animal Farm*, *The Great Gatsby*, *Hamlet*, *The Catcher in the Rye*, *A Separate Peace*, *Fahrenheit 451*, and *Brave New World*. Each novel guide provides a chapter-by-chapter novel summary, character profiles, metaphor analysis, theme analysis, a list of top 10 quotes, and a biography of the author. Information is provided by IGD Solutions Corporation.

417.   **Voice of the Shuttle: Web Page for Humanities Research**

http://vos.ucsb.edu

Voice of the Shuttle is an excellent meta-list of links to humanities and humanities-related resources on the Internet. The Web site is searchable and browseable through an easily accessible table of contents. Some of the areas of interest include history, classical studies, art and art history, media studies, women's studies, minority studies, and religious studies. The English Literature subpages have information about literature taught in many English and American literature classes. High school English teachers will want to check out the section on American 19th-century literature for a surprisingly long list of sites. The literature-by-genre section contains an extensive Drama and Theater Studies list, along with Fiction Studies and Poetry Studies. Created and maintained by Alan Liu (ayliu@humanitas.ucsb.edu), professor of English, University of California, Santa Barbara.

Lesson Plans

See also "Interactive Learning and Telecommunications Across the Curriculum" (entries 28–32) and "Lesson Plans Across the Curriculum" (entries 33–44).

418.   **CyberGuides for Literature**

http://www.sdcoe.k12.ca.us/score/cyberguide.html

CyberGuides (teacher guides and student activities) are supplementary units of instruction based on core works of literature, requiring students to use the World Wide Web. CyberGuides contain Web-searching activities that lead to a student product. They may be used in a classroom with one computer, connected to the Internet. Almost 100 titles are available to choose from in this K-12 collection of literature organized by grade level. Some of the titles include: *The Very Hungry Caterpillar* by Eric Carle and *Frog and Toad Are Friends* by Arnold Lobel (grades K–3); *From the Mixed-up Files of Mrs. Basil E. Frankweiler* by E. L. Konigsburg and *Dragonwings* by Laurence Yep (grades 4–6); *Tuck Everlasting* by Natalie Babbit and *Pyramid* by David Macaulay (grades 6–8); and *To Kill a Mockingbird* by Harper Lee, *The Crucible* by Arthur Miller, and *Night* by Elie Weisel (grades 9–12). General comments should be addressed to Don Mayfield (donmayfi@sdcoe.k12.ca.us) and Linda Taggart-Fregoso (ltaggart@mail.sandi.net), directors of the SCORE Language Arts Project.

419.   **K-12 Language Arts Lesson Plans from the Boulder Valley (Colorado) School District**

gopher://bvsd.k12.co.us
Path: **Main Menu/Educational_Resources/Lesson_Plans/Big Sky/language arts**

There are more than 60 teacher-written lesson plans in this collection. All lessons include goals and objectives and step-by-step instructions. When looking for a little dash of classroom zest, consider choosing lessons from titles like these: Horrid Homonyms, Becoming a Logophil, Euphemisms, Learning Propaganda Techniques Through Advertisements, Zoo Animal Poetry, Busy as a Bee Similes, and a whole-language experience using Ernest Lawrence Thayer's classic poem *Casey at the Bat* (written in 1888).

420. **Maine Samplers**

http://www.umcs.maine.edu/~orono/collaborative/collaborative.html

Provides literature-based activities for the classroom. Maine Samplers are activity guides and suggestions for lesson plans that incorporate language arts and across-the-curriculum integration of the Maine Student Book Awards. Guides for more than 75 books are online. Book titles include picture books and chapter books for elementary and young adult. Each guide gives a summary of the book, suggested grade level, themes, activities, and resources.

421. **Teachnet.Com Language Arts Lesson Ideas**

http://www.teachnet.com/lesson/index.html

These lesson plans focus on the general study of language arts as well as specific studies of reading, writing, and terminology.

Grammar and Vocabulary

See also "Dictionaries and Writing Reference Tools" (entries 1388–1395).

422. **A.Word.A.Day**

http://www.wordsmith.org/awad/index.html
or
wsmith@wordsmith.org

Instructions: On the subject line type:
subscribe [your first name and last name]
Leave the body of the message blank.

E-mail subscribers receive a daily message containing a word and its definition. The Web page also changes daily; both today's and yesterday's words and definitions are posted. An archive of vocabulary words is available from March 14, 1994, the debut of A.Word.A.Day. Look for an interesting FAQ section and links to other word resources on the Internet, like Crossword Puzzle and The Word Wizard. See also the Anagram Server and the Wordserver at (http://www.wordsmith.org). A.Word.A.Day is maintained by Anu Garg (anu@wordsmith.org).

423. **On-Line English Grammar**

http://www.edunet.com/english/grammar/

On-Line English Grammar is an excellent and concise British English grammar resource. The table of contents reads like a good grammar textbook, and the contents are searchable through the subject index. The Grammar Clinic section offers a bulletin board for discussion and a FAQ list. Links are provided to other English grammar sites. Note: The sound files for the English alphabet use British English pronunciation (that is, "zed" for the letter "z") . The site is copyrighted and maintained by Anthony Hughes (ahughes@edunet.com).

424. **Vocabulary University**

http://www.vocabulary.com

Students have fun and learn vocabulary words at Vocabulary University. This is the place to practice vocabulary skills, learn roots to words, and brush up on synonyms and antonyms. In addition to enhancing students' personal vocabularies, exercises and puzzles at three levels of difficulty are especially useful for helping students prepare for tests such as the SSAT, GED, PSAT, SAT, and ACT. Vocabulary quizzes are immediately graded, and students receive good feedback. Students can register for free; use e-mail to set up an account that automatically records every submission and sends the student a virtual Vocabulary University degree after 12 sessions. Webmaster is Carey Cook (rich@vocabulary.com).

Key Pals

425. **CyberFriends**

http://www.cyberfriends.com

CyberFriends, a registry for key pals, is growing daily. At the time of publication of this book, the site counted 12,188 registered members representing all age groups, professions, and more than 200 nationalities and ethnicities. Ages range from 3 to 84. The database is updated every week. Listings can be searched by age, gender, nationality, and ethnicity, or it can be keyword searched. You can use CyberFriends to find a key pal for free. To be included in the database costs US $10 per year.

426. **ePals.com Classroom Exchange**

http://www.epals.com

A clearinghouse for classroom exchanges, ePals.com provides free teacher-monitored e-mail exchanges between students and classrooms. Teachers can sign up for a free e-mail account and so can students. Teachers can search to find other classrooms with which to exchange e-mail or work collaboratively on various projects. Teachers must register their classrooms to be included in the searchable database. Information is available in French, Spanish, and English. A translator is available and automatically translates six different languages so classes can communicate with students who speak and write in a language other than their own.

427. **Intercultural E-Mail Classroom Connections**

http://www.iecc.org

The Intercultural E-Mail Classroom Connections (IECC) mailing lists are provided by St. Olaf College as a free service to help teachers and classes link with partners in other countries and cultures for e-mail classroom pen-pal and project exchanges. IECC is intended for teachers seeking partner classrooms for international and cross-cultural electronic mail exchanges. This list is not for discussion or for people seeking individual pen/key pals.

428. KidsCom Key Pal Locator

http://www.kidscom.com/orakc/keypal/pwdkeypal.html

KidsCom describes itself as a communication playground for kids ages 4 to 15. Students can start on the KidsCom home page (http://www.kidscom.com) by specifying a language preference; options are English, French, Spanish, and German. Students indicate a key-pal preference by clicking on gender; age; country or U.S. state; and interests, such as ice skating, baseball, gymnastics, and reading. KidsCom members are allowed full access to the site and are entered on the key-pal database. To register, students fill out the registration form located at (http://www.kidscom.com/orakc/registration.html).

429. The Penpal Network

http://www.penpal-network.com

Before joining the Penpal Network, students agree not to use obscene language. Parents have the option of having duplicate e-mail messages sent to them as part of a parent protection plan. The database is searchable to help in finding a compatible pen pal/key pal.

430. The Student Center

http://www.studentcenter.org/cyberpals.html

High school students, college students, and teens looking for key pals add their entries to the database by filling out an online form. (They can change or edit their entries later if they want to.) A search engine allows students to search for cyberpals with common interests. Students can choose cyberpals from these categories: high school, college, gaming, music, and sports. Also visit the Student Homepage Directory (http://studentcenter.org/homepages/) for more information about free e-mail accounts and home pages.

Writing

Publishing

431. CRAYON: CReAte Your Own Newspaper

http://crayon.net

CRAYON: CReAte Your Own Newspaper helps students create newspapers using preselected Internet sites. Using the forms provided, students select information they want to appear in their newspapers. Sections include national news, world news, weather, business, technology, entertainment, sports, comics, tabloid information, and WWW news. Sections are in a predetermined order, but students can customize them. Step-by-step directions are given, and once the links are saved, students can access current information updated directly from the Web each day. Newspapers personalized to reflect individual or classroom needs should be saved on a computer's hard drive for easy accessibility. Doing so does not create a Web presence or Web page. This interactive newspaper experience is perfect for beginning and experienced student journalists as well as an elementary class project. The creators and Webmasters are Jeff Boulter (boulter@netpressence.com) and Dave Maher (maher@netpressence.com).

432. KidNews

http://www.kidnews.com

KidNews, a free news and writing service for students and teachers around the world, provides a great site on which to publish student writing online. Teachers are encouraged to submit special student publishing projects, and individual students may submit news stories, feature stories, reviews, sports stories, creative writing, poetry, or fiction using the online submission form. To date, more than 2,000 young people have published their work on the KidNews site. Students will enjoy reading other students' work, and possibly be inspired to write and publish their own work. KidNews also encourages writing through correspondence with electronic pen pals, and on a Kids Talk bulletin board system (not a live chat). Students who wish to have their e-mail addresses posted must first have their parent or guardian fill out a permission form and mail it to KidNews. Dr. Peter Owens (powens@cape.com), an English and professional writing professor at the University of Massachusetts, Dartmouth, is the editor and publisher of KidNews.

433. Scriptito's Place

http://members.aol.com/vangarnews/scriptito.html

Scriptito's Place is for young people ages 7 to 15 who are interested in creative writing for fun. Here you will find information about creative writing contests, a creative writing newsletter, story starters, and tips for creative writers. Books that contain entries from past contests are listed with annotations. This is Vangar Publishing Company's Creative Writing Resource Center. Scriptito is the mascot of Vangar Publishers, a publisher of young writers located in Baltimore, Maryland.

Reference Tools

434. Inkspot for Young Writers

http://www.inkspot.com/young/

Aspiring young writers and their parents can find useful information and resources at this site. An index includes links to workshops and associations, tips for young writers by young writers, publications seeking young writers, e-zines and online writing by and for young people, information about online contests (including guidelines), and books and articles about writing.

435. The Writers' Workshop: Online Resources for Writers

http://www.english.uiuc.edu/cws/wworkshop/index.htm

The Writers' Workshop at the University of Illinois at Urbana-Champaign maintains an online Writing Guide that includes a Grammar Handbook, a Bibliography Styles Handbook, and a Writing Process Handbook. The Bibliography Styles Handbook summarizes and illustrates the bibliographical formatting rules for three citation styles: the American Psychological Association (APA), the new Modern Languages Association (MLA) style, and the old MLA style. There is also an annotated list called Best Web Sites for Writers organized by topic: teachers of writing, sites offering online critiques of writing, Web-based self-help for writers, information for business and technical writers, and help for students and teachers of English as a second language.

Tutorial Service

436.   **Online Writing Tutorial Service (OWL)**
http://owl.english.purdue.edu
or
owl@sage.cc.purdue.edu

OWL is the Purdue University Online Writing Lab. This lab provides online materials on such topics as grammar, resumes, formats for citing sources (MLA, APA, and Sociology), and non-sexist language. There are links to other sources of information, including other writing labs.

Discussion Groups

437.   **High School Scholastic Journalism**
E-mail: listproc@LaTech.edu
Instructions: On the first line of the body of the message, type:
subscribe HSJOURN [your first name and last name]

438.   **Writing Across the Curriculum Discussion Forum**
E-mail: listserv@postoffice.cso.uiuc.edu
Instructions: On the first line of the body of the message, type:
subscribe WAC-L [your first name and last name]

Literature

American Literature

439.   **African American Women Writers of the 19th Century**
http://digital.nypl.org/schomburg/writers_aa19/

African American Women Writers of the 19th Century is a digital collection of 52 works (published prior to 1920) by 19th-century black women writers. This online collection contains the first book of poetry by an African American, *Poems on Various Subjects, Religious and Moral*, by Phillis Wheatly (1773); the first book of essays by an African American, *Essays*, by Ann Plato (1841); and the first novel published by a black person in the United States, *Our Nig*, by Harriet Wilson (1859). The database is browseable and searchable by keyword, so users can find out what these women had to say about family, religion, slavery, or any other keyword. Sponsored by the Schomburg Center, The New York Public Library.

440.   **American Literature**
E-mail: listproc@lists.missouri.edu
Instructions: On the first line of the body of the message, type:
subscribe AMLIT-L [your first name and last name]

The American Literature online discussion list promotes the exchange of ideas, opinions, and information related to American literature.

441. Hypertexts

http://xroads.virginia.edu/~HYPER/hypertex.html

Students at the University of Virginia have put more than 50 American literature works online in hypertext format. Some online books have been extended and enriched by linking them to other materials or adding comments relating them to the cultural context in which they were written. Some online works include *My Twenty Years at Hull House* (Jane Addams), *The Red Badge of Courage* (Stephen Crane), *Uncle Remus* (Joel Chandler Harris), *Incidents in the Life of a Slave Girl* (Harriet Jacobs*)*, *Uncle Tom's Cabin* (Harriet Beecher Stowe), *Walden* (H. D. Thoreau), and *American Slave Narratives* (WPA). Some of the other authors represented in the collection are Mark Twain, Alexis de Tocqueville, Sinclair Lewis, Upton Sinclair, Edgar Allan Poe, and Herman Melville. The Webmaster's address is (asgrp@virginia.edu).

442. The Nineteenth-Century American Women Writers Web

http://www.unl.edu/legacy/19cwww/19cwww.html

The Nineteenth-Century American Women Writers Web site contains a collection of poetry, novels, and short stories; biographical material; documents; and sites devoted to the study and appreciation of 19th-century American women writers. Links are provided to other related information, such as online journals, author Web pages, and documents. Sharon M. Harris (sharris@unllinfo.unl.edu) is the editor of this Web site and *Legacy*, a journal of American women writers (http://www.unl.edu/legacy/legacy.htm).

Nineteenth-Century Magazines

443. Godey's *Lady's Book*

http://www.history.rochester.edu/godeys/

Louis A. Godey published the first *Lady's Book* in Philadelphia in the 1830s. It was a novel idea, and became one of the most popular lady's books, or magazines, of the 19th century. Each issue contained poetry, beautiful engravings, and articles by some of the best-known authors in America. The January through April and November 1850 issues are available online at this University of Rochester site. The *Lady's Book* makes for interesting reading and definitely opens the door to a bygone era. In the January 1850 issue, for example, ladies are told to inform their gentlemen that at the theater, "loud thumping with canes and umbrellas, in demonstration of applause, is voted decidedly rude." As to fashion, readers are told that, for the 1850 season, a "long sharp boddice is the mark of a Parisian evening dress." For issues of Godey's *Lady's Book* dating from 1855 to 1858, see Hope Greenberg's excellent collection at the University of Vermont (http://www.uvm.edu:80/~hag/godey/index.html).

Stephen Crane (1871–1900)

444. Stephen Crane: Man, Myth, and Legend

http://www.cwrl.utexas.edu/~mmaynard/Crane/crane.html

Biographical information, photos, and original sound clips from selected works by Stephen Crane are featured at this site. Links are provided to critical analyses of Crane's work, including literary techniques. This site was created collaboratively for Michele Maynard's (mmaynard@mail.utexas.edu) Masterworks of American Literature class at the University of Texas at Austin.

William Faulkner (1897–1962)

445. William Faulkner on the Web

http://www.mcsr.olemiss.edu/~egjbp/faulkner/faulkner.html

Visitors are welcomed to virtual Yoknapatawpha County, a county in northern Mississippi and the setting for most of William Faulker's novels and short stories. This comprehensive multimedia Web site is a guide to the life and works of William Faulkner. Extensive information is divided into areas covering Faulkner's writings; biography; his hometown of Oxford, Mississippi; his relationship to Hollywood; Faulkner trivia; and links to other Faulkner-related information on the Internet. The site was created and is maintained by John Padgett (egjbp@ olemiss.edu), graduate instructor of English at the University of Mississippi in Oxford. John credits his interest in Faulkner to his 10th-grade English teacher, who used reverse psychology to challenge him to read *The Sound and the Fury* without *Cliff's Notes*.

F. Scott Fitzgerald (1896–1940)

See also The Great Gatsby (entry 1177).

446. F. Scott Fitzgerald Centenary Home Page

http://www.sc.edu/fitzgerald/index.html

Originally created as a centenary birthday commemoration, this site provides comprehensive information about the life and literary works of F. Scott Fitzgerald, who is best known for his classic novel *The Great Gatsby*. Information about his writing, life, and relationship with other writers of the 20th century is well organized and easily accessible. This site draws extensively on books, photographs, and related materials from the Matthew J. and Arlyn Bruccoli Collection of F. Scott Fitzgerald at the Thomas Cooper Library, University of South Carolina, Columbia, South Carolina.

Ernest Hemingway (1899–1961)

447. Picturing Hemingway: A Writer in His Time

http://www.npg.si.edu/exh/hemingway/

Marking the 100th anniversary of Ernest Hemingway's birth, this exhibition focuses on one of America's most influential writers of the 20th century with a pictorial biography that also includes paintings, letters, first editions, manuscripts, and personal memorabilia. Of the many photographs available, an early photograph shows Hemingway (at the age of six) fishing in Michigan; a later photograph shows him receiving the Nobel Prize for literature in 1954 for *The Old Man and the Sea*.

Zora Neale Hurston (1891–1960)

448. Zora Neale Hurston

http://falcon.jmu.edu/~ramseyil/hurston.htm

Best known for her novel, *Their Eyes Were Watching God* (1937), Zora Neale Hurston was one of the Harlem Renaissance writers. This site provides a brief biography, a selected bibliography, and a list of selected works. Look for links to lesson plans using Hurston's works. There is an excellent collection of links to other resources about Hurston on the Internet, including literary criticism, essays on the roles of African American women, poetic images in Hurston's works, and other general-information Web sites. The site administrator is Inez Ramsey (ramseyil@ jmu.edu).

Stephen King (1947–)

449. The Official Stephen King Web Presence

http://www.stephenking.com

Find out more about the popular author of horror who was the first major author to publish a book, *Riding the Bullet*, in electronic format only. In addition to biographical information, this Web site gives a bibliography of King's novels and other works and discusses his current and future projects.

Jack London (1876–1916)

450. The Jack London Collection

http://sunsite.berkeley.edu/London/

Jack London was a prolific writer who produced more than 50 volumes of stories, novels, and political essays. He is best known for his novels, *The Call of the Wild*, *White Fang*, and *The Sea-Wolf*; and for such short stories as "The White Silence." This Web site provides comprehensive information about London and his works. When he died at age 40 from kidney disease, in addition to writing, he was creating a new model for farming on his Beauty Ranch in California, using techniques he had observed in Japan, such as terracing and manure spreading. Information is available specifically for school reports, with warnings about some sites with incorrect information. Look for images of Jack London, documents, full-text works in HTML, and other information, including links to additional sites.

Herman Melville (1819–1891)

451. The Life and Works of Herman Melville

http://www.melville.org

Biographical information includes observations by friends and family members as well as Melville's own reflections on his life and work. Melville's letters to Nathaniel Hawthorne are included in the section devoted to Melville's works. Links lead to literary criticism, museums with exhibits that relate to Melville's life or some aspect of his work, geography related to Melville's works, whales, the age of sailing, and other 19th-century authors.

James A. Michener (1907–1997)

452. James A. Michener: Tales of the Storyteller

http://www.jamesmichener.com

Using links to newspaper articles, interviews, photos, videos clips, and interactive maps, this site takes a comprehensive, multimedia approach to presenting the life and works of James A.

Michener. A complete timeline shows the release dates of the author's works. A photo file includes video clips of the author at his home in Austin, Texas. An interactive map of the world allows students to click on an area to discover the books Michener wrote about that area. Instructions for joining the Michener online discussion group (michener-l) are given, as are links to related sites. Eric Johnston (johnston@ir-gpn.com) is site administrator.

Toni Morrison (1931–)

453. Toni Morrison's *Beloved*

http://www.cwrl.utexas.edu/~mmaynard/Morrison/home.html

Students at the University of Texas at Austin created this site to provide information about Toni Morrison and her book, *Beloved*. See also Anniina Jokinen's (anniina@luminarium.org) Web page (http://www.luminarium.org/contemporary/tonimorrison/toni.htm).

Edgar Allan Poe (1809–1849)

454. CyberTour: Edgar Allan Poe

http://dcls.org/x/archives/poe.html

Edgar Allan Poe fans will enjoy this opportunity to take a virtual pilgrimage to Poe sites located in Maryland (Baltimore and Annapolis), Virginia (Richmond and Charlottesville), and Pennsylvania (Philadelphia). Links lead to the Edgar Allan Poe Society of Baltimore, the Edgar Allan Poe National Historic Site in Philadelphia, and the Raven Society at the University of Virginia. Information on this Web page originally appeared in a newsletter for patrons at the Dauphin County (Pennsylvania) Library System.

455. Edgar Allan Poe

http://www.gothic.net/poe/

Through selected links, students can access online the complete works of Edgar Allan Poe as well as other resources pertaining to the author and his works, including biographies, movies, Web sites honoring Poe, FTP sites, and links to the Baltimore Poe House. The creator and Webmaster is Jamison Novak (talon@gothic.net).

456. *The Fall of the House of Usher*

http://www.cwrl.utexas.edu/~mmaynard/Poe/poe.html

Classes studying Edgar Allan Poe's masterful short story "The Fall of the House of Usher" will find plenty to help them here. Look for in-depth analyses of Poe's characters, imagery, and themes of fear, death, and freedom. Learn more about the stories within the story. The full text of the story and brief biographical information about Poe are included. Students at the University of Texas at Austin published this site based on their study of the story.

457. The House of Usher: Edgar Allan Poe

http://www.comnet.ca/~forrest/

The House of Usher home page offers an extensive, eclectic, multimedia collection of information about and related to Edgar Allan Poe. Students will find links to some of Poe's online works arranged in alphabetical order. This site also offers links to serious research resources, including information on how to write essays and term papers on Edgar Allan Poe. A link to the Internet Movie Database provides a wealth of information about Poe-related filmography. Favorite Haunts allows visitors to virtually visit a number of places, including the Poe Museum in Richmond, Virginia, and the Poe House and Museum in Baltimore, Maryland. Students will enjoy the graphics and flights of fancy, such as Poe's favorite felines. Don't miss Poe's virtual library page, with more than 50 links categorized by topics such as photographs, exhibits, criticism of poetry and short stories, and humor. The Web page author for The House of Usher is Peter Forrest (forrest@comnet.ca).

Anne Rice (1941–)

458. Anne Rice's Official Home Page

http://www.annerice.com

Anne Rice, best known for the five books in the Vampire Chronicles series, has her own Web site, with more than 100 pages of information about her life (timeline and photo gallery); fan club; new books; new television series; projects; and business venture, Kith & Kin. Visitors are asked to always check The Scoop, the announcements section, to see what's new. Don't miss the You Asked, Anne Answered section, where Anne answers fans' questions. Signing the guest register (using either online forms or e-mail address) automatically subscribes visitors to an irregularly published, free newsletter, *Commotion Strange*, written by Anne. Archives of past newsletters are available for browsing. Instructions for joining the Anne Rice Vampire Lestat Fan Club (ARVLFC) are provided. Cathy Corbitt of Corbitt Designs (us037509@mindspring.com) is the site administrator.

For a lengthy list of unofficial Anne Rice home pages and related sites, including links to Anne's publishers and *Interview with the Vampire* movie pages (scripts, pictures, sounds from the film, reviews, and interviews with the actors and actresses), see Shay Mitchell's (shay@earthsystems.org) Web page located at (http://earthsystems.org/~shay/commotion.html).

Mark Twain [Samuel Clemens] (1835–1910)

459. Mark Twain Resources on the WWW

http://marktwain.miningco.com

Intended to be both educational and enjoyable, this comprehensive directory of online resources by or about Mark Twain offers everything from texts of his books to an analysis of the appearance of his character on *Star Trek: The Next Generation*. Links lead to a collection of Mark Twain quotes and scholarly studies; online discussion groups; a readers' theater adaptation of *The War Prayer* (appropriate for grades 7 and up); and a database of information about films based on Twain's novels and stories, including *A Connecticut Yankee in King Arthur's Court*.

Twain has long been the target of censors. Students can find out more by reading summaries of incidents of censorship since 1876 related to *The Adventures of Tom Sawyer* and *The Adventures of Huckleberry Finn*, and by following a full page of links to the controversy surrounding Huckleberry Finn, with historical background, news of recent challenges, and various perspectives on the book.

This site is maintained by Syracuse University professor Jim Zwick (marktwain.guide@miningco.com), author and editor of various articles and works on Mark Twain.

Walt Whitman (1819–1892)

460.   **Walt Whitman's Notebooks**
http://lcweb2.loc.gov/ammem/wwhome.html

Four notebooks by Walt Whitman have been scanned for online publication. One of Whitman's earliest notebooks is still under construction, but others ("Perceptions or Senses," "1862," and "Hospital," about his visit to Civil War hospitals) are complete. Students can read Walt Whitman's notes in his own penmanship. The notebooks have been described by the Library of Congress staff as "typical writer's notebooks in which Whitman jotted down thoughts in prose and expressions in poetry." These four notebooks are part of the collection of forty Whitman notebooks in the Thomas Biggs Harned collection at the Library of Congress.

British and Irish Literature

461.   **Nineteenth-Century British and Irish Authors**
http://lang.nagoya-u.ac.jp/~matsuoka/19th-authors.html

Nineteenth-century British and Irish authors are listed in chronological order by birth date, with links to online resources that include full-text works and Web sites. This comprehensive listing is maintained by Mitsuharu Matsuoka, associate professor of English at Nagoya University in Nagoya, Japan (matsuoka@lang.nagoya-u.ac.jp).

462.   **Victorian Web Site**
http://www.stg.brown.edu/projects/hypertext/landow/victorian/victov.html

As a resource for courses in Victorian literature at Brown University, this searchable database contains comprehensive information about science, politics, gender, technology, economics, religion, philosophy, visual arts, and literature in the Victorian era. George P. Landow (George_Landow@brown.edu), professor of English and art history, is the Webmaster.

Nineteenth-Century Magazines

463.   ***The Penny Magazine***
http://www.history.rochester.edu/pennymag/

The Penny Magazine was a weekly illustrated magazine for the working class. Part of the liberal reform movement of the 1830s, the magazine published poetry and information about subjects of general interest, such as tea and coffee; well-known places in England; animals and birds of Great Britain; and stagecoaches. The first issue (March 31, 1832) and 11 other issues (through October 31, 1835) are collected here.

Jane Austen (1775–1817)

464.   **Jane Austen Information Page**
http://www.pemberley.com/janeinfo/janeinfo.html

Providing both educational and "just for fun" information, this site is a comprehensive collection of links to Jane Austen's works, biographical and family life, and some recent popular humor.

Students will enjoy reading The Jane Austen Top Ten Song List and will want to make up their own entries for Austen characters, such as *Papa Don't Preach* by Maria and Julia Bertram and *Girls Just Want to Have Fun* by Lydia and Kitty Bennet. There are also links to information about the movies *Persuasion* and *Sense and Sensibility*, other film/video adaptations, and articles about "Austenmania." Notes, quotes, letters, and genealogy charts for characters in her novels are all here.

Lewis Carroll [Charles Lutwidge Dodgson] (1832–1898)

465. Lewis Carroll Home Page

http://www.lewiscarroll.org/carroll.html

Commemorating the centenary of Lewis Carroll's death, this online exhibition provides comprehensive information about the man and his works. A table of contents divided into four topics makes navigation relatively easy. Students can access links to online texts, graphics and photography, biographical information, Carroll societies, publications, reference materials, and references to Carroll's work (mostly *Alice in Wonderland*) in popular culture. Look for links to online games, riddles, and math problems written by Carroll, whose real name was Charles Dodgson, a mathematician of distinction as well as a literary author. The Webmaster is Joel M. Birenbaum (birenbau@netwave.net).

466. Lewis Carroll, Illustrated

http://www.rust.net/~kdonohue/aliceidx.html

A compilation of Carroll-related graphics makes this site visually entertaining and informative. Find illustrations by Sir John Tenniel and others, including book covers. Look for photographs actually taken by Charles Lutwidge Dodgson. The Biography section has pictures of Lewis Carroll's house in Guildford, the cemetery where he is buried, and photographs of Carroll and the English countryside (including a treacle well). Also available is a picture of an Alice tangram at (http://www-groups.dcs.st-andrews.ac.uk/~history/Diagrams/Alice_tangrams.jpeg). The Costumes/Performances section has links to graphics from stage and TV. Created and maintained by Kathy Donohue-Vredevoogd (kdonohue@rust.net).

Charles Dickens (1812–1870)

467. Charles Dickens: A CyberGuide Author Study

http://www.west.net/~cybrary/Dickenstg/

As an author study, this is an excellent supplemental unit providing resources for classes studying one or all of the works of Charles Dickens. Students use Internet resources to take a virtual tour of one of Dickens's homes, read a letter written by Dickens, study a chronology of his life and works, and read descriptions of Dickens written by his family and friends. From their online research, students can then participate in a number of activities, including creating a chart comparing life in Dickens's era to their own; illustrating a timeline of Dickens's life; writing a diary entry; making a storyboard; and translating one of Dickens's letters into contemporary language. Written by Lucy Lynne Davis (cybrary@west.net) of Chaparral Middle School in Moorpark, California. For more CyberGuides, see (http://www.sdcoe.k12.ca.us/score/cyberguide.html).

468. The Dickens Page

http://lang.nagoya-u.ac.jp/~matsuoka/Dickens.html

The Dickens Page is a comprehensive collection of essays, critiques, and articles about Dickens and his works. It includes links to biographies, bibliographies, and full-text e-texts. Information is available on the Dickens Fellowship, the Dickens Society, mailing lists, and academic resources. The site is maintained by Mitsuharu Matsuoka, associate professor of English at Nagoya University, Nagoya, Japan (matsuoka@lang.nagoya-u.ac.jp).

469. The Dickens Project

http://humwww.ucsc.edu/dickens/index.html

The Dickens Project of the University of California, a scholarly consortium, promotes study and enjoyment of the life, times, and work of Charles Dickens. The Dickens Project Web site includes information about conferences, publications, news, summer workshops, teaching resources, and people interested in Dickens. The Dickens Electronic Archive offers resources for reading, teaching, and study. The Latest Arrivals area highlights new additions to the archive. The Webmaster's address for the Dickens Project is (dpj@cats.ucsc.edu).

Arthur Conan Doyle (1859–1930)

470. 221B Baker Street

http://members.tripod.com/~msherman/holmes.html

It's "Elementary, my dear Watson," to read online most of the stories by Sir Arthur Conan Doyle recounting the adventures of Mr. Sherlock Holmes and his companion in crime-solving, John H. Watson, M.D. Also provides illustrations and links to related sites. Created and maintained by Michael Sherman (msherman@erols.com). Another good Web site for Sherlock Homes is the Baker Street Connection (http://www.citsoft.com/holmes3.html) by David Carroll (dwcar@netcom.com).

Clive Staples Lewis (1898–1963)

471. Into the Wardrobe: The C. S. Lewis Web Site

http://cslewis.drzeus.net

C.S. Lewis fans and scholars alike will appreciate this comprehensive site, which provides information about Lewis's life and writing (fiction, nonfiction, and poetry). There is a collection of secondary works, papers, speeches, and some random quotes. Each day a quote by C.S. Lewis is featured. The Photograph Album contains pictures of Lewis and significant places in his life, such as Oxford and Magdalen College. The Sound Like Lewis files contain several clips of Lewis speaking about literary topics. The online discussion list devoted to Lewis, Mere-Lewis, is archived at this site.

To subscribe, send an e-mail message to:
listserv@listservaol.com

Leave the subject line blank, and in the body, type:
subscribe merelewis [your first and last name]

This C.S. Lewis Web site is maintained by John Visser (DrZeus@yahoo.com).

The C.S. Lewis newsgroup (alt.books.cs-lewis) discusses anything to do with the life and works of Clive Staples Lewis. To obtain the newsgroup's FAQ list, go to (http://cslewis.DrZeus.net/faq.html).

George Orwell (1903–1950)

472. George Orwell's Life
http://www.levity.com/corduroy/orwell.htm

George Orwell, the pen name of Eric Arthur Blair, is best known for two books reflecting his distrust of autocratic government: *Animal Farm* (1945), a modern fable attacking Stalinism, and *Nineteen Eighty-Four* (1949), a dystopian novel depicting an intrusively bureaucratized state. This page gives a short biographical sketch of Orwell's life.

473. Orwellian & Animal Farm Studies Resources
http://dewey.chs.chico.k12.ca.us/orwell.html

The Chico High School Library (California) provides a page of Internet links related to the study of George Orwell's *Animal Farm*. Through Internet resources, students learn about Orwell's use of allegory and how the novel relates to the Russian Revolution from 1917 to 1943. Links are also provided to information about propaganda, "Newspeak," and utopias. See also George J. Lamont's comparison of *Animal Farm* characters to personalities involved in the Russian Revolution (http://pages.citenet.net/users/charles/af-comp.html).

William Shakespeare (1564–1616)

See also "The Renaissance" (entries 1264–1268), The Art of Renaissance Science (entry 680), and The Sistine Chapel (entry 1304).

474. *The Complete Works of William Shakespeare*, Searchable
http://www-tech.mit.edu/Shakespeare/works.html

The Complete Works of William Shakespeare, consisting of more than 30 plays and a large body of poetry, is keyword-searchable, accessible by category, and browseable by chronological or alphabetical order. The full texts of plays are given, with highlighted words linked to a glossary designed to help students understand some of the vocabulary words used in Elizabethan England (1558–1603). The search engine for this database is excellent. The phrase *all the world's a stage* returned the result *As You Like It*, act 2, scene 7. Links are then given to the play, the scene, or to the text beginning "All the world's a stage."

An interesting media link is to a movie database, which lists several films based on Shakespeare's plays, such as *Cleopatra* (1917) and *Much Ado About Nothing* (1993).

Jeremy Hylton (jeremy@cnri.reston.va.us), an employee of the Corporation for National Research Initiatives, is the creator and Webmaster of this outstanding site.

Another searchable database of Shakespeare's complete works is located at (http://www.gh.cs.usyd.edu.au/~matty/Shakespeare/index.html). Full-text versions of the Bard's plays are available in either HTML or plain-text formats, and links lead to other Shakespeare sites. This second searchable database of Shakespeare's complete works is maintained by Matty Farrow (matty@cs.usyd.edu.au). See also the Internet Public Library's Shakespeare Bookshelf (http://www.ipl.org/reading/shakespeare/shakespeare.html). Shakespeare's works are organized on a bookshelf by comedy, tragedy, history, and poetry. Clicking on a book, opens it and the text for each book includes in-text links to definitions for some of the words.

475. The Macbeth Home Page

http://www.falconedlink.com/Macbeth.html

Students who think *Macbeth* is boring should read this summarized version written by English teacher Rodger Burnich (rburnich@localnet.com). Believing that this Shakespearean play has everything a modern audience could wish for (witches, treachery, murder, and lots of blood), as well as current themes (faithlessness, deception, and ambition), Burnich explains each act using his gift as a storyteller to make the action in *Macbeth* come alive for today's students. Throughout all five acts, Burnich mixes storytelling and teaching, interjecting questions and pointing out the importance of special lines. He ends each act with an interesting "hook" to keep students reading to find out what's going to happen next. This is a wonderful resource to use when introducing *Macbeth*. Burnich treats *Hamlet* in much the same manner at (http://www.falconedlink.com/htable.html).

476. Mr. William Shakespeare and the Internet

http://daphne.palomar.edu/shakespeare/

Mr. William Shakespeare and the Internet provides an annotated guide to scholarly Shakespeare resources on the Internet, making it an excellent research site. Information is well organized into categories such as Shakespeare the Man, which includes biographical materials; Literary Journals and Renaissance Resources; Primary and Secondary Sources; and Aspects of Elizabethan Performance, which includes links to music, dance, staging, and sites for those interested in producing authentic Elizabethan productions. Links are also provided to educational sites and the best of the best Shakespeare sites according to compiler, Terry A. Gray (tgray@palomar.edu).

477. Shakespeare and the Globe Theatre, London

http://www.rdg.ac.uk/globe/

Find out about the original Globe, and visit the New Globe Theatre in London. See recent photographs of the New Globe, officially opened by the Queen in June 1997. The Shakespeare in Performance database compares the staging in the original Globe to staging in the New Globe. Information is available about the season's schedule of performances. Links are provided to other Shakespeare sites. Dedicated to the New Globe and to Shakespearean staging, this page is produced by Chantal Miller-Schütz (c.miller-schutz@reading.ac.uk), a Leverhulme Research Fellow at the University of Reading (England) Renaissance Texts Research Centre.

478. Shakespeare Illustrated

http://www.cc.emory.edu/ENGLISH/classes/Shakespeare_Illustrated/Shakespeare.html

Shakespeare Illustrated explores 19th-century paintings, criticism, and productions of Shakespeare's plays and their influences on one another. Paintings are listed for each of Shakespeare's plays, and there is a separate alphabetical list of artists who based paintings on various plays by Shakespeare. Students can see how artists interpreted Shakespeare's works and read information about the art. Created and maintained by Harry Rusche (enghr@emory.edu.), professor of English, Emory University, Atlanta, Georgia.

479. Shakespeare Sonnet Quiz

http://exp.psychologie.uni-kassel.de/cgi-bin/quiz.pl

Students can use this interactive quiz to test their knowledge of Shakespeare's 154 sonnets. A couplet from one of the Bard's sonnets is randomly presented with the last word missing. Students are asked to type in the correct word and then check their response by clicking on "Check." Students can either pause online to read the full text of the sonnet or click on "Next" to proceed to the next puzzle. A cumulative score is given. This site was written and created by Michael Hildebrandt (hilde@hrz.uni-kassel.de).

480. Shakespearean Insults

http://alabanza.com/kabacoff/Inter-Links/cgi/bard.cgi

Students will enjoy creating their own language-rich insults that sound like Shakespearean English. For many students, this might provide an interesting "hook" for studying Shakespeare's works. Some examples from this site include: "Thou mammering rude-growing whey-face," "Thou gleeking dizzy-eyed miscreant," and "Thou spleeny fool-born lewdster."

These insults are not from Shakespeare's works. They are random phrases generated from a set of nouns and adjectives that reflect the language of Elizabethan England. Each time the page is loaded, a new phrase is constructed by cgi-bin PERL script. This site was created and is maintained by Robert I. Kabacoff.

481. Webspeare

http://cncn.com/homepages/ken_m/shakespeare.html

Aimed at high school students, this Web site serves a variety of interests related to the study of Shakespeare's plays. Look for links to study guides, *Bartlett's Familiar Quotations*, Shakespeare on film, art inspired by Shakespeare's plays, the complete works with in-text links to definitions, and the Folger Shakespeare Library in Washington, D.C. Created and maintained by Kenneth Mathews of Brick Tree Designs (webspeare@cncn.com).

Mary Wollstonecraft Shelley (1797–1851)

482. Mary Shelley and *Frankenstein*

http://www.desert-fairy.com/maryshel.shtml

Biographical information is given for Mary Shelley and Percy Bysshe Shelley. Links are provided to literary sources of *Frankenstein* and other Mary Shelley and *Frankenstein* sites. Interesting information is available on the summer of 1816, literary sources that inspired her writing, and a critical analysis of the birth of a monster. Webmaster is Kim Woodbridge (webmaster@desert-fairy.com).

Robert Louis Stevenson (1850–1894)

See also "Pirates" (entries 1274–1275).

483.   ***Treasure Island***

http://www.ukoln.ac.uk/services/treasure/

Stevenson wrote *Treasure Island* for his stepson in 1881. A tale of pirates, a treasure map, a mutiny, and a one-legged sea cook, it remains one of literature's best-loved adventure stories. Written especially for children, this site offers information on the author, the book, related links, and suggestions for fun things to do. Links lead to true stories about treasure and how to find it; tropical islands to visit; ships used by pirates; and more information about pirates. Students are invited to use e-mail to send in reviews of the book, participate in an online treasure hunt, and answer pirate questions.

This excellent site, produced by the U.K. Office for Library and Information Networking (UKOLN), shows how the Internet and books can be made to complement each other. Written by Information Officers Steve Hill and Sarah Ormes (lisslo@ukoln.ac.uk); Ms. Ormes has an M.A. in librarianship.

John Ronald Reuel Tolkien (1892–1973)

484.   **Grey Havens: The Ultimate J. R. R. Tolkien Resource Web Page**

http://tolkien.cro.net

Grey Havens is dedicated to J.R.R. Tolkien's magnum opus. Three main areas of information include Middle-Earth, songs and tales, and pictures. Find out more about hobbits, elves, dwarves, orcs, balrogs, and Tolkien. The site is mirrored on two Web servers. Webmaster is Cirdan (cirdan@fesb.hr).

485.   **The J. R. R. Tolkien Information Page**

http://www.csclub.uwaterloo.ca/u/relipper/tolkien/rootpage.html

Since 1993, this site has provided one-stop shopping for all the Tolkien information available on the Internet. Find out more about the life and works of J.R.R. Tolkien, and access lists and links to other WWW pages, FAQs, mailing lists, and games. Links are also provided to Tolkien newsgroups, such as (alt.fan.Tolkien) and (rec.arts.books.Tolkien), and various Tolkien newsletters and societies, such as the Oxford Tolkien Society Home Page. Information is available on Tolkien films *The Hobbit, Lord of the Rings*, and *Return of the King*. This site was created and is maintained by Eric Lippert (Eric_Lippert@uwaterloo.ca) at the University of Waterloo in Canada. There are five mirror sites in Canada, the United States, Austria, and Australia.

Children's and Young Adult Literature

See also "Library Service to Children and Young Adults" (entries 1443–1452) for more information on children's literature and award-winning children's books, the Caldecott and Newbery Awards, and notable children's Web pages.

General Resources

486. Carol Hurst's Children's Literature Site

http://www.carolhurst.com

Look for rated reviews of children's books and ideas for integrating books and literature into the curriculum. Lists of recommended books can be browsed or searched by author, title, type of book, and grade level. Across-the-curriculum units tie literature to history, math, geography, and science. Twenty themes and topics on which to focus class work, research projects, and discussion groups are listed with related books, activities, and links to related sites. Topics and themes range from Appalachia or Colonial America to the Middle Ages, Patterns, Quilts, Rivers, Time, and Trains.

487. Children's and Young Adult Literature

E-mail: **listserv@bingvmb.cc.binghamton.edu**
Instructions: On the first line of the body of the message, type:
subscribe KIDLIT-L [your first name and last name]

488. Children's Literature: Electronic Resources

gopher://lib.nmsu.edu:70/11/.subjects/Education/.childlit
or
gopher://lib.nmsu.edu
Path: **Main Menu/Resources by Subject/Education/Children's Literature: Electronic Resources**

Designed for students and teachers of children's literature at the college level, as well as children's literature enthusiasts, this site provides information in seven areas: links, books, authors, awards, reviews, criticism, and pedagogy. The content consists of a collection of databases, bibliographies, scholarly papers, announcements, and syllabi. Links are provided to author information, awards, electronic journals and book reviews, and electronic children's books. Donnie Curtis (dcurtis@lib.nmsu.edu) at the New Mexico State University Library maintains this Gopher site.

489. The Children's Literature Web Guide

http://www.acs.ucalgary.ca/~dkbrown/index.html

Comprehensive and well organized, this Web site provides a guide to Internet resources related to books for children and young adults. Information is available about conferences and book events, children's book awards, lists of recommended books, online children's stories, authors of children's books, characters and settings, current movie tie-ins, and electronic journals and discussion groups. There is also information for parents, teachers, storytellers, writers, and illustrators. Links are provided to children's publishers and booksellers on the Internet and related sites. Webmaster is David K. Brown (dkbrown@acs.ucalgary.ca) of the Doucette Library of Teaching Resources, University of Calgary. This is an excellent site for finding information about children's literature.

490. Electronic Resources for Youth Services

http://planetpostcard.com/childlit/childlit.html

Electronic Resources for Youth Services is a comprehensive compilation of annotated Web resources related to children's literature and youth services. Categories include book reviews, reading and storytelling, listservs, newsgroups, associations, awards, information about authors, publishers, and booksellers. The information on this Web site is keyword-searchable. Maintained by Erez Segal (aa331@ccn.cs.dal.ca), a student at the Dalhousie University Library School in Halifax, Nova Scotia.

491. Fairrosa Cyber Library

http://www.dalton.org/libraries/fairrosa/

The Fairrosa Cyber Library is a personal cybercollection of materials found on the Web related to children's literature, and is intended for adults who study children's literature. The bookshelves in the Reading Room are labeled Classics, Fairy and Folk Tales, Stories and Rhymes, and Magazines. There is an alphabetical list of authors and illustrators. Links are provided to articles, reviews, and sites related to Lewis Carroll. Created and maintained by Roxanne Hsu Feldman, aka Fairrosa (fairrosa@yahoo.com).

492. Kay Vandergrift's Children's Literature Page

http://mariner.rutgers.edu/special/kay/childlit.html

Vandergrift discusses the importance of literature in children's lives, ways to select the best literature, and characteristic features of various genres. Links are provided to articles and bibliographies of children's books. Created and maintained by Kay E. Vandergrift (kvander@scils.rutgers.edu), professor of children's literature at Rutgers University.

Multicultural Children's Literature

See also "Multicultural Resources" (entries 1213–1236), "Folklore: Fables, Folktales, and Fairy Tales" (entries 536–541), "Legends" (entries 542–546), "Myths and Mythology" (entries 547–548), and Norse Mythology (entry 1273).

African American

See also Kids Zone (entry 575).

493. Access the Africa Access Review Database

http://filemaker.mcps.k12.md.us/aad/

Africa Access Review provides an electronic guide to children's materials about Africa, which are reviewed by authorities on the subject. Reviews are written by university professors, librarians, and teachers, most of whom have lived in Africa and have graduate degrees in African Studies. Reviews look closely at materials to discern accuracy, bias, and possible stereotyping. It is hoped that educators will use the information provided in Africa Access Review to build quality collections on Africa and to avoid biased and stereotypical materials. Brenda Randolph (brendar@umd5.umd.edu), librarian at Parkland Middle School in Rockville,

Maryland, was the coordinator, compiler, and editor of this project, which produced an extensive number of in-depth and evaluative reviews of children's materials on Africa. A search engine allows keyword searches.

494. African American Images in Picture Books

(Part One)
http://www.scils.rutgers.edu/special/kay/afro.html
(Part Two)
http://www.scils.rutgers.edu/special/kay/afro1.html

African American Images in Picture Books is a two-part unannotated bibliography of picture books arranged alphabetically by author. Criteria for inclusion are strong, positive, visual images of African American children, their friends, and their families, with emphasis on realistic stories, folktales, and legends. Created and maintained by Kay E. Vandergrift (kvander@scils. rutgers.edu), professor of children's literature at Rutgers University.

Asian American

See also "History and Culture of China" (entries 299–305) and "History and Culture of Japan" (entries 359–368).

495. Asian American Literature

http://falcon.jmu.edu/~ramseyil/asia.htm

Look for a compilation of links related to teaching Asian American literature on this page from the Internet School Library Media Center (ISLMC) Web site. Bibliographies are available for K-6 and young adults on fiction, nonfiction, and poetry. Reviews of books, articles, and Asian American literature criticism resources are also listed.

See also Kay E. Vandergrift's (kvander@scils.rutgers.edu) bibliography of picture books featuring folktales and stories portraying realistic images of Asian and Asian American children (http://www.scils.rutgers.edu/special/kay/asian.html).

Jewish Culture

See also "Jewish Americans and Jewish Culture" (entry 1236).

496. Bibliography of Jewish Culture in Children's Books

http://www.armory.com/~web/jbooks.html

Wendy E. Betts, editor of *Notes from the Windowsill,* has compiled an annotated bibliography of children's books about Jewish religion and culture. More than 30 titles are organized in three categories: picture books, chapter books, and intermediate and young adult books. Most titles are linked to reviews in *Notes from the Windowsill,* an online journal of children's books (entry 500). Created and maintained by Wendy E. Betts (web@armory.com).

Latino and Hispanic

See also "History and Culture of Mexico" (entries 394–398); "History and Culture of Spain" (entries 399–401); and "History and Culture of Spanish-Speaking Peoples" (entries 402–409).

497. Latino and Hispanic Images in Picture Books

http://www.scils.rutgers.edu/special/kay/hispanic.html

Looking for a list of Latino and Hispanic picture books? This bibliography helps teachers and librarians find literature that reflects positive images of Latino and Hispanic people and cultures. Books are listed (without annotations) in alphabetical order by author. Compiled by Kay E. Vandergrift (kvander@scils.rutgers.edu), professor of children's literature at Rutgers University. See also Seattle Public Library's bibliography for Latino culture and tradition in books for children (http://www.spl.lib.wa.us/children/latino.html).

Native American

See also Native American Poetry (entry 555) and "Native Americans" (entries 1223–1234).

498. Native American Images in Picture Books

http://www.scils.rutgers.edu/special/kay/native.html

Listed in alphabetical order by author, this is a non-annotated bibliography of powerful Native American images revealed in picture books. Compiled by Kay E. Vandergrift (kvander@scils.rutgers.edu), professor of children's literature at Rutgers University.

499. Native American Literature Units

http://www.carolhurst.com/subjects/nativeamericans.html

Taken from an article by Carol Otis Hurst that first appeared in the "Library Corner" column of *Teaching K-8 Magazine*, the information on this Web page offers suggestions for using literature (nonfiction, poetry, novels, picture books, and myths) in Native American studies. Ideas appropriate for both classroom use and library programming include how to create displays, how to use picture books as starters, and how to make charts to organize research information. Created and maintained by Carol Otis Hurst (carolhurst@aol.com). See also Native American Lore (http://www.ilhawaii.net/~stony/), for hundreds of pages of stories.

Book Reviews and Book Discussions

500. *Notes from the Windowsill*

http://www.armory.com/~web/notes.html

Notes from the Windowsill (formerly *The WEB Online Review*) provides reviews of children's books. Reviewers are volunteers who love children's literature and have professional or personal experience evaluating it. Past issues are archived at this site. Wendy E. Betts (web@armory.com) is the editor.

501. YALSA-BK

E-mail: **listproc@ala1.ala.org**
Instructions: On the first line of the body of the message, type:
subscribe yalsa-bk [your first name and last name]

YALSA-BK is an online discussion list open to young adults and adults who are interested in discussing specific titles, as well as other issues concerning young adult reading and young adult literature. This discussion group is sponsored by YALSA (Young Adult Library Services Association), a division of the American Library Association. For more information on YALSA, see (http://www.ala.org/yalsa/).

Favorite Children's Authors and Illustrators

See also Laura Ingalls Wilder: Frontier Girl (entry 1146) and "Caldecott and Newbery Awards" (entries 1445–1446).

502. Index to Internet Sites: Children's and Young Adults' Authors and Illustrators

http://falcon.jmu.edu/~ramseyil/biochildhome.htm

The Internet School Library Media Center's (ISLMC) index to author and illustrator Internet sites is a metasite designed to foster easy access to curriculum-related sites for authors and illustrators of children's and young adult literature. Authors and illustrators are listed alphabetically. As an example, for the author Beverly Cleary, links are provided to a biography and two lesson plans, one for *Dear Mr. Henshaw* (grades 7–8) and another for a fourth-grade author study. Additionally, the Name Index has a See reference that refers to other pages in the ISLMC as well as other author pages on the Internet. Site administrator is Inez Ramsey (ramseyil@jmu.edu), professor of library science at James Madison University, Harrisonburg, Virginia.

Judy Blume (1938–)

503. Welcome to Judy Blume's Home Base

http://www.judyblume.com/index.html

From Judy Blume's home base, readers will find lots of links to biographical information and photographs, helpful hints on how to write your own stories, Judy's serious and thoughtful comments on censors, a bibliography of her published books, and what is currently new. Judy answers readers' questions, shares her thoughts from being on tour, and provides interesting details about her life and her books.

Jan Brett (1949–)

504. Jan Brett Home Page

http://www.janbrett.com

Jan Brett's home page is a colorful complement to her picture books, filled with creative energy. Craft projects include directions for making a sailor's bracelet, an armadillo, and a troll pencil topper. To send cyber-postcards to friends by e-mail, choose from more than 26 different designs drawn by Jan Brett. Colorful animal masks from *The Mitten* and *Town Mouse, Country Mouse* make ideal props for use in dramatic productions and are easy to download. There are lots of coloring pages to print out for coloring, including Comet's *Nine Lives*, *The Owl and the Pussycat*, and *Berlioz the Bear*. Because she likes to tell children about the fun and hard work that goes into writing and illustrating children's books, Jan Brett has written online letters to children about each of her picture books, explaining how she got the ideas for the stories, characters, and what to include in the illustrations. Links help students and teachers locate biographical information and a complete list of published books. Jan Brett (janbrett@ janbrett.com) loves to write to teachers and children who read her books, and she will send teachers or librarians a free teacher's pack upon request.

Eric Carle (1929–)

505. Eric Carle

http://www.eric-carle.com

The official Eric Carle Home Page provides a brief biography, a FAQ section, and a list of his books published since 1967. The Caterpillar Exchange bulletin board encourages users to exchange ideas about how to use Carle's books. A What's New section previews Carle's newest books. There is a postal service (snail-mail) address for Carle and links to the town where he lives, Northampton, Massachusetts.

Beverly Cleary (1916–)

506. The Unofficial Beverly Cleary Home Page

http://www.teleport.com/~krp/cleary.html

Each month a different book by Beverly Cleary is featured. Look for biographical information about this award-winning author, creator of characters such as Henry Huggins, Beezus Quimby, Ramona Quimby, Ellen Tebbits, Ralph S. Mouse, and Leigh Botts. Provides a bibliography and FAQs. Created and maintained by Karen R. Pederson (krp@teleport.com).

Susan Cooper (1935–)

507. Susan Cooper

http://missy.shef.ac.uk/~emp94ms/

Susan Cooper is a diversified and talented writer who is best known for the Dark Is Rising series, stories of high fantasy for children and young adults. In these stories, Arthurian and Celtic myths and legends are interwoven in an ongoing battle between Dark and Light. One title in this series, *The Grey King,* published in 1975, won the Newbery Medal. Biographical information; pictures; a FAQ section; and information about her books, picture books, plays, and films make this an excellent glimpse into Susan Cooper's life and work. Created and maintained by Mark Scott (EMP94MS@Sheffield.ac.uk).

See also a bibliography of print and nonprint resources from ERIC (http://www.indiana.edu/ ~eric_rec/ieo/bibs/cooper.html).

Jean Craighead George (1919–)

508. Jean Craighead George

http://www.jeancraigheadgeorge.com

Find out more about Jean Craighead George, known best for *My Side of the Mountain* and its sequel, *On the Far Side of the Mountain*; the Julie trilogy, *Julie of the Wolves, Julie,* and *Julie's Wolf Pack; Who Really Killed Cock Robin?: An Ecological Mystery;* and *There's an Owl in the Shower.* The author shares tips for how to write good stories, photographs, answers to readers' questions, and news about her plans and current endeavors.

Virginia Hamilton (1936–)

509.   Virginia Hamilton
http://www.virginiahamilton.com

Virginia Hamilton is an award-winning writer of more than 30 children's books. Just a few are: *M. C. Higgins, the Great* (Newbery); *The People Could Fly; Sweet Whispers, Brother Rush* (Newbery Honor); *A Little Love* (Coretta Scott King); and *The House of Dies Drear* (Edgar Allan Poe). She was the Laura Ingalls Wilder Award recipient in 1995, and the recipient of the international Hans Christian Andersen prize in 1992. This site offers biographical information, a schedule of the author's major appearances and events, a photo gallery, links to all her books, and a collection of articles and interviews. Hamilton shares her newest books, just released and to be released. Look for more information on the annual Virginia Hamilton Conference on Multicultural Literary Experiences for Youth. Created and maintained by Virginia Hamilton (bodeep@ aol.com).

Brian Jacques (1939–)

510.   Redwall: The Official Brian Jacques Homepage
http://www.redwall.org

The first book in the popular fantasy series, *Redwall* (Philomel Books 1986), was written for children at the Royal Wavertree School for the Blind in Liverpool, England. For them, Brian Jacques (pronounced "jakes") painted pictures with his words so that they could easily imagine the story through settings, characters, and action. Since the publication of the first book in 1986, 12 more books in the Redwall series have been published; 2 more are scheduled for publication in 2000. Stories in the series center around Redwall Abbey during the medieval period. The heroes are peace-loving mice, moles, shrews, squirrels, and their friends, all of whom exhibit human characteristics. They face the dark side of the animal world, represented by rats, weasels, stoats, foxes, and their villain allies, in the day-to-day struggle of good versus evil, life versus death.

This site provides information about Brian Jacques as an author and his Redwall Fan Club. Look for biographical information about Jacques; a list of books in the Redwall series, with links to further information and fan reviews; and a gallery of illustrations from the series. Fans can join the Redwall Club and visit Redwall Abbey, the club's home on the Web; send e-mail to Jacques; talk to one another via the Internet; subscribe to the Redwall Newsletter by e-mail; and try their hand at completing Redwall-related crossword puzzles. Don't miss the Redwall Encyclopedia and the Molespeech/English Dictionary and Translator. Fans share their artwork, poetry, fiction, and recipes based on Redwall books. Created and maintained by David Bruce Lindsay, a devoted Redwall fan!

A.A. Milne (1882–1956) and Ernest H. Shepard (1879–1976)

511.   A. A. Milne: The Page at Pooh Corner
http://www.electrontrap.org/jmilne/Pooh/

Dedicated to the stories written by A.A. Milne and illustrated by E. H. Shepard, this page offers a good bibliography, a map of Cotchford Farm in the Ashdown Forest area, and a picture of

Poohsticks Bridge. A chronology of Milne's life and biographies of both Milne and Shepard are also provided. Creator and Webmaster is James Milne (jmilne@electrontrap.org).

For two other Web sites about A.A. Milne and Winnie the Pooh, see A. A. Milne: Pooh Home Page (http://www.Pooh-Corner.com) and A. A. Milne: The Pooh Pages (http://worldkids.net/pooh/welcome.html), originally created by Katie Prunka when she was a seventh-grade student as a book report for her English class. This "Expotition" to a Wonderful Place is fun in itself and is great to show to other students as a model of how a book report can be written in HTML.

Patricia Polacco (1944–)

512. **Patricia Polacco**

http://falcon.jmu.edu/~ramseyil/polacco.htm

Learn more about children's author and illustrator, Patricia Polacco. In addition to biographical information, there are a list of her books and links to related sites. For *Rechenka's Eggs*, a link leads to a site about Ukrainian Easter eggs and directions for making them. See also Patricia Polacco's new home page (http://www.patriciapolacco.com).

Beatrix Potter (1866–1943)

513. **Beatrix Potter: More Than Just a Rabbit's Tale!**

http://www.wwwebguides.com/authors/society/potter/beatr.html

Beatrix Potter earned enduring fame as the author of *The Tale of Peter Rabbit* and other nursery tales, but she was also a farmer and landowner, a breeder and judge of prize sheep, and one of the great benefactors of England's National Trust. Links are provided to Lake District sites related to her various achievements.

514. **Beatrix Potter: The Peter Rabbit Web Site**

http://www.peterrabbit.co.uk

Click on Peter to enter this official Frederick Warne (Penguin Group) Beatrix Potter site enhanced by Potter's original illustrations. Potter's biography with photographs is divided into the early years, the book years, and the Lake District years. Her artist's sketchpad shows examples of childhood sketches, natural history, landscapes, picture letters, and imaginary art. Students can find out more about characters from Potter's books such as Mrs. Tiggy-winkle, Squirrel Nutkin, the Tailor of Gloucester, Peter Rabbit, Tom Kitten, and Jemima Puddle-Duck. The Playground contains puzzles and games based on Beatrix Potter's books.

Arthur Ransome (1884–1967)

515. **The Arthur Ransome Society Home Page (Swallows and Amazons Forever!)**

http://humboldt1.com/ar/

English writer Arthur Ransome is known for his series of books, Swallows and Amazons. This Web site provides information on Ransome's books, his life, the locations and identities featured in his writings, and other Ransome-related information. Links are provided to Virtual

TARS, the electronic branch of the Arthur Ransome Society, and information about how to join TARS is available. There is a bibliography of books by Ransome, books about him, and archived materials. A guide to the Swallows and Amazons series is helpful, containing information about characters, plots, and settings.

The Arthur Ransome slide show displays a collection of photographs taken by members and friends of TARS. Some of the scenes include Wild Cat Island, the Amazons, the lake, the hills, and the boats.

Maurice Sendak (1928–)

516. **Maurice Sendak**
http://homearts.com/depts/relat/sendakf1.htm

In an illustrated online interview, Maurice Sendak reflects on: Stories My Father Told Me, Childhood Books I Remember, and Getting Kids to Read. Sendak, who produced more than 80 books since 1951, is probably best known for *Where the Wild Things Are*, which won the Caldecott Medal in 1964.

Dr. Seuss [Theodore Geisel] (1904–1991)

517. **Cyber-Seuss!**
http://www.afn.org/~afn15301/drseuss.html

Cyber-Seuss! is the place to find all things related to the genius and memory of Dr. Seuss (Theodore Geisel), who in 1956 published *The Cat in the Hat*. The book, which contained only 220 rhyming words, effectively ushered boring Dick and Jane out the door. Discover lists and links to Dr. Seuss everywhere! There are lists of Beginner Books, stories online, and Dr. Seuss books in print. Links are provided to graphics, CD-ROM products, and early Seuss writings. Also available are articles on the Grinch, Seuss wisdom, Seuss quotes, and his obituary.

Janet Stevens (1953–)

518. **Janet Stevens**
http://www.janetstevens.com

Janet Stevens explains why her e-mail address (rhinoink@aol.com) might seem a little strange but is perfect for her. There are lists of her books published by Holiday House and Harcourt Brace and important information about how to prepare for her to visit your school, classroom, or library.

Robert Lawrence Stine (1943–)

519. **R. L. Stine and the Goosebumps Series**
http://place.scholastic.com/goosebumps/indexa.htm

For R.L. Stine and his fans, reading is a scream. R.L. Stine, creator of the Goosebumps and Fear Street series, has his own home page. Find out what Stine looks like, read a brief biography, and get his address. Links lead to information about books in the Goosebumps series and television shows based on the books. Find out how to join the R.L. Stine Fan Club and learn more about audio books, home videos, games, and CD-ROMs. A photo gallery completes this Web site, which cautions those who dare to enter!

Chris Van Allsburg (1949–)

520. **Chris Van Allsburg**

http://www.eduplace.com/rdg/author/cva/index.html

Houghton Mifflin puts author Chris Van Allsburg in the spotlight. Look for a biography, links to his books, and information on how to integrate them into the curriculum. Student reviews of Van Allsburg's works are listed, along with readers' questions and answers and an interview.

See (http://www.wondersociety.com/rws/art/illusbk/) for another site about Chris Van Allsburg's books, including *The Garden of Abdul Gasazi*, *Ben's Dream*, *The Wreck of the Zephyr*, *The Mysteries of Harris Burdick*, *The Widow's Broom*, *The Sweetest Fig*, and *Two Bad Ants*, as well as *Jumanji* and *The Polar Express*.

Laura Ingalls Wilder (1867–1957)

521. **My Little House on the Prairie Home Page**

http://vvv.com/~jenslegg/

Laura Ingalls Wilder wrote nine books in the Little House series. Fans will be delighted to discover a collection of Wilder family photographs and accompanying biographical information. In-text links provide additional information about museums and historical sites. This comprehensive site includes information about the new Little House books written by Maria D. Wilkes (Brookfield Years) and Roger Lea MacBride (Rocky Ridge Years), the Little House on the Prairie movie (Universal Pictures), and information on the Laura Ingalls Wilder Medal. Created and maintained by Jennifer Slegg (jenslegg@pinc.com). *See also* Laura Ingalls Wilder: Frontier Girl (entry 1146).

Audrey Wood and Don Wood

522. **The Audrey Wood Clubhouse**

http://www.AudreyWood.com

Find out more about children's authors and illustrators, Audrey and Don Wood, by visiting their specially designed Clubhouse. Look in Secrets for FAQs about the illustrators' work. Read their biographies and find out about the books they write and illustrate. Explore the Clubhouse to find out more interesting things such as computer art.

Publishers

523. **HarperCollins: The Big Busy House**

http://www.harperchildrens.com/index.html

The Big Busy House is a frequently updated activity center and Web site devoted to children's and young adult books published by HarperCollins. The search engine at this site allows searching for any children's book in the HarperCollins catalog by title, author, or ISBN. The advance search feature allows for searching according to grade levels, subjects, themes, and holidays. The Author section provides brief biographical information about children's and young adult authors. Aliki's *How a Book Is Made* is featured. The Awards section highlights HarperCollins books that have won awards such as the Newbery and Caldecott Medals, the National Book Award, ALA Notable Children's Books, ALA Best Books for Young Adults, and ALA Quick Picks for Young Adults. Summaries (some accompanied by color images of the book jackets) are provided for each award-winning book. Look to the Games section for some "just for fun" activities, and stop by the Features section, which focuses on a changing tableau of authors, illustrators, and the latest books published by HarperCollins for children and young adults. Check back often to see what's new.

HarperCollins also has a children's literature discussion group:
HarperCollins Children's Discussion List

For a subscription in digest format, e-mail: **lists@info.harpercollins.com**
Instructions: On the first line of the body of the message, type:
subscribe childrenslibrary-digest

For a subscription in single-message format, e-mail: **lists@info.harpercollins.com**
Instructions: On the first line of the body of the message, type:
subscribe childrenslibrary

HarperCollins Children's Books' electronic news subscription serves K-12 teachers and librarians. Information is provided on HarperCollins children's books as they are nominated for state awards and other awards; author appearances in local areas when authors are interested in school or library visits; and biographical information about children's book authors and illustrators. This list accepts questions addressed to a particular author. Both questions and answers are posted to the list. The list is archived, which is particularly useful in finding biographical sketches. Just send a message to the list requesting a list of filenames; after you select the filename you want, send another e-mail message to get the file.

524.   **Houghton Mifflin's Education Place**
        http://www.eduplace.com/School.html

Houghton Mifflin offers an excellent variety of outstanding instructional materials for K-8 at this Web site. Resources in the Reading/Language Arts Center correlate to the reading program called Invitations to Literacy, but those not using the program will also find this site extremely useful because of its contents, which include dozens of activities and bibliographies organized by theme, theme-based links to Internet sites, and interactive games. The Mathematics Center offers a directory of math links and a collection of fun and challenging brain-teasers updated weekly for grades 3 and above. The Social Studies Center includes a directory of social studies links; professional articles; and GeoNet, an online geography game. Also available are more than 25 political and physical outline maps with a special note to teachers: "Feel free to print or download any of these maps for your personal use in activities, reports, or stories." Teachers can search the Project Center to find out how to participate in online projects or contribute their own project ideas to this continuously growing resource. The activity search feature is helpful for finding classroom activities by grade level and subject area. Parents are invited to explore Parents' Place to find articles on various parenting issues, education, and children and the Internet. The Just for Kids area provides links to many parent-approved sites, where students can go to play interactive games, access online magazines, and travel the globe via Internet field trips. The Link Library organizes resources by topic. The What's New section is updated weekly to point out additions and changes, so be sure to check back often.

525. Penguin Putnam Young Readers Web Site

http://www.penguinputnam.com/yreaders/index.htm

The Penguin Putnam Young Readers Web Site is bright and very appealing. It offers a number of interesting activities to engage young readers with books. Stories for All Seasons provides links to Penguin Putnam books related to holidays. *Jamie O'Rourke and the Big Potato* by Tomie de Paola and *Daniel O'Rourke* by Gerald McDermott are suggested for St. Patrick's Day. Links connect students to books, authors, and illustrators. Each author/illustrator biography is accompanied by a color photograph and a list of books published by Penguin Putnam. Most books are linked to additional information, including a color graphic of the front cover of the dust jacket and a summary "booktalk." There are reproducible activities and activity suggestions in the Toy Box. Some Teacher's Guides include Discovering Math in Literature, Jean Fritz's American History, *Goldilocks and the Three Hares* by Heidi Petach, Poke & Look Learning Books, and Patricia Polacco Teacher's Guide for *Babushka Baba Yaga*, *Boat Ride with Lillian Two Blossom*, *Pink & Say*, and *Chicken Sunday*. Teacher's Guides are located in the Educational Section.

526. Random House Teacher's Resource Center

http://www.randomhouse.com/teachersbdd/

Random House provides more than 100 Teacher's Guides for children's literature titles published by Random House to help integrate these books into the curriculum. For example, Phyllis Reynolds Naylor's *Shiloh* is listed under Careers in the Interdisciplinary Index. Suggested classroom activities include relating the main character's contemplation of growing up to be a veterinarian to asking readers to find out more about a career as a veterinarian and identifying colleges in their states that offer a degree in veterinary medicine. The Authors and Illustrators Index has an alphabetical listing of author and illustrator names linked to biographies, some audio interviews, and the Teacher's Guide for information on how to use one or more books by each author or illustrator. The Grade Index and the Thematic Unit Index suggest books by appropriate grade level and broad topic of study. A Reluctant Reader list of books, a list of award-winning books, a special monthly Spotlight on authors, and a link to Random House news make this an indispensable site for teachers and librarians who want to incorporate more literature titles into their lessons.

527. Scholastic's Internet Center

http://scholastic.com

Scholastic's home page, Scholastic Place, provides information about joining the fee-based Scholastic Network, as well as links to free information for students and teachers. Kids can find out more about Goosebumps, The Magic School Bus, The Babysitters Club, the Animorphs, and the Dear America series. Teachers can gain access to the online magazines *Instructor* and *Electronic Learning*. Find out more about Scholastic book clubs and Scholastic book fairs. Also look for special reports, articles, and interviews with favorite authors.

528.   Simon & Schuster's SimonSays Kids

http://www.simonsays.com/kids/

SimonSays Kids is a special Web area just for kids and the children's books published by Simon & Schuster. An extensive alphabetical listing of authors and illustrators allows students to locate biographical information and a photograph of their favorite author or illustrator. A Search For Titles By This Author feature lets students access an index of current books in print by Simon & Schuster for each author and illustrator listed. The Teacher's Lounge has guides to reading for a few titles, incorporating discussion questions, writing exercises, and research projects. Simon & Schuster's children's book catalog is available online and is both browseable and searchable by keyword, title, or author.

Young Adults

529.   Young Adult Librarian's Help Home Page

http://yahelp.suffolk.lib.ny.us

From the table of contents you can link to a comprehensive list of sites appropriate for young adults. Starting Points are links to sites and documents concerning young adults and young adult literature. The Reading Pages section provides links to information about young adult reading, publishing, and various lists and bibliographies; Reading Pages also provide links to home pages for authors Michael Crichton, Dean Koontz, Christopher Pike, and Stephen King. The Professional Pages give links to adolescent behavior, welfare, and education. The Teen Pages give links for teens, including online magazines and sites of special interest. Ending Points offers information of interest to young adult librarians. Finally, a What's New section provides annotated links to new pages. The Young Adult Librarian's Home Page was created by Patrick Jones and is currently being maintained by Tracey Firestone (tfiresto@suffolk. lib.ny.us) at Suffolk Cooperative Library System, New York.

Discussion Groups

530.   Children's Literature: Criticism and Theory

E-mail: **listserv@email.rutgers.edu**
Instructions: On the first line of the body of the message, type:
subscribe CHILD_LIT [your first name and last name]

For more information, see (http://www.rci.rutgers.edu/~mjoseph/childlit/about.html).

531.   Children's Literature Newsgroup

Newsgroup: **rec.arts.books.childrens**

Parents, teachers, librarians, and others discuss children's literature.

Electronic Books

532.   Bibliomania

http://www.bibliomania.com

Bibliomania provides full-text online versions of fiction, nonfiction, poetry, and Shakespeare's works written in HTML. All text is fully searchable, making it simple to find specific passages, themes, or words. The database is also browseable. Text can be read online or printed for personal use and study. New works are continually being added.

533. Classic Short Stories

http://www.bnl.com/shorts/

Access is provided to a collection of full-text short stories written in HTML. More than 80 short stories are available, written by authors such as Guy de Maupassant, Edgar Allan Poe, Anton Chekhov, O. Henry, Rudyard Kipling, Nathaniel Hawthorne, and Charles Dickens. Maintained by Gary Lindquist (shorts@bnl.com).

534. The On-line Books Page

http://digital.library.upenn.edu/books/

On-line Books allows you to search by author or title, browse by author or title, browse new book listings, and browse subject listings. Special exhibits have included "Banned Books On-Line" and "A Celebration of Women Writers." Links are provided to other general English repositories, such as the CMU English Server and the Internet Wiretap book collection, and to specialty or foreign-language repositories, such as ARTFL and the Fourth World Documentation Project.

535. Project Gutenberg

http://www.promo.net/pg/

Project Gutenberg is a vast library of public-domain literature, mirrored at FTP and Web sites around the globe. Project Gutenberg aims to create and distribute 10,000 electronic texts (e-texts) in "plain vanilla ASCII" by the end of 2001, giving readers and scholars online access to the classics at no cost. These e-texts are available from FTP servers as TXT files or TXT files using ZIP compression. Dante's *La Divina Commedia* became the thousandth e-text in the Gutenberg archives during late summer 1997. The Project Gutenberg Library holds three categories of e-texts: Light Literature, such as *Alice in Wonderland*, *Peter Pan*, and *Aesop's Fables*; Heavy Literature, such as the Bible, Shakespeare, *Moby Dick*, and *Paradise Lost*; and References, such as *Roget's Thesaurus*, almanacs, an encyclopedia, and various dictionaries. Books are cataloged by author and title, and the database is keyword-searchable. Information is available on how to become one of the Project Gutenberg volunteers (nearly 1,000 from around the world), and links lead to other e-text archives. Monthly progress reports on Project Gutenberg are also posted on this site.

Project Gutenberg is the brainchild of Michael Hart. When he was told that he had basically unlimited account privileges at the University of Illinois in 1971, he decided to put the full text of books on the Internet so that everyone could have access to the world's greatest literature. Hart has been quoted as saying, "I personally believe that you can't have democracy without freedom of choice . . . and the foundation of democracy is literacy." He adds, "You can't burn these books."

Folklore: Fables, Folktales, and Fairy Tales

See also "Multicultural Children's Literature" (entries 493–499) and 19th-Century German Stories (entry 331).

536. Aesop's Fables

http://www.pacificnet.net/~johnr/aesop/

Reverend George Fyler Townsend (1814–1900) and Ambrose Bierce (1842–1914) translated most of the 655 fables by Aesop, indexed in table format with morals, available on this site. Also included are fables by Jean de la Fontaine, fairy tales by Hans Christian Andersen, and other literature selections. A dictionary is provided to find meanings for words used in the fables. Created and maintained by John R. Long (johnr@pacificnet.net) with RealAudio narrations by daughter Heather.

537. Hans Christian Andersen (1805–1875)

http://HCA.Gilead.org.il

Born in Odense, Denmark, Hans Christian Andersen is best known for his fairy tales. This Web site lists all 168 of Andersen's stories in the chronological order of their original publication. Most are in the public domain and are available online in full text, with the original illustrations by Vilhelm Pedersen and Lorenz Frølich. The English translations were done by H. P. Paull in 1872. Some of Andersen's best-known stories are "The Princess and the Pea," "Thumbelina," "The Little Mermaid," "The Ugly Duckling," "The Emperor's New Suit," and "The Little Match Seller." A Webography provides annotated links to related information. Created and maintained by Dr. Zvi Har'El (rl@math.technion.ac.il), senior lecturer in the Department of Mathematics at the Technion, Israel Institute of Technology, in memory of his son, Gilead Har'El (1977–1996).

538. Myths and Fables from Around the World

http://www.afroam.org/children/myths/myths.html

From *Kids Zone* (entry 575), sponsored by the African-American Newspapers, Inc. (entry 1414), this site offers myths and fables from around the world. Each month features a new myth or fable. Stories of African origin include the Anansi tales. "How Coyote Stole Fire" has a Native American origin; "The Tea Kettle of Good Luck" is Asian; and "The Tiger, the Brahman, and the Jackal" is from India. The Webmaster's e-mail address is (matt@afroam.org).

539. The Realm of Books and Dreams

http://www.bconnex.net/~mbuchana/realms/page1/

The Realm of Animal Fables and Fairytales contains a collection of Aesop's fables. Other "realms" of stories are also available, including the Realm of Nursery Rhymes, Realm of Fairytales, Realm of Adventure, Realm of Poetry and Verse, and Realm of Laughter. The Web site creator is Marlene Buchanan (mbuchana@bconnex.net).

540. Snow White

http://www.scils.rutgers.edu/special/kay/snowwhite.html

Kay E. Vandergrift's Snow White Pages provide in-depth coverage of this fairy tale, with an online hypertext version of the story, illustrations from various versions of the story, and information about films, videos, and recordings. Scholars will appreciate discussions of issues related to the study of fairy tales in general and of Snow White in particular, as well as excerpts of criticism of Snow White. This scholarly resource allows users to study this traditional tale "in different versions and variants published over an extended time frame." There are two bibliographies. One contains resources about folklore, fairy tales, and Snow White; the other is a guide to the versions of Snow White used in this study.

541. Tales of Wonder

http://members.xoom.com/darsie/tales/index.html

Tales of Wonder is a collection of tales from around the world, and is an excellent multicultural reading resource. Links are provided to full-text stories, and most tales also have links to reference material.

Legends

542. Arthurian Legends: Interdisciplinary Approach

http://www.ncsa.uiuc.edu/Edu/RSE/RSEblue/arthur/artidu.html

Educators will appreciate the depth and creativity in this Web-based interdisciplinary approach to the study of Arthurian legends. Lesson plans allow students to increase their proficiency in using the Internet and to learn about Arthurian England. Links lead to a dictionary of feudal terms, pictures of armor, images and art (including Celtic clip art), a history of English money, Celtic music, and essays about the Arthurian legend. Created by Katherine A. Eisenhower (keisenho@pen.k12.va.us) at Hylton High School in Woodridge, Virginia. See also The Mystic Realm of King Arthur (http://www.public.iastate.edu/~camelot/arthur.html).

543. The Camelot Project, The University of Rochester

http://www.lib.rochester.edu/camelot/cphome.stm

The Camelot Project provides a database of Arthurian texts, images, bibliographies, and basic information. The main menu lists Arthurian characters, symbols, and sites. Links lead to submenus offering basic information, texts, images, and a bibliography about each subject. Alan Lupack (alupack@rcl.lib.rochester.edu), curator of the Robbins Library, a branch of Rush Rhees Library, is the creator and Webmaster.

See also the *Annotated Guide to Arthurian Resources on the Internet* (http://jan.ucc.nau.edu/~jjd23/arthur/), written by John J. Doherty (John.Doherty@nau.edu), undergraduate reference services librarian at Cline Library, Northern Arizona University (Flagstaff, Arizona).

544. Legends

http://www.legends.dm.net

Legends explores the history, literature, and lore surrounding King Arthur, Robin Hood, swashbuckling characters of balladry fame, and characters from films such as the Queen of Elfland and Zorro. Legends also contains information about Shakespeare, fairy tales, and Beowulf. A collection of excellent links is provided to legendary resources on the Internet. Paula Katherine Marmor (pkm@dn.net), the editor and Web designer, is assisted by Donald G. Keller and Elizabeth Willey in bringing legends and legendary characters to life.

545. *The Many Realms of King Arthur*

http://bcn.boulder.co.us/library/bpl/child/booklook/booklook.html

The first online edition of *Booklook,* a publication of the Boulder (Colorado) Public Library intended to connect kids with books, focuses on Arthurian legends. *The Many Realms of King Arthur* traces the development of the Arthurian legends from their origin in the Middle Ages to their latest adaptations in the 20th century. The material in Classroom Connections is from Barbara Elleman's article "The Days of Camelot," which appeared in the American Library Association's bimonthly publication, *Book Links,* in September 1991. The paper version can be viewed online using Adobe Acrobat Reader.

546. The Robin Hood Project, The University of Rochester

http://www.lib.rochester.edu/camelot/rh/rhhome.stm

The Robin Hood Project provides a database of texts, images, bibliographies, and basic information about the Robin Hood stories and other outlaw tales. The menu of stories is arranged alphabetically by author, but most ballads are listed under the heading Anonymous. There is a bibliography of Robin Hood literature and films. Alan Lupack (alupack@rcl.lib.rochester.edu), curator of the Robbins Library, a branch of Rush Rhees Library, is the creator and Webmaster.

Myths and Mythology

See also Encyclopedia Mythica (entry 1340) and Norse Mythology (entry 1273).

547. Bulfinch's Mythology *The Age of Fable or Stories of Gods and Heroes*

http://www.webcom.com/shownet/medea/bulfinch/welcome.html

The Age of Fable or Stories of Gods and Heroes by Thomas Bulfinch is now online as an illustrated, annotated, and hyperlinked edition. This is an excellent online resource for studying mythology. In-line text links assist readers by providing additional information. This reformatted online rendition of Bulfinch's text is also searchable using keywords, names, or phrases. The Webmaster is Bob Fisher (webmaster@showgate.com).

548. Mythology on the Web

http://www.angelfire.com/mi/myth/

Mythology on the Web is an index of links to myths and mythology Internet resources. Categories are broad and include African Mythology, Mythology of the South Pacific, Mythology of Scandinavia, and Eastern European Mythology. Use this site to find out more about Native American myths and legends as well as the mythology of the Ancient Middle East. The Webmaster is Richard L. Koshak (rkoshak@unm.edu).

Poetry

General Interest

549. **A Collection of Poetry**
http://eserver.org/poetry/

Part of the English Server (http://english.hss.cmu.edu), with more than 18,000 works online, this poetry collection contains original and classic verse as well as literary and poetic theory. Poems can be searched by title, author, or keyword. Poems are listed alphabetically by author. A few of the poems in this collection include Tennyson's *The Charge of the Light Brigade*, Longfellow's *Song of Hiawatha* (with introductory note), Coleridge's *The Rime of the Ancient Mariner*, Pope's *Rape of the Lock*, Homer's *Iliad*, and Whitman's *Leaves of Grass*.

550. **The Internet Poetry Archive**
http://metalab.unc.edu/ipa/

The Internet Poetry Archive makes available selected poems by contemporary poets. The initial unit features eight living poets, including Philip Levine and Nobel Prize winners Seamus Heaney and Czeslaw Milosz. Project coordinator is Paul Jones (paul_jones@unc.edu).

551. ***Poetry Magazine***
http://www.poetrymagazine.com

Poetry Magazine publishes monthly. Poets submit their work using a convenient online submission form. Archives (beginning with 1997) can be browsed by month or poet's name. Selected poetry from 1996 is also available. There is a separate section of children's work. Mary Barnet is the editor.

552. **Twentieth Century Poetry in English**
http://www.lit.kobe-u.ac.jp/~hishika/20c_poet.htm

Students will find the poetry of 159 20th-century poets compiled on this Web site and listed alphabetically by author to make access easy.

American Poetry

553. **The American Verse Project**
http://www.hti.umich.edu/english/amverse/

The American Verse Project is an electronic archive of volumes of American poetry prior to 1920, created as an ongoing collaborative project between the University of Michigan Humanities Text Initiative (HTI)) and the University of Michigan Press. To date, most of the archive is made up of 19th-century poetry, with some 18th- and 20th-century texts. Students can find online poetry written by Alcott, Benét, Emerson, Longfellow, Millay, Poe, Sandburg, and Whitman, to name just a few. The archive is both searchable and browseable.

554. Literary Kicks

http://www.charm.net/~brooklyn/LitKicks.html

Some of the Beat poets highlighted here are Jack Kerouac, Allen Ginsberg, Neal Cassady, William S. Burroughs, Gary Snyder, Lawrence Ferlinghetti, Gregory Corso, and Michael McClure. Find out more about the Beat Generation, Beat Connections in Rock Music, films about the Beats, Buddhism as a Beat religion, and the origin of the term *Beat*. This site was created and is maintained by Levi Asher (brooklyn@netcom.com).

555. Native American Poetry

http://www.sdcoe.k12.ca.us/score/nampoet/poettg.htm

Appropriate for upper elementary and older students, this mini-unit uses Internet Web sites as resources for students to read and study free-verse Native American poetry. Students learn to identify free verse and sensory language, and to write their own original free-verse poems. Teacher background information, student activities, and links to Internet resources are all provided. This Native American Poetry CyberGuide was written by Luella Stilley (lstilley@ mail.sandi.net). For other CyberGuides, see (http://www.sdcoe.k12.ca.us/score/cyberguide.html).

556. Poetry and Prose of the Harlem Renaissance

http://www.nku.edu/~diesmanj/poetryindex.html

Provides a collection of selected full-text works by poets and authors of the Harlem Renaissance. Look for work by Gwendolyn Bennett, Arna Bontemps, Countee Cullen, Jessie Redmon Fauset, Langston Hughes, James Weldon Johnson, Claude McKay, Esther Popel, and Jean Toomer. Collected and maintained by Jill Diesman (diesmanj@nku.edu).

American Poets

Maya Angelou (1928–)

557. Maya Angelou Home Page

http://www.cwrl.utexas.edu/~mmaynard/Maya/maya5.html

Written by students at the University of Texas at Austin for a literature class, this page offers biographical information and selected full-text poems. There is a list of Angelou's books and links to audio and video files. For two other sites about Angelou, go to (http://www.chron.com/ content/chronicle/special/99/1pmaya/1pmaya.htm) and (http://www.mayaangelou.com).

Emily Dickinson (1830–1886)

558. The Emily Dickinson Page

http://userweb.interactive.net/~krisxlee/emily/

The Emily Dickinson Page provides links to information about the poet's life, e-mail discussion groups, the Emily Dickinson International Society, references, a FAQs section, books and on-line reviews, and related sites. Links are provided to more than 460 of Dickinson's poems located online. Students can also access a photograph of Emily Dickinson. Originally created by Paul E. Black (paul.black@nist.gov), this site is now maintained by Kris Selander (ksel4052@

uriaccuri.edu). For another site on Emily Dickinson, go to (http://www.bartleby.com/113/index.html).

Nikki Giovanni (1943–)

559.　**Nikki Giovanni**

http://athena.english.vt.edu/Giovanni/Nikki_Giovanni.html

Nikki Giovanni, an English professor at Virginia Polytechnic Institute and State University, is featured with her picture; a brief biographical timeline; and a list of her publications, honorary degrees, and awards.

Langston Hughes (1902–1967)

560.　**The Poetry of Langston Hughes**

http://www.sdcoe.k12.ca.us/score/langhu/langhutg.html

Following this CyberGuide from the San Diego County Office of Education, which incorporates the use of Internet resources, students will find out more about Langston Hughes as a poet and the influence of Africa and African American history on his work. After researching the Web using suggested links, students create products such as an author brochure, bookmarks, and an image map. Written by Barbara Garrison (Blair56@inet1.inetworld.net). For more CyberGuides, see (http://www.sdcoe.k12.ca.us/score/cyberguide.html). See also a Langston Hughes Web site created by students at the University of Texas at Austin (http://www.cwrl.utexas.edu/~mmaynard/Hughes/hughes.htm).

British and Irish Poetry

561.　**British Poetry 1780–1910: An Archive of Scholarly Electronic Editions**

http://etext.lib.virginia.edu/britpo.html

The Electronic Text (Etext) Center at the University of Virginia has compiled a hypertext archive of scholarly editions of British poetry from 1780 to 1910. Links are provided to works in the Project Bartleby collection at Columbia University as well as the Electronic Text Center. Other British poetry available online, outside the period 1780–1910, includes *Beowulf*, Milton's *Paradise Lost*, and Spenser's illustrated *Shepheardes Calendar*. Additional works of British and American literature can be found in the Etext Center's Modern English Collection (http://etext.lib.virginia.edu/modeng/modeng0.browse.html). Webmasters are Jerome McGann (jjm2f@lizzie.engl.virginia.edu) and David Seaman (etext@virginia.edu).

British and Irish Poets

William Blake (1757–1827)

562.　**The William Blake Archive**

http://jefferson.village.virginia.edu/blake/

Begun in 1995, as an online project to create an electronic hypermedia archive of William Blake's works, this Web site contains digitized images of Blake's paintings, drawings, engravings, and commercial illustrations, as well as illustrations and text from his illuminated books. Upon completion, this searchable archive will include a major portion of Blake's writings and artwork (19 illuminated books and 3,000 images) and a bibliography of more than 500 critical articles and books about Blake's work, allowing students to study Blake as printmaker, artist, and poet.

563. The William Blake Page
http://members.aa.net/~urizen/blake2.html

William Blake, an English Romantic poet, was also a painter, engraver, and printer. Here students can view several of his paintings and read full-text versions of *The Songs of Innocence*, *The Songs of Experience*, and *The Marriage of Heaven and Hell*. Links lead to related sites. One of these sites, The Blake Digital Text Project (http://virtual.park.uga.edu/~wblake/), allows users to search Blake's works; it also offers many illustrations and a map. The William Blake Page is maintained by Richard Record (urizen@aa.net).

Robert Burns (1759–1796)

564. Robert Burns: A Literary Feast
http://www.geocities.com/Paris/3294/

A Literary Feast honors Robert Burns, the Bard of Scotland. Poems and songs are divided into categories, such as Regarding the Lassies, Patriotism and Freedom, Drinking and Good Times, Wit and Wisdom, and so on. Links lead to other Robert Burns resources, as well as links to pages on Scotland and Scottish interests. Alexander J. Hay III (ahay@ghgcorp.com) is creator and Webmaster.

565. Robert Burns, Poet: A Celebration
http://www.innotts.co.uk/~asperges/burns.html

Robert Burns died July 21, 1796. This site celebrates the bicentenary of his death. The home page includes text and graphics about his life, along with some critical analysis. Text and sound files feature some of his works, such as "To a Mouse," "Up in the Morning Early," and "For a' That." Links lead to other resources about Burns. Creator and Webmaster is Jeremy Boot (asperges@innotts.co.uk), who lives in Nottingham, England.

Rudyard Kipling (1865–1936)

566. Complete Collection of Poems by Rudyard Kipling
http://www.poetryloverspage.com/poets/kipling/kipling_ind.html

Kipling's poems have been compiled into a searchable and browseable archive. A brief biography includes in-text links to poems and additional information. Created and maintained by Edward Bonver (exb1874@grace.isc.rit.edu).

Edward Lear (1812–1888)

567.   Edward Lear Home Page

http://www2.pair.com/mgraz/Lear/index.html

Students will find out why Lear might be the inventor of the term "snail mail" as they discover some of his nonsense poetry, limericks, and artwork. A table of contents and a poem index make navigation easy through this collection of Web pages. Biographical information about Lear includes pictures and bibliographies. Also look for essays on the history and origins of the limerick.

Recommended Poetry for Children and Young Adults

568.   A Bibliography of Poetry for YAs

http://falcon.jmu.edu/~ramseyil/yapoetrybib.htm

What type of poetry might appeal to young adults? This page lists poetry that is both multicultural and diverse. For more African American and Native American poetry suitable for YAs, see the Middle and Secondary Language Arts page (http://falcon.jmu.edu/~ramseyil/yalit.htm). These two pages are part of the excellent Internet School Library Media Center site (http://falcon.jmu.edu/~ramseyil/index.html) maintained by Inez Ramsey (ramseyil@jmu.edu), with the library science program at James Madison University in Harrisonburg, Virginia.

569.   Poetry for Upper Elementary Students

http://falcon.jmu.edu/~ramseyil/poemiddle.htm

Need some poems for intermediate elementary grades? This page offers a list with links to some full-text classics. Students will appreciate reading some of these poetry favorites: *Casey at the Bat* by Ernest Lawrence Thayer; *Daffodils* by William Wordsworth; *The Highwayman* by Alfred Noyes; *The Raven* by Edgar Allan Poe; *Trees* by Joyce Kilmer; *The Tyger* by William Blake; *The Village Blacksmith* by Henry Wadsworth Longfellow; and *The Walrus and the Carpenter* by Lewis Carroll. This poetry list is a page from the Internet School Library Media Center site (http://falcon.jmu.edu/~ramseyil/index.html), maintained by Inez Ramsey (ramseyil@jmu.edu), with the library science program at James Madison University in Harrisonburg, Virginia.

Japanese Poetry

Haiku

570.   Haiku for People

http://www.toyomasu.com/haiku

Find out what *haiku* is and learn the difference between *haiku, hokku,* and *haikai.* Though it recognizes that there is no consensus on how to write haiku poems in languages other than Japanese, this site nevertheless provides helpful tips for writing them. Links are provided to many other sites related to haiku poetry. Examples of haiku poems are listed.

Turkish Poetry

Mevlana Jelaluddin Rumi (1207–1273)

571. Jelaluddin Rumi: Poet and Mystic

http://www.chattanooga.net/baylor/academic/english/studentwork/rumi/rumi.html

Thirteenth-century Persian poet and spiritual master Mevlana Jelaluddin Rumi's life, poetry, and religious beliefs are highlighted on this Web site. Rumi was the founder of the Mevlevi Sufi order, a leading mystical brotherhood of Islam, and instituted devotional dances, notably those of the whirling dervishes. Rumi's modern disciples have their headquarters at Konya, Turkey. Over the centuries, Sufism has influenced many poets to write Sufi poetry, especially in Iran (ancient Persia), where there are still about 100 Sufi orders. After reading Rumi's poetry, students wrote essays, created art to accompany specific poems, wrote original music for piano and guitar, and participated in a whirling dervish ceremony. Created by Baylor School high school students in Chattanooga, Tennessee.

Science Fiction and Fantasy

572. Future Fantasy Bookstore

http://futfan.com/home.html

The Future Fantasy Bookstore is a commercial site, but it offers free useful information for science fiction, fantasy, and mystery readers. Some books are listed by series, and new releases are listed monthly. The database is searchable by author; title; type of book (science fiction, fantasy, mystery, horror, and vampire); and special categories, such as series. Results can be sorted by author, title, or publication date. A list of links to science fiction, fantasy, and mystery resources on the Internet is helpful. Links are also provided to online magazines, original fiction, and publishers.

573. Science Fiction and Fantasy Network

http://www.sff.net/sff/index.htp

The Science Fiction and Fantasy Network provides a comprehensive collection of science fiction and fantasy-related sites on the Internet. Links lead to authors, publishers, e-zines, literary agents and agencies, general interest links, and new listings. Maintained by Jim Macdonald (yog@greyware.com).

Electronic Periodicals for Students

See also the *Hanabi* home page (entry 370), CRAYON: CReAte Your Own Newspaper (entry 431), Sports Illustrated for Kids Online (entry 1354), Time for Kids (entry 1412), and "Magazines" (entries 1408–1413).

574. *CyberKids*

http://www.cyberkids.com

Written for kids by kids, *CyberKids* ' regular features include stories, artwork, puzzles, and miscellaneous tips, such as how to get the Dracula font. For information about submitting materials, send e-mail to (cyberkids@mtlake.com).

575.   *Kids Zone*

http://www.afroam.org/children/children.html

Kids Zone is a fun and educational monthly magazine with an African focus for *all* students. It is an excellent site for students who are studying African geography. Regular features each month include "Fun and Games," "Brain Teasers," "Myths and Fables," and "Discover Africa," which features the geography of a different African country each month. Sponsored by African-American Newspapers, Inc. (*see also* entry 1414).

576.   *MidLink Magazine:* The Electronic Magazine for Kids in the Middle Grades

http://longwood.cs.ucf.edu/~MidLink

Published bimonthly by students at Discovery Middle School in Orlando, Florida, this online magazine is aimed at students aged 10 to 15. Issues are filled with school news of interest to *MidLink* readers, such as an online project with the research ship *Malcolm Baldrige*. (Students at Discovery Middle School plan to chart the ship's course and study marine biology from the daily postings by the crew.) The WriteSpot encourages students to submit their writings for publication.

MidLink describes itself as a "cooperative project developed by middle school students from the global community with a little help from adults." It truly has become a collaborative effort by middle school students around the world.

Archives of back issues are available online. The first issue was published September 19, 1994. Since then, issues have featured a virtual haunted house, folklore and storytelling, multicultural December holiday information, famous African Americans, Civil War portfolios, and various environmental issues.

577.   *Smithsonian Magazine's Kids' Castle*

http://www.kidscastle.si.edu

Kids' Castle features articles written for kids ages 8 to 16 on topics such as animals, personalities, sports, history, the arts, travel, science, and air and space. Interestingly written articles are accompanied by photographs and links to related Internet sites. After reading an article, kids are encouraged to post their own messages and read those from others at the Message Board in response to specific questions, such as "What special tricks can your pet do?" "Do you know anyone who remembers World War II?" and "What is your favorite book?" Interactive games and contests make this a fun site. Links are also provided to magazines in the Cricket Group, *Muse*, and the *Smithsonian Magazine*.

578.   *The Vocal Point*

http://bvsd.k12.co.us/cent/Newspaper/Newspaper.html

A unique student newspaper created by students from Boulder Valley School District in Colorado, *The Vocal Point* is, for the most part, written by students at Centennial Middle School. Each month the writers choose a theme. Students then write stories and find links to related sources on the Internet, which they append to each issue. Past topics have included censorship, violence, the environment, water, poverty, animal rights, the Internet, technology, and education. These are great articles; the students explore and study tough issues and subjects.

579.   **Weekly Reader Galaxy**

http://www.weeklyreader.com

Weekly Reader Galaxy complements *Weekly Reader* in the classroom. The Web site provides on-line information by grade level for prekindergarten through sixth grade, with a Teen Trek category for older students. Links are provided to special information for teachers and parents. Reference is made to *Weekly Reader* articles in recent previous issues, and links to other resources on the Internet are then added as a way to extend student interest and learning. The Webmaster's address is (galaxy@weeklyreader.com).

Mathematics

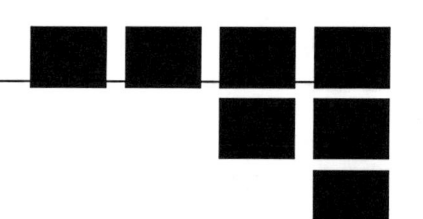

All URL addresses in this chapter are checked and updated monthly. If a link does not work, please refer to the Directory Update Web page located at (http://www.lu.com/lu/irdupdates.html).

There are general mathematics resources as well as resources specific to geometry, algebra, and calculus. The Geometry Junkyard (entry 639) is a collection of Junk (Internet resources) sorted into "piles," including such topics as spirals, fractals, origami, tiling, and circles and spheres. Students can improve their problem-solving skills with Word Problems for Kids (entry 623) and Algebra Word Problems Online (entry 625).

Many mathematics lesson plans are available on the Internet. The Houghton Mifflin Mathematics Center (entry 587) has a variety of lesson plans appropriate for K–8, as do The Math Forum Home Page (entry 590) and the mathematics lesson plans (entries 610–616). The history of mathematics (entries 599–601), the Biographies of Women Mathematicians (entry 594), and Biographies of Mathematicians (entry 593) should provide fresh materials for lesson planning.

Math resources enable students to communicate with other students and teachers to collaborate on projects and to develop higher-order thinking skills. Higher-level math students may participate in a discussion about fractals; elementary, middle school, and high school students may use e-mail to ask questions of Dr. Math (entry 603). Teachers will want to search some of the calculus resources available at the Geometry Center (entry 629).

Teachers will also want to take advantage of discussion groups. Many of the discussion groups listed in this chapter are extremely helpful for developing lesson plans and ideas to promote general curriculum development and innovative classroom teaching.

World Wide Web sites, such as MathMol (entry 608), offer exciting interactive participation for students. Be sure to check out Cool Math (entry 604) for brain teasers, problems, and puzzles. Sites such as The Explorer Page for Mathematics (entry 610) make teaching and learning about mathematics more exciting.

National Standards

580. Illuminations: Principles & Standards for School Mathematics
http://www.illuminations.nctm.org

The National Council of Teachers of Mathematics designed this site to "illuminate" the new *NCTM Principles and Standards for School Mathematics* and improve the teaching and learning of mathematics for all students. Grade-level focuses includes preK–2, 3–5, 6–8, 9–12, and Across the Grades. There are four sections for each grade band. These comprise selected Web resources; Internet-based lesson plans; a searchable, interactive version of the updated NCTM standards; and I-Math investigations, which are online, interactive multimedia math investigations designed to inspire and teach. This Web site is invaluable for teaching preK–12 mathematics.

581.   Standards 2000

http://www.nctm.org/standards2000/index.html

Written by the National Council of Teachers of Mathematics (NCTM) and revised for the year 2000, this document presents standards for school mathematics, divided among grade catego- ries Pre-K–12. Today's businesses no longer seek workers with "shopkeeper" arithmetic skills; instead, they seek workers who have mathematical literacy. To this end, the standards incor- porate five goals for all students: to learn the value of mathematics, to become confident in their ability to do mathematics, to become mathematical problem solvers, to learn to communi- cate mathematically, and to learn to reason mathematically. A fully linked table of contents al- lows easy access to all the standards for each grade level. At the time of publication, the 1989 standards were located at (http://standards-e.nctm.org/1.0/89ces/Table_of_Contents.html).

Professional Associations

582.   American Mathematical Society

http://www.ams.org

As the Web site of the American Mathematical Society (AMS), e-MATH provides the latest news of interest to mathematicians, including information on legislative funding, conferences, publications, and employment and career opportunities in mathematics. Of particular interest is the What's New in Mathematics section, a compilation of information of interest to the gen- eral public. Reference is made to television programming, movies, columns, tributes, awards, and exhibitions associated with math. The AMS helps to sponsor National Mathematics Aware- ness Week each year during the last week of April. Links are provided to related online muse- ums and exhibitions and other math Web sites.

583.   National Council of Teachers of Mathematics

http://www.nctm.org

Access is provided to the *NCTM News Bulletin*, journals, and the NCTM catalog. Hot Topics high- light areas of interest. Conference announcements and jobs are posted. Information is avail- able on how to join and get involved.

General Interest

584.   Children's Literature Books for Math

http://www.enc.org/classroom/focus/childlit/nf_31.htm

Provides a list of children's trade books that support the study of mathematics. Books are grouped by subject, including number sense, counting books, measurement, multiplication and division, geometry, applied math, and puzzles and game books. Gives the title of the book, author, publication date, publisher, and a brief annotation. Information is provided by the Eisenhower National Clearinghouse for Mathematics and Science Education.

585. Frequently Asked Questions in Mathematics

http://www.cs.unb.ca/~alopez-o/math-faq/math-faq.html

The FAQ site for the newsgroup (sci.math) provides authoritative mathematical information. It is a compilation of frequently asked questions about mathematics and their answers. Topics range from trivia and the trivial to advanced subjects, such as Wiles's recent proof of Fermat's Last Theorem. From the fully linked table of contents, information is available on algebraic structures, numbers, number theory, special numbers and functions, famous problems, mathematical games, and awards, competitions, and the Fields Medal. This page is maintained by Alex Lopez-Ortiz (alopez-o@daisy.uwaterloo.ca), a professor of computer science at the University of New Brunswick (Canada).

586. A Homepage for New Math Teachers

http://people.clarityconnect.com/webpages/terri/terri.html

Practical advice and relevant information make this a must-read Web page for new math teachers. Topics covered include classroom management, how to make clear lessons, multicultural mathematics, and math myths. Links are provided to Great Sites for Math Teachers, a collection of selected online resources. Created and maintained by Terri Husted (terri@clarityconnect.com), math teacher at DeWitt Middle School in Ithaca, New York.

587. Houghton Mifflin Mathematics Center

http://www.eduplace.com/math/index.html

Houghton Mifflin has created an online Mathematics Center for grades K-8. A math activities database allows searching by grade level. For example, a grade 5–8 math activity is to have students create a rating system for evaluating 19th-century presidents, based on important issues of the time. Math Projects is a collection of projects using math and telecommunication, such as Mighty M&M® Math in which students compare and analyze their class average percentages of each color candy to those of other participating classes, use spreadsheets, and make graphs. Useful links to other math-related Internet resources are categorized by topics such as lesson plans, problems and puzzles, and history of math and biographies. Brain Teasers, entertaining and mentally challenging problems, are posted each week, one at each of three grade levels. Solutions are published the following week. Archives of past Brain Teasers are available, along with hints and solutions.

588. K-12 Teaching Materials

http://archives.math.utk.edu/k12.html

The Math Archives located at the University of Tennessee in Knoxville, Tennessee, has a collection of annotated links to K-12 teaching materials, organized into categories that include lesson plans, software, and mathematics topics. Links are provided to other related K-12 math sites on the Internet. Be sure to visit the Math Archives Home Page located at (http://archives.math.utk.edu).

589. Math.com

http://math.com

Follow one of four pathways into the world of math online: students, teachers, parents, and everyone. Students can access homework help; references such as dictionaries, converters, and online equation solvers; math lessons and interactive exercises in pre-algebra, algebra, and geometry; test-taking tips and advice; and puzzles and mathematical tricks. Teachers can find lesson plans and classroom resources, generate algebra worksheets, and access other practice worksheets to print out and use with students. Parents will find online articles from the U.S. Department of Education on how to help develop a child's ability to do mathematics and encourage positive attitudes toward mathematics. Mathematics for Everyone emphasizes lifelong learning, recreational math, and math used every day around the home and on the job.

590. The Math Forum Home Page

http://forum.swarthmore.edu

The Math Forum is a center for math education on the Internet funded by the National Science Foundation and sponsored by Swarthmore College (Swarthmore, Pennsylvania). By clicking on Math Resources by Subject, K-12 teachers will be able to locate extensive resources for arithmetic, algebra, geometry, precalculus, calculus, probability and statistics, and discrete math. Each subject includes links to classroom materials, software, Internet projects, and other related Internet resources, including discussion groups. Classroom materials contain annotated lists of lesson plans, activities, and interactive resources.

591. Platonic Realms

http://www.mathacademy.com

Platonic Realms is a collaborative effort of math graduate students and educators to provide comprehensive math resources online. It includes a collection of links, quotations, and an encyclopedia. The Math Links Library houses more than 1,000 links to Web resources. Sites are divided into categories and the entire database of links can be searched. The Quotes Collection is a collection of mathematical quotations and is browseable by author. The Platonic Realms' Interactive Mathematics Encyclopedia is searchable. The Webmaster's address is (webmaster@mathacademy.com).

592. South Carolina SSI Math and Science Resources

http://scssi.scetv.org/mims/ssrch2.htm

The South Carolina Statewide Systemic Initiative (SC SSI) sponsors a math and science database of annotated Internet resources. Browseable by categories (18), the resources are also keyword searchable. Some of the Web sites offer specific lesson plans, whereas others are helpful in developing lesson plans. Math categories encompass numeration systems, algebraic concepts, patterns and relationships, measurement, geometry and spatial sense, probability, and statistics. Find interesting lesson plans with titles such as Number Bracelet Game, Metrics in Space, The Cake Problem, and How Big Is a Million? This is a treasure trove of Internet resources for math and science teachers.

Biographies of Mathematicians

593. Biographies of Mathematicians
http://www-groups.dcs.st-and.ac.uk/~history/BiogIndex.html

Chronological indexes range from 1680 B.C. to A.D. 1947. There is also a full alphabetical index. Mathematicians of the Day is a section that highlights mathematicians who were born or died on the current date, with links to their individual biographies. There is a separate section on female mathematicians. The entire database is searchable. Most biographies are accompanied by a photograph, a map showing where the mathematician was born, a reference list of books and articles, links to other mathematicians, and sometimes links to other Web sites for more information. Interesting information and graphics are liberally interspersed throughout. For example, there is a graphic of the Rhind Papyrus in the British Museum, showing how Egyptians multiplied numbers. There is also a graphic illustrating Pythagoras's theorem.

594. Biographies of Women Mathematicians
http://www.agnesscott.edu/lriddle/women/women.htm

Biographies of Women Mathematicians is part of an ongoing project by students in mathematics classes at Agnes Scott College in Atlanta, Georgia, to illustrate the many achievements of women in mathematics. Women mathematicians are presented in both alphabetical and chronological order. Hypatia (370–415) of Alexandria is the first known woman mathematician. She edited the work *On the Conics of Apollonius*, which divided cones into different parts by a plane; this forms the underlying concept of hyperbolas, parabolas, and ellipses.

Ada Byron, daughter of Lord Byron, was a contemporary of Charles Babbage and a pioneer in the work that laid the foundation for the Computer Age. When Ada translated a French article about Babbage's calculating engine (a forerunner of the computer), Babbage suggested that she add her own notes—which ended up being three times the length of the original article. Byron predicted that such a machine might be used to compose complex music and to produce graphics. She was correct, and in 1979 the U.S. Department of Defense named a software language Ada in her honor.

Calculators

595. The Abacus: The Art of Calculating with Beads
http://www.ee.ryerson.ca:8080/~elf/abacus/

The abacus was an ancient calculator used by the Chinese as early as 500 BC. By clicking on the colored beads, students are able to operate this Java abacus to perform addition, subtraction, division, and multiplication calculations. Unlike a real abacus, the numeric value for each column is shown and updated in the top frame with each bead movement. For a more hands-on approach, information is provided on how to build an abacus from LEGO building blocks. Comparisons are made between the Japanese, Chinese, and Aztec abacuses and the abacus and the electronic calculator. A visit to the virtual abacus museum (http://www.soroban.com/museum/index_eng.html), presented by the Tomoe Soroban Co., Ltd. (makers of abacuses since 1921), is well worthwhile. This site was created and is maintained by Luis Fernandes (elf@ee.ryerson.ca). *See also* Tomoe Soroban Co., Ltd., Abacus Makers (entry 368).

596. The Texas Instrument Calculator Home Page

http://www.ti.com/calc/

The Texas Instrument (TI) Calculator Web site provides helpful information for educators about workshops, training, conference notification, workbooks, discussion forums, and classroom activities for elementary and middle school students using calculators. Information is also available for educators working with high school students using calculators in algebra, precalculus and calculus, differential equations, linear algebra, geometry, statistics, physics, biology, and chemistry.

Encyclopedias for Mathematics

597. Eric Weisstein's World of Mathematics (MathWorld)

http://mathworld.wolfram.com

MathWorld is a comprehensive and interactive mathematics encyclopedia from A to Z, or from A-Integrable to the Zsigmondy Theorem. Examples are given with explanations and references. MathWorld is searchable or browseable by topic, such as discrete mathematics, geometry, number theory, recreational mathematics, algebra, and applied mathematics. It is also browseable by alphabetized index. Created and maintained by Eric E. Weisstein (mathworld@wolfram.com).

598. Mathematics Encyclopedia

http://www.mathacademy.com/platonic_realms/encyclop/encyhome.html

The Mathematics Encyclopedia, PRIME, is a comprehensive resource for students and educators. It is searchable and cross-indexed with in-text links to glossary explanations. The main encyclopedia can be subsearched by categories such as biography, history, languages, and subjects. Illustrations and graphics accompany some entries. Created and maintained by Math Academy Online (webmaster@mathacademy.com).

History of Mathematics

599. History of Mathematics Home Page

http://aleph0.clarku.edu/~djoyce/mathhist/mathhist.html

The History of Mathematics is an extensive site divided into topic areas: Web resources, regional mathematics, subjects, books and other resources, chronology, timelines, and an index of files. Web resources is a linked listing of resources related to the history of mathematics. Information is divided into categories, such as multimedia exhibits, books online, biographies of mathematicians, mailing lists, newsletters, and other history-of-mathematics pages on the Web. This site was created and is maintained by David E. Joyce (djoyce@clarku.edu), professor in the Department of Mathematics and Computer Science at Clark University.

600. The History of Mathematics Web Pages

http://www.maths.tcd.ie/pub/HistMath/HistMath.html

Developed by the School of Mathematics, Trinity College, Dublin, this comprehensive history-of-mathematics site offers many links to unique information, such as Egyptian Fractions, Babylonian Mathematics, Mayan Numbers, and Archimedes Home Page. Links are also provided to biographies of 17th- and 18th-century mathematicians and to individual mathematicians' home pages. Maintained by Dr. David R. Wilkins (dwilkins@maths.tcd.ie), lecturer in mathematics.

601. The MacTutor History of Mathematics Archive

http://www-groups.dcs.st-and.ac.uk/~history/index.html

The MacTutor History of Mathematics Archive contains an index of important math discoveries, as well as biographies of more than 1,000 mathematicians. Several hundred are fairly detailed, and most are accompanied by pictures. Access is available through alphabetical or chronological indexes. There is also a series of articles on the development of mathematical ideas, cross-referenced to the biographies; these can be accessed through a History Topics index. The archive is part of the Mathematical MacTutor system developed at the School of Mathematical and Computational Sciences of the University of St. Andrews, Scotland, for learning and experimenting with mathematics. This Web page is maintained by John O'Connor (joc@st-andrews.ac.uk) and Edmund F. Robertson (efr@st-andrews.ac.uk).

Interactive Math

See also Quia! (entry 293).

602. 3D-Filmstrip: A Mathematical Visualization Program

http://rsp.math.brandeis.edu/3D-Filmstrip_html/3D-FilmstripHomePage.html

Mathematicians have always used the "mind's eye" to visualize abstract objects and processes in mathematical research. The computer allows students to see classical textbook concepts not only in three dimensions (3-D), but also in rotation and morphing animations that can bring the known mathematical world to an exciting precipice of new insights and conjectures. 3-D visualization allows mathematicians to do mathematical experiments with greater ease and offers a bridge toward understanding more difficult mathematical concepts. Richard Palais (palais@math.brandeis.edu) is the author of 3D-Filmstrip, an excellent mathematical visualization program that is constantly being updated. The latest release (version 7.1) is designed to run on Macintosh computers, system 7, or PowerMacs. It downloads in Binhex format. 3D-Filmstrip helps students visualize various mathematical objects in two or three dimensions. The current version allows visualization of plane curves, space curves, surfaces, polyhedra, conformal maps, waves, and various kinds of differential equations in a plane or in space. More categories will be added to later versions of the program. To take advantage of the stereo vision features, you will need sufficient RAM, a color monitor, and a pair of red/green or red/blue stereo glasses.

Those who do not want to download the software can use the main catalogue of 3D-Filmstrip Visualizations to access a limited number of color visualizations (including stereo versions and rotating morphing versions) with their Web browsers. This Gallery of Surfaces includes general surfaces such as Steiner's Roman Surface; minimal surfaces such as the Catalan Surface; and pseudospherical surfaces such as the Kuen Surface. With QuickTime, students can see Helicoid-Catenoid Morph, Dini Family Morph, and a rotating Klein Bottle. A Gallery of Curves is forthcoming. Look for a collection of links to other galleries of mathematical objects on the Internet.

603. Ask Dr. Math!

http://forum.swarthmore.edu/dr.math/

Dr. Math has been helping students online with answers to their math questions since November 1994. This site is a project of Geometry Forum, a National Science Foundation-funded program housed at Swarthmore College in Swarthmore, Pennsylvania. Elementary, middle school, and high school students are encouraged to write to the Swat Team, which is made up of more than 175 college students, college professors, and current or retired math teachers from all over the globe. Members of the Swat Team are listed, some with links to personal home pages, a few with pictures (http://forum.swarthmore.edu/dr.math/staff.html).

Look for the Dr. Math Archives with questions and answers. The information is organized by grade level and topic; it also may be searched by keyword, such as *decimal, fractal, pi,* or *proof.* If you don't find the answer to your question in the FAQs, use the provided online form to send your question.

604. Cool Math

http://www.coolmath.com

Cool math activities and concepts are packaged with really cool mathematical graphic designs. Find out more about functions, limits, and tessellations. Students will enjoy teasing their minds with possible solutions to online math puzzles and problems. How to Succeed in Math provides helpful steps for studying for math tests and succeeding as a math student. The Fractal Gallery has more than 30 images of fractals and is connected to the Infinite Fractal Loop. A list of links to mathematics career information will help interested students plan for their futures. Created and maintained by an artist who is a math teacher (coolmath2@aol.com).

605. GCSE Mathematics Review for High School

http://www.gcse.com/Maths/pre.htm

Review problems have the correct answers and step-by-step solutions to the problems. Problems start off easy and become progressively more difficult. These online interactive tutorials, written in Java, cover algebra, fractions, functions, and sequences, graphs, probability, ratios and proportions, and trigonometry. It is suggested that students complete the tutorials before practicing their math skills using the online problems.

606. Manipula Math with JAVA

http://www.ies.co.jp/math/java/index.html

Interactive program and animation help middle and high school students grasp mathematical ideas. Java applets use Web technologies to illustrate basic and advanced math concepts. Manipula Math with JAVA has more than 222 math applets and continues to grow. The site is in both English and Japanese. Information is provided by International Education Software (IES).

607. **MathDEN**

http://www.actden.com

Login ID: **guest**
Login Password: **guest**

Select MathDEN and use "guest" as the ID and password. MathDEN has sets of math problems for older students that roughly correspond to these grades: stage 1 (grades 7 and 8); stage 2 (grades 9 and 10); stage 3 (grade 11); and stage 4 (grade 12). After completing any of the problem sets, students submit their answers, which are immediately checked. The response informs students which problems they answered correctly or incorrectly. Solutions accompany all answers so students can learn from their mistakes. This is a great interactive way to learn math.

Other activities on the site are equally engaging. Math Challenge offers several logic-based questions each week. Students e-mail their solutions to Minus, the resident math shark, who posts his five favorite solutions the following week. Hot Math Tips shows students how to use basic addition and multiplication skills to increase their calculating speeds. Math on the Net provides links to other really good math sites on the Internet.

To set up a personal progress report file or participate in discussion groups and online polls, students must register. Registration and access to DEN are free.

608. **MathMol Home Page**

http://www.nyu.edu/pages/mathmol/

MathMol provides the K–12 educational community with information and materials dealing with the rapidly growing fields of molecular modeling and 3-D visualization. Using molecular modeling, scientists are better able to design new and more potent drugs to fight diseases such as cancer, AIDS, and arthritis. Molecular modeling has also aided discovery of new materials, such as fullerenes. One of the important reasons for studying molecular modeling is to adapt to changing career opportunities.

Color graphics illustrate the similarities between math structures and molecular structures. Activities provide interaction for students. MathMol activities center around specific themes that reinforce the K–12 science and mathematics curricula. Information is provided for teachers.

609. **Webmath**

http://www.webmath.com

Webmath gives sample problems for many different kinds of math, from simple to complex, and explains how to solve the problems. Uses interactive software to perform mathematical processes. Look for sample problems in everyday math, personal finance, fractions, scientific notation, quadratic equations, polynomials, word problems, solving equations, trigonometry, and calculus.

Lesson Plans for Mathematics

See also K–12 Internet Geometry Resources (entry 640) and "Lesson Plans Across the Curriculum" (entries 33–44).

610. The Explorer Page for Mathematics

http://unite.ukans.edu

The Math Section of the Explorer Page is divided into general mathematics, problem solving and reasoning, whole numbers and numeration, fractions, decimals, ratio and proportion, percent, measurement, geometry, statistics and probability, and algebraic ideas. Information is further divided by grade-level appropriateness. Teacher resources available for downloading include lesson plans, software, downloadable files (physical media), HyperCard and Claris-Works files, Adobe Acrobat files, news resources, thematic units, lab activities, professional development resources, field trip resources, guest speaker resources, and student-created material resources. Users may browse through the math curriculum by viewing either individual subject folders or outlines.

611. Mathematics Lesson Plans

http://math.rice.edu/~lanius/Lessons/

Students and teachers will enjoy using some of these exciting, original math lessons that incorporate problem solving, student interaction, and online resources. Developed and maintained by Cynthia Lanius, math teacher (lanius@math.rice.edu).

612. Maths Ideas

http://www.teachingideas.co.uk/maths/contents.htm

Provides a list of math activities to use in elementary classrooms. Some activities are designed to improve mental arithmetic skills, practice recognizing number patterns, and teach decimals. Worksheets can be printed and used in the classroom. Part of the Teaching Ideas for Primary Teachers Web site created and maintained by Mark Warner (mark@teachingideas.co.uk).

613. Maths Resources

http://www.primaryresources.co.uk/maths/maths.htm

Provides math lesson plans, worksheets, and ideas for use with students ages 5 to 11 (primary school in the United Kingdom). Adobe Acrobat Reader is required to view and print out worksheets. Topics cover number literacy and arithmetic operations as well as measurement, shape, and space. Created and maintained by Gareth Pitchford (gareth@primaryresources.co.uk).

614. MegaMath

http://www.c3.lanl.gov/mega-math/welcome.html
or
http://www.cs.uidaho.edu/~casey931/mega-math/welcome.html

MegaMath is a fun way to introduce elementary mathematics. MegaMath's projects bring unusual and important mathematical ideas to elementary school classrooms so that students and teachers can think about them together. Some of the math lessons involve colors, graphs, knots, and ice cream. Math stories are attention-getting and high-interest, with titles such as "Pizza Producers," "Permuto Man's Revenge," "Mort and Nort," "Gertrude and the Superperson Series," and "The Young Map Colorer." Teachers will find additional information on ideas, concepts, and definitions. Links are provided to other Internet math sites. The project was created by the Computer Research and Applications Group at the Los Alamos National Laboratory in Los Alamos, New Mexico.

615. New York Times Mathematics Lesson Plans

http://www.nytimes.com/learning/teachers/lessons/mathematics.html

Lesson plans are appropriate for grades 6–12 and include lessons that require students to collect data to perform simple manipulations and create graphs or discuss the role of mathematics in everyday life. For example, in "Census Sensibility," students are asked to gather statistical data from the Census Bureau's Web site to create graphs comparing state and national populations, and to compose written reflections on why the census is necessary. In "Using Your Melon for Math," students use recipes to practice their fraction multiplication and division skills. Lessons are linked to *New York Times* articles, copies of worksheets, Web resources, and academic content standards. Lesson format is thorough, including overview; objectives; materials and resources needed; activities, including a warm-up and a wrap-up; further questions; evaluation; vocabulary; extension activities; interdisciplinary connections; and additional related articles and Web resources. There is a printer-friendly version for each lesson. New lessons are continually being added.

616. *Pi* Mathematics, a Multidisciplinary Project

http://www.ncsa.uiuc.edu/Edu/RSE/RSEorange.html

Studying the concept of *pi* in this multidisciplinary project incorporates math, history, English, and critical-thinking skills for fifth- through eighth-graders. It allows students to discover the approximate value of *pi*, an irrational number, using measurement and reporting the data, applying formulas, and doing problem solving. This is a fun, collaborative project using Internet references. Teacher resources are available.

Middle School Math Competitions

617. MATHCOUNTS® Home Page

http://206.152.229.6

MATHCOUNTS is the national math coaching and competition program for seventh- and eighth-grade students. Find out about the program and the competition and learn how to register. The Problem Solving area offers a problem of the week and an archive of past problems. Problem-solving strategies and algebraic reasoning are discussed. Other problems and extended activities are available as workouts and warm-ups.

Problems, Puzzles, Games, Trivia, and Quotes

618. Interactive Mathematics Miscellany and Puzzles

http://www.cut-the-knot.com

If learning starts from wondering, then this collection of curious things related to mathematics will certainly have students learning. Look for games and puzzles and interesting questions and possibilities. For example, students are asked, "Did you know that . . ." there are imaginary and surreal numbers, there are shapes of constant width other than the circle, and that one can cut a pie into eight pieces with three movements. A list of impossible things is discussed and the concept of probability is explored. Available also is an archive of past and current "Cut The Knot!" columns, written by Alex Bogomolny for publication in *MAA Online*, the online Web site of the Mathematical Association of America. These columns provide interactive opportunities using Java applets. Created and maintained by Dr. Alex Bogomolny (alexb@cut-the-knot.com), former associate professor of mathematics at the University of Iowa.

619. **Math Comics**

http://www.csun.edu/~hcmth014/comics.html

Students and teachers alike will get a laugh from reading these math-related comics and cartoons. The collection is browseable and searchable. Collected and maintained by Bamdad Samii (bsamii@csun.edu), a math professor at the University of California, Northridge.

620. **Math in the Movies**

http://world.std.com/~reinhold/mathmovies.html

Math in the Movies provides a list of movies (with links to the Internet Movie Database) in which mathematics or mathematicians are accurately portrayed. For example, the movie *Big* is listed because in it Tom Hanks helps the young son with his homework during a dinner party, offering a nice explanation of basic algebra. In *The Mirror Has Two Faces*, math professor Jeff Bridges explains the Twin Prime Conjecture to English professor Barbara Streisand. Links are provided to the Charles Babbage Institute's "Hollywood and Computers," a list of 42 movies featuring computers. This site was created and is maintained by Arnold G. Reinhold (reinhold@world.std.com).

621. **Mathematical Quotation Server**

http://math.furman.edu/~mwoodard/mqs/mquot.shtml

Start off math lessons with a math-related quotation. This site, located at the Furman University (Greenville, South Carolina) math department, offers a collection of mathematical quotations that are keyword-searchable and browseable alphabetically by author's last name. Or select a quotation using the random quotation generator. Each week a different quotation is featured. Webmaster is Mark Woodard (Mark.Woodard@furman.edu).

622. **Rubik's Online Home Page**

http://www.rubiks.com

Go directly to the Play Online area and choose one of the Java-required interactive games, including the classic Rubik's Cube. Other available online games are Smallest Number, WPC Puzzles, Sideview, Connection 2, and Anglers. These games are fun and test problem-solving skills and eye-mouse coordination.

623.   Word Problems for Kids

http://juliet.stfx.ca/people/fac/pwang/mathpage/math2.html

Students can improve their problem-solving skills by working through these carefully selected word problems, which are divided into grade levels from grade 5 to grade 12. Each word problem has a helpful hint and the correct solution so that students can check their answers. There are more than 40 problems for each grade, making this an excellent online tutorial for gaining proficiency in solving word problems. The Web editor's address is (pwang@juliet.stfx.ca).

Algebra

624.   Algebra Online

http://www.algebra-online.com

Using e-mail, students receive free personal help with algebra problems. Eight volunteer tutors answer questions and coach students. There is also an online mailing list and online chat for algebra students.

625.   Algebra Word Problems Online

http://www2.hawaii.edu/suremath/intro_algebra.html

Students learn the fundamentals of how to solve word problems at this site devoted to creating problem-solving literacy. Using the 3 Rs of Request, Response, and Result, the process of solving word problems is emphasized. Many illustrative examples are provided, involving problem solving through the calculation of age, speed, distance, length, sales, salaries, and depreciation.

Arithmetic

626.   Math in Daily Life

http://www.learner.org/exhibits/dailymath/

How do numbers affect everyday decisions? People around the world use the same math every day, regardless of their native language, because math is the universal language of numbers. This Annenberg/CPB Project Exhibit demonstrates how numbers are important in ordinary circumstances such as playing games, cooking, making decisions as to whether to buy or lease a car, and decorating a home. Be sure to look at the Related Resources section for Web sites and books.

Calculus

627.   AP Calculus

http://www.seresc.k12.nh.us/alvirne/

Alvirne High School (Hudson, New Hampshire) invites students to join them in preparing for the AP Calculus exam. Each week, sample problems are posted, along with problems from the archives and detailed solutions. Links are provided to information about the previous year's exam and the AP Calculus AB/BC free-response questions with commentary and scoring guides from the College Board Online. This is an excellent site for AP calculus students and teachers.

628. Graphics for the Calculus Classroom

http://www.math.psu.edu/dna/graphics.html [GIF version]

http://www.math.psu.edu/dna/graphics-j.html [Java version]

Provides selections from a collection of graphical demonstrations of first-year calculus. Some of the graphics illustrate differentials and differences, computing the volume of water in a tipped glass, the intersection of two cylinders, measuring the height and velocity of a bouncing ball, and Archimedes's calculation of *pi*. Created and maintained by Douglas N. Arnold (dna@psu.edu), professor, Mathematics Department, Penn State University, State College, Pennsylvania.

629. The University of Minnesota Calculus Initiative

http://www.geom.umn.edu/education/calc-init/

The Geometry Center helps to develop interactive technology-based modules for engineering calculus. These modules emphasize the geometric concepts of calculus while examining applications of mathematics to the physical and life sciences. Topics include how rainbows are formed in the Rainbow Lab; testing a fundamental theorem of calculus in the Numerical Integration Lab; how different methods of supporting a beam contribute to the beam's ability to support loads in the Beams, Bending, and Boundary Conditions Lab; and exploration of powerful techniques for geometric analysis of differential equations (phase space, equilibria, and stability) while modeling population growth.

Discrete Mathematics

630. AMOF: The Amazing Mathematical Object Factory

http://www.schoolnet.ca/vp-pv/ECOS/index.html

Discrete mathematics studies combinatorial objects, and this site explores nine combinatorial objects, including magic squares, Fibonacci sequences, partitions, permutations of a multiset, pentominoes, 8-Queens Problem, permutations, combinations, and subsets. After learning more information about a combinatorial object by clicking on the purple icon, students and teachers can click on a green icon to generate a combinatorial object using their custom specifications. Sponsored by the Computer Science Department of the University of Victoria, Canada.

631. Math Forum—Discrete Math

http://forum.swarthmore.edu/discrete/discrete.html

Discrete mathematics is concerned with relations among fixed rather than continuously varying quantities, such as combinatorics and probability. It is the mathematics that underlies computers and telecommunications. This site provides materials for teachers and students to use in the classroom. Includes Internet resources with activities and interactive resources. Also gives links to software, Internet projects, and mailing lists and newsgroups that focus on the topic of discrete mathematics.

Fractals

632.   Chaos in the Classroom

http://math.bu.edu/DYSYS/chaos-game/chaos-game.html

Easy-to-teach topics involving ideas from fractal geometry are presented. The Chaos Game is explained with a resulting Sierpinski triangle, one of the basic fractal shapes. From chaos, students understand the construction of the Sierpinski triangle. To play the game online using Java applets, go to (http://math.bu.edu/DYSYS/applets/chaos-game.html). Created and maintained by Robert L. Devaney (bob@bu.edu), professor of mathematics, Boston University, Boston, Massachusetts.

For nine online games using Java applets to understand fractals, chaos, and iteration, including the classic game Towers of Hanoi, go to (http://math.bu.edu/DYSYS/applets/index.html).

633.   Fractals

http://math.rice.edu/~lanius/frac/

A fractals unit for elementary and middle school students provides lesson plans, teaches how to make different kinds of fractals, explores fractal properties, and gives a rationale for studying fractals. Lessons are aligned with the NCTM national standards. Created and maintained by Cynthia Lanius (lanius@rice.edu), a math professor at Rice University, Houston, Texas.

634.   The Fractory

http://library.thinkquest.org/3288/fractals.html

The Fractory is an interactive tool for creating and exploring fractals. By demonstrating that there is order in seemingly random things, fractals can help us understand the order in the chaos of life—perhaps even the weather! Information is presented in five steps of increasing difficulty, from basic to complex. The first step is to enjoy the beauty of fractals in the Fractal Gallery. The next steps involve understanding fractals; knowing how fractals are generated; comprehending the math behind fractals; and, finally, continuing to study fractals by programming them or reading further from the provided bibliography. Created by David Green (Davidthe8@aol.com), Alex Kulesza (kulesza@math.gmu.edu), and Keith Bergstresser (kberg3@aol.com), ThinkQuest Team 3288.

635.   NCSA Fractal Microscope

http://www.ncsa.uiuc.edu/Edu/Fractal/Fractal_Home.html

The Fractal Microscope is an interactive tool for exploring the Mandelbrot set and other fractal patterns. Students and teachers from all grade levels can engage in a discovery-based exploration that focuses on the art as well as the science of mathematics. This focus can help students with scientific notation, coordinate systems and graphing, number systems, convergence, divergence, and self-similarity.

Geometry

636. Connected Geometry

http://www.edc.org/LTT/ConnGeo/

Connected Geometry is a curriculum development project funded by the National Science Foundation. It is designed to help teachers and students engage in meaningful mathematical activity by offering students a chance to understand and appreciate the connections and unifying themes within mathematics and to build on the connections between students' backgrounds and mathematics. Available on this site are Geometer's Sketchpad sketches. Interactive Java allows students to explore concepts such as constant areas of rectangles and constant perimeters of rectangles.

637. Geometry

http://library.thinkquest.org/2918/

ThinkQuest team 2918 invites students to practice their geometry with lots of online problems. Provides an interactive glossary with explanatory text and diagrams and illustrated geometry theorems and geometry proofs. Gives a timeline for geometry.

638. The Geometry Center

http://www.geom.umn.edu

Students explore four-dimensional space through interactive manipulation of mathematical objects. Some of the programs allow students to examine a mathematical model of light passing through a water droplet to discover how rainbows are formed; generate Penrose tilings or nonperiodic tilings of the plane; or explore the effects of negatively curved space in Orbifold Pinball, a pinball-style game. In addition to manipulable math, there are also multimedia documents, video productions, course materials, and student work. This site was created by the Center for the Computation and Visualization of Geometric Structures at the University of Minnesota.

639. The Geometry Junkyard

http://www.ics.uci.edu/~eppstein/junkyard/

The Geometry Junkyard is a collection of Internet resources related to discrete and computational geometry. Junk sorted into piles includes topics such as spirals, fractals, origami, tiling, and circles and spheres. Geometry in Action is a categorized collection of links to real-world applications of geometry, such as architecture, video game programming, and biochemical modeling. Recreational Math leads to links for fun, including puzzles, games, toys, and cartoons. Created and maintained by David Eppstein (eppstein@ics.uci.edu), Department of Information and Computer Science, University of California, Irvine (Irvine, California).

640. K–12 Internet Geometry Resources

http://forum.swarthmore.edu/geometry/k12.geometry.html

Math Forum at Swarthmore College has compiled a comprehensive listing of K–12 Geometry resources on the Internet. Classroom materials for teachers and students provides a long list of lesson plans, activities, and interactive resources. Look for problems and puzzles as well as selected lesson plans. There are links to publicly available software for geometry and fun and challenging Internet activities and projects. Links are also provided to other geometry-related Internet resources, including newsgroups and online discussion groups.

Statistics

641. The Data and Story Library (DASL)
http://lib.stat.cmu.edu/DASL/

The Data and Story Library, known as DASL and pronounced "dazzle," is an online library of datafiles and stories that illustrate the use of basic statistics methods. Provides stories and sets of data in different subject areas. Teachers can use these examples to illustrate statistics concepts, with the idea that good examples can make a lesson on a particular statistics method more vivid and relevant for students. Stories and data sets can be accessed in a number of ways: alphabetically by story topic, alphabetically by statistical method, alphabetically by datafile subject, and via a site search engine. The data can be downloaded as a space- or tab-delimited table of text, easily read by most statistics programs. Paul Velleman is the Webmaster (pfv2@cornell.edu).

642. Statistics
Polls: What Do the Numbers Tell Us?

http://www.learner.org/exhibits/statistics/activity0/frontpoll.phtml

Each day, and especially during elections, numbers are used to describe information from polls and surveys. What do these numbers actually tell us? This interactive web site explores statistics and explains terms such as random sampling, margin of error, confidence intervals, and margin of error. Gives opportunities for hands-on activities in determining whom voters will choose in a hypothetical mayoral election. Provides links to related sites such as the U.S. Census Bureau to discover how census data is collected. The address for the Webmaster for Annenberg/CPB Exhibits is (exhibits@learner.org).

Trigonometry

643. Dave's Short Trig Course
http://aleph0.clarku.edu/~djoyce/java/trig/

Provides an introductory guide to learning trigonometry; assumes a knowledgeable background in algebra and geometry. Gives exercises with short answers. Interactive Java allows diagrams to be adjusted to illustrate mathematical concepts. Created and maintained by David E. Joyce (djoyce@clarku.edu), Department of Mathematics and Computer Science, Clark University, Worchester, Massachusetts.

Science

Science resources on the Internet offer exciting and dynamic opportunities for collaborative, hands-on learning and problem solving that closely resemble real-life problem solving in the scientific community. In addition, the Internet allows students and teachers to communicate with scientists and to use scientific resources that cannot be brought into the classroom any other way. For example, color images from the Hubble telescope can be downloaded; weather maps allow students to track major weather developments. Lesson plans written with a gender equity goal are interesting for both boys and girls (entry 677).

The World Wide Web offers weather maps and satellite images that can be viewed as individual graphic images or as time-elapsed video clips. Free software, such as Blue-Skies (entry 859), offers a graphical interface to weather and environmental information. Students can interact with projects, such as the virtual frog dissection (entry 780) and the virtual dissection of a cow's eye (entry 748).

NASA provides daily news, frequent updates on shuttle launches, and educational information to enhance the curriculum. Images and sounds of the rain forest can be downloaded from the Australian National Botanic Gardens (entry 984). Students can visit the University of California Museum of Paleontology to view images of dinosaur specimens (entry 836). The vast resources of the Library of Congress and the Smithsonian Institution are available for student research. Don't miss gem and mineral collections from A Gem of a Story (entry 820). The science resources on the Internet truly bring the world into the classroom, and the multimedia features of the Web make learning exciting and interactive.

National Standards

644. *The National Science Education Standards*

http://bob.nap.edu/readingroom/books/nses/html

The National Science Education Standards are guidelines designed to ensure that all students graduate from high school with a specific knowledge of science and intellectual abilities based on a standardized science curriculum. The *Science Standards* are organized into seven chapters. Chapters 3 and 4 outline the standards for science teaching and professional development. The content standards for students are found in chapter 6, and are organized by K–4, 5–8, and 9–12 grade levels. These standards provide expectations for the development of student understanding and ability over the course of their K–12 education. A fully linked table of contents allows easy navigation of the document and the standards by grade level.

General Interest

645. Cornell Theory Center Math and Science Gateway

http://www.tc.cornell.edu/Edu/MathSciGateway/

The Cornell Theory Center Math and Science Gateway provides links to resources in mathematics and science for educators and students in grades 9–12. There are links to resources in high school math and science subject areas, information on grades 9–12 curriculum, lesson plans, software for the classroom, and instructions for setting up Web servers in the schools.

Curriculum topics include astronomy; biology; chemistry; computers; the Earth, the ocean, and the environment; engineering; health and medicine; mathematics; and physics. Links are provided to journal and research articles, schools on the Net, virtual field trips and museums, and more.

646. The Explorer Page for Science

http://unite.ukans.edu

The science section of the Explorer Page is divided into general natural science, life science, plants, animals, heredity, evolution, ecosystems, physical science, matter and energy, force and motion, waves and vibrations, electricity/magnetism, earth science, geology, atmosphere, hydrosphere, outer space, and common themes. Information is further divided into grade-level appropriateness.

Teacher resources available for downloading include lesson plans, computer software, downloadable files (physical media), HyperCard files, ClarisWorks files, Adobe Acrobat files, news resources, thematic units, lab activities, professional development, field trips, guest speakers, and student-created material resources. Users can browse through the curriculum by viewing either individual subject folders or outlines. This is an excellent resource to help teachers and students in the classroom.

647. Helping Your Child Learn Science

http://www.ed.gov/pubs/parents/Science/index.html

Simple hands-on science activities are described for parents and educators. These activities can be done at home or school and are planned for children to do with an adult. Teachers can find interesting ideas for classroom experiments in these activities, which include complete instructions and a list of materials needed. Some activities include working with bubbles, sticky things, and crystals. Celery Stalks at Midnight and Moldy Oldies are science activities sure to interest children.

648. The History of the Light Microscope

http://www.utmem.edu/personal/thjones/hist/hist_mic.htm

The History of the Light Microscope explores the early history of the microscope, beginning with simple lens microscopes used in ancient times, the first compound microscope used in the late 16th century, and microscopes used in the 19th century. Interesting illustrations and photographs accompany the text. Created by Thomas E. Jones (thjones@utmem1.utmem.edu).

See also the WWW Virtual Library Microscopy (http://www.ou.edu/research/electron/www-vl/noframes.shtml) for links to other Internet resources related to microscopes.

649. The National Science Foundation

http://www.nsf.gov

The National Science Foundation (NSF) is an independent agency of the federal government that was established in 1950 to promote the progress of science and engineering. This page has pointers to an overview of the NSF, its organization, staff, and programs. Information is also available about grants and publications. Links are provided to other science resources on the Internet, such as the national supercomputer centers and NSF science and technology centers, as well as other federal agencies. News of Interest includes hot topics, NSF tip sheets, press releases, and features. If you are considering writing a grant, don't miss the Grant Proposal Guide.

650. Quest: Internet in the Classroom (NASA's K-12 Internet Initiative)

http://quest.arc.nasa.gov

The mission of Quest is to provide support and services for schools, teachers, and students to fully use the Internet, and its underlying information technologies, as a basic tool for learning. One major feature is the Live from ... series of projects. Live from the Stratosphere allows students to join airborne astronomers during their research. Past projects have included Live from Antarctica and Live from Other Worlds. The site provides links to NASA scientists, researchers, and engineers so that students can participate in online interactive projects, such as TOPEX/Poseidon (an ocean topography experiment) and Systems Research Aircraft Online (to modify and test an F-18).

651. Sci4Kids

http://www.ars.usda.gov/is/kids/

Science is everywhere you look, not just something in a laboratory. Sponsored by the Agricultural Research Service (ARS), Sci4Kids is a series of stories about what scientists do at ARS. Look for information on a variety of topics, such as animals, nutrition, plants, insects, water, transportation, and weird science. Looking for a science project idea? This site has ideas to get you started and tips on how to do a good science project.

652. SciCentral

http://www.scicentral.com

Professional scientists review science Web sites and maintain links to more than 50,000 sites in more than 120 specialties in science and engineering. A special K–12 Science subsection indexes sites into many categories applicable to the K–12 curriculum, such as science fair projects, rain forests, zoos and aquariums, weather, and endangered species. SciCentral's Web editors may be contacted at (scicentral@scicentral.com).

653. Science Bytes

http://ur.utenn.edu/ut2kids

University of Tennessee scientists have written about various science topics and problems with a K–12 audience in mind. Geologist Dr. Tom Broadhead presents an interesting look at rocks and minerals in He's Nothing but a Rock Hound, A Diggin' All the Time. He explains the types of geologists, why scientists study rocks, the types of rocks, where you can look for rocks, and rock-hunting safety tips. Dr. Hap McSween explains about analyzing rock from Mars in MarsRocks! Vicki Johns searches for spring in Antarctica and finds phytoplankton. In Rhinos and Tigers and Bears—Oh My!, a biology student explains how he designed animal enrichment activities so that the bears and other wild animals at the Knoxville Zoo don't get bored. A cartographer explains how maps are drawn in Mapmaker, Mapmaker, Make Me a Map. In The Future Is Yours!, three women scientists (geochemist, physicist, and chemist) describe their careers. Learn how UT students and scientists are working to restore four endangered species of fish to Abrams Creek, Tennessee, in Struggling Upstream. Maintained by Tina Jones (tina@novell.ur.utk.edu), computer coordinator, and Vicki Slagle Johns (vickij@novell.ur.utk.edu), editor.

654. Science Resource Center

http://chem.lapeer.org

Provides a way for science teachers to share labs, demonstrations, and other information related to classroom teaching. Information is available for teachers of biology, chemistry, life sciences, and physics. Teachers are encouraged to submit information. Links are provided to teachers' home pages and to additional science resources. Patrick Gormley (patrickg@mail.si.umich.edu) is the creator and Webmaster.

655. Science Tracer Bullets

http://lcweb2.loc.gov/sctb/

Science Tracer Bullets are literature guides prepared by the Library of Congress for K–12 students who are working on science projects and undertaking other research-oriented science studies. The guides are finding aids for materials in areas related to science and technology. This informal series helps readers locate published materials on subjects about which they have only general knowledge. Most Science Tracer Bullets provide a list of weighted subject headings to be used in searching card, book, or computer catalogs; lists of basic texts, bibliographies, reports, conference proceedings, and government publications; a list of abstracting and indexing services useful in finding journal articles and technical reports; and the names and addresses of organizations to contact for additional information. Examples of a few topics of Science Tracer Bullets are dolphins, environmental science, freshwater ecology, UFOs, women in science, and desalination.

Print copies of LC Science Tracer Bullets not online are available by request, without charge, from: Science and Technology Division, Reference Section, Library of Congress, 10 First Street, SE, Washington, DC 20540-4750. Include a self-addressed mailing label with requests. For a complete list with accompanying order numbers, see the folder/menu labeled "Available Tracer Bullets."

Museums and Exhibits

656. The Exploratorium (San Francisco) Home Page

http://www.exploratorium.edu

The Exploratorium, located in San Francisco, is a prominent science education museum offering more than 650 interactive exhibits in the areas of science, art, and human perception. A few of these exhibits are online. These online exhibits are effective demonstrations that help students learn scientific concepts.

657. Franklin Institute Science Museum (Philadelphia)

http://sln.fi.edu

The Franklin Institute Science Museum's missions are to stimulate interest in science, to promote public understanding of science, and to strengthen science education. Its purpose since its founding in 1824 has been to honor Ben Franklin and advance the usefulness of his inventions. The online museum offers many resources for science and health education as well as astronomy, aviation, electricity, math, mechanics, and biology. Teacher resources and activity lesson plans are provided. Benjamin Franklin: Glimpses of the Man is an online exhibit that includes video clips and links to color graphics and sound files outlining his achievements. Science activities are suggested for specific grade levels. These lesson plans include purposes, objectives, materials needed, activities, and step-by-step procedures. Another popular multimedia exhibit is The Heart: An Online Exploration (entry 749).

658. The Nanoworld Image Gallery

http://www.uq.oz.au/nanoworld/images_1.html

The Nanoworld Image Gallery is sponsored by the Centre for Microscopy and Microanalysis at the University of Queensland, Australia. It provides a visit to a world invisible to the naked eye. A few of the many images available include reproductive parts of plants; pollen and spores; insects, such as ants and mosquitoes; the leg of a fly; human hairs of various ethnic origins; a mouse hair; and blood cells. Magnification varies (67,000 times, 25,000 times, 1,000 times, 22 times) and the sizes of the image files are listed. Kids will love these exciting, up-close images taken from electron microscopes. Duncan Waddell (D.Waddell@mailbox.uq.oz.au) is the scientific officer for this site.

659. Natural History Museum (London)

http://www.nhm.ac.uk

The Natural History Museum, located in London, opened in 1881. The museum houses a large collection of information related to life and earth sciences. Also part of the museum are the Walter Rothschild Zoology Museum at Tring and Down House, Charles Darwin's home. The Natural History Museum's library holds one of the largest collections of published materials on earth and life sciences. The library's online catalog is searchable by author, title, and keyword.

660. Ocean Planet Home Page

http://seawifs.gsfc.nasa.gov/ocean_planet.html

It is everyone's responsibility to conserve the ocean planet, as 99 percent of the space on Earth is ocean. Students can find out what sea products in addition to seafood are used every day. From seafarers' stories, students learn about various maritime communities and the social and economic concerns facing those who need to make decisions about conserving the oceans. Endangered marine habitats are highlighted. Reports on ocean pollution outline the threats of oil spills, overfishing, agricultural runoff, dumping of sewage and toxic wastes, and coastal development. Profiles of ocean conservationists let students know what others are doing to conserve oceans and what action students themselves can take.

Be sure to take advantage of the six interdisciplinary lesson plans for middle and high schools that were created especially to complement Ocean Planet (http://educate.si.edu/resources/lessons/currkits/ocean/main.html). Sea Secrets explores ocean geography, Sea Connections looks at the plants and animals that live in various marine ecosystems, Ocean Market identifies and explains the value of many products of the seas, Pollution Solution examines the effects of an environmental crisis, Stranded Along the Coast explores both natural and human causes of animal strandings, and Reflections on the Sea explores the influence of oceans on language and literature.

Each lesson plan has a statement of learning objectives; a list of required materials; step-by-step procedures; student handouts; and a list of additional resources, including connections to the online version of the Ocean Planet exhibition. Lesson plans are downloaded in Adobe Acrobat format. Guiding students to a better understanding of the diversity and importance of the seas, these lesson plans are an excellent enhancement to the curriculum in biology, mathematics, geography, and social studies.

661. Smithsonian Institution's Natural History Web

http://www.mnh.si.edu/nmnhweb.html

The Smithsonian Natural History Web is an Internet resource compiled and maintained by the staff of the National Museum of Natural History. Information is given on anthropology, botany, entomology, invertebrate zoology, mineral sciences, paleobiology, and vertebrate zoology. The fabulous Smithsonian Gem and Mineral Collection (http://galaxy.einet.net/images/gems/gems-icons.html) can be accessed as a link from Other Natural Science Resources. Enlargeable thumbnail sketches of color graphics are accompanied by descriptions. In addition to uncut and unset gems and minerals, there are also pictures of the Hope Diamond, a dragon vase carved from rare lavender jade, and Marie Antoinette's earrings.

662. Theater of Electricity

http://www.MOS.org/sln/toe/toe.html

Through pictures and text, the Theater of Electricity explains the concepts of static and current electricity. A Teacher's Resource provides helpful background information. Students can take a lightning safety quiz after their self-guided tour of the exhibit. Links are provided to other lightning sites on the Internet. A picture gallery and video gallery provide additional materials. Created and maintained by the Museum of Science in Boston, Massachusetts (http://www.MOS.org/mos/).

Question-and-Answer Services

663. Ask a Scientist/Expert Page

http://www.k12science.org/askanexpert.html

Students can pose questions directly to scientists and experts in scientific fields. Physicists, population geneticists, meteorologists, geologists, hydrologists, bird experts, horticulturists, diamond and gem experts, and astronomers volunteer their time to answer curriculum-related e-mail questions from K-12 students. Links are also available to Dr. Math and Ask the Engineer, as well as other experts in math, science, and technology.

664. MAD Scientist Network

http://www.madsci.org

A series of Web interfaces allow users visiting this site to ask questions, view recently submitted questions and answers, or search the archive of more than 2,000 question-and-answer files. More than 500 scientists from around the world answer questions in 25 areas, including chemistry, physics, astronomy, engineering, computer science, earth science, and the biological sciences. Previous questions range from: "Why is the sky blue?" and "Do ants sleep?" to "Why do astronomers believe meteorites from Mars suggest the planet once supported life?" There is also a library of science-related Internet links. Network administrators are Lynn Bry (lynn@pharmdec.wustl.edu) and Joe Simpson (simpson@npg.wustl.edu).

Television Programs

665. *Beakman's World*

http://www.spe.sony.com/tv/kids/beakman/beakmain.html

Beakman is an irreverent and inquisitive scientist who has dedicated himself to answering kids' science questions. *Beakman's World* is a 30-minute, Saturday-morning television program. This Web site has pictures of Beakman and the set, video clips, and audio from this wacky but educational television show that makes science fun. Look for experiments to do at home and fast facts.

666. *Bill Nye the Science Guy*

http://nyelabs.kcts.org

Bill Nye the Science Guy is a popular television science show that airs daily on PBS and weekly on almost 200 syndicated television stations. This Web site contains information about the television show, experiments, and links to science-related Internet sites. Bibliographies for students are available on various science topics. Bill Nye makes science fun for both students and teachers. Note: Only browsers installed with the latest version of Macromedia Shockwave may access this site. Shockwave plug-ins are free and easy to install. See (http://www.macromedia.com/shockwave/download/) for downloads.

667. The Magic School Bus

http://place.scholastic.com/magicschoolbus/index.htm

Want to know more about that wacky science teacher named Ms. Frizzle who takes her class of enthusiastic, inquisitive students on educational field trips in the Magic School Bus? This home page provides information on the television show and the book series by Joanna Cole and Bruce Degan. Links are provided to more information about the author and illustrator. Find out what's new, more about an art gallery students can add to, news about the Magic School Bus Traveling Exhibits, and more. Questions on science and the *Magic School Bus* television show can be sent to (msbsci@aol.com).

668. *Newton's Apple*

http://ericir.syr.edu/Projects/Newton/

Newton's Apple is an award-winning, fast-paced, magazine-format, family science program, which began its 17th season in October 1999. Check your local PBS listings for exact air dates and times. Predicated on the hands-on discovery approach, *Newton's Apple* focuses on basic scientific concepts and can be used with any curriculum approach.

From this page, you can access the current season's lesson pages as well as lessons from some of the past years. Each lesson (25 to 26 per season) includes insights about the topic, connections to encourage classroom discussion, resources, and vocabulary. Lessons also include a main activity and several hands-on activities related to each topic. *Newton's Apple* allows three-year off-air record rights and encourages duplication of materials for educational purposes.

669. You Can with Beakman and Jax

http://www.beakman.com

Beakman and Jax, from the TV show *Beakman's World*, have a place on the Web: You Can with Beakman and Jax. At You Can, students find out that a good question is a very powerful thing! Answers are given to 50 good questions asked by students. Answers are accompanied by instructions for hands-on activities. Find out how soap works, how a remote control works, and why the moon looks bigger on the horizon. Some activities require Netscape (2.0 or higher) and Shockwave. Created and maintained by Jok Church (jok@nbn.com).

Activities, Projects, and Lesson Plans

See also "Virtual Field Trips and Online Projects"(entries 839–845); "Sport Science"(entries 1007–1010); and "Lesson Plans Across the Curriculum" (entries 33–44).

Activities

670. The Exploratorium Science Snacks

http://www.exploratorium.edu/snacks/snackintro.html

These snacks are not to eat, but to have fun with and learn from. Exploratorium Science Snacks are miniature versions of some of the most popular exhibits at the Exploratorium (San Francisco, California). Each Snack begins with a photograph of itself, a short introduction, and a list of the materials needed. Other sections give assembly instructions, describe how to use the completed exhibits, and explain the science behind them. More than 100 Science Snacks cover topics such as a magnetic pendulum, handheld heat engine, fog chamber, water spinner, and squirming palm. More Snacks are added on a regular basis. Check back often. *See also* The Exploratorium Home Page (entry 656).

671. IIow to Make Recycled Paper

http://www.beakman.com/paper/paper.html

Making paper is a messy project that is lots of fun. Use the directions provided on this Web site, or try using window screening, heavy-duty rubber bands, and #10 cans. Save pieces of construction paper left over from classroom use to make the paper pulp. This project is easily tied to literature by reading and showing Denise Fleming's books, such as *Where Once There Was a Wood* (Henry Holt, 1996), which includes information on how to create a backyard habitat; or *In the Small, Small Pond* (Henry Holt, 1993*); In the Tall, Tall Grass* (Henry Holt, 1991); *Lunch* (Henry Holt, 1992); *Count* (Henry Holt, 1997); and *Barnyard Banter* (Henry Holt, 1994). Henry Holt also has produced a How to Make Paper kit in conjunction with Denise Fleming, and the publishing company provides a free video entitled *A Visit with Denise Fleming*, which shows the author demonstrating her paper-making skills.

672.   How to Make Rock Candy

http://www.beakman.com/rock-candy/rock-candy.html

Making rock candy is a great way to find out more about crystals. This delicious experiment from Beakman and Jax absolutely requires adult supervision because of high-temperature cooking.

Collaborative Projects and Interactive Learning

673.   Athena: Earth and Space Science for K-12

http://www.athena.ivv.nasa.gov
or
http://athena.wednet.edu
or
http://inspire.ospi.wednet.edu:8001

Project Athena is one of NASA's Public Use of Earth and Space Science Data Over the Internet projects, in cooperation with Science Applications International Corporation (SAIC). It engages students in observing phenomena using remote-sensed data to construct knowledge about the world. Curriculum materials are available on topics such as oceans, earth resources, weather and atmosphere, and space and astronomy. Lesson plans and classroom management strategies are available for teachers.

674.   Journey North

http://www.learner.org/jnorth/

Journey North is a global study of wildlife migration. More than 200,000 students from all 50 states and seven Canadian provinces, representing 4,000 schools, participated collaboratively during the spring of 1999, helping to track wildlife migration and sharing signs of spring. This annual project begins each fall as teachers incorporate inquiry-based teaching and learning into the curriculum in preparation for four months of spring tracking from February 2 to June 1. Students monitor the migrations of robins, monarch butterflies, loons, and gray whales, and share signs of spring through sightings of earthworms, frogs, and tulips. Classroom lesson plans and teacher tips assist teachers with integrating this project into their classrooms. There is a teacher discussion area, and news is published weekly about sightings and activities. Sponsored by the Annenberg/CPB (Corporate Public Broadcasting) Math and Science Project, this site won a 1999 Webby Award (*see* entry 1365).

675.   Science Learning Network Home Page

http://www.sln.org

How can I do inquiry science? How can I collaborate and share ideas? These questions and others are answered on the Science Learning Network, where students can explore resources and see inquiry in action. Some of the resources available include: introducing the physics of water by investigating and creating fountains; understanding hurricanes by investigating a storm center, reading survivors' stories, and making a weather station; investigating wind by building a wind-powered machine; investigating the anatomy of the eye by dissecting a cow's eye (with step-by-step instructions and a glossary of terms); and investigating powerful magnification with an electron microscope. Teacher background information is provided for each investigation.

Lesson Plans

See also South Carolina SSI Math and Science Resources (entry 592) and "Lesson Plans Across the Curriculum" (entries 33–44).

676.   CIESE Online Classroom Projects

http://www.k12science.org/currichome.html

CIESE (Center for Improved Engineering and Science Education of the Stevens Institute of Technology) sponsors and designs interdisciplinary projects that focus on utilizing real-time data available from the Internet. These collaborative projects involve participating classes from all over the world. Each project is listed with a brief description and links to the National Science Standards and NCTM Math Standards. Past projects are available in an archive. Registration is required to join a project; there is no fee.

677.   Gender Equity Science Lesson Plans

http://www.apase.bc.ca/unmixed/unhome.html

Unmixed Messages Strategies for Equitable Science Education is part of an educational initiative in British Columbia, Canada, sponsored by the Association for the Promotion and Advancement of Science Education. This Web site contains science activities geared toward elementary students' interests. The activities are designed to bring about gender equity in the classroom with topics of interest to both boys and girls. Although their primary focus is science, these activities naturally lead into other subject areas. Some of the lesson plans include:

Engineering Toothpaste

http://www.apase.bc.ca/unmixed/una1.html

By making a tasty natural toothpaste that cleans and protects teeth from decay, students learn that many health care products, such as toothpaste, shampoo, and skin lotion, are made by chemical engineers. By making an everyday product from scratch, students learn about biochemistry and the importance of our natural world.

Glorious Garbage

http://www.apase.bc.ca/unmixed/una13.html

What is true garbage? By thinking creatively, students discover a fourth R, "Re-vision," that complements "Reduce, Reuse, and Recycle."

The Hidden Jewels of Geometry

http://www.apase.bc.ca/unmixed/una12.html

Making jewelry involves thinking about symmetry and shapes, much like engineers think when they design and build buildings, cars, and even medical or farming equipment. Students learn about geometry by experimenting with various shapes and sizes to make attractive jewelry.

Ice Energy

http://www.apase.bc.ca/unmixed/una2.html

Students discover how science affects foods by preparing two homemade ice cream recipes.

Positively Paper

http://www.apase.bc.ca/unmixed/una3.html

Students learn that recycling some types of paper requires bleaching agents, which are harmful to the environment. By experimenting with different kinds of paper and bleaching agents, students determine what kinds of paper recycle best and are the most environmentally friendly.

Robot Game

http://www.apase.bc.ca/unmixed/una9.html

Introduces the two stages of computer operation—command and decision making based on yes-or-no answers—using students' knowledge of a favorite video game.

Sounds Like Science: Bottle Organ

http://www.apase.bc.ca/unmixed/una7.html

To understand notes as the ABCs of music and the musical scale, students make and fine-tune bottle organs to experiment with variables that affect pitch.

Sounds Like Science: Drums

http://www.apase.bc.ca/unmixed/una4.html

By experimenting in groups with the concepts of force, pitch, and volume, using handmade drums, students explore the field of sound engineering and the science of instrument design and construction.

Sounds Like Science: Guitars

http://www.apase.bc.ca/unmixed/una5.html

Students explore inaudible and audible sounds, high and low frequencies, and vibrations using homemade guitars.

Sounds Like Science: Kazoo

http://www.apase.bc.ca/unmixed/una6.html

Using different sizes of toothed combs, waxed paper, and a variety of other kinds of paper, students learn about force, energy, and energy transfer.

Stop, Thief!

http://www.apase.bc.ca/unmixed/una10.html

Students learn about careful observations and to distinguish the difference between observations and conclusions.

Whodunit?

http://www.apase.bc.ca/unmixed/una11.html

Working in teams, students observe the geometric patterns in their own fingerprints to develop their own systems of classification and nomenclature; only then do they look at a standardized system.

678. Project Primary

http://www.owu.edu/%7emggrote/pp/

Project Primary is a collaboration of university professors and K-3 teachers producing hands-on activities for teaching science to primary-grade students. Science topics covered include botany, chemistry, geology, physics, and zoology. Activities are designed to follow the principles for constructivist learning. An online article explains the appropriate use of the various activities. For more information contact Michael Grote (Mggrote@cc.owu.edu), Ohio Wesleyan University, Delaware, Ohio.

679. What on Earth Are You Doing for Earth Day?

http://www.education-world.com/a_lesson/lesson059.shtml

Looking for cool Earth Day projects on the Internet? You'll find 28 interesting ideas and activities to involve students in learning more about saving the Earth, as well as using the Internet as a communication and research tool. This Web site from Education World (http://www.education-world.com) was written in 1998. For current information about Earth Day, see (http://www.earthday.net). An 11-page coloring book on Earth Day is available in .pdf format (requires Adobe Acrobat Reader) from the Environmental Protection Agency (http://www.epa.gov/docs/Region5/happy.htm).

History of Science

680. The Art of Renaissance Science

http://www.crs4.it/Ars/arshtml/arstitle.html

The Art of Renaissance Science traces the origins of modern science to mathematics practiced during the scientific revolution of the 16th and 17th centuries, especially Galileo's mathematics, or "new science." The site also explores how Galileo's work was related to the works of painters and architects during the Italian Renaissance. This is an excellent site for older students studying Galileo. Incorporating interdisciplinary studies of science, math, history, and art, it effectively demonstrates how the interaction of artists and scientists in the Renaissance changed human perspective and contributed greatly to human knowledge. Information is accurate, interesting, and attractively illuminated with color graphics. This Web site was created by Joseph W. Dauben (jdx@cunyvms1.gc.cuny.edu), professor of history and history of science at Lehman College, City University of New York, and is based on a videotape by Professor Dauben entitled *The Art of Renaissance Science: Galileo and Perspective*.

Science Fairs

681. Battlefield Middle School's Science Fair Page

http://www.spotsylvania.k12.va.us/bms/bmssf.htm

Students in grades 6–8 at Battlefield Middle School in Fredericksburg, Virginia, have put together a nifty page of helpful tips for starting and completing award-winning science fair projects. Science fair topics are listed by topic as well as alphabetical keyword. Sixth-, seventh-, and eighth-grade science fair award winners are showcased. Pictures of the tabletop cardboard display boards for the projects are available for viewing as well. For students creating a science fair display, a picture *is* worth a thousand words! Links are provided to other related sites on the Internet. This site is maintained by Jackie Keith (jkeith@pen.k12.va.us).

682. Getting Started: Some Helpful Hints for Science Fair Projects

http://www.scri.fsu.edu/~dennisl/special/sf_hints.html

Having trouble thinking of a science fair topic or getting started? This page provides helpful hints on how to get started thinking about a science fair project. Students are encouraged to begin early and to find projects they can enjoy while learning.

683. Science Fair Project Ideas

http://www.stemnet.nf.ca/sciencefairs/

Canada's Stem Net is a high-quality computer network for educators in Newfoundland and Labrador; it supports the teaching curriculum and professional development. The network is a great source of ideas for science fair projects for both students and teachers.

Ideas for primary projects (grades 1–4) are suitable for beginners and for encouraging personal observations. Elementary (grades 4–6) science fair project ideas focus on making displays and conducting experiments, with emphasis on making models and conducting demonstrations. Junior high (grades 7–8) ideas encourage experimental projects by asking questions, such as "How strong is a toothpick?" Senior high (grades 9–12) ideas promote experimentation. For the latter students, ideas are grouped by category (i.e., engineering, biology [life sciences], physical science, earth science and meteorology, environmental, and computer science).

684. Step-by-Step Guide for How to Do a Science Project

http://www.isd77.k12.mn.us/resources/cf/SciProjIntro.html

David Morano (dmorano@vax1.mankato.msus.edu), associate professor at Mankato State University, has posted two guides for students who plan to do an experiment-based science project. One is an introductory guide and the other is an intermediate guide to doing experimental science projects. An example science project is also posted so that students can read through the various steps while following an actual fourth-grade project, The Effect of Salt on the Boiling Temperature of Water. These guides are appropriate for students in grades 3 and up.

685.   Virtual Science Fair

http://www.parkmaitland.org/Science_Expo/science_fair_home_page.htm

First- through sixth-grade students at Park Maitland Elementary School in Maitland, Florida, have put their science fair projects online. Experiments are listed by grade level. Each student used a template, so presentation of information is standardized. Pictures of displays, photos, drawings, and links to relevant resources on the Internet are interesting. Grades 3 and 5 have listed their inventions as well as their poems and stories about inventors and inventions. Maintained by Laura Cohn (LACohn@socrates.parkmaitland.org), technology coordinator.

Aeronautics

686.   The K-8 Aeronautics Internet Textbook

http://wings.ucdavis.edu/index.html

Students can explore the principles of aeronautics at this exciting Web site. A complete multimedia text on aeronautics can be accessed at different reading levels (beginner, intermediate, and advanced). There is a separate instructor text. Accompanying lesson plans are composed of fun experiments and exercises to help students understand the contents of the textbook. Curriculum Bridges suggests activities as bridges to cross-curricular studies. Links are provided to NASA tours and a career guide with a descriptive listing of the many possible careers in aeronautics. Be sure to investigate the link to aerodynamics in sports technology. This is an excellent learning site from the cooperative efforts of NASA's Learning Technologies Project and Cislunar Aerospace, Inc.

687.   Ken Blackburn's Paper Airplane Page

http://www.geocities.com/CapeCanaveral/1817/

Blackburn is the coauthor of *The World Record Paper Airplane Book* (Workman, 1994), the *Kids' Paper Airplane Book* (Workman, 1996), and the *1997 Paper Airplane Calendar*. His home page provides links to his work at McDonnell Douglas, instructions on how to fold simple paper airplanes, and a very brief history of paper airplanes and paper airplane aerodynamics.

688.   Off to a Flying Start

http://ltp.larc.nasa.gov/flyingstart

Off to a Flying Start is a K-4 online telecommunications project that uses worldwide collaboration and aeronautics to provide learning opportunities for students in math and science. Collaborative participation is free and limited from October 1 to May 31. Teachers are asked to register their classes (e.g., C. L. Hass's Flight Crew based at The New City School). Material is presented as sequential Learning Modules. Module 1 covers the parts of an airplane and how and why airplanes fly. Module 2 provides hands-on activities. Students and teachers actually construct models of the Falcon Flyer from the instructions and templates provided. Then, predicting flight distances, they fly their airplanes and collect, record, and graph the data. In Module 3, students design, construct, and fly their own planes. Participating classes share their data, their artwork, and their writings online. Produced by NASA Langley Research Center as a Learning Technologies Project, e-mail about this project should be addressed to Project Coordinator, Jeff Seaton (flyingstart@k12unix.larc.nasa.gov).

Astronomy, the Solar System, and Space Exploration

See also Athena: Earth and Space Science for K-12 (entry 673). For space robotics, *see* NASA's Intelligent Mechanism Group (entry 903).

Astronomy

689.   The Astronomy Cafe

http://www2.ari.net/home/odenwald/cafe.html

At the Astronomy Cafe you can find out more about being an astronomer. You can ask an astronomer a question and read about careers in astronomy. You can also find out about hyperspace, black holes, time travel, and quantum cosmology. There is a collection of essays on Big Bang cosmology and links to related Internet sites.

690.   Astronomy Picture of the Day

http://antwrp.gsfc.nasa.gov/apod/astropix.html

NASA helps students discover the cosmos with this interesting Web site. Each day a different image or photograph of the universe is featured, along with a brief explanation written by a professional astronomer. Selected vocabulary words in the text are hyperlinked to definitions. A nice feature for teachers is the preview announcing tomorrow's picture (for example, "Tomorrow's Picture: Aurora Crowns the Earth") . This is an excellent way to begin a day or class with a view to the cosmos.

691.   Classifying Galaxies: An Interactive Lesson

http://www.smv.org/hastings/galaxy.htm

Classifying Galaxies is an interactive lesson on the Hubble system of classifying galaxies, written for grades 5–9 by George and Jane Hastings, both teachers of astronomy in Richmond, Virginia. This lesson covers what a galaxy is, explains the Hubble classification of galaxies, and provides students with practice in using the Hubble classification system as an example of how scientists classify objects in nature. All materials required to complete this lesson are available online. Created and maintained by George Hastings (ghasting@pen.k12.va.us) and Jane Hastings (jhasting@pen.k12.va.us).

692.   Star Journey

http://www.nationalgeographic.com/features/97/stars/index.html

National Geographic provides its popular Star Chart with overlays of Hubble Space Telescope images. Take a closer look at the Hubble Space Telescope using a model and guide. An interactive feature allows students to take charge of the telescope to plot their own course. Also available is National Geographic's Star Attractions, with some highlights of the heavens.

693. The Web Nebulae

http://www.seds.org/billa/twn/

The night sky: a black void, or a brilliant universe inhabited by spectacular objects known as gaseous nebulae? Intended to intrigue viewers with their heavenly beauty, 25 photographs, taken with the aid of a telescope, show gaseous nebulae in amazing detail and color. Types of nebulae are identified. For each object there is a corresponding page of information. Created and maintained by Bill Arnett (billa@znet.com).

694. Windows to the Universe

http://windows.engin.umich.edu
or
http://windows.ivv.nasa.gov

Sponsored by NASA, Windows to the Universe is an innovative and interactive Web site that includes documents, images, movies, animations, and data sets for the exploration of earth and space sciences, with an emphasis on the human experience. Many categories are available for exploration, including News; Space Missions; Myths; Our Solar System; The Universe; and Art, Books and Films, a bibliography of related books, films, art, poetry, and fiction. The People section allows students to find out more about scientists from ancient times to the present, including NASA's astronauts. Students can discover how stars are formed and view, in real time, pictures of the sun and the aurora. Teacher Resources provides suggested classroom activities, links to educational resources, and an online bulletin board for discussion. All information in Windows to the Universe is available on three reading levels: beginner, intermediate, and advanced. The default is intermediate. Look for the menu bar in the upper right-hand corner to change levels. Links are provided to Ask a Scientist and the Ulysses Mission. A table of contents and menu links at the bottom of each page make navigation through this plethora of information relatively easy.

Aurora Borealis

695. Northern Lights Planetarium

http://www.uit.no/npt/homepage-npt.en.html

From this home page, pointers are given to information about the Northern Lights (aurora borealis). There are pictures, reading lists, and explanations.

Comets

696. Comet Hale-Bopp

http://www.jpl.nasa.gov/comet/

What does Comet Hale-Bopp look like? This site contains more than 2,400 images. Students can read what Alan Hale, the discoverer of Comet Hale-Bopp, writes of his discovery. (Hale credits Tom Bopp for independently discovering the same comet.) Links are provided to other Hale-Bopp sites, including media accounts.

697. Comet Shoemaker-Levy 9 (SL9) Collision with Jupiter

http://www.jpl.nasa.gov/sl9/sl9.html

NASA maintains this site for research purposes. Background information is provided as well as the latest conclusions about the comet's collision. Students will find more than 1,444 images from 64 observatories around the world, as well as impact images, artists' renditions of the impact, general information, and computer animations. Links are provided to other SL9-related World Wide Web pages.

Space Studies for Younger Children

698. NASA Kids

http://kids.msfc.nasa.gov

Young children will enjoy this site's puzzles, such as unscrambling space-y pictures and word finds. There are six word-finds that you can either work online (if you have Java) or print out and solve on paper. Students who complete the puzzles online are rewarded with "You Win!!" There is an animated story entitled "Our Summer Vacation," and readers are asked to help Ashley and Travis solve some puzzles during their adventures. Those without Futuresplash can enjoy the non-animated version. The picture gallery has great images, and the coloring book section has pages to print out and color. Students can calculate their weight on other planets and the moon and explore what zero gravity means. Information is available on the Space Cadet Academy, and there is a fun Kid's Quiz. NASA Kids was created and is maintained as a volunteer project by Becky Bray (Becky.Bray@msfc.nasa.gov), Patrick Meyer (Patrick.Meyer@msfc.nasa.gov), and John Jaap (John.Jaap@msfc.nasa.gov).

699. The StarChild Project

http://starchild.gsfc.nasa.gov/docs/StarChild/

StarChild is a learning center for young astronomers. Information and activities are presented on two levels for the solar system, space, and the universe. To learn more about the planets, younger students can play Tic-Tac-Toe Planets; older elementary students can calculate their age and weight on each planet. Links are provided to a glossary and interesting new information. Sponsored by NASA, the Webmaster's address is (starchild@heasarc.gsfc.nasa).

Multimedia Resources

700. Astronomical Pictures and Animations

http://graffiti.u-bordeaux.fr/MAPBX/roussel/astro.english.html

Astronomical Pictures and Animations is a comprehensive compilation (more than 4 gigabytes) of photographs and video clips related to astronomy. Students will find pictures of eclipses, images from the Hubble Space Telescope, planets, and views of the Shuttle. More than 2,300 space animations representing approximately 4,000 MB of compressed data are in this Space Movie archive. A database of more than 500 movies of space imagery is archived and is keyword searchable. Digital movie files include clips from the 11 days of the Mir-Atlantis encounter; the 1991 eclipse; and a massive, 14-MB tour of Deanna Troi's quarters on the starship *Enterprise* (from *Star Trek: The Next Generation*). Links are provided to information on how to uncompress .gz files and to resources for obtaining animation players for specific platforms. Created and maintained by French astronomer, Dr. Frank Roussel (Astro@pegase.unice.fr).

701. **Exploration In Education**

http://www.stsci.edu/exined/exined-home.html

Exploration In Education (ExInEd) is a NASA-supported program that provides a library of free Electronic Picture Books, multimedia publications incorporating the results of astronomy and planetary research as well as images from the Hubble Space Telescope, interplanetary spacecraft, and astronaut-held cameras. Available titles are compatible with Color Macs, System 7 or higher, using HyperCard Player 2.1, or for Windows using WinPlus Runtime. The software to run these HyperCard stacks is provided if needed. This ongoing initiative currently includes 16 titles. Some of the available titles are: Gems of Hubble (3.9 MB); The Red Planet (3.6 MB); Clementine Explores the Moon (2 MB); and The Planetary System (with more than 100 images. 6.4 MB). Electronic tutorials and reports requiring Adobe Acrobat Reader are also available. A CD-ROM version of The Hubble Library of Electronic Picture Books can be ordered for a fee from NASA CORE (Central Operation of Resources for Educators). See (http://core.nasa.gov) for more information.

The Solar System

702. **Cyber-Center Planetary Research Center**

http://www.nasm.edu/ceps/SIIMAGES/

The National Air and Space Museum's Cyber-Center is a planetary online research center with activities for middle school students and lesson plans for teachers. Students are invited to explore the mysteries of the solar system and experience the excitement of planetary research. Why does the moon have so many craters? What causes storms on Jupiter? The first assignment is an introduction to the solar system, in which students describe the planets and their features after observing them in this simulated research center. The Webmaster's address is (vportway@ceps.nasm.edu).

703. **The Nine Planets: A Multimedia Tour of the Solar System**

http://www.seds.org/billa/tnp/

The Nine Planets is an overview of the history, mythology, and current scientific knowledge of each of the planets and moons in our solar system. A multimedia collection of information about the solar system, it includes 60 WWW pages with pictures, facts, and links to related sites. There are also sound files and links to video clips of objects in space. A glossary is included, as is a history of planetary science and spacecraft.

The Express Tour allows students to jump among the main objects in the solar system. The full tour is an overview of the solar system that includes all the planets and their moons, the sun, and small bodies (i.e., comets, asteroids, and meteors), including Halley's Comet and Comet Shoemaker-Levy 9. Created and maintained by Bill Arnett (billa@znet.com).

704.   **The Science Education Gateway**

http://cse.ssl.berkeley.edu/segway/

The Science Education Gateway (SEGway) is a collaborative NASA project that brings together the expertise of NASA scientists, science museums, and K-12 educators to produce NASA science-based Earth and space science curricula for classroom and public use via the World Wide Web. Educators can use a virtual resource cart to collect and design a custom collection of resources. Selections placed in the cart are converted to links in a custom Web page listing all the items chosen. A lesson plan template is provided to help create lesson plans from the resources on this site. Additionally, an excellent collection of lesson plans is available on space science, earth science, and the solar system. The Grab Bag contains high-quality images, movies, games, online quizzes, and more. Get a resource cart and fill it with these quality goodies for your classroom!

705.   **The Sun—A Multimedia Tour**

http://www.astro.uva.nl/demo/sun/kaft.htm

How long does it take to travel to the sun? This online journey to the sun takes about 20 minutes and contains several MPEG movies. Students can click on clearly labeled diagrams to learn more about the layers of the sun or click on images of solar flares and solar winds to enlarge them for detailed study. The sun's current influence on the Earth is examined, as is the sun's future influence on Earth when all the hydrogen in the sun's core is consumed. Created by Michiel Berger, graduate student in astronomy at the Astronomical Institute of the University of Amsterdam. Another excellent site written especially for K-12 is The Sun: Man's Friend & Foe (http://library.thinkquest.org/15215/). For one application of solar energy, *see also* the Solar Cooking Archive (entry 957).

706.   **Welcome to the Planets**

http://pds.jpl.nasa.gov/planets/

Welcome to the Planets is a multimedia tour of the nine planets taken from a NASA CD-ROM. The tour consists of 190 images acquired during 20 years of NASA planetary exploration, in addition to information on the Hubble Space Telescope, *Galileo, Magellan, Voyager 1* and *2, Viking 1* and *2,* and *Mariner 10.* There are annotated pictures of the ion and dust tail of Halley's Comet, the asteroid 243 Ida, a chondrite meteorite, an achondrite meteorite, and an iron meteorite.

Sky Maps

707.   **Earth and Moon Viewer**

http://www.fourmilab.ch/earthview/vplanet.html

Students can choose to view the Earth showing day and night regions in real time or any location above the planet by latitude, longitude, and altitude; from a satellite in Earth's orbit; or from above various cities around the globe. The Earth can also be viewed from the sun or from the moon. The moon can be viewed above any named formation on the lunar surface as well as from Earth and the sun. The moon's night side can also be viewed.

708. Home Planet

http://www.fourmilab.ch/homeplanet/homeplanet.html

Home Planet is a comprehensive astronomy, space, satellite-tracking package for Microsoft Windows 95 and Windows NT 4.0 and above. It is freeware that allows unique imaging of the Earth and sky, including orbits of asteroids and comets, stars at the horizon, and views of the Earth, the moon, and planets. The "lite" version is 1,411 KB and the full edition is 7,221 KB. Installation instructions are clear and concise for both versions, and there is a North American download site.

709. Your Sky

http://www.fourmilab.ch/yoursky/

Your Sky is an interactive planetarium that allows students to create star maps for any location on Earth at any date and time. Sky Map allows students to view the entire night sky from a given location and a specified time and date, using latitude, longitude, north/south, and east/west settings. Horizon Views requires the same settings as Sky Map plus a viewing direction or azimuth to produce a map showing a specified view toward the horizon of the night sky. Students can aim the Virtual Telescope by entering coordinates, and they can also select to track a number of various astronomical objects, such as planets, constellations, navigation stars, named stars, and named asteroids.

Space Exploration

710. Basics of Space Flight

http://www.jpl.nasa.gov/basics/

The Basics of Space Flight Learner's Workbook was designed by the Jet Propulsion Laboratory at Cal Tech (*see* entry 723). There are a table of contents and a glossary of terms and abbreviations. Students can browse the workbook by selecting specific topics from the table of contents.

711. Challenger Center Online

http://www.challenger.org

Educational Resources, Current News, Educational Programs, and Teacher Training are all part of the Challenger Center Online, part of the Challenger Center for Space Science Education, a not-for-profit organization committed to promoting science literacy. Using the theme of space exploration, the center hopes to create positive learning experiences; foster interest in science, math, and technology; and motivate young people to explore.

The Education Resources area has activities, clip art, and links to educational sites. One of the Challenger Center projects is an electronic field trip entitled "The Theory of Wow! A Kid-Size Exploration of the Solar System." A detailed program overview and teacher's guide are freely available online; videos of this previously televised program are for sale.

712. The Galileo Europa Mission (GEM)

http://www.jpl.nasa.gov/galileo/gem/gem1.html

Ice, water, and fire aptly describe the Galileo Europa Mission (GEM), during which the Galileo spacecraft began a new mission to spend two more years at Jupiter studying the icy moon Europa, the thunderstorms of Jupiter, and the fiery volcanoes of the moon Io. Originally scheduled to end its exploration on December 7, 1997, NASA and Congress have extended Galileo's studies until December 31, 1999. This site provides the latest news, images, and information. In the K-12 Education section, NASA provides background information for educators on Galileo, suggested educational activities for the classroom, teaching materials, and links to related educational resources. Students can download and build a scale model of the Galileo spacecraft. A FAQ section and glossary are also provided. *See also* Project Galileo: Journey to Jupiter (entry 719).

713. **Human Spaceflight (NASA)**

http://spaceflight.nasa.gov

NASA's Human Spaceflight Web site provides links to comprehensive information about the space shuttle, space station, missions to explore Mars, and space history. A searchable gallery contains images, video, and sound clips. Real-time data show the exact position of the space station and its altitude, speed, and path. The same real-time data are provided for shuttle missions.

714. **The Ice and Fire Preprojects: Europa, Pluto, and the Sun**

http://www.jpl.nasa.gov/ice_fire/

In its Ice and Fire Preprojects group, NASA is proposing three missions in the next decade as part of the Outer Planets/Solar Probe Program. These missions would explore the hottest, coldest, and hardest-to-reach regions of our solar system. The Pluto-Kuiper Express is planned as a robotic reconnaissance mission to Pluto and its moon Charon around 2010 or later. If the encounter with Pluto is successful, the mission may be extended to encounter one or more icy, asteroid-sized objects in the Kuiper Disk. (The recently discovered Edgeworth-Kuiper Disk of ice dwarfs or minor planets lies beyond Pluto.) The Europa Orbiter spacecraft will measure the thickness of the surface ice on Jupiter's moon, Europa, and detect an underlying liquid ocean if it exists. If liquid water exists on Europa, it would not be unreasonable to speculate that life also exists there, perhaps near undersea volcanic vents; such life, which requires no sunlight and thrives on chemical nutrients, is found on Earth in the depths of the ocean. The Solar Probe would go directly into the atmosphere of the sun. With a heat shield that can withstand temperatures of 2,200 Kelvins, the probe would take close-up measurements (3 solar radii from the surface) in hopes of revealing some of the sun's secrets. Web page maintained by Stephen C. Brewster (stephen.c.brewster@jpl.nasa.gov). For more information on educational resources for the Pluto-Kuiper Express mission, *see* entry 718. For more information on the Solar Probe, *see* entry 720.

715. **International Space Station**

http://spaceflight.nasa.gov/station/

The International Space Station (ISS) is an ambitious project that will require cooperation and planning between the United States and its four international partners during 44 flights over a period of 4.5 years, beginning in June 1998. The ISS is a remarkable example of the world's countries united for a common goal: building an international community and science institute in space. This Web site is designed to communicate the progress of the space station during its development and assembly and to answer questions. Educational resources are available, including a FAQ section; an ISS image library with scale-model drawings; QuickTime VR videos; and color graphics, fact sheets, and related links.

716.   Magellan Mission to Venus

http://www.jpl.nasa.gov/magellan/

The Magellan Mission Web site contains much information, including press releases and lots of images. In addition, it includes the last status reports before Magellan's planned crash in October 1994, as well as 1995 reports and releases. This is a comprehensive page. Some high-resolution versions of the images require as much as 39.3 MB, but many images are 200 KB or less.

717.   Mars Exploration Mission

http://mpfwww.jpl.nasa.gov

Provides information about the Mars Pathfinder mission, Mars Global Surveyor, Polar Lander, and Surveyor 2001, including history, architecture, and press materials. Photographs and images are available. Suggestions are given for topics of study, such as the biological potential of Mars, the Martian interior, water and ice on Mars, surface materials, and Mars mapping. Supportive materials are provided for each topic. Students and teachers who would like to stay current on space topics should visit Space Scientists Online (http://quest.arc.nasa.gov/sso/index.html) for live chats, news, featured events, and e-mail addresses for asking specific questions.

718.   The Pluto-Kuiper Express Educational Outreach

http://www.jpl.nasa.gov/ice_fire/edout.htm

The Pluto-Kuiper Express is planned as a robotic reconnaissance mission to Pluto and its moon, Charon, around 2010 or later. If the encounter with Pluto is successful, the mission may be extended to encounter one or more icy, asteroid-sized objects in the Kuiper Disk. The recently discovered Edgeworth-Kuiper Disk of ice dwarfs or minor planets lies beyond Pluto. The Pluto Express Educational Outreach page hopes to engage students and teachers as active participants during all phases of the mission, including development, cruise, encounter, and data analysis. Curriculum guides and news releases are available. In exchange for an unopened V-120 VHS videotape, teachers can request a videotape entitled, "JPL Computer Animation," which includes an overview of the Pluto-Kuiper Express mission.

719.   Project Galileo: Journey to Jupiter

http://www.jpl.nasa.gov/galileo/

The Galileo spacecraft arrived at Jupiter on December 7, 1995. After sending a probe into Jupiter's atmosphere, which relayed information back to scientists, the spacecraft's orbiter spent the next two years orbiting the planet and studying Jupiter and its moons. The probe results, as well as images, are available on this Web site. There are educational resources for the classroom in the Galileo K-12 Education area. NASA provides background information for educators on Galileo, suggested educational activities for the classroom, teaching materials, and links to related educational resources. Students can download and build a scale model of the Galileo spacecraft.

New images of Europa are posted on this site, as Galileo extended its mission until December 1999, to intensively study Europa and gather data during fly-bys of Io. For more information on the Galileo Europa Mission (GEM), *see* entry 712.

Galileo status reports and press releases are now available via e-mail. To subscribe, e-mail: **majordomo@sender.jpl.nasa.gov**
Instructions: On the first line of the body of the message, type:
subscribe galileo

720.   The Solar Probe

http://www.jpl.nasa.gov/ice_fire/sprobe.htm

NASA's Solar Probe is a proposed mission scheduled to start development in 2001. The probe will fly through the sun's corona to try to answer some of these questions:

> What heats the solar corona and accelerates the solar wind?
> What are the sources of the solar wind in the corona?
> What roles do turbulence and waves play in the coronal heating process?
> What are the characteristics of the structures in the polar regions of the sun?

National Aeronautics and Space Administration (NASA)

721.   Biographies of NASA Astronauts

http://www.hq.nasa.gov/office/pao/History/nauts.html

Biographical sketches are available for current, former, and deceased NASA astronauts. This site has everything from an astronaut's scouting record to how many astronauts were born in each state. Biographical information about former and deceased astronauts, as well as the *Astronaut Factbook*, are in PDF format, requiring Adobe Acrobat Reader. *See also* Women of NASA (entry 726).

722.   The Educator Resource Center for NASA Langley

http://www.vasc.org/erc/

The Educator Resource Center (ERC) for NASA Langley houses information on print resources, video resources, and Internet resources by subject area. For example, the subject area, Living and Working in Space, offers a list of Internet resources that includes links to the International Space Station Home Page, the Shuttle-Mir Web, and the Space Station Mir Home Page.

To help disseminate NASA educational materials to educators, NASA's Education Division has established the NASA Educator Resource Center Network. This network is composed of Educator Resource Centers, Regional Educator Resource Centers (RERCs), and the NASA Central Operation of Resources for Educators (CORE). Regional Educator Resource Centers are located in most states throughout the United States. These facilities are the principal distribution points where educators may obtain NASA publications, get video and computer materials, and participate in training workshops on the use of NASA educational products.

723.   Jet Propulsion Laboratory, California Institute of Technology

http://www.jpl.nasa.gov

The Jet Propulsion Laboratory (JPL) Web site contains an image information archive, various FAQs, and news flashes with recent news from the JPL, such as updates on the Galileo Mission to Jupiter, the Martian Chronicle, and space radar images. Links are provided to Welcome to the Planets (entry 706) and Basics of Space Flight (entry 710).

724. NASA Home Page

http://www.nasa.gov/NASA_homepage.html

NASA provides extensive information related to its aeronautics and space research. Sidebar navigation allows for easy access to the NASA Centers, Educational Resources, Public Affairs News and Information, NASA History, Research Opportunities, and Space Shuttle Launches. Links are also provided to Frequently Asked Questions, Hot Topics, a Multimedia Gallery, NASA Television, and Today@NASA.

725. NASA Spacelink

http://spacelink.msfc.nasa.gov/home.index.html

NASA Spacelink is an electronic information system available for use by the entire educational community. The system offers a wide range of materials, such as computer text files, software, and graphics related to the space program. Documents include science, math, engineering, and technology education lesson plans; historical information related to the space program; current status reports on NASA projects; news releases; information on NASA educational programs; NASA educational publications; and other materials.

Taking full advantage of all the NASA resources online requires various computer applications for playing sounds, displaying images, and showing movies on your computer. NASA provides links for downloading all the essential applications, including sound, image/graphics display, video, live audio/video, and portable documents. Software such as Adobe Acrobat Reader, RealPlayer audio, MpegPlay, and QuickTime are freely available for Windows, Macintosh, or UNIX platforms. For more information on downloading software, see (http://www.nasa.gov/hqpao/user_tips.html).

Educators may use NASA imagery, video, and audio material for educational or informational purposes, including photo collections, textbooks, public exhibits, and Internet Web pages, without copyright restrictions. This general permission does not include the NASA insignia logo, the NASA logotype, and the NASA seal. These are copyrighted and are used only by NASA employees or products (including Web pages) that are NASA-sponsored. For more information on NASA copyright guidelines, see (http://www.nasa.gov/gallery/photo/guideline.html). The NASA Spacelink database is maintained by the Education Programs Office at the NASA Marshall Space Flight Center in Huntsville, Alabama.

726. Women of NASA

http://quest.arc.nasa.gov/women/intro.html

One of the goals of the Women of NASA project is to provide a resource for teachers and others interested in learning more about gender bias in math and science and methods of teaching that reduce inequity in the classroom. More than 45 women are profiled in Women of NASA. In addition, students can follow the daily routines of various NASA women through their online journal entries. Students can find out what aerospace engineers, environmental public relations specialists, and K-12 technical assistants do. Suggestions are given on how to integrate Women of NASA into the curriculum.

Magazines and Newsletters

727. AIR&SPACE Magazine
http://www.airspacemag.com

AIR&SPACE Magazine is an extension of the Smithsonian Institution's National Air and Space Museum and contains articles that try to convey the adventure of flight and space travel to readers with a special interest in the history and technology of aerospace. Abstracts of articles in the current issue are provided. Feature articles from back issues are archived and are searchable. The Web site has an AIR&SPACE Web Directory with comprehensive links to aviation- and space-related Web sites.

728. Earth & Sky
http://www.earthsky.com

Earth & Sky is an award-winning daily science radio series by Deborah Byrd and Joel Block. The Web site contains the script of the day's show as well as the week's shows. There is a searchable archive of past Earth & Sky topics and resources for teachers.

Earth & Sky programs inform listeners about popular science subjects, including the night sky, earth science, and environmental science. Students' questions are answered from those sent to the commentators by mail, not e-mail.

The series airs on more than 950 stations in the United States and on many stations around the world, and is produced in association with the American Geophysical Union and made possible by a grant from the National Science Foundation.

Subscribe to the Earth & Sky mailing list to receive scripts and other information.

E-mail: **earthandsky-request@earthsky.com**
Instructions: On the first line of the message, type:
subscribe

Earth & Sky also posts to these newsgroups: (sci.geo.geology), (sci.space.new), and (sci.astro). Write to Earth & Sky, P.O. Box 2203, Austin, TX 78768, or e-mail Marc Airhart at (mairhart@earthsky.com) to ask Earth & Sky a question.

Biographies of Scientists

See also "Biographies of Physicists" (entries 894–896); Exploring Leonardo (entry 878); Women of NASA (entry 726); and Biographies of NASA Astronauts (entry 721).

729. 4000 Years of Women in Science
http://www.astr.ua.edu/4000WS/4000WS.html

4000 Years of Women in Science includes biographies of women from antiquity to the present, but emphasizes women scientists from the past. Biographies can be accessed alphabetically, from a time-ordered list, and from a field-of-study ordered list. Students will find biographies

for En Hedu'anna (ca. 2354 B.C.E.), a Babylonian moon priestess responsible for creating a calendar for religious events, and Deborah Crocker (1957–), a 20th-century astronomer.
Students can try the interactive quiz on the History of Women in Science. Those who
score perfectly win the Hypathia Award. Deborah Crocker (crock@kudzu.astr.ua.edu) is the
Webmaster.

730. African American Women in the Sciences

http://lcweb2.loc.gov/sctb/
Instructions: **Using African American Women as keywords, search Tracer Bullet titles**
or
gopher://marvel.loc.gov
Path: **Main Menu/Research and Reference (Public Services)/LC Reading Rooms/Science
and Technology/Bibliographies and Guides/Science Tracer Bullets/African American
Women in the Sciences**

African American Women in the Sciences is a Library of Congress document, Tracer Bullet (TB
93-4), compiled by Gail T. Austin (August 1993). This guide lists sources documenting the
contributions of African American women in science, technology, medicine, and related disciplines. Of possible interest to users of this compilation are "Blacks in Science and Related Disciplines"(TB 89-9) and "Women in the Sciences"(TB 90-6). Not an exhaustive treatment of the
subject, this Tracer Bullet, as the name of the series implies, is designed as a guide to put the
reader "on target."

731. Faces of Science: African Americans in the Sciences

http://www.lib.lsu.edu/lib/chem/display/faces.html

African American scientists are featured, with pictures and biographical information, in this
resource. Originally prepared for Martin Luther King Jr. Day and Black History Month 1995, the
biographies are divided into scientists of the past and present, with commentary about the future. Graphs illustrate the number of Ph.D. recipients from the 1800s to the present. Links are
provided to graduate-level educational opportunities for African Americans in chemistry.

Biology

General Interest

732. Access Excellence

http://www.accessexcellence.org

Access Excellence is a place in cyberspace for biology teaching and learning provided by Ge-
nentech, Inc., an international biotechnology company. This site is designed for high school
biology teachers. Lesson plans and activities are shared. There is a weekly science report, interviews with news-making scientists, and a place for teachers to discuss topics of interest
with their colleagues and share their teaching ideas, strategies, and activities.

733. Cell Biology

http://mindquest.net/biology/cell-biology/cell-biology.html

This site provides in-depth cell biology study guides, sample exams, and interactive quizzes for high school biology studies. It covers such topics as cell theory and cell types, cell arrangements and tissues, cell structure and function, cell membrane transport, cell replication, cell genetics, cell chemistry, and cell metabolism. The Multimedia Gallery includes photographs, clip art, and video clips which require a Java-enabled browser. Provided and maintained by MindQuest.net. *See also* the online version of *The Dictionary of Cell and Molecular Biology*.

734. Cells Alive!

http://www.cellsalive.com

Featuring color graphics, animated GIFs, and downloadable QuickTime video (.mov) files, the Web site explores dynamics of cells and cell structure. Cells Alive! looks at the cytoskeleton of living cells; some of the complexities of the HIV virus; how bacteria multiply; the difference in size among virus, bacterium, and human cells; how penicillin kills bacteria; and other related topics on the study of cells. Great images help make this topic interesting. Created and maintained by James A. Sullivan at Quill Graphics (quill@comet.net).

735. DNA From The Beginning

http://vector.cshl.org/dnaftb/

Provides an animated primer on the basics of DNA, genes, and heredity. Information is organized around three categories—classical genetics, molecules of genetics, and organization of genetic material—and comprises 32 concepts or facts. The science behind each concept is explained by animation, images, video interviews, biographies, problem solving, and links to related information for further study. Requires Flash Player from Macromedia. Created by the DNA Learning Center.

736. DNA Graphics

http://grserv.med.jhmi.edu/~paul/PovChem.html

As part of his doctoral research, graduate student Paul Thiessen has written a software program, PovChem, to help students visualize chemical structures. This software combines chemistry, ray tracing, and a little art to make high-quality molecular graphics. Be sure to visit the DNA Gallery. Created and maintained by Paul Thiessen (paul@grserv.med.jhmi.edu), who is doing his postdoctoral work at Rose Lab, Johns Hopkins University (http://grserv.med.jhmi.edu).

737. Living Things

http://www.fi.edu/tfi/units/life/

Living Things is a comprehensive unit on biology that provides hands-on activities and is easily accessible to elementary as well as older students. Before using this site, you may want to try an Orientation Activity. You may also want to review the Keyword Index to get an overview of the topics. Content is categorized into four main areas: Individuals, Families, Neighborhoods, and the Circle of Life. "Individuals" deals primarily with the anatomy and physiology of plants and animals. Cells, structure, systems, and adaptations are a few of the subject areas. "Families" addresses the systems for classification of plants and animals. Observed characteristics are emphasized as a primary means of classification. "Neighborhoods" considers the interactions of living things with the world around them. Ecosystems, habitats, and biomes are introduced. "Circle of Life" features the daily survival needs of plants and animals. Plant and animal life cycles are detailed, including birth, growth, reproduction, and death. Activities are aligned with national science standards. A keyword index, crossword references, career connections, and teacher tips are provided. A Curriculum Connections index helps identify resources in Living Things with the National Science Education Standards. Sponsored by the Franklin Institute Science Museum, Philadelphia, Pennsylvania.

738. Microbe Zoo

http://commtechlab.msu.edu/sites/dlc-me/zoo/

Microbes (microorganisms) are extremely diverse and represent all the great kingdoms of life (including animals, plants, fungi, protists, and bacteria), yet these small organisms are too tiny to be seen with the naked eye. Viruses, and the recently discovered prions, are also considered microbes. Major attractions at the Microbe Zoo include DirtLand, Animal Pavilion, Snack Bar, Space Adventure, and Water World. Students also learn what microbial ecologists do. This is a well-designed, colorful, and interesting educational Web site from the Michigan State University Center for Microbial Ecology (microbes@commtechlab.msu.edu).

739. The MIT Biology Hypertextbook

http://esg-www.mit.edu:8001/esgbio/7001main.html

The Biology Hypertextbook has chapters on Chemistry Review, Large Molecules, Cell Biology, Enzyme Biochemistry, Photosynthesis, Mendelian Genetics, Immunology, Recombinant DNA, and Prokaryotic Genetics and Gene Expression. Words in chapters are hyperlinked to definitions, and sections are accompanied by graphics and diagrams. This would be useful as supplementary material in a high school biology class.

740. Stanford University Human Genome Education Program Resources

http://www-shgc.stanford.edu/bio-ed/

The Human Genome Education Program Resources at Stanford University is an extensive list of both general and specific resources and references for biological studies. Categories include educational resources for biology teachers, experiments, demonstrations, museums, and places of exploration. Genetics and molecular biology is a category, as are botany, zoology, ecology, evolution, and medicine.

741. The Tree of Life

http://phylogeny.arizona.edu/tree/phylogeny.html
or
http://ag.arizona.edu/tree/phylogeny.html

The Tree of Life is a project designed to contain information about the phylogenetic relationship and characteristics of organisms, to illustrate the diversity and unity of living organisms, and to link biological information available on the Internet in the form of a phylogenetic navigator. It seeks to show how all forms of life are related. One of the goals of The Tree of Life is to aid education about and appreciation of biological diversity by providing a means to find taxon-specific information on the Internet, both taxonomic and otherwise. Still under development, the Tree has more than 1,270 pages housed on 18 computers in 3 countries. The Tree provides a map to biological information that can be used by researchers, teachers, and students. Some of the outstanding pages nearing completion include information on beetles, jumping spiders, sac fungi, frogs, and vertebrates. The Tree of Life project is a multiauthored, hierarchically coordinated project created by Wayne Maddison, Department of Ecology and Evolutionary Biology, and David Maddison, Department of Entomology, University of Arizona (tree@ag.arizona.edu).

742. Virtual Cell

http://ampere.scale.uiuc.edu/~m-lexa/cell/cell.html

Using a mouse, students can manipulate this virtual plant cell environment by using *zoom* to get a closer look; *cut* to open and reveal the contents of the next layer; *turn* to show the object from a different angle; *EM* to show a black-and-white electron micrograph illustrating a real image of the main object; or *write* to get more written information.

Anatomy

743. Anatomy and Physiology for High School Students

http://www.msms.doe.k12.ms.us/biology/anatomy/apmain.html

Students at the Mississippi School for Mathematics and Science (entry 25) have collaboratively created an anatomy and physiology site especially for other high school students. Their illustrated pages provide complementary information for exploring the body's systems—lymphatic, nervous, respiratory, circulatory, digestive, reproductive, skeletal, muscular, and integumentary—as well as the concept of artificial intelligence. William R. Odom, Ph.D., is the teacher, and the Webmaster for this page is student Nathan Dixon (ndixon@msms.doe.k12.ms.us).

744. Human Anatomy On-Line

http://www.innerbody.com/htm/body.html

As an introduction to anatomy, students can select any of 10 pictured anatomy systems, such as the digestive, reproductive, muscular, or nervous systems. After the image is fully loaded, students can run their mouse over the image. For each pick point, an eyeglass icon appears, along with the name of the item. By clicking on these pop-up labels, students can find out more information. This site is under construction. General lessons on the human anatomy and the skeletal system are online and contain more than 75 pages. More human anatomy lessons are planned. Human Anatomy On-Line uses Java applets to show images and select anatomy parts. Developed by Informative Graphics. The Webmaster's e-mail address is (info@innerbody.com).

745. Your Gross and Cool Body

http://www.yucky.com/body/

Kids will love this newest addition to the Yuckiest Science sites on the Internet. *See also* Cockroach World (entry 787) and Worm World (entry 795). Wendell, the Web's ace worm reporter, and his friend Dora find out what makes the human body work by investigating dandruff, sweat, zits, ear wax, snoring, gas, bad breath, snot, funnybones, and more. Graphics-rich and linked to sounds, this site is sure to interest kids in learning more about their bodies.

The Brain

746. Neuroscience for Kids
http://faculty.washington.edu/chudler/neurok.html

Created especially for elementary and secondary school students and teachers, Neuroscience for Kids provides comprehensive information about the nervous system. This is an excellent reference resource for students studying any topic related to neuroscience. Experiments, activities, and games are available to help learn more about the brain and the spinal cord. Graphics and text explain the brain, the spinal cord, the peripheral nervous system, and neurons. Extended information covers the Sensory Systems, providing a wonderful enhancement for units on the senses. The page called Safety Tips for Eyes includes an online quiz. The effects of drugs on the nervous system are explored, as are future careers in neuroscience. Links are provided to other neuroscience resources on the Internet and to commercial resources for kits, charts, and software. An online/offline bibliography of books, magazine articles, and newspaper articles is provided for further reading. This excellent site was created and is maintained by Eric H. Chudler, Ph.D. (chudler@u.washington.edu), research assistant and professor in the Department of Anesthesiology at the University of Washington in Seattle.

The Eye

See also B-EYE: The World Through the Eyes of Bees (entry 784).

747. The Closeup Galleries
http://www.theimage.com/closeup/closeup.html

What is it that the eye really sees? At this site, students look at close-up images of common objects and try to guess what they really are. This is an excellent interactive exercise in comparing close-up views with normal perspectives. This site was created and is maintained by Ron Gibbs (theImage1@aol.com).

748. Dissecting a Cow's Eye
http://www.exploratorium.edu/learning_studio/cow_eye/

Providing step-by-step instructions on how to dissect a cow's eye, this Web site allows students to study the anatomy of the eye. In addition, there is a Cow's Eye Primer, an interactive program that provides a tutorial on the parts of the eye, a glossary of terms, and links to other eye resources on the Internet. This virtual dissection from the Exploratorium, a science museum in San Francisco, attempts to satisfy students' curiosity about what is inside an eye. The material at this site is not intended to replace the act of dissection in the classroom, but to enhance the experience.

The Heart

749. The Heart: An Online Exploration
http://sln2.fi.edu/biosci/heart.html

The Heart is a multimedia exhibit at the Franklin Institute Science Museum in Philadelphia (entry 657), which supports learning through inquiry-based exploration. Students explore the heart by studying its development and structure. They can follow the blood through the blood vessels and wander through body systems. The exhibit also explains how to maintain and monitor your heart's health. A section on the history of heart science is available, along with resource materials, enrichment activities for students, and a brief glossary.

Before you begin your tour of the heart, visit the Heart Preview Gallery, which offers lists of things to see, do, hear, and learn, as well as places to go. For example, you can view open-heart surgery in a short QuickTime movie; see four echo views of the heart using echocardiography; see an animation of a beating heart; and listen to various heart sounds. These are a few of many multimedia enrichment activities based on the study of the human heart.

The Lungs

750. Lung Tour
http://www-itg.lbl.gov/ImgLib/COLLECTIONS/lung_tour.html

Lung Tour is a set of images of the lung made with the scanning electron microscope and organized in hyperimage format to allow you to travel through and, see in more and more detail, the structure of the lung. You begin with a whole lung that has been opened to show the branching airway; you can zoom in to the surface of this airway at different points using varying powers of magnification. This interactive tour of the lung was developed by the Lawrence Berkeley National Laboratory, University of California, Berkeley.

The Five Senses

751. Come to Your Senses
http://tqjunior.advanced.org/3750/

To learn more about the five senses, students can click on Mr. Potato Head's eyes, nose, hands, mouth, or ears, or use a convenient side navigation bar. Find out some sense-sational facts and follow some sense-sational links for how the body sees, hears, tastes, feels, and smells. There is a glossary of terms and a recipe activity for involving all the senses. Come to Your Senses was created by fifth- and sixth-graders at Burlington Day School (Burlington, North Carolina) for a ThinkQuest Junior competition.

Skeletal and Muscular Systems

752. Lobster Lab: Muscles at Work
http://juliet.stfx.ca/~edemont/lobster.htm

The Lobster Lab, produced at St. Francis Xavier University, is a virtual laboratory exploring how muscles often function in a system of levers, using simple principles from physics to show how they work. This site requires a Shockwave plug-in. If you have not already downloaded Shockwave, you may do so from this site by clicking on the Shockwave icon at the bottom of the page.

Animals

See also "Environmental Sciences and Ecology" general-interest sites (entries 860–866).

General Interest

753. Animal Information Database: Sea World/Busch Gardens

http://www.seaworld.org/animal_bytes/animal_bytes.html

The Animal Bytes database includes scientific classification, facts, and biological information. Some of the animals listed include the African lion, American alligator, Bengal tiger, bottlenose dolphin, California sea lion, chimpanzee, gorilla, Grevy's zebra, killer whale, penguin, red rat snake, sea otter, shark, South American ornate horned frog, and walrus.

Information booklets on baleen whales, bottlenose dolphins, gorillas, manatees, killer whales, and walruses contain in-depth information about habitat, behavior, diet, and reproduction, plus a bibliography and index. Of special note is the section called Books for Young Readers, which suggests fiction and nonfiction books about specific animals. The baleen whales list includes 20 books; the bibliography is not annotated but has complete citations.

Sea World has developed teacher's guides with specific lesson plans that integrate science, mathematics, geography, art, and language arts into the study of ocean environment, ocean resources, and ocean creatures. Complete teacher's guides may be ordered from the education department at Sea World. A few activities from each teacher's guide are posted on this Web site.

754. National Zoological Park Home Page

http://www.si.edu/natzoo/

The home page for the National Zoo in Washington, D.C., provides a wealth of information on the animals who make the National Zoo their home. Maps of the Zoo are available as well as an online audio tour with pictures. Students can find out information about new Zoo births and special Zoo events. Educational games, such as crossword puzzles, word searches, and a symbolic language memory game based on ongoing studies with the Zoo's orangutans, accompany and complement some of the online information. Links to various Web cameras allow students to actually see some animals in the Zoo. Using either RealAudio or True Speech players, students can download and listen to illustrated slide shows on a range of topics, including pollination, animals of the Amazon, and baby elephants.

755. NetVet and The Electronic Zoo

http://netvet.wustl.edu

NetVet and The Electronic Zoo are two interrelated areas of veterinary and animal-related Web sites created by Dr. Ken Boschert, DVM (ken@wudcm.wustl.edu), associate director of Washington University's Division of Comparative Medicine, St. Louis, Missouri. Animal-related information on the Internet is categorized and organized in an easy-to-use format. Lists are maintained of relevant publications, organizations, mailing lists, newsgroups, telnet sites, FTP sites, Gopher sites, and WWW sites.

The Electronic Zoo lists all animal-related information on the Internet. Zoo animals, farm animals, marine mammals, invertebrates, common and unusual pets, wildlife, and more are available for individual study and research. There is even a section on fictional animals, such as Babe, Miss Piggy, and Danger Mouse! Pick of the Litter features a different animal, pet, or veterinary science Web page each week, and links are available to past picks as well as the current pick.

NetVet has information on veterinary medicine as a career. What's New focuses on news in veterinary science, animal research and animal rights, public health, biotechnology companies, and U.S. pharmaceutical companies. Past news is archived. Both the NetVet and The Electronic Zoo databases are keyword-searchable.

Farm Animals

756. Barnyard Palace
http://www.agr.state.nc.us/cyber/kidswrld/general/barnyard/barnyard.htm

By clicking on an aerial photo of the Teaching Animal Unit at the NCSU Veterinary Medicine College, students can easily visualize a real farm and find out more about farm animals, such as beef cows, poultry (turkeys and chicken), sheep, goats, pigs, dairy cows, and horses. Gives good information about life cycles, dietary facts, what the species produces, what distinguishes the species from others, and what is unique about the species—and includes plenty of photographs. Because many of the animals are raised primarily for consumption, and the text states that some animals are fed for slaughter and others are processed for their meat and hides at varying ages, caution is advised for use with very young students. *See also* the Montana Kids page on Livestock (http://kids.state.mt.us/db_engine/subcat.asp?Subcat=The+ Livestock) with information about swine, sheep, milk cows, horses, emus and ostriches, chickens, and cattle.

Dairy Cows

757. MooMilk
http://www.moomilk.com

MooMilk provides a photographic tour of the dairy industry for primary students by explaining how cows are milked, how milk is transported to processing plants, and how raw milk is treated. Gives facts about what cows eat, and how often, and how much milk they can produce in one day. Questions are answered in a FAQs section, a MooMilk quiz tests readers' knowledge of dairy cows, and Dairy Cuisine features recipes that use milk and milk products. Find out more about the benefits of milk consumption at All About Milk (http://www.whymilk. com/about/index.html) and an accompanying Teaching Master from Education World (http:// www.education-world.com/a_lesson/TM/WS_got_milk.shtml). For a lesson plan tie-in, see Newton's Apple and MooooMath (http://ericir.syr.edu/Projects/Newton/11/dairyfrm.html).

Pigs

758. Farmtastic Voyage

http://www.nppc.org/ForKids/farmtastic.html

Bethany and Michael, a young girl and boy, take students on a photographic tour of their pig farm in Iowa. Primary-age students find out what pigs like to eat and drink, how pigs' skin feels, what color pigs are, what *farrowing* means, what piglets in a litter look like, and the difference between pot-bellied pigs and American pigs. Sponsored by the National Pork Producers Council.

Mammals

Bats

759. Bats: A Thematic Resource for Teachers and Students

http://intergate.cccoe.k12.ca.us/bats/

Did you know that bats are the only mammal that can fly? This searchable Web site integrates the study of bats into science, art, sports, literature, environmental studies, and conservation. Suggested projects and activities include directions on how to build a bat house, a bat word search and crossword puzzle, and a BatQuest. A reading bibliography is provided as part of a list of bat resource materials. Students can take an interactive quiz to test their bat knowledge. Created by teachers enrolled at the Hayword's Educational Technology Leadership Graduate Program at California State University. Contact Doug Prouty (dprouty@cccoe.k12.ca.us), technology specialist for Contra Costa County Office of Education.

Bears

760. The Bear Den

http://www.nature-net.com/bears/

Students learn to appreciate bears and discover how bears are classified according to taxonomic criteria. Information is provided on the eight species of bears. There is a bibliography, a photo gallery, and information on bear conservancy organizations. Links are provided to wildlife, conservancy, and backcountry Web sites. This Web site and The Cub Den (entry 761) are maintained by Don Middleton (dmiddlet@nature-net.com), who welcomes questions from students.

761. The Cub Den

http://www.nature-net.com/bears/cubden.html

The Cub Den is a companion site to The Bear Den (entry 760). The Cub Den encourages younger children to find out more about bears. This site contains Ten Facts About Bears; Amazing Facts About Bears; and Books for Young Readers. Students learn interesting facts (for instance, there are eight kinds of bears; baby bears in cold climates are born while the mother bear is hibernating).

Wolves

762. The Searching Wolf

http://www.iup.edu/~wolf/wolves.htmlx

The Web page has information on all things wolfish. Here you can find facts about wolves, from family life and pups to communication. Learn how to growl and howl. Good information and excellent pictures are available. A test on basic wolf facts can be downloaded as a zipped DOS program. Created and maintained by Bill Forbes (wolf@grove.iup.edu), professor of biology, Indiana University of Pennsylvania (Indiana, Pennsylvania).

Marine Life

See also Ocean Planet Home Page (entry 660) and "Submarine Geology" (entries 824–829).

Cephalopods

763. The Cephalopod Page

http://is.dal.ca/~ceph/TCP/index.html

Octopuses, squid, cuttlefish, and the chambered nautilus all belong to class *Cephalopoda*. Find out more about these amazing invertebrates that live in all the oceans of the world, including the abyss. Provides FAQs, photographs, and information about different species. Created and maintained by James B. Wood (deph@is.dal.co) at Dalhousie University, Halifax, Nova Scotia, Canada.

Deep-Sea Ecology

See also Ocean Planet Home Page (entry 660) and "Submarine Geology" (entries 824–829).

764. Into the Abyss

http://www.pbs.org/wgbh/nova/abyss/

NOVA details an expedition to the Pacific Northwest coast to retrieve several black smokers from the seafloor. Black smokers are places where bizarre life forms thrive on volcanic chemicals rather than sunlight. Shows the body parts of tube worms, animals with no mouths, no stomachs, no intestines, and no way to eliminate waste. Discusses other life forms with common names such as "basketball fish," "fangtooth," and "umbrellamouth gulper," and what it is like for creatures to live at extremes.

765. Meet the Creatures: Where Life Began

http://www.discovery.com/stories/science/seavents/creatures.html

Meet the Creatures is part of an online report of a 1998 Discovery Channel Expedition to Nine North on the East Pacific Rise, a portion of the Earth's midocean ridge where tectonic plates separate. This causes lava to seep up, adding layers to the Earth's crust, and hydrothermal vents to blow out the superheated sea water, saturated with chemicals and minerals, that supports life around the vents. Some of the deep-sea creatures highlighted with color photographs and brief text are tube worms, Jericho worms, mussels, clams, amphipods, Zoarcid fish,

Galatheid crabs, Brachyuran crabs, and Alvinellid worms. These amazing deep-sea creatures use chemosynthesis rather than photosynthesis. Links to other sections of this Discovery Web site lead to maps and more information about Nine North.

Fish

766. Fish FAQ

http://www.wh.whoi.edu/faq.html

Everything you ever wanted to know about fish can probably be accessed from this page, which is a link from the U.S. Department of Commerce, National Oceanic and Atmospheric Administration, National Marine Fisheries Service. The National Marine Fisheries Service annually answers thousands of questions about oceans and marine life. More than 100 frequently asked questions are answered at this site.

The URL for the Northeast Fisheries Science Center Woods Hole (Massachusetts) Laboratory is (http://www.wh.whoi.edu/noaa.html). The URL for the Northeast Fisheries Science Center Headquarters Home Page is (http://www.wh.whoi.edu).

Turtles

767. Turtle Trax

http://www.turtles.org

Turtle Trax, a Web site devoted to marine turtles, gives people the chance to become familiar with the wonder and beauty of turtles. Information is available on pending legislation that affects sea turtles and things you can do to help.

Whales

768. Whale Songs

http://whales.ot.com

Whale Songs is an online whale education center. It links classrooms with the Song of the Whale Project and the crew of *Song of the Whale*, a research ship sponsored by the International Fund for Animal Welfare. Find out more about the ship and its crew members. Students can click on an interactive map showing the Azores Islands to follow the ship's adventures in search of cetaceans (whales, dolphins, and porpoises). A Pennsylvania bioethics teacher, who joined the *Song of the Whale* in the spring of 1995, shares his onboard experiences assisting the crew with their research. Cetacean Information provides links to images of cetaceans to scale and pictures and information on various species of whales and dolphins.

769. WhaleNet

http://whale.wheelock.edu

WhaleNet is a teacher-enhancement project funded by the National Science Foundation and sponsored by Wheelock College and Simmons College, both in Boston. The purpose of WhaleNet is to enhance science education and environmental awareness using interdisciplinary learning through telecommunications. Whale watching data is collected, compared, and used for student research. For more information, educators can contact WhaleNet coordinator Michael Williamson (mwilliamson@vmsvax.simmons.edu).

770. Whales: A Thematic Unit

http://curry.edschool.Virginia.EDU/go/Whales/

Teacher resources include guides from the Sea World Education Department. These guides are appropriate for K-8. Other teacher resources include a bibliography; book reviews; a glossary; homework suggestions; and lesson plans, such as one on whale songs that helps students in grades 3–5 understand echolocation. Student activities include whale research and units of study across the curriculum (math, science, language arts, and social studies). Links are provided to helpful Internet resources such as Charlotte, the Vermont Whale, and Sea World. Kimberlye P. Joyce (kjoyce@richmond.edu) is curator of this site.

771. WhaleTimes

http://www.whaletimes.org

WhaleTimes is an ocean adventure aimed at early elementary students. Here students can find out about some of the animals that live in the sea including what they eat, how they live, and more. The WhaleTimes library has information on river dolphins, elephant seals, California sea lions, penguins, gray whales, and killer whales. A bibliography is provided.

772. Whale-Watching-Web

http://www.physics.helsinki.fi/whale/

The Whale-Watching-Web site has information on commercial whale watching as well as all aspects of whale study. A clickable world map shows whale watching areas. Areas of interest for study include categories on interspecies communication, bioacoustics, and art. There is a gallery of pictures. There is also information on oceanographic research and a cetacean encyclopedia. Links are provided to whales in literature, music, video, and film. There is a special link to whale information especially designed for children. Maintained by Rauno Lauhakangas (Rauno.Lauhakangas@helsinki.fi) at the Research Institute for High Energy Physics, University of Helsinki, Finland.

Birds

General Interest

773. Audubon's Multimedia Birds of America

http://employeeweb.myxa.com/rrb/Audubon/

The online version is a replica of the complete John James Audubon's *Birds of America* (1840–1844), and includes the full text, color plates, and figures. Each of seven volumes has its own hypertext table of contents. Family and genus are given for each wild bird native to North America, along with detailed descriptive text and a color plate. For some birds, a sound file is available, giving the bird call. As an extension of Audubon's work, the HTML version gives a list of birds that have become extinct since Audubon published *Birds of America*, and a list of birds now on the endangered list. Students can click on extinct birds to see what they looked like when Audubon was alive. There is also a list of state birds. Created and maintained by Rich Buonanno (rrb@myxa.com).

774. **The Barn Owl**

http://www.rain.org/~sals/barnowl.html

The Western Regional Office of the National Audubon Society, in cooperation with RRR, a non-profit wildlife conservation center in Simi Valley, California, and Patagonia, Inc., a corporation that supports wildlife habitat protection and restoration, has prepared a brochure on how to build barn owl nest boxes. Instructions are accompanied by illustrations. This is a great extension activity for science classes studying owls.

775. **Common Birds of the Australian National Botanic Gardens**

http://155.187.10.12/anbg/birds.html

For each of the birds that make the Australian Botanical Gardens home, there is a drawing accompanied by the bird's name and a brief description. For many birds there is an accompanying sound file of the bird's call.

776. **National Audubon Society**

http://www.audubon.org

Although most of the pages are still hatching, there is a great deal of information available here for birdwatchers. Links to bird conservation initiatives are provided, as are interesting facts. For example, coffee plantations now support more than 150 species of birds, although rapid changes in these habitats are causing many species to be added to the WatchList. Links are provided to ornithological information sources on the Web and to national campaigns.

777. **The Owl Pages**

http://www.owlpages.com

Find out more about owls around the world. Different species are represented by color pictures with accompanying information detailing the description, size, mortality, habitat, breeding, and hunting habits of each owl. Sound files allow students to hear the individual voices of owls. A map shows the distribution of species. Some categories for investigation include Australian owls, North American owls, owls of the world, physiology, reproduction, owl art, and mythology. Find out more about owls in American Indian legend and lore, as well as how other cultures view owls. For example, Zuni mothers placed an owl feather next to their babies to help them sleep; in the Sierras, native peoples believed the Great Horned Owl carried souls of the dead to the underworld. The Webmaster's address is (deane@owl.au.cd).

Penguins

778. **Pete & Barb's Penguin Pages**

http://ourworld.compuserve.com/homepages/Peter_and_Barbara_Barham/pengies.htm

Students can look at small photographs with brief descriptions of each of the 17 different species of penguins, such as the Adelie, emperor, rockhopper, and king. Categories for the investigation and study of penguins include Species Notes, Breeding Behavior, Ecological Threats,

Life Cycle, and Teaching Ideas and Activities. Where To See Penguins has information on where to go to see penguins in the wild in their natural geographical habitats as well as in captivity. A FAQs section and reading bibliography are also available. Created and maintained by Dr. Peter Barham and Barbara Barham (peter.barham@bris.ac.uk). See also Kevin C. Welch's The Penguin Page (http://www.vni.net/~kwelch/penguins/).

Frogs and Toads

779. The Froggy Page

http://frog.simplenet.com/froggy/

The Froggy Page has links to all things pertaining to frogs. Information ranges from the scientific to Kermit the Frog. There are sound files of various frogs, stories, lots of pictures, songs, and plenty of scientific information to go along with the fun. For activities, students can make an origami jumping frog or use one of Dr. Frog's recipes to make an "appetizing" meal for a frog.

780. Interactive Frog Dissection

http://teach.virginia.edu/go/frog/

Designed for high school biology students, this multimedia tutorial for the dissection of a frog might also appeal to some middle school and elementary school students. Students are shown exactly what to do, and at each step they are given the opportunity to practice. Both correct and incorrect responses are recognized. Students go through the process of preparation, skin incisions, muscle incisions, and the identification of internal organs.

781. The Whole Frog Project

http://george.lbl.gov/ITG.hm.pg.docs/Whole.Frog/Whole.Frog.html

From the Lawrence Berkeley National Laboratory at the University of California at Berkeley, the Whole Frog is an interactive resource that demonstrates the benefits of imaging and networking in science, education, and industry. The ITG Whole Frog Project is intended to introduce the concepts of modern, computer-based, 3-D visualization, and at the same time to demonstrate the power of whole-body, 3-D imaging of anatomy as a curriculum tool. High school biology classes can explore the anatomy of a whole frog using 3-D visualizations of the intact anatomical structures.

Insects

See also Bugfood! (entry 953) for insect-themed food.

782. Bee Research Center

http://gears.tucson.ars.ag.gov

The Carl Hayden Bee Research Center, located near the University of Arizona, offers information on all aspects of bees. This resource contains an Internet Classroom section that answers such questions as: "Just what are bees, anyway?" and "How do bees help make apples?"

783. Beekeeping Home Page

http://www.hive-mind.com/bee/

Find out about regular honey bees and killer bees (Africanized honey bees). This comprehensive site has everything about bees and beekeeping, including links to commercial sites. There are beekeeping FAQs, archived articles, newsletters, images, and links to other related Internet sites. Created and maintained by Jordan Schwartz (jordan@hive-mind.com).

784. B-EYE: The World Through the Eyes of Bees

http://cvs.anu.edu.au/andy/beye/beyehome.html

How do other creatures see the world? Here you can find out how honey bees see the world or at least how scientists think the world looks to bees. B-Eye is an interactive program showing what some grayscale patterns look like to bees. Created and maintained by Andrew Giger (andrew@cvs.anu.edu.au), a neuroscientist doing research on bee vision and training bees to discriminate between visual patterns.

785. The Bug Club

http://www.ex.ac.uk/bugclub/main.html

The Bug Club is for children who are interested in bugs and other creepy-crawlies. Membership is payable in British pounds, which includes the cost of mailing a newsletter from the United Kingdom. However, without becoming a member, you can still access a great deal of information from this site. Selected articles from the newsletter are posted. Care sheets for a few insects, such as praying mantises, stick insects, cockroaches, crickets, and tarantulas, are available. (The care sheet for crickets informs us that they are omnivorous and can be fed a combination of rolled oats with fresh fruit and vegetables. If not well fed, crickets will prey on one another.) There is a key pal page for people interested in bugs and a submission form to be listed as a key pal. Links are provided to The Wonderful World of Insects (http://www.insect-world.com/main/six.html). This site explores bugs in more depth by including topics like insect anatomy and the order of insects.

786. The Butterfly Web Site

http://www.butterflywebsite.com

Students will learn about butterfly gardening, farming, and ecology at this comprehensive site. The Education Center contains an annotated bibliography of butterfly and moth books for children and space for individual classes to share their butterfly-oriented projects. Information is available on how to attract butterflies to a backyard wildlife habitat and how to build butterfly houses. The picture gallery contains hundreds of clearly identified pictures of butterflies. Links are provided to online public butterfly gardens and zoos around the world. The Webmaster's address is (butterfly@mgfx.com).

787. Cockroach World

http://www.yucky.com/roaches/

Some have described this site as the "yuckiest" on the Internet. Kids will love learning about cockroaches using a multimedia format. They can click on different parts of a roach body to learn interesting facts. An interactive multiple-choice quiz tells them the correct answers and scores their responses. Activities include tips on how to catch and keep a cockroach, along with a writing journal. Students are encouraged to write and submit their own cockroach stories, which are posted for other students to read. A list of cockroach facts, a glossary, and a searchable database are all helpful additions to the seriously fun study of cockroaches on this wonderfully icky Web site.

788. The Wonderful World of Insects

http://www.insect-world.com/main/six.html

The Wonderful World of Insects has an impressive index linked to the information on this Web site. Information is available on everything from Africanized honeybees to wasps and walking sticks. This site contains some very interesting insect facts sure to please students: the biggest, the smallest, the most numbers in a species, the fastest flyer, the most tolerant of cold, the smallest eggs, and the most tolerant of drying out (desiccation). There are links to basic anatomy, a glossary, classification, and evolution. Information is given on how to keep some insects, such as crickets, praying mantises, and cockroaches. Links are also provided to other insect-related sites on the Internet.

Snakes and Reptiles

See also "Snakebites" (entries 1004–1006).

789. Crocodilians

http://crocodilian.com

Students can find out detailed information about all 23 crocodilian species, including both alligators and crocodiles. Information is available on breeding, behavior, and communication sounds (distress calls, threatening adult hisses, and courtship bellows), and there are pictures and distribution maps. A list of links is provided to crocodilian information resources on the Internet covering conservation, management, bibliographies, scientific research, and commercial use. Created and maintained by Dr. Adam Britton (crocodilian@ibm.net), a professional zoologist currently working with Wildlife Management International. This site is more scientific than The Gator Hole listed below (entry 790).

790. The Gator Hole

http://www.magicnet.net/~mgodwin/

Students can find out interesting facts about the American alligator and look at photographs of nests and hatchlings. Pictures reveal the difference between an alligator's snout and a crocodile's snout. Information is given on alligator farming in Florida. Links are provided to both alligator and crocodile resources on the Web. Created and maintained by Floridian Mike Godwin (mgodwin@magicnet.net). Another good American alligator site is (http://www.geocities.com/Heartland/5960/alligator.html).

791. Jason's Snakes and Reptiles

http://www.snakesandreptiles.com/index.html

Jason's collection of herpetological Web sites includes links to boas, pythons, chameleons, turtles, crocodiles, iguanas, geckos, frogs, and more. Created and maintained by Jason Shade (jason.shade@snakesandreptiles.com).

Spiders

792. Arachnida, Spiders of NW-Europe

http://www.xs4all.nl/~ednieuw/Spiders/spidhome.htm

House spiders and web spiders are divided into two groups, the hunters and the catchers. Catchers spin webs and wait to catch their prey in the sticky threads. Hunters actively seek out and hunt for their prey. More than 100 color photographs of spiders commonly found in Northwestern Europe, along with explanatory text, allow students to study the anatomy of spiders, including their spinnerets and fangs; web construction; and use of silk strands. Interesting spider facts are available, as is information on habitats and spider sizes.

793. Spider Homepage

http://www.powerup.com.au/~glen/spiders1a.htm

Incy Wincy spider went up the water spout, and the children in Year 5A at Rochedale State School in Australia have written a great Web site filled with interesting facts and information about black widow spiders, orb weavers, wolf spiders, and more. Find out about the anatomy of a spider, their habitats and prey, and what to do if a spider bites you. Student work includes examples of poems, stories, letters, and art. Links are provided to other spider resources on the Internet. Glenda Crew (glen@powerup.com.au) is the Web editor.

794. Tarantulas

http://www.nationalgeographic.com/features/97/tarantulas/intro1.html

Find out about the life cycle and anatomy of tarantulas. Look at colorful images of some of the numerous species, estimated at 800 to 900. Other interesting facts are presented about mating, the young, and molting. Interesting pictures and text explain how tarantulas hunt and kill their prey. Tarantulas have few natural enemies, and students can find out more about these daring predators. To learn about the tarantula's anatomy, students can click on a diagram for more information on each labeled part. Those with computer capability for QuickTime can download a video of a tarantula and compare it to the diagram. This excellent site devoted to tarantulas is sponsored by National Geographic.

Worms

795. Worm World

http://www.yucky.com/worm/

Learn the worm's inside story. Meet different kinds of worms, such as Eddie the Earthworm, Bearded Bobby Worm, Larry Leech, Paulette Planaria, and Tommi Tapeworm. Students can see a worm's five hearts beating, look at a labeled diagram, and learn how worms and the rest of the decomposition team chew up food and other organic waste. Worm pictures, jokes, poetry, and stories are also available on this Web site. Submission of student work is encouraged.

Here's just one amazing fact: The Australian Gippsland earthworm grows to 12 feet long and can weigh 1-1/2 pounds.

Botany

See "Horticulture" (entries 984–987).

Discussion Groups for Biology

796. **Discussion for Biology Curriculum Innovation Study**

E-mail: **listserv@sivm.si.edu**
Instructions: On the first line of the body of the message, type:
subscribe BIOCIS-L [your first name and last name]

797. **Secondary Biology Teacher Enhancement PI Discussion Group**

E-mail: **listserv@ksuvm.ksu.edu**
Instructions: On the first line of the body of the message, type:
subscribe BIOPI-L [your first name and last name]

Chemistry

See also DNA Graphics (entry 736) and DNA From The Beginning (entry 735).

General Interest

798. **Chem4Kids**

http://www.chem4kids.com

Explores five topics related to chemistry, including matter, elements, atoms, math, and reactions. Chemistry quizzes are available to test your knowledge after reviewing the online information.

799. **ChemEd: Chemistry Education Resources**

http://www-hpcc.astro.washington.edu/scied/chemistry.html

Some of the categories on this page include software, educational organizations, the history of chemistry, a science reference desk, chemical safety, and other chemistry links. ChemEd is a link from the SciEd Home Page (http://www-hpcc.astro.washington.edu/scied/science.html), which has links to many science disciplines.

800. **Chemist's Art Gallery**

http://www.csc.fi/lul/chem/graphics.html

Chemist's Art Gallery contains visualizations and animations in chemistry from around the world. Some images are taken with electron microscopes. Movies and animation show rotations and reactions, creating multimedia learning in some areas of chemistry.

801.   **ChemViz**

http://www.ncsa.uiuc.edu/Edu/ChemViz/index.html

The ChemViz group at the National Center for Supercomputing Applications (NCSA) has developed computing and communication tools so that high school teachers and their students can do their own research by visualizing atomic and molecular orbitals using computational methods. Software, documentation, and classroom materials are available. There are also examples of ChemViz images. The Curriculum Materials section provides lesson plans that ChemViz teachers have used successfully in their classrooms. Each teacher will need an NCSA account, which is free. Questions or comments should be directed to (chemvizhelp@ncsa.uiuc.edu).

802.   **MathMol: Mathematics and Molecules K-12**

http://www.nyu.edu/pages/mathmol/

The purpose of MathMol is to provide the K-12 educational community with information and materials dealing with the rapidly growing fields of molecular modeling and 3-D visualization. In the K-12 Activities section, a water module allows middle and high school students to calculate the density of water and ice online. Students can review concepts in mass, volume, and density; view the structure of the Photosynthetic Reaction Center; and more.

803.   **The Mole Hole**

http://www.chemmybear.com

Provides a collection of resources helpful for chemistry high school teachers, including information about AP Chemistry. Chemistry study cards can be downloaded using Adobe Acrobat Reader. Written and maintained by Paul Groves (Pgroves@aol.com), chemistry teacher at South Pasadena High School, South Pasadena, California.

804.   **The pH Factor**

http://falcon.miamisci.org/ph/

The pH Factor is an interactive resource to help elementary and middle school teachers introduce acids and bases to their students. Information is organized around the six Es: Excite, Explore, Explain, Extend, Exchange, and Examine. For each E there are lesson plans and an interactive activity sheet that can be used by individual students or groups. Excite tries to stimulate the learner's curiosity through activities such as tongue tasting, secret messages, and magic liquids. Sponsored by the Miami Museum of Science (Miami, Florida), the Webmaster's address is (webmaster@miamisci.org).

The Periodic Table of Elements

805.   **The Periodic Table of Elements**

http://pearl1.lanl.gov/periodic/

The Web site presents a colorful table of elements. For each of the elements, a hyperlink provides extensive information. For example, the symbol Mg is linked to a page with the following information: the element's name (magnesium), the atomic number, atomic symbol, atomic weight, and electron configuration. Additional information on the same page includes: Magnesium's History, Sources, Properties, Uses, Compounds, and Handling. To help create a visual link for students, an image of a bicycle appears next to the name Magnesium with the text: Used in bicycles. For calcium, there is a picture of the Statue of Liberty with the text: For cement and plaster of paris. The CRC Handbook of Chemistry and Physics and the American Chemical Society are cited as references.

806. The Periodic Table of Elements for K–12
http://www.chemicalelements.com

Each element is linked to a list of basic information and a colorful diagram of the atomic structure suitable for projecting in class. Students can choose to list elements by atomic number, element name, chemical symbol, or date of discovery. This site was created by Yinon Bentor (webmaster@chemicalelements.com) as a science fair project in 1996, while she was an eighth-grade student at Rawlinson Road Middle School in Rock Hill, South Carolina; it is now an ongoing project. Yinon is currently a high school student in Boone, North Carolina.

807. Web Elements
http://www.webelements.com

For each element, there is a pronunciation sound file. All elements have key data, description, historical information, and use. In addition, each element can also be researched according to its chemical, crystallographic, physical, nuclear, electronic, biological, and geological properties. Created and maintained by Dr. Mark Winter (webelements@sheffield.ac.uk) of the Chemistry Department, University of Sheffield, England.

Earth Science

See also Athena: Earth and Space Science for K–12 (entry 673); Natural History Museum (London) (entry 659); Quest: Internet in the Classroom (entry 650); and "Environmental Sciences and Ecology" (entries 860–866).

General Interest

808. Amber: Window to the Past
http://www.amnh.org/exhibitions/amber/

Amber is the hardened resin of coniferous and angiospermous trees. As resin oozes from cuts in these trees, unsuspecting insects are sometimes trapped much like they are in flypaper. Amber has preserved ancient life in such detail that scientists are able to capture fragments of DNA from organisms entrapped in it. This online exhibition from the American Museum of Natural History provides a look at some different varieties of amber and how amber is used as art. Students can click on 10 pieces of amber to find out what is locked inside and what clues it provides about ecosystems from the prehistoric past. *See also* Amber, a View of the Past (http://academy.d20.co.edu/kadets/lundberg/amber.html); Amber Inclusions (http://alg.zfn.uni-bremen.de/~il8m/amber.html) for 24 images of inclusions that can be viewed using stereoscope Java applets; and Organic Fly Paper from the Why Files (http://whyfiles.news.wisc.edu/008amber/index.html), featuring a quiz and reading list. The Smithsonian Institute also has a nice collection of four inclusions, including a spider, termite, feather, and tree leaf and flower (http://www.150.si.edu/150trav/discover/fossil.htm).

809.   **The Earth Science Learning Web**

http://www.usgs.gov/education/

The U.S. Geological Survey Web site has created the Learning Web to foster the study of earth science in K-12 classrooms. It is a pathfinder for Earth Science educational information. Lesson plans, teaching activities, and links to appropriate sites have been chosen to enrich and enhance the study of subjects such as volcanoes, tree rings to determine past climates, plate tectonics, acid rain, and radon gas.

Geology

810.   **Neill's Geology for Kids!**

http://www.geocities.com/Athens/Parthenon/8991/

Describes geology as a huge area of science that encompasses the history of earth, especially the history of rocks. Students can learn more about gemology and what gemologists do; glaciology and what glaciologists do; marine geology and what marine geologists do; paleontology and what paleontologists do; seismology and what seismologists do; and volcanology, including what volcanologists do. Created and maintained by Ciara Neill (cneill@hotmail.com).

811.   **U.S. Geological Survey Home Page**

http://www.usgs.gov

The U.S. Geological Survey (USGS) was established, by an act of Congress in 1879, as an agency of the Department of the Interior. The USGS is a scientific fact-finding and research organization. It is the principal source of scientific and technical expertise in the earth sciences within the federal government. Links are provided to environmental research, publications, geographic information systems and databases, USGS Fact Sheets, and What's New.

Caves

812.   **United States Show Caves Directory**

http://www.goodearthgraphics.com/showcave.html

Looking for a complete guide to U.S. caves that are open to the public? This directory lists the locations, operating hours, and telephone numbers for all caves in the continental United States. Look for maps, photographs, and links to related Web sites.

813.   **The Virtual Cave**

http://www.goodearthgraphics.com/virtcave.html

Some of the features from caves around the world have been collected to make this virtual cave experience memorable. A click of the mouse starts the tour through stunning images, some with accompanying sound files. While virtually underground, explore more than 30 different cave phenomena, such as canopies, bathtubs, columns, draperies, flowers, pearls, stalactites, stalagmites, and soda straws. Djuna Bewley (djuna@earthsci.ucsc.edu) is the Webmaster.

Earthquakes

814.   *Earthquake ABC*

http://www-socal.wr.usgs.gov/ABC/index.html

Earthquake ABC: A Child's View of Earthquake Facts and Feelings by Dr. Lucy Jones, USGS, was published by Sirius Productions in 1994, and was written to help second- and third-graders understand earthquakes. Children's artwork accompanies each of the 26 facts and feelings. Students investigate such earthquake-related terms as *aftershock*, *earth's crust*, and *epicenter*. This online version of *Earthquake ABC* includes an introduction, a parents' guide, and a guide for teachers. Paperback copies of the book can be ordered from Sirius Productions. Royalties benefit the San Rafael Elementary School in Pasadena, California.

815.   Earthquake Engineering Center

http://www.eerc.berkeley.edu

The University of California at Berkeley Earthquake Engineering Research Center provides links to information services related to earthquake engineering, earthquake hazard mitigation, earthquake disaster response, and related disciplines. This server provides information about recent earthquakes as well as past earthquake disasters. The Loma Prieta Data Archive is a rich resource on the earthquake that rocked the greater San Francisco Bay area in 1989, and the Kobe Earthquake Archive is devoted to information on the earthquake that struck Kobe, Japan, on January 17, 1995. Links are given to other earthquake centers and research centers on the Internet.

816.   National Earthquake Information Center

http://earthquake.usgs.gov

On the National Earthquake Information Center (NEIC) WWW server located in Golden, Colorado, students can find current earthquake information, general earthquake information, and seismograph station codes and coordinates. They can search the earthquake database or report an earthquake. Links are also provided to other earthquake lists, the Albuquerque Seismological Laboratory Home Page, and other earthquake information sites. The National Earthquake Information Center is a part of the Department of the Interior, U.S. Geological Survey, and the NEIC Web site is maintained by Madeleine Zirbes (zirbes@usgs.gov).

817.   Surfing the Internet for Earthquake Data

http://www.geophys.washington.edu/seismosurfing.html

Seismic information located on the Internet is compiled on this Web site. The SeismoSurfing index contains selected current news about earthquakes and the science of seismology. This home page is maintained by Steve Malone (steve@geophys.washington.edu).

Plate Tectonics

818.   Global Earth History

http://vishnu.glg.nau.edu/rcb/globaltext.html

Provides a series of plate-tectonic reconstructions to show the patterns of Phanerozoic Earth history. The presentation consists of 14 paleogeographic maps with global, North America, and Europe reconstructions; 21 maps that show the sedimentologic, tectonic, and paleogeographic evolution of the North Atlantic region; and 28 maps that display the major tectonic elements such as plates, oceans, ridges, subduction zones, and mountain belts through time. Information can also be accessed through a time period such as the present, Triassic, Jurassic, and Cambrian. These time slices show the movement of the supercontinent Rodinia, the formation of Pangaea from the collision of Rodinia and Laurasia, and the movement and breakup of Pangaea. Created and maintained by Ron Blakey (ronald.blakey@nau.edu), professor of geology, Northern Arizona University, Flagstaff, Arizona.

819. Plate Tectonics
http://www.ucmp.berkeley.edu/geology/tectonics.html

From the Museum of Paleontology of the University of California at Berkeley and the Regents of the University of California, information is provided on the history and the theories of plate tectonics. This exhibit, with animation and QuickTime files, shows simulated movement of the Earth's continents over millions of years from prehistoric times. Links are provided to other Web sites focused on the modern theory of plate tectonics, including a lesson from Volcano World (entry 830) and the PLATES Project from the Institute for Geophysics at the University of Texas at Austin. Additional links are provided to a geological timeline; glossary; and a taxa section, including bacteria, viruses, fungi, plants, animals, and vertebrates, from the University of California's Museum of Paleontology (entry 836).

Rocks, Gems, and Minerals

820. A Gem of a Story Online
http://www.bsu.edu/teachers/academy/gems/index.html

A Gem of a Story provides a virtual field trip to the Janet Annenberg Hooker Hall of Geology, Gems, and Minerals at the Smithsonian National Museum of Natural History in Washington, D.C. Though designed to supplement a fee-based electronic field trip broadcast, this site serves as a self-contained Web-based guide for the study of terrestrial gems, crystals, and minerals. Provides close-up views of individual gems and minerals in the archives, activities, resources, and a virtual tour through the Smithsonian exhibits.

See also the Smithsonian Gem and Mineral Collection (http://galaxy.einet.net/images/gems/gems-icons.html) for color graphics of gems and minerals. Each graphic is identified with a brief description. Thumbnail images can be enlarged. In addition to uncut and unset gems and minerals, there are also pictures of the Hope diamond, a dragon vase carved from rare lavender jade, and Marie Antoinette's earrings. A complementary set of lesson plans, titled "Minerals, Crystals, and Gems: Stepping-Stones to Inquiry," was published in the December 1998 issue of *Smithsonian in Your Classroom* (http://educate.si.edu/resources/lessons/siyc/gems/start.html). Lesson plans are aligned to standards. *Smithsonian in Your Classroom* is published four times annually; subscriptions are free (http://educate.si.edu/about/contact.html).

821. Mineral Gallery and Gemstone Gallery
http://www.theimage.com

The Mineral Gallery has more than 125 high-quality photographs of more than 70 different mineral varieties. For each mineral there is an image, its chemical makeup, color, hardness, crystal composition, and more. For example, the mineral pyrite is described as being pale-yellow metallic with a greenish/brownish black streak. It is found in Spain; Portugal; Italy; and Wyoming and New York, United States. A note informs students, "soluble in nitric acid, known as 'fools gold,' the name 'Pyrite' means 'firestone' in Greek. The name firestone came from the common belief that pyrite held fire (inside) and was used by ancients as a sparking source."

The Gemstone Gallery has more than 150 photographs of more than 20 gem minerals in different colors and variations. Complete information is given for each gem. Students can find out interesting facts, such as that the majority of garnets are used in the manufacture of sandpaper. This site was created and is maintained by Ron Gibbs (theImage1@aol.com).

822. Rock Hound

http://www.fi.edu/fellows/payton/rocks/

Follow Rocky, the rock hound, in discovering some of earth's treasures by examining rocks online. First read about rock collecting safety, and then learn how sedimentary, metamorphic, and igneous rocks are formed. Online interactive quizzes and puzzles test your knowledge. The teacher resource area contains lesson plans, literature tie-ins, activities, and collaboration ideas. This Web site was submitted by Tammy Payton of Loogootee Elementary School West (Loogootee, Indiana), one of nine Online Fellows at the Franklin Institute Science Museum, as part of the Wired@School project. To find lessons appropriate for K-8 by other Online Fellows, see (http://www.fi.edu/qa98/wiredindex.html).

823. Rockhounds Information Page

http://www.rahul.net/infodyn/rockhounds/rockhounds.html

Established and supported by the members of the Rockhounds discussion group, this is a comprehensive Web page with links to rocks, gems, and minerals. Other categories of links include general earth science information; paleontology-related sites; collecting sites and trips; earth-science-related groups, clubs, and societies; software; and personal home pages of collectors.

Rockhounds Discussion List

E-mail: **rockhounds-request@infodyn.com**
Instructions: On the first line of the body of the message, type:
subscribe rockhounds [your e-mail address]

Submarine Geology

See also Ocean Planet Home Page (entry 660) and "Deep-Sea Ecology" (entries 764–765).

824. Black Smokers

http://www.amnhonline.org/expeditions/blacksmokers/home.html

The Black Smoker Expedition Web site chronicles the adventures of scientists, engineers, and educators who extracted black smoker sulfide chimneys from the ocean floor as a project of the American Museum of Natural History. Three of the chimneys are on view at the museum to-day. Features photographs, graphics, interpretive text, underwater film footage, and a 3-D model of the section of the midocean ridge where the black smokers were harvested.

825. Dive and Discover
http://science.whoi.edu/DiveDiscover/

Provides details about a series of planned diving trips to the midocean ridge, thousands of meters deep, to explore underwater volcanoes, black smokers, and the amazing animals that live in hydrothermal vent communities. The first expedition traveled to the Gulf of California, to the Guaymas Basin, where the seafloor is spreading apart and creating large fractures. The second expedition explored the East Pacific Rise, where the Earth's crust is constantly being created. Maps, images, and photographs are accompanied by explanatory text. Concepts such as plate tectonics, geophysics, midocean ridges, hydrothermal vents, and vent biology are ex-plained. Dive and Discover is a joint project by the Woods Hole Oceanographic Institution and the National Science Foundation.

826. "Getting to the Bottom"
http://www.scientificamerican.com/explorations/1998/062998atlantis/index.html

Find out how the research ship *Atlantis* and her companion submersible *Alvin* explore the mi-docean ridges, using this article from *Scientific American* (June 29, 1998). Provides maps and diagrams of ridges and vents. Links are provided to the real-time whereabouts of the dynamic duo, *Alvin* and *Atlantis*. *Alvin*, one of only six submersibles in the world capable of diving more than 4,000 meters, can accommodate a pilot and two passengers, and has ferried more than 10,000 people to the ocean floor since 1963. *Atlantis* was launched in 1997, and features state-of-the-art laboratories, computer labs, and a special heavy-duty A-frame for launching and retrieving *Alvin*. For more information about *Alvin*, see (http://www.marine.whoi.edu/ships/alvin/alvin.htm). For more information about *Atlantis*, see (http://www.marine.whoi.edu/ships/atlantis/atlantis.htm).

827. The Oceans Chimneys—Hydrothermal Vents
http://tiger.chm.bris.ac.uk/cm1/AlexandraG/Welcome.htm

Explains hydrothermal vents—what they are, where they are found, how they work, and why they are important. Provides a diagram and color pictures to illustrate the nature of hydrother-mal vents. Written by Alexandra Louise Gulliver, School of Chemistry, University of Bristol, Bristol, England. Webmaster is Professor John Maher (john.maher@bristol.ac.uk).

828. REVEL Project
http://www.ocean.washington.edu/outreach/revel/

REVEL (Research and Education: Volcanoes, Exploration and Life) promotes interaction be-tween science teachers and scientists working on cutting-edge research. REVEL explores the relationship between different types of volcanoes and life, as well as encompassing scientific problems ranging from the origin of life to new aspects of biotechnology. There are detailed descriptions of two separate expeditions to the ocean floor, conducted in 1999 with deep-submergence vehicles, by people from numerous institutions and countries working together. Links to additional resources are available.

829. RIDGE Program Homepage

http://ridge.oce.orst.edu

Midocean ridges are plate boundaries along which new volcanic material is continually being added to the Earth's surface. RIDGE (**R**idge **I**nter-**D**isciplinary **G**lobal **E**xperiments) is a National Science Foundation initiative that promotes and fosters interdisciplinary scientific study, communication, and outreach related to all aspects of this globe-encircling, midocean ridge system. RIDGE scientists explore the volcanology and geology of the ocean's crust; the chemistry and biology associated with hydrothermal vents; the physics and chemistry of the resulting hydrothermal plumes and surrounding waters; and the unique, complex ecosystems sustained by this hydrothermal activity. Links to related resources on the Web are listed for nonscientists.

Volcanoes

830. Volcano World

http://volcano.und.nodak.edu

Rocky welcomes students to Volcano World, a K-12 volcano site supported by NASA. Some topics for exploration include: currently erupting volcanoes; volcano images and information; volcanic parks and monuments; volcanoes of other worlds (planetary volcanoes); and how to become a volcanologist.

Students can e-mail questions directly from this page to volcanologists, who answer questions within 24 hours. Students can also access a bulletin board archive to read previously asked questions and their answers. Lesson plans about volcanoes involve collaborative problem-solving and interdisciplinary studies (e.g., science, social studies, language arts). Goals, objectives, summaries, materials needed, and instructional sequencing are provided.

The color graphics of current and recent eruptions and other images of volcanoes, along with informational text, help students understand volcanoes as complicated phenomena that necessitate the understanding of a number of sciences, especially geology.

Paleontology

See also "Prehistoric Humans"(entries 1240–1243).

Mesozoic Era (Triassic, Jurassic, and Cretaceous Periods)

See also Amber: A View of the Past (entry 808).

Dinosaurs

831. Dino-Mania: Read, Write Now—Dinosaurs

http://www.marshall-es.marshall.k12.tn.us/jobe/Read-Write/dinosaur/maindino.html

Learning activities for primary language arts abound in this Web unit planned on the topic of dinosaurs. Look for fiction and nonfiction Web-based book activities, crossword puzzles, Dino-dots, Dino-word searches, and Dino-hidden messages. Student work is posted in the Dino-mite writing center, and the Teacher Page contains suggested activities, bibliographies, online resources, and related links. Created and maintained by Hazel Jobe (jobeh@ten-nash. ten.k12.tn.us), first- and second-grade Title 1 reading and language arts teacher at Marshall Elementary School in Lewisburg, Tennessee, and a Franklin Institute Science Museum Online Fellow. See also Jobe's homepage for other teaching ideas (http://www.marshall-es.marshall. k12.tn.us/jobe/index.html).

832. Dino Russ's Lair

http://www.isgs.uiuc.edu/isgsroot/dinos/
or
http://www.isgs.uiuc.edu/dinos/dinos_home.html

Geoscientist Russ Jacobson is the Webmaster for this page. His purpose is to promote an awareness of the importance of geoscience, particularly in the field of paleontology. Through the Educational Extension program at the Illinois State Geological Survey, Jacobson provides links to all known public geoscience servers and selected dinosaur and paleontological materials. Requests for volunteer help with summertime dinosaur digs are posted. Families and teachers are especially welcome to volunteer. Some of the information available is a 3.6 MB Macintosh HyperCard file on dinosaurs developed by Jim Reynolds; this requires Stuffit Expander and HyperCard Player.

833. Dinosaur Eggs

http://www.nationalgeographic.com/features/96/dinoeggs/
or
http://www.nationalgeographic.com/dinoeggs/

Dinosaur Eggs is a teaching guide that takes students behind the scenes *of National Geographic* magazine's May 1996 article "The Great Dinosaur Egg Hunt" to show how fossil researchers "hatched" fossilized dinosaur eggs to reveal the embryos inside. The Museum area has more information about dinosaur babies and parents.

834. The Dinosauria: Truth Is Stranger than Fiction

http://www.ucmp.berkeley.edu/diapsids/dinosaur.html

In an attempt to dispel some of the myths about dinosaurs, this Web site allows students to compare the rumors from the media with facts and current research on topics such as how fast dinosaurs could run, whether they were warm-blooded, why they became extinct, and whether they are related to birds or reptiles or both. Information about some of the more popularly known dinosaurs is available. Students can actually see pictures of dinosaur fossils, and a glossary of terms is provided. Links are available to information about dinosaur digs in the United States.

835. Hadrosaurus *foulkii:* The First Dinosaur Discovery

http://www.levins.com/dinosaur.html

William Parker Foulke discovered the first complete dinosaur skeleton in Haddonfield, New Jersey, in 1858, establishing the first real proof of the existence of dinosaurs. This Web site contains pictures of the 30-foot-deep ravine, a former marl pit, where Hadrosaurus *foulkii* was discovered, as well as the history leading up to and the meaning of this archaeological find. Links are provided to related sites, including the Philadelphia Academy of Natural Sciences, where Hadrosaurus *foulkii* is on display today. Site created and maintained by Hoag Levins (hoag@levins.com).

836. The Museum of Paleontology

http://www.ucmp.berkeley.edu

The Museum of Paleontology at the University of California at Berkeley is the fourth largest in the United States. The museum conserves paleontological materials and supports research and instruction. In the online exhibits area, Paleontology Without Walls, students find out that paleontology is more than the study of fossils. Students can explore the exhibits from three points of view: phylogeny, geological time, and evolutionary thought. One of the links from the Mesozoic Era is to The Dinosauria: Truth Is Stranger than Fiction (entry 834).

Cenozoic Era (Quaternary Period)

The Ice Age

837. The Mammoth Saga

http://www.nrm.se/virtexhi/mammsaga/welcome.html.en

The Mammoth Saga is a virtual exhibition of mammoths, wooly rhinoceroses, reindeer, saber-toothed cats, and plants of the Ice Age, based on an earlier exhibition held at the Swedish Museum of Natural History in Stockholm, Sweden. Through pictures and text, students can discover more about the major climatic cycles that were particularly intense during the Pleistocene Epoch when continental ice sheets shifted, spreading from the poles to cover as much as one-third of the Earth's surface (as compared to one-tenth today), and then retreating.

838. Midwest U.S. 16,000 Years Ago

http://www.museum.state.il.us/exhibits/larson/larson_top.html

Sponsored by the Illinois State Museum, *Midwest U.S. 16,000 Years Ago* is an excellent, fact-filled online exhibition with accompanying photographs, images, drawings, maps, and animated maps focusing on the landscape, plants, and animals of the late Pleistocene Epoch, specifically in Illinois and the American Midwest. Students are invited to make scientific observations from online pictures and text. Evidence of the Ice Age in Illinois is established by examining the thickness of loess deposits, which are more extensive in areas bordering large, continental glaciers. Drawings and photographs of archaeological finds bring to life many different animals, such as mastodons, peccaries, and musk oxen. At the end of the late Pleistocene Epoch, a variety of animals became extinct across North America. These were mostly mammals larger than 100 pounds, such as saber-toothed cats, mammoths, and mastodons. Although medium to large mammals also became extinct on other continents during this period approximately 11,000 years ago, the most severe extinction occurred on the North American continent. Students are asked to consider the possible causes for this extinction: environmental causes due to climate change and human hunting and overkill. The Webmaster is Project Director, Rickard S. Toomey, III (toomey@museum.state.il.us).

Virtual Field Trips and Online Projects

Annual Scientific Expeditions

839.   **The JASON Project**

http://www.jasonproject.org

The JASON Project was founded in 1989 by Dr. Robert D. Ballard. Each year a two-week scientific expedition is mounted in a remote part of the world and broadcast in real time, using technology to network around the world. This annual scientific expedition is the focus of original curriculum developed for grades 4–8. The JASON Project emphasizes an advanced approach to teaching and learning in which teachers are facilitators in the learning process. Information is provided to help teachers incorporate projects into the curriculum.

Information on current and past projects is available. In 1997, Jason VIII: Journey from the Center of the Earth explored Iceland and Yellowstone, studying two of the Earth's unique geological locations. Some past JASON Project expeditions have included the Florida Keys to study coral reefs, sharks, and the behavior of crocodiles; the Big Island of Hawaii to observe the largest surface lava flow and to look for other volcanic activity in the solar system using NASA's infrared telescope; and Central America to study the health of our planet by looking at the canopy of a rain forest and a barrier reef.

Antarctica and the South Pole

840.   **Antarctica: A Resource for Teachers and Students**

http://www.anta.canterbury.ac.nz/Subfolder/education/resource/homepage/homepage
.htm

The International Centre for Antarctic Information and Research (ICAIR), in association with Antarctica New Zealand, provides an educational Web resource page. Content covers many topics related to the Antarctic, including the ice-and-rock composition of the continent; how plants, penguins, seals, whales, and invertebrates survive the cold; tourism in Antarctica; living and working in Antarctica; a history of the Ross Dependency; and an overview of the New Zealand science program in Antarctica. There are three student self-study units on diseases in Antarctic fish, Antarctic weather, and the ozone issue. A glossary and bibliography are helpful. The address for the home page to this Web site, Gateway Antarctica, is (http://www. anta.canterbury.ac.nz/). Site maintained by Paul Bealing (p.bealing@anta.canterbury.ac.nz).

841.   **Live from Antarctica**

http://quest.arc.nasa.gov/antarctica/
and
Live from Antarctica 2
http://quest.arc.nasa.gov/antarctica2/index.html

Live from Antarctica is now available on videotape, and resources for studying what life is like in the coldest place on the planet are located on these two Web sites. Some of the topics include information on the hole in the ozone layer above Antarctica, a bibliography of resources, a field journal by scientists, and links to other sites. There are teachers' guides, classroom activities, and additional National Science Foundation resources relating to Antarctica and this project. Live from Antarctica 2 was an active project from January to March 1997, and Live from Antarctica was active December 1994 to January 1995.

842. South Pole Virtual Tour

http://astro.uchicago.edu/cara/vtour/pole/

Students can take a virtual tour of the Amundsen-Scott South Pole Research Station. Look for a brief history; images of the Ceremonial Pole, the South Pole Station, and McMurdo; and a lot of cold facts.

843. Virtual Antarctica

http://www.terraquest.com/antarctica/

TerraQuest, which made a voyage to Antarctica in December 1995, was the first commercial travel expedition to make live uplinks to the Internet from Antarctica. Enter this Web site to experience a virtual expedition. Great graphics! Some topics include history, science, ecology, and the expedition. In the Guide section, there is an Antarctica glossary, a checklist of birds and animals, a reading list, and links to other Web sites on Antarctica.

The Arctic and the North Pole

See also Arctic Circle (entry 1287).

844. Animals of the Arctic

http://tqjunior.advanced.org/3500/

The Arctic has many animals that are unique to the North. Students will learn more about 12 of these animals, look at pictures, and read stories, including a true story about a walrus hunt told by a Cup'ik. The arctic animals highlighted on this site include Dall sheep, the arctic fox, caribou, collared lemmings, arctic terns, narwhals, polar bears, snowy owls, walruses, wolverines, and arctic hares. Hands-on activities for students include making scrimshaw and blubber mittens, using soap for animal carvings, examining owl pellets, and conducting experiments to investigate arctic adaptations in animals. Lots of information is available in the Resources section. This site was created as a ThinkQuest Jr. project.

Galápagos

845. Virtual Galápagos

http://www.terraquest.com/galapagos/index.html

Virtual Galápagos was a virtual field trip for students during May 1996. Relive the adventure by visiting this site. Interactive maps let students travel down the Rio Aquarico, through the Avenue of the Volcanoes, to the islands on the Galápagos itinerary with David Brower and a ship filled with adventurers and scientists. Sections on the history of the islands, the issues, and the wildlife are well presented. The Education Workbook provides excellent educational resources and classroom activities.

Weather

General Weather Resources

846. The Daily Planet

http://www.atmos.uiuc.edu

The Department of Atmospheric Sciences at the University of Illinois maintains this Web site. Information includes current weather data, pointers to climate data, hypermedia instructional modules, and links to other resources. Some of the teaching modules include a thematic unit on weather for grades 2–4 and a unit on forces and winds. Of interest is a slide series titled A Look at Thunderstorms and Their Severe Weather Potential.

847. Florida EXPLORES!

http://www.met.fsu.edu/explores/explores.html

Since its beginnings in 1992, Florida EXPLORES! has been an ongoing yearly precollege outreach program designed to bring weather satellite imagery into K-12 classrooms. EXPLORES! is an acronym for **EXP**loring and **L**earning the **O**perations and **R**esources of **E**nvironmental **S**atellites! The EXPLORES! program seeks to integrate the National Oceanic and Atmospheric Administration (NOAA) direct-readout satellite data into Florida's elementary, middle, and high school classrooms. At the time of publication of this book, there were more than 158 satellite ground stations in Florida schools. From Florida State University (Tallahassee) meteorology faculty, teachers learn the how-tos of content acquisition of satellite-derived meteorological data, as well as the data's application to earth, environmental, and space science. The EXPLORES! site is rich in meteorological information. The Teacher's Guide area has links to helpful classroom information. The Satellite Resource Guide provides a historical summary of each weather satellite launched by the United States, both polar orbiting satellites and geostationary satellites. For more information, contact Webmaster Steven Graham (graham@met.fsu.edu), who is with the Florida State University Department of Meteorology.

848. Unisys Weather

http://weather.unisys.com

The Unisys Weather site provides a complete source of graphical weather information. Images are generated using Weather Processor (WXP), a special weather visualization software tool. Weather information from the National Weather Service via the NOAAPORT satellite data service is presented using comprehensive color graphics that visually display meteorological data and satellite images. WXP allows users to visualize near-real-time and archived meteorological data. An interactive North America weather map displays the current satellite image and surface map (background is elevation relief) and allows students to click anywhere on the map to get local data and forecast. Data is also available as an enhanced infrared satellite image, a four-panel ETA surface forecast, a MRF nine-panel forecast plot, and a composite satellite surface map. The Webmaster for this site is Dan Vietor (devo@ks.unisys.com).

849. The Weather Channel

http://www.weather.com/homepage.html

Up-to-date weather information is available for all U.S. states and major cities, as well as most countries and major cities around the world. Weather maps and satellite images help students visualize the weather. A glossary is helpful for students who want to understand meteorology terms, such as Kelvin, Celsius, and Fahrenheit. The safety section addresses the importance of preparedness and having an emergency plan. This section also provides safety tips for extreme heat, floods, hurricanes, lightning, and tornadoes.

850. Weather Here and There

http://www.ncsa.uiuc.edu/Edu/RSE/RSEred/WeatherHome.html

Weather Here and There is an integrated weather unit incorporating interaction with the Internet along with hands-on, collaborative problem-solving activities for students in grades 4–6. The unit is divided into six lessons. Math, science, geography, and language arts are integrated into the process of learning about weather phenomena. This project was designed by Brenda Foster (Dr. Howard Elementary School), Evelyn Walton (Wiley Elementary School), and Deborah S. H. Foertsch (Carrie Busey Elementary School).

851. The Weather Underground

http://groundhog.sprl.umich.edu

The University of Michigan Weather Underground Web site makes weather information available to K-12 teachers and students. Weather imagery, current conditions and forecasts, and curriculum activities are available. A searchable, frequently updated weather database allows students to search for weather anywhere in the United States by city, township, state, zip code, or airport. SkyMath, a project using atmospheric data as an aid in learning mathematics concepts, and Shocking Blue-Skies are a new generation of talking weather maps. For Blue-Skies software, *see* entry 859.

Severe Weather

Hurricanes

852. Hurricane Hunters Home Page

http://www.hurricanehunters.com

The 53rd Weather Reconnaissance Squadron, known as the Hurricane Hunters of the Air Force Reserve, is one of a kind, the only Department of Defense organization flying into tropical storms and hurricanes on a routine basis. Students can take a cyberflight into the eye of a hurricane with the crew of one of the 10 Lockheed WC-130 aircraft. A FAQs section addresses questions about hurricane hunting. There is a section on how to become a hurricane hunter and a history of the 53rd Weather Reconnaissance Squadron. E-mail to the 53rd WRS should be addressed to (info@hurricanehunters.com). Major Val Schmid (valerie@hurricanehunters.com) is responsible for the development and maintenance of this page.

853. Hurricanes: Storm Science

http://www.miamisci.org/hurricane/

Appropriate for elementary science classes studying hurricanes, this site from the Miami Science Museum (Miami, Florida) lets students explore questions such as: "What is a hurricane like?" "How does a hurricane work?" "What happens when a storm comes?" and "What paths do hurricanes take?" Students are encouraged to write about their own personal disaster stories and to share these stories online.

854. National Hurricane Center

http://www.nhc.noaa.gov

The National Hurricane Center at the Florida International University campus in Miami, Florida, issues all official tropical weather outlooks and advisories for storms in the Atlantic and Eastern Pacific basins. Current information is always available through satellite and radar imagery. Students can also find historical data on hurricanes, such as the deadliest and the most expensive. The Webmaster's e-mail address is (webmaster@nhc.noaa.gov).

855. *USA Today Hurricane News Center*

http://www.usatoday.com/weather/whur0.htm

Created by USA Today, the *Hurricane News Center* is a comprehensive yet easily accessible guide to hurricane information. This site answers such questions as: "What is a hurricane?" "Where do they form?" and "Why are hurricanes named?" Students can find out more by reading the history of hurricanes and checking the glossary of terms. A section on hurricane safety and preparedness helps students understand how severe hurricanes can be and how important it is to be prepared. As an interesting informational sidebar, there is a link to William Gray of Colorado State University, who since 1983 has been predicting what will happen during the hurricane seasons. Students can access his most recent forecast, find out the factors he uses, and see for themselves how well Gray has done in the past with his predictions. Links are provided to the National Hurricane Center and other related resources on the Internet. This guide is maintained by Chris Cappella of the USA Today Information Network. Address suggestions to him via the Ask Jack feedback page (http://www.usatoday.com/weather/askjack/wjack1.htm).

Tornadoes

856. Tornado Project Online

http://www.tornadoproject.com

Tornado stories, myths, a top ten chart, and a FAQs section will answer students' questions about tornadoes. Colorful pie charts illustrate the percentage of all tornadoes from 1950 to 1994 based on the Fujita Scale, a system for rating the intensity of tornadoes by linking damage to wind speed. An F5 on this scale is the most destructive. The Tornado Safety page tells students what to do at home, at school, and to and from school or work in case of a tornado. A link leads to an online article titled, "Closet, Car, or Ditch? The Mobile Home Dilemma During a Tornado." Students can find out how to locate Tornado Alley on a map and how Doppler radar in the NEXRAD (NEXt generation weather RADar) system helps to detect and track tornadoes in the United States. See also "Turn! Turn! Turn!," an article (*Scientific American*) exploring how scientists are trying to unravel the mysteries of tornadoes (http://www.sciam.com/explorations/052096explorations.html) and a current tornado information index from *USA Today* with all the latest tornado watches and reports (http://www.usatoday.com/weather/wtwist0.htm).

857. **Tornadoes and Twisters**

http://www.movies.warnerbros.com/twister/

From Warner Brothers came the movie *Twister*, and now comes a chance for students to study and learn more about tornadoes. Click to continue, and then click to read the computer message after a successful log-on. Next, go to the Severe Weather Institute Research Lab for further briefing and information on becoming a volunteer storm chaser. To qualify for the storm-chasing team, students must successfully complete a five-question Storm Chaser's Test. To prepare for the test, students are given safety information, a general glossary, a tornado intensity scale, warning definitions, severe event location codes, tornado statistics listed by state (1950–1994), a list of 1995 killer tornadoes, and a storm chaser's guide.

858. **TORRO: The Tornado and Storm Research Organisation**

http://www.torro.org.uk

TORRO's Web site is a more scholarly, British look at tornadoes and severe storms. British intensity scales for tornadoes are different from those used in the United States. Information is current and contains actual photographs. This U.K. site cautions that the movie *Twister* gives a very misleading representation of storm chasing and technically inaccurate information about tornadoes. Students should be able to compare the movie to the facts to discover for themselves how removed from reality the film really is.

Software

859. **Blue-Skies**

http://groundhog.sprl.umich.edu/blueskies.html

Blue-Skies software is a unique graphical interface for weather and environmental information that incorporates user input features. Blue-Skies features the graphics protocol IIF (Interactive Image Format). This software is available for Macintosh and Windows platforms as well as a Java version for those running Java-compliant browsers (e.g., Netscape and Internet Explorer).

Environmental Sciences and Ecology

See also What on Earth Are You Doing for Earth Day? (entry 679); "Nuclear Physics and Nuclear Power" (entries 899–900); and Ocean Planet Home Page (entry 660).

General Interest

860. **Ecoregions Home Page**

http://www.sierraclub.org/ecoregions/

The Sierra Club has mapped out 21 plans for restoring ecological health to the United States and Canada, region by region. Provides a clickable map of the regions, including the Alaskan rain forest, the boreal forest, Hawaii, the Atlantic coast, and the North American prairie. Find out more about each of these regions and what must be done to protect the "web of life," ensure biodiversity, and prevent extinction of species.

861.   The Environment Page from the WWW Virtual Library

http://earthsystems.org/Environment.shtml

Look for a comprehensive collection of links to environmental resources on the Internet. Links are browseable and searchable; they are also categorized by subject and sorted alphabetically. Maintained by Shay Mitchell (shay@earthsystems.org).

862.   Environmental Education

http://eelink.net

The EE-Link is a project of the National Consortium for Environmental Education and Training (NCEET), which is funded by the U.S. Environmental Protection Agency. Through EE-Link, NCEET provides free online access to resources of special interest to educators who teach about the environment. These resources include instructional materials, articles, funding sources, and networking opportunities. Activities and lesson plans appropriate for K-12 environmental studies are provided, along with articles, newsletters, and information on grants and awards. Also available are bibliographies, catalogs of educational materials (including audiovisual), and software. Regional resources, such as the North Carolina Teacher's Guide to Environmental Education, are listed. Links are provided to projects and teaching resources for studying the ozone hole, recycling, wildlife, whales, and solid waste. The Web site is searchable.

863.   Environmental Protection Agency

http://www.epa.gov

The EPA provides comprehensive access to its documents containing environmental information. Pointers are provided to What's New and What's Hot as well as major public data holdings. The information on the Web server is keyword-searchable. The EPA supplies information on standards, rules, regulations, and legislation. Links are given to newsletters and journals, software, and databases. The Students and Teachers area has many documents on topics such as: Are schools environmentally safe? Look also for facts about the environment and teaching aids and curriculum guides. Fun Things for Kids includes tips on how kids can help with recycling. The EPA online library is compiled by the EPA library network and comprises the National Catalog, Hazardous Waste, Clean Lakes, EPA Regions, and Chemical Collection System.

864.   National Institute of Environmental Health Sciences

http://www.niehs.nih.gov

The National Institute of Environmental Health Sciences (NIEHS) Web directory contains an overview and mission statement along with a list of current events, press releases, newsletters, phone/fax directories, organizational structures, and maps. Other resources available include the *EHP On-line Journal,* the National Toxicology Program (NTP), Research Grants and Contracts (DERT), Intramural Research (DIR), and the NIEHS Library.

865. The National Oceanic and Atmospheric Administration

http://www.noaa.gov

The National Oceanic and Atmospheric Administration (NOAA) is part of the Department of Commerce. With the underlying premise that oceanic, atmospheric, and related earth science issues are interrelated, the NOAA routinely collects environmental information from 10,000 locations around the world. It has the largest environmental data archive in the world. To help access this information, the NOAA provides searchable databases, connections to NOAA online data and information systems, other environmental data systems, NOAA satellite information, weather information and images, NOAA periodicals, and other useful information.

866. National Wildlife Federation

http://www.nwf.org

Find out about some environmental issues and how to take action in the areas of endangered habitats, land stewardship, water quality, wetlands, and international issues. Learn how to create backyard wildlife habitats and access Animal Tracks Teacher Resources. Special-issue reports are available, as are photos and full-length articles from *Ranger Rick*, *National Wildlife*, *International Wildlife*, and *Your Big Backyard*. The latest environmental news and Action Reports are posted. In the Just for Kids section there are games and virtual cool tours related to the topics of our public lands, endangered species, water, and wetlands. Students "follow the tracks" to more information. The National Wildlife Federation maintains an extensive database that is keyword- and concept-searchable.

Biomes

General Biome Resources

867. Biome Basics

http://www.richmond.edu/~ed344/webunits/biomes/biomes.html

Introduces the seven kinds of biomes in the world: tundra, taiga, temperate forest, tropical rain forest, desert, grassland, and ocean. A color-keyed map of the world shows where these biomes are located. The characteristics of each biome are discussed, including climate, plants, animals, and interesting facts. Additional links are provided for further study of each biome.

868. Biomes of the World

http://mbgnet.mobot.org/sets/index.htm

Find out more about six of the world's major biomes: rain forest, tundra, taiga, desert, temperate, and grasslands. Also provides links to freshwater and marine ecosystems. Shows where various biomes are located. Gives the characteristics for each biome and discusses animals and plants indigenous to these six biomes. Look for stories and virtual field trips. Produced by The Evergreen Project, Inc.

The Rain Forest

869. An Amazon Adventure

http://jajhs.kana.k12.wv.us/amazon/

An Amazon Adventure invites students to explore a small portion of the upper Amazon basin through text and graphics. Covering an area approximately three-fourths the size of the United States (draining parts of Colombia, Peru, Ecuador, Bolivia, and Brazil), and including an enormous variety of plants and animals, the Amazon rain forest is one of the largest and most diverse habitats in the world.

The Amazon adventure depicted on these Web pages is part of an ongoing Earthwatch project (http://www.earthwatch.org/ed/home.html). Each year since 1996, small teams of volunteers (mostly high school and college students) and scientists conduct field research in the Amazon basin. The Amazon katydid project (http://www.earthwatch.org/ed/pm/nickle.html) has identified more than 360 species of katydids in the Peruvian Amazon in the last 10 years. Be sure to check out the colorful image collection of unidentified (for now) specimens photographed near Iquitos, Peru.

Elementary, middle, and high school students from around the world have also contributed to this site, and the submission of additional materials, such as artwork and research, is continually encouraged. This Amazon adventure includes maps and pictures as well as information on Amazon animals, plants, the Amazon River, and the rain forest. The Webmaster for this site is Robert Frostick (bfrostic@access.k12.wv.us).

870. Live from the Rain Forest

http://passporttoknowledge.com/rainforest/intro.html

Live from the Rain Forest is a Passport to Knowledge project, supported in part by the National Science Foundation and NASA. Although the real-time electronic field trip has ended, information on this site is still valuable for students studying rain forests. Look for seven maps showing rain forests around the world, as well as descriptions of different types of rain forests. There is a gallery of images and information about various trees, plants, birds, animals, and insects found in the rain forest. A teacher's guide is provided, with background information and suggested lesson plans. A bibliography and list of additional Web resources are also available.

871. Nature's Pharmacy

http://www.nwf.org/nwf/endangered/value/g4pharm.html

Forty percent of all prescriptions written today are either based on or synthesized from natural compounds from various species of plants and animals. Sixty-eight percent of the 250,000 species of the world's flowering plants are found in the world's tropical rain forests, which are being destroyed at an estimated worldwide rate of 41.7 million acres per year. This report describes a few of the medical benefits we've obtained from animal and plant species and under scores the rapid destruction and extinction of species before their benefits to mankind can be studied. Footnotes and a bibliography are attached. See also Wealth of the Rainforest: Pharmacy to the World (http://rain-tree.com) for more comprehensive and scholarly coverage.

872.   The Rain Forest Workshop

http://kids.osd.wednet.edu/Marshall/rainforest_home_page.html

The Rain Forest Workshop was developed by educator Virginia Reid and seventh-grade students at Marshall Middle School in Olympia, Washington. This excellent site addresses temperate rain forests as well as tropical rain forests. Educational resources for teachers and students include lesson plans. Information is available on animals, plants, people, travel, and more. This site is well organized for classroom use.

873.   Rainforest Action Page for Kids

http://www.ran.org/ran/kids_action/

Using an eight-step guide, this page explains what kids can do to change the world. There is a good overview of life in a rain forest, as well as a question-and-answer section and a glossary. Information is available on the Animals of the Rainforest and Native Peoples. Resources are available for teachers.

The Kids' Page is a link from the Rainforest Action Network (RAN) home page, which older students and adults will also want to access (http://www.ran.org/ran). The mission of RAN is to protect the Earth's rain forests and support the rights of their inhabitants through education, grassroots organizing, and nonviolent direct action. RAN has been working toward this goal since it was organized in 1985.

874.   Tropical Forests

http://www.seaworld.org/tropical%5Fforests/amaztf.html
and
http://www.seaworld.org/tropical%5Fforests/endangtf.html

The Conservation Information Department at Busch Gardens provides a Tropical Forests study unit that explains tropical forests as ecosystems. A bibliography is provided, along with information, activities, and suggestions for how students can help stop rain forest destruction. Appreciation of nature and commitment to conservation are prevalent themes in this unit, as reminders of naturalist John Muir's words, "When one tugs at a single thing in nature, he finds it attached to the rest of the world."

Endangered and Threatened Species

875.   Endangered and Threatened Species Home Page

http://eelink.net/EndSpp.old.bak/Endangered.html

The EE-Link Endangered Species Web site provides information to help incorporate the topic of endangered species into the classroom curriculum. Look for lesson plans, ongoing collaborative projects, and information about conservation efforts. There are endangered and extinct species lists for the United States and the entire world.

Be sure to link to the Endangered and Threatened Species Factsheet (http://eelink.net/EndSpp.old.bak/factsheet.html). This listing, which is updated periodically, contains information on threatened and endangered mammals, birds, amphibians, reptiles, fish, mollusks, insects, crustaceans, and plants. The name of each species is linked to additional information.

For example, information about the bottlenose dolphin is linked to a Sea World Education Department resource. Sea World provides extensive information on individual animal habitats, physical characteristics, diet, and reproduction. *See also* Animal Information Database: Sea World/Busch Gardens (entry 753).

876. Vanishing Species Curriculum

http://www.rice.edu/armadillo/Vanishing/index.html
or
gopher://riceinfo.rice.edu:1170/11/Texas/Vanishing/

Developed for a middle school (grades 5–8) curriculum in Texas, the purpose of the Vanishing Species Curriculum is: "In the end, we will conserve only what we love; we will love only what we understand; and we will understand only what we are taught." The curriculum is intended to be used as a framework or guide. Customizing the curriculum to individual classrooms to involve local cultural or educational groups and address local problems is recommended as most effective.

Inventors and Inventions

Inventors

Alexander Graham Bell (1847–1922)

877. Alexander Graham Bell's Path to the Telephone

http://jefferson.village.virginia.edu/albell/introduction.html

Follow Alexander Graham Bell's path toward the invention of the telephone through a number of experiments. Pictures and diagrams help students understand the technology of the telephone. For example, diagrams illustrate how sound can be reproduced. Students will be able to find out more about the Helmholtz transmitter and receiver, the science of bidirectional sound, and a number of experiments leading to Bell's first patent in 1876, a copy of which is available online for students to read and study. A linked table of contents makes navigation easy, and an excellent bibliography is provided. See also the Alexander Graham Bell Family Papers at the Library of Congress (http://memory.loc.gov/ammem/bellhtml/bellhome.html).

Leonardo da Vinci (1452–1519)

878. Exploring Leonardo

http://www.mos.org/sln/Leonardo/LeoHomePage.html

Leonardo da Vinci is used as a topic of study in a creative, hands-on science unit designed for students in grades 4–8, although many activities can be adapted for younger or older students. As a Renaissance man, da Vinci is an excellent role model for applying the scientific method creatively in every aspect of life, including art and music. Web content is divided into four areas. Leonardo: Right to Left explores da Vinci's curious habit of writing in reverse. What, Where, When? is a brief biography with images. Leonardo's Perspective introduces da Vinci's way of looking at the world and explores Renaissance techniques for representing the three-dimensional world on two-dimensional surfaces. Inventor's Workshop highlights some of da Vinci's futuristic inventions, introduces the elements of machines, lets students explore how these elements can work together to perform new functions, and gives students a chance to try analyzing da Vinci's inventions and designing their own.

Opportunities are provided for students to communicate their ideas electronically, experiment with interactive elements, and extend their learning with hands-on classroom activities. This science Web site was created by the Science Learning Network staff at the Museum of Science, Boston, Massachusetts (sln@mos.org).

Thomas Alva Edison (1847–1931)

879. Thomas Alva Edison

http://www.si.edu/lemelson/edison/html/thomas_alva_edison.html

Thomas Edison was an optimist who always looked on the bright side and did not become discouraged, because he felt that "every wrong attempt discarded is another step forward." He said that he was successful because he was not a clock-watcher and felt that "if we all did the things we are capable of doing, we would literally astound ourselves!" Students can find out more about Edison's life, his inventions, his thoughts, and how to make a light bulb. Links are provided to other resources on the Internet about Edison. Created and maintained by the Smithsonian National Museum of American History's Lemelson Center for the Study of Invention and Innovation (http://www.si.edu/lemelson/).

Inventions

880. Invention Dimension

http://web.mit.edu/invent/

A different inventor is profiled each week, with a biographical sketch covering his or her accomplishments and their impact upon society. An archive of almost 150 inventors featured in past weeks is available, listed alphabetically by inventor's last name. You can also search the archive by the name of the invention. Links are provided to invention-related resources. The Webmaster's e-mail address is (invent@mit.edu).

881. Inventure Place, The National Inventors Hall of Fame

http://www.invent.org

Inventure Place is a hands-on science museum located in Akron, Ohio. Students will want to visit The National Inventors Hall of Fame to find out more about inventors and their inventions. Inventors are listed alphabetically and by date of induction. For each inventor, there is a short biographical sketch, a picture, and patent information. The Online Links area provides a list of links in categories such as Hands-on Museums, On-line Exhibits, Creativity Sites, Invention Sites, Invention Competitions and Awards, Kids Stuff Sites, and African-American Inventors Site.

Materials Science

882. **MicroWorld**

http://www.lbl.gov/MicroWorlds/

MicroWorld is an interactive tour of current research in materials science for grades 9–12. The Advanced Light Source (ALS) produces the world's brightest light in the ultraviolet and soft X-ray regions of the spectrum. This powerful tool can help scientists probe the inner structure of materials to find out what it is about a material that makes it hard, brittle, or a good electrical conductor. ALS reveals the details of Kevlar's structure to show why the material is strong enough to stop bullets. Students are invited to find out how materials science helps scientists to understand environmental problems; how infinitesimal quantities of trace elements can change a material for better or worse; what polymers are and why they are so useful; and what it is like to work at the ALS, a national user facility located at Ernest Orlando Lawrence Berkeley National Laboratory of the University of California at Berkeley.

Physical Science

Engineering

883. **Engineering Resources**

http://www.educationindex.com/engineer/

Compiled and annotated by Education Index, this Web page comprises a list of engineering resources on the Internet in alphabetical order. Links are to professional organizations and societies, standards, resources for design engineers, engineering case studies, and journals. The Online Learning Environment is a Web site developed by Ed Schmidt of Putnam County High School (Illinois) for the purpose of using the Internet as part of his technology/engineering curriculum. This site is aimed at students in grades 8–12 who are interested in science and junior engineering. See also Introduction to Technology and Principles of Technology (http://www.geocities.com/Baja/8205/robotenter.htm).

Bridge Building

884. **Bridge Building Contest**

http://www.iit.edu/~hsbridge/

The construction and testing of model bridges promotes the study and application of fundamental principles of physics, and also helps high school students develop hands-on skills. International contests are held annually. A regional contest locator helps schools find out about regional contests. Tips are given on organizing and conducting school contests. A few pictures of past model bridge entries are posted along with links to other bridge-building information. For further information, contact Carlo Segre (segre@iit.edu) at the Illinois Institute of Technology.

885. **Build a Bridge**

http://www.pbs.org/wgbh/nova/bridge/

In this companion Web site created to accompany a *NOVA* special (produced by the Public Broadcasting Service) on super bridges, students learn about the four major types of bridges and then test their knowledge by matching bridges to the correct sites. Links are provided to the history of the Golden Gate Bridge, bridge research, and other bridge engineering sites. *See also* "Secrets of Lost Empires: China Bridge" (http://www.pbs.org/wgbh/nova/lostempires/china/). In this *NOVA* special, students see the efforts by scholars and construction workers to design and build an authentic Chinese bridge from wood and bamboo known only from an ancient painting. In the Hot Science section, there is a hands-on activity to reinforce learning about the four major types of bridges: arches, beams, suspension, and cable-stayed.

Physics

General Interest

886. Frequently Asked Questions About Physics

http://math.ucr.edu/home/baez/physics/faq.html

Frequently Asked Questions About Physics is one of many FAQs sites. This FAQs site is recommended reading for anyone, especially before they post to the (sci.physics) newsgroup. Some of the general physics questions in this FAQs site include: "Why are golf balls dimpled?" "Why does hot water freeze faster than cold?" "Why do mirrors reverse left and right?" "Is glass a solid or liquid?" and "Why do stars twinkle and planets do not?" Maintained by Philip Gibbs (pg@pobox.com).

887. Fusion: Physics of a Fundamental Energy Source

http://FusEdWeb.pppl.gov/CPEP/Chart.html

The opening page of this Web site contains an interactive fusion chart. Each main area of the chart is linked to additional information. A guided tour begins with Energy Sources and Conversions. Other main features of the tour are How Fusion Reactions Work, Two Important Fusion Reactions, Plasmas (fourth state of matter), Creating the Conditions for Fusion, and Fusion Research. Each stop on the guided tour contains links to additional information and teacher resources. Fusion at the sun's core is explained with a colorful diagram. This site is under construction. Robert F. Heeter (rfheeter@pppl.gov) is the Webmaster.

888. Glenbrook South Physics Home Page

http://www.glenbrook.k12.il.us/gbssci/phys/phys.html

Teachers and students will want to explore all the physics resources on this Web site. Course outlines, tutorials, online reviews, curriculum aids, and project information are available online as integrated resources for various physics courses taught at Glenbrook South High School (Glenview, Illinois). The Quiz Room provides specific suggestions on how to study for upcoming quizzes. The Laboratory contains information about how to make up missed labs. Additional links provide opportunities for extra practice with physics problems. Created and maintained by Tom Henderson (THenderson@glenbrook.k12.il.us), physics teacher, Glenbrook South High School.

889.   Physics Zone

http://207.10.97.102/physicszone/

High school physics teachers will want to take the time to study this well-organized and information-packed Web site in depth. Students will want to take advantage of the complementary online information to assist them in their studies. Course outlines and homework assignments with solutions are provided for three high school physics classes: conceptual physics, physics, and AP Physics. Physics lessons and review questions are posted along with "101 Physics Phacts." Links to related Internet resources are provided for help with physics research as well as for "Phamous Phaces" and "Phun Links." You need the Shockwave plug-in installed on your Web browser to see the HomeWork Solutions. Created by physics teachers Steve Wirt (swirt@icsd.k12.ny.us) and Ken Wright (kwright@icsd.k12.ny.us), Ithaca High School, Ithaca, New York.

890.   Playground Physics

http://lyra.colorado.EDU/sbo/mary/play/

Playground Physics is an introduction to physics for grades 4–7. Students relate experiences on the playground to basic physics concepts. Teacher guides are provided with sufficient information to allow elementary teachers with little or no experience with physics to be successful in introducing physics concepts through hands-on activities and experiments. Reproducible handouts are available.

See also other science-related educational materials written by the same author, Mary Urquhart, at (http://lyra.colorado.edu/sbo/mary). This site is created and maintained by Mary Urquhart (urquhart@argyre.colorado.edu), a doctoral student in the Astrophysical, Planetary, and Atmospheric Sciences Department at the University of Colorado, Boulder.

Atoms and Subatomic Particles

891.   The Atoms Family

http://www.miamisci.org/af/sln/

The Atoms Family online resource is based on a current exhibit at the Miami Museum of Science, and contains educational activities relating to different forms of energy. Frankenstein's Lightning Laboratory explores electricity; Dracula's Library looks at the properties of light; the Wolf Man's Ghostly Graveyard addresses fuel conservation; the Phantom's Portrait Parlor peeks at atomic matter; and the Mummy's Tomb digs into potential and kinetic energy. The Webmaster's address is (webmaster@miamisci.org).

892.   Life, the Universe, and the Electron

http://www.iop.org/Physics/Electron/Exhibition

Sponsored as a collaborative project between the Science Museum in London and the Institute of Physics, this site is an online exhibition celebrating the centenary of the discovery of the electron in 1897. Some of the topics covered include an explanation of electrons as the first subatomic particle and a timeline highlighting important discoveries about the electron and the atom from 1897 to the present. A section on Seeing with Electrons focuses on the electron microscope to magnify the smallest objects; the Hubble Space Telescope to observe distant galaxies (faint objects); the large electron-positron collider to investigate atomic structures; and synchrotron radiation to probe the structure of matter. Links are provided to particle physics laboratories; museums with related collections, galleries, and displays; general physics sites; and a bibliography.

893. The Particle Adventure
http://ParticleAdventure.org

The Particle Adventure is an excellent interactive tour of the inner workings of the atom. Quarks, leptons, fermions, bosons, baryons, mesons, force carriers, and more are explained with colorful diagrams. The Standard Model of Fundamental Particles and Interactions explains the whys of physical interactions, but still leaves many mysteries unexplained today. A brief history of particle physics is available. Activity sheets for students are provided, and teachers are encouraged to print out and reproduce these pages for classroom use. Sponsored by the Contemporary Physics Education Project and Particle Data Group.

Biographies of Physicists

See also "Biographies of Scientists" (entries 729–731), Biographies of NASA Astronauts (entry 721); Women of NASA (entry 726); and "Biographies" (entries 1333–1336).

894. Contributions of 20th Century Women to Physics
http://www.physics.ucla.edu/~cwp/

Contributions of 20th Century Women to Physics is a historical archive created to help celebrate the centenary of the American Physical Society in 1999. This archive contains information about women who have made original and important contributions to physics in this century through 1975.

Albert Einstein (1879–1955)

895. Einstein: Image and Impact
http://www.aip.org/history/einstein/

Einstein: Image and Impact is an online biographical tribute with more than 100 pages of text and pictures devoted to all aspects of Albert Einstein's life. There are three ways to approach the exhibit. The index gives quick access to topics and special features. Einstein in Brief gives a quick sketch of high points of Einstein's life, with some pictures and quotes. The Main Exhibit can be navigated by accessing rooms off halls, with each hall representing a different aspect of Einstein's life. Some of the halls are Formative Years, E=mc², Quantum and Cosmos, The Nuclear Age, and An Essay: The World As I See It. This is a premiere Web site paying tribute to Albert Einstein's life and contributions presented by the Center for History of Physics, a division of the American Institute of Physics.

Stephen W. Hawking (1942–)

896. Welcome to Professor Stephen Hawking's Website
http://www.hawking.org.uk/home/hindex.html

Stephen Hawking is the current Lucasian Professor in the Department of Applied Mathematics and Theoretical Physics at Cambridge University, United Kingdom, a post once held by Sir Isaac Newton. Hawking is a British theoretical physicist who has devoted much of his life to explaining space-time described by general relativity and the singularities where it breaks down. He has done most of his work while confined to a wheelchair with a progressive neurological disease, amyotrophic lateral sclerosis (ALS or Lou Gehrig's disease). This official Web site of Stephen Hawking provides a brief autobiography, information about his disability, a glossary of terms, and the latest news about Hawking and his lecture schedule.

History of Physics

897. Center for History of Physics Exhibits
http://www.aip.org/history/

The Center for History of Physics has collected and organized exhibits that help students understand the important role physics has played over time. Find out about the Nobel Prizes in physics and the recent winners. Learn more about people in physics, such as Marie Curie and Richard Feynman. The histories of useful devices cover light microscopes, fiber optics, the telephone, and quartz watches. Information is provided on the history of astronomy and the history of space exploration. Picture files contain images of various physicists.

Interactive Physics

898. Amusement Park Physics
http://www.learner.org/exhibits/parkphysics/

Roller coasters create a sense of dangerous excitement for riders by hurling them around tight curves with incredible force and plummeting them down sheer drops. Amusement park builders use the laws of physics to simulate danger on roller coaster rides that are actually very safe. At this Web site, students are given the opportunity to design and test their own roller coaster. Students can also investigate the physics of other amusement park rides, including pendulum and free-fall rides, carousels, and bumper cars. A glossary is available to help explain physics terms. Links to related sites are provided. This interactive learning site is created and maintained by the Annenberg/CPB Projects.

Nuclear Physics and Nuclear Power

See also "Nuclear Weapons, Realities of Nuclear War, and Peace Efforts" (entries 1197–1201).

899. Nuclear Physics: Past, Present, and Future
http://tqd.advanced.org/3471/index.html

Students and staff of the Thomas Jefferson High School for Science and Technology and the New Plymouth High School have put together a very informative site that deals with nuclear physics, the science that forms the basis for the development of nuclear power. This site also deals with the pros and cons of nuclear energy and offers the opportunity to participate in a forum. Designed for a general audience, students successfully explain the physics behind the technology of the atom and connect this technology to popular history, current issues, and prospects for the future.

900. U.S. Quick Virtual Nuclear Power Plant Tour

http://www.cannon.net/~gonyeau/nuclear/tour-a.htm

Students can find out how nuclear power compares to other ways of generating electricity by looking at pictorial comparisons, as well as different types of nuclear power plants used in the United States. Nuclear wastes, environmental effects, and radiation safety are also addressed. Nuclear power-related links are listed for government agencies, universities, corporations, individuals, and professional associations. A link is also provided to another virtual tour of nuclear power plants around the world (http://www.cannon.net/~gonyeau/nuclear/index.htm). Created and maintained by Joseph Gonyeau (gonyeau@cannon.net), senior nuclear consultant (engineering) with Northern States Power at the Prairie Island Nuclear Generating Plant.

Discussion Groups

901. High School Physics Teachers Sharing Resources

E-mail: listserv@lists.psu.edu
Instructions: On the first line of the body of the message, type:
subscribe PHYSHARE [your first name and last name]

Robots and Artificial Intelligence

902. Annual Robotics Competitions for High School Students

http://www.usfirst.org

For Inspiration and Recognition of Science and Technology (FIRST) is a nonprofit organization whose mission is to generate interest in science and engineering among today's youth by providing an opportunity for students to experience the excitement of engineering and competition. Since 1992, its primary means of doing so has been to sponsor an annual robotics competition, usually in early April at the Epcot Center in Orlando, Florida. Radio-controlled robots created by more than 200 teams across the United States (made up of high schools and corporate sponsors) competed in the 1998 competition. Links are provided to many of the individual teams' home pages. General competition information includes procedures for registering a team.

For each year, beginning with 1992, teachers, students, and sponsors can explore an online scrapbook of pictures and descriptions of the competitions, as well as lists of teams and sponsors. Links are provided to FIRST news articles and to other robotics-related information on the Internet. Webmaster's e-mail is (webmaster@usfirst.org).

903. Intelligent Mechanism Group (IMG)

http://img.arc.nasa.gov

The Intelligent Mechanism Group (IMG) is developing planetary and space-based robotics systems. This group does research on a variety of architectures for intelligent mechanisms and tests the complete systems under field conditions. This site has information on IMG's projects and current activities as well as data from its archive.

One of the past projects, Dante II (a cooperative project with Carnegie Mellon University), developed a tethered walking frame robot that explored an active volcano (Mt. Spurr, Alaska) in

July 1994, via teleoperation. The pages for Dante II contain hundreds of images of this mission into the volcano on Mt. Spurr. Also look for information on Ranger, Trov, Pathfinder, Nomad, and Marsokhod.

Science Journals and Magazines

904. *Discover Magazine*
http://www.discover.com

Discover Magazine is an award-winning, self-proclaimed leading-edge science magazine targeting science educators and published by the Walt Disney Company. The Archive Library contains back issues from 1993. For each month's issue the table of contents is given, along with selected full-text articles. Look for the *Discover Magazine* television series schedule on this site.

905. *DRAGONFLY*
http://www.muohio.edu/Dragonfly/index.htmlx

DRAGONFLY is a theme-based, bimonthly journal that features children's research, art, and creative writing. *DRAGONFLY* also allows children to interact directly with renowned researchers who are writing about their own investigations and the process of discovery. A joint project of the National Science Teachers Association and Miami University, *DRAGONFLY* links third- to sixth-grade children, scientists, teachers, and parents.

906. *Scientific American*
http://www.sciam.com

Since its first publication in 1845, *Scientific American* has continued to track and report key changes in technical and scientific development. The online edition highlights at least two full-text articles and some features from the print issue each month and uses the capabilities of the WWW to augment these articles with links to the researchers and their work. The online edition has weekly features not found in the print version, such as Explorations, Interviews, and Ask the Experts. The Web site opens to the current month's online issue, and previous issues are archived from January 1996.

907. *The Why Files: Science Behind the News*
http://whyfiles.news.wisc.edu

The Why Files is a weekly science news magazine that explores the science, math, and technology lurking behind the daily headlines. Supported by the National Science Foundation, *The Why Files* is published solely on the Web, and takes advantage of the Web's capability to provide links to definitions of scientific jargon, bibliographies, and other relevant sites. Each weekly feature contains 5 to 15 pages of text, drawings, and photographs. Past stories are stored in file cabinet drawers labeled environmental science, health, physical science, social science, sports, and technology. There is also a search engine for these archived stories. Cool Images is another weekly feature, offering unique and interesting graphics related to the scientific world, from microscopic to satellite and telescope images, from the unusual to the bizarre and beautiful.

Applied Arts and Sciences: Vocational Education, Driver's Education, Family Life Education, Health & Safety, Horticulture, Physical Education, Sport Science, and Sports

All URL addresses in this chapter are checked and updated monthly. If a link does not work, please refer to the Directory Update Web page located at (http://www.lu.com/lu/irdupdates.html).

It's never too early to learn how to develop a healthy lifestyle and good eating habits. Two sites target younger students: the National Dairy Council's Chef Combo's Fantastic Adventures in Tasting and Nutrition (entry 981) focuses on general nutrition, and the Dole 5 A Day site (entry 959) provides students with information about the importance of eating fruits and vegetables. Older students can calculate their life expectancy based on their current lifestyles and can compute the caloric, fat, cholesterol, and sodium content of typical fast-food meals from a variety of nationally known restaurants.

Safety is a major concern for young people, and various sites address these concerns, such as the Teen New Drivers Homepage (entry 931), the Bicycle Helmet Safety Institute (entry 996), and the International In-Line Skating Association's page of in-line skating tips (entry 1001).

Family, Career and Community Leaders of America (entry 932) has its own Web site. Look for great recipes at the Betty Crocker Web site (entry 952), the Campbell's Soup site (entry 954), the Kraft Interactive Kitchen (entry 955), and Sally's Place (entry 956). Martha Stewart's site (entry 934), a companion to her weekly television program and magazine, *Martha Stewart Living*, provides ideas, tips, and suggestions for entertaining, home decorating, gardening, and food preparation. Simplicity offers online pattern catalogs to make pattern selection a breeze (entry 936).

Physical education teachers will want to visit PE Central (entry 991) for lesson plan ideas and links to various individual and team sports. Golfers will want to access GolfWeb (entry 1017), and tennis players will want to read the tennis news that's posted daily to The Tennis Server (entry 1020). Information about the Olympics (entries 1024–1027) includes the history of the Games; the summer games in Sydney, Australia, in 2000; and the 2002 winter games in Salt Lake City, Utah.

Vocational Education

General Interest

Tech Prep and School-to-Work

908. School-to-Work National Office
http://stw.ed.gov

The School-to-Work National Office Web site provides information about STW grants, initiatives by state, and resources and tools. Find out what's new in school-to-work topics. Read the research and evaluations. Post messages and chat with others involved in this area of education. This comprehensive site is searchable.

Automobile Mechanics

909. Automotive Learning On-Line
http://www.innerauto.com/innerauto/htm/auto.html

Automotive Learning On-Line is an interactive reference site, training tool, and educational program for those considering a career in automobile mechanics, as well as those who would like to know more about cars in general so that they can be more knowledgeable when having their vehicles serviced. Students can choose from 10 automotive systems, such as AC/heat, electrical, and exhaust. Text labels and icons of magnifying glasses appear when students run the mouse pointer over pick points on the different pictures of automobile systems. A click on the text reveals a link to additional information. Clicking on the magnifying glass gives a closer view of the area or object, with additional pick points to choose from. Students can also access information from an animation library to help them understand certain engineering concepts, and there is a hyperlinked index that includes automotive terminology and the history of automobiles. This Java-enriched site, with hundreds of illustrations and thousands of descriptive text links, was created by Informative Graphics. E-mail can be addressed to the Webmaster at (innerauto@innerbody.com). *See also* Informative Graphics' Human Anatomy On-Line (entry 744) for a similar reference for students studying human anatomy.

Agriculture, Farm, and Ranch

910. AgWeb.com
http://www.agweb.com

AgWeb is a news Web site for those interested in agriculture, and includes information provided by *Farm Journal, Proud Farmer, Top Producer, Beef Today*, and *Dairy Today*. Content covers federal government analysis from Washington, D.C.; market news such as prices and auctions; and commodities, including corn, soybeans, wheat, cotton, beef, pork, and dairy. Registration is free and required. Site users can customize their agricultural news to specific topics.

911. **Farm and Ranch Business Center**

http://www.traderivers.com/farmranch/index.html

The Farm and Ranch Business Center Web site provides comprehensive agricultural information. Look for links to all the U.S. Department of Agriculture (USDA) livestock reports; crop reports; USDA-National Agricultural Statistics Service (USDA-NASS) reports; and the markets for
crops, cattle, dairy, hogs, poultry, lumber, fruits, and vegetables. Includes state-by-state crop
and weather information updated weekly. Find out what crops are doing well or not doing well
in each state. This is an excellent site for finding out more information about one's own state
or making comparisons among various states. See also Agricultural Resources from Education
Index (http://www.educationindex.com/ag/).

912. **Today's Market Prices**

http://www.todaymarket.com

Today's Market Prices is a commercial site devoted to agricultural information from around the
world. It includes a Market Prices Service, an agricultural databank dedicated to growers, shippers, wholesalers, researchers, scholars, and all others interested in up-to-date information
on agribusiness. Students can find the daily selling prices of 120 different fruit and vegetable
products sold at the wholesale markets of the United States, Canada, Mexico, Europe, and Japan. Prices are on fresh fruit and vegetables, including onions, potatoes, herbs, and tropical
fruits. A free password registration is required. The weekly Rotterdam fruit and vegetable exchange auction prices are posted, as is the twice-a-week Tokyo Central Wholesale Ota Market
report. Green links provide the most comprehensive links to agribusiness on the Internet.

Business Education

See also "Economics" (entries 1091–1096) and "News Sources" (entries 1405–1419) for links
to CNN, *Fortune*, and *The Wall Street Journal*.

National Standards for Business Education

913. **Business Education Standards**

http://www.nbea.org/curfbes.html

The National Business Education Association has posted online the business education standards for accounting, business law, career development, communications, computation, economics and personal finance, entrepreneurship, information systems, international business,
management, and marketing. Each standard is listed with resources and links to Web sites to
assist in implementing the standards in the curriculum. The Web address for the National Business Education Association, NBEA Online, is (http://www.nbea.org).

General Interest

914. **Business Nation: Small Business Services**

http://www.businessnation.com/smallbiz.html

Business news is updated daily. Links are provided to stock quotes, Biz-Tech news wires, and
industry news. Business directories and databases are available. Look for a listing of the Best

Business sites on the Internet by category. Comprehensive information is available for class-room discussion and research on topics such as Women in Business, Legal Information, Banking, Minorities, Web Marketing, and International Trade. Research materials relevant to small business issues can be obtained through links to online articles, newsletters, statistical reports, databases, and directories.

915. The Dow Jones Business Directory

http://bd.dowjones.com

The Dow Jones Business Directory provides listings of high-quality business Web sites. Categories of interest include: Careers; Companies in the Dow; Economy; Financial Markets; Government & Politics, Industries; and Law.

916. From Carbons to Computers: The Changing American Office

http://educate.si.edu/scitech/carbons/start.html

The Smithsonian Institution explores American offices and makes some comparisons between the modern business workplace and that of 20, 50, or 100 years ago. Looks at how inventions and technological changes affect daily life. Highlights office organization, the concept of the global office, and what the office environment will be like in the 21st century. Includes a historical timeline, lesson plans, and resources.

917. Start Your Own Business

http://www.tax.gov/kids/business.htm

The U.S. Treasury Department has created this site to show students what's involved in starting a business and how employers file their taxes. Students can find out more about starting three specific businesses: a lemonade stand, a lawn-mowing service, and a music band. Links are provided to a glossary of terms, tax information, government functions, tax forms, and related links.

Professional Associations

918. Future Business Leaders of America

http://www.fbla-pbl.org

Future Business Leaders of America-Phi Beta Lambda (FBLA-PBL) is a nonprofit educational association of students preparing for careers in business and business-related fields. Information is available on membership, awards, scholarships, and competitions. Links are provided to business publications, internship opportunities, and career resources as well as resume, cover letter, and interview tips.

International Business

919. Biz/Ed

http://bizednet.bris.ac.uk

Located in the United Kingdom, Biz/Ed is a dedicated business and economics information gateway for students and teachers. Links are provided to some British companies to use as case studies. Links are also provided to economics data and financial and business data. Students can use data from the Office for National Statistics, Penn World Data, and the U.S. Census Bureau. The Company Report Browser summarizes company reports for some 20 leading firms, and the Company Report Profiler helps students to analyze, interpret, and compare the company reports.

920.   The Business Bureau (United Kingdom)

http://www.businessbureau-uk.co.uk

The Business Bureau Web site provides comprehensive information for the small business. Some of the topics include sales and marketing; finance and accountancy, with a glossary of accounting terms; and links to the best British business Internet resources. Excellent advice on how to start a new business, including how to write a business plan, is given.

Consumer Education

General Interest

921.   Calculators

http://www.bankrate.com/brm/pop_calc.asp

Bankrate.com provides calculators to help determine rates and costs. Includes calculators for credit cards, savings, mortgages, moving, auto financing, and loans. Calculate your payment on any loan. Compare credit cards and find out which is the best; calculate the real cost of your debt. Evaluate auto leasing deals and compare interest rates and rebates. Compare the cost of living between cities. Find out how to reach a savings goal and how to save for college. Find out how much house you can afford and what your payment and prepayment options are.

922.   The Mortgage Qualifier

http://www.homefair.com/usr/qualcalcform.html

An online mortgage calculator from Homefair.com helps to determine the maximum loan amount for which someone would qualify based on standard lender rules. By filling in amounts for income, savings, monthly debt payments, and interest rate, the mortgage calculator calculates the maximum house price affordable for the given data. The total monthly mortgage payment is then broken down to show the amounts for principal and interest, taxes and insurance, and mortgage insurance.

923.   The Salary Calculator

http://www.homefair.com/calc/salcalc.html

The Salary Calculator compares the cost of living in hundreds of cities in the United States and other countries. For any specific salary, find out what comparable salary would be required in another location. Compare cost of living, crime rates, and other pertinent city information. Pick the best cities to live in based on climate, cost of living, and other factors. Find out crime indexes for U.S. and Canadian cities, compare demographic information between two Zip Codes, and select information about local public schools in other communities.

New and Used Car Information and Buying Guides

924. Edmund's Automobile Buyer's Guides

http://www.edmunds.com

Edmund provides information about new cars, new trucks, and used cars. Safety information is provided for most vehicles. Results of road tests of selected automobiles are posted. A list of current incentives and rebates is given. Check Edmund's Guide before purchasing your next new or used car.

925. Kelley Blue Book

http://www.kbb.com

Want to know what the Blue Book suggested retail or trade-in value is of a specific used car? Look at the Kelley Blue Book Web site. The first *Blue Book of Motor Car Values* was published in 1918 by Les Kelley, a California used car salesman. Blue Book values are listed for new cars and used cars.

926. *New Cars and Trucks Buyers Guide 2000*

http://www.popularmechanics.com/popmech/auto3/2000CBG/2000CBGP.html

This buyers guide for new, year-2000 vehicles, from *Popular Mechanics*, is divided into two sections: Be a Smart Consumer and Catalog of Vehicles. The catalog has detailed information, specifications, and visuals for each of the more than 200 cars, minivans, vans, sport utility vehicles, and pickup trucks that are available for 2000. Be a Smart Consumer contains articles on how to take a test drive, whether you should buy or lease, which is safer (cars or trucks), and how to purchase a car.

927. *Popular Mechanics Homepage*

http://popularmechanics.com

The PM Zone, the online edition of *Popular Mechanics*, has regular articles on topics related to automobiles, home improvement, science and technology, electronics, outdoors, movies, shopping, and more. The annual *New Car and Truck Buyers Guide* and a car cost calculator are available (http://popularmechanics.com/carcost.html). Students can figure out their monthly car payments by filling in the blanks with appropriate financial data.

Driver's Education

928. Minot High School Driver's Education Department Home Page

http://www.misu.nodak.edu/library/de_bookmarks_1.html

From buyer's guides to motor oil and how to find your way under the hood of a car, this site has a comprehensive listing of links to Web sites related to driver education. Online information provides links to crash information, maps and travel, motorcycles, substance abuse, traffic issues, automobiles, and government agencies. The Webmaster is driving instructor, Howard Theige (theige@minot.ndak.net).

929. **National Highway Traffic Safety Administration**

http://www.nhtsa.dot.gov

Find out a car's crash test rating and comparative safety information by model and year. Reports list safety features and give crash test ratings of frontal protection for new and used cars. The National Highway Traffic Safety Administration (NHTSA) maintains a database of vehicle and equipment information, including recalls and customer complaints, accessible from this site. Information is available on child safety seats, air bags, and traffic safety/occupant issues. Statistical data is also given. The NHTSA is responsible for reducing deaths, injuries, and economic losses resulting from motor vehicle crashes.

930. **Online Drivers License Study Guide**

http://www.golocalnet.net/drive/

Designed as an enrichment for drivers and students studying for a learner's permit or driver's license, this site is a wonderful asset for license-test students or for those researching traffic laws and rules of the road in different states. To individualize the online study guide for a specific state and county within the state, scroll down to the bottom of the page and select your state. On the next page, select your county. In-text links are provided to a table of contents with chapter information about passing, intersections and turning, sharing the road, what to do if you have an accident, motorcycles, parking, and defensive driving. Practice tests with a database of 80 questions are available. Tests can be scored online. All questions are linked to the study material and there is a printable list of all questions at the end. A Java-enabled browser is required to access information on this site. Tip: Use the navigation buttons inside the frames instead of the Back button on your browser to move from frame to frame. Sponsored by GoLocalnet, the Webmaster's address is (webmaster@golocalnet.net).

931. **Teen New Drivers' Home Page**

http://www.ai.net/~ryanb/

Ryan Buckholtz wrote this collection of safety tips for new teen drivers while he was a senior at Glenelg High School in Harrowed County, Maryland. Tips are categorized into driving around school, driving around town, driving in the country, driving in bad weather, general tips, parallel parking, passing, major factors in accidents, danger signs for fatigue, buying a used car, and links to other driver information sites. Teen drivers have shared their tips, usually from firsthand experience, and other teens are encouraged to e-mail Ryan with their own driving safety tips. One teen shared this tip: "Make sure your garage door is completely open before you back out of it." Another wrote, "When starting out in bad weather, test your brakes to see how far it takes you to stop." Still another good tip is, "Don't leave valuables like wallets, shoes, leather jackets, or sports equipment in your cars where they can be seen because they invite break-ins." Ryan is maintaining this Web page as a continuing community service project while attending the University of North Carolina at Chapel Hill. His e-mail address is (ryanb@ lightst.com).

Family Life Education

General Interest

932. Family, Career and Community Leaders of America

http://www.fcclainc.org

Family, Career and Community Leaders of America (FCCLS) is a national career and technical student organization for young men and women in family and consumer sciences education in public and private schools through grade 12. Formerly the Future Homemakers of America, founded in 1945, the FCCLS has broadened its approach and now includes young men and young women, with a commitment to build strong leaders in families, careers, and communities. Chapter projects focus on a variety of youth concerns, including teen pregnancy, parenting, family relationships, substance abuse, peer pressure, nutrition and fitness, teen violence, and career exploration. Information is available about the national organization, membership, programs, and conferences.

933. *HomeArts*

http://www.homearts.com

HomeArts is an online home and gardening journal published by Hearst Communications Inc. Feature articles and Web pages cover food, gardening, health, family, recipes, shopping, home, money, makeovers, fashion, relationships, and fiction. Information can be located by keyword-searching or clicking on a topic. Links are provided to other Hearst magazine sites.

934. Martha Stewart Living

http://www.marthastewart.com

The Martha Stewart Living Web site highlights information from Martha Stewart's weekly television series, *Martha Stewart Living*. Look for selected recipes, crafts, and techniques and tips from each week's television programs. Get to know Martha Stewart through an online biography, scrapbook with color pictures, and a frequently asked questions with answers section covering decorating, entertaining, and gardening. Also available is subscription information for the magazine, *Martha Stewart Living*, and how to order the catalog, *Martha by Mail*.

Clothing and Textiles

935. *The History of Costume* by Braun & Schneider—c. 1861–1880.

http://www.siue.edu/COSTUMES/history.html

The History of Costume was originally printed in Germany between 1861 and 1880, and is an excellent source both for students who are studying the history of fashion and for costume designers. The online edition has images of 500 color plates illustrating historic costume, from ancient Egypt through the end of the 19th century. Created and maintained by Charles Otis Sweezey (osweeze@siue.edu).

936. **Simplicity Pattern Company, Inc.**

http://www.simplicitypatt.com

Simplicity offers online pattern catalogs complete with color images. The Easy Way to Perfect Fit provides information about identifying your correct pattern size. Simplicity also offers sewing tips. This is a great site to use when looking for a perfect pattern.

937. *Threads Online*

http://www.taunton.com/th/index.htm

Threads Online is a technical garment-sewing magazine for enthusiastic sewers of all skill levels. For people who love to sew, *Threads Online* provides instruction on a variety of sewing topics, including design, fitting, alterations, fabric, embellishment, supplies, notions, and tools. Learn ways to improve your sewing and discover ideas for creative projects. Subscription information is also available for the print version of *Threads*.

938. **Vy's Sewing Site**

http://www.geocities.com/Heartland/4456/sewingpage.html

Vy's Sewing Site provides an extensive collection of links to sewing resources on the Web, from bridal veils to T-shirts, slipcovers, cross-stitch, and embroidery. Links are organized by categories such as fabric, notions, patterns, sewing home pages, sewing machines, sewing organizations, and sewing tips and techniques. Also look for laundering tips, including stain removal tips, and how-to information for preparing fabric before sewing. The Webmaster's address is (vysews@geocities.com).

Early Childhood Education and Child Care

Early Childhood Education

See also Yahooligans! (entry 1376).

General Resources

939. **Early Childhood Education/Young Children (Ages 0-8)**

E-mail: **listserv@postoffice.cso.uiuc.edu**

Instructions: On the first line of the body of the message, type:
subscribe Ecenet-L [your first name and last name]

The Early Childhood discussion list, Ecenet-L, is an online forum for the consideration of issues related to the development, education, and care of children from birth through age eight. It is intended for teachers, teacher educators, researchers, policy makers, students, and parents.

How to Access the ECENET-L archives:

http://www.askeric.org/Virtual/Listserv_Archives/ECENET-L.html

940. Early Childhood Educators' and Family Web Corner

http://users.sgi.net/~cokids/

Teachers and parents will find a plethora of information about working with young children. Early Childhood in the News is a collection of articles from newspapers, magazines, and e-zines concerning early childhood issues, such as transition from preschool to kindergarten, child development, literacy, advocacy, and using the Internet as a teaching tool. Maintained by Beth Conant (cokids@nauticom.net), consultant with Early Intervention Technical Assistance (EITA).

941. Hall of Early Childhood

http://www.tenet.edu/academia/earlychild.html

The Texas Education Network (TENET) has compiled and sorted more than 50 online resources related to early childhood into four categories: Resources for Educators, Resources for Parents, Resources for Special Populations, and Kids' Corner. Look for arts and crafts activities, computer skills lesson plans for primary grades, lullaby and song lyrics, reading activities, and links to activity and game pages.

Educational and Fun Sites for Early Learners

942. Billy Bear's Playground

http://www.billybear4kids.com

Read online versions of Billy Bear's adventures, and have fun with pages of children's songs, games, puzzles, and activities. Holiday pages are a special feature. Kids can access pages about New Year's Day, Easter, St. Patrick's Day, Mother's Day, Father's Day, the Fourth of July, Thanksgiving, Christmas, Halloween, April Fools Day, and Valentine's Day. Billy Bear clip art is available.

943. Crayola Crayon Home Page

http://www.crayola.com

Find out the history of Crayola crayons, made by Binney & Smith Company, makers of slate pencils, dustless chalk, and barn door red paint pigment. Take a virtual tour of the Crayola factory in Easton, Pennsylvania, and find out how Crayola crayons are made, as well as how to remove Crayola stains. Enjoy Crayola crayon trivia questions and find out what's new in Crayola products. Girls can do their own "jazzy thing" at the Girls Only Net Club.

944. Kids Web

http://www.kidsvista.com/index.html

Kids Web is a World Wide Web digital library for students. They can link to information on the Web in curriculum areas such as social studies, science, and art. A miscellaneous section contains references, sports, and fun and games. The purpose of Kids Web is to present a subset of the WWW that is very simple to navigate and contains information targeted at the K-12 level.

945. *Little Explorers Picture Dictionary*

http://www.EnchantedLearning.com/Dictionary.html

The *Little Explorers Picture Dictionary* has more than 1,000 illustrated dictionary entries. By clicking on a letter of the alphabet, preschoolers can access a page of words with pictures beginning with that letter. Most entries have links to related Web sites that have all been carefully chosen as appropriate for young children. Links are to connect-the-dots, nursery rhymes, stories, arts and crafts projects, zoos, museums, and more. Versions of this dictionary are available in English only, English-French, English-German, English-Portuguese, English-Spanish, and Japanese. Created by Enchanted Learning Software.

946. **The Mother Goose Pages**

http://www-personal.umich.edu/~pfa/dreamhouse/nursery/rhymes.html

Find the words to nursery rhymes about Daffy Down Dilly, Georgie Porgie, Simple Simon, Jack and Jill, and Little Bo Peep, as well as many others. In addition to an alphabetical listing of Mother Goose rhymes, there is a section on tips for reading Mother Goose to various age groups, and an annotated list of recommended books and resources. Rhymes are further grouped by theme such as bedtime, food, holidays and seasons, and weather. Created and maintained by Pat Anderson (pfa@nwu.edu), media librarian at the Galter Health Sciences Library Learning Resources Center, Northwestern University.

947. **Theodore Tugboat Online Activity Centre**

http://www.cochran.com/theodore/

Theodore Tugboat is a popular TV program for younger children. Parents and teachers can review synopses of the programs, read descriptions of the characters, and find out how the Big Harbour works. Kids can work in the online coloring book and listen to a Theodore story using RealAudio. There are two illustrated online interactive stories created especially for the Internet.

Berit Erickson, online librarian at the Theodore Tugboat Online Activity Centre, has compiled a list of links to more than 600 places of interest to kids on the Internet. Each site has been carefully selected, reviewed, and given a rating. This database of Internet sites is searchable and is also grouped by topic for easy browsing.

Child Care

948. **The ABC's of Safe and Healthy Child Care**

http://www.cdc.gov/ncidod/hip/ABC/abc.htm

The Hospital Infections Program of the National Center for Infectious Diseases has prepared a handbook to help the child care provider reduce sickness, injury, and other health problems in the child care facility, regardless of whether that setting is a center or a private home. Coverage includes how infectious diseases are spread; what to do to prevent diseases and injury; and what the most common childhood diseases are, how to recognize them, and what to do when they occur. Alphabetized fact sheets allow quick access to childhood diseases and conditions such as chickenpox, head lice, impetigo, pinkeye (conjunctivitis), and ringworm. Includes bibliographical references.

949. Baby Place

http://www.baby-place.com

Baby Place is a resource for new and expectant parents, providing information on pregnancy and baby care. Pregnancy and Birth FAQs and Parenting FAQs answer many common questions. Links are provided to information on baby product hazards, breastfeeding resources, child health, and newsgroups related to child care and parenting.

950. Babysitting Safety Tips

http://www.scpd.org/babysitting_safety_tips.htm

The Santa Clara Police Department provides these babysitting safety tips, including an information template to print out to use on each babysitting job. This information sheet should be filled out by the employers before they leave the house. Babysitting safety tips include things to know and do before accepting a job, what to do in case of fire, what to do when leaving the house during the daytime with the child(ren), and what to do when the employer returns home. See also Captain Bud Gundersen's (Los Angeles City Fire Department) Guide for Babysitters (http://www.sosnet.com/safety/babysitters.tips.html).

Meal Planning, Cooking, and Foods

See also "Nutrition" (entries 978–983).

Meal Planning and Cooking

951. Aunt Edna's Kitchen

http://www.cei.net/~terry/auntedna/

Aunt Edna's Kitchen provides information on preparing and cooking meals. Students can view the USDA food pyramid and find out more about nutrition. The cooking utilities section contains information on measurements, conversions, and spices and their uses. Links are provided to other food and cooking resources on the Internet, including brand-name food pages, recipes, and kitchen products. This site is designed and maintained by Terry and Edna Campbell (auntedna@aol.com).

952. Betty Crocker

http://www.bettycrocker.com

What's for dinner? This Betty Crocker site assists in planning dinners by the week. Menus can be adjusted for different cooks: those with kids, those who love to cook, those on a healthful diet, those who are adventurous, and those with little time. After you collect the menus that appeal to you and your family, ask Betty to print a shopping list created specifically from the selected menus. No time to go to the grocery store? Betty allows time-pressured cooks to type in ingredients on hand, and from these ingredients produces a list of recipes. Click on a recipe that sounds tempting, and Betty provides the complete recipe, including preparation time, cooking time, calories per serving, fat, cholesterol, sodium, carbohydrates, and protein. Betty Crocker Kitchens keeps a 75-year tradition alive on this Web site by providing reliable, creative cooking and baking advice.

953.   Bugfood!

http://www.uky.edu/Agriculture/Entomology/ythfacts/bugfood/bugfood.htm

Insect-themed recipes (no insects are actually eaten) can be made for fun, to enliven a party or an insect or nutrition unit. In Bugfood I, find out how to make Ants-on-a-Log, Bee Bread, Spider Cake, and Butterfly Snacks. Some color photographs allow visualization of the final products. Recipes compiled by Stephanie Bailey, Entomology Extension Specialist, University of Kentucky. In Bugfood II, find out more about insects as food. Discover how insects can be a good source of nutrition and how many bugs you might already be eating as microscopic parts of processed foods purchased in grocery stores. Bugfood III discusses different countries where insects have been eaten and enjoyed in the past and are eaten and enjoyed currently. For example, in Japan, you might find these items on a restaurant's menu: *hachi-no-ko* (boiled wasp larvae), *zaza-mushi* (aquatic insect larvae), *inago* (fried rice-field grasshoppers), *semi* (fried cicada), and *sangi* (fried silk moth pupae). Bugfood II is written by Stephanie Bailey and Bugfood III is written by Lana Unger, Extension Entomology Specialist, University of Kentucky.

954.   Campbell's Soup Home Page

http://www.campbellsoupco.com

Campbell's Creative Kitchen will help you create a delicious meal in minutes using ingredients you have on hand. Nutrition information is available, as are easy-to-make recipes and cooking tips. Crossword puzzles, the Alphabet Soup Game, and instructions for arts and crafts projects are located in the Campbell's Fun and Games Park. You'll find the history of the Campbell Soup Company at the Community Center.

955.   Kraft Interactive Kitchen

http://www.kraftfoods.com

Tired of the same old meals? Kraft Foods provides an online menu planner. No time to plan a meal? Kraft suggests recipes using ingredients you have on hand. The Kraft Cookbook lets you create your own Recipe Box online to store your favorites. Each day, a new recipe is highlighted on the Web site; or, to receive recipes directly, sign up for Kraft's Recipes by E-Mail. Feature articles are seasonal. The Kraft Career Site informs students about different jobs at Kraft and what it's like to work at Kraft Foods.

956.   Sally's Place

http://www.sallys-place.com

Sally's Place proclaims itself as the premier Internet site for food, beverage, and travel enthusiasts. The Food section offers tips for beginning cooks; background about each season's produce, with shopping and cooking tips and recipes; and a closer look at farmers' markets. You'll discover recipes to help celebrate a German Christmas or the Paris chocolate scene; you'll find recipes from many other countries as well. Cookbooks are reviewed. The site is searchable. Created and maintained by Sally Bernstein (sally@bpc.com).

957. **The Solar Cooking Archive**
http://solarcooking.org

Solar cooking benefits the environment because it doesn't use any type of fossil fuel. There is very little difference between conventional cooking and cooking in a solar box except for doubling the cooking time and leaving out water when cooking fresh vegetables or meats. This site shows illustrated construction plans for the three basic solar cookers (box, panel, and parabolic), and provides links to the latest news and topics on solar cooking. Look for links to K-12 lesson plans (http://www.sbgschool.com/teacher_activities/reading/world_around_us/sunny.html) and the physics of solar cooking (http://www.stanford.edu/group/syesp/activities/projects/engineer/physics.html). Webmasters for this site are Tom Sponheim (tsponheim@accessone.com) and Elizabeth Mann (mannifest@worldnet.att.net). See also Solar Cooks Do It in the Sun (http://www.solarcook.com).

To join the Solar Cooking online discussion group:
E-mail: **majordomo@igc.org**
Instructions: On the first line of the body of the message, type:
subscribe solarcooking-l

Foods

958. **Broccoli Town USA**

http://www.broccoli.com/mainpage.htm

Enter Broccoli Town USA for a tour of how broccoli is grown, harvested, and packaged at Mann's Farm. Find out the history of broccoli and the health benefits of including broccoli in your diet. Broccoli recipes are ripe for the picking. An interactive image of a broccoli plant helps students identify the plant parts. This Web site is sponsored by Mann Packing Company, Incorporated, one of the largest shippers of fresh broccoli in the world.

959. **Dole 5 A Day**

http://www.dole5aday.com

This is an excellent site developed by the Dole Food Company. The fruit and vegetable nutrition center discusses the importance of fruits and vegetables. Fruit and vegetable characters, such as Bobby Banana, are appealing, as are the music and catchy lyrics. Cool Stuff gives interesting facts about individual fruits and vegetables, their histories, where they are grown, how they are grown and harvested, how they are transported, tips for selecting the best fruits and vegetables, and important nutritional information. Recipes are also available. Lists of fruits and vegetables high in Vitamin A, Vitamin C, and fiber are given. Dole's 5 A Day Adventures CD-ROM is the first to encourage children to eat five servings of fruits and vegetables each day. Information about how elementary schools can order the CD-ROM free of charge is available.

960. **The Strawberry Facts Page**

http://www.jamm.com/strawberry/facts.html

The Strawberry Facts Page has all kinds of facts about strawberries. Learn how to pronounce *strawberry* in languages other than English, find a delicious strawberry recipe, and learn about the nutritional value of strawberries. There is information about growing and tending strawberry plants and the history of the plants. Links are provided to strawberry icons, images, clip art, and festivals. Discover the world capital of strawberries. Peruse lists of music, movies, and literature with a strawberry flavor. Links are available to other berry and fruit resources.

Health

National Associations

961. The American Cancer Society

http://www.cancer.org
or
http://www.cancer.org/noframes.html

The home page for the American Cancer Society (ACS) provides information about the ACS and its efforts against cancer. Cancer information is given in a very readable format. Find out about new guidelines, programs, events, and publications.

962. The American Heart Association

http://www.americanheart.org

Students can find out if they are at risk for heart disease by taking a simple test. Then they can find out how to reduce their risk of heart disease. The American Heart Association (AHA) has declared war on fad diets. Tips on how to lose weight and keep it off and how to recognize a fad diet are just two of the articles in the online *Heart and Stroke A-Z Guide* (http://www.americanheart.org/Heart_and_Stroke_A_Z_Guide/). The American Heart Association Diet is also online. It is an easy-to-follow guide to healthy eating with dietary guidelines for both children and adults.

963. The American Lung Association

http://www.lungusa.org

Since 1904, the American Lung Association (ALA) has been a leader in public education about lung health. This site provides easy access to information about a variety of lung health issues, including asthma, asthma and children, smoking and tobacco control, lung disease and related diseases, and environmental health. All information is keyword-searchable.

964. American Red Cross

http://www.redcross.org

Each month a new health and safety tip is posted on this site. The American Red Cross sponsors CPR (cardiopulmonary resuscitation) training, first aid, and other health and safety services, including water safety. The Red Cross publishes safety information about general water safety, home pool safety, and ocean safety. Find out about these and other Red Cross health and safety services.

General Interest

965.   BioRAP® (Biological Research for Animals and People)

http://www.biorap.org/core.html

Using an inquiry approach, this site addresses a number of health issues, such as Aging and Genetics, Product Safety, Healthy Skin, and AIDS. Careers are suggested in related fields, with information guaranteed to interest students. There are Teacher Guides, Rap Sheets, Bio Words, and links to research information and resources. Topic explorations are aimed at engaging students in an interactive study of health sciences and consumer sciences. BioRAP® is an educational project published by Connecticut United for Research Excellence, Inc. (CURE). E-mail may be directed to (cure@nso1.uchc.edu).

966.   Healthtouch®: Online for Better Health

http://www.healthtouch.com

The Healthtouch® site is divided into areas of health-related information. In Drug Information, students can look up information about prescription or over-the-counter medications to find out about common drug uses, proper use of medicines, and possible side effects. The Health Resource Directory lists selected health organizations and government agencies that can be contacted for more information about specific health topics, diseases, and illnesses. Health Information offers up-to-date information about a variety of health concerns, including allergies, asthma, diet and nutrition, drug and alcohol abuse, eye diseases, eating disorders, headaches, mental health, poison prevention, sexually transmitted diseases, and HIV and AIDS.

967.   The Longevity Game

http://www.northwesternmutual.com/games/longevity/

Students fill in their lifestyle habits and family history to calculate how long they can expect to live, based on life insurance industry research. Everyone starts with the average life expectancy of 73 years. This Web site is maintained by Northwestern Mutual Life Insurance Company.

968.   MEDLINE

http://www.nlm.nih.gov/databases/freemedl.html

During 1997, the National Library of Medicine began allowing free Web-based access to its MEDLINE database of more than 9 million references to articles published in 3,800 biomedical journals. Access is provided by either PubMed or Internet Grateful Med. Through PubMed, students can also access GenBank DNA Sequences, GenBank Protein Sequences, Biomolecule 3D Structures, and Complete Genomes databases. Internet Grateful Med can be used to access other databases, such as AIDSLINE, HealthSTAR, AIDSDRUGS, AIDSTRIALS, DIRLINE, HISTLINE, HSRPROJ, OLDMEDLINE, and SDILINE. Complete citations and abstracts are given for each article.

969. SciCentral's Gateway to Health Sciences

http://www.scicentral.com/H-02heal.html

Students can investigate more than 45 different health sciences categories, from AIDS/HIV to Virology. This is a good resource to use for research into current issues and topics related to health sciences, such as infectious diseases, nutrition, and cancer research, as well as career exploration into nursing, dentistry, physical therapy, pharmacy, and public health. Informational Web sites and full-text articles, including selected articles from professional journals, special reports, and software reviews, are accessible by specialty areas. Links are provided to a number of health-related Web sites, including the World Health Organization, the National Library of Medicine, and MedWeb.

Health for Kids

970. KidsHealth.org

http://www.kidshealth.org

A broad range of excellent health information is available for parents, teens, and kids. Some of the topics in the Kids section discuss feelings, health problems, how to stay healthy, everyday illnesses and injuries, and how the body works. Some of the topics in the Teen area cover what to do if your friend shoplifts, how to eat healthy on the go, sexual questions, school violence, prom stress, how to stay safe, and how to get along with your teachers. The Parent section contains topics on general health, medical problems, growth and development, emotions and behavior, nutrition and fitness, infections, first aid and safety, pregnancy and newborns, and positive parenting. This site is enhanced with color photographs, diagrams, and interactive Java applets, as well as being keyword-searchable. Created by the pediatric medical experts at The Alfred I. duPont Hospital for Children, The Nemours Children's Clinics, and maintained by The Nemours Foundation.

Question-and-Answer Services

971. Ask a Medicine/Health/Fitness Expert

http://k12science.ati.stevens-tech.edu/curriculum/aska/medicine.html

This page offers a list of links to experts in the fields of medicine and health. Students can ask questions of a doctor, a nurse, an optometrist, an immunologist, a pharmacist, a dietitian, and an STD specialist.

972. Go Ask Alice!

http://www.goaskalice.columbia.edu

Go Ask Alice! is an interactive question-and-answer service by Healthwise, the Health Education division of Columbia University Health Services. The service answers questions from the university's student population, but is open to the general public. Each week, Alice answers questions about health, including all types of questions about sexuality, sexual health, sexual relationships, general health, fitness and nutrition, emotional well-being, stress, and alcohol and other drugs. Questions are answered publicly but anonymously (without identifying who asked the question) in Alice's New Questions and Answers of the Week. This allows students to ask questions they might be too embarrassed or unwilling to ask in person.

Usually if one person has a question, so do many others. Past questions and answers are archived and searchable. Check the archives before asking a question, because it could take up to a month for Alice to answer a question, and there is no guarantee that Alice will answer any one specific question. Go Ask Alice! is for educational purposes only, and its contents are not intended to diagnose, treat, or provide a second opinion on a health problem or disease.

Addiction: Alcohol, Drugs, and Tobacco

973. The Smoking Handbook

http://www.westnet.com/~rickd/smoke/smoke1.html

The Smoking Handbook was written by eighth-grade students at Eastchester Middle School (Eastchester, New York) after they studied the hazards associated with tobacco in their health classes. The handbook's target audience is middle-school kids, because the rationale is that most smokers develop the habit during their teen years. Students will discover what tobacco and nicotine are, the reasons why people begin to smoke, the particular allure of smoking for teenagers, the consequences of smoking, methods of quitting, and the effects of secondhand smoke. The handbook can be read sequentially by chapters or nonsequentially by clicking on links to topics of interest at the bottom of each page. The Webmaster is Rick Donahue, computer technology teacher (MrDonahue@aol.com).

974. Web of Addictions

http://www.well.com/user/woa/

The Web of Addictions provides accurate information about alcohol and other drug addictions. Click on Facts, a collection of fact sheets and other materials arranged by drug. All the fact sheets are in the public domain, and students and teachers are encouraged to copy and distribute them. This site was created and is maintained by Dick Dillon (Razer@ix.netcom.com), who is associated with a nonprofit counseling agency in St. Louis, Missouri, and Andrew L. Homer, Ph.D. (AHomer@mail.coin.missouri.edu).

Diseases

975. AIDS Handbook

http://www.westnet.com/~rickd/AIDS/AIDS1.html

Selected as a related resource by the Discovery Channel for the program, "The Science of HIV," the AIDS Handbook is a thorough guide written by Eastchester Middle School (Eastchester, New York) students in Linda Sokol's eighth-grade health classes. Students can read the information online sequentially or click to link to topics of their interest, such as Prevention, Transmission, Symptoms, Treatment, and How the Immune System Fights Disease. A list of AIDS-related links on the Web is provided. The Webmaster is Rick Donahue, computer technology teacher (MrDonahue@aol.com).

976. HIV InSite

http://hivinsite.ucsf.edu

HIV InSite is a gateway to AIDS knowledge, providing the latest medical information and research findings. International reports are available, as well as state-by-state information about HIV/AIDS. The section on prevention and education has information on what works and what doesn't for preventing HIV infection. HIV InSite is a project of the University of California at San Francisco AIDS Program at San Francisco General Hospital.

Fitness

977. The Fitness Files

http://rcc.webpoint.com/fitness/fundhome.htm

Sponsored by Racine County, Wisconsin, and the All Saints Health Care System, this site provides excellent information about fitness fundamentals, the benefits of an active lifestyle, and health dos and don'ts. Find out your target heart rate and take a fitness quiz. Get the truth about fitness myths, such as "no pain, no gain," and "women who lift weights will develop big, bulky muscles." Pick up some stretches and exercises to use in home workouts. The Injurenet section offers tips on preventing injuries, and the Fuel for Fitness section discusses nutrition and diet. As a fun and informative activity, students can build and analyze a meal using the Fat & Calorie Counter.

Nutrition

978. Center for Science in the Public Interest Home Page

http://www.cspinet.org

The Just for Kids CHOW Club lists the 10 best and worst foods for kids, tips for good eating, and some nutritional recipes. There is a diner's guide to health and nutrition claims on restaurant menus, Booze News, and nutrition quizzes. Links lead to other health and nutrition sites, including associations and organizations and U.S. government sites, such as the FDA, the FDA's Center for Food Safety and Applied Nutrition, and the Food Nutrition Information Center. The Center for Science in the Public Interest is a nonprofit education and advocacy organization that focuses on improving the safety and nutritional quality of our food supply and on reducing the carnage caused by alcohol abuse.

979. Fast Food Facts

http://www.olen.com/food/book.html

Based on the book *Fast Food Facts* by the Minnesota attorney general's office, this site provides information about calories, fat, cholesterol, and sodium. Examples of typical fast-food meals from McDonald's, Domino's, Kentucky Fried Chicken, and Taco Bell are compared to better meal choices from the same establishments.

980. Fast-Food Finder

http://www.olen.com/food/index.html

The Fast-Food Finder was created with the Minnesota attorney general's office. Students can type in a food item from one of many fast-food restaurants to find out the calories, fat, cholesterol, and salt content.

981. National Dairy Council's Chef Combo's Fantastic Adventures in Tasting and Nutrition

http://www.chefcombo.com/index.html

Preschool children's eating habits develop between the ages of two and five. This site attempts to help early childhood educators formulate strong nutrition education components in their curriculum. Activities are broader than nutrition; they include, for example, Sergeant Hanky Germ Buster, to demonstrate how invisible germs stick to your hands.

982. Nutrition and Diet

http://www.osu.edu/units/osuhosp/patedu/homedocs.pdf/nut-diet.pdf/nutframe.htm

"Lite" recipes are accompanied by lists of foods high in iron, hidden sources of sugar, information on cholesterol, tips for successful weight reduction, the importance of including fiber in your diet, and simple ways to change a recipe. Adobe Acrobat Reader is needed to view these PDF (portable document format) documents.

983. The Nutritionist's Tool Box

http://www.fsci.umn.edu/tools.htm

This page is from the University of Minnesota's Department of Food Science and Nutrition. The kCal-culator allows students to calculate their energy needs. There is a K-12 Nutrition Expedition with a Trail Guide for teachers. Links are provided to other food and nutrition sites.

Horticulture

984. Australian National Botanic Gardens

http://155.187.10.12/anbg/

The purpose of the Australian National Botanic Gardens, located in Canberra, Australia, is to grow, study, and promote Australia's flora. While maintaining a scientific collection of native plants and cultivating plants threatened in the wild, the gardens are also open for the enjoyment and education of visitors. Students can access the gardens' botanical and horticultural databases and photographic collection, as well as sections on the use of plants by Australian Aborigines and various birds and animals indigenous to Australia.

985. Gardening.com

http://www.sierra.com/sierrahome/gardening/

The plant encyclopedia has listings for more than 1,500 plants. Students can search by plant name or attributes. The encyclopedia is fully illustrated. To hear Latin pronunciations of plants, you need RealAudio capabilities. A search for daisies returned nothing; a search for daisy returned 16 hits. Each hit was accompanied by a color thumbnail picture, Latin name, and common name, all linked to an entry surprising in its coverage and depth of information. Other features of this Web site include an Ortho problem solver, which helps in diagnosing and treating 700 pest and disease problems; and an annotated garden site directory, which can be searched by keyword or subject. This Web site is an excellent reference for gardeners.

986. Missouri Botanical Garden

http://www.mobot.org/welcome.html

The home page has a virtual tour of the garden. In the Education area, a clickable map of Costa Rica provides images and information on tropical plants. A Tropical Feast provides information about food products grown in the tropics, with images of each product. Links are provided to other botanical resources on the Internet, such as the Flora of North America Project, the Flora of China Project, and the Flora Mesoamericana Project.

987. School Gardens

http://aggie-horticulture.tamu.edu/kindergarden/index.html

Students and teachers will find out more about the benefits of school gardening at this Web site. Resources are available so that teachers can integrate the topic of gardening into curriculum areas such as history, economics, poetry, math, and science. Because gardens are a big responsibility, there is a step-by-step guide and some things to consider before undertaking a school gardening project. Information is given on plant growth, terrariums, and the relationship between plants, air, water, and light. Available resources include a bibliography for teachers and links to related Internet resources. Links are also provided to schools with gardens created by students, as well as to schools in various climates and regions throughout the world so that students can virtually visit a school located in the grasslands or the desert. See also Margaret Beeks Elementary School Gardening Project (http://www.hort.vt.edu/faculty/relf/4984/Mbelem.html).

Physical Education

National Standards

988. Adapted Physical Education National Standards

http://teach.virginia.edu/go/apens/NATSTND.html

The purpose of the Adapted Physical Education National Standards (APENS) project is to ensure that physical education instruction for students with disabilities is provided by qualified physical education instructors. Information is available on the components of the national standards, as is information on the national examination (including exam applications and a study guide).

General Interest

989. Games Kids Play

http://www.corpcomm.net/~gnieboer/

Remember all the games that kids have played for generations in backyards and on playgrounds? Games and rules are most often passed down through generations, but sometimes are lost. This site gives the rules and describes how to play more than 250 games, including Red Rover, Duck Duck Goose, Four Square, Marco Polo, Crack the Whip, Mother May I?, Simon Says, and Steal the Bacon. Look for circle games, team games, and games that are both active and passive. This is an excellent site for classroom teachers and for physical education (PE) teachers. Many games are ideal for use on rainy days. Created by Geof Nieboer (gnieboer@ corpcomm.net).

990. P.E. and Health Teachers Discussion Group

Newsgroup: **k12.ed.health-pe**

991. PE Central

http://pe.central.vt.edu

Sponsored by the Virginia Tech Health and Physical Education Program, PE Central is a site for physical education teachers, students, and interested parents and adults. This site, which is updated frequently, provides the latest information about contemporary, developmentally appropriate physical education programs for children and youth. Links are provided to lesson ideas for the classroom teacher, PE lesson ideas, health lesson ideas, and assessment ideas. Lesson plans are available for pre-K, elementary, middle, and high school. The Top Web Sites section offers links to various individual and team sports, fitness, health, dance, and outdoor Web sites. Information is available on how to purchase equipment, job listings, conferences, workshops, and online discussion groups. Links are provided to supplementary instructional resources on the Internet.

992. Sports Media International

http://www.sports-media.org

Sports Media International is a comprehensive sports site for physical education teachers, coaches, and athletes. Provides lesson plans, drills, exercises, and games. Look for medicine-ball drills for gymnastics, line dances, step-aerobic patterns, exercises for back care, basket-ball drills, and general lesson plans. The Coaching & Training section has information from Aerobics to Yoga, including tips for coaching beginning badminton players, a 10-week intensive training for "Ultimate," and information on how to coach table tennis. There is a list of links to sports-related sites around the world and a pen-pal section for those who want to communicate about sports. Guy VanDamme (guy.vandamme@sports-media.org) is the Webmaster.

Safety and First Aid

General Safety and Personal Safety

993. Children's Safety Center

http://legal.firn.edu/kids/kids.html

Provides a series of slides with questions and answers to help young children protect themselves and handle emergencies. Answers questions such as what to do if a bully picks on you; what to do if someone offers you drugs; what to do if you find drugs or drug needles; what to do when someone picks a fight; and what to do if you get lost. Created by the Attorney General's Office for the state of Florida.

994. National SAFE KIDS Campaign

http://www.safekids.org

The National SAFE KIDS Campaign is the first and only national organization dedicated solely to the prevention of unintentional childhood injury, the leading killer of children aged 14 and under. Information is available about the national office and state and local coalitions. There is a Family Safety Check List and Frequently Asked Questions and Answers. Facts sheets highlight childhood injuries, such as scalding burns, poisoning, drowning, shopping cart, sports, and unintentional injuries from firearms. A bicycle injury fact sheet states that 75 percent of bicycle-related fatalities among children could be prevented by a bicycle helmet.

995. Personal Safety

http://www.softport-co.com/safety/

This site is sponsored by the Los Angeles County Deputy Sheriff's office. Some of the categories of tips for personal safety include how to protect yourself while walking at night, while using an automated teller machine, while shopping, and while in a parking garage. Tips for preventing a carjacking are also given.

Bicycle Safety

996. Bicycle Helmet Safety Institute

http://www.bhsi.org/index.htm

Learn about bicycle helmet safety and how to organize bicycle helmet programs. Articles are available on helmet laws, standards, and statistics. There is a FAQs section and links to pages related to helmets and bicycles. A good literature tie-in is *Mick Harte Was Here*, a fictional story, by Barbara Park (Knopf, 1995). Not wearing a helmet, Mick dies in a bicycle accident. His sister Phoebe describes her brother, Mick, and the effect his death has on the family. In an author's note, Park pleads with kids to wear their bike helmets to prevent such a needless tragedy in real life.

997. Welcome to Kevin's Road Safety Page

http://www.roadsafety.net/Kids/Menu/fs.html

Queensland Transport in Queensland, Australia, sponsors this Web site on road safety for kids. Covers walking on roads, riding on buses and in cars, and riding bicycles and helmet safety. Find out more about how to do these things safely with a "down under" flair—and be sure to take the bicycle safety test. Walking and bicycle rules apply for countries where automobiles are driven on the right-hand side of the road.

Fire Safety

998. Current Stories and Safety Bulletins

http://www.sosnet.com/safety/fire.safety.index.html

Provides current stories about fires and safety bulletins on topics such as using the correct fire extinguisher; using 911 properly; using the stop, drop, and roll technique; and smoke detectors. Provided by the Los Angeles City Fire Department. The Webmaster is Ed Swift (sos@sosnet. com).

999. **Fire Safety**

http://www-personal.umd.umich.edu/~jobrown/fire.html

Suggested student projects can be done individually, in small groups, or as an entire class. All projects help students become knowledgeable about fire safety so they can inform and educate others in their community. Lots of links to fire safety information sites revolve around the theme of fighting fire with facts. Specific fire safety tips are given. Links are provided to the National Fire Protection Association and the Firehouse Museum, with displays of firefighting equipment and memorabilia from across the country and around the world. This fire safety site is for middle school students, grades 5–8. Written and maintained by Joan Marie Brown, School of Education, University of Michigan-Dearborn (jobrown@umich.edu).

1000. **Smokey Bear's Official Web Site**

http://www.smokeybear.com

Smokey tells younger students how to prevent forest fires and how to correctly make camp fires. Shockwave v.5 is necessary to take advantage of the puzzles and animations.

In-Line Skating Safety

1001. **International In-Line Skating Association**

http://www.iisa.org/icp/gu-intro.html

This site promotes the Gear Up! Take a Lesson program, a nationwide, public-service in-line skating safety program that encourages skaters to don protective gear before skating. Skaters wearing protective equipment are far less likely to become injured. Helmets, knee pads, elbow pads, and wrist protection are discussed. Free consumer Gear Up! information is available at (800) 56-SKATE or by e-mail using the forms provided on the Web site. The guide features articles such as "Gearing Up to Go Skating," "The State of In-Line Safety," "How to Get the Most Out of an In-Line Lesson," "The World of In-Line Skating," and "Becoming a Certified In-Line Instructor." The guide also includes listings of certified instructors by region so that those interested in taking a lesson will have immediate access to qualified professionals.

Sun Safety

1002. **Safe Sun Tips**

http://www.aad.org/SkinCancerNews/SafeSunTips/index.html

The American Academy of Dermatology presents sun safety tips, the benefits of using lots of sunscreen, and special advice for those going to summer camp.

Find out how skin-savvy you are. Take the academy's true/false quiz "What Do You Know About the Skin You're In?" at (http://homearts.com/depts/health/winsunb2.htm).

General First Aid

1003. **Rescue 411**

http://library.advanced.org/10624/index.html

Do you know what to do when faced with an unexpected life-or-death situation that requires quick action? This site recommends that you be certified in Standard First Aid and CPR. Find out what first aid is appropriate for sudden illness and accidents and injuries. What is the difference between CPR and rescue breathing? Find out how to treat burns, frostbite, broken bones, choking, and poisoning. Before leaving this site, take an interactive mini-quiz to find out how much you know about first aid. This site was developed by Julia Becker and Daina Lieberman, students at Cranford High School (Cranford, New Jersey), for the 1997 ThinkQuest competition.

Snakebites

See also Jason's Snakes and Reptiles (entry 791).

1004. **Clinical Toxinology Home Page**

http://www.wch.sa.gov.au/paedm/clintox/

Discusses the science of clinical toxinology, which deals with injury to humans from venoms and poisons produced by animals, plants, fungi, and bacteria. Provides a link to a Web version of the CSL Antivenom Handbook used by doctors in Australia to treat snakebites, spider bites (as well as other arthropod bites and stings), and marine bites and stings. CSL Ltd. provides antivenins for use by doctors and hospitals. Maintained by Dr. Julian White (toxinaus@ wch.sa.gov.au), Toxinology Department, Women's and Children's Hospital, North Adelaide, Australia.

1005. **Snakebite Emergency First-Aid Information**

http://www.xmission.com/~gastown/herpmed/snbite.htm

This site offers advice on what to do and what not to do if you are bitten by a venomous snake. Emphasis is on being prepared and what to include in a snakebite kit. Links are provided to sites with related information. The Webmaster's address is (grenard@con2.com).

1006. **Treating and Preventing Venomous Bites**

http://www.fda.gov/fdac/features/995_snakes.html

About 8,000 people a year receive venomous bites in the United States, and 9 to 15 of those people will die. This article, written by the U.S. Food and Drug Administration, explains how to prevent and treat venomous bites. Information is given about the types of poisonous snakes in the United States and how to avoid them. Treatment dilemmas are discussed, with emphasis on current controversies. First aid for snakebites as recommended by the American Red Cross is outlined.

Sport Science

See also Science of Hockey (entry 1018).

1007. Aerodynamics in Sports Technology

http://wings.ucdavis.edu/Tennis/index.html

Focusing on tennis data, how the tennis ball flies, its speed, how it spins, how it moves through the air, what happens when the ball hits the court, and the strokes of the players, Aerodynamics in Sports Technology is designed to help K-12 students understand aerodynamics, physics, and mathematics. Short video clips of experiments and animations allow students to interact in a virtual laboratory. Students and classes can participate in three ways: sharing in live video conferences and chats over the Internet, conducting guided research projects on their own, and proposing experiments for the NASA team to test and then following those results. Each lesson plan is designed to meet the national science standards and includes tips to educators on how to integrate the lessons into the classroom curriculum. Once a month, new information, activities, curriculum, and research results are posted to this Web site. Look for a Tennis Science online textbook, curriculum bridges (cross-curriculum activities), lesson plans, and feature stories. Created by NASA's Learning Technologies Project and Cislunar Aerospace, Inc., students are encouraged to understand the exciting career possibilities of combining an interest in science with an interest in sports.

1008. Slam Dunk Science

http://www.scire.com/sds/sdsmenu.html

Intended to provide an introduction to many aspects of sport science as they relate to shoe design, this guide allows students in grades 5 through 12 to see how some science careers are actively involved in sports. Shoe Design 101 highlights the parts of a shoe and how science affects shoe design. Lab Tools demonstrates how impact test machines measure the cushioning characteristics of a material, and what those measurements mean. Hands-on activities are suggested for students, most requiring a computer with QuickTime and other hardware and software, such as Measurement in Motion, Logger Pro using a universal laboratory interface (ULI), and Force Probe. Without computers, students can set up a low-cost sport research lab, calculate VO_2 (volume of oxygen) max, and create a shoe design poster. A glossary of terms is provided, and a list of print and Internet resources helps students to find additional information for further research.

1009. Sport! Science @ The Exploratorium

http://www.exploratorium.edu/sports/

Sport! is the world's largest and most interactive exhibition; it's found at the Exploratorium science museum in San Francisco. It is devoted entirely to the science of athletics. The exhibit focuses on how science and technology can make a difference in the games people play. A question-and-answer section allows students to learn the answers to such questions as "Why do your muscles burn when you work out?" Sport science bibliographies and links are provided for a wide variety of sports.

1010. *Sportscience*

http://www.sportsci.org

Sportscience is a peer-reviewed journal of the Internet Society for Sport Science. The journal is published online every few months, and features news articles as well as opinion and perspective articles. Regular feature columns focus on topics such as biomechanics, training, nutrition, kinesiology, and history-makers in sport science. To submit articles, contact the editor (editor@sportsci.org).

Sports

See also ESPNET SportsZone News (entry 1352); Women's National Basketball Association (entry 1353); *Sports Illustrated Online* (entry 1355); and *Sports Illustrated for Kids Online* (entry 1354).

General Interest

1011. **Sports Central: The History of Sports**

http://library.advanced.org/10480/index.html

Students can find out more about the history of football, soccer, basketball, baseball, and hockey. They can then take an interactive quiz to see how much they know about these sports. Links are provided to other sports-related information on the Internet. Created by Jeffrey Tierney, Daniel Springer, and David Polonitza, students at Cranford High School (Cranford, New Jersey), for the 1997 ThinkQuest competition. The Webmaster's address is (Madmooch@aol.com).

Participation and Coaching

Baseball

1012. **Home State Bank Team Manual**

http://webscores.com/zdr/tm/jzm.html

Provides an online copy of the team manual used by coaches and players involved with Little League and All Star teams in Crystal Lake, Illinois. The manual is used as a text of baseball instruction by players and as a guide by coaches. It explains skills with writing aimed at 10- to 12-year-olds. Both team offense and team defense are explained. Player conduct is outlined with specific responsibilities of players listed. The Parent Handbook is also available to outline expectations of parents. Written and copyrighted by Coach Joe Zander (zdr@dls.net).

1013. **Total Baseball Online**

http://www.totalbaseball.com

Total Baseball Online is the online home of the Official Encyclopedia of Major League Baseball. There are daily features and news stories about major and minor league baseball, as well as player biographies and statistics, official box scores, line scores, and game accounts. Find out team histories, awards, and team rosters. Look up batting, pitching, fielding, and base-running records. Additional interesting features include a baseball calendar, baseball FAQs, and an Ask the Baseball Expert online question-answering service. Produced by Total Sports, a sports information company; the Web editor is Sarah MacDougall (sarahm@totalsports.net).

Basketball

1014. Basketball Coaching Information Web Page

http://hometown.aol.com/coachmjw/pp22.htm

Coach Wells has compiled a fantastic collection of links to Internet resources on basketball coaching. Look for links to rules, governing associations, coaching resources, and high school basketball tournaments. Be sure to check out The Mental Game Plan, Hoop Tech, StatKeeper, and Hooplinks. Some of Coach Wells's pages for online reading include "3 Out–2 In Motion Offense," "The Tipping Zone," and "4 Out and 1 In Motion Offense." Coaches will want to join the Basketball Coaching online discussion list directly from the Web site. Created and maintained by Michael J. Wells (coachmjw@aol.com), varsity boys' basketball coach, Keswick, Christian High School (St. Petersburg, Florida).

1015. Basketball Highway

http://www.bbhighway.com

Basketball Highway is a resource for basketball coaches and enthusiasts. It offers information about events, schedules, results, clinics, learning materials, camps, travel, training sites, job information, and even ways for coaches to electronically communicate with other coaches around the world using the Coaches Bulletin Board. Links are provided to NBA, CBA, men's college, and women's college news and statistics. Other links are to officiating resources and rules.

Football

1016. Toby's Football Coaching Site

http://members.aol.com/tbran1996/private/tobys.htm

Coaches will want to check out the Playbook for defensive and offensive plays, as well as the Links section. Find out more about the "Multiple Tight Slot Offense." Links are provided to football coaching books. A Message Board and Trading Center allow coaches to communicate with one another. Created and maintained by Tom Brandow (tbran1996@aol.com). See also Team Discovery's football coaches Web site (http://www.teamdiscovery.com/football/).

Golf

1017. GolfWeb

http://www.golfweb.com/index.html

GolfWeb ambitiously states that it includes everything about golf on the World Wide Web. Students will be interested in the golf news and the online golf instruction. John Jacobs's instruction page covers the basics, the swing, troubleshooting, and some special shots.

Hockey

1018. Science of Hockey

http://www.exploratorium.edu/hockey/

The Science of Hockey takes you inside the sport and explains the science behind the world's fastest game. This site was developed by the Exploratorium science museum in San Francisco and the National Hockey League's (NHL) San Jose Sharks. Contains RealVideo and Audio interviews with scientists and NHL players and coaches.

Soccer

1019. Soccer Center

http://www.teamdiscovery.com/soccer/

Check out the collection of soccer drills and games for kids in the Coaching Library. If you have a question, ask one of the online coaches! The Soccer Board is a place to discuss coaching issues, get advice, and talk soccer. Soccer Chat is open 24 hours a day. Links are provided to other soccer sites on the Internet.

Tennis

See also Aerodynamics in Sports Technology (entry 1007).

1020. The Tennis Server

http://www.tennisserver.com

Plan to visit this site regularly or subscribe to the free e-mail newsletter to find out the latest tennis news. Each month new information is posted on tennis equipment, playing tips by USPTA Pro John Mills, and news about internationally developing juniors. Links are provided to daily tennis news sources, and regular columns discuss current issues and topics in the tennis community.

1021. TennisONE

http://www.tennisone.com

TennisONE features an in-depth series of tennis lessons. Past lessons are stored in the TennisONE Library. Tennis players and enthusiasts can post questions and comments on the Global Bulletin Board.

Volleyball

1022. Schneid's Volleyball Page

http://www.xnet.com/~schneid/vball.shtml

Information about volleyball is divided into categories including general, rules and statistics, strategy, drills, skills, training, fun, equipment, publications, and links to other sites of interest. In addition to information about volleyball, this site provides information about exercise and fitness, sports medicine, and nutrition.

Wrestling

1023. USA Wrestling Coaches Corner

http://www.usawrestling.org/coaches.htm

Coaching tips are shared along with nutrition and training tips. Information is available on the U.S. National Wrestling Team (which includes the Freestyle Team, the Greco-Roman Team, and the Women's Team), its event schedule and results, daily trivia, and a photo gallery. Questions (600 words or less) may be e-mailed to the USA Wrestling Coach using an online template. The Web site e-mail address is (USAW@concentric.net).

International Competitions

Olympics

1024. 2000 Olympic Summer Games in Sydney, Australia

http://www.sydney.olympic.org

These pages contain information concerning the Games of the XXVIIth Olympiad to be held in Sydney in the year 2000, from September 15 to October 1. Athletes from 200 countries are expected to compete in 28 sports. The News area contains recent news as well as archived news releases. Find out more about Sydney and Australia.

1025. 2002 Winter Olympic Games in Salt Lake City, Utah

http://www.SLC2002.org/home.html

The XIX Olympic Winter Games will be held on February 8–24, 2002, in Salt Lake City, Utah. Competition is scheduled in 7 sports with 70 medal events, more than those in previous Games. There is a section for news with the latest headline news and a news release archive. An interactive area for children is planned. This site is under construction.

1026. The First Olympic Games, Athens, 1896

http://orama.com/athens1896/

This site, which documents the first modern-day Olympic Games, opens with a graphic of the cover of the 1896 Olympic Games program and links to its contents. Find out how the ancient Olympic Games were revived and what they were like in 1896 from the original writings of the Olympic Committee. Pierre de Coubertin shares his ideas about the Olympic Movement and how he came up with the idea of reviving the ancient Olympic Games. Information on the history of the Panathenean Stadium, where the 1896 Olympics were held, is written by Professor Nicholaos G. Politis. Secretary of the Games, Timoleon J. Philemon, writes about the organization of the first Olympics in Athens, and Charalambos Anninos writes a day-by-day description of the games. The 1896 medal winners are listed, with some links to their pictures and biographical information. This is an excellent page to use to begin an integrated unit with the Olympics as a theme.

1027. **The Olympic Movement Home Page**

http://www.olympic.org

This is the home page for the International Olympic Committee (IOC), the authority for the Olympic Movement. It is a multimedia site filled with sounds and sights, enhanced by Shockwave's Flash (plug-in) software. The extensive information on the past, present, and future includes lists of where the games have been held, the various games of the Olympiad, documents about Olympic solidarity, the medical commission, the Olympic program, and much more. There are links to the Olympic Museum in Lausanne, Switzerland. The address for the non-Shockwave version of this Web site is (http://www.olympic.org/flat/index.html).

Social Studies and Geography

All URL addresses in this chapter are checked and updated monthly. If a link does not work, please refer to the Directory Update Web page located at (http://www.lu.com/lu/irdupdates.html).

The social studies and geography resources in this chapter will be of interest to historians, teachers, and students of social studies, world history, U.S. history, political science, government, and geography.

The section on geography has information about the national standards and provides activities, lesson plans, and resources to aid in geography education, including resources for maps and globes. Outline maps are available from the Houghton Mifflin Company (entry 1321), lesson plans are provided by National Geographic (entry 1317), and geography and map-reading lessons (entry 1318) have been designed by the U.S. Geological Survey (USGS).

Many resources available on the Internet are not available in print format, making these resources unique. For example, students can read letters written during the Civil War (entry 1156). *The Prairie Traveler: A Hand-Book for Overland Expeditions* (entry 1144), written in 1859, was an essential guidebook offering practical advice—still sound today—to the many emigrants heading west, most of whom were poorly informed and ill-prepared for such a journey. The entire text is now available online, including maps, illustrations, and itineraries of the principal routes between the Mississippi and the Pacific.

The American Presidency by Grolier Online (entry 1052) is a great way to learn more about the presidents and also have fun. Some government Web sites have been designed with younger constituents in mind, notably Welcome to the White House for Kids (entry 1056), the South Carolina Government Kids Page (entry 1102), and the U.S. Department of the Treasury's Kids Page (entry 1077).

Many social studies resources are updated daily. For example, the White House posts news releases daily. Supreme Court decisions are available on the Internet within a few hours of their public reading. Congressional Gophers and the Library of Congress online system (LOCIS) maintain up-to-the-minute information about legislation in both the Senate and the House of Representatives.

World Wide Web sites have pictures of state flags and senators and representatives to Congress. Be sure to look at The 50 States of the United States (entry 1097), and listings of individual Web pages created by members of the U.S. House of Representatives (entry 1063) and the U.S. Senate (entry 1064).

To maximize its usefulness, the organization of this chapter reflects how subjects are taught and how students and teachers research topics in social studies. Alphabetical order and hierarchical organizations are adapted to meet the needs of readers. For example, information about the United States precedes information about other countries of the world. Browse through this chapter to discover for yourself how the Internet is helping to bring history to life!

National Standards

1028. ***Expectations of Excellence: Curriculum Standards for Social Studies***

http://www.ncss.org/standards/

The National Council for the Social Studies published *Expectations of Excellence: Curriculum Standards* in 1994, as a framework for K-12 social studies program design through the use of 10 thematic strands. It also serves as a guide for curriculum decisions by providing performance expectations for all students and practice examples for classroom teachers.

Biographies

See "Biographies" (entries 1333–1336), and consult the subject index for individuals.

General Interest

1029. **Economics and Geography Lessons for Grades 1-5**

http://www.mcps.k12.md.us/curriculum/socialstd/Econ_Geog.html

Excellent lessons in economics and geography have been prepared using 32 children's picture books. For example, in reading *Uncle Jed's Barbershop* by Margaree Mitchell (Simon & Schuster, 1993), students discover the differences between life now and long ago. In the early 1900s, Uncle Jed is saving his money to buy his own barbershop, but because his niece needs an operation, and because he loses his $3,000 savings during a Great Depression bank closure, he must save much longer than he had once planned. Some of the other titles in this unit are *Sarah, Plain and Tall; Mama Is a Miner, Grandma Essie's Covered Wagon*, and *Can't You Make Them Behave, King George?*

1030. **The History Channel**

http://www.historychannel.com

The History Channel's Web site provides a gold mine for social studies teachers. Classroom materials pages (written to accompany The History Channel classroom programs) are copyright-free, and educators are encouraged to print these pages for classroom use. This Day in History highlights past events that happened on each day of the year. Students can search the database by specifying the month and day. Each month a different exhibit is featured in an online history museum. Some of the past exhibits include Ellis Island; a Twentieth Anniversary Celebration of *Roots;* the History of Woman's Suffrage in America; Jerusalem: Three Religions, One Holy City; and the Great Sioux Nation. The History Hotlist lists Internet resources easily located by category. In the Great Speeches Archive, students can listen to "words that changed the world." (This requires the RealAudio plug in.) A few of the audio clips in this archive include "That's one small step for [a] man, one giant leap for mankind," by astronaut Neil Armstrong; "This was their finest hour," by Prime Minister Winston Churchill; "The future of flying is filled with promise," by Amelia Earhart; and "Old soldiers never die, they just fade away," by General Douglas MacArthur. TV listings are provided, as is a 12-month calendar of history events.

1031. The History Classroom

http://www.thehistorychannel.co.uk/classroom/

Sponsored by the History Channel in the United Kingdom, the History Classroom provides information for high school students in the United Kingdom taking either the GCSE (General Certificate of Secondary Education) or A-level (advanced-level) examinations. Study guides relate to television programming on the History Channel. Some topics include the French Revolution, the American Revolution, the American Civil War, the Luddites, Tsarist Russia, Henry VIII, Bismarck's Policies, and the Rise of the Nazis.

1032. The History Place

http://www.historyplace.com

The History Place moves the past into the present and the future with an extensive database of information that includes a diversity of essays and opinions by established scholars and historians, as well as photos, speeches, and timelines. This Month in History is one of the featured sidebar items. Each day of the month is filled with interesting facts, and in-text links provide further information. History in the USA provides links to tourist Web sites for most states. For example, Arizona has a link to the Grand Canyon Web site and California has links to Alcatraz, Death Valley, the Hearst Castle, and the San Diego Aerospace Museum. Featured exhibits include the American Revolution, Abraham Lincoln, the U.S. Civil War, World War II in the Pacific, Apollo 11, a photo history of John F. Kennedy, Nazi Germany, and a Holocaust Timeline. These detailed treatments of historical topics provide interesting content that incorporates the Web's multimedia capabilities through the successful interweaving of text, pictures, sound files, and links to other related Internet resources. Comments may be addressed to (comments@ historyplace.com).

1033. History/Social Studies Web Site for K-12 Teachers

http://www.execpc.com/~dboals/boals.html

By providing links to selected history and social studies resources on the Internet, this site encourages use of the World Wide Web as a tool for learning and teaching history and social studies.

1034. The Library of Congress

http://www.loc.gov
or
http://lcweb.loc.gov

The Library of Congress presents information about its collections on the World Wide Web. Some of the current offerings include historical collections from American Memory, several LC exhibits, the POW/MIA database, country studies, and links to LC MARVEL and LOCIS.

Some of the LC exhibits available online include Rome Reborn: The Vatican Library and Renaissance Culture; Revelations from the Russian Archives; Scrolls from the Dead Sea; 1492: An Ongoing Voyage; African American Culture and History; The Russian Church and Native Alaskan Cultures; The Gettysburg Address; and Temple of Liberty: Building the Capitol for a New Nation.

1035. National Museum of American History Homepage

http://americanhistory.si.edu

The National Museum of American History, a bureau of the Smithsonian Institution, is responsible for the collection, care, and preservation of more than 17 million artifacts, including 14 million stamps housed in the National Postal Museum. The collections represent material evidence of the nation's heritage in the areas of science, technology, and culture; they include coins and medals, automobiles, First Ladies' gowns, the John Bull locomotive, presidential campaign items, musical instruments, military weapons, the Star-Spangled Banner (the flag), Thomas Edison's phonograph, early digital and electronic computing machines, ship models, steam engines, and innumerable artifacts of everyday life. In addition to virtual tours of the museum, there are virtual exhibitions. This section presents electronic displays of materials that are not currently being shown in the museum. Some virtual exhibits preserve displays formerly shown at the museum; others are of exhibits that were developed solely for electronic display. Some virtual exhibitions are: Magic Lanterns/Magic Mirrors: A Centennial Salute to Cinema; Tool Chests: Symbol and Servant; Life in Ancient Greece Reflected in the Coinage of Corinth; Surviving Images: Forgotten People (Native Americans, Women, and African Americans on Early United States Bank Notes); The 1804 U.S. Dollar: The King of American Coins; Quilts, Counterpanes, and Throws: A Selection from the National Collection; and Produce for Victory: Posters on the American Home Front 1941–1945.

1036. Patterns of Our Lives: American History

http://metalab.unc.edu/cisco/tour2.html

Patterns of Our Lives contains a collection of American history education resources on the Internet. Internet resources are divided into newsgroups and Web resources. Each resource is briefly annotated. Look for some unusual resources on this page, with an emphasis on multicultural sites.

1037. SCORE History and Social Science Resources

http://score.rims.k12.ca.us

The SCORE (Schools of California Online Resources for Education) Web site has resources and lessons by grade level, by topic, and by keyword. Lessons and activities follow the California frameworks and standards, which are similar to those in many states. For example, the principles of economics are addressed in the 12th grade. Sixth-grade world history addresses ancient civilizations, such as India, China, Greece, Rome, Mesopotamia, and prehistoric peoples. For each topic, there are resources and activities. This is a treasure trove for K-12 social studies teachers.

1038. This Day in History from the History Channel

http://www.historychannel.com/thisday/

This Day in History from the History Channel highlights various past events for each day of the year. Students can search the database to travel in time to any date by specifying the month and day. Also see the National Park Service's Today in History Web site (http://www.cr.nps.gov/history/today.html) for history related to monuments, parks, and historic places managed by the National Park Service.

1039. Today In History

http://www.scopesys.com/anyday/

For any given month and day, Today In History's database provides information on famous historical birthdays, deaths, historical events, lists of those reported missing in action, holidays, religious observances, religious historical events, and a thought for the day. This site is provided by Scope Systems, a worldwide industrial electronics repair and services company (Scope@ScopeSys.com).

Lesson Plans

See also "Lesson Plans Across the Curriculum" (entries 33–44).

1040. The Library of Congress Learning Page

http://memory.loc.gov/ammem/ndlpedu/index.html

Look for activities and lesson plans using the resources at the Library of Congress, such as George Washington: First in War; First in Peace; and First in the Hearts of His Countrymen and Port of Entry: Immigration. Additionally, there are lesson plans created by American Memory Fellows, outstanding media specialists, and humanities educators who are selected to attend the annual National Digital Library Educators Institute. Lessons in this collection are based on primary sources from the American Memory collections at the Library of Congress, as well as other print resources and Internet resources. Look for lessons such as: To Market to Market (sharpening student observation and interpretation skills by critically examining visual images from the turn of the centuries, circa 1900 and circa 2000); Doing the Decades (studying themes in 20th-century U.S. history); The Conservation Movement at a Crossroads: The Hetch Hetchy Controversy; and From Jim Crow to Linda Brown: A Retrospective of the African-American Experience from 1897 to 1953.

Tips are given on how to use primary sources in the classroom; there is also a framework for using primary resources in lesson plans. Thematic topics are available for units on presidents, elections, Thanksgiving, women pioneers, inaugurations, and immigration. The New page highlights what has recently been added to this growing Web site.

Question-and-Answer Services

1041. Ask a Historian

http://www.cr.nps.gov/history/askhist.htm

The National Park Service has provided a list of historians who will answer questions via e-mail. American history experts are identified by subject area of expertise. Use this list to locate experts on Alaska and the Klondike Gold Rush; Aviation; the Civil War; Military, Mining, and Maritime History; Native American History; and Western and Women's History.

Special Topics for Unit Studies

Crime

1042. Bonnie and Clyde

http://www.fbi.gov/yourfbi/history/famcases/clyde/clyde.htm

From the FBI Famous Cases files, find out more about Clyde Barrow and Bonnie Parker, a legendary pair of murderers, who were finally killed while trying to escape in 1934. Look for other cases in the FBI files, including those of Al Capone, John Dillinger, Baby Face Nelson, Tokyo Rose, and Ethel and Julius Rosenberg (http://www.fbi.gov/yourfbi/history/famcases/famcases.htm).

1043. The Crime Library

http://www.crimelibrary.com

This database of crime is divided into four areas: classic crime; mass and serial murders; gangsters, outlaws, and G-men; and terrorists, spies, and assassins. Classic crime entries include Lizzie Borden, the Lindbergh kidnapping, and Sacco and Vanzetti. Gangsters includes the well-known members of 1920s and 1930s crime gangs, as well as Wyatt Earp and Jesse James.

1044. Famous Trials

http://www.law.umkc.edu/faculty/projects/ftrials/ftrials.htm

Students studying famous trials in the United States will want to check this site first. Famous trials include the Salem Witchcraft trials in 1692; Amistad trials (1839–1840); Dakota Conflict trials (1862); Johnson Impeachment (1868); Oscar Wilde (1895); Bill Haywood trial (1907); Leopold and Loeb (1924); Scopes "Monkey" trial (1925); Scottsboro trials (1931–1937); Hauptmann "Lindbergh Kidnapping" trial (1935); Rosenberg trials (1951); Mississippi Burning (1967); Chicago Seven Conspiracy (1969–1970); My Lai court martial (1970); and O. J. Simpson (1994–1995). Links are available to other famous trials. Created and maintained by Douglas O. Linder (linderd@umkc.edu), professor of law, University of Missouri, Kansas City, Missouri.

1045. Historical Investigation into the Past: The Lizzie Borden/Fall River Case Study

http://ccbit.cs.umass.edu/lizzie/intro/home.html

By providing late 19th-century primary source materials from the Lizzie Borden axe murder trial and from Lizzie Borden's home town (Fall River, Massachusetts), this project allows students to conduct research, formulate hypotheses, and state their findings. Students study what it was like to live during this time period and what societal expectations were for women. Look for census information, documents from the trial, photographs, maps, diagrams, Borden family history, and links to related 19th-century literature. Jointly co-produced by the History Department and the Center for Computer-Based Instructional Technology at the University of Massachusetts at Amherst.

Disasters

Earthquakes and Fires

See also "Earthquakes" (entries 814–817).

1046. Before and After the Great Earthquake and Fire: Early Films of San Francisco, 1897-1916

http://memory.loc.gov/ammem/papr/sfhome.html

The 1906 San Francisco earthquake and fire rivaled the Chicago fire of 1871 in the annals of urban disasters in America. This American Memory collection contains 26 films representing early film production in the United States. Of these, 17 show the city before the 1906 disaster; 7 document the earthquake and fire; and 2 provide views of the city in 1915 and 1916 after it was rebuilt. Be sure to see the Learn More About It! feature for integrating this into the social studies and language arts curricula. American Memory film collections are available online in three formats: QuickTime, .mpg (Motion Pictures Experts Group or MPEG), and .rm (Real Media).

1047. The Great Chicago Fire and the Web of Memory

http://www.chicagohs.org/fire/intro/

This online commemorative exhibition, created by the Chicago Historical Society and North-western University, is divided into two parts. The Great Chicago Fire has five chronologically organized chapters focused on the city before the fire, during the fire, and during the recovery afterward. The Web of Memory contains six chapters, each examining a way in which the fire has been remembered, including eyewitness accounts. These primary resources are compared to the legend of Mrs. O'Leary. This multimedia exhibition takes advantage of Shockwave to provide a 360-degree view of Chicago in 1858 prior to the fire, MIDI music files, 3-D stereo-graphs of the city after the fire, and a QuickTime video. A bibliography of print and Web re-sources is provided for further study, and a table of contents makes it easy to access information on this comprehensive Web site.

The Sinking of the RMS Titanic (April 14, 1912)

See also a WebQuest on this topic titled The Titanic: What Can Numbers Tell Us About Her Fatal Voyage? (http://asterix.ednet.lsu.edu/~edtech/webquest/titanic.html).

1048. Encyclopedia Titanica

http://www.encyclopedia-titanica.org

The largest section of this site comprises the passenger and crew lists and their associated bi-ographies. The passenger lists are organized alphabetically and the crew lists are categorized by individual occupation. Deck plans are interactive schematics of the ship's decks. When you move your mouse over the deck plans, labels appear. By clicking on the highlighted rooms and areas, you will be linked to additional information. For cabins, you will be linked to a biogra-phy of the person who occupied the cabin. Lifeboats contain listings of passengers and crew who were saved, along with their individual biographies. The Encyclopedia Titanica aims to be the most comprehensive source of information on the *Titanic*. Created and maintained by Philip Hind (philip.hind@virgin.net).

1049. *R. M. S. Titanic* (April 14, 1912)

http://www.lva.lib.va.us/pubserv/vnp/titanic/titanic1.htm

The Virginia Newspaper Project examines how the sinking of the *Titanic* was reported in newspapers. Links are provided to the passenger list, a map of the disaster, and the actual headline from the Richmond (Virginia) *Times-Dispatch*. Information is available on inaccurate or misleading reporting, headline coverage of the disaster, editorial cartoons, and the aftermath and inquiry. A bibliography is provided. Site maintained by catalog librarian, Clay-Edward Dixon (ced4g@virginia.edu). See also David Clarke's 3D Titanic (http://home.interlynx.net/~dclarke/Titanic.html), RMS Titanic, Inc. (http://www.titanic-online.com), and The Titanic Information Site (http://www.skarr.com/titanic/).

Student Essays

1050. The Concord Review

http://www.tcr.org

The Concord Review, a journal for the academic work of secondary students, founded in March 1987, publishes exemplary history essays by high school students in the English-speaking world. Information is available on how to subscribe to *The Concord Review* and how to submit essays for publication. Students who submit and have their essays published have often sent reprints of their articles with their college applications. Although subscriptions are not free, there are 28 sample student essays available online, which serve as wonderful models for students learning how to write excellent history essays, including those for AP History. Each sample essay is well written and fully documented with footnotes and a bibliography. These sample essays are benchmarks for other students to use to measure their own writing and research skills. Some of the titles of those available online include: "Kamikaze Pilots," "Czechoslovak Radio in the Soviet Occupation," "Negro Leagues," and "Hamilton and Burr." The Webmaster's e-mail address is (fitzhugh@tcr.org).

Discussion Groups

1051. Online Discussion for K-12 Social Studies Teachers

E-mail: mailserv@hcca.ohio.gov
Instructions: On the first line of the body of the message, type:
subscribe SOCSTUD-L [your first name and last name]

K-12 social studies teachers have an online forum in which they share lesson plans, keep current, and discuss the teaching of social studies with other professionals in the field. Topics of discussion also include research and new approaches to organization and teaching, state and national frameworks, and commission-recommended standards.

U.S. Government

Executive Branch

1052. The American Presidency by Grolier Online

http://gi.grolier.com/presidents/preshome.html

The American presidency comes alive at Grolier Online's comprehensive site devoted to the history of presidents, the presidency, politics, and related subjects. Information is based on three sets of encyclopedias: *The New Book of Knowledge* (grades 3–8), *The Academic American Encyclopedia* (grades 5–up), and *Encyclopedia Americana* (grades 6–up). After students finish reading all the articles on the American presidency in any one set of encyclopedias, they may take a 25-question, multiple-choice quiz that is automatically scored. In addition to the encyclopedia information, there is an Online Exhibit Hall of Presidents with pocket documentaries on the presidents and sound bytes from speeches, as well as the music of the presidency, available for downloading. Students can access a complete list of results of American presidential elections from 1789 to 1996. Virtual flash cards can be printed out or projected in class. The front side of each card shows a president's picture; the back side (displayed by clicking with the mouse) reveals the president's name, his presidential career highlights, and fun facts. Using these online flash cards, students can find out that James Madison was the first president to wear trousers rather than knee britches; that Millard Fillmore didn't meet his running mate Zachary Taylor until after they were elected; and that, while in high school, Bill Clinton played saxophone in a trio called the Three Blind Mice (all three musicians wore dark glasses while performing). The Webmaster for Grolier's Online can be reached at (webmaster@grolier.com).

1053. The American Presidents and First Ladies

Presidents
http://www2.whitehouse.gov/WH/glimpse/presidents/html/presidents.html
First Ladies
http://www.whitehouse.gov/WH/glimpse/firstladies/html/firstladies.html

For each president there is a color image; one fun fact; and links to his inaugural address(es), biographical highlights, and presidential library, if available. What makes these pages so interesting are the pictures and biographies of the First Ladies. Students can learn that Martha Washington burned her correspondence with the first president to ensure their privacy. Frances Folsome Cleveland was the first White House bride. She married President Grover Cleveland, a man 27 years her senior. Lucy Hayes, a temperance advocate married to "Rud," was a popular White House hostess despite her ban on serving liquor. Students will enjoy these personal glimpses into the lives of American presidents and First Ladies.

1054. POTUS: Presidents of the United States

http://www.ipl.org/ref/POTUS/

Created by the Internet Public Library, POTUS provides background information, election results, names of cabinet members, presidency highlights, and some odd facts about each president. Links to biographies, historical documents, audio and video files, and other presidential sites make this a comprehensive and interesting site guaranteed to enrich the teaching curriculum. Links to presidential information are chronological, and there is additional access through name, subject, and topic indexes. E-mail the Webmasters at (potus@ipl.org).

1055. Welcome to the White House

http://www.whitehouse.gov/WH/Welcome.html

A virtual tour of the White House is just one activity available at this Web site. Students can send e-mail to the president, vice president, First Lady, or Mrs. Gore. There is a portrait and biographical sketch of each president and each First Lady (entry 1053). A section called First Families at Home provides a glimpse into the lives of families who have lived in the White House. Art in the White House—A Nation's Pride provides a historical perspective of selected pieces from the White House collection. The Virtual Library contains White House documents, sound files of speeches, and a collection of photographs. The Briefing Room contains the current day's press releases and hot topics. *Inside the White House* is a newsletter for young people.

1056. Welcome to the White House for Kids

http://www.whitehouse.gov/WH/kids/html/kidshome.html

Socks, the First Cat, is your guide to the White House. The tour is divided into six sections: Where Is the White House?, The History of the White House, Our President, Children in the White House, Pets in the White House, and How to Write to the President. Socks is an excellent tour guide, and this site is informative and easy to use for younger (and older) students who want to find out more about the White House.

Judicial Branch

1057. The Oyez Project

http://oyez.nwu.edu

Oyez Oyez Oyez, pronounced "o-yay" or "o-yez" or "o-yes," is called out three times in succession to introduce the opening of a court of law. The Oyez project is a multimedia database about the U.S. Supreme Court, featuring digital audio (RealAudio) of the oral arguments in many important cases, announcements of the Court's opinion, and speeches by several Justices. Students will find abstracts of key constitutional cases, and brief biographies and portraits of all 108 Justices who have served on the Supreme Court. Look for a virtual tour of the Supreme Court building. Created by Jerry Goldman (J-goldman@nwu.edu), a political scientist at Northwestern University (Evanston, Illinois).

1058. Supreme Court Collection

http://supct.law.cornell.edu/supct/

Under the auspices of Project Hermes, the Supreme Court's electronic-dissemination project, this archive contains nearly all opinions of the Court since May 1990 and more than 600 of its most important historical decisions. Historical cases can be accessed by browsing through topics, party names, or opinion authors. This makes it easy to find the Supreme Court cases for topics such as abortion, censorship, and capital punishment. The database of cases is also searchable. For each case, there is a syllabus, the Justice's opinion, and the concurring and dissenting opinions. Provides a court calendar; a gallery of the current Justices, including pictures, biographies, and lists of decisions; a gallery of former Justices; Supreme Court rules; and a glossary of legal terms. The Supreme Court does not have its own Web site. This is the unofficial Web site from the Legal Information Institute at Cornell Law School, Cornell University, Ithaca, NY. Requires Adobe Acrobat Reader.

Legislative Branch

1059. Congressional Web Sites

http://www.lib.umich.edu/libhome/Documents.center/congweb.html

Who's currently serving on the Senate and U.S. House of Representatives Committees on Appropriations? What are the committees' responsibilities, and what have these committees accomplished during the current session? Look for the answers to these questions as well as many others about other Senate and House committees. Standing committees are listed in alphabetical order for each congressional house. There are also links to the Joint Committees. Web pages created by members of the U.S. Senate and House of Representatives are listed alphabetically by the states they represent. Maintained by Grace York (graceyor@umich.edu), coordinator, Documents Center, University of Michigan Library.

1060. The Internet Guide to the U.S. Congress

http://www.capweb.net/classic/index.morph

CapWeb provides an unofficial guide to the U.S. Congress and congressional information on the Internet. Links are provided to articles from the weekly newspaper *The Hill* and to "Capitol Hill Diaries," a regular news column featuring personal views on politics and life on Capitol Hill by congressional staff members, as well as current events and comical stories. Find out what is happening today on Capitol Hill, and enjoy the sights and sounds. Students can compare information on this site with information on the official congressional Web site, THOMAS (entry 1066). Webmasters are Chris Casey (chris@casey.com) and Jeff Hecker (Jeff_H@cais.com).

1061. The U.S. Legislative Branch

http://www.loc.gov/global/legislative/congress.html

The Library of Congress has provided a comprehensive Internet resource Web page focused on information related to the legislative branch of the federal government. Categories include: About Congress; Congressional Mega Sources; Members; Committees; Congressional Organizations; E-Mail Addresses; Calendars & Schedules; Floor Proceedings; Legislation; House and Senate Rules; Congressional Record; Voting Records; Executive Business of the Senate; Legislative Process; Congressional News and Analysis; Congressional Internet Services; The History of Congress; and Visitor Information.

Directories and Listings

1062. Congress.org: Congressional Directories

http://congress.org

Congress.org is updated for the 107th Congress. This site allows Internet users to access a complete and reliable directory of information about the members of the U.S. House of Representatives and the U.S. Senate. For every member of the Senate and the House of Representatives, Congress.org includes contact information (office room number and mailing address, D.C. office telephone and fax number, and e-mail address); staff information; and committee assignments. Each entry includes a picture, a brief biographical sketch, and a link to a listing of the state delegation. The directory is accessible by alphabetical listing of last name, state delegation, or committee. A search engine allows you to find your representative by typing in your zip code. Congress.org is a joint venture of two Washington, D.C., area firms with expertise in communicating with Congress: Issue Dynamics Inc., a leader in developing public affairs strategies, and Capitol Advantage, the nation's largest publisher of congressional directories.

1063. Individual Web Pages for Members of the U.S. House of Representatives

http://www.house.gov/house/MemberWWW.html

Members of the U.S. House of Representatives who have created Web pages are listed in alphabetical order by last name, with links to their respective Web pages. Each member's page is different and individualized, but most include a picture, biographical information, summaries of congressional work, press releases, constituent services, and links to state and district information. For links to representatives' Web pages listed alphabetically by state, see (http://www.house.gov/house/MemStateSearch.htm).

1064. Individual Web Pages for Members of the U.S. Senate

http://www.senate.gov/senators/senator_by_state.cfm

Senators are listed alphabetically by the states they represent. Each senator's page is different, reflecting individual interests and state constituencies. Most include a picture, biographical information, links to bills sponsored and cosponsored, press releases, and summaries of committee work. For an alphabetical listing of all U.S. senators by last name, see (http://www.senate.gov/senators/index.cfm).

Legislation

1065. How to Search Congressional Legislation

telnet://locis.loc.gov

No login required. Choose #2, Federal Legislation.

Note: LOCIS operates with restricted hours: Monday through Friday (24 hours; not all files are available after 9:30 P.M.); Saturday (until 5 P.M.); Sunday (after 11 A.M.). Maintenance is possible any evening Sunday through Friday from 5 P.M. to 8 P.M. All times are USA Eastern Standard. Closed on holidays.

LOCIS is the Library of Congress Information System service. Among other information, this site contains summaries, abstracts, chronologies, and status information about legislation (bills and resolutions) introduced in the U.S. Senate and House of Representatives since 1973. Information about the current Congress is updated within 48 hours of its creation.

See also THOMAS (entry 1066), the U.S. legislative information World Wide Web home page and The Library of Congress (entry 1034).

1066. THOMAS: Legislative Information on the Internet

http://thomas.loc.gov

THOMAS provides a daily account of the proceedings on the House and Senate floors, which is searchable by keyword. The site was established in the spirit of Thomas Jefferson and is a service of the U.S. Congress through its library. The full texts of all versions of House and Senate bills are searchable by keyword or by bill number for Congresses beginning with the 103d. The full text of the *Congressional Record* is available for Congresses beginning with the 103d.

This site is constantly adding new legislative information. For example, it has an easy-to-understand explanation of how laws are made, written by the House Law Revision Counsel. There is a link to the U.S. House of Representatives (entry 1067), which has directory information for House of Representatives members and committees, the House calendar, the daily committee hearing schedule, the current week's floor schedule, and visitor information.

U.S. House of Representatives

1067. U.S. House of Representatives
http://www.house.gov

The U.S. House of Representatives Web page provides access to the full text and status of bills and resolutions being considered by Congress; current information on the House floor debates; summaries of recent House floor and committee actions; House floor and committee meetings schedules; names, addresses, phone numbers, e-mail addresses, and Web page addresses (if available) of members; educational information; visitor information; the House ethics manual; and the *U.S. Code* and *Code of Federal Regulations*, which are full-text searchable. Today in Committee gives up-to-the-hour information on each vote and a record of how each representative voted. This Web page provides a place for citizen feedback through e-mail.

U.S. Senate

1068. U.S. Senate
http://www.senate.gov

Students can learn more about the Senate's history, procedures, and terminology, and they can take a virtual tour. Legislative Activities includes information about recent legislative actions, scheduled activities, and other records. Other Resources contains statistical information and FAQs, as well as links to other related information. All the files are keyword-searchable.

Departments, Agencies, and Other Government Entities

Census Bureau

1069. Basic Tables and Trends Reports from the 1990 Census
http://oseda.missouri.edu/usinfo.html

The Missouri State Census Data Center's Web site provides both Missouri and U.S. census information. Basic tables are provided for states, counties, cities, and metropolitan areas. Census trends compare 1980 census data with 1990 data for states, counties, and cities. Under the U.S. Census by Cities/Places, statistics are given for total population, race, age, income, types of household, education levels, labor force, and housing. In Trends, data are compared between 1980 and 1990, showing changes in both raw figures and percentages to indicate either an increase or decrease for each entry.

1070. U.S. Census Bureau Home Page

http://www.census.gov

The Census Bureau provides information about its history and responsibilities, as well as news hot off the press and highlights from the latest reports. Use the population clock to find out the current estimated population of the United States and the world, as well as other population statistics. The Main Data Bank holds a wealth of information. This page allows students to access a large variety of databases. A small sampling of the sources: county business patterns, population data, genealogy, GeoWEB (making data available geographically), county and city data, and *Statistical Abstract of the United States*.

Be sure to see Census in Schools (http://www.census.gov/dmd/www/schindex.htm) for information on how to incorporate census information into the K-12 curriculum. Links are provided to free materials and lesson plans.

Central Intelligence Agency

1071. CIA Home Page

http://www.odci.gov/index.html

The Central Intelligence Agency provides the president and senior advisors with foreign intelligence relating to national security. This page provides information about the CIA and links to the *World Factbook* and the *Factbook on Intelligence*. Pointers are included to hundreds of maps of various countries.

Departments

Commerce

1072. U.S. Department of Commerce

http://www.doc.gov

The U.S. Department of Commerce Web site has information from the office of the secretary of Commerce, including speeches, press releases, commerce publications, and additional information about the Department of Commerce. Links are provided to U.S. Department of Commerce agencies, such as the Bureau of Export Administration, Bureau of the Census, International Trade Administration, Minority Business Development Agency, Patent and Trademark Office, National Telecommunications and Information Administration, the National Oceanic and Atmospheric Administration (including Environmental Information Services), and U.S. Travel and Tourism Administration. There are also data on the budget of the United States, the Economic Conversion Information Exchange, and the Information Infrastructure Task Force.

Defense

For individual home pages for each of the armed forces and Web sites for military academies and armed forces recruiting, *see* "Careers in the Armed Forces" (entries 68–75).

Interior

1073. U.S. Department of the Interior

http://www.ios.doi.gov

The U.S. Department of the Interior's Web site gives historical information about the department, an organizational chart, and a list of bureaus within the department. Also available are job announcements and budget information.

Justice

1074. U.S. Department of Justice

http://www.usdoj.gov

The Justice Department's Web site has information about the attorney general and the Department of Justice, such as its purpose and duties. Links are provided to information within the Department of Justice and to other federal government information sources. The annual report from the Office of the Attorney General, the *Federal Bureau of Investigation Crime Bulletin*, reports from the Antitrust Division and the Civil Rights Division, and the Crime Bill are located on this Web site.

State

See also The Geographic Learning Site (entry 1309), a K-12 educational site sponsored by the U.S. Department of State.

1075. U.S. Department of State

http://www.state.gov/index.html

The U.S. Department of State is the lead U.S. foreign affairs agency and is responsible for implementing the president's foreign policies. The United States has diplomatic relations with more than 170 countries and maintains no fewer than 250 embassies, consulates, and missions around the world. This site offers a FAQs section and an e-mail address you can use to send your opinions to the secretary (secretary@state.gov). The Hot Topics area has links to press statements and briefings as well as some of the current international topics. International Policy is divided into regions, such as the New Independent States of the Former USSR. A special ancillary Web page has been added for students and their teachers. Information is available on the Secretary of State, careers, the history of the State Department (including a timeline), and information about countries and embassies around the world. A link is provided to the Geographic Learning Site (GLS) which focuses on geographic Hot Spots and international issues. To view GLS pages, you'll need Flash, a free software available for downloading at the GLS site. Foreign policy comments and questions should be addressed to (usdosweb@uic.edu).

Treasury

1076. U.S. Department of the Treasury

http://www.treas.gov

The U.S. Department of the Treasury's mission is to manage, protect, and continue to build for the future the government's financial system; to promote prosperous and stable economies in the United States and the world; and to foster a safe and drug-free America. The Briefing Room contains news releases, speeches, statements, and photographs updated daily. The Virtual Library houses Treasury reports and an archive of press releases from January 1996 to the present. Students will want to check the What's New section to find reports and press releases of current news to help them with class discussions and research. For example, students can locate online full-text reports (in PDF [portable document format] requiring Adobe Acrobat Reader) such as *The Treasury Study on the Sporting Suitability of Modified Semiautomatic Assault Rifles* (April 1998) and *The Economic Costs of Smoking in the United States and the Benefits of Comprehensive Tobacco Legislation* (March 1998). As an added feature, the entire Web site is searchable. Also available are a history of the U.S. Treasury, a virtual tour of the U.S. Treasury building, a FAQs section, and downloadable tax forms.

1077. U.S. Department of the Treasury's Kids Page

http://www.treas.gov/kids/

Students will learn about the history of the Treasury Department and its role in the federal government. They can take a virtual tour to find out more about the U.S. Treasury Building, the Cash Room, and the Burglar Proof Vault. The History section gives information on the history of the Secret Service, the U.S. Mint, and frequently asked questions (with answers) about the U.S. tax system. Dog of the Month features a dog working in the Canine Enforcement Program. Information is also available on U.S. savings bonds. The Bureau of Printing and Engraving provides resources and activities for students and teachers to help in understanding money and math-related skills.

Federal Bureau of Investigation

1078. FBI: Federal Bureau of Investigation

http://www.fbi.gov

The FBI Web site contains very thorough and in-depth information about the Federal Bureau of Investigation. If students would like to know more about becoming an FBI agent, there is career and employment information. There is also a FAQs section about the FBI and a short description of general facts. One section contains information about FBI investigations, such as the Centennial Olympic Park Bombing; TWA Flight 800 Investigation; and Rogue Brokers, a securities fraud initiative. There is another section on FBI crime statistics. Links are provided to the FBI *Law Enforcement Bulletin*, a monthly publication. Current issues are available, as is an archive of back issues.

Check out the frequently asked questions (FAQs) about the FBI's Top Ten (http://www.fbi.gov/mostwant/topten/tenlist.htm). To be considered for the Top Ten, criminals must have a lengthy record of committing serious crimes or be considered a particularly dangerous menace to society. Also, nationwide publicity must be seen as a way of apprehending the fugitive. As of August 1999, there have been 458 fugitives on the list; 7 of these have been women. For each name on the list, there is a photograph, a description, and other information that might lead to identification. Because of citizen cooperation, 134 fugitives from this list have been located. Citizens are warned not to try to apprehend any of these fugitives themselves. A list of the FBI field offices is included.

Government Printing Office

1079. U.S. Government Printing Office

http://www.access.gpo.gov

The U.S. Government Printing Office (GPO) provides free electronic access to a wealth of information produced by the federal government, such as the *Congressional Record*. *GPO Access* provides free online use of more than 1,000 databases of federal information and allows searching in multiple databases, as well as searching of more than 1,350 official U.S. federal agency and military Internet sites using keywords. Through the GPO, more than 7,500 individual federal agency files, in a variety of formats, are available for free download from the Federal Bulletin Board (FBB). Information retrieved from *GPO Access* can be used without restriction, unless specifically noted.

National Debt

See also WebQuest: Look Who's Footing the Bill! (http://www.kn.pacbell.com/wired/democracy/debtquest.html).

1080. U.S. National Debt Clock

http://www.brillig.com/debt_clock/

The U.S. National Debt Clock is maintained by Ed Hall (edhall@brillig.com). The clock continuously updates the amount of the national debt, which went over $5 trillion in February 1996 and continues to increase at a rate of more than $171 million every day. Use the reload button on Netscape to see how much the debt increases in just one minute! Using figures from the U.S. Treasury Department and the Census Bureau, the population is figured along with the debt, showing how much each citizen's share of the debt is. There is a graph of the national debt since 1940 in the Here Are Some Answers section. Links are provided to other sites concerning the national debt.

National Park Service

1081. National Park Service WWW Server

http://www.nps.gov

Find out more about the National Park Service. This Web site gives the historical background of the National Park Service with its Links to the Past. There are also links to information about individual national parks and cultural and natural resources. There is an alphabetic list of national parks by region and an interactive National Park System map. For sites devoted to the Grand Canyon, *see* entries 1104–1106.

Office of Management and Budget

1082. Budget of the U.S. Government, Fiscal Year 2001

http://w3.access.gpo.gov/usbudget/index.html

Budget publications and reports are available online from this U.S. Government Printing Office site. Documents are available in .pdf format or as spreadsheets. *A Citizens' Guide to the Federal*

Budget for Fiscal Year 2001 can be downloaded as a .pdf file or viewed online in its entirety at (http://w3.access.gpo.gov/usbudget/fy2001/guidetoc.html). *A Citizens' Guide to the Federal Budget* helps to make the federal budget more accessible and understandable. A table of contents is helpful for locating information on how the government creates a budget, what the budget is, where the money comes from, and where it goes. A glossary helps students understand terms such as *surplus*, *revenue*, *federal debt*, and *deficit*. The problems of the budget deficit and federal debt are addressed. Diagrams are also helpful.

This site is searchable and provides information about past budgets beginning with 1996.

Postal Service

1083. U.S. Postal Service
http://www.usps.gov

The U.S. Postal Service provides a virtual post office with information on Zip Codes, postage rates, stamps, State Department passport information, and more. In ZIP Code Lookup, you can locate the Zip Code for a specific address. The Postage Calculator helps you calculate postage for letters, postcards, packages, and international mail. Find out what stamps are available for collecting and mailing in the Stamps section.

Smithsonian Institution

1084. Smithsonian Institution Home Page
http://www.si.edu

The Smithsonian Institution was established in 1846 with funds bequeathed to the United States in 1829 by James Smithson, an English scientist, who wanted to found an institution for the "increase and diffusion of knowledge." As an independent trust instrumentality of the United States, the Smithsonian now holds some 140 million artifacts and specimens in trust, preserving the heritage of the country as well as disseminating knowledge. The Smithsonian has fondly been called the "nation's attic." The Institution is also a center for research dedicated to public education, national service, and scholarship in the arts, sciences, and history. This page provides links to the 16 Smithsonian museums, research centers, and the National Zoo, as well as educational outreach programs, exhibitions, and educational resources. Information is also provided to help in planning a trip to Washington, D.C. Many graphics help bring this virtual tour of the Smithsonian to life. Information on this server is searchable to enable visitors to find and explore all online aspects of the institution.

1085. Smithsonian Magazine
http://www.smithsonianmag.si.edu

Monthly issues of *Smithsonian* are online from January 1995 to the present. These issues are browseable and searchable. Online issues are enhanced with color graphics and in-text links. Information can be searched using keywords or suggested categories, such as Ecology, History, the Animal Kingdom, and the Arts. A database of back issues, January 1995 to the present, is available, and results provide full-text articles with color photographs. Back issues from 1989–1994 are searchable as well, but only bibliographic citations are given as results. This is an excellent reference resource for the classroom.

Social Security Administration

1086. **Social Security Online**

http://www.ssa.gov

Students will find out about the history of the Social Security Administration (SSA) and why it was created, as well as the benefits provided by Social Security. Links are available to press releases, congressional testimony, and President Clinton's State of the Union Message on the topic, "What Is the Future of Social Security?" Special features include a FAQs section, This Month in SSA History, and Research and Data. Younger students will want to visit the Social Security Kids' page (http://www.ssa.gov/kids/kids.htm), and older students will want to go to the Hot Questions for Cool Teens page (http://www.ssa.gov/kids/teens.htm).

U.S. Politics

1087. **CNN's All Politics Home Page**

http://cnn.com/ALLPOLITICS/

CNN and *Time* magazine cosponsor this page, which features daily national news entirely related to the political arena. Top stories are summarized on the home page, with links to full-text stories. The Analysis and In-Depth sections provide closer looks at issues and events. This all-politics news database is searchable.

1088. **The Democratic National Committee**

http://www.democrats.org

The Democratic National Committee (DNC) has a comprehensive online Web site. Find out about the history of the party and how the donkey came to be used as a party symbol during Jackson's campaign for the presidency. There is a Democratic Party FAQs section and information about the past chairs of the DNC, as well as the party charter and bylaws. Links are provided to Democratic state parties, the 1996 platform, and other sites related to the Democratic Party.

1089. **The Republican National Committee**

http://www.rnc.org

From the Republican Main Street, students can access information by clicking on various buildings or text. The Republican headquarters has information about the history of the Republican Party, the 1996 Republican platform, the rules of the Republican Party, and a list of state GOP offices.

In the school building, students will discover that the GOP elephant was created by Thomas Nast, a famous illustrator and caricaturist for *The New Yorker*. When a rumor that animals had escaped from the New York City Zoo was simultaneously discussed with the concern that Grant might run for a third term, Nast chose to represent the Republicans as elephants, because elephants were clever, steadfast, and controlled when calm but unmanageable when frightened. Other categories of information are the newsstand, travel, What's New, speeches, and the convention center.

1090. Third Party Central

http://www.3pc.net

Third Party Central provides information about the third-party movement in American politics. Third parties are listed in an index, and links are provided to each party's Internet site. Parties with national organizations include the Libertarian Party, Green Party, U.S. Taxpayers Party, Reform Party, and Natural Law Party. There is a list of smaller, established third parties such as Alaskan Independence Party, American Party of Oregon, Grassroots Party, New Party, Patriot Party, Peace and Freedom Party, Socialist Party USA, and Workers World Party. There are also links to third parties in formation. The Webmaster's address is (info@3pc.net).

Economics

See also "Business Education" (entries 913–917) and "News Sources" (entries 1405–1419) for links to CNN, *Fortune*, and *The Wall Street Journal*.

1091. Economics Resources

http://mel.lib.mi.us/education/edu-econ.html

The Michigan Electronic Library includes a collection of excellent links to economics education resources. Look for a link to the Economic Education Web, filled with lesson plans and resources to use in K-12 classrooms. Teachers will also want to investigate EconEdLink, where they will find several useful resources, including EconomicsMinute, designed to help students explore the economics behind the news of the week through links to newspapers and suggested classroom activities and discussion questions. Available from this page are links to the national content standards in economics and the National Council on Economic Education. Peter Butts (pbutts@mel.org) is the selector and collection librarian for the Michigan Electronic Library (http://mel.lib.mi.us/main-index.html).

1092. EduStock

http://library.advanced.org/3088/

EduStock provides information to help students understand what the stock market is and how it works. It includes tutorials on the stock market and how to pick good stocks. Information about a select group of companies is provided to help students begin their research and build individual portfolios. Students can also look up stock quotes in real time (with a 20-minute delay).

1093. Good News Bears Stock Market Project

http://www.ncsa.uiuc.edu/edu/RSE/RSEyellow/gnb.html

Good News Bears Stock Market Project is an excellent interdisciplinary project specifically designed for middle school students and teachers. This project revolves around an interactive stock market competition between classmates using real time stock market data from the New York Stock Exchange and NASDAQ. Lessons related to a variety of subject areas give students a better understanding of how the stock market is an integral part of their everyday life and future security. Teachers will find reproducible pages in the Teacher Resources section. Links are provided to current data on the stock markets.

1094. Investing for Kids

http://tqd.advanced.org/3096/

After reviewing stocks, bonds, mutual funds, and the principles of saving and investing, and after trying different investment activities, students will be ready to test their financial skills with a financial quiz and a stock simulation game. Work with the online financial goals calculator to graph a single goal or to do multiple-goal calculations. A glossary of investment terms is helpful. Created by David Leung, Steven Ngai, and Hassan Mirza as a ThinkQuest project.

1095. The MONEY Page

http://www.trib.com/MONEY/

New York Stock Exchange prices are available and updated every 3 minutes, with a 15-minute delay from the tape. There is a graph of the Dow Jones Industrial Average. There are links to business news from CNN and NandoNet. A current currency converter and current oil prices are also provided.

1096. Quote Server from Security APL

http://www.secapl.com/cgi-bin/qs/

At what price is a stock currently trading? This server provides information (updated every 3 minutes, with a 20-minute delay, Monday through Friday from 8 A.M. to 6 P.M. EST) to indexes such as Standard and Poor's; the NASDAQ; the Canadian Exchange; and other indexes from London, Paris, and Japan.

By putting the ticker symbol in the search box, students can find information about a stock, including the day's high and low, the 52-week high and low, the volume of trades, number of trades, date and time of last trade, and ask and bid prices.

Students who do not know the ticker symbols should consult the Ticker Lookup searchable database (http://www.secapl.com/secapl/quoteserver/search.html). See also Yahoo! Finance (http://finance.yahoo.com).

State-by-State Information

General Information About the 50 States

1097. The 50 States of the United States

http://www.50states.com

Find out information and facts about all 50 states. Each state has its own separate link, and information is presented in a standardized format. Some of the facts available for each state include: a color graphic of the state flag, capital city, bird, flower, tree, motto, nickname, population, maps, song, date of statehood, and names of the representatives to both the U.S. House of Representatives and the U.S. Senate. Some states have special pages designed for younger constituents. *See* The South Carolina Government Kids Page (entry 1102). The 50 States of the United States was created by Ray Weber (scvol@scvol.com) of Santa Clarita, California.

Kids' Pages to State Information

1098. Official Student Information Guide to Alaska

http://www.dced.state.ak.us/tourism/student.htm

Designed especially for students researching information about Alaska, this site has everything you always wanted to know about Alaska, and more! Click on the question-mark icon to
discover photographs, facts, and maps, including a map of Alaska's five regions. Links are provided to a history of the Gold Rush, current Alaskan communities, and the Alaska State Home
Page.

Here are some more Kids' Pages to State Information:

(Arizona) Governor Jane Hull's Kids Page

http://www.governor.state.az.us/kids/index.html

Colorado's Kids Page

http://www.state.co.us/kids/index.html

Delaware's Kids' Page

http://www.state.de.us/kidspage/index.htm

Florida Kids

http://dhr.dos.state.fl.us/kids/

Idaho's Just For Kids Page

http://www2.state.id.us/justforkids/index.htm

Discover Illinois

http://www.state.il.us/kids/

(Indiana) Little Hoosiers—Kids' Page

http://www.state.in.us/sic/HTML/kids.html

Louisiana Information for Students

http://www.state.la.us/state/student.htm

Maine Kid's Page

http://www.state.me.us/sos/kids/ (entry 1101)

Maryland Kids' Page

http://www.sos.state.md.us/sos/kids/html/kidhome.html

Massachusetts Kids' Page

http://www.state.ma.us/gov/funstuff.htm

Michigan Kids Korner

http://www.mda.state.mi.us/kids/index.html

Missouri Kids Page

http://www.gocampingamerica.com/kidspage/

Montana Kids!

http://kids.state.mt.us

Nebraska Kid's Net

http://www.nol.org/kids/kidsnet.html

New York's Kids' Room

http://www.dos.state.ny.us/kidsroom/menupg.html

North Carolina Kids' Page

http://www.secretary.state.nc.us/kidspg/homepage.asp

Ohio—Oh! Kids

http://www.oplin.lib.oh.us/products/oks/

South Carolina Government Kids Page

http://www.lpitr.state/kids.htm (entry 1102)

Tennessee Kids' Pages

http://www.state.tn.us/kids.html

Texas SenateKids

http://www.senate.state.tx.us/kids/

Washington State Kids' Page

http://www.leg.wa.gov/common/kids/default.htm

Wyoming Kids Page

http://www.state.wy.us/text_kids.html

Alaska

1099.   **The Official Iditarod Web Site**
http://www.Iditarod.com

The Iditarod International Sled Dog Race covers 1,150 miles from Anchorage to Nome, Alaska. Students can easily find the rules, history, facts, and fiction of the Great Race. Students can follow trail maps and calculate mileage, keep up with the mushers and their dogs, and follow the weather. Press releases are posted daily. This site is sponsored by the Iditarod Trail Committee, Inc. (iditarod@iditarod.com). See also Dogsled.com for more information on mushers and their dogs (http://www.dogsled.com).

1100.   *Woodsong* Integration Unit

http://www.ticon.net/~rziol/

Woodsong by Gary Paulsen (Bradbury Press, 1990) is the centerpiece of this interdisciplinary unit focusing on the Iditarod, Alaska, dogs and dogsledding. Activities are outlined for language arts, math, reading, science, and outdoor learning. A bibliography of resources is provided. Pictures and a PowerPoint slide presentation, "Mushing on the Internet," are also available. For more information, e-mail (rziol@eudoramail.com).

Maine

1101.   Maine Kid's Page

http://www.state.me.us/sos/kids/

This is the place to come and learn about Maine. Symbols, famous people, history, government, schools, and places to visit are easily accessible from this site. Look for homework helpers, children's books, essay contests, citizenship awards, old photographs, and the Maine tree of facts. Have some fun and learn more about Maine, the pine tree state that each year produces the largest blueberry crop in the nation!

South Carolina

1102.   The South Carolina Government Kids Page

http://www.lpitr.state.sc.us/kids.htm

The South Carolina General Assembly has created a Web site that is extremely kid-friendly in its explanation of how state government works and what the general assembly does. To learn more about the South Carolina general assembly, students can tour the state house complex, e-mail members, participate in interactive online quizzes and puzzles, and have fun with the Official SC State House coloring book. The South Carolina Kids Page was created and is maintained by Legislative Printing & Information Technology Resources (lpi@legis.lpitr.state.sc.us).

Texas

1103.   The Texas Studies Armadillo: Not Just for Texans!

http://riceinfo.rice.edu/armadillo/
or
gopher://riceinfo.rice.edu:1170/1/

The Texas Studies Server (Armadillo) was designed with middle school teachers and students in mind. It presents information about Texas natural and cultural history to support an interdisciplinary course of study around themes of interest to students. Menu items include Texas history and geography; famous Texans and immigrants to Texas; The Texas Environment: A Shared Past; Texas and the U.S. Since Reconstruction; Texas community profiles; Texas county demographics; vanishing species from the Texas Memorial Museum; multicultural themes; and AskERIC lesson plans.

Student projects have been posted and are continually updated. Teachers have shared projects ranging from holiday recipes and stories to international ecology art projects. Some projects are networked. All are cross-curriculum, linking science, math, physical education, language arts, history, and communication and technology.

U.S. National Parks

See also the National Park Service WWW Server (entry 1081).

1104. Grand Canyon Explorer

http://www.kaibab.org

Students can access general information about the Grand Canyon National Park, its history, and maps of the area. Excellent graphics accompany a virtual visit to the Grand Canyon area and a river trip down the Colorado River through the Grand Canyon Park. Park services are listed, and there is a bibliography of books, guides, and reference resources. Links are provided to other resources about the Grand Canyon. This is a good starting point for all types of information about the Grand Canyon. Maintained privately by Bob Ribokas (ribokas.bob@ teradyne.com).

1105. Grand Canyon River Running

http://www.azstarnet.com/grandcanyonriver/

Students can experience a virtual rafting experience on the Colorado River in the Grand Canyon. This page is an unofficial guide to rafting on the Colorado River, complete with maps, photographs, sounds, and video clips. Also provided are reading lists for more information and links to other sites relevant to the Grand Canyon and rafting on the Colorado River. Maintained by Leonard Thurman (thurman@azstarnet.com).

**1106. *The River That Flows Uphill*: A Two-Week Diary
by William H. Calvin**

http://faculty.washington.edu/wcalvin/bk3/index.htm

Real-life high adventure makes exciting and informative reading for students. This book was published by Sierra Club Books in 1987 and can be read in English, Dutch, or German through this site. It details Calvin's two-week river journey through part of the Grand Canyon and his musings on evolution. Maps and photos are available as well.

U.S. History

Historical Documents

1107. Historical Text Archive

http://www.geocities.com/Athens/Forum/9061/index.html

The Historical Text Archives from Mississippi State University contain information by country/area, including Canada, Latin America, France, the United Kingdom, and the United States. Historical documents are also organized under topics such as Discoverers, Journals, War, and Women. Resources include addresses, bibliographies, journals, photographs, and links to history servers, university history departments, and journals.

Historical texts in the History of the United States archive are organized by periods: Colonial, Revolutionary War, Early Republic, Nineteenth Century, and Twentieth Century. The Historical Text Archives are maintained by Don Mabry (djm1@ra.msstate.edu), professor of history at Mississippi State University.

Discussion Groups

1108. Teaching American History Discussion List

E-mail: **listserv@lists.wayne.edu**
Instructions: On the first line of the body of the message, type:
subscribe TAMHA [your first name and last name]

The Age of Exploration

1109. Age of Exploration Curriculum Guide

http://www.mariner.org/age/1ndex.html

One of the largest international maritime museums in the world, the Mariners' Museum (http://www.mariner.org) located in Newport News, Virginia, is a nonprofit, educational institution dedicated to "preserving and interpreting the culture of the sea and its tributaries, its conquest by man, and its influence on civilization." The Age of Exploration curriculum guide provides teachers with materials that address maritime discovery from ancient times to Captain Cook's voyage to the South Pacific in 1768. It complements the Age of Exploration Gallery, a permanent exhibition at the museum. Online materials available include lesson plans, vocabulary, links to related Web sites, and guides to other reference materials. Students may explore the curriculum guide through either a menu or a timeline. Also available are student activities, teacher activities, a list of explorers with brief biographical information, and a suggested reading bibliography. Students will find pictures of Egyptian ships; methods of navigation used by the Vikings; information on the Portuguese, English, and French sailors and explorers; and what life was like on board ship for Columbus's crew. With provided directions, students can create a compass, an astrolabe, a quadrant, and a globe. They can identify parts of a ship and navigational instrument, decide what they would take to sea, and find out more about common diseases and health-related problems of sailors. Questions and comments should be directed to (tmmedu@infi.net).

1110. Columbus and the Age of Discovery

http://muweb.millersv.edu/~columbus/

The main portion of this huge database (with more than 700 files) dates from the 1992 Quincentennial, the 500th anniversary of Columbus's discovery of the New World, but new information has been added. Materials include speeches, conference papers, newsletters, magazine and journal articles, reviews, bibliographies, letters, and the like, divided into topics such as history, geography, fine arts, archaeology, and literature. Under the topic of history is a collection of full-text articles from a wide range of journals and magazines, such as *National Geographic, Washington Post National Weekly Edition, Natural History, Newsweek,* and *The New York Times Magazine.*

1111.   **The Columbus Navigation Homepage**

http://www1.minn.net/~keithp/index.htm

By examining the history, navigation, and landfall of Christopher Columbus, this Web site encourages students to develop critical-thinking skills. For example, along with a map of the Bahamas the question is asked, "Where was Columbus's first landing place in the New World?" It is known that Columbus visited five islands, but four are still in dispute more than 500 years later. Students are encouraged to read the facts (clues) and then the theories. Math joins this history/ geography puzzle when students must figure the difference between leagues and miles.

Students gain a better understanding of Columbus's four voyages by studying the difference between dead reckoning navigation and celestial navigation. Information is available on longitude and the ships Columbus used. A timeline, select bibliography of Columbus literature, and links to related sites are provided. Created and maintained by Keith A. Pickering (keithp@minn.net).

1112.   **Discoverers Web Home Page**

http://www.win.tue.nl/cs/fm/engels/discovery/index.html

The Discoverers Web site has a comprehensive collection of links to resources about voyages of discovery and exploration. It is far more encompassing than the traditional "age of discovery" time period. Information is available about ancient explorers, explorers during the Middle Ages, South American explorers, explorations to the polar regions, oceanographic expeditions, nonwestern explorers, and more. There is an alphabetical list of explorers. There is also a list of primary and semiprimary sources. *Primary Sources* are the texts the travelers wrote on their voyages. Students can read extracts from Christopher Columbus's 1492 journal from the *Medieval Sourcebook;* John Pory's *Description of Plymouth;* and Thomas Jefferson's letter to Meriwether Lewis. Maintained by Andre Engels (engels@win.tue.nl), a Dutch historian.

1113.   **Explorers of the World**

http://www.bham.wednet.edu/explore.htm

Explorers of the World is a Bellingham Public Schools (Bellingham, Washington) project that explores the kinds of persons who choose a life of exploration, challenge, and discovery. Areas of exploration include land, ideas, sky, and art. Explorers of the arts include modern dancer Alvin Ailey, composer Ludwig van Beethoven, poet Emily Dickinson, and painter Vincent van Gogh. Explorers of ideas are defined as those who dare to challenge old ways of thinking. In this category are Benjamin Banneker, Rachel Carson, Jonas Salk, and Louis Pasteur.

1114.   ***1492: An Ongoing Voyage***

http://metalab.unc.edu/expo/1492.exhibit/Intro.html

The 1492: An Ongoing Voyage exhibit raises the question: "What was the effect of Columbus's 1492 voyage on the Americas throughout the Western Hemisphere?" Accompanying text provides invaluable historical insights. The exhibit is divided into six sections:

1.   What Came To Be Called America
2.   The Mediterranean World
3.   Christopher Columbus: Man and Myth

4. Inventing America
5. Europe Claims America
6. Epilogue

The online exhibit includes 22 objects from more than 300 in the original exhibit.   The exhibit attempts to describe the Americas before and after European contact; the 15th-century Mediterranean world, including navigation skills; and the facts and myths surrounding Christopher Columbus. The exhibit also highlights some of the differences and similarities between European and American worldviews at the time of contact.

Some of the objects online include a page from Oviedo's 1535 description of a hammock bed; a terrestrial globe with armillary sphere designed by Caspar Vopel (1511–1561); a color graphic of Columbus's coat of arms; the first map of America to include the name of California (Gutierrez, 1562); a photograph of a church in Cuzco constructed on top of the remains of an Incan temple, showing the combination of Christian, Muslim, and Incan cultures; a winter count calendar by Batteste Good of the Dakota-speaking people (Brule); and a Mexican calendar.

The American Colonial Period

1115. **Archiving Early America**

http://earlyamerica.com

Archiving Early America provides a look at 18th-century America through primary resources such as newspapers, maps, magazines, and writings. Students can read online a handwritten receipt for nine guns and nine bayonets signed by a Continental Army officer on July 5, 1776, and the story of the creation of the first copper penny, which appeared in the *Columbian Centinel* (Boston, MA) newspaper on June 20, 1792. Pages from the Past offers examples of some typical newspapers from the 1700s, including the scanned front page of the *Boston Gazette* with news of the Revolutionary War (October 7, 1776). This Day in Early America highlights historical events from the 1700s for the current month and day. The Gallery of Early American Portraits includes digitized images of black-and-white engravings made from original oil paintings of statesmen, activists, politicians, and military leaders. The Lives of Famous Americans includes the *Autobiography of Benjamin Franklin* (entry 1128) and David Ramsay's *The Life of George Washington* (entry 1134). The interactive crossword puzzle tests students' knowledge of early American history and can be solved either online or printed out for pencil-and-paper solution by an entire class. This Web site is searchable, and links are provided to the current and archived issues of the *Early American Review*, a journal of fact and opinion on the people, issues, and events of 18th-century America. Don Vitale (devcom@devcom.seanet.com) is the curator for this site.

1116. **Colonial America: 1600-1776**

http://www.carolhurst.com/newsletters/newsletters11f.html

Carol Hurst's *Children's Literature Newsletter* (April 1996) features colonial America as a topic for integrating literature into the curriculum. Discussion Starters, Research Starters, Activities, an annotated bibliography of books (picture books, novels, and nonfiction) set in the colonial period, and an annotated list of Internet links assist teachers and students with their studies of colonial America.

1117.   **Resources for Arts of Colonial America**

http://artsedge.kennedy-center.org/student/colonyfinal.html

Available from ARTSEDGE at the Kennedy Center (Washington, D.C.), Resources for Colonial America is a Student Research Page that guides students in their research of the arts of
colonial America. Annotated Internet resources are grouped into categories: Architecture, Literary Arts, Music, Theater, Visual Arts, and Folk Arts, Life, and Culture. A Teacher's Guide to
American Art and lesson plans on Colonial American Paintings are also available.

Jamestown

1118.   **Jamestown Rediscovery Archaeological Project**

http://www.apva.org

Jamestown Rediscovery is a 10-year interdisciplinary project searching for, finding, and exca-
vating the remains of James Fort (1607) on Jamestown Island, Virginia. The project is sponsored by the Association for the Preservation of Virginia Antiquities (APVA), the oldest
statewide preservation organization in the nation founded in 1889 and one of three institutions that interprets history at Jamestown. The APVA owns the area known as Old Towne,
which is the location of the first fort at Jamestown. Students can take a virtual field trip to
Jamestown Island to see the remains of the fort. A map is included. There are photographs of
the current exhibit by APVA and a history of Jamestown. One of the other institutions that interprets Jamestown history is the Colonial National Historic Park, which owns the area known
as New Towne, into which the settlement expanded during the 17th century. There are a visitor's center and a seasonal living history museum featuring glassblowers in a re-creation of
the Glasshouse of 1608. The third institution is Jamestown Settlement, founded in 1957. It is
a state-run facility featuring full-sized replicas of the three ships that arrived in 1607, a re-
creation of James Fort, and a re-created Native American village.

1119.   **Virtual Jamestown**

http://jefferson.village.virginia.edu/vcdh/jamestown/

Virtual Jamestown is an ongoing project in preparation for the 400th anniversary of the
founding of the fort, in 2007. The site is divided into four areas and provides primary documents, including firsthand accounts, letters, laws, state papers, contracts such as the Inden-
ture Contract of William Buckland, and census data. Two searchable databases are available:
the Bristol Registers of 17th-century indentured servants and an 18th-century runaway slave
advertisement. In Jamestown Remembered, accounts and analyses by modern historians, written on the 300th and 350th anniversary celebrations, have been posted. Jamestown Resources
has virtual panoramas of the fort and views from the fort (requires Apple QuickTime plug-in),
maps, teaching materials, bibliographies, and links to other Web resources. This is a work in
progress to explore the legacies of the Jamestown settlement and "the Virginia experiment."

New England

1120. The Colonial History of Lexington, Massachusetts

http://hastings.ci.lexington.ma.us/Colonial/Colonial.html

Students at the Maria Hastings Elementary School in Lexington, Massachusetts, started this project in 1994 and have continued to add to the site each year. There is a spider diagram of their studies. Students have researched and posted their work on such topics as colonial crafts, Lexington family history, historic homes, the battle, colonial life, British soldiers, the old graveyard, Paul Revere's ride, and the people who lived in Lexington before it was colonized. See the lantern at the Concord Museum, which hung in the steeple of Christ Church (the Old North Church), which was Boston's tallest building at the time. Information is shared about Colonial Days, when three fourth-grade classes at this school tried their hands at authentic colonial crafts. Future classes plan to work on sections about the colonial militia, appreciation and understanding of a colony, and the events leading to revolution. See also lesson plan resources on the Revolutionary War provided by the Discovery Channel (http://discoveryschool.com/lessonplans/themes/americanrevolution.html).

1121. *Mayflower* Web Page

http://members.aol.com/calebj/mayflower.html

Caleb Johnson's *Mayflower* Web Page is a definitive site for finding information about the *Mayflower* and its passengers, addressing both genealogy and history. There is a link to every passenger on the *Mayflower,* with genealogical information. Not only are there full texts of early Plymouth documents, but also books, letters, wills, and journals written by the *Mayflower* Pilgrims. There are also sections about the girls and women of the *Mayflower,* clothing worn by the Pilgrims, their religious beliefs, and the weapons they used. The ship's history includes information about the ship's dimensions, inventory, and crew; a complete passenger list includes links to interesting biographical information. Students can locate information on the history of Thanksgiving and Native Americans, including a biography of Tisquantum (Squanto). Links are provided to lists of *Mayflower* museums, *Mayflower*-specific genealogy research resources, and passengers with descendants living today. Created and maintained by Caleb Johnson (mayfloweb@aol.com).

1122. Seventeenth-Century Native Americans in New England

http://www.nativeweb.org/NativeTech/

NativeTech is devoted to Native American technology and art in the 1600s. Illustrations and diagrams accompany informative and interesting information about the life and culture of Native Americans in New England during the colonial period. Find out more about beadwork, pottery, feathers, clothing, metalwork, weaving, and the use of plants and trees. Poetry and stories are available, as are essays and articles. Excellent links are provided to the Nipmuc Indian Association of Connecticut, as well as other Native American resources on the Internet. Tara Prindle is the Webmaster (prindle@uconnvm.uconn.edu).

1123. **A Walking Tour of Plimoth Plantation**

http://archnet.uconn.edu/topical/historic/plimoth/plimoth.html

Take a virtual field trip to Plimoth Plantation as it was in the 1600s. Plimoth (Plymouth) Plantation was the first permanent European settlement in southern New England (1620). This site allows students to visit Plimoth's living museum via color photographs and descriptive text. The living museum is dedicated to re-creating 17th-century life in the New World. People in period costumes socialize and work, carrying out the daily tasks of farming, husbandry, construction, and craft production. The museum is divided into two areas, the village occupied by the Pilgrims and the reconstructed Native American hamlet known as Hobbamock's Homesite.

Williamsburg

1124. **The Official Colonial Williamsburg Home Page**

http://www.history.org

Sponsored by the Colonial Williamsburg Foundation, this site offers rich resources for the classroom. Color photographs bring to life colonial Williamsburg of yesterday and today. The Education Resources area has lesson plans and electronic field trips. Some titles of the teacher's guides and lesson plans include Mathematics with a Mob Cap; Choosing Revolution: Political and Family Turmoil in the 18th Century; Don't Wanna Slave No More: African-American Choices in the American Revolution; Let America Speak: Our Voice as Our Vote; Order in the Court: Juvenile Justice in the Eighteenth Century; and Of Kith and Kin: The Trials and Triumphs of African-American Family Life. Students are invited to Meet the People, See the Places, and Experience Colonial Life. Additionally, there is an excellent timeline with links and a historical almanac.

The American Revolution and the Early Republic

The Revolutionary War

1125. **American Revolution in South Carolina**

http://www.anderson1234.k12.sc.us/d3/StarrElem/rev/rev.htm

Did you know that more Revolutionary battles and skirmishes were fought in South Carolina than in any other state? Research this site to discover more about the battles at Camden, Kings Mountain, Cowpens, and Sullivan's Island. Find out more about South Carolina generals who fought in the Revolutionary War, such as Francis Marion, Andrew Pickens, William Moultrie, and Thomas Sumter. Created and maintained by Martha Taylor (josh@carol.net), media specialist at Starr Elementary School, Anderson, South Carolina.

1126. **The Revolutionary War: Journey Towards Freedom**

http://library.advanced.org/10966/

Students might understand how it was to be a soldier at the time of the Revolution after taking an illustrated tour of Valley Forge, where Washington and his men wintered and later crossed the Delaware River. Find this virtual tour in the Infopedia section, along with links to historical documents, biographical profiles, maps, major battles, and colonial-period recipes (with modern instructions). The Fun Zone contains Revolutionary War games, matching card games, word searches, and a timed quiz to help guide Paul Revere on his legendary ride to Lexington and Concord. The Teacher's Corner has lesson plans and activities. A bibliography of resources is available, and links are provided to related sites on the Internet. Created as a ThinkQuest project by Andrew Spencer (sndworm@juno.com), Pad Haney (paien@juno.com), and Melissa Caine (MLC615@aol.com).

Revolutionary War and Early Republic Biographies

1127.   Biographies of Historical Persons Related to American History
http://odur.let.rug.nl/~usa/B/index.htm

From Revolution to Reconstruction, a WWW project of collective writing in hypertext (http://odur.let.rug.nl/~usa/), provides more than 80 online biographies of historical persons related to American history, including extensive biographies on John Adams (1735–1826), Benjamin Franklin (1706–1790), Alexander Hamilton (1755–1804), and Andrew Jackson (1767–1845), as well as autobiographies of Frederick Douglass and Geronimo. This is a good beginning resource for students researching the founding fathers and members of the Continental Congress. Students will find readable text with in-line links to further information helpful.

Benjamin Franklin (1706–1790)

1128.   *The Autobiography of Benjamin Franklin*
http://earlyamerica.com/lives/franklin/index.html

A year after Benjamin Franklin's death, his autobiography, entitled *Memoires de la Vie Privee de Benjamin Franklin*, was published in Paris (March 1791). The English translation was published in London two years later. This work, consisting of 12 chapters, is now online. Franklin ended his account of his life in 1757 when he was 51 years old. His autobiography portrays a fascinating picture of life in Philadelphia as well as Franklin's shrewd observations on the literature, philosophy, and religion of the time. Considered to be the greatest autobiography produced in colonial America, Franklin's autobiography is a wonderful primary resource for students.

1129.   Benjamin Franklin: Glimpses of the Man
http://sln.fi.edu/franklin/rotten.html

The Franklin Institute Science Museum in Philadelphia, Pennsylvania, hosts an excellent multimedia exhibit on Benjamin Franklin. Students can find out more about Franklin as a scientist, an inventor, a statesman, a printer, a philosopher, a musician, and an economist. Resource materials, enrichment activities, and a brief glossary are provided, as is Franklin's family tree. There are electricity and balloon hands-on enhancement activities in science, as well as reading and writing activities. In one writing project, students compare Franklin's two epitaphs (one written when he was 22 and the other when he was 84) and then write their own epitaphs.

Thomas Jefferson (1743–1826)

1130. Monticello, Home of Thomas Jefferson

http://www.monticello.org

Students can visit Monticello, Thomas Jefferson's home, online to find out what a day in the life of Thomas Jefferson was like by following a typical schedule from early morning to an evening spent in the parlor. Color photographs and in-text links to fun facts and suggestions for activities (like baking breakfast muffins and pressing flowers) make this an engaging and informative site for students to learn more about Thomas Jefferson, his home, and life in America around the turn of the 19th century. Dig Deeper and Matters of Fact links connect students to more interesting factual details, and Personality Profile links provide fascinating human insights into the people who visited and lived at Monticello during Jefferson's lifetime.

1131. Thomas Jefferson: Online Resources at the University of Virginia

http://etext.virginia.edu/jefferson/

Students can explore the Jeffersonian resources compiled by the Electronic Texts Center at the University of Virginia. These resources include a bibliography of significant writing by and about Jefferson from 1826 to 1990. Electronic texts by and to Jefferson include some manuscript images as well as typed text. There are more than 2,100 excerpts from Jefferson's writings, including selected quotations that represent Jefferson's principles of government. Links are provided to other Jefferson resources on the Web, online exhibitions with Jefferson content, Jefferson organizations, and virtual tours of the University of Virginia.

George Washington (1732–1799)

1132. George Washington and Mount Vernon

http://www.mountvernon.org

Students can take a self-guided virtual tour of the Mount Vernon grounds and buildings that were George Washington's home. Accessible information from this site includes an image gallery and George Washington's views on slavery. The George Washington Lesson Plan is available at (http://www.mountvernon.org/education/biography/index.html). Written at the fifth-grade level, this Biography Lesson contains more than a dozen images, an interactive quiz, and a timeline. A bibliography of suggested reading for both students and teachers is available, with a list of additional classroom resources. A linked table of contents makes navigation easy. Sponsored by the Historic Mount Vernon Museum.

1133. George Washington Papers at the Library of Congress

http://lcweb2.loc.gov/ammem/gwhtml/gwhome.html

The Manuscript Division of the Library of Congress has placed online 41 of George Washington's letter books (about 8,000 pages). The collection is a rich source for almost every aspect of colonial and early American history. Also available is an illustrated timeline with in-text links. Included in Washington's letters is one to his mother after an engagement in the French and Indian War when he was only 23. Washington wrote, "I luckily escaped without a wound, tho' I had four bullets through my Coat, and two Horses shot under me. I was not half recovered from a violent illness that confined me to my Bed, and a Waggon, for above ten Days."

1134. ***The Life of George Washington* by David Ramsay**

http://earlyamerica.com/lives/gwlife/index.html

The Life of George Washington was published by David Ramsay eight years after George Washington's death. Ramsay was a contemporary of Washington and an active participant in the events leading to the establishment of the United States. (He was twice elected a delegate to the Continental Congress.) Ramsay's book is part of the Keigwin and Mathews Collection. Thirteen chapters cover Washington's life from his early years to his death in 1799. Each month a new chapter will be added until the online work is complete. Ramsay's insights provide students with an insider's perspective.

1135. **The Papers of George Washington**

http://minerva.acc.Virginia.EDU/gwpapers/

The Papers of George Washington project was established in 1969 at the University of Virginia, under the joint auspices of the University and the Mount Vernon Ladies' Association of the Union; its mission is to publish a complete edition of Washington's correspondence. The finished project will be contained in 85 volumes. Selected documents are online, including Washington's Farewell Address, an entry about the Whiskey Insurrection from Washington's diaries, and his Thanksgiving Proclamation in 1789.

The Early 1800s

Society and Culture

1136. **19th Century Schoolbooks**

http://digital.library.pitt.edu/nietz/nietz2.html

Part of the Nietz Old Textbook Collection at the University of Pittsburgh is available online. Look for 30 online full-text volumes of textbooks used in schools in the United States during the 19th century. Included in the collection are several examples of William Holmes McGuffey's readers. The collection is browseable and searchable.

1137. ***Democracy in America* by Alexis de Tocqueville**

http://xroads.virginia.edu/~HYPER/DETOC/home.html

Tocqueville's *America* is a project of the American Studies Programs at The University of Virginia. The full-text version of the book is online, in HTML format. Supplementary text has been added to ground the work specifically in America between 1831–1832. Look for articles on topics such as everyday life, American women, American religion, and race relations. Other articles give European perspectives of American democracy and European travelers' commentaries on American modes of transportation, habits, physical appearance, manners, and education. Maps from the 1840 census show population distribution, the slave population, transportation, and occupations.

Westward Expansion and the Gold Rushes

Westward Expansion

1138.   The American West
http://www.americanwest.com

The American West consists of 17 states (west of the Mississippi River). This site presents comprehensive information about the history and development of the American West. Students will be able to find out more about westward expansion; western trails; cowboys; Indians/Native Americans; pioneers; gunslingers; outlaws; ghost towns; and famous people, such as Doc Holliday, Kit Carson, Wyatt Earp, Wild Bill Hickok, Davy Crockett, Daniel Boone, Billy the Kid, Jesse James, and Buffalo Bill. A graphics library provides photographs of the Wild West, and links are given to popular films with Western themes. Bengt Lindeblad (Webmaster@AmericanWest.com) is the Webmaster.

1139.   In the Steps of Esteban: Tucson's African American Heritage
http://dizzy.library.arizona.edu/images/afamer/homepage.html

In the Steps of Esteban: Tucson's African American Heritage is an online exhibit documenting the history of Tucson, Arizona's African American community, which was founded by homesteaders, cowboys, and soldiers. A photograph gallery complements the histories recorded on this site, including biographies and oral histories. This site is a tribute to the early African American settlers who came to Arizona Territory searching for freedom and opportunity. Rising above the hardships and racial discrimination they experienced, African Americans helped build the city by contributing to the vitality of the early Tucson community, as family members, businessmen, and citizens. The first recorded African American settlers to follow in the footsteps of Esteban, a slave on one of the 16th-century Spanish expeditions, arrived in the Tucson area in the mid-1800s. By 1900, 86 persons who lived in Tucson identified themselves as people of African descent. This site gives a rare insight into the history of African Americans who were part of the American West. Questions and comments can be sent to Stuart Glogoff (sglogoff@bird.library.arizona.edu), assistant dean of Library Information Systems, University of Arizona Libraries.

For more information about African Americans and the American West, *see* The African-American Mosaic (entry 1216).

1140.   The Kansas Collection
http://www.ukans.edu/carrie/kancoll/

The Kansas Collection is an online collection of primary resources relevant to Kansas history and the settling of the American West. Students can access books, letters, diaries, photographs, maps, and other materials. Some exhibits include Orphan Trains, Heroes and Villains, and Bleeding Kansas. On the Trail highlights materials about the many trails crossing Kansas: the Oregon, Santa Fe, Smoky Hill, Military, and others. Created by Lynn Nelson, professor of history at the University of Kansas (lhnelson@raven.cc.ukans.edu).

1141. Lewis & Clark: The Journey of the Corps of Discovery

http://www.pbs.org/lewisandclark/

In 1804, an expedition of 33, including the captains, Meriwether Lewis (Thomas Jefferson's secretary), and Lewis's friend William Clark, set out to explore the western lands of the United States. This Corps of Discovery came into contact with nearly 50 native tribes during their 28-month travels. Students will meet 16 of those tribes at this Web site. Students can also listen to experts answer questions by using RealAudio to access sound files. Excerpts from the journals of different members of the Corps are available in the Archive for online reading. Seventeen lessons are provided (http://www.pbs.org/lewisandclark/class/idx_les.html) for meaningful classroom learning. Students can participate in an interactive fictionalized story titled "Into the Unknown," in which they lead the expedition. In this site, the Public Broadcasting Service (PBS) provides an interesting and comprehensive companion to *Lewis & Clark: The Journey of the Corps of Discovery*, a film by Ken Burns.

For original maps and a press release in Jefferson's hand, see the Library of Congress American Treasures exhibit (http://lcweb.loc.gov/exhibits/treasures/trr001.html). *National Geographic* has a great site with a kids' section, Go West Across America with Lewis & Clark (http://www.nationalgeographic.com/lewisclark/index.html). See also Lewis & Clark in North Dakota (http://www.ndlewisandclark.com).

1142. Museum of Westward Expansion Tour

http://www.nps.gov/jeff/mus-tour.htm

The Museum of Westward Expansion Tour charts the entire history of the 19th-century American West, from the Louisiana Purchase to the closing of the frontier in 1890. A timeline allows students to put specific events into perspective. Students can click on a floor plan or a location index to take a virtual tour of the museum, which is located in St. Louis, Missouri, and is part of the Jefferson National Expansion Memorial maintained by the National Park Service. Some of the areas for student exploration include Mountain Men and Trappers, American Indians, Farmers, Buffalo Hunters, Miners, and Cowboys. Audio clips using RealAudio (also available as online text) feature narratives from prominent figures in America's pioneering history.

1143. Oregon Trail: The Trail West

http://www.ukans.edu/kansas/seneca/oregon/mainpage.html

For 25 years during the mid-19th century, the Oregon Trail was a primary route for emigrants moving to the western territories of the United States. The trail was used by so many people before the Central Pacific and Union Pacific railroads were joined at Promontory Point, Utah, in 1869, that even today the ruts from thousands of Conestoga wagons are still visible along various parts of the trail. Students will find trail maps, trail diaries, and links to information about other trails, such as the Overland Trail, the California Trail, and the Missouri Trail. Don't miss the links to (http://www.over-land.com/trore.html) for additional information about the Oregon Trail, including a chronology (1841–1866) and the annual reenactment of the crossing of the Snake River (Utah). Sponsored by the KANZA Chapter of the Oregon California Trail Association, the Web editor for this site is Marcia Philbrick (pioneer@parod.com). See also the Wagon Train of 1843, to find out more about some of the pioneers who traveled the Oregon Trail during the early years (http://www.peak.org/~mransom/pioneers.html).

1144.   The Prairie Traveler: A Hand-Book for Overland Expeditions

http://kuhttp.cc.ukans.edu/carrie/kancoll/books/marcy/index.html

In 1859, the War Department, which had become alarmed about the flood of inexperienced pioneers setting out for the western frontier, directed Randolph Barnes Marcy, a captain in the U.S. Army with much experience in the West, to write *The Prairie Traveler: A Hand-Book for Overland Expeditions*. A bestseller in its day, *The Prairie Traveler* was an essential guidebook offering practical advice (which is still sound today) to the many emigrants heading west, most of whom were poorly informed and ill-prepared for such a journey. As a guide for traveling and surviving in the West, *The Prairie Traveler* saved many lives. The entire text is now available online, including maps, illustrations, and itineraries of the principal routes between the Mississippi and the Pacific. Students will enjoy reading Marcy's book, which is written with a dry sense of humor and contains interesting details on how to survive. From a fully linked table of contents, chapters may be easily accessed either sequentially or nonsequentially.

Students and teachers should also plan to explore other books, letters, diaries, and photographs in the Kansas Collection (http://kuhttp.cc.ukans.edu/carrie/kancoll/), an online collection of primary and historical materials created by Lynn Nelson (lhnelson@raven.cc.ukans.edu), professor of history at the University of Kansas.

1145.   WestWeb

http://scholar.library.csi.cuny.edu/westweb/

WestWeb is a topically organized Web site on the study of the American West. Each of the more than 30 topic headings contains collections of primary and secondary documents, biographical and bibliographical resources, and lists of links to other related sites. Students can explore the history and culture of ancient and native peoples of the American West, as well as the roles played by women, Asians, African Americans, immigrants, and Chicanos. Students may become involved in the study of Western maps, how the West was measured, and the history of transportation in the West. Links are provided to a three-dimensional model of the Great Kiva in Chaco Canyon, an online photo exhibition of wild plants of the Pueblo Province, and Washington State University's Multicultural History of the American West (http://www.wsu.edu:8080/~amerstu/mw/). Created and maintained by Catherine Lavender (lavender@postbox.csi.cuny.edu), Department of History, College of Staten Island, City University of New York.

Laura Ingalls Wilder

See also Laura Ingalls Wilder's books in the *Little House on the Prairie* series (entry 521).

1146.   Laura Ingalls Wilder: Frontier Girl

http://webpages.marshall.edu/~irby1/laura.htmlx
or
http://ourworld.compuserve.com/homepages/p_greetham/ingalls/home.html

Little House fans will love this site. This is Laura's real story, told with in-text links to pictures and more information about the family's move westward, complete with a map. Laura and her family were pioneers of the American West. In 1868, the family moved to the prairies of Kansas; in 1874, the family tried to settle in a sod house on a farm near Walnut Grove, Minnesota; and in 1879, they moved to the Dakota Territory. Biographical information is from *Laura Ingalls Wilder—A Biography* (HarperCollins, 1992) by William Anderson. In Laura's Classroom, students can click on objects to find out more about Laura and her family. Students will find Pa's fiddle, a Bible kept by Laura, and a quiz about Laura's books. Developed by Rebecca Irby and Phil Greetham. E-mail Irby (irby1@marchall.edu), and she will try to answer your questions about Laura and her family. Check the FAQs first to see if someone else has asked your question. See also Travel the Prairie with Laura and Caddie (http://web.isbe.state.il.us/mshride/index.htm), an ongoing Internet project by third- and fifth-graders at Arthur Elementary School in Arthur, Illinois, for information on the growth of prairie cities in six states.

California

1147. California History
http://www.jspub.com

All fourth-graders in California are required to study California history. Click on the button labeled "Students" on the map of resources to go to information about the California history text, *Oh, California*. Students will find information about California missions, Mexican California, the Donner party, and the Bear Flag Revolt. Only some of the chapters are online to date, but eventually all chapters will be online. The Teacher/Parent page provides detailed instructions for constructing a model of a mission. Other links are available to general history and California history on the Internet. The Webmaster's address is (jsp@jspub.com).

The Gold Rushes

Alaska

1148. The Great Klondike Gold Rush
http://www.gold-rush.org

The Great Klondike Gold Rush Web site is rich with nuggets of information. Gold was first discovered in 1849, followed in 1880, by a major gold strike on Gold Creek near Juneau. However, it was the discovery of gold on Bonanza Creek in 1896 that set off the great Klondike Gold Rush, or Klondike Stampede. *Ghosts of the Klondike Gold Rush*, created by the Gold Rush Centennial Task Force, is a commemoration of this event in Alaskan history. This site is full of interesting history about the Gold Rush and the opening of the Yukon Territory. Students will find out about gunslingers, the mounted police, the completion of the White Pass and Yukon Route Railway, the Chilkoot Pass and killer avalanche, and the founding of the Iditarod Trail. In 1897, the North West Mounted Police set up a border crossing into Canada at the summit of the Chilkoot. They ordered every stampeder to carry a year's worth of supplies. Students can access the actual list to find out what was required. There are also interviews with descendants of Gold Rush miners. A good literature tie-in for older students is *Klondike: The Last Great Gold Rush, 1896-1899* (revised edition now in paperback; McClelland and Stewart, 1994) by Canadian author Pierre Berton. An Events Calendar has dates of various festivals, parades, and celebration activities through the year 1999. Databases are searchable by name.

California

1149.   **"California as I Saw It": First-Person Narratives of California's Early Years, 1849-1900**

http://lcweb2.loc.gov/ammem/cbhtml/cbhome.html

This collection from American Memory at the Library of Congress consists of the full texts and illustrations of 190 works documenting the formative era of California's history, through eyewitness accounts by such individuals as Mark Twain, Robert Louis Stevenson, and William Tecumseh Sherman. These primary resources, including journals, diaries, and letters, provide insight into the everyday life of the period, as well as offering descriptions of the development of urban centers such as San Francisco and Los Angeles.

1150.   **John A. Sutter's Account of the Discovery of Gold**

http://www.sfmuseum.org/hist2/gold.html

Students can read firsthand John A. Sutter's account of the discovery of gold and find out how he tested the metal with *aqua fortis* from his apothecary shop. Students will also learn that Sutter considered this sudden discovery of gold the cause of his financial ruin. Other features of this site include the article about gold from the *Encyclopedia Americana* and links to other information about the discovery of gold in California.

1151.   **Treasure in the Stream CyberGuide**

http://www.sdcoe.k12.ca.us/score/treasure/treasuretg.html

Treasure in the Stream: The Story of a Gold Rush Girl (Silver Burdett, 1991) by Dorothy Hoobler, Thomas Hoobler, and Nancy Carpenter is used as a focus for this CyberGuide, which integrates literature and Internet resources into the curriculum. Using the story of an ordinary farm family caught up in the gold frenzy and a young girl named Amy Harris, students find out about mining camps, gold-crazed miners, disappointments, and riches. This unit provides objectives, worksheets, and links to relevant Internet resources, with suggested student research activities. Written by Ann Nemerouf (Anemrouf@telis.org). For other CyberGuides, see (http://www.sdcoe.k12.ca.us/score/cyberguide.html).

Slavery and the Underground Railroad

1152.   **The North Star: Tracing the Underground Railroad**

http://www.ugrr.org

In the years before the Civil War, a secret network of people and places, known as the Underground Railroad, helped slaves to escape to freedom. This network was neither "underground" nor a "railroad"; rather, it was a loose organization of aid and assistance to fugitives from slavery. Escaping slaves had to travel hundreds of miles to freedom, and depended on abolitionists and sympathizers to give them shelter and assistance along the way. Perhaps as many as 100,000 enslaved persons may have escaped in the period between the American Revolution and the Civil War. Be sure to look in the Learning Center at the Teacher Resources for links to lesson plans, annotated reading lists, classroom projects, and activities. The Montgomery County Public School Underground Railroad Assignments are particularly excellent (http://www.mcps.k12.md.us/curriculum/socialstd/UGRR.html).

1153. The Underground Railroad

http://www.nationalgeographic.com/features/99/railroad/index.html

Students follow Moses (Harriet Tubman) on the Underground Railroad to Delaware, Rochester, and Canada in this interactive journey produced by the National Geographic Society. The site allows visitors to make choices along the way and is illustrated with photographs and sound. A map shows the route to Canada, and a slavery timeline runs from 1501 to 1865. Provides classroom ideas, links to related Web sites, and brief biographies of 12 abolitionists.

The Civil War

1154. The American Civil War Home Page

http://sunsite.utk.edu/civil-war/

Offering comprehensive links to electronic files about the American Civil War (1861–1865), The American Civil War Home Page includes timelines, graphic images, letters, accounts, diaries, other documentary records, modern histories, and bibliographies. Also included are rosters of combatants, miscellaneous military information, and links to other information sites. Of special note are photographs taken by Matthew B. Brady during the Civil War. This Web site is an invaluable research resource for students studying the Civil War. Maintained by Dr. George H. Hoemann (hoemann@utk.edu).

1155. Civil War Resources on the Internet: Abolitionism to Reconstruction (1830s-1890s)

http://www.libraries.rutgers.edu/rulib/socsci/hist/civwar-2.html

Using a table-of-contents format to present information, this page serves as a subject archive for the American and British History page maintained at Rutgers University. The table of contents covers the 1830s to 1890s: the years leading up to the Civil War, the actual war years, and Reconstruction. It includes online bibliographies. The section on War Years is divided into general sites; a collection of diaries, letters, and papers; military histories; and state studies. This site is well organized and allows access to comprehensive information and primary documents.

1156. Letters of an Iowa Soldier in the Civil War

http://www.civilwarletters.com/home.html

Newton Scott was a 21-year-old clerk in the Union Army during the Civil War. He was enlisted in the 36th Infantry of Iowa Volunteers. This page provides access to his letters, which were written during a three-year period. Most were written to his neighborhood friend Hannah Cone, who lived in Albia, Monroe County, Iowa. (Scott later married Hannah.) Scott's letters are rich in detail about the war and the living conditions in Union camps in Mississippi, Missouri, Iowa, and Arkansas.

1157.   **Mr. Lincoln's Virtual Library at the Library of Congress**
        http://lcweb2.loc.gov/ammem/alhtml/alhome.html

Four of more than 26,000 papers in the Library of Congress's Lincoln collections are now on-line. Among them is a first draft, in Lincoln's his own hand, of the Emancipation Proclamation, written more than five months before he issued it on September 22, 1862. More papers from the Lincoln collection will go online in the near future. In addition to papers, students can view an image of the items found in the 16th president's pockets after he was assassinated. The artifacts include two pairs of spectacles and a penknife.

1158.   **Poetry and Music of the War Between the States**
        http://www.erols.com/kfraser/

The author of this Web site believes that if you want to understand the thoughts and emotions of the men who faced each other across the Civil War battlefields, and those who waited for them at home, you must look at the poetry and songs written during the era. Students will find sound files (MIDI) and text files so that they can listen to the music as they follow the words. Links from each poem and song lead to historical notes and references. Songs and poetry are categorized as either Confederate or Union. In addition, songs and poems can be accessed through indexes of titles, first lines, and authors. Created and maintained by Kathie Fraser (kfraser@erols.com).

1159.   **The Valley of the Shadow: Living the Civil War in Virginia and Pennsylvania**
        http://jefferson.village.virginia.edu/vshadow2/

Described as a dynamic interactive exhibit, this is an outstanding WWW site on the Civil War and its effects on two close communities: Staunton in Augusta County, Virginia, and Chambersburg in Franklin County, Pennsylvania. The communities are adjacent to one another along the Shenandoah or Great Valley that stretches through Pennsylvania, Maryland, Virginia, and Tennessee. An impressive team of experts has developed this dual community study project, designing databases of census information; charting troop movements; analyzing newspapers, diaries, and military rosters; and mapping the area. Edward L. Ayers, the Hugh P. Kelley Professor of History at the University of Virginia and author of *The Promise of the New South* and other books about southern history, decided to pursue this project using hypermedia rather than traditional means of research because of the exciting possibilities of creating and linking information using various databases, illustrations, maps, census records, diaries, newspaper articles, letters, and biographical data. The project is planned for three installments. The first installment is online and covers the period between John Brown's raid and the beginning of the Civil War in April 1861.

This Web site is well organized and has information specifically for classroom use. Lesson plans and assignments are available from various teachers. Examples of completed student papers and projects are also posted. Using The Valley of the Shadow as primary research on a local study, students can consider broader questions, such as the inevitability of war, the centrality of slavery, economic and social differences, and political miscalculations.

The Late 1800s and Early 1900s

Conservation of Western Lands

1160.   John Muir Exhibit

http://sierraclub.org/john_muir_exhibit/

The John Muir Exhibit features the life and legacy of John Muir (1838–1914), naturalist, writer, conservationist, and founder of the Sierra Club. This comprehensive exhibit includes pictures and audio files. Information is also available about the National Park System and individual parks. This page is hosted by the Sierra Club. Be sure to access the *John Muir Day Study Guide* (http://www.sierraclub.org/john_muir_exhibit/john_muir_day_study_guide/). Suggested activities and lessons for grade levels K-12 include the John Muir Geography Cards.

The Gilded Age and the Progressive Era—1890 to World War I

See also Alexander Graham Bell's Path to the Telephone (entry 877), Thomas Alva Edison (entry 879), "Inventions" (entries 880–881), and Historical Investigation into the Past: The Lizzie Borden/Fall River Case Study (entry 1045). See also a WebQuest on this topic: The Gilded Age: Documenting Industry in America (http://www.oswego.org/staff/tcaswell/wq/gildedage/student.htm).

1161.   Coal Mining in the Gilded Age and Progressive Era

http://www.history.ohio-state.edu/projects/Lessons_US/Gilded_Age/Coal_Mining/default.htm

Describes the working conditions in coal mines. Provides information about mine workers' lives, anthracite coal mining communities, child labor, and strikes. *Coal Creek Rebellion* by Jamie McKenzie (mckenzie@fno.org) is a online, full-text novel about how the state of Tennessee brought convict labor to Coal Creek to break the miners' union in 1891. Coal Creek is now Lake City, Tennessee, north of Knoxville. Provides a map and introductory notes.

1162.   The Richest Man in the World: Andrew Carnegie

http://www.pbs.org/wgbh/amex/carnegie/index.html

This Web site places Andrew Carnegie in a time period called by some historians a "Gilded Age," a time of ostentatious spending by a privileged few, notably the extremely wealthy in New York City. Provides a biography of Carnegie, an in-depth look at Carnegie's philanthropy, information about the steel and railroad industries, and the strike at the Homestead Mill. A QTVR (QuickTime VR technology) tour of The Elms, one of the Gilded Age mansions, is available, providing interactive, 360-degree color views of four rooms. Also provides information about the houses that were built on Millionaire's Row: Carnegie Mansion, Frick Mansion, Vanderbilt Chateau, and Mrs. Astor's house. Look for a timeline to put events into historical perspective.

1163. **Technology in 1900**

http://www.pbs.org/wgbh/amex/kids/tech1900/

What were some of the technology predictions for the future at the turn of the century in 1900? Where were some of the popular technological developments that would affect daily life? Find out more about the first telephone operators, early automobiles, and video music from the 1900s. Part of the WayBack: U.S. History for Kids online feature series sponsored by The American Experience television series and Web site produced by the Public Broadcasting Service (PBS).

Immigration

1164. **The Ellis Island Immigration Museum**

http://www.ellisisland.org/ellis.html

The Ellis Island Immigration Museum opened in 1990 as a nonprofit organization for educa- tion and commemoration. Because more than 40 percent of all living Americans can trace their roots to an ancestor who came through Ellis Island, the American Immigrant Wall of Honor has been created. Students who search for names in the Wall's online database might be able to find their ancestors and their immigrant roots.

1165. **Ellis Island Photographs, 1900-1920**

http://cmp1.ucr.edu/exhibitions/immigration_id.html

The University of California at Riverside has a small online collection of stereoscopic photo- graphs taken of Ellis Island in the early 20th century. These black-and-white images may be enlarged for projection in the classroom or for study in greater detail. One photograph shows the SS *Lusitania* docked in the harbor; others show scenes of medical examinations; the exami- nation of immigrants' luggage; a group of immigrants after they had successfully passed their tests; and Ellis Island from a distance, as immigrants on arriving ships would have seen it.

1166. **Immigration in American Memory**

http://lcweb2.loc.gov/learn/features/immig/immig.html

The American Memory collections at the Library of Congress offer rich and varied primary re- sources pertaining to immigration. This Web site addresses immigration in the United States as a topic for historical study and current debate. Divided into four sections for easy access, il- lustrations, sound files (.wav format), and in-text links help students understand the history of immigration and its role in building a nation. Students can link directly to current legisla- tion and recent bills in Congress to learn more about arguments supporting and opposing im- migration. The Library of Congress American Memory collections are searchable and contain hundreds of items about migration, immigration, and emigration.

1167. **Port of Entry: The American Journey of Immigration**

http://lcweb2.loc.gov/ammem/ndlpedu/activity/port/start.html

Students use their detective skills to uncover the stories of immigrants to the United States. Traveling back to the beginning of the twentieth century, they search for clues to the past in images and primary source documents from the American Memory collections at the Library of

Congress. Teacher materials are available for this sample lesson, and include curriculum use suggestions and classroom management ideas.

1168.   RootsWeb

http://www.rootsweb.com

The RootsWeb project has two missions: to make large volumes of data available to the online genealogical community at minimal cost, and to provide support services to online genealogical activities such as the ROOTS-L online discussion group. Genealogists can post information directly to online registries and find home pages of genealogical and historical societies, such as the Olive Tree Genealogy Homepage, which includes ship lists and other resources.

ROOTS-L: Genealogy Discussion List

E-mail: **ROOTS-L-request@rootsweb.com**
Instructions: On the first line of the body of the message, type:
subscribe

ROOTS-L is one of the oldest and largest genealogical online discussion groups, with more than 10,000 subscribers. For more information, go to the ROOTS-L home page (http://www.rootsweb.com/roots-l/). To search more than 11 years of ROOTS-L messages, go to the online archives at (http://searches.rootsweb.com/roots-l.html).

Orphan Trains (1856–1930)

1169.   History for Children: Orphan Trains

http://www.suite101.com/article.cfm/history_for_children/18538

Read this series of three articles to find out more about the work of Charles Loring Brace, with the Children's Aid Society, and orphan trains in the United States. The first article, "Street Arabs," describes the situation in New York City in 1853, when the city harbored more than 10,000 homeless children. The second article, "Westward Ho! All Aboard the Orphan Train," discusses how the Children's Aid Society "placed out" more than 100,000 children between 1854 and 1929 to families in 47 states and Canada. Most of these children went to homes in Ohio, Indiana, Michigan, Illinois, Iowa, Missouri, and Kansas. Be sure to link to individual state sites about orphan trains: Kansas (http://www.ukans.edu/carrie/kancoll/articles/orphans/index.html) and Nebraska (http://www.rootsweb.com/~neadoptn/Orphan.htm). The third article, "The Last Orphan Trains," tells why the orphan train movement ended and gives links to further information, including primary documents. Written by Meg Greene Malvasi (malvasi@home.com) for Suite 101.com.

Woman Suffrage (1848–1920)

1170.   Suffrage Photographs: 1850-1920

http://lcweb2.loc.gov/ammem/vfwhtml/vfwhome.html

The Library of Congress has created an online exhibit of 38 pictures, including portraits of individuals, suffrage parades, picketing suffragists, an anti-suffrage display, and editorial cartoons commenting on the movement. This exhibit creates a visual representation of the debate on woman suffrage during this period of time. Look for pictures of Lucy Stone, Lucretia Mott, Susan B. Anthony, Sojourner Truth, and Elizabeth Cady Stanton. This collection of photographs is a pictorial partner for the text documents in "Votes for Women: Selections from the National American Woman Suffrage Collection, 1848–1920." For a bibliography of the suffrage movement and a chronology of events leading to women's right to vote, see (http://www.rochester.edu/SBA/hisindx.html).

1171. Woman Suffrage and the 19th Amendment

http://www.nara.gov/education/teaching/woman/home.html

By the mid-1800s, woman suffrage supporters were lecturing, writing, marching, lobbying, and practicing civil disobedience in a battle to achieve Constitutional change allowing women the right to vote. These efforts continued until August 24, 1920, when the 19th Amendment to the Constitution was ratified. The National Archives and Records Administration has created a Web site of primary sources, activities, and links to related Web sites for educators and students to commemorate this struggle. This is an excellent Web site, allowing students access to primary resources for their research.

The Spanish-American War

1172. National Parks History of the Spanish-American War

http://www.cr.nps.gov/history/1spamwar.htm

The National Park Service has created a Web site for the centennial of the Spanish-American War. Students can find links to National Park sites related to the war, links to Spanish-American War sites on the Internet, a selected bibliography of books, and links to Spanish-American War conferences and events. Questions about the centennial of the Spanish-American War at the National Park Service should be directed to Harry Butowsky (Harry_Butowsky@nps.gov).

1173. What Really Sank the *Maine*?

http://www.usni.org/Naval_History/NHallen.htm

What caused the explosions that sank the USS *Maine*—an accident or a mine? The National Geographic Society commissioned a study to answer this question. Students can read this special online report printed in *Naval History*, a publication of the U.S. Naval Institute. Written by military historian Thomas B. Allen, students can explore the evidence and view diagrams. Was it an explosion from a coal-dust fire, or was it a mine? See also "Remember the *Maine*?," an article by Allen that appeared in the February 1998 issue of *National Geographic* magazine.

World War I

1174. The Great War

http://www.pitt.edu/~pugachev/greatwar/ww1.html

This collection of links to poetry, images, and art provides powerful insight into the human realm of the Great War, from the hope of ending all wars in 1914 to the disillusionment with that plan by 1916. Students will find a chronology of the major events during the Great War, to help put some of the names, dates, and places into an understandable context. Interesting links are provided to sites such as My Mother's War (http://www.geocities.com/Athens/ Acropolis/4144/mom/wwlinks.html); My Mother's War is the story of Helen Burrey, one of the first volunteer Red Cross nurses to be sent to France to work on the hospital trains of the American Expeditionary Forces. The Webmaster is Tony Novosel (novosel+@pitt.edu).

1175. World War I Document Archive

http://www.lib.byu.edu/~rdh/wwi/

Primary documents from World War I have been collected by volunteers of the World War I Military History List (WWI-L), and are accessible by year and category such as Conventions and Treaties. In addition to personal reminiscences, there is a biographical dictionary with brief biographical sketches and photographs of prominent persons of the Great War era. The Web administrator in charge of content is Jane Plotke (cd078@dogbert.xroads.com).

1176. World War I: Trenches on the Web

http://www.worldwar1.com

Trenches is an evolving project on World War I with a reference library and a searchable database. Information includes photographs, documents, maps, timelines, artwork, and an exhibit of weapons and military equipment. Interesting articles to date include Jack London on the Great War, the Red Baron, and the battlefield art of Mary Riter Hamilton. Site developed and maintained by Mike Lavarone (mikeei@mcs.com).

The 1920s: The Roaring Twenties and the Jazz Age

See also Poetry and Prose of the Harlem Renaissance (entry 556), F. Scott Fitzgerald Centenary Homepage (entry 446), Jazz Dance Homepage (entry 156), and "Jazz Music" (entries 175–176).

1177. The Great Gatsby

http://www.wshs.fcps.k12.va.us/academic/english/1project/99gg/toc.htm

Students in three English classes at West Springfield High School have posted their papers about the 1920s and F. Scott Fitzgerald's novel, *The Great Gatsby*, on this Web site. There are summaries of chapters as well as illustrated essays on a wide variety of topics, such as clothing in the 1920s, Prohibition, art of the 1920s, the stock market, the Harlem Renaissance, and characters in the novel.

1178. The Harlem Renaissance

http://encarta.msn.com/schoolhouse/Harlem/harlem.asp

Find out more about the Harlem Renaissance from this Microsoft Encarta Web site. African American culture flourished during the 1920s in Harlem, an all-black neighborhood in New York City. This period of history is brought to life through photographs and multimedia. Explores the music and writers of the period, as well as providing related Encarta articles, Web links, and lesson plan suggestions. See also Rhapsodies in Black: Art of the Harlem Renaissance (http://www.iniva.org/harlem/).

The 1930s: Depression and the New Deal

1179. **America from the Great Depression to World War II: Photographs from the FSA-OWI, 1935-1945**

http://lcweb2.loc.gov/ammem/fsowhome.html

Some of the most famous documentary photographs of the Great Depression are now online from the Library of Congress, including 55,000 black-and-white photographs and 1,600 color photographs. Photographs taken by U.S. government photographers show Americans in every part of the nation. These often poignant images emphasize rural life and the negative impact of the Great Depression, farm mechanization, and the Dust Bowl. In the same collection are photographs taken in the 1940s, when the nation turned its attention to the mobilization effort for World War II. These later photographs focus on factories and women employees, railroads, and aviation training. All photographs are part of the Farm Security Administration-Office of War Information (FSA-OWI) Collection at the Library of Congress, and are available online at the Library's American Memory Web site.

1180. **New Deal Network**

http://newdeal.feri.org

Sponsored by the Franklin and Eleanor Roosevelt Institute, this site provides primary resources for students studying the Depression and the New Deal. Some of the online Features spotlight the Civilian Conservation Corps (CCC); the photoessays of Rondal Partridge, documenting the lives of the youth of California gripped by the Depression; the photoessays of Imogen Cunningham, documenting the homeless and indigent in Oakland, California's tent cities or "Hoovervilles"; and the Milwaukee WPA Handicraft Project. The Image Library contains hundreds of photographs. Students can match wits with Professor Puzzler, an expert on the New Deal. Also available are lesson plans, including one that challenges students to understand political cartoons and the TVA, and another that asks students to analyze letters written to Mrs. Roosevelt by children during the Depression.

1181. **Radio Days**

http://www.otr.com/index.shtml

Radio Days features radio broadcast history in both sound and text. Allows students to hear excerpts from radio broadcasts, including news reporting with Edward R. Murrow; mystery series and private-eye stories such as *The Shadow*; comedy with Burns and Allen, Fibber McGee and Molly, and Amos 'n' Andy; and science fiction programs featuring Buck Rogers and Flash Gordon. Look for feature articles that explore the history of radio. The Web site is searchable and requires RealPlayer. See also WebQuest: Radio Days (http://www.branson.k12.mo.us/langarts/radio/radio.htm).

World War II

General Interest

1182. **HyperWar: A Hypertext History of the Second World War**

http://metalab.unc.edu/hyperwar/

This is an ongoing project to provide a primarily military history of the Second World War, using mostly U.S. government documents and materials. Gives military histories of participation in the war by the Army, Air Force, Navy, and Marine Corps. Divides discussion of combat into two theaters of operations, the Pacific and the European. There is a listing of online diplomatic and political documents, including FDR's "Day of Infamy" speech, given on December 8, 1941, and German and Japanese surrender documents. Provides a glossary of terms with links to the *Glossary of U.S. Naval Code Words* and the Department of Defense's *Dictionary of Military and Associated Terms*. Created and maintained by Patrick Clancey (patrick@akamail.com).

1183. *USS Arizona*—"that terrible day"

http://dizzy.library.arizona.edu/images/USS_Arizona/USS_Arizona.shtml

The battleship *Arizona* served in the U.S. Navy from 1916 until 1941, when it was sunk during the Japanese attack on Pearl Harbor with a loss of more than 1,100 crew members. The University of Arizona Library Special Collections has made available online papers, photographs, and memorabilia of the *USS Arizona*. There is also a brief history of the battleship and links to Web resources about the *USS Arizona* and the attack on Pearl Harbor. This Web site is one of the University of Arizona Library's Web Exhibits.

1184. **What Did You Do in the War, Grandma?**

http://www.stg.brown.edu/projects/WWII_Women/tocCS.html

Students in the ninth-grade honors English program at South Kingstown High School have written an oral history project of Rhode Island Women during World War II. The 30 interviews online make interesting reading. Also included is a glossary and a brief timeline of World War II events. This site provides a good model for how oral history projects bring history alive.

1185. **World War II Commemoration from Grolier**

http://gi.grolier.com/wwii/wwii_mainpage.html

Grolier Online has put together a very complete collection of World War II historical materials on the Web. Articles and biographies are from *Encyclopedia Americana*. In-text links and a 25-question multiple-choice test make this site interactive for students engaged in their learning. The Photo Gallery allows students to access photographs from the National Archives. Pictures are labeled and dated, providing a pictorial history. Photographs can be enlarged to full screen for projected viewing by an entire class. Three films taken by combat photographers in Europe have been edited and can be downloaded and viewed using QuickTime. Links are provided to other sites on the Internet related to World War II. The Webmaster for this site can be reached at (webmaster@grolier.com).

Japanese American Internment

See also WebQuest: Japanese Internment (http://php.ucs.indiana.edu/%7Eeciernia/wq.html).

1186. Children of the Camps
http://www.pbs.org/childofcamp/

This Web site was created as complementary and ancillary materials for the PBS documentary, "Children of the Camps," which focused on the experiences of six Americans of Japanese ancestry who were confined, as children, in internment camps by the U.S. government during World War II. Provides a timeline and links to historical documents. See also A History of the Japanese-American Internment (http://www.fatherryan.org/hcompsci/), researched and written by students at Father Ryan High School in Nashville, Tennessee.

1187. Japanese American Internment
http://www.geocities.com/Athens/8420/main.html

President Franklin D. Roosevelt signed Executive Order 9066 in February 1942. Under this order, approximately 110,000 Japanese Americans were forced from their homes and assembled at various internment camps surrounded by barbed wire and armed guards. They would live in these prison camps for three years until the end of World War II. This Web site provides a comprehensive overview of Japanese American internment, with information easily accessible from a table of contents. Provides photographs, a glossary, a map of all the prison camps, and links to Web sites and Web documents. Created by C. John Yu (CJohnYu.96@alum.mit.edu) when he was a student at Massachusetts Institute of Technology. See also War Relocation Authority Camps in Arizona, 1942–1946 from the University of Arizona Library (http://www.library.arizona.edu/wracamps/).

The Holocaust

1188. Anne Frank Homepage
http://www.annefrank.nl

Students can find out more information about Anne Frank, her diary, and the house where she and her family lived in secret from July 6, 1942, until August 4, 1944. An interesting FAQs section answers students' questions, such as "When did Anne receive her first diary notebook?" "When did Anne come to live in Amsterdam?" and "What are the names and birthdays of the helpers, and are any of them still alive?" A glossary of keywords helps students to understand terms like *anti-Semitism*, *fascism*, and *resistance*. The Web page for the Anne Frank House in Amsterdam is located at (http://www.channels.nl/amsterdam/annefran.html).

1189. An Auschwitz Alphabet
http://www.spectacle.org/695/ausch.html

Links are provided from A to Z to show the grim horrors of Auschwitz. A is for *Arbeit Macht Frei* ("Work Brings Freedom"—the sign over the gates of Auschwitz); F is for filth; I is for injections; K is for krematoria; and V is for victims. Links are provided to other Holocaust-related sites on the Internet and a bibliography for further reading. Created and maintained by Jonathan Blumen (jblumen@spectacle.org).

1190.   **Cybrary of the Holocaust**

http://www.remember.org

Divided into sections, this site focuses on Holocaust research, survivor stories, photographs, and educational resources. Remembering Lest We Forget makes student-written poetry and artwork available, as well as feedback from classes studying the Holocaust. Extensive links to Holocaust information are provided. The Webmaster is Michael Dunn (dunn@webletter.net).

1191.   **Do You Know? Will You Remember?**

http://www.euronet.nl/users/jubo/holocaust.html

Young adults studying the Holocaust will find an annotated bibliography of books and links to other Web sites to help with their research. Karen L. Simonetti is the creator and Webmaster (klsimonetti@earthlink.net).

1192.   **Holocaust Archives**

http://www.shamash.org/holocaust/

Historical photographs, some graphically detailed, accompany text by Daniel Keren. Historical documents include excerpts from rulings and verdicts of German courts regarding Treblinka and Auschwitz-Birkenau and a short statistical summary of the Holocaust by German historians. A bibliography is provided.

Arguments denying the reality of the Holocaust are refuted. A nine-part report documents the infiltration of neo-Nazi groups in Germany, which took place between October 1992 and April 1993.

1193.   **Holocaust Pictures Exhibition**

http://www.fmv.ulg.ac.be/schmitz/holocaust.html

Each picture located on this Web site is labeled and annotated with the source. Most of these pictures document the terrorizing of men, women, and children and the horrific treatment of the human beings who were systematically exterminated in concentration camps operated by the Nazis. These historical photographs are definitely for older students.

1194.   **The Nizkor Project**

http://www1.us.nizkor.org

The Nizkor Project is dedicated to the nearly 12 million victims ruthlessly destroyed by Adolf Hitler and his Nazi regime. It monitors the falsehoods and misinformation distributed via the Internet and other media by individuals and organizations that are fascist, racist, and anti-Semitic. The project uses nonviolent methods to refute these lies and to document and expose materials expressing hate. It seeks to educate with truth and to provide teachers with curricula to bolster democratic, multicultural, and multiracial learning. Nizkor maintains a listing of other sites on the Internet that relate to the Holocaust, its denial, racism, and fascism.

1195. To Save a Life: Stories of Jewish Rescue

http://www.humboldt.edu/~rescuers/

To Save a Life: Stories of Jewish Rescue is an entire book, available online, in which personal narratives and photographs reveal how certain individuals acted upon their own moral convictions, disregarding the danger to themselves and their families, to save the lives of Jewish persons during the Nazi regime. Six true stories of rescues in Holland, Czechoslovakia, and Poland are brought to life by the narrations of both the rescuers and the people they rescued. Each story is illustrated with photographs and maps. Students studying the Holocaust will benefit from reading these personalized accounts of history and learning about the conditions of Jewish people in countries controlled by the Nazis. Ellen Land-Weber, a professor in the Art Department at Humboldt State University in Arcata, California, is the author and photographer (eel1@axe.humboldt.edu).

1196. The U.S. Holocaust Memorial Museum

http://www.ushmm.org/index.html

The U.S. Holocaust Memorial Museum opened in April 1993 on the fiftieth anniversary of the Warsaw ghetto uprising. The museum asks all who enter to remember the 6 million Jews and the millions of others who were murdered by the Nazis during the Holocaust.

The museum presents the facts of the Holocaust. Jeshajahu Weinberg, director of the museum, writes in *The World Must Know*, "[A] visit to the museum will be an interesting and challenging learning experience but, at the same time, it also will be a thought-provoking, disturbing, and personally upsetting one. And so it should be."

This WWW server will be continually expanded as new sections are added. Sections available for online access and exploration include:

1. General information for visiting the museum
2. Background information
3. Educational programs
4. The research institute
5. Calendar of community programs at the museum
6. Links to the Association of Holocaust organizations

Nuclear Weapons, Realities of Nuclear War, and Peace Efforts

See also "Nuclear Physics and Nuclear Power" (entries 899–900).

Nuclear Weapons

1197. A-Bomb WWW Museum

http://www.csi.ad.jp/ABOMB/

Little Boy and Fat Man were dropped on the cities of Hiroshima (August 6, 1945) and Nagasaki (August 9, 1945) respectively.   The creators of this site believe that education and understanding are the keys toward building lasting global peace. They, along with those interviewed, hope that atomic bombs will never be used again—never again will weapons of total destruction be unleashed on humanity. Students will benefit from exploring this compilation of facts, photographs, and interviews, including the voices of survivors. Created by Mitsuru Ohba and John Benson (abomb-admin@sel.cs.hiroshima-cu.ac.jp).

Realities of Nuclear War and Peace Efforts

1198. 1,000 Cranes Project Home Page

http://www.csi.ad.jp/suzuhari-es/1000cranes/index.html

This site chronicles the Thousand Cranes project at Suzuhari Elementary School in Hiroshima, Japan. For background information about Hiroshima and the atomic bomb, see (http://www. scrtec.rtec.org/track/tracks/s01634.html).

Sadako and the Thousand Paper Cranes (Putnam, 1990), written by Eleanor Coerr, is the true story of a courageous 12-year-old Japanese girl who died of leukemia, a result of the radiation from the atomic bomb dropped on Hiroshima when she was 2 years old. Today, children around the world celebrate peace and make peace cranes by folding pieces of paper. Directions for creating origami cranes can be found at these three sites:

(http://www.csi.ad.jp/suzuhari-es/1000cranes/paperc/index.html)
(http://www.jwindow.net/KIDS/SCHOOL/ART/origami/kids_origami_crane1.html)
(http://www.sadako.org/foldingcranes.htm)

1199. Hiroshima Peace Site

http://www.pcf.city.hiroshima.jp/peacesite/

Contents include the reality of the A-bomb disasters, the current status of nuclear weapons, and efforts to create peace. The first atomic bomb, Little Boy, was dropped on the city of Hiroshima on August 6, 1945. Students can read about some of some of the horrors of nuclear bombs and see photographs and artifacts. Looks at the evolution of nuclear weapons and ways to promote peace. Provides links to additional information, including a series of nonprofessional artworks by survivors of the bomb. Gives a virtual tour of the Hiroshima Peace Memorial Museum.

1200. Remembering Nagasaki

http://www.exploratorium.edu/nagasaki/

Remembering Nagasaki is an exhibition at the Exploratorium, a science museum and one of San Francisco's most prominent museums. The contents of this exhibition include the photographs of Yosuke Yamahata, a section devoted to memories of the atomic blast, commentary, and commemorations.

On August 10, 1945, the day after the bombing of Nagasaki, Yamahata started to take photographs of the devastation. His black-and-white photographs, interspersed with his firsthand personal comments, give unwavering testimony to the grim realities of the aftermath of the Nagasaki bombing.

As part of an investigation into the nature of memory, the Exploratorium in 1995 invited people, old and young, to share their recollections of learning about the bombing of Hiroshima and Nagasaki. These candid memories are from persons who did not directly experience the bombings; however, their thoughts help students see the bombings from many individual perspectives.

1201. Sadako and the Thousand Cranes

http://www.sdcoe.k12.ca.us/score/crane/cranetg.html

The San Diego County Office of Education has produced a Teacher CyberGuide for use in studying *Sadako and the Thousand Paper Cranes* (Putnam, 1990) by Eleanor Coerr. CyberGuides are supplementary units of instruction based on core works of literature, requiring students to use the World Wide Web. Three activities are suggested as catalysts for student research: (1) a poster to help respond to the question, "Was the atomic bomb a necessary evil?"; (2) a brochure on the positive benefits of nuclear energy; and (3) original poems on world peace, a Web page on organizations promoting world peace, or a Peace Web Page (a tribute to the victims of the atomic bomb with links to related Internet resources).

Korean War

1202. The Korean War Project

http://www.koreanwar.org

The Korean War Project includes information on the Korean War (1950–1953) and the DMZ War in Korea from 1966 to 1969. The History and Reference page provides overview information as well as specific information on battles, events, and memorials. An online database provides information about those killed in action (KIA), missing in action (MIA), and prisoners of war (POWs). Links are provided to individual veterans' home pages, newspaper articles, photographic travelogues to North Korea and Heartbreak Ridge, and personal recollections. Students will be able to access personal photographs taken by veterans during the war, as well as maps from the Library of Congress and other sources. Created and maintained by Hal Barker (hbarker@onramp.net) and Ted Barker (tbarker@onramp.net).

The Cold War and the 1950s

1203. CNN: Cold War

http://www.cnn.com/SPECIALS/cold.war

This comprehensive, multimedia Web site complements the award-winning CNN documentary series on the Cold War; it looks at five decades of history and comprises more than 1,000 pages of information. Summaries are available for each of the 24 episodes in the series. To experience the Cold War era, ancillary feature materials have been gathered into four categories: culture, technology, espionage, and the bomb. An educator's guide is provided.

The Culture section provides a 14-chapter online Cold War thriller written just for this Web site, as well as information about movies, the Red Scare, television, music, fashion, and drama. The Technology section gives a timeline showing the space race, but also focuses on how this competition fueled creativity among scientists and inventors, eventually giving birth to inventions such as the computer and the microwave oven. Find out more about spies, nuclear secrets, and the KGB in the Espionage section. Follow a nuclear timeline and find out about the development of nuclear weapons from pre-World War II to Pakistan and find out more about the fear, cost, science, and opposition surrounding the bomb, as well as nuclear accidents.

Viewing this site requires Java-enhanced browsers. Interviews require Microsoft's Windows Media Player for video streaming. Apple's QuickTime 3 is required to view excerpts of the Cold War series and experience QTVR interactive images. IPX is needed to view photographs in an interactive spherical format, and Cult 3-D is needed to view models in the Space Race section. A section on required plug-ins is available.

1204. The Literature and Culture of the American 1950s

http://www.english.upenn.edu/~afilreis/50s/home.html

Links to online information associated with and related to the American 1950s is alphabetically organized along with a glossary of terms. Who were Senator Joe McCarthy, Betty Friedan, James Dean, and Mario Savio? Why did Arthur Miller write *The Crucible*? Learn more about the American 1950s, including communism, the Cold War, the feminist movement, the Beats, Black consciousness, and psychoanalysis. This list of links was created for an English course, The Literature and Culture of the 1950s, taught by Al Filreis (afilreis@english.upenn.edu), professor of English at the University of Pennsylvania.

The 1960s

1205. Popular Culture in the 1960's

http://www.d.umn.edu/cla/faculty/tbacig/hmcl3270/

"The times they are a-changing," "I dig Rock and Roll music," and "Go ask Alice—when she's ten feet tall" are excerpts from some of the full-text sixties rock music lyrics found on this Web site. Although the history and culture of the sixties is intricately intertwined and reflected in the music of the era, this site is best used to explore some of the ideas at the center of the sixties counterculture. Supplemental lists of links, used in teaching Popular Culture in the 1960s as a humanities course, are organized into the following categories: music and musicians; films and the actors in them; literature and authors; drugs; art and artists; the Vietnam War; the Hippie lifestyle; and carryovers from the sixties to the nineties. Created by Tom Bacig (tbacig@umn.edu), professor of humanities and classics at the University of Minnesota Duluth.

1206. The Sixties Project

http://lists.village.virginia.edu/sixties/

The Sixties Project is an ongoing collaborative humanities project, which collects and makes available primary and secondary sources for researchers, students, teachers, and others interested in the 1960s. Links are provided to Sixties-L, an online discussion group; bibliographies; primary documents; a glossary of Vietnam War military terminology and slang; and book, film, music, and multimedia reviews. Students can read personal narratives submitted by ordinary individuals writing about their personal experiences during the 1960s. Links are provided to other Internet resources with related sixties information, as well as to sites related to the Vietnam War. The Web site is keyword-searchable. The Sixties Project Web site is sponsored by the Institute of Advanced Technology in the Humanities at the University of Virginia (Charlottesville, Virginia) and by Viet Nam Generation, Inc. (Tucson, Arizona). The Web editor is Kali Tal (Kali.Tal@yale.edu).

Vietnam War

1207. Images of My War by Ron Heller
http://www.ionet.net/~uheller/vnbktoc.html

Ulf R. "Ron" Heller writes about what it was like to be a young first lieutenant in the infantry of the U.S. Army going through Jungle Warfare Training School and then serving in Vietnam from July 1968 to January 1970. Some chapter titles include: "Ambush," "The Dead Man in the O-Club," "Recon Platoon," "13 Days at Phu Hoa Dong," "Company C," and "Discipline and Morale." This makes for interesting reading and a highly personalized view of the Vietnam era. Ron Heller's e-mail address is (uheller@ionet.net). His home page is located at (http://www.ionet.net/~uheller/index.html).

1208. Vietnam Archives
http://www.geocities.com:80/Athens/Forum/9061/USA/Vietnam/vietnam.html

Mississippi State University's Historical Text Archive contains materials and links to resources about the Vietnam War. Look for combat art, songs, and photographs. Information is available about combat casualties and the Soviets in Vietnam. Links lead to publications on Vietnam, National Archives records, a few Vietnam newsletters, and more information about the Soviet role in Vietnam.

1209. The Vietnam Veterans Home Page
http://grunt.space.swri.edu

The purpose of the Vietnam Veterans Home Page is to honor veterans, living and dead, who served their country during the Vietnam conflict. This is a place where veterans and friends of veterans can share stories, pictures, songs, art, poetry, and experiences using the multimedia capabilities of the World Wide Web.

Contributions to this page span the period from the early war years through present-day Vietnam. A section of remembrances includes many that are funny, tragic, or poignant.

A Visit to Vietnam is a virtual trip with pictures of contemporary Vietnam. Visitor's Reports is a series of entertaining stories and useful tips written by recent travelers to Vietnam. Maps of Vietnam provides a multimedia geography lesson, and links are provided to Vietnam WWW sites with beautiful pictures, artwork, poetry, and useful information about the country. There is also a compendium of information on the people of Vietnam and the country. Links are provided to Vietnam veterans' organizations and support groups.

This home page is dedicated to Lewis B. Puller, Jr. (1945–1994), who was seriously wounded in the Vietnam War as point man for his patrol, and who went on to win the Pulitzer Prize for biography for his book *Fortunate Son: The Autobiography of Lewis B. Puller, Jr.* (Grove Press, 1991). The site is maintained by Bill McBride (billm@swri.edu).

1210. The Vietnam Veterans' Memorial Wall Page
http://thewall-usa.com/index.html

The Vietnam Veterans' Memorial in Washington, D.C., lists the names of veterans who lost their lives during the Vietnam War. This page provides access to an online, searchable database of the names listed on the Memorial Wall. Names can be searched by first name, last name, home-town, home state, service number or Social Security number, birthday, and rank. By clicking on Complete Information you can find out the known facts about the person's service record, birth date, and death. Links are provided to other wall sites and literary works. Created and maintained by Alan Oskvarek (webmaster@TheWall-USA.com), a Vietnam veteran.

1211. **Vietnam War Page**

http://www.shss.montclair.edu/english/furr/vietnam.html

As a supplement to an English course titled The Vietnam War and American Culture, this page provides a comprehensive list of annotated links to Internet resources related to the Vietnam War. Students can view a large-scale map of Vietnam showing the unified Democratic Republic of Vietnam as of 1985. One link leads to Lessons of the Vietnam War, a lesson plan appropriate for use at the secondary level (http://members.aol.com/jmstarr/). Created and maintained by Grover Furr (furrg@alpha.montclair.edu), professor of English at Montclair State University (Upper Montclair, New Jersey).

Contemporary World History Issues

1212. **The Beast Within: An Interdisciplinary Unit**

http://www.fred.net/nhhs/html/beast.htm

From North Hagerstown High School in Hagerstown, Maryland, The Beast Within unit involves a study of the darker side of human nature as explored by 20th-century literature and history. This ninth-grade U.S. government course calls for an examination of authoritarian government as com-pared with a democratic system. To achieve this goal, students examined the human rights abuses of such regimes as Nazi Germany, Iraq under Saddam Hussein, Cuba under Fidel Castro, and China under the Communist Party. They also examined the Holocaust as the epitome of evil of which man is capable, so that they were able to apply the lessons of the Holocaust to discussions about cur-rent events and examples of modern-day genocide, including the tragedy in Bosnia. Some stu-dents have published their poetry, pencil sketches, and fiction stories on this site in response to their class field trip to the Holocaust Memorial Museum. Also included are pages written by social studies teacher George Cassutto, telling the story of his parents, who were survivors of the Holo-caust from the Netherlands. Literature suggestions for use with this unit include *Lord of the Flies*, *The Invisible Man*, *The Elephant Man*, *Night*, *Fahrenheit 451*, and *The Diary of Anne Frank*. Sugges-tions are also given for incorporating English, science, and mathematics lessons.

Multicultural Resources

See also "Multicultural Children's Literature" (entries 493–499) and "Holidays Around the World" (1399–1402).

General Interest

1213. **Multicultural Calendar**

http://www.kidlink.org/KIDPROJ/MCC/

KIDLINK's KIDPROJ has developed a Multicultural Calendar for use in classrooms, using sub-missions from KIDLINK kids from around the world. Entries reflect an international celebration of holidays and festivals. These entries, rich in local customs, contain recipes for holiday foods, historical background, significance of the holidays, and the special ways in which these days are observed. Students can browse or search the Multicultural Calendar by month, country, holiday, or author. Searching can be narrowed by creating a search statement using two indexes. For example, searching the holiday New Year and the country Spain produces all the entries about the New Year holiday in Spain. This ongoing KIDLINK project provides an authentic writing/language arts assignment for students. For more information, contact Patti Weeg (pweeg@shore.intercom.net) or Grant Dougall (dougallg@duke.usask.ca), KIDPROJ WWW contact.

1214.   The Multicultural Home Page

http://pasture.ecn.purdue.edu/~agenhtml/agenmc/

Foreign students at Purdue University have created Web pages to share information about their home countries. This site will be constantly under construction, and some pages will be left behind by students who graduate and move on. This is a great model for students at other schools to use in studying and sharing information about various countries around the world. Country pages cover a wide range of information: geography, history, arts, weather, recipes, tourist information, and so on. The Webmaster can be reached at (embleton@ecn.purdue.edu).

1215.   Multicultural Pavilion, University of Virginia

http://curry.edschool.Virginia.EDU/go/multicultural/

The University of Virginia's Multicultural Pavilion provides resources for educators interested in multicultural issues. The entire site is searchable by keyword. The Teacher's Corner has resources for K-12 teachers, including reviews of children's music, multicultural activities, online archives, and links to multicultural Web sites. The Multicultural Activity Archives provides tested and proven activities that help foster awareness of multiculturalism and diversity. Multicultural Paths: Other Sites contains hundreds of categorized links to Internet sites, resources, document archives, and special topics. Other areas include links to international projects, research, and online discussion groups. Created and maintained by Paul Gorski (pcg9r@virginia.edu).

African American Studies and Black History

See also "Africa" (entries 1282–1286); "Ancient Egypt" (entries 1248–1251); In the Steps of Esteban: Tucson's African American Heritage (entry 1139); *AFRO-Americ@*'s Newspapers Home Page (entry 1414); BlackBaseball's Negro Baseball Leagues (entry 1351); "African American" children's literature (entries 493–494); *Kids Zone* (entry 575); "Folklore: Fables, Folktales, and Fairy Tales" (entries 536–541); "Legends" (entries 542–546); and "Myths and Mythology" (entries 547–548).

1216.   The African-American Mosaic

http://lcweb.loc.gov/exhibits/african/intro.html

The African-American Mosaic is a Library of Congress Resource Guide for the study of Black History and Culture. The exhibit is a sampler of the kinds of materials and themes covered by the publication and the library's collections. Covering the nearly 500 years of Black experience in the Western Hemisphere, the Mosaic surveys the full range, size, and variety of the library's collections, including books, periodicals, prints, photographs, music, film, and recorded sound. The exhibit currently covers only four areas—colonization, abolition, migrations, and the WPA—but will be expanded in the future. In 1998, the library will mount a major exhibition and cultural program examining the impact of African American history and tradition in the formation of American national identity.

1217. **African Missouri**

http://www.umsl.edu/~libweb/blackstudies/

African Missouri is a compilation of information about the history of African Americans in Missouri. Links lead to articles and narratives from a number of resources, including *The African-American Heritage of St. Louis: A Guide,* published by the St. Louis Public Library; *Preservation Issues*, a publication of the Historic Preservation Program; and Missouri slave narratives from the WPA Project. The complete text of *The Role of the Negro in Missouri History, 1719-1970* is online and can be accessed through a hyperlinked table of contents. This history traces the accomplishments of African Americans throughout the history of the state of Missouri. Maintained by Anne Taylor (ataylor@umsl.edu), reference librarian at Thomas Jefferson Library, University of Missouri-St. Louis.

1218. **Interesting Dates in Black History**

http://www.ai.mit.edu/~isbell/HFh/black/bhist.html

For each day of the year, interesting facts about the history of African Americans are presented. As an example, for January 3, one of the interesting facts is that William Tucker, the first African American child born in America, was baptized in Jamestown in 1624. This source would be useful when incorporating the study of African Americans into the curriculum, as well as when planning a library program or bulletin board display for months other than Black History Month (February).

1219. **Stamp on Black History**

http://library.advanced.org/10320/

Stamp on Black History features African American men and women who have been commemorated on U.S. postage stamps. The collection begins in 1940 when Booker T. Washington became the first African American to be so honored. The names of people on stamps are listed alphabetically and by curriculum area. In the arts section you can find Henry O. Tanner; under mathematics, Benjamin Banneker; under science, George Washington Carver, Bessie Coleman, Charles R. Drew, Percy Lavon Julian, and Ernest E. Just. For each listing there is a biography with bibliography and a color image of the postage stamp commemorating the person. To place these individuals within the perspective of history, a section on the history of Blacks and African Americans is given from the period of African Heritage (300–1619) to Black Americans in the 1990s. In-text links to all the African Americans honored on postage stamps are included in this history. This Web site won third place in the social studies category of the 1996 ThinkQuest contest.

Dr. Martin Luther King, Jr. (1929–1968)

1220. The Dr. King Timeline Page

http://pps.k12.or.us/district/depts/itss/buckman/timeline/kingframe.html

After reading Faith Ringgold's biography of Dr. Martin Luther King, Jr., students in a K-2 class at Buckman Elementary School in Portland, Oregon, created The Dr. King Timeline Page. They have created more than 30 colorful drawings to accompany dates from King's birth on January 15, 1929, to his assassination on April 4, 1968.

1221. The Martin Luther King Jr. Directory

http://www.stanford.edu/group/King/

The Martin Luther King Jr. Directory contains secondary documents written about Martin Luther King, Jr., as well as primary documents written during King's life. There is a brief biography and a chronology with links to information from highlighted years. The site also provides information about the King Center in Atlanta, Georgia. The MLK Papers Project at Stanford University has published an authoritative, annotated, 14-volume edition of Dr. King's most significant correspondence, sermons, speeches, published writings, and unpublished manuscripts.

1222. A Tribute to Martin Luther King

http://www.seattletimes.com/mlk/

The *Seattle Times* created this site as a tribute to Martin Luther King, Jr. "Few have had as much impact upon the American consciousness as Dr. Martin Luther King Jr. A Baptist minister and passionate fighter for civil rights through non-violent action, he was the closest this country has come to producing a leader with the moral stature of Mohandas Gandhi." In addition to biographical information, there is information about the civil rights movement, King's legacy, and the holiday commemorating his birthday. The Electronic Classroom has resources for teachers and students, including a study guide, an interactive quiz, links to other Internet sites, and an archive of student dialog about King.

Native Americans

See also Seventeenth-Century Native Americans in New England (entry 1122), "Native American" children's literature (entries 498–499), and Native American Poetry (entry 555).

1223. Index of Native American Resources on the Internet

http://www.hanksville.org/NAresources/

Categories of information on all topics related to Native American culture and life, past and present, are listed in table format, making it easy to access Native American resources on the Internet from this Web site. The index provides links to information on museums, artists, archaeology, legal resources, music, personal home pages of Native Americans, and bibliographies. Be sure to read the frequently asked questions with answers. Resources listed in the index are keyword-searchable. This site is maintained by Karen M. Strom (kstrom@hanksville.phast.umass.edu).

1224. Native Americans Collection from the Augustana College (Illinois) Special Collections

http://www.augustana.edu/libraryold/native1.html

The online archives at this site include photographs of western Illinois Native Americans, including descendants of Chief Black Hawk, taken by John Hauberg. Also included are interviews and biographies. Some photographs in the Fort Armstrong Centennial collection are of Fort Armstrong 25 years after the Black Hawk War.

1225. NativeWeb

http://www.nativeweb.org

NativeWeb's indexed and searchable database contains hundreds of links related to Native, aboriginal, and indigenous Internet resources from all parts of the world. This Web site provides a comprehensive collection of information organized according to subject categories, geographic regions, cultural groups, literature, language, journals, and organizations. Information is also available regarding news, events, announcements, and job listings. A list of online discussion groups, each focused on interests related to native peoples, is provided.

Cherokee

1226. The Cherokee Nation

http://www.cherokee.org

The Cherokee Nation's official Web site provides information on treaties, government legislation and policies, in addition to tribal culture and history. An interesting feature is Weekly Photos, which includes photographs along with accompanying current news briefs. The Webmaster's address is (rgallegos@cherokee.org).

Ken Martin (martikw@phoenix.net) maintains a History of the Cherokee Web site (http://pages.tca.net/martikw) that provides excellent historical information, images and maps, genealogy for research, and links to other Cherokee history resources.

1227. Trail of Tears

http://ngeorgia.com/history/nghisttt.shtml

As a north Georgia history site, Trail of Tears gives the facts leading up to the forced removal of the Cherokee in the winter of 1838–1839 and the legend of the Cherokee Rose, now the official flower of the state of Georgia. On a forced march of 1,200 miles, an estimated 4,000 Cherokee lost their lives. This became known as the Trail Where They Cried, or the Trail of Tears. The descendants of the survivors of the forced removal constitute today's Cherokee nation in Oklahoma; the nation has a membership of more than 195,000. They are separate from the Eastern Band of Cherokee Indians of Cherokee, North Carolina (http://www.cherokee-nc.com). For more information about the history of the Cherokee Nation in Georgia, see Cherokee History in Georgia, Part I and Part II (http://ngeorgia.com/history/cherokeehistory.shtml). A literature tie-in for older students is *Trail of Tears: The Rise and Fall of the Cherokee Nation* (Anchor Books, 1988) by John Ehle, an excellent historical source and intense reading.

Cheyenne

1228. Eagle Wing: A Northern Cheyenne Web Site

http://members.xoom.com/eaglewing/

When the Cheyenne were subdued in the late 1800s, they were sequestered on a reservation in Oklahoma. The northern branch of the Cheyenne longed for their homeland in the north, and despite armed conflict, they were led by Sweet Medicine Chief to Montana, where they eventually secured a separate reservation. Today the Cheyenne Nation is divided between Montana and Oklahoma, but it remains one people tied by traditional beliefs, culture, language, and relations. This site provides links to a Cheyenne Word of the Week with a sound file (.wav format), lists of movies, books, and research. Explanations are given for the origins of colorful names like Eugene Little Coyote.

Hopi

1229. Hopi Basketry

http://www.nativeweb.org/pages/baskets/

In this special online version of a presentation on Hopi basketry, students are able to find out more about the various Hopi symbols. Color images show close-ups of the intricate designs. The presentation includes sections on History and Meaning and Manufacture and Decoration. A bibliography is included for further research and study. The Webmaster is Frank Provo (mosaic@u.washington.edu).

1230. Hopi Information Network

http://www.infomagic.com/~abyte/hopi

Five hundred years ago, the Hopi built adobe homes on mesas, 600-foot-high windswept cliffs in northern Arizona. Today there are 11 villages on the Hopi reservation, 350 miles north of Phoenix. Find out more about the Hopis today as they struggle to maintain their culture and way of life.

Iroquois Confederacy

1231. Oneida Indian Nation

http://oneida-nation.net

The Oneida (People of the Standing Stone) Nation is one of the original members of the Iroquois Confederacy. This sovereign Indian nation, located in central New York, helped George Washington's troops at Valley Forge. Find out more about the Polly Cooper Shawl and how it is linked to the Revolutionary War, as well as other cultural and historical information. Webmaster is Dan Umstead (umstead@oneida-nation.org).

Pueblo

1232.　**Pueblo Indians**

http://nmaa-ryder.si.edu/education/guides/pueblo/main.html

Pueblo Indian Watercolors: Learning by Looking is a National Museum of American Art online teaching guide and lesson. All images of Pueblo Indian watercolors are from the museum's collection, and biographies of the artists are provided. The stated goals are for students to understand and appreciate the diversity of cultural traditions; develop skills in researching local, ethnic, and family traditions; and find out more about the social customs, religion, and history of the Pueblo peoples. A map shows the location of *pueblos*, or towns. A glossary, bibliography, suggested fiction reading list, and suggested activities are helpful in integrating this unit into the curriculum.

Seminole

1233.　**The Seminole Tribe of Florida**

http://www.seminoletribe.com

To find out more about the Seminole of Florida, read the FAQs. Information is available about Seminole tribe education; tourism; hunting adventures and safaris; 4-H opportunities; rodeos; the Seminole tribal library system; and the *Seminole Tribune,* the official newspaper of the Seminole Tribe of Florida. A sample story, "Gray Bear," from *Legends of the Seminoles* (Pineapple Press, 1994), written by Betty Mae Jumper and Peter Gallagher, illustrated by Guy LaBree, is available for online reading. The Webmaster's e-mail address is (semtribe@gate.net).

Sioux

1234.　**The Sioux Nation, South Dakota**

http://www.state.sd.us/state/executive/tourism/sioux/sioux.htm

The home page of the Sioux Nation provides links to topics relevant to all the tribes in the Sioux Nation, such as legends, artifacts, art, powwows, a historical overview, and graphics of famous landmarks. The seven original bands of the Great Sioux Nation were joined in an alliance called the Oceti Sakowin or Seven Council Fires. There are links to individual tribes as well.

Asian Americans

See also "History and Culture of China" (entries 299–305); "History and Culture of Japan" (entries 359–368); and "Japanese American Internment" (entries 1186–1187).

1235.　**Asian American Resources**

http://www.ai.mit.edu/people/irie/aar/

Asian American Resources is a compilation of Internet resources related to Asian Americans. Links to resources are grouped by categories such as Clubs and Organizations, Events, Media, Personal Home Pages, and Information and FAQs. Under the heading Media, information is available on Asian art, bands, literature, music, and theater. Maintained by Robert Irie (irie@mit.edu).

Jewish Americans and Jewish Culture

See also "The Holocaust" (entries 1188–1196); "Israel" (entries 1297–1298); and Bibliography of Jewish Culture in Children's Books (entry 496).

1236. Judaism and Jewish Resources
http://www.shamash.org/trb/judaism.html

With 30 items listed in the table of contents, this resource page provides links to a wealth of Jewish information and Internet resources related to Judaism. A few sample topics include museums and exhibits, books, calendars, Jewish communities, the State of Israel, the Holocaust, Yiddish, FTP archives, mailing lists, products and services, Jewish learning, libraries, Jewish studies, travels, and archaeology. Maintained by Andrew Tannenbaum (trb@shamash.org).

Latinos and Hispanics

See "History and Culture of Mexico" (entries 394–398); "History and Culture of Spain" (entries 399–401); "History and Culture of Spanish-Speaking Peoples" (entries 402–409); and Latino and Hispanic Images in Picture Books (entry 497).

World History

For resources about the history or culture of specific countries, *see* the listings for each country under the heading "Countries and Regions of the World" (entries 1279–1306).

General Interest

1237. Mr. Dowling's Virtual Classroom
http://www.mrdowling.com

Browse the world in an online geography and history class. Each topic is presented in an easy-to-understand format, and most are accompanied with study guides, homework assignments, and tests. Teachers are encouraged to use all resources, and a download page is provided (requires Windows and Word 97). This Web site is a must for world history teachers and other social studies teachers. Some of the topics include The Earth, Western Religions, The Crusades, Conflicts in the Middle East, Colonial Africa and Africa Today, Europe Today, Russia and Communism, The Caribbean, Mexico and Central America, The Middle Ages, and The Renaissance. Created and maintained by Mike Dowling, a sixth-grade geography teacher at Roosevelt Middle School (a math/science/technology magnet school in Palm Beach County, Florida).

1238. Pages Through the Ages: The Building Blocks of Civilization
http://www.fcps.k12.va.us/OakViewES/harris/96-97/agespages/index.html

Fifth-grade students at Oak View Elementary School in Fairfax, Virginia, have learned that the ancient civilizations were the foundation or building blocks of later cultures. They have created Web pages for the prehistoric era, Ancient Egypt, Ancient Greece, Ancient Rome, the Middle Ages, the Renaissance, and the Age of Discovery. Maintained by fifth-grade teacher, Miss Harris (kharris@fc.fcps.k12.va.us).

1239.   World History Links Page

http://historyoftheworld.com

Links related to world history are organized by interesting headings: Africa, Asia, Australia, Canada, Europe, Ireland, Israel, Japan, Middle East, Poetry, Russia, United States, Women Writers, and World Cams. Other links are to California history and U.S. history.

Prehistoric Humans

See also "The Ice Age" (entries 837–838).

1240.   The Arago Cave and the Tautavel Man (Tautavel, France)

http://www.culture.fr/culture/arcnat/tautavel/en/index.htm

From the skeletal remains discovered in 1971 at Tautavel, France, the Tautavel Man has been identified and estimated to be 450,000 years old. Tautavel Man was the first to be discovered in Europe with a complete front section of the skull of a *Homo erectus*. Students can study pictures and diagrams of the Arago Cave, the stages of discovery and reconstruction of the Tautavel Man, and archaeological information that explains the daily life of a prehistoric human as a hunter in this area of France.

1241.   The Chauvet Cave, France

http://web.culture.fr/culture/arcnat/chauvet/en/gvpda-d.htm

The Chauvet Cave, located at Vallon-Pont-d'Arc in the Ardèche region of France, is a recent (December 1994) archaeological discovery of more than 300 paintings and engravings dating to the Paleolithic era (between 32,000 and 30,000 years ago). These cave drawings depict a rich variety of prehistoric animals, including rhinoceroses, felines, bears, owls, and mammoths. In addition to the paintings, the cavern also contains numerous traces of human activity, including remains of hearths, flintstones, and human footprints.

1242.   Flints and Stones: Real Life in Prehistory

http://museums.ncl.ac.uk/flint/menu.html

In this online exhibition, students are welcomed to the world of the late Stone Age hunter-gatherers of Britain and Northwest Europe. Shaman, the leader of the Stone Age people, tells students about his people, their homes, art, ceremonies, food, and way of life. Students also meet the archaeologist, who explains how he was able to look at evidence and determine what life was like for prehistoric peoples living in this area. One section of this exhibition sheds light on some misconceptions, such as the stereotype of cave dwellers as club-wielding, barely human savages. Another section puts world history into perspective with a timeline. Students can take an online interactive food quiz to determine if they would have survived as hunter-gatherers by living off the plants that grew around them, selecting plants good to eat rather than poisonous ones. Flints and Stones: Real Life in Prehistory is produced by the Museum of Antiquities of the University and Society of Antiquaries of Newcastle upon Tyne.

1243. What's the Point? Identifying Flint Artifacts

http://www.oplin.lib.oh.us/products/flint/

Ohio has been home to humans for at least 15,000 years, since the end of the last Ice Age. These prehistoric groups did not leave any written record, but each group developed a distinctive style of tool making. By studying these flint tools, students gain a better understanding and appreciation of the accomplishments of these ancient cultures. Students examine and compare different flint tools to learn that some groups were hunters and gatherers, moving from camp to camp as the seasons changed; whereas others were gardeners and farmers, settling in more permanent communities. Lessons are available about the prehistoric peoples of Ohio, and an online program with illustrations helps in the identification of different types of flint artifacts such as blades, drills, points, and scrapers. An online glossary is most helpful. This site is sponsored by OPLIN (Ohio Public Library Information Network) and the Ohio Historical Society.

Ancient History and World Cultures

1244. The Ancient World Web

http://www.julen.net/aw/

Information is divided into three indexes. The Meta Index lists all sites. The Geographic Index organizes resources into categories: Africa, Americas, Asia, Europe, Mediterranean Region, and Mid- and Near East sites. The Subject Index organizes information into broad topics, such as Ancient Documents, Art and Art History, and Architecture. Links are provided to other Internet resources and related indexes. Maintained by Julia Hayden (Julia@Virginia.edu).

1245. Dead Sea Scrolls Exhibit

http://metalab.unc.edu/expo/deadsea.scrolls.exhibit/intro.html

The online exhibition of the Scrolls from the Dead Sea: The Ancient Library of Qumran and Modern Scholarship is from an exhibit at the Library of Congress. The exhibition describes the historical context of the scrolls, the Qumran community where the scrolls might have originated, and the story of their discovery 2,000 years later.

The online exhibit includes images of 12 scroll fragments and 29 other objects loaned by the Israel Antiquities Authority for this exhibition. Resource materials given for teachers include a selected annotated bibliography, a selected annotated list of films, and an annotated list of organizations that can provide a variety of information related to archaeology and Near East history and geography. A glossary and selected readings are included.

Scholars agree on the significance of the Dead Sea Scrolls, and carbon-14 testing has confirmed their age. However, debate continues on who wrote the Dead Sea Scrolls, what the Qumran library was, and why the scrolls were hidden in caves. This exhibit allows students to see for themselves a significant sampling of the scrolls and to explore their history and meaning. A map of the Dead Sea and many graphics are provided. The exhibition hopes to encourage a better understanding of the challenges and complexities connected with scroll research.

1246. Exploring Ancient World Cultures

http://eawc.evansville.edu/index.htm

Exploring Ancient World Cultures provides in-depth information on eight cultures: ancient Near East, ancient India, ancient Egypt, ancient China, ancient Greece, ancient Rome, early Islam, and medieval Europe. This site is enhanced with links to Argos, a search engine dedicated to ancient and medieval worlds. There is a link to an Educator's Resource Page, which is under construction but promises to be a wonderful resource. Already online are some links to maps, interactive computer quizzes on the ancient world, print and film resources, and an index of related sites.

1247. The Seven Wonders of the Ancient World

http://ce.eng.usf.edu/pharos/wonders/

The original list of the Seven Wonders of the Ancient World was destroyed with the Alexandrian library. The list used today was compiled during the Middle Ages; it remains the canonical list. These impressive structures are listed chronologically and geographically. Through excellent descriptions, watercolor renditions, and histories, students can learn more about the Great Pyramid of Giza, the Hanging Gardens of Babylon, the statue of Zeus at Olympia, the Temple of Artemis at Ephesus, the Mausoleum at Helicarnassus, the Colossus of Rhodes, and the Lighthouse of Alexandria. There is a geographic map, a list of other wonders of the world, and related links. This site was created collaboratively, with Alaa K. Ashmawy (ashmawy@ geosystems.gatech.edu) as principal editor.

Ancient Egypt

See also Duke University's Papyrus Archive page (entry 372), which provides electronic access to texts about and images of 1,373 papyri from ancient Egypt. *See also* The Institute of Egyptian Art and Archaeology (entry 131).

1248. Akhet Egyptology

http://www.akhet.co.uk

Akhet Egyptology contains information on many aspects of ancient Egyptian culture. Students can find out more about the mummification process by using the Clickable Mummy. The Egyptian Mythology section provides a beginner's guide to Egyptian gods and goddesses. Look for information on Isis, Osiris, and Anubis. The Art and Sculpture section provides links to color graphics of jewelry, coffin art, mummy masks, and grave models. The King List is under construction and contains the names of pharaohs by dynasties, with brief biographical information. For example, Tutankhamen is listed in Dynasty 18 of the New Kingdom. Created and maintained by Iain Hawkins (akhet@iname.com).

1249. Egyptian Mummies

http://www.si.edu/resource/faq/nmnh/mummies.htm

Egyptian Mummies is an entry from the *Encyclopedia Smithsonian* that discusses the mummification process. There is a bibliography.

1250. **Egyptian Pyramids**

http://www.si.edu/resource/faq/nmnh/pyramid.htm

The Egyptian Pyramid is another entry from the *Encyclopedia Smithsonian*. The text answers questions frequently asked about pyramid history, facts, and construction. A bibliography is included.

1251. **Egyptology Resources**

http://www.newton.cam.ac.uk/egypt/

Egyptology Resources is a directory of Internet resources of interest to Egyptologists sponsored by the University of Cambridge (England). Links to information are divided into categories: Journals and Magazines; Institutions; Museums; Organizations and Societies; Personal Egypt Pages; and Other Egyptology Pages. For a guide to introductory readings on the peoples and cultures of the ancient Near East, see (http://www-oi.uchicago.edu/OI/DEPT/RA/RECREAD/REC_READ.html). Maintained by Nigel Strudwick (ncs3@cam.ac.uk).

Ancient Greece

See also "Latin and Greek" foreign language (entries 372–374).

1252. **Perseus Project**

http://www.perseus.tufts.edu

The Perseus Project is an evolving digital library of resources for the study of the ancient world, located in the Department of the Classics, Tufts University. The Web site is searchable and contains an encyclopedia and an atlas. Information can be searched in Latin, Greek, and English. The English index allows for searching all in English. There is a wealth of information, including texts, translations, images, essays, and catalogs. The historical overview provides a brief summary of the history of ancient Greece from approximately 1200 B.C. to 323 B.C. and the death of Alexander the Great. In-text links provide additional information. Professor Gregory Crane (gcrane@tufts.edu), is the editor-in-chief of the project.

Ancient Rome

1253. **Forum Romanum**

http://www.geocities.com/~stilicho/

Explore ancient Roman society through its history, culture, religion, and language. Students can take a virtual walking tour through the center of the eternal city via 80 photographs linked to histories of some of the major buildings. Find out about Roman life and major Roman festivals (224 days each year!). Learn about Roman funeral customs, the importance of togas, and the Latin language that lives today in quotations, abbreviations, and mottoes. Links are also provided to a dictionary of mythology and a picture index of people, mythological characters, and places. Another link connects students to Latin literature online. This site was created and is maintained by David Camden (dcamden@hotmail.com), an award-winning Latin-language high school student in Lynchburg, Virginia. See also The Forum Romanum (http://library.thinkquest.org/11402/), a ThinkQuest site.

Archaeology

1254. ***Archaeology* Magazine**

http://www.he.net/~archaeol/index.html

Archaeology is an official publication of the Archaeological Institute of America. The print magazine is published six times each year; the Web site provides a table of contents, abstracts, and selected articles for each issue online. Online back issues are available beginning with the January/February 1996 issue. Links are provided to archaeological Internet sites, including museum exhibitions around the world.

1255. **ArchNet: WWW Virtual Library for Archaeology**

http://archnet.uconn.edu

Internet resources about archaeology are categorized by geographic region and subject. Links are provided to academic departments, museums, archaeological news, and journals and publishers. The database is searchable.

1256. ***Current Archaeology***

http://www.cix.co.uk/~archaeology/

Current Archaeology is a full-color magazine devoted to British archaeology. It is published six times each year. This site highlights some of the articles from past and current issues and provides additional information about archaeology. There is a cybertour of some of the major recent discoveries in British archaeology. There is also a directory of British archaeology, a guide to British archaeological excavations, an index to current archaeology, and a guide to some other Internet resources. A career guide offers advice about how to become an archaeologist.

Eastern Cultural Regions

See also "History and Culture of India" (entries 347–350).

1257. **The Islamic and Arabic Arts and Architecture**

http://www.islamicart.com

Islamic and Arabic artifacts are used to explain in detail the historical and cultural aspects of Islamic and Arabic culture. The site, created and maintained by the Islamic and Arabic Arts and Architecture Organization, is illustrated with photographs of dozens of works of art, from massive Islamic shrines and buildings to small silver coins. The online chronology of historic events covers a time period beginning with the birth of the Prophet Muhammad in A.D. 570 to the end of the dynasty of the Great Mughals in India in 1858. A continuation of historic events from 1858 to the present is proposed as a future update to this site. In-text links to an encyclopedia provide further information about rulers and explanations for specific terms such as *muezzin* and *hegira*. The Webmaster's address is (Info@islamicart.com).

Medieval History

See also a WebQuest on this topic: The Medieval Faire (http://www.manteno.k12.il.us/drussert/WebQuests/LeschMartinWynnWilson/MEDIEVAL%20FAIR.HTML)

1258. Castles of Britain

http://www.castles-of-britain.com

Find out more about the castles of Great Britain by exploring this Web site. Castles are defined as properly fortified military residences. Most in Wales, England, Ireland, and Scotland were built between 1000 and 1600. The Learning Center has articles on how to build and defend castles, as well as descriptions of what it was like to live in a castle. Lists are provided of "haunted" castles and castle shams. A photo gallery provides photographs and each month a different castle is highlighted. Written and maintained by Lise Hull, a medieval researcher and castle expert (CastlesU@harborside.com). For more on the Castles of Wales, see (http://www.castlewales.com/home.html).

1259. Castles on the Web

http://www.castlesontheweb.com

Castles on the Web is a directory of castle-related Internet resources. Links are provided so that students can tour individual castles from around the world and find indexes and pictures of castles. The Castles for Kids section has links to castle information selected for interest and appeal to children, including Journey Through the Middle Ages, a ThinkQuest Junior Web site created by fourth-graders (http://tqjunior.advanced.org/4051). In addition, there are a question-and-answer section, a glossary, and a bibliography. Webmaster is Ted Monk (tmonk@fox.nstn.ns.ca).

1260. Labyrinth: Medieval Studies WWW Server

http://www.georgetown.edu/labyrinth/labyrinth-home.html
or
http://www.georgetown.edu/labyrinth/

Labyrinth provides worldwide access to electronic resources in medieval studies through a Web server located at Georgetown University. Some of the countries and areas included in the Labyrinth are the British Isles, France, Germany, Scandinavia, and Italy. Special topics include Arthurian Studies; Heraldry, Arms, and Chivalry; Medieval Women; and Vikings, Runes, and Norse Culture. There are links to online bibliographies and pedagogical resources.

1261. The Middle Ages

http://www.learner.org/exhibits/middleages/

What was it really like to live in the Middle Ages? This exhibit from the Annenberg/CPB (Corporation for Public Broadcasting) multimedia Web Projects Collection explores the feudal system, town life, religion, housing, clothing, health, arts, and entertainment. Students have the opportunity to treat three patients for various ailments to learn more about the health problems and healing methods of the time. They are invited to contribute a story about a medieval tapestry and to listen to sound files to hear the difference among musical instruments, such as a recorder, a cittern, and a shawm. Hats were an important part of medieval garb and varied as to one's occupation and the time of the year. Students are asked to identify five different hats. This site provides an interesting look at the Middle Ages, and students will enjoy exploring topics such as garbage disposal and discovering which great medieval cathedral collapsed because it was not structurally sound. Links are provided to related Web sites. See also Aaron Rice's (ricej@ed.byu.edu) Middle Ages Internet Links (http://www.byu.edu/ipt/projects/middleages/).

1262. On-Line Text Materials for Medieval Studies

http://orb.rhodes.edu

On-Line Text Materials for Medieval Studies (ORB) is an academic site, written and maintained by medieval scholars. The ORB Encyclopedia is an index of original essays arranged by topic. The Medieval Studies for the Nonspecialist section contains links to Internet resources addressing the historical accuracy of the Middle Ages represented in movies, television, and historical fiction. From the ORB Reference Shelf, Web Sites Relevant to Medieval Studies provides links to Web sites related to medieval studies and to graphics, literature, manuscripts, journals, and newsletters. Students can see the Bayeux Tapestry, the Lindisfarne Gospels, and some illuminated images from the Bodleian Library at Oxford. Manuscripts include one of Leonardo da Vinci's notebooks, the *Magna Carta*, Saint Patrick's *Autobiography*, and Scriptorium: Medieval Manuscripts. Some of the links in the history category provide more information about Gregorian chants, alchemy, the age of King Charles V, and Genghis Khan. The ORB Web site, a collaborative effort by scholars of the medieval era, is maintained by Carolyn Schriber (schriber@rhodes.edu), a professor of history at Rhodes College (Memphis, Tennessee) and current editor of ORB.

1263. Plague: The Black Death

http://www.discovery.com/stories/history/blackdeath/blackdeath.html

"I am bit by fleas and plagued by family. That is all there is to say," is the first diary entry written by Birdy in *Catherine, Called Birdy* by Karen Cushman (Clarion, 1994), the story of a young-teenage girl in the last decade of the 12th century. At the instruction of her older brother, Birdy reluctantly agrees to keep a diary. At first, she has nothing more interesting to write than how many fleas she has picked off herself. Fleas were a common problem for humans in the medieval period, and infected fleas carry the deadly bubonic plague from rats to humans. Traveling along the trade routes from China, Mesopotamia and Asia Minor, the disease reached Europe in 1348. Five years later, 25 million people were dead—almost one-third of Europe's population. Large outbreaks of the plague continued until the early 1600s, and the plague still exists today. Since 1900, there have been incidents of bubonic plague every few years. Fleas from infected rats, squirrels, rabbits, and skunks still carry the disease. However, since the development of penicillin and other antibiotics, the plague is curable if treated quickly.

With current news of AIDS, the Ebola virus, and flesh-eating bacteria, students will be interested in studying about the bubonic plague. The Discovery Channel's Web site is an excellent multimedia look at the Black Death. An interactive map of the trade routes of the 14th century allows students to click on red dots to visit the cities, villages, and towns affected by the plague. RealAudio provides online interviews and comments from experts. Students click on an image of a rodent to follow the story of the plague. As an excellent primary resource, students should read a description of the Black Death written by Giovanni Boccaccio (1313–1375) in the *Decameron* (http://www.brown.edu/Departments/Italian_Studies/dweb/plague/plague.html). For a modern comparison to the Black Death, students can locate information about the influenza epidemic of 1918–1919, which killed 25 million people, at (http://home.nycap.rr.com/useless/bubonic_plague/bubonic.html).

The Renaissance

See also "William Shakespeare (1564–1616)" (entries 474–481), The Art of Renaissance Science (entry 680), and The Sistine Chapel (entry 1304).

1264. The Lives of Renaissance Women

http://www.bced.gov.bc.ca/equity/renhome.htm

The Lives of Renaissance Women is a cooperatively planned humanities unit for secondary school students, designed by teachers and librarians in British Columbia, Canada. This unit illuminates the lives and contributions of all classes of women who lived between 1350 to 1650 in Western Europe and England. The unit asks, "Did Renaissance women enjoy a Renaissance?" Ten activities with handouts are available online, as is a bibliography. Students can explore such topics as Female Renaissance Artists, Elizabeth I: Renaissance Rules, Marriage in the Renaissance, and Renaissance Witch Trials. These lesson aids are sponsored by the British Columbia Teachers' Federation (BCTF).

1265. Renaissance

http://www.learner.org/exhibits/renaissance/

What inspired this age of balance and order following the stagnation of the Middle Ages? This exhibit from the Annenberg/CPB (Corporation for Public Broadcasting) multimedia Web Projects Collection explores the forces that drove this rebirth in Europe, and in Italy in particular. Topics include Rise of the Middle Class and Resurgence of Cities, Exploration and Trade, Printing and the Humanist Philosophy, Life in Florence, and Florentine Art and Architecture. Students are invited to become spice traders and make decisions based on a fictionalized journey. If they are successful, they will be wealthy; if they fail, they will be bankrupt, lose their ship, and ruin their reputation as a trader. Students are also asked to solve the puzzle of the seashell spiral, by following a series of numbers developed by Italian mathematician Leonardo Fibonacci. Links are provided to related Web sites.

1266. Rome Reborn: The Vatican Library and Renaissance Culture

http://metalab.unc.edu/expo/vatican.exhibit/exhibit/Main_Hall.html

The original exhibit was on display in the Jefferson Building of the Library of Congress in early 1993. The exhibit is divided into nine sections: Vatican Library; Archaeology; Humanism; Mathematics; Music; Medicine and Biology; Nature Described; Orient to Rome; and Rome to China. Each section contains exhibit text and separate image files for each object. The exhibition presents the untold story of the Vatican Library as the intellectual force behind the emergence of Rome as a political and scholarly superpower during the Renaissance. Rare manuscripts, books, and maps are featured, many of which played a key role in the humanist recovery of the classical heritage of Greece and Rome.

1267. Virtual Renaissance: A Journey Through Time

http://www.twingroves.district96.k12.il.us/Renaissance/VirtualRen.html

Virtual Renaissance is an excellent interdisciplinary project by teachers and students at Twin Groves Junior High School in Illinois. Visitors can teleport throughout Virtual Renaissance by location or by character. A clickable map takes travelers to all the major locations within

Virtual Renaissance. Some of the highlights include: Cathedral of Santa Maria, Sistine Chapel, Tower of London, University of Padua, Globe Theatre, Hospital of the Innocents, and VirRen Castle. There is a chronology, which lists major events by topic; a glossary; and links to Internet resources grouped by subject category. The Reference section provides links to resource materials to be used in conjunction with the Virtual Renaissance Web site and links to student projects completed as a result of exploring Virtual Renaissance. Travel back in time to learn more about the Renaissance period.

1268. **Welcome to the Renaissance Faire**

http://www.renfaire.com/index.html

How did Elizabethans speak? What did people wear during the Renaissance? Find out at the Renaissance Faire. Sound files help with pronunciation and vocabulary lists increase awareness of speech. Items of clothing and clothing accessories are identified and accompanied by color pictures. Gives a timeline and interesting information about the Elizabethan period, including insight into the structure and organization of Elizabeth I's household. Find out more about today's Renaissance faires as historical reenactments and showcases of typical life in the late Elizabethan period. Created and maintained by John M. Vinopal (banshee@resort.com).

Eighteenth Century

1269. **Eighteenth-Century Resources**

http://andromeda.rutgers.edu/~jlynch/18th/

Eighteenth-Century Resources is a directory of links to Internet resources focused on the 18th century. The collection includes information on literature (particularly British literature), history, art, music, religion, economics, and philosophy. Links are available to online texts of 18th-century authors. Information is accessible through subject headings and keyword searches. Maintained by Jack Lynch (jlynch@english.upenn.edu).

Discussion Groups

1270. **Medieval Siege Weaponry List**

E-mail: **listserv@morgan.ucs.mun.ca**
Instructions: On the first line of the body of the message, type:
subscribe SIEGE [your first name and last name]

Siege is a forum for the discussion of pre–black-powder defense and attack of fortified positions, such as castles. Discussions include the science, mechanics, construction, and transportation of siege equipment and its use in war.

Archives of past discussions include diagrams and directions for constructing siege engines in the classroom for demonstrations and science projects. Instructions include mathematical calculations. To get archived e-mail messages, send an e-mail message to:

listserv@morgan.ucs.mun.ca
Instructions: On the first line of the body of the message, type:
index siege

You will be sent a list of the available archive files. You can then order these files with a **GET SIEGE LOGxxx** command, where xxx is the name of the file.

The Vikings

1271. The Viking Home Page

http://www.control.chalmers.se/vikings/

The Viking Home Page is a comprehensive collection of Internet resources on the topic of Vikings. Information is available on Viking ships and sailing; warfare; Norse religion; Runes; and old Norse Eddas and sagas. Look for information on Viking feasts, festivals, and sports. A map of Vinland links Vikings to the New World, and Viking explorations are also linked to Denmark, Sweden, Norway, England, France, and Spain. Links are provided to Viking parks and exhibitions such as the Jorvik Viking Centre in York, England. The creator and Webmaster is Lars Jansson of Chalmers University of Technology, Gothenburg, Sweden (lj@s2.chalmers.se).

1272. The World of the Vikings

http://www.pastforward.co.uk/vikings/index.html

Describing itself as the definitive guide to Viking resources on the Internet, this Web site lives up to its billing. The Internet sites are divided into 13 categories, and each site is briefly annotated. Some of the categories are Runes, Mead, Sagas, Museums, Ships, Reenactments, and Exhibitions. Links lead to Web sites that allow access to Viking mythology; how to make mead; old literature; Icelandic sagas; saga characters; the electronic Beowulf Project; Viking genealogy; and the World of the Vikings, an international project led by the National Museum of Denmark. Information is available on Viking expeditions from central Sweden, 700–1000. *The Raid*, a story by fifth-graders in Ireland, brings the Vikings to life. Visit various museums and exhibits, such as the Jorvik Viking Centre in the United Kingdom. There is also excellent information about the Viking navy and the Leif Ericson Viking Ship. This page should be bookmarked for every class studying the Vikings.

Mythology of the Vikings

For other mythology resources, *see* Encyclopedia Mythica (entry 1340) and "Myths and Mythology" (entries 547–548).

1273. Norse Mythology

http://www.pantheon.org/mythica/areas/norse/

The Norse Mythology Web site has more than 104 articles on the collective myths of the people of Scandinavia, including Sweden, Denmark, Norway, and Iceland. Information is presented in an easy-to-access, alphabetical format. The old Icelandic collections of texts known as Edda (1065–1220) are the main sources for Norse mythology, and some of these are included. The entry for Thor, the Norse god of thunder, is several paragraphs long, with a number of links to additional information. He is compared to the Roman god Jupiter.

Pirates

See also Treasure Island (entry 483).

1274. PIRATES!

http://www.nationalgeographic.com/features/97/pirates/maina.html

Learn more about Blackbeard and his crew of pirates, who terrorized sailors on the Atlantic Ocean and Caribbean Sea from 1716 through 1718. An excellent bibliography of books about pirates is given. Links are provided to other pirate sites, including Pirates of the Bahamas; a Discovery Channel site about two female pirates, Mary Read and Anne Bonny; and information about the recovery of the *Whydah*, the only known pirate shipwreck. This is a colorful and well-researched site for kids from *National Geographic*.

1275. Pirates Homepage

http://www.powerup.com.au/~glen/pirate.htm

Students at Rochedate State School in Australia have researched pirates and posted their work at this site. Their work is divided into topic areas: famous pirates, pirate terminology, a summary of *Treasure Island* by R. L. Stevenson, student-written pirate stories, student-written limericks, and pirate questions and answers. Younger students are pictured participating in Pirate Dress Up Day. Links are provided to other pirate resources on the Internet. Glenda Crew (glen@powerup.com.au) is the Web editor.

International Organizations

1276. North Atlantic Treaty Organization (NATO)

http://www.nato.int

In response to the Soviet Union's consolidated political and military power in Central and Eastern Europe following World War II, 10 European countries joined with the United States and Canada to form the North Atlantic Treaty Organization (NATO). Following the end of the Cold War, the alliance was restructured; today it works alongside other international organizations and undertakes peacekeeping missions and crisis-management tasks. For example, a NATO-led multinational force operating under a UN mandate was established to implement the military aspects of the Bosnian peace agreement.

This searchable database contains basic texts, contact points, communiqués, speeches, press releases, military committee press releases, the NATO *Handbook*, NATO fact sheets, newsletters, and information sheets. Other menu items have information about academic fellowships, biographies, and scientific and environmental affairs; links lead to the Allied Command Europe (ACE) and other commands and organizations.

NATO has a Public Data Service Distribution List. You may subscribe free of charge to automatically receive press releases, speeches, and communiqués via e-mail: **listserv@cc1.kuleuven.ac.be** Instructions: On the first line of the body of the message, type: **subscribe NATODATA [your first name and last name]**

1277. United Nations

http://www.un.org

The United Nations home page has many categories of information. There is an overview of the UN Charter and organization. Global Issues is an introduction to the substantive work of the United Nations. Daily highlights, press releases, and the *UN Journal* can be found in UN News. UN Documents offers selected documents from the Secretary General, General Assembly, Security Council, and Economic and Social Council. UN Photos is an archive of newly released and historical UN photographs. There are links to each of the UN departments as well as to UN publications. A What's New section provides links to new Web pages and special events.

1278. The United Nations CyberSchoolbus

http://www.un.org/Pubs/CyberSchoolBus/

The United Nations CyberSchoolbus Web site is designed to help K-12 students understand the work of the United Nations, including a virtual tour. Geography activity tie-ins are linked to the UN's Country At A Glance database. Classroom resources include Global Trends topics, such as population, food, education, and health. InfoNation is an easy-to-use database with more than 30 different fields of information about 185 countries. More than 20 cities around the world are profiled in City Profiles. The Curriculum Corner suggests teaching modules on world issues. Look for games and activities, news updates, and links to the Model UN Discussion forum. Information on how to subscribe to a free online newsletter is also available.

Countries and Regions of the World

See also Yahooligans' listing of countries for K-12 at (http://www.yahooligans.com/ Around_the_World/Countries/). *See also* the CIA *World Factbook* (entry 1424); "Atlases" (entries 1420–1423); and Flags of the World (entry 1425).

General Interest

1279. Bureau of Consular Affairs Home Page

http://travel.state.gov

U.S. citizens who plan to travel abroad should access this Web site. Links are provided to the U.S. Customs Home Page, the Immigration and Naturalization Service, passport and visa information, travel warnings and consular information sheets, and health information. Links are provided to the home pages of all U.S. embassies around the world.

1280. Countries.com

http://www.countries.com

Students can locate information on more than 200 countries; this includes flags and statistical data as well as links to culture, travel, weather, and government. Countries are listed alphabetically and by region. Younger students will appreciate each country's concise statistical data; older students will want to use the provided links to the more detailed information published in the *World Factbook*. The countries.com database is also searchable using keywords. The Webmaster's address is (webmaster@countries.com).

Comparative Cultures

1281. **The Global Gazette**

http://library.advanced.org/18802/

Three students from different countries (China, Norway, and the United States) collaborated to compare the cultures in their respective countries. Information covers sports and governments as well as traditions, special symbols, recipes, art, music, and everyday life. The students have included maps, short stories, poems, and hand-drawn illustrations. After exploring this Web site, students can test their knowledge with an online quiz. References and links to other related information on the Internet are provided. The Global Gazette was created as a ThinkQuest project by Nicki Mahncke (nicki1@mindless.com) from Hong Kong and Germany, Ali Bronsdon (cbronsdon@aol.com) from the United States, and Kiki Kuhnle (kiki205@iname.com) from Norway.

Foreign Embassies and Consulates in the United States

For foreign embassies and consulates in the United States with Web pages, see Yahoo's directory, (http://dir.yahoo.com/Government/U_S__Government/Embassies_and_Consulates/Foreign_Embassies_and_Consulates_in_the_United_States/).

A Sampling of Countries, Geographic Areas, Regions, and Territories

Africa

See also the Discover Africa section of *Kids Zone* (entry 575); "Ancient Egypt" (entries 1248–1251); "African American Studies and Black History" (entries 1216–1222); "Folklore: Fables, Folktales, and Fairy Tales" (entries 536–541), "Legends" (entries 542–546); and "Myths and Mythology" (entries 547–548).

1282. **The African Cookbook**

http://www.sas.upenn.edu/African_Studies/Cookbook/about_cb_wh.html

Find out more about different African countries and their individual customs and traditions by studying how native dishes are prepared and served. Menus and authentic recipes from Africa can be accessed on this Web site by country or by dishes such as appetizers, soups, fish entrees, and desserts. Available from the University of Pennsylvania's African Study Center, this information is extracted with permission from *The African Cookbook,* edited by Bea Sandler, illustrated by Leo and Diane Dillon, and first published in 1970 by the Carol Publishing Group, New York. Web editor is Ali B. Ali-Dinar, Ph.D. (aadinar@mail.sas.upenn.edu).

1283. **African Story Project**

http://www.umich.edu/~aaps/africa_stories/

As part of their interdisciplinary studies at Huron High School in Ann Arbor, Michigan, ninth-grade students wrote short stories set in Africa. Before writing, the students studied African culture and geography and practiced fiction writing. African readers were invited to respond to the stories; their comments are online as a method of intercultural exchange. The 10 stories represent a variety of African countries, settings, and time periods.

1284. African Studies Web Resources (University of Pennsylvania)

http://www.sas.upenn.edu/African_Studies/AS.html

The African Studies home page at the University of Pennsylvania provides links to online information about Africa, African news, and country-specific pages for Africa. Links are also provided to pictures from Africa, the Smithsonian Institution, maps and satellite images, flags, CIA maps, and pictures from some of the countries. The Egypt files contain more than 50 color images, including pictures of the Sphinx, the Karnak Temple in Luxor, King Tutankhamen, and a contemporary Egyptian with his camel. The Web editor is Ali B. Ali-Dinar, Ph.D. (aadinar@mail.sas.upenn.edu). *See also* K-12 Electronic Guide for African Resources on the Internet (entry 1285).

1285. K-12 Electronic Guide for African Resources on the Internet

http://www.sas.upenn.edu/African_Studies/Home_Page/AFR_GIDE.html

K-12 teachers, librarians, and students will want to use this guide to help locate online resources that can be used in the classroom for research and studies about Africa. Information is available on travel in Africa, the environment, and languages. Links are provided to African resources in libraries around the world. The Multimedia Archives contain images of maps, flags, African dress, African masks, and African animals.

1286. The Kennedy Center African Odyssey InterActive

http://artsedge.kennedy-center.org/odyssey.html

Provides information about African and African American arts and cultural events taking place at the Kennedy Center, in metropolitan Washington D.C, and around the world. The Arts and Education Resources section has information about visual and performing arts, history and geography, and K-12 arts and teaching. Look for links to online projects.

Amazon: South American Rain Forest

See "The Rain Forest" (entries 869–874).

Antarctica

See "Antarctica and the South Pole" (entries 840–843).

The Arctic

See also "The Arctic and the North Pole" (entry 844).

1287. Arctic Circle

http://arcticcircle.uconn.edu

Addressing the political, economic, and cultural issues currently facing the Arctic rim countries and the indigenous populations of the Arctic and subarctic regions, this is an excellent site about the Arctic Circle. Discussions on the topic are comparative in approach and grounded in historical context. The creators of this site remind us to consider all facets before making any decisions. Discussion topics include natural resources, history and culture, social equity, and environmental justice. The virtual classroom has case studies titled Arctic National Wildlife Refuge; Corporate Strategies and Village Values; and Project Chariot: The Nuclear Legacy of Cape Thompson, Alaska. Also included for study are geographic maps, information on the Arctic Circle, and links to related information on the Internet.

Canada

See also the CIA *World Factbook* entry for Canada, (http://www.odci.gov/cia/publications/factbook/).

Nunavut Territory

1288. **Welcome to Nunavut**
http://www.inac.gc.ca/nunavut/Nunavut/welcome.html

Nunavut became Canada's third territory on April 1, 1999. In Inuktitut, the Inuit language, *Nunavut* means "our land." The Nunavut Territory covers a territory of 2 million square kilometers, one-fifth the total size of Canada, and is inhabited by 25,000 people, most of whom are Inuit. Maps, photographs, and interesting facts help introduce this new territory so that students can learn more about the geography and people of Nunavut. This site can be accessed in either English or French.

China

See "History and Culture of China" (entries 299–305); and the CIA *World Factbook* entry for China, (http://www.odci.gov/cia/publications/factbook/).

Egypt

See "Ancient Egypt" (entries 1248–1251); and the CIA *World Factbook* entry for Egypt, (http://www.odci.gov/cia/publications/factbook/).

England, Scotland, and Wales

See "Ireland"(entries 1294–1296) for information about Northern Ireland.

1289. **Britannia: British History**
http://britannia.com/history/

Students studying the history of England and Wales will find a timeline of British history, biographies of Britain's monarchs, and information on understanding British titles and royal family names. The Magical History Tour allows students to click on a map of southern England to travel back in time to explore legendary history at Stonehenge, Tintagel, Glastonbury, Canterbury, and Leeds Castle. Sketches of prime ministers of Britain as political leaders since 1721 are available. In exploring the role of the church in Britain, students can find lists and photos of the great cathedrals. A three-part series on the English medieval castle is filled with facts and photographs. A collection of full-text and excerpted versions of important historical documents is also available, as is an Arthurian timeline and history. This site is searchable and easy to navigate. Created by *Britannia Internet Magazine*, the contact address for this Web site is (rhampton@britannia.com).

1290. British Isles: Early English History

http://www.georgetown.edu/labyrinth/subjects/british_isles/british_isles.html

Part of the Labyrinth Web site, this early history of England focuses on the Anglo-Saxon culture and the 14th century. In the Teaching Resources area, look for a map of Anglo-Saxon England and sound recordings of Old English poetry (RealAudio). The Living History section has links to pictures of Anglo-Saxon clothing, Anglo-Saxon and medieval recipes, the Regia Anglorum Web site (http://www.regia.org/), and West Stow Country Park and Anglo-Saxon Village (http://www.stedmunds.co.uk/west_stow.html). Important events in the 14th century are highlighted starting with 1338, the beginning of the Hundred Years' War, and ending in 1399, the year Richard II was arrested. Illustrations accompanying this text are from a 15th-century manuscript of the chronicle of Jean Froissart, a contemporary of Chaucer's. Also, look for links to Middle English bibliographies, literature, and pedagogical resources.

1291. BritSpeak: English as a Second Language for Americans

http://pages.prodigy.com/NY/NYC/britspk/main.html

BritSpeak is home to the BritSpeak Dictionary and the Best of Britain. The dictionary can be accessed either as British-American or American-British. Some words are problems because they mean the reverse on opposite side of the Atlantic. For example, *bomb* means a failure in the United States and a great success in the United Kingdom; *public schools* are state-supported in the United States and private in the United Kingdom; and *tabling* something in the United States means to set it aside, whereas in the United Kingdom it means to bring it to a vote. Look for the phrase of the fortnight and links to other British-American dictionaries on the Internet.

The Best of Britain category provides links to most things British, including newspapers such as the *Guardian*, the *Times*, the *Telegraph*, and the *Financial Times*. There are links to the Royal Botanic Gardens at Kew, the Tube, the BBC, the Natural History Museum, and more. The Webmaster's address is (ukmark@aol.com).

1292. The UK Travel Guide

http://www.uktravel.com

The UK Travel Guide is helpful for visitors planning virtual and real trips to the United Kingdom. It consists of UK A-Z, the UK Active Map, and The London Guide. UK A-Z has brief informational entries for travelers on topics such as currency and banking hours, VAT refunds, public holidays, and locations of cybercafés. Look for links to online railway timetables for the entire United Kingdom, as well as the current weather forecasts. The UK Active Map allows point-and-click access to more than 100 areas of interest, including color photographs. The London Guide also has a clickable map. Clicking on tube stations produces information on nearby tourist attractions, and clicking on railway stations returns train information. The London Transport Company has made available a map of the Underground system with travel news, travel advice, and fares and pricing information (http://www.londontransport.co.uk/info/lul_index.htm).

France

See "History and Culture of France and French-Speaking Peoples" (entries 311–322); and the CIA *World Factbook* entry for France, (http://www.odci.gov/cia/publications/factbook/).

Germany

See "History and Culture of Germany and German-Speaking Peoples" (entries 331–340); and the CIA *World Factbook* entry for Germany, (http://www.odci.gov/cia/publications/factbook/).

Greece

See also "Ancient Greece" (entry 1252); and the CIA *World Factbook* entry for Greece, (http://www.odci.gov/cia/publications/factbook/).

1293.   Embassy of Greece (Washington, D.C.)

http://www.greekembassy.org

The Greek Embassy in Washington, D.C., provides general information about the Hellenic Republic and its capital, Athens. Students who seek more information on Greece's foreign policy should read online statements from the Hellenic Republic's Ministry of Foreign Affairs about Greek-U.S. relations, Greece's relations with the Balkan countries, and with the European Union. A history of Greece is divided into time periods for easy access. Links to archaeological sites and museums are available, as are links to the Greek National Tourist Organization office in Athens and other offices around the world. Software is provided for those who want to download and install Greek fonts. Most information is in English, but some texts are in Greek.

India

See "History and Culture of India" (entries 347–350); and the CIA *World Factbook* entry for India, (http://www.odci.gov/cia/publications/factbook/).

Ireland

See also the CIA *World Factbook* entry for Ireland, (http://www.odci.gov/cia/publications/factbook/).

1294.   *Irish Times Online*

http://www.irishtimes.com

The Irish Times is a daily online news Web site that gives students current news from an Irish perspective. Archives of past issues are searchable. Look for special news features and the entertainment guide to Dublin. See also a new weekly online magazine, *Ireland's Eye*, for insight into the culture, traditions, and history of Ireland (http://www.irelandseye.com).

1295.   The Northern Ireland Information Page

http://www.interknowledge.com/northern-ireland/index.html

The official home page of the Northern Ireland Tourist Board provides information on the 5,500 square miles (approximately the size of Connecticut) that make up Northern Ireland. Though aimed at tourists, students will find information about the city of Belfast and surrounding counties as well as the ancestral heritage and industrial heritage. This site also provides a link to the *Belfast Telegraph Online* for current news. A section of Belfast Impressions & Dublin Thought provides some factual, thought-provoking articles on the issues in Ireland.

1296.   Sinn Fein

http://sinnfein.ie

Updated daily, this is the official Sinn Fein Web site. Sinn Fein is the legal political party of Northern Ireland and the Republic of Ireland. The party's objective is to end British rule in Ireland, and to seek national self-determination and the unity and independence of Ireland as a sovereign state. The Webmaster's address is (sfweb@irlnet.com).

Israel

See also the CIA *World Factbook* entry for Israel, (http://www.odci.gov/cia/publications/factbook/).

1297.   Israel Foreign Ministry Home Page

http://www.israel.org/mfa/home.asp
or
gopher://israel-info.gov.il

Established and maintained by the Information Division of the Israel Foreign Ministry, the Web site and Gopher site contain information about the Ministry of Foreign Affairs, recent developments in Israel, and general background about various facets of Israeli government and life. Information is updated daily. Links are provided to the Guide to the Mideast Peace Process and Facts About Israel, including information about Israel's history, its land and people, education, health and social services, culture, society, and economy. Graphics include many color maps and pictures of Israel and the Middle East from antiquity to the present. This is an invaluable source for students researching Arab-Israeli relations. The Centenary of Zionism (1897–1997) page includes a timeline with in-text links to historical documents such as the Balfour Declaration (1917) and the Israel-Jordan Peace Treaty (October 26, 1994).

The Israeli Consulate in New York prepares daily postings (Monday through Friday) of English summaries from the Israeli press. These are available online or by free e-mail subscription.

How to Access:

E-mail: listserv@pankow.inter.net.il
Instructions: On the first line of the body of the message, type:
subscribe israeline [your first name and last name]

1298.   The Jerusalem Mosaic

http://www1.huji.ac.il/jeru/
or
http://jeru.huji.ac.il/jerusalem.html

The Jerusalem Mosaic is a living museum project that provides information and exhibits about Jerusalem, a city with 4,000 years of recorded history. Students can enter Jerusalem through any of four gates:

1.   The Faces of Jerusalem Gate
2.   The Maps of Jerusalem Gate
3.   The Views of Jerusalem Gate
4.   The Paintings of Jerusalem Gate

Also included is a section titled Main Events in the History of Jerusalem, which contains a timeline that begins in the 19th century B.C. and extends to A.D. 1967. This is an excellent reference for history students.

The Faces of Jerusalem is a collection of photographs taken in the last 100 years that provide insight into the people living in Jerusalem. Thirteen pictures are from 1867–1918, and 17 are from 1994. Maps of Jerusalem includes 23 maps; 2 were drawn before the advent of printing, 12 were printed between 1575 and 1870, 4 are topographical maps of Jerusalem, and 5 were printed between 1967 and 1994. Views of Jerusalem is a collection of pictures of various views of the city, including the Wailing Wall, the Church of Gethsemane, and the surrounding countryside. Paintings of Jerusalem is a colorful collection taken from the book *Painting Palestine in the Nineteenth Century* (Yerushalayim: Yad Yitshak Ben-Tsevi: Yediot aharonot: Sifre hemed, 1992) by Professor Yehoshua Ben-Arieh.

Italy

See "History and Culture of Italy" (entries 352–355); and the CIA *World Factbook* entry for Italy, (http://www.odci.gov/cia/publications/factbook/).

Japan

See "History and Culture of Japan" (entries 359–368); and the CIA *World Factbook* entry for Japan, (http://www.odci.gov/cia/publications/factbook/).

Malaysia

See also the CIA *World Factbook* entry for Malaysia, (http://www.odci.gov/cia/publications/factbook/).

1299.   Malaysia
http://www.visitmalaysia.com/main.html

Students can locate Malaysia on the map provided at this Web site and find out more about Malaysia's people, culture, cuisine, music, and art. An illustrated timeline, beginning with ancient Malaysia (35,000 B.C.–100 B.C.) helps to put historical events into perspective. Explore the Mulu Caves and look at Borneo's unique "villages" to find out what it's like to live in a longhouse. Malaysia's varied environment is home to the world's oldest rain forest and the world's rarest and most remarkable animals, such as the Sumatran rhinoceros, clouded leopard, sun bear, monitor lizard, and the orangutan. Created by the Malaysia Tourism Promotion Board, New York, New York.

Mexico

See also "History and Culture of Mexico" (entries 394–398); "History and Culture of Spanish-Speaking Peoples" (entries 402–409); Aztec Calendar (entry 1426); and Latino and Hispanic Images in Picture Books (entry 497). See also the CIA *World Factbook* entry for Mexico, (http://www.odci.gov/cia/publications/factbook/).

Oceania

Oceania includes: American Samoa; Ashmore and Cartier Islands; Australia; Baker Island; Brunei; Cook Islands; Coral Sea Islands; Fiji; French Polynesia; Guam; Howland Island; Indonesia; Jarvis Island; Johnston Atoll; Kingman Reef; Kiribati; Macau; Malaysia; Marshall Islands; Micronesia (Federated States of); Midway Islands; Nauru; New Caledonia; New Zealand; Niue; Norfolk Island; Northern Mariana Islands; Pacific Islands (Trust Territory of the Palau); Palmyra Atoll; Papua New Guinea; Philippines; Pitcairn Islands; Solomon Islands; Taiwan; Tokelau; Tonga; Tuvalu; Vanuatu; Wake Island; Wallis and Futuna; and Western Samoa.

1300. Guam: Where America's Day Begins

http://tqjunior.advanced.org/5129/

Fifth-grade students from Guam worked together as a ThinkQuest Jr. team to create this information-packed Web site on Guam. Topics include geography, climate, and weather; culture and traditions; indigenous animals; and Chunk (one of the smallest Micronesian island groups in the Pacific Ocean). Learn more about the KoKo bird and the fruit bat. Read The Coconut Legend that explains why Guam has so many coconuts and compare the legend of Sirena to the European Little Red Riding Hood story. After learning more about Guam, students are invited to take an online interactive quiz to test their knowledge.

1301. New Zealand Embassy (Washington, D.C.)

http://www.nzemb.org

The New Zealand Embassy's Web pages provide lots of factual information as well as insights into the way of life of New Zealanders (known as Kiwis). Find out more about the self-sufficient people of New Zealand, who enjoy being active out-of-doors in a country where the water is fresh and the air is clean, and who value education, the "overseas experience," and entrepreneurial pursuits. Find out more about the Maori, the indigenous tribal people. Students will learn that in New Zealand, a country in the southern hemisphere, the seasons are opposite to those in North America. January is the warmest month of the New Zealand summer, and July is the coolest month of winter. They will also discover that due to New Zealand's isolation, strange species of animals have survived and peculiar ones have evolved, such as the tuatara, a mini-dinosaur; and the kakapo, a heavy, flightless parrot. See also New Zealand on the Web (http://nz.com).

Russian Federation and East European Countries

See "History and Culture of Russia and Former Soviet Union Countries" (entries 377–385); and the CIA *World Factbook* entries for countries in the Russian Federation and Eastern Europe, (http://www.odci.gov/cia/publications/factbook/).

South Africa

See also the CIA *World Factbook* entry for South Africa, (http://www.odci.gov/cia/publications/factbook/).

1302. South Africa Online

http://www.southafrica.co.za

Information abounds on all aspects of South African life at this Web site. Students can locate information on businesses, education, government, health, lifestyles, sports, and more. Game park and safari information is available, as are links to daily newspapers and online magazines.

1303. Virginia Hamilton's Visit to South Africa: Images of a New South Africa

http://www.virginiahamilton.com/pages/safricamain.html

Virginia Hamilton records online, with music, pictures, and captions, some of what she saw as a member of a delegation of children's specialists who extensively toured South Africa in November 1996. Images from Johannesburg, Soweto, Capetown, Peace Park, and the Kruger National Park show schools, libraries, children, storytelling, squatter shanties, African landscape, jacaranda trees, and African animals in this personalized look at South Africa.

A link is provided to Mandela and the African National Congress Home Page (http://www. anc.org.za). See also Virginia Hamilton's Home Page at (http://www.virginiahamilton.com).

Spain

See "History and Culture of Spain" (entries 399–401); "History and Culture of Spanish-Speaking Peoples" (entries 402–409); Artistas Españoles (entry 119); and the CIA *World Factbook* entry for Spain, (http://www.odci.gov/cia/publications/factbook/).

Vatican City

See also Rome Reborn: "The Renaissance" (entries 1264–1268).

1304. The Sistine Chapel

http://www.christusrex.org/www1/sistine/0-Tour.html

The Sistine Chapel was built between 1475 and 1483 and is the exact dimensions of the Temple of Solomon as given in the Old Testament. Architecturally, the Sistine Chapel is rectangular, with a barrel vault ceiling, smaller side vaults over the centered windows, and a flattened exterior roof. The wall paintings were executed by a number of artists, including Sandro Botticelli. Pope Julius II commissioned Michelangelo to repaint the ceiling between 1508 and 1512. A master plan of the chapel is provided, which makes locating each painting relatively easy through an alphanumeric code. Eighty-six separate images of the wall paintings are available for viewing. There are 18 images of Michelangelo's ceiling showing the overview, followed by more than 100 separate images of individual scenes. These close-up images show such famous sections of the ceiling as the Creation, Adam and Eve being expelled from the Garden of Eden, and the individual prophets and sibyls around the edges of the ceiling. Each scene has multiple images from different perspectives, including long and medium shots, close-ups, and right and left views. Also included in this collection is Michelangelo's *Last Judgement*, painted on the altar wall between 1535 and 1541. This is truly an impressive and awe-inspiring Web site.

1305. Vatican City

http://www.christusrex.org/www1/icons/vatican.html

Find out more about the Vatican City as a separate and independent country located inside Italy. This Web site has the state flag of the Vatican, a map, the official languages, a brief historic background, and information about the government.

Yugoslavia (the former)

1306. A Beginner's Guide to the Balkans

http://abcnews.go.com/sections/world/balkans_content/

This ABC News Special Report Web site focuses on the civil war in the former Yugoslavia during the early 1990s, and on the 1995 peace treaty; one of its aims is to help students to understand that in some parts of the world ethnic identity is more important than political citizenship. Students can click on a map of the Balkans to find out more about Slovenia, Croatia, Bosnia-Herzegovina, Montenegro, the Federal Republic of Yugoslavia, Serbia, Kosovo, and Macedonia. Today, the Federal Republic of Yugoslavia (FRY) is only a part of the former Communist Republic of Yugoslavia, established by Josef Broz Tito after World War II. Led by Slobodan Milosevic, the FRY consists of the republics of Serbia and Montenegro. Serbs dominate the government, army, and state administration. Kosovo is officially a province of Serbia. An illustrated timeline from circa 7,000 B.C. puts events into historical perspective. This Web site provides a good foundation for understanding the subsequent conflict in Kosovo. A section about Wiping People Off the Map addresses "ethnic cleansing" and its weapons.

Geography

See also "Atlases" (entries 1420–1423).

National Standards

1307. National Geography Standards and the Five Themes

http://www.nationalgeographic.com/resources/ngo/education/standardslist.html

The goal of the National Geography Standards is to produce a geographically informed person who sees meaning in the arrangement of things in space and applies a spatial perspective to life situations. The standards address six areas of competency: the world in spatial terms, places and regions, physical systems, human systems, environment and society, and the uses of geography. The five themes of geography education are defined and each theme is accompanied with activity ideas at this site (http://www.nationalgeographic.com/resources/ngo/education/themes.html). The five themes of geography are location, place, human environment interaction, movement, and regions. More resources for teachers, including how to participate in the National Geography Bee, can be found at this location (http://www.nationalgeographic.com/resources/ngo/education/resources.html).

1308. Geo-Globe: Interactive Geography

http://hyperion.advanced.org/10157/

Students who are curious about world geography will enjoy this site filled with facts and inter-active games. Students can choose six areas of geography to explore. In Geo-Find, students can select one of three skill levels to find the locations of countries, cities, rivers, lakes, and mountains. Using animals from around the world, Geo-Quest is a version of the game "Twenty Questions." Geo-Tour gives clues that lead to some of the Earth's most interesting landmarks. Geo-Seas allows students to follow a maze through the ocean. Geo-Layers lets students dis-cover the layers of the globe both below and above the Earth's surface. In Geo-Adapt, students find out how plants have adapted to various habitats all over the world.

1309. The Geographic Learning Site

http://geography.state.gov/htmls/plugin.html

Sponsored by the U.S. Department of State, this site allows students and teachers to learn more about the world of current international affairs. Students explore countries where U.S. diplomats work; places where the Secretary of State travels; and international affairs and im-portant international issues (divided into three grade levels: K-4, 5–8, and 9–12). World Geo-graphic News covers geographic issues; natural disasters (floods, fires, volcanic eruptions); and disasters caused by people (expanding cities, new infrastructure, war). Addressing the frequency of changes in the political map of the world, The Changing World lists changes since 1990 with accompanying maps. Hot Spots features geopolitical issues currently in the news—countries where such issues as peacekeeping, famine, population, environment, refu-gees, and humanitarian assistance are important. This is an excellent site for students study-ing geographical relationships among peoples of the world and their environments.

1310. The Great Globe Gallery

http://hum.amu.edu.pl/%7Ezbzw/glob/glob1.htm

More than 70 different views of Earth are part of the collection on this Web site. Some of the images include views of Earth from various projections and views from space showing El Niño, ozone from 1979 to 1994, land temperatures, clouds, terrestrial impact structure, and sea temperatures. Other globes presented are 3-D, ancient globes, and medieval globes.

1311. How Far Is It?

http://www.indo.com/distance/

How Far Is It? uses the University of Michigan Geographic Name Server and a supplementary database of world cities to find the latitude and longitude of two places, and then calculates the distance between them (as the crow flies). It also provides a map showing the two places, using the Xerox PARC Map Server. As the crow flies, it is 643 miles (1,036 km) from London to Prague. This activity will help children learn more about geography and reinforce map locating skills.

1312. K-12 Internet Resources for Geography Education

http://members.carol.net/josh/geoindex.html

K-12 teachers and students will find links to resources that support geography education and the National Geography Standards. Especially interesting on this Web page is the list of links provided for the Uses of Geography, one of the six areas of competencies outlined in the Geography Standards. In addition, look for an extensive collection of lesson plans, grouped by geography theme and grade level. Created and maintained by Martha Taylor (josh@carol.net), KidsConnect volunteer and media specialist at Starr Elementary School in Anderson, South Carolina.

1313. National Geographic: Round Earth, Flat Maps

http://tectonic.nationalgeographic.com/2000/exploration/projections/
or
http://tectonic.nationalgeographic.com/2000/exploration/projections/intro1.html

National Geographic helps students to understand how maps are created by exploring the science of cartography as defined by projections, objectives, and map tools. Planar, conic, and cylindrical projections are compared, as well as different focuses involving area, shape, distance, direction, and world reference. In-text links with accompanying diagrams clearly illustrate mapmaking skills and tools such as interruptions, centering, and Tissot's Indicatrix. For more information on mapmaking, go to National Geographic's Map Machine, located at (http://www.nationalgeographic.com/resources/ngo/maps).

1314. Physical Geography Resources on the Internet

http://feature.geography.wisc.edu/resources/phys.html

Physical Geography Resources on the Internet is a compilation of links to such topics as weather, climate, topography, oceans, stream flow, vegetation, and solar and atmospheric conditions and data.

1315. Ptolemy's Geography

http://www.ncsa.uiuc.edu/SDG/Experimental/vatican.exhibit/exhibit/d-mathematics/Ptolemy_geo.html

Ptolemy's Geography is part of the Library of Congress Vatican Exhibit and focuses on Ptolemy's science of the Earth's surface. Ptolemy offered instruction in great detail on how to draw maps. Ptolemaic maps incorporated latitude and longitude and provided drawings using different methods of projection from thousands of coordinates.

1316. U.S. Geological Survey

http://www.usgs.gov

The U.S. Geological Survey (USGS) home page provides a wealth of information, including links to geographic information by state. Each state has a fact sheet and links to articles and reports. Information covers the history of the USGS, floods, volcanoes, earthquakes, extreme weather and hurricanes, water data, maps, and photographs. Links lead to Ask-A-Geologist, regional information, nongeographic resources, and resources beyond the United States. The Web site is searchable; teachers will appreciate being able to search for specific information from such a large database.

Geography Lesson Plans and Projects

1317. National Geographic Lessons and Activities

Grades K–4
http://www.nationalgeographic.com/resources/ngo/education/ideask4/index.html

Grades 5–8
http://www.nationalgeographic.com/resources/ngo/education/ideas58/index.html

Grades 9–12
http://www.nationalgeographic.com/resources/ngo/education/ideas912/index.html

National Geographic provides online lesson plans and activities that address specific geography themes and standards. For younger students, lesson plans are available using story maps and identifying locations of stories from clues. Older students can become engaged in activities that introduce the concept of global interdependence by exploring the origins of many of the goods that they wear and use every day, and by understanding how mapping techniques can be used to understand social issues and to solve problems.

1318. Working With Maps

http://www.usgs.gov/education/learnweb/wwmaps.html

Created by the U.S. Geological Survey (USGS), this home page contains step-by-step lesson plans, reproducible map packets, and activity sheets—everything necessary to teach map skills to students in grades K-12. Map Adventures is appropriate for grades K-3, and focuses on how to understand and use maps. What Do Maps Show? is a teaching packet for grades 5–8, and Exploring Maps is an interdisciplinary set of materials on mapping for grades 7–12. For more information, contact Maura Hogan (mhogan@usgs.gov).

Maps

See also "Sky Maps" (entries 707–709).

1319. Mapmaker, Mapmaker, Make Me a Map

http://ur.utenn.edu/ut2kids/maps/map.html

Will Fontanez and the University of Tennessee at Knoxville Cartographic Services Laboratory explain different maps, their uses, map projections, and the role of atlases and latitude and longitude in mapmaking. This site helps students learn more about cartographers and the science of mapmaking.

1320. MapQuest

http://www.mapquest.com

MapQuest allows you to freely create maps showing driving routes in the United States from one destination to another. You can zoom in or out of a specific location and pinpoint an exact address. There is also an interactive atlas that allows students to find any place by using a large database of worldwide maps. Students can type in the country, city, street, or name of business, or just click on a continent to view an interactive map. This information is provided by MapQuest Publishing Group of Denver, Colorado, and Lancaster, Pennsylvania. See also Yahoo! Maps (http://maps.yahoo.com/py/maps.py).

1321. Outline Maps from Houghton Mifflin Company

http://www.eduplace.com/ss/ssmaps/index.html

The Houghton Mifflin Company has made available online more than 32 outline maps. These maps may be freely downloaded and used in homes and schools. Maps are available for the United States as well as other areas of the world. Teachers and students may choose outline maps of the United States that feature political, physical, climate, historical, state capitals, or no labels.

1322. Road Maps *Road Trip USA*

http://www.moon.com/road_trip/

The full text of *Road Trip USA*, a travel guide to the United States, is online, along with a clickable map of the United States. Eleven different road trips are featured, including one trip along US 93 from Montana to Mexico and one along the Great River Road, traveling through 10 states bordering the Mississippi River. Students will learn geography and history as they take virtual trips throughout the United States using this travel guide. The paperback edition by James Jansen was published in July 1996 by Moon Travel Handbooks.

1323. Xerox PARC Map Viewer

http://pubweb.parc.xerox.com/map/

Students can point and click on this interactive globe. They can zoom in or out, include borders and rivers, elect to view in color, change the projection from elliptical to rectangular, change the database to the United States only, and much more. This is an excellent learning tool for geography students.

Reference

All URL addresses in this chapter are checked and updated monthly. If a link does not work, please refer to the Directory Update Web page located at (http://www.lu.com/lu/irdupdates.html).

The Internet offers many reference resources. Most major universities offer virtual reference desks with searchable databases of dictionaries and thesauri. Keyword-searchable resources allow quicker access and more accurate retrieval of information. The searchable databases listed in this chapter may be used without cost (other than the cost of Internet access). The CIA *World Factbook* (entry 1424) is keyword-searchable, as are *Webster's Dictionary and Thesaurus* (entry 1394), *Roget's Thesaurus* (entry 1398), and a dictionary of acronyms and abbreviations (entry 1388).

Four quality online, searchable encyclopedias are included in this chapter. Microsoft's Encarta Concise Encyclopedia (entry 1344) is an abridged online version of *Encarta Encyclopedia*. It contains 16,000 articles and more than 2,200 photos, illustrations, maps, charts, and tables. Encyclopedia Mythica (entry 1340) is an encyclopedia of mythology, folklore, and mysticism. Encyclopedia Smithsonian (entry 1342) is a collection of FAQs related to the collections at the Smithsonian museums. Encyclopedia.Com from Electric Library (entry 1339) has more than 17,000 articles from *The Concise Columbia Electronic Encyclopedia, Third Edition*, which are cross-referenced with links to related Web sites, lists of related books from BarnesandNoble.com's database, and extensive articles and pictures from the Electric Library.

The "Biography" section of this chapter is rich in resources. More than 15,000 entries are available from A&E's Biography Database (entry 1333), 18,000 from the Biographical Dictionary (entry 1334), and 400 from Celebrity Biographies (entry 1335).

Students will appreciate all the homework resources: B. J. Pinchbeck's Homework Helper (entry 1362), Homework Central (entry 1363), and Study Web (entry 1364).

Valuable resources include those that are updated daily, such as *The New York Times* (entry 1416). These resources are also keyword-searchable. *Time* magazine has placed on the Internet all the Man of the Year covers, along with the cover stories and an archive of the last 52 issues of *Time* (entry 1411). This is an incredibly rich resource for K-12 libraries. With these kinds of resources, both rural and urban schools with access to the WWW will be able to offer the same resources to all students, thus leveling the playing field for students in rich and poor districts across the country.

The Millennium

1324. Time 100: The Most Important People of the 20th Century
http://www.time.com/time/time100/index.html

Who has had the greatest impact on the 20th century? Time profiles 100 people who have changed the world, for better or worse, during the last 100 years, using 5 different categories: Leaders & Revolutionaries, Artists & Entertainers, Builders & Titans, Scientists & Healers, and Heroes & Inspirations. The Time Person of the Century was announced in December 1999.

General Interest

1325. Infoplease.com
http://www.infoplease.com

Infoplease.com provides a fast way to find answers in its almanacs, dictionary, and encyclopedia databases. The home page has daily news, weather, and feature articles. Information is searchable and the biography database and almanacs are also browseable. Find information about disasters, flags, people, holidays, recent elections, geography, and inventions and discoveries.

1326. Kids' Almanac
http://kids.infoplease.com

Provides a kids' version of Infoplease.com with subject headings and articles written for K-12 students. Information is available from Infoplease.com's almanacs, dictionary, and encyclopedia. Subjects such as people, science, math & money, the United States, and the world are filled with facts and statistics. For example, the Disaster Digest, part of the "World" section, highlights both natural disasters and disasters caused by accidents. Links are provided to Word of the Day, Today in History, Facts Behind the News, Feature Articles, Homework Center, and Fun Facts.

1327. *The Old Farmer's Almanac*
http://www.almanac.com

The Old Farmer's Almanac has been continuously published every September since 1792. It provides useful information with a touch of humor for everyone: monthly calendars with links to "red-letter days," tide tables, sunrise and sunset tables, moon phases charts, planting charts and gardening advice, recipes and cooking tips, and weather predictions and weather proverbs. Find out what to substitute for vanilla extract in a recipe, how to sterilize toothbrushes, and why Halloween is National Magic Day in the United States. *The Old Farmer's Almanac* can be used for general reference or as a wonderful resource in language arts, science, home economics, and agriculture/horticulture classes.

Question-and-Answer Services

1328. Ask an Expert
http://www.k12science.org/askanexpert.html

Using this site, students can take advantage of experts in areas such as science and technology, literature, personal and college advisory, economy and marketing, and computing and the Internet. There is also a list of people to contact for online library reference.

1329. Pitsco's Ask an Expert
http://www.askanexpert.com

Experts are available in career and industry, health, science and technology, Internet and computer science, education, recreation, entertainment, personal development, the arts, money and business, international, law, and religion. Pitsco's Ask an Expert is a directory of links to persons who have volunteered their time to answer questions. More than 300 Web pages and e-mail addresses are provided in 12 subject/topic areas.

Ready Reference

1330. Needle in a CyberStack—the InfoFinder
http://members.home.net/albeej/

Using an easy-to-navigate table format, this site is an alphabetized listing of links to useful research, study, and writing resources on the Internet. Look for links to news, reference, business and career tools, multisearch tools, the very Best of the Web, museums, law and justice, cybrarians' favorites, and popular magazines. Created and maintained by John Albee (albee@ revealed.net), a teacher in Davenport, Iowa.

1331. Research-It!
http://www.iTools.com/research-it/research-it.html

Research-It! has myriad access points to various types of references, providing a one-stop virtual reference desk. Included are dictionaries (Merriam Webster, rhyming, computing, and pronouncing); thesauri; foreign language translators; a French conjugator; acronym and anagram servers; quotations; King James Bible searches; world map searches; CIA *World Factbook*; currency converters; stock quotes and symbol lookup; U.S. postal codes; and AT&T's toll-free Internet directory.

1332. The University of California at Irvine's Research Resources A-Z
http://www.lib.uci.edu/rraz/genref.html

The UCI Library's Virtual Reference Collection provides ready access to the most important and useful reference resources currently available on the World Wide Web. Information is available by alphabetized category for easy access, such as almanacs, biographies, dictionaries, encyclopedias, language translators, and style manuals.

Biographies

See also "Biographies of Mathematicians" (entries 593–594); "Revolutionary War and Early Republic Biographies" (entries 1127–1135); Biographies of NASA Astronauts (entry 721); Women of NASA (entry 726); "Biographies of Scientists" (entries 729–731); Contributions of 20th Century Women to Physics (entry 894); and Einstein: Image and Impact (entry 895).

1333. A&E's Biography Database

http://www.biography.com

A&E has a searchable database of more than 15,000 names of some of the world's greatest individuals, past and present. You can choose from an alphabetical listing, select a letter, or enter a name to search. Entries are from the *Cambridge Biographical Encyclopedia* (Cambridge University Press, 1994). Entries are brief, usually no more than 100 words. Each entry states whether the person was male or female and gives the birth date (and death date for those who are deceased).

1334. Biographical Dictionary

http://www.s9.com/biography/

The Biographical Dictionary contains more than 18,000 entries of notable men and women from ancient times to the present day. Information includes birth and death years, professions, positions held, literary and artistic works, and other achievements. The dictionary is searchable by name, date, or keyword. Students can search on topics, such as greenhouse effect or dinosaur, or on professions, such as astronaut. Students are invited to take the online interactive Master Biographer Challenge to see if they can attain the "summit" by accumulating a score of 100 points. Created and maintained by Eric Tentarelli (TENTARELLI@iiiv.tn.cornell.edu).

1335. Celebrity Biographies

http://mrshowbiz.go.com/celebrities/index.html

Biographies of more than 400 stars are searchable and browseable by last name and category such as actress, actor, athlete, TV personality, and musician. Each celebrity's listing includes a photograph and brief biographical sketch. If more information is available online, links are provided to selected news articles and stories as well as other Web sites. A birthday list of stars changes daily. Each day, a different celebrity is featured as Today's Star.

1336. Spotlight: Biography

http://educate.si.edu/spotlight/

Using images from the National Portrait Gallery, the Smithsonian Institution has created an excellent biography Web site for famous and not-so-famous American artists and athletes, soldiers and scientists, inventors and social reformers, and other interesting people. Each biography is two to three paragraphs long, and in-text links connect the reader to relevant pages within the Smithsonian's Web site. Links at the bottom of each biography have been carefully selected to provide additional information from related Internet resources around the world. Larger images of each portrait can be created by clicking on the small thumbnail portraits. Biographies can be accessed by using an alphabetized index. Biographies can also be accessed by subject, such as Western Expansion, Labor Reform, Musical Theater, Inventors, Artists, Athletes, and Founding Fathers. This is an excellent compilation of information from the Smithsonian and other sources about the lives and times of some notable Americans. When reviewed, this site featured 60 biographies.

Encyclopedias

1337. Compton's Encyclopedia Online
http://www.optonline.com/comptons/

Compton's Encyclopedia Online has more than 37,000 articles with cross-referenced text; more than 1,000 color pictures, flags, maps, and charts; and tables and MIDI and other sound files. The encyclopedia is browseable and searchable by articles, by pictures and graphics, or by both. Icons help students determine if information is a sound file, flag, related article, main article, or graphic.

1338. The Encyclopaedia Britannica Guide to Black History
http://blackhistory.eb.com

This comprehensive site offers pictures and biographies of famous African Americans, accessible from an alphabetical listing that includes more than 450 names. The audio and video section has movie clips and sound files such as Gwendolyn Brooks reading one of her poems and Dizzy Gillespie and Charlie Parker performing "Hot House" in 1952. A timeline covers black history through five eras, from 1517 to the present. There are a bibliography, links to related Web sites, and a teacher's guide.

1339. Encyclopedia.Com from Electric Library
http://www.encyclopedia.com

More than 17,000 articles from *The Concise Columbia Electronic Encyclopedia, Third Edition,* are available for browsing using an alphabetical index or searching using keywords. Entries are short, but are cross-referenced, and links are provided to related Web sites, lists of related books from BarnesandNoble.com's database, and extensive articles and pictures from the Electric Library. This is a great ready reference resource.

1340. Encyclopedia Mythica
http://www.pantheon.org/mythica/

Encyclopedia Mythica is an encyclopedia on mythology, folklore, and mysticism. It contains entries for gods, goddesses, supernatural beings, and legendary creatures and monsters. It also has some definitions of mysticism and the occult. This Web site is currently under construction. If you are looking for more information on such things as unicorns, dragons, gnomes, leprechauns, fairies, or imaginary places (such as Atlantis and Avalon), this Web site is for you.

1341. Encyclopaedia of the Orient

http://i-cias.com/e.o/index.htm

The Encyclopaedia of the Orient focuses on the countries and people of North Africa and the Middle East. It is both searchable and browseable. Original articles and photographs provide reference materials for high school and university-level students. A sidebar with alphabetical links to articles makes browsing easy.

1342. Encyclopedia Smithsonian

http://www.si.edu/resource/faq/

Encyclopedia Smithsonian is a compendium of FAQs on various topics, such as anthropology, mineral sciences, musical history, physical sciences, transportation history, and vertebrate zoology. Each FAQ addresses the topic and provides a bibliography for further reading. Students can find out more about such diverse topics as carrier pigeons used by the military during World War I, the Hope diamond, the Stradivarius violin, the RMS *Titanic*, the Loch Ness Monster, endangered and threatened vertebrates, and sharks.

1343. How Stuff Works

http://www.howstuffworks.com

Have you ever wondered how things like cell phones, televisions, or light sabers work? What are MP3 files? Why do we celebrate St. Patrick's Day and St. Valentine's Day? This is the place to come to find out. This Web site is searchable and browseable by topics such as engines, music, around the house, and telecommunications. Clearly written text and actual photographs and diagrams make this site accessible for elementary students and interesting enough for adults. Created and maintained by Marshall Brain (comments@howstuffworks.com).

1344. Microsoft's Encarta Concise Encyclopedia

http://encarta.msn.com

The Microsoft Encarta Concise Encyclopedia is an abridged, online version of *Encarta Encyclopedia*. It contains 16,000 articles and more than 2,200 photos, illustrations, maps, charts, and tables. The Schoolhouse contains a collection of lesson plans, topic archives, and information of interest for teachers (in the Teachers' Lounge).

Entertainment

1345. *Entertainment Weekly* Online Magazine

http://www.ew.com/ew/

What's happening in entertainment this week? This magazine reports it all. Look for good film and video reviews, daily news and notes, TV guides for Tonight's TV, and feature stories. Weekly charts cite the top films, TV shows, albums, videos, and books.

1346. Mr. Showbiz

http://mrshowbiz.go.com

Mr. Showbiz, sponsored by ABCNews.com, provides information about stars and celebrities. Daily headlines feature news about actors, actresses, movies, musicians, TV personalities, and athletes. The Movie Reviews section incorporates what's new at the theater as well as video releases, DVDs (digital video discs), critics' picks, and box office statistics. Links to music information provide news, CD reviews, chart statistics, feature stories, and biographies of selected artists, as well as biographies of more than 400 celebrities and stars. Updated daily.

Movies

1347. The Academy of Motion Picture Arts and Sciences

http://www.oscars.org

Information, press releases, and the history of the Oscar are available here. Questions such as "Who is Oscar?" are answered. Information is posted about the first celebration of the Annual Academy Awards, May 16, 1929.

1348. American Film Institute Fan Sites

http://www.afionline.org/corps/links/welcomes/hello.html

With more than 25,000 links, the American Film Institute's directory of film and media claims to be the Internet's largest. The database is searchable and browseable. Links are provided to radio, cinema, news media, and television. Links are also provided to journals and magazines, studios, festivals, actors, research, and more. You'll find movie and sound clips as well as links to cinema and media schools.

1349. Current Movie Reviews

http://mrshowbiz.go.com/reviews/moviereviews/

Weekly reviews are given for new movie releases. This is just one page from the Mr. Showbiz site (http://www.mrshowbiz.com). Movie Reviews highlights what's new at the theater as well as video releases, DVDs (digital video discs), critics' picks, and box office statistics. There is also a searchable database of movie reviews. Students may search by film title, star, or director.

1350. The Internet Movie Database

http://www.imdb.com

Self-proclaimed as the largest database of movie information freely available online, the Internet Movie Database has more than 100,000 movies and 1.5 million filmography entries—and continues to expand. The goal of the creators is to capture any and all information associated with movies from across the world, starting with the earliest cinema, going through to the very latest releases and even movies still in production. It covers filmographies for all professions in the industry; plot summaries; character names; movie ratings; year of release; running times; movie trivia; quotes; goofs; soundtracks; personal trivia; alternative names; certificates; color information; country of production; genres; production companies; distributors; special effects companies; sound mix; reference literature; filming locations; sequel/remake information; release dates; advertising tag lines; detailed technical data;

alternative versions; laserdisc availability; languages; reviews; links to official studio pages, fan pages, and image and multimedia archives; direct purchase links for movies and associated merchandise; box office grosses; movie posters; and Academy Award information. A complete history of the Oscars is available for the 1927 films to the present.

Sports

See also "Sports: Participation and Coaching" (entries 1012–1023).

1351. BlackBaseball's Negro Baseball Leagues

http://www.blackbaseball.com

Learn about the origins of the Negro Baseball Leagues. Find out what the leagues were, why they were founded, and why they no longer exist, all in the History and Introduction section. The Players section has photos and sound clips of players who are in the National Baseball Hall of Fame, as well as those who aren't but should be. There is a listing of the teams of the era and a comprehensive listing of the best books on the subject. An additional literature tie-in is *Black Diamond: The Story of the Negro Baseball Leagues* (Scholastic, 1994) by Patricia C. McKissack and Frederick McKissack, Jr. Links are provided to more information for further research and other Web sites with information on the Negro Leagues. The Negro Leagues at (blackbaseball.com) is edited by James A. Riley, Director of Research at the Negro Leagues Baseball Museum in Kansas City, Missouri. He is the author of many books on the subject, including *The Negro Leagues* (Chelsea House, 1996) in the African-American Achievers series. The Webmaster's e-mail address is (webmaster@blackbaseball.com).

1352. ESPNET SportsZone News

http://espn.go.com

Use ESPNET SportsZone to find news about major sports. Pointers are provided to the top sports news stories, feature stories, and scores. Other features include the ability to select a specific sport for more in-depth coverage, participate in live chats on specific sports, and submit questions to ESPN's Up Close interview program. Links are provided to the ESPN Studios for up-to-the-minute program updates, TV listings, and network releases. Zoned Out! offers This Date in Sports History, news, and yesterday's stories from the Zone. Trivia and Quick Facts complete Zoned Out!

1353. Women's National Basketball Association

http://www.wnba.com

Updated daily, this official site of the Women's National Basketball Association features news, the players, scores and stats, schedules, and information about the WNBA. Check it out to find out what's what in women's basketball.

Sports Journals and Magazines

1354. *Sports Illustrated for Kids Online*

http://www.sikids.com

The online version of *Sports Illustrated for Kids* contains some of the same articles as the print version, and more. Kids can enter their birth date to find out the names of sport personalities who share their birthday. The SIFK Library has article archives. Readers are encouraged to submit their sports art and questions by e-mail.

1355. *Sports Illustrated Online*

http://CNNSI.com

Sports Illustrated Online offers some of the same features as the print version, and more. A link to the swimsuit issue has all the photos selected for the magazine as well as additional ones. It's easy to locate news, scores, statistics, and photos. *SI Online* is searchable. Archives of back issues are available.

Television

See also "News Sources" (entries 1405–1407) for news related television programming such as CNN.

1356. *Cable in the Classroom*

http://www.ciconline.com

The online version of *Cable in the Classroom* magazine is available and is searchable. Each month's issue features more than 540 hours of commercial-free viewing for the classroom. Copyright restrictions are given, and supplementary teacher resource materials are listed.

1357. **CBS**

http://www.cbs.com

The Columbia Broadcasting System provides information about its television programming as well as *CBS News* (http://cbsnews.cbs.com). Information is accessible for primetime, daytime, late night, and specials. There is a link to programming for children.

1358. **Discovery Channel Online**

http://www.discovery.com

The Discovery Channel home page encourages teachers, learners, and educational partners to use Discovery Channel programs in new ways. News stories about relevant and current topics contain links to additional information. Be sure to see Discovery Channel School (http://school.discovery.com) for information for teachers, students, and parents and Discovery Kids (http://www.discoverykids.com) for lots of personalized adventure.

1359. NBC

http://www.nbc.com

The National Broadcasting Company provides news and complementary information for prime-time viewing. Television shows are listed in alphabetical order and are also listed as daytime, primetime, and late night. A special teens section gives previews and provides information of interest to the teenage viewing audience. NBC news and sports are located at this link (http://www.nbc.com/msnbc/news/).

1360. Public Broadcasting Service

http://www.pbs.org

In addition to information about regular programming, look for PBS Kids for access to home pages of popular kids' programming on PBS, such as *Arthur, Barney, Mister Rogers, Teletubbies,* and *Theodore Tugboat.* Teacher Source provides teachers with lesson plans and activities, a listing of television programs by subject area, previews of future programming, and information about copyright. Links are provided to ways to teach with technology, including tutorials and Web-based lessons.

1361. Ultimate TV

http://www.ultimatetv.com

Find out what's on TV tonight on American channels, as well as channels around the world. Daily television listings are posted along with TV news and feature stories.

Homework Web Pages

1362. B. J. Pinchbeck's Homework Helper

http://school.discovery.com/students/homeworkhelp/bjpinchbeck/

Pinchbeck's Homework Helper is a collection of more than 570 Internet resources categorized by topic. In addition to general subject areas, links can be found for Playtime, News and Current Events, Reference, and Computer Science and the Internet. Created and maintained by B. J. Pinchbeck (BJPinchbeck@discoveryschool.com).

1363. Homework Central

http://www.homeworkcentral.com
or
http://www.homeworkheaven.com

Thousands of links are divided by school subjects to make homework an easier task. Study collections are divided into three age categories: grades 1–6, middle and high school, and college and beyond. Teachers Resources has links to lesson plans by subject and grade, professional resources, and Web instructions. The Parents Only section has links to articles and resources on child development, studying at home, and health and family issues.

Homework Central provides two free weekly newsletters delivered via e-mail. *Top 8* is sent out on Mondays with a list of the best, newly discovered, academic sites. *Weekend on the Web*

(*W.O.W.*) is sent by e-mail every Friday. *W.O.W.* is a list of the most entertaining and educational sites. All sites are selected and annotated by Homework Central editors. To subscribe to either newsletter or both, fill out the online form located at (http://www.homeworkcentral.com/top8/vsl_top8_list.asp).

1364. Study Web
http://www.studyweb.com

Study Web is a place where students can find links for curriculum-based research. Students can browse or search through more than 53,000 quality URLs. Each link has a brief annotation, an approximate grade-level designation, and an evaluation of visual content, using a scale of one to four apples.

Internet

Awards

1365. The Webby Awards
http://www.webbyawards.com

Move over Oscars and Tonys—here come the Webbies! The 1999 Webby Awards were presented on March 18, 1999, in San Francisco, California. Awards are given for 22 categories such as education, news, fashion, science, and weird. A total of 110 awards constitute the Best Sites of the Year, but only 22 are the best of the best. For 1999, Journey North (entry 674) was the best of the best in the Education category, along with Kathy Schrock's Guide for Educators (entry 1456), The Global Schoolhouse (entry 10), The Math Forum (entry 590), and Web66 (entry 16). For archives of Best Sites of the Year, see (http://www.webbyawards.com/nominees/archives.html). Webby Award nominees and winners are chosen by the distinguished International Academy of Digital Arts and Sciences.

Citing Electronic Sources

1366. Citing Internet Addresses
http://www.connectedteacher.com/newsletter/citeintres.asp

"Citing Internet Addresses: How Students Should Reference Online Sources in Their Bibliographies" is an updated electronic version of an article that appeared in the March 1996 issue of *Classroom Connect*. This excellent article addresses how to cite information from electronic mail, Gopher, FTP, telnet, WWW, USENET newsgroups, and IRC (Internet Relay Chat), as well as graphics, sounds, and video clips. Explanations are succinct and clearly understandable and are illustrated with examples. With permission, printouts of this how-to guide for referencing online sources in student bibliographies may be posted in classrooms and at school computers to aid students in correctly citing online resources in their research work.

1367. *The Columbia Guide to Online Style*
http://www.columbia.edu/cu/cup/cgos/idx_basic.html

Janice R. Walker (jwalker@chuma.cas.usf.edu), a professor of English at the University of South Florida, and Todd Taylor have written a guide to citing electronic sources, *The Columbia Guide to Online Style*. This guide addresses how to cite FTP sites; WWW sites; telnet sites;

Gopher sites; e-mail; listservs; newsgroups; synchronous communications, such as MOOs (multiuser object-oriented systems), MUDs (multiuser dimension/domain/dungeon), and IRCs (Internet Relay Chat); and so on. See also MLA Style at (http://www.mla.org/style/sources.htm).

E-mail Addresses

1368. The Electronic Activist

http://gemini.berkshire.net/~ifas/activist/

The Electronic Activist lists e-mail addresses for the U.S. president, U.S. vice president, U.S. representatives and senators, state elected officials, media, and some governmental committees and groups. Use this list when you would like to write a letter (e-mail message) to an elected official.

1369. Yahoo! People Search

http://people.yahoo.com

The Yahoo! People Search directory is a free online search and listing service that includes more than 10 million e-mail addresses and more than 100 million names for U.S. residential telephones. For both the e-mail directory and the telephone directory, search parameters include first and last names, street, city, and state to help narrow the search. Other directories are available, including national and state governments and some international listings.

Finding Tools for Discussion Groups and Newsgroups

1370. Diane K. Kovacs Directory of Scholarly and Professional Discussion Lists

http://www.n2h2.com/KOVACS/

Diane K. Kovacs has compiled a directory of scholarly and professional e-conferences. Discussion groups are browseable through subject/category and alphabetical lists. The directory is searchable. The Webmaster is Diane K. Kovacs (diane@kovacs.com).

1371. Tile.Net: Finding Listserv Discussion Groups

http://www.tile.net/listserv/

Listserv discussion groups are listed alphabetically by description, by name, and by subject. The database is searchable. This WWW site is a reference to all the listserv discussion groups on the Internet. It contains only discussion groups run by listserv software, not discussion groups run by majordomo, listproc, or other list-management software.

Directories, Search Engines, and Other Internet Search Tools

Directories

1372. Google

http://www.google.com

Google is a relatively new search directory and search engine that organizes search results into hierarchical categories. Browsing is also easy by categories. Google's search engine was named after the mathematical term "googol," which stands for 10^{100} (1 followed by 100 ze-roes). As a different approach to searching the Web, Google analyzes the words around the link to make sure they are relevant to the original query, and ranks search results by how often other pages on the Web link to the page using that term. For most search engines, one must remember to put quotation marks at the beginning and the end to have a sequence of words treated as one phrase (e.g., "Grand Cayman Islands") . With Google, phrase searching is auto-matic. However, the hierarchical categories in Google are not as deep or thorough as those of Yahoo! For example, Google lists the Grand Cayman Islands as Regional Caribbean Cayman Is-lands and Yahoo! lists the Grand Cayman Islands as Regional Countries United Kingdom De-pendent Areas Cayman Islands. The authors and managers of this database and search engine are Larry Page (larry@google.com) and Sergey Brin (sergey@google.com).

1373. Yahoo!

http://www.yahoo.com [Home Page]
or
http://search.yahoo.com/search/options/ [Optional Search Page]

If you are tired of using a search engine only to receive irrelevant hits, use Yahoo! (Yet An-other Hierarchically Officious Oracle of WWW sites). Yahoo! makes searching easy and your search results will be returned in organized categories and subject headings.

Yahoo! is a massive, keyword-searchable database of resources on the Web. Updated daily, it is a hierarchical hotlist that primarily targets HTML documents, but other URLs are also selec-tively included. Use Yahoo!'s optional page (http://search.yahoo.com/search/options) for easy advanced keyword searching, such as limiting searches to a person's name, specifying ex-act phrases without using quotation marks, using multiple keywords, using wild cards (*) to extend a word or when you are unsure of the spelling of a word, and excluding or including in-formation that must appear in the result documents (e.g., (bridges -contractors) or (sting +police)). These capabilities are extremely helpful in finding specific information on the Internet. Yahoo! also automatically transfers search queries to various search engines, such as AltaVista, Excite, and HotBot, if further searching is desired.

Yahoo!'s home page offers a short list of WWW sites divided into broad categories for easy ac-cess and browsing, as well as separately featured links to stock quotes, maps, sports scores, the current day's top news stories and weather forecasts, and lists to both New and Cool Web sites. From Yahoo!'s home page, you can also access free Yahoo! e-mail and My Yahoo!, a page you can customize to keep track of personal stock holdings, specific news, weather, and more. The authors and managers of this database and search engine are David Filo and Jerry Yang.

Directories for Children

Directories with search-engine capabilities are designed to guide children to selected Web sites that are age- and quality-appropriate for learning and satisfying natural curiosities. Util-izing Internet directories created especially for children represents a more positive approach to searching for information on the Internet than the use of filtering technologies.

1374. Ask Jeeves for Kids

http://www.ajkids.com

Imagine using a search engine that takes you to one and only one Web site that answers your question, instead of 43,256 matches or more. Using natural-language queries, students can type in questions to Ask Jeeves, such as, "How tall is the Empire State Building?" Ask Jeeves for Kids repeats the question for clarification and presents a short list of matched questions. After selecting the closest match, Ask Jeeves for Kids takes the student to one Web site with the appropriate answer. For the question, "Who is the king of Siam?," Ask Jeeves for Kids responds, "Who is the head of state of Thailand?" When the student clicks on that question, Ask Jeeves for Kids provides one Web page with the answer. Ask Jeeves for Kids responds to real kid questions, such as "What's the capital of Vermont?" "Where can I see the flag of Peru?" "How do I use a semicolon?" "Where can I see a map of Russia?" "Where can I hear the national anthem of Canada?" "What does a tuba sound like?" "Where can I learn yo-yo tricks?" Let Jeeves (inspired by the unflappable British servant in the stories of Jeeves and Wooster by P. G. Wodehouse) act as your very own information valet.

1375. KidsClick!

http://sunsite.berkeley.edu/KidsClick!/

KidsClick! was created by a group of librarians at the Ramapo Catskill Library System (RCLS), to address the need for public librarians to guide their young users to valuable and age-appropriate Web sites. KidsClick! contains all the sites listed in the American Library Association's Great Sites!, as well other evaluated and selected Web resources, organized around subjects. Students can access subjects by a letter search or by browsing through topics such as Current Events, Weird & Mysterious, Popular Entertainments, Sports & Recreation, Machines & Transportation, Literature, and Fine Arts. Each Web site in KidsClick! is annotated with a suggested reading level, notes about Web page graphics, and the subject. To find other entries in the same subject, just KidsClick! The Webmaster is Jerry Kuntz (jkuntz@rcls.org), RCLS Electronic Resources Consultant. Funded by a grant under the federal Library Services and Technology Act (LSTA), KidsClick! does not contain commercial advertising banners.

1376. Yahooligans!

http://www.yahooligans.com

Yahooligans! is a searchable and browseable Web directory, just for kids, from Yahoo! The database is structured hierarchically just like Yahoo! but with links to child-oriented "safe" sites. Some of the Yahooligans categories to browse include: Around the Word, with information about countries and history; Art Soup, with information on books and reading as well as the arts; and Science & Oddities, with information about space, animals, and robots. School Bell has more than 220 sites to help children with homework questions. Yahooligans is highly recommended as a search engine for use by elementary students. It is also an excellent database for elementary classroom teachers to consult when looking for Internet resources to integrate into curricular studies.

Internet Search Engines

1377. AltaVista

http://www.altavista.com

AltaVista is the most extensive Internet index, with more than 21 million Web pages. It is very fast and can handle millions of users at once. AltaVista cannot accommodate plain English queries, though. AltaVista uses the same search features as Yahoo! (entry 1373).

1378. Excite

http://www.excite.com

Excite searches Web and Usenet newsgroups. It is a fast search engine with a very large Web content index that returns search results by a percentage ranking system. In theory, this concept makes it much easier to find the search results that most closely match your query.

1379. HotBot

http://www.hotbot.com

HotBot is a fast search engine with a large index. Customized searching and a percentage ranking system allow more accurate searching.

1380. InfoSeek

http://infoseek.go.com

InfoSeek is a search engine with a comprehensive index. InfoSeek accepts plain English queries as well as keywords and phrases. It works well on word searches, especially case-sensitive searches.

1381. Lycos

http://www.lycos.com

Lycos is a search engine that also has a searchable directory. You can use the search engine to search Lycos's comprehensive index or directory. Advanced searching allows the designation of specific types of documents such as FTP files, newsgroups, music, multimedia, and recipes. SearchGuard is a free filter that can be set up for use with Lycos.

1382. WebCrawler

http://webcrawler.com

Part of the WebCrawler project at the University of Washington, WebCrawler searches Web document titles and content, and provides a quick response.

Meta Search Engines

1383. MetaCrawler

http://www.go2net.com/search.html

MetaCrawler links to more than a dozen Internet search engines. Enter your keyword search, and MetaCrawler sends the search to many search engines at the same time.

Guides to Selected Internet Resources

See also the Webby Awards (entry 1365).

1384. In the Limelight

http://www.osu-okmulgee.edu/limelite.htm

Each month, Oklahoma State University at Okmulgee (Oklahoma) highlights outstanding Web sites in the categories of technology, interactive innovations, history, humanities, math and science, communication, social culture, business, information, fun, health, and travel. Sites are annotated, and Web sites from previous months are archived by month for two years.

1385. The WWW Virtual Library

http://vlib.org/Overview.html

The WWW Virtual Library is a subject catalog of Web sites. Subjects are broadly diverse, such as museums, culture, demography and population studies, environment, languages, and medieval studies. These A–Z subjects lead to interesting information, from Aboriginal Studies to the Whale Watching Web.

File Transfer Protocol (FTP) Search Tool

1386. List of Hypertext Archie Servers

http://archie.emnet.co.uk

Archie servers allow you to search FTP sites. This Web site lists the Archie services or gateways on the Web. Form-based Archie services are listed by continent. A list is also provided for those who use browsers that do not support forms.

Language Arts

Online Bookstores

1387. Amazon.com

http://www.amazon.com

Claiming to be the "world's largest bookstore," with more than 3 million titles, Amazon.com's database is searchable by subject keyword, author, and title. Searches may be limited to various categories, such as juvenile. This resource can be used as a *Books in Print* type resource, but is limited to those titles in the Amazon.com database. Also available are reviews, author interviews, and related articles. All titles are discounted by at least 10 percent, with some discounted as much as 40 percent.

Dictionaries and Writing Reference Tools

See also LOGOS Dictionary (entry 291) and "Dictionaries and Glossaries" (entries 219–221).

Dictionaries

1388. Acronym and Abbreviation Dictionary, Searchable

http://www.ucc.ie/info/net/acronyms/index.html

For the purposes of this database, an *acronym* is any string of characters formed from the initial letters (or occasionally from other letters) of several words, regardless of whether the result is pronounceable or not. This is a good way to search for or look up acronyms and abbreviations. You can either enter the acronym and search for the expansion or enter in one of the words in an expansion to find out the acronym or abbreviation. The Webmaster is Peter Flynn (webmaster@www.ucc.ie).

1389. ArtLex

http://www.artlex.com

ArtLex is a dictionary of visual art. More than 2,600 terms are defined, many with pronunciation notes and illustrations. Names of artists and titles of works are not listed as terms. Go to the index to find links to some of the longer articles on topics such as Cubism, Impressionism, Mythology, and Pop Art. Created and maintained by Michael Delahunt (delahunt@artlex.com).

1390. One Look Dictionaries

http://www.onelook.com

Similar to a meta-search engine, One Look Dictionaries allows you to type in a word and search in multiple dictionaries at the same time. Search results tell you in what type of dictionary your term was located, by subject area. For example, your word might be found in automotive terms under Technology, botanical terms under Science, or a phrase-and-fable dictionary under Arts and Humanities. Locates words in 598 dictionaries found online.

1391. The Semantic Rhyming Dictionary

http://www.link.cs.cmu.edu/dougb/rhyme-doc.html

Need help writing poetry, song lyrics, or witticisms? Use this rhyming dictionary to help find a perfect rhyme. Type a word to search the database. A list of rhyming words is returned. Each word in the list is linked to definitions from *Webster's Dictionary*. Searches can be tailored to match a last sound only, find a homophone, or find a synonym.

1392. Voycabulary

http://www.voycabulary.com

Turn an entire Web page or a page of typed text into one where all the words are hyperlinked to definitions. Sound impossible? Not with Voycabulary. You can choose to apply this service using Merriam-Webster's online dictionary, Merriam-Webster's online thesaurus, a medical dictionary, a computer dictionary, and an acronym dictionary. This Web site also acts as a language translator for both Web pages and typed text. Provided by Voyager Info-Systems. Think about using Voycabulary with difficult reading assignments such as Shakespeare's works, technical reports, and foreign languages.

1393. A Web of On-Line Dictionaries

http://www.facstaff.bucknell.edu/rbeard/diction.html

More than 400 dictionaries and thesauri, representing more than 130 different languages, are available from this Web site. Look for multilingual and specialized dictionaries, thesauri, language identifiers and guessers, an index of dictionary indices, and a link to the Web of On-Line Grammars. Robert Beard (http://www.departments.bucknell.edu/russian/index.html), professor at Bucknell University, is the compiler and Webmaster for this site.

1394. ***Webster's Dictionary and Thesaurus,* Searchable**

http://www.m-w.com/netdict.htm

Merriam-Webster's online dictionary is searchable and provides a thesaurus with antonyms and synonyms. If you enter a misspelled word, you are offered some similar words, which may or may not be helpful. For the misspelled word *eclaire*, the list of similar words included: *aglare, eagle ray,* and *Eau Claire.* An added feature is the Word of the Day, which includes a definition, pronunciation guide, example sentence, and a Did You Know? section for added interest. For example, the word *jovial* derives its meaning from the Roman god Jupiter (also called Jove), a "majestic, authoritative type who was the source of happiness."

1395. **Word Central**

http://www.wordcentral.com

Word Central is a fun and interactive place for students to learn about words and the English language. Students can type in a word to search in the Student Dictionary. If they misspell the word, a short list of suggested words appears. Entries are brief and contain a pronunciation guide, part of speech, and short definition. Using a school building theme, students can navigate down hallways to the music room to find a rhyming dictionary and a verse composer. The computer room lets students encode and decode messages. The science lab provides experiments with words. On the first-floor hallway, a daily buzzword is posted. There is a teacher's resource area with suggested lesson plans. Created by Merriam-Webster.

Quotations, Poetry, and Literary Works

1396. ***Bartlett's Familiar Quotations***

http://www.bartleby.com/99/
or
http://www.columbia.edu/acis/bartleby/bartlett/

Familiar Quotations: Passages, Phrases and Proverbs Traced to Their Sources in Ancient and Modern Literature by John Bartlett, ninth edition, published in 1901, is online as a searchable database. The database is searchable by keyword. Access Search Hints to learn about search options; for example, using a comma without a space represents the Boolean OR, and a semicolon without a space represents the Boolean AND. By typing in the keyword *stage*, this author learned that the phrase "All the world's a stage" is from Shakespeare's *As You Like It,* line 194.

1397. **Project Bartleby**

http://www.bartleby.com
or
http://www.columbia.edu/acis/bartleby/

Project Bartleby is a literary site originating from New York City's Columbia University. All works are searchable and keyed by paragraph or verse. Material published at this site is usually out of copyright (published prior to 1920). This site is a premiere online library for poems, books, and reference materials. The full text of Eugene O'Neill's *Beyond the Horizons* is on this

Web site, as is *The Mysterious Affair at Styles* by Agatha Christie, F. Scott Fitzgerald's *This Side of Paradise*, and *The History of the Civil War 1861–1865* by James Ford Rhodes. Look for Einstein's *Theory of Relativity* in the near future. Poetry fans will be able to locate selected poems by Emily Dickinson, T. S. Eliot, Robert Frost, Thomas Hardy, G. M. Hopkins, John Keats, Edna St. Vincent Millay, Carl Sandburg, Siegfried Sassoon, Percy Bysshe Shelley, Walt Whitman, Oscar Wilde, William Wordsworth, and William Butler Yeats. This site includes *Modern British Poetry* edited by Louis Untermeyer, including biographies of the poets. The next big poetry release from Project Bartleby will be the *Oxford Book of English Verse*.

Also included is the full text of *Bartlett's Familiar Quotations* (entry 1396). An ongoing goal of Project Bartleby is the publication of excerpts and complete texts of Pulitzer Prize materials. Steven van Leeuwen is the editor in chief of Project Bartleby (publications@columbia.edu).

Thesauri

1398. *Roget's Thesaurus*, Searchable

http://web.cs.city.ac.uk/text/roget/thesaurus.html

Using a version of the 1911 edition of *Roget's Thesaurus*, this Web site allows full-text searching of one of Project Gutenberg's e-texts. Another online thesaurus with a different search software is located at (http://www.thesaurus.com).

Holidays Around the World

See also Multicultural Resources (entries 1213–1236); The 100th Day of School Web Site (entry 15); and What on Earth Are You Doing for Earth Day? (entry 679).

1399. Celebrate America! Independence Day—July 4

http://henson.austin.apple.com/edres/ccenter/america/celebrate.shtml

Celebrate America! is one of the curricular thematic lesson plan suggestions in Apple Computer Company's K-12 Curriculum Center. Using Independence Day in the United States as a jumping-off point, teachers will find guidelines and suggestions for student activities on presidents, immigration, colonial America, the American Revolution, the Declaration of Independence, and much more. Lists of grade-appropriate Web sites are also available. A great grade 3 Independence Day lesson plan written by Joe Williamson (colusa@yolo.k12.ca.us), Colusa Community School, California, can be found at: (http://score.rims.k12.ca.us/activity/indepday/index.html).

1400. Christmas Around the World

http://christmas.com/worldview/

Click on the world map to find out how Christmas is celebrated in specific countries. (*Note:* Some countries are currently works in progress.) Find out the origins of Christmas and ancient festivals coinciding with Christmas. Learn the name for Christmas in several countries. Find out the legends of Santa Claus around the world and Christmas recipes from different countries. Listen to Christmas carols (.mid files) and sing along with the lyrics, both browseable in alphabetical order. This site is an excellent source for a December holidays unit focused on multiculturalism.

1401. Diversity Calendar

http://www3.kumc.edu/diversity/

The Diversity Calendar was created to foster an environment in which people appreciate, value, and respect diversity in their communities. Holidays can be accessed by month or by type, such as ethnic, religious, national (United States), and other. Each holiday is linked to a historical explanation, most with several paragraphs and in-text links to further information. For example, Presidents' Day is linked to an explanation of its beginning with a law passed in 1968, and links are provided to further information about George Washington and Abraham Lincoln. Religious holidays reflect some of the major holidays associated with Western Christianity, Eastern Orthodox, Islam, Hinduism, and Judaism. This is a wonderful site to find out more about Diwali, Purim, Rosh Hashanah, Kwanzaa, Tet Nguyen Dan, Labor Day, and Valentine's Day. Created and maintained by the Kansas University Medical Center. The Web site administrator is Alisa Lange (alange@kumc.edu), Diversity Coordinator in the Department of Human Resources. See also Holidays on the Net (http://www.holidays.net).

1402. The Worldwide Holiday and Festival Site

http://www.HolidayFestival.com

National and religious holidays are organized through an alphabetical listing of countries. Holiday names and dates are listed for both fixed and moveable holidays (many holidays occur on different dates each year). Holidays are listed by religion, such as Hinduism, Islam, Jainism, Judaism, and Zoroastrianism. Christian holidays are further listed by the three calendars of the Christian faith: the Western, the Orthodox New Calendar, and the Orthodox Old Calendar. The database of holidays is searchable. Links are provided to other calendar and holiday sites. Explanations of holidays are not given. Created and maintained by Brian Prescott- Decie (webmaster@HolidayFestival.com). See also Earth Calendar (http://www.earthcalendar.net).

Libraries

See also "School Libraries on the Web" (entries 1462–1464).

1403. The Internet Public Library

http://www.ipl.org

The lobby of this virtual library is divided into areas such as reference, youth, and librarian services. From the lobby you can also access the exhibit hall, the reading room, or the classroom. Ready reference covers main topic areas and is keyword-searchable. An experimental e-mail form is provided for patrons to use in posting reference questions.

The IPL's Youth Division offers a story hour, Dr. Internet to help with math and science homework, and Ask the Author bulletin boards. Authors Avi, Natalie Babbit, Matt Christopher, Robert Cormier, Lois Lowry, Phyllis Reynolds Naylor, Jill Paton Walsh, Jane Yolen, and Charlotte Zolotow have agreed to answer questions from children. Bookie the Bookworm moderates online discussions by children about books they are reading. There is also a section where children can submit and publish original creative stories.

The virtual public library is hosted by the School of Information and Library Studies at the University of Michigan.

1404. The Michigan Electronic Library (MEL)

http://mel.lib.mi.us/main-index.html

The Michigan Electronic Library (MEL) is a virtual library of Internet resources evaluated and selected by librarians to serve as a comprehensive electronic information tool. MEL includes more than 18,000 resources in 14 major subject areas, and is browseable and keyword-searchable. MEL has a Michigan state focus centered on information about Michigan's government, libraries, schools, and history. Michigan for Kids is designed to help students with their studies about the state. However, most of the information in MEL will be of value to anyone who is interested in finding quality Web sites. The Webmaster's address is (webmaster@mel.org).

News Sources

See also "Television" (entries 1356–1361).

1405. BBC Online

http://www.bbc.co.uk

Look at news from a British perspective by accessing the BBC Online (British Broadcasting Corporation), which incorporates news with a directory of Web sites. Be sure to jump to such categories as Education, History, and Kids (as well as others) to find information to use in the classroom.

1406. CNN Interactive

http://cnn.com

Cable News Network's (CNN) Web site features news information that is updated often throughout the day. News stories are accompanied by photos. Top news articles for the day appear in a special digest section for easy access. Coverage includes the United States, world, sports, entertainment, politics, business, weather, and technology. News stories are archived and the database is searchable. Information about CNN TV is also available.

1407. The News Page

http://www.trib.com/NEWS/

The News Page provides many links to current news resources. Some of the links include:

> Associated Press National and International News
> Today's headlines and world news briefs from Reuters and Clairinet.com
> *Time Daily*
> Local news in the United States and Canada
> European newspapers from most countries (e.g., Russia, Poland, Germany, Great Britain)

Magazines

See also "Education Journals and Magazines" (entries 96–102); "Computer Science Journals and Magazines" (entries 275–282); "Electronic Periodicals for Students" (entries 574–579); *Scientific American* (entry 906); *AIR&SPACE Magazine* (entry 727); *Entertainment Weekly* Online Magazine (entry 1345); "Sports Journals and Magazines" (entries 1354–1355); and "Staying Current" (entries 1494–1508).

See also these Web sites:

American Heritage

http://www.americanheritage.com

Astronomy

http://www.kalmbach.com/astro/astronomy.html

Audubon Online

http://magazine.audubon.org

Discover Magazine

http://www.discover.com/current_issue/index.html

Ebony

http://www.ebony.com

Field & Stream

http://www.fieldandstream.com

Golf

http://www.golfonline.com

Motor Trend Online

http://www.motortrend.com

Mountain Bike

http://www.mountainbike.com

National Geographic

http://www.nationalgeographic.com/media/ngm/index.html

Newsweek.com

http://newsweek.com

Popular Science

http://www.popsci.com

Prevention

http://www.prevention.com

RollingStone.com

http://rollingstone.tunes.com

Runner's World

http://www.runnersworld.com

Science News Online

http://www.sciencenews.org

Seventeen

http://www.seventeen.com

Sky & Telescope

http://www.skypub.com/skytel/skytel.shtml

1408. Fortune

http://www.fortune.com/fortune/

Fortune Magazine's online Web site provides daily news about markets, investing, stocks, and the stock market. Provides a list of the Fortune 500, with links to data and company home pages. Some of the topics in the navigational sidebar include stock indexes, small businesses, business life, and technology.

1409. *LIFE* Magazine

http://www.lifemag.com/Life/

LIFE provides a picture of the day and selected feature stories. This Day in *LIFE* shows *LIFE* covers from the past and gives birthdays and history for the date. Be sure to browse all the *LIFE* covers from 1936 to 1972, the years when *LIFE* was published weekly. *LIFE* has appeared monthly since 1978.

1410. *People* Magazine

http://people.aol.com/people/index.html

People Magazine focuses on personalities and people of interest in the news. Provides daily news, weekly features, and special features, along with photographs. Archives are online beginning with 1995.

1411. *Time* Daily and *Time* Magazine

http://www.time.com/time/daily/

You'll definitely want to bookmark this site for the latest in daily news! *Time* Daily is an excellent resource for the top national and international news stories. A search box accessible on the page allows students to search further in the *Time* Daily archives by using keywords. By using an advanced search feature (http://cgi.pathfinder.com/time/search/index.html), students can expand their searches to *Time* magazine.

Time magazine is also available at this Web site. This Week's *Time* shows the cover and a contents page with links to the full-text cover story and to selected other stories. Approximately 10 stories per issue cover all aspects of the news, even arts and media. In the *Time* magazine archive, color covers of each magazine are presented in chronological order from the current issue back to 1994. Each issue includes the full-text cover story and selected full-text articles.

The Man of the Year (http://cgi.pathfinder.com/time/moy/index.html) has been a special feature of *Time* magazine since Charles Lindbergh was named in 1927. Man of the Year Archives provide a retrospective look at recipients. The cover of *Time* with the picture of the Man of the Year and the accompanying cover story are available for each year beginning with 1927. A scrollable timeline is provided, as is an index to issues by decade. Man of the Year Archives are available at (http://cgi.pathfinder.com/time/special/moy/moypast.html).

1412. *Time for Kids*
http://www.pathfinder.com/TFK/

Time for Kids provides weekly news information for kids from September through May each year. Past issues are archived and are also available online beginning with September 15, 1995. In addition to cover stories and news articles, *Time for Kids* encourages responses from readers via e-mail or U.S. mail in Kids Talk Back. Who's News highlights interesting personalities in the news, and Top 5 features the five top items in a category such as the most popular flower gardens and the youngest singers to have a number-one hit.

1413. *U.S. News & World Report* Online
http://www.usnews.com/usnews/home.htm

Topics listed on the home page include This Week's Issue, News Watch, Washington Connection, News You Can Use, College Fair, Town Hall, and Corporate Links. This Week's Issue online contains the same information as the print version of *U.S. News & World Report*, but does not have a date, so you don't know which issue you are reading online. A small thumbnail picture of the cover appears at the beginning of the story, and the names of the authors appear at the end. Stories are enhanced with color photos. Links are provided to related stories. Sound files are available courtesy of Mutual/NBC Radio.

Newspapers

1414. *AFRO-Americ@'s* Newspapers Home Page
http://www.afroam.org

AFRO-Americ@, the online edition of the African-American Newspapers, Inc., provides news from around the nation of interest to the African American community. The Black History Museum section has a number of interactive exhibits. Students studying African American history will find helpful information in some of the exhibit areas, such as This Is Our War, a compilation of articles written by AFRO correspondents while following African American troops during World War II. Jackie Robinson highlights his struggle to be the first African American in the major leagues. Black Resistance to Slavery in the U.S. focuses on dispelling the myth that all African American slaves were quiet, docile workers. Also, students can find information about the Tuskegee Airmen, the first African American combat pilots; the Black Panther Party; the Million Man March; the Scottsboro Boys; and a look at Black advertising in the 1920s and 1930s, which focused on "Black is not Beautiful." The Culture section has links to all aspects of modern African American culture. *Kids Zone* (entry 575) is a monthly magazine feature with an African focus.

1415. *Los Angeles Times*

http://www.latimes.com

The *Los Angeles Times* has local, national, and international news as well as a searchable database of movie reviews beginning January 1995 to the present. Full-text reviews are searchable by keyword or title, rating, director, producer, cast member, or character name. Browsing the *Los Angeles Times* archives is free, as is printing lists of story citations, including the headline, the first few sentences of the story, the date, author, and length. Other searches, including the display, printing, or downloading of full-text stories (without graphics) are fee-based and require a credit card.

1416. *The New York Times*

http://www.nytimes.com

Although some *New York Times* services are fee-based (such as downloading articles from the archives and subscribing to a clipper service), access to *The New York Times* daily online version is free. The online version has some extremely helpful features. Quick Read Summaries on the Front Page offer summaries of the paper's front-page stories, as well as other selected news stories. If a summary interests you, the full text is just a click away. Full-text articles include the reporter's byline and links to related articles in *The New York Times*. *The New York Times* Books section is available daily, and there is an archive of more than 50,000 *New York Times* book reviews searchable by author and title. Also available are selected first chapters from best-sellers and recently reviewed books, as well as some RealAudio readings by famous authors.

1417. *USA Today*

http://www.usatoday.com

Updated daily, *USA Today Online* provides pictures and full-text news stories in its Front Page, News, Sports, Money, Life, Weather, and Marketplace sections. The current day's news is searchable, as is an archive of past issues. However, there is a per-article fee to download articles from the archive. Top news stories are highlighted along with feature articles on the home page.

1418. **The Wall Street Journal Interactive Edition**

http://interactive.wsj.com

The no-cost version of the online daily edition of *The Wall Street Journal* is a limited edition. Links are provided to a few top news stories, reports, and the Dow Jones Industrial Average at market close on the previous day. Information is also available on careers, personal technology, and travel.

1419. *The Washington Post*

http://www.washingtonpost.com

The Washington Post, a daily newspaper from the nation's capital, provides news about the Washington metro area, as well as national and international news. Daily Book World features news about books and reviews. A business glossary and Federal Job Finder provide helpful information.

Social Studies and Geography

See also "State-by-State Information" (entries 1097–1103) and "Geography" (entries 1307–1323).

Atlases

1420.   3D Atlas Online

http://www.3datlas.com

Provides information about countries of the world with map links, images of country flags, Web links, and glossary terms. Provides different views of Earth from space. The Glossary is interlinked with in-text links. Information provided by The Learning Company, Inc.

1421.   Atlapedia Online

http://www.atlapedia.com

Atlapedia Online contains full-color physical and political maps, as well as key facts and statistics for each individual country of the world.

1422.   Color Landform Atlas of the United States

http://fermi.jhuapl.edu/states/states.html

For each state there are maps showing the satellite image, 1895 state maps showing railroads, black-and-white maps, county maps, and shaded relief maps created from arrays of elevation data. To use any of these maps for a project, first contact Ray Sterner (sterner@ tesla.jhuapl.edu) for permission. Include your educational purpose, name, and e-mail address.

1423.   World Atlas

http://cliffie.nosc.mil/~NATLAS/

The Atlas of the World Web site contains maps of continents and geographical regions as well as individual countries.

CIA World Factbook

1424.   CIA *World Factbook*

http://www.odci.gov/cia/publications/factbook/

Information on all the countries and regions of the world is compiled annually by the Central Intelligence Agency in the *World Factbook*. This online version is divided so that users can access information from an alphabetical listing or an A–Z letter index, as well as by geographical reqion such as North America, Africa, Oceans, and Europe. Reference maps are available. This version of the database is not searchable.

Flags

1425.   Flags of the World

http://fotw.digibel.be/flags/

Flags of the world are listed alphabetically, and searching is available for country flags, U.S. state flags, special flags, and flags of territories. This site has all the Russian Federation flags. In addition to current flags, historical flags are also available. Each flag is presented as a color image. This site is updated frequently.

Calendars and Time

Calendars

See also the Multicultural Calendar (entry 1213) and "Holidays Around the World" (entries 1399–1402).

1426.   Aztec Calendar

http://www.aztecalendar.com

The Aztecs used two different calendars. One calendar, called the *xiuhpohualli*, has 365 days. It describes the days and rituals related to the seasons, and is the agricultural year. The second calendar is the sacred calendar, the *tonalpohualli*, or the day-count, with 260 days. A day (*tonal*) consists of a number and a symbol, or day sign. Each day sign is dedicated to a god. Students can use the calendar calculator to convert any modern calendar date to the corresponding Aztec *tonalpohualli* calendar date. Links are given to Aztec-related information and Mesoamerican calendar sites. Created and maintained by Reneé Voorburg (voorburg@xs4all.nl).

1427.   Education Calendar and WWW Sites

http://home.earthlink.net/~mediadesigns/Calendar.html

The Education Calendar features significant dates and events in history that occurred during the current month. Each date is accompanied by a descriptive entry and a link to a related Web site. For example, for the month of February, links were provided to honor African American History Month, Groundhog Day, the anniversary of the Mexican Constitution, St. Valentine's Day, Susan B. Anthony's birthday, Presidents' Day, and Frederick Douglass Day. The calendar is updated monthly. The Education Calendar is published as a service to the educational community by Media Designs. Robert Rede (mediadesigns@earthlink.net) is the Web creator.

1428.   Perpetual Calendar

http://www.mnsinc.com/utopia/Calendar/Virtual_Calendars.html

Perpetual Calendars are set up so that you are able to choose a 12-month calendar by the first weekday in the year for either a leap year or non-leap year. Calendars can be selected in two formats, three columns across or four columns across. A special holiday calendar shows holidays in the United States and Canada from the present to 2010. For example, in 2010, Thanksgiving Day in the United States will be celebrated on Thursday, November 25. A glossary of time measurement is available to explain terms such as *fortnight* and *millennium*. A seasons charts has dates for the beginning of spring, summer, fall, and winter for the Northern Hemisphere, Southern Hemisphere, and Australia. The Webmaster is Mark J. Smith (AblonDain@ aol.com).

Time

1429. The Directorate of Time, U.S. Naval Observatory
http://tycho.usno.navy.mil

The Directorate of Time is the official source of time used in the United States. Find out the history of U.S. Naval Observatory timekeeping, the times the sun and moon rise and set, and the phases of the moon. Read the list of frequently asked questions. Use the scrollable window to find out times in various cities in the United States, and double-click to find out the time in time zones across the United States. Links are available to world time zones, as well as other time information.

1430. Local Times Around the World
http://www.hilink.com.au/times/

Times in various cities and countries around the world are compared to Greenwich Mean Time.

1431. A Walk Through Time
http://physics.nist.gov/GenInt/Time/time.html

The National Institute of Standards and Technology, an agency of the Technology Administration of the U.S. Department of Commerce, is responsible for A Walk Through Time, a Web site on the history and evolution of time measurement. Journey from prehistoric times and ancient calendars to the earliest clocks, mechanical clocks, and finally to atomic timekeeping. Links are provided to the world's time zones and a bibliography.

1432. World Clock
http://www.timeanddate.com/worldclock/

You will need Netscape 2.0 or higher to view this grid showing the local time in more than 100 cities and places worldwide. This site can be set to update automatically every minute or every five minutes.

Converters

General Converters

1433. Convert It!
http://microimg.com/science/

An easy-to-use conversion table allows students to convert values of length, area, volume, mass, velocity, acceleration, pressure, energy, power, metrology, and liquid or U.S. fluid to find equivalents. For example, a conversion table for length allows conversions of inches, feet, yards, meters, chains, kilometers, and miles. How many inches are there in a mile? How many drams are there in a pint? How many U.S. dry quarts are there in a U.S. bushel? How many kilograms are in a metric ton? Convert It!, sponsored by Micro Images, makes math conversions like these as simple as a click of the mouse.

Currency Converters

1434.   The OANDA Currency Converter

http://www.oanda.com/converter/classic

The OANDA Currency Converter converts 164 different currencies. When you choose a country, all other countries' currencies are converted to the chosen country's equivalent. You can determine the amount to be converted. Rates are updated daily, Monday through Friday, when the market is open.

1435.   The Universal Currency Converter

http://www.xe.net/currency/

The Universal Currency Converter does not convert as many currencies as the OANDA Currency Converter, but it is updated daily and is easy to use. Tables can be generated for most currencies.

Temperature Converters

1436.   WWW Temperature Converter

http://students.washington.edu/kyle/temp.html

The weather station just predicted a high of 30 degrees Celsius/centigrade. Should you wear a coat or a bathing suit? If you need to convert degrees in either Celsius or Fahrenheit, use this handy temperature converter. The converter also converts to kelvins and Reaumur. The Webmaster's address is (kyle@u.washington.edu).

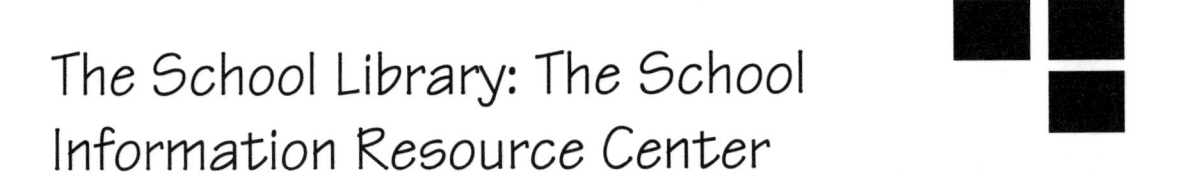

The School Library: The School Information Resource Center

All URL addresses in this chapter are checked and updated monthly. If a link does not work, please refer to the Directory Update Web page located at (http://www.lu.com/lu/irdupdates.html).

The school library media center is the information resource center for the school. This chapter contains information for teacher-librarians, media specialists, and school librarians, but is also of value to K-12 administrators and classroom teachers, computer science lab teachers, and technology coordinators. The resources listed cover, among other things, acceptable use policies (entries 1465–1466), copyright (entries 1467–1470), intellectual freedom and censorship (entries 1471–1474), and technology planning (entries 1491–1493). Those responsible for selecting materials for classroom use and the school library will want to refer to the American Library Association (ALA) School Media Specialist Workbook for Writing Selection Policies (entry 1476). Teachers, school library media specialists, and administrators serving on technology planning committees will want to examine school technology plans posted by the National Center for Technology Planning (entry 1491) for new ideas, solutions to problems, and helpful checklists for planning or revising technology plans.

More and more school library media specialists are assuming the responsibility of developing in-service staff development programs. A new section has been added this year to help media specialists in their roles as technology trainers. Look for online tutorials on desktop publishing, Microsoft Windows, Adobe Photoshop, and Adobe Acrobat Reader (entries 1478–1490). Adobe Acrobat Reader is necessary to download documents from the Internet in PDF (portable document format).

Online discussion groups (entries 1509–1515), such as LM_NET, are tremendous resources for school library media specialists. Working closely together, the members of LM_NET use the power of e-mail to help one another with reference and technical questions and to provide professional support and development.

Web pages created by and for librarians (entries 1453–1461) offer a wealth of organized information. *See* Mr. Moore's Library and Information Seeking Page (entry 1464) for how one media specialist personalizes school Web pages as information resources for specific class assignments and research. KidsConnect (entry 1438) offers a question-and-answer e-mail service for students, teachers, and parents. KidsConnect volunteers respond within 48 hours to curriculum-related questions. These KidsConnect volunteers, mostly media specialists, have done much to humanize the Internet and assist students with their research. To find out how to become a KidsConnect volunteer, *see* the entry for KidsConnect.

There are a number of ways to stay current on new Internet resources appropriate for integration into the curriculum, and on developments in technology. Be sure to look at "Staying Current" (entries 1494–1508).

General Interest

Future of Libraries

1437. Building, Books, and Bytes

http://www.benton.org/Library/Kellogg/buildings.html

Building, Books, and Bytes is a report published in November 1996. It compiles what the general public and library leaders have to say about the future of libraries in the digital age. The entire report is online and easily accessible through a table of contents with links.

Question-and-Answer Services

1438. KidsConnect

http://www.ala.org/ICONN/kidsconn.html
or
E-mail: AskKC@iconnect.syr.edu

KidsConnect is a question-answering, help, and referral service for K-12 students on the Internet. The goal of this free service, sponsored by ICONnect, a technology initiative from the American Association of School Librarians (AASL), a division of the American Library Association, is to help students access and use curriculum-related information available on the Internet effectively and efficiently.

Professional Organizations

1439. American Library Association Home Page

http://www.ala.org

The American Library Association (ALA) home page provides information about the Association with links to its offices; chapters; round tables; and divisions, such as the American Association of School Librarians (AASL), the Association for Library Service to Children (ALSC), and the Young Adult Library Services Association (YALSA). Hot Topics in the News focuses on current issues and news affecting the library community. The Events section contains information on conferences and library promotional events. Other areas of interest include Library Advocacy and Support, Education and Employment, the ALA Bookstore and Graphics Shop, and Membership.

1440. American Association of School Librarians

http://www.ala.org/aasl/

The American Association of School Librarians is a division of ALA (the American Library Association). AASL is interested in the general improvement and extension of library media services for children and young people. Information is available about the division, membership, and publications. Links are provided to AASL programs, ICONnect, Count on Reading, and the National Library Power Program.

1441.   International Federation of Library Associations and Institutions (IFLA)

http://www.ifla.org

IFLA is a worldwide organization created to provide librarians around the world with a forum for exchanging ideas, promoting international cooperation, and fostering research and development in all fields of library activity. Founded in 1927, IFLA represents members in more than 143 countries around the world. The IFLA Journal is published six times a year, and articles are online in .pdf format. The membership database is searchable. Find out more about activities, services, membership, and annual conferences at this Web site.

To join the IFLA list:

E-mail: **listserv@infoserv.nlc.bnc.ca**
Instructions: On the first line of the body of the message, type:
subscribe IFLA-L [your first name and last name]

Lesson Plans

1442.   Lesson Plans and Teaching Activities for School Librarians

http://www.libertynet.org/lion/lessons.html

LION (Librarians Information Online Network) provides links to library and information skills curriculum documents and related books and periodicals, as well as to lesson plans and activities designed for use in the school library. Links are annotated and are applicable for elementary, middle, and senior high school. Most lesson plans are written and shared by practicing school librarians; some are written and compiled by university professors. There is a list of library curriculum books and periodicals, with links to publishers and individual publications. The link to *School Library Media Activities Monthly* leads to more than 40 lesson plans previously published in this periodical. To submit additions to this collection, e-mail (lion@libertynet.org).

Library Service to Children and Young Adults

See also "Children's and Young Adult Literature: General Resources" (entries 486–492); "Multicultural Children's Literature" (entries 493–499); and "Book Reviews and Book Discussions" (entries 500–501).

Authors, Illustrators, and Guides to Children's Literature

See also "Favorite Children's Authors and Illustrators" (entries 502–522).

1443.   Children's Authors and Illustrators, and Their Books

http://www.acs.ucalgary.ca/~dkbrown/authors.html

Authors and illustrators are listed alphabetically. Information is also available on series books, folklore, myths, and legends. Links are provided to other Internet sites with author and illustrator information.

1444. *Children's Literature: A Guide to Criticism*

http://www.unm.edu/~lhendr/

Children's Literature: A Guide to Criticism, written by Linnea Hendrickson (G. K. Hall/Macmillan, 1987), is an annotated bibliography that draws together significant articles, books, and dissertations on children's literature criticism. Compiled from a wide variety of popular and scholarly sources, this reference work is now online as well as in print. Both Part A, Authors and Their Works, and Part B, Subjects, Themes and Genres, are keyword-searchable. Questions, comments, and suggestions should be sent to Linnea Hendrickson (lhendr@unm.edu).

Awards and Award-Winning Children's Materials

Caldecott and Newbery Awards

1445. **The Caldecott Medal Home Page**

http://www.ala.org/alsc/caldecott.html

The official American Library Association page for the Randolph Caldecott Medal Winners and Honor Books displays book jackets of the current winners and honor books, along with plot summaries and links to award-winning illustrators. Past medal and honor winners are listed, with some pictures and links. Information is given about the medal and how it is awarded.

1446. **The John Newbery Medal Home Page**

http://www.ala.org/alsc/newbery.html

The official American Library Association page for John Newbery Medal Winners and Honor Books displays book jackets of the current winners and honor books, with summaries and links to authors. A list of previous winners and honor books is available, with some pictures and links to authors. Information is given about the medal and how it is awarded.

Other Book Awards

1447. **Children's Book Awards**

http://www.acs.ucalgary.ca/~dkbrown/awards.html

Children's Book Awards is one of the most comprehensive guides to English-language children's book awards on the Internet. This page from The Children's Literature Web Guide lists children's book awards presented in the United States, Canada, Great Britain, New Zealand, Australia, and internationally.

Notable Web Sites for Children and Young Adults

1448. **ALA's 700+ Great Sites**

http://www.ala.org/parentspage/greatsites/amazing.html

Compiled by the Children and Technology Committee of the Association for Library Service to Children, a division of the American Library Association, 700+ Great Sites is self-proclaimed as a recommended and annotated collection of "amazing, spectacular, mysterious, colorful Web sites for kids (preschool to age 14) and the adults that care about them." Some of the categories include Arts and Entertainment, Literature and Language, People Past and Present, Planet Earth and Beyond, and Science and Technology.

1449. The Librarians' Guide to Cyberspace for Parents and Kids, 50+ Great Sites

http://www.ala.org/parentspage/greatsites/guide.html

Parents will appreciate this Web guide from the American Library Association. Addressed to parents, there is an introduction, definition of terms, safety tips, and an explanation of selection criteria as to what makes a great Web site. Parents are provided with an e-mail address and sources of additional information, including how to contact KidsConnect (entry 1438), an online question-and-answer service for homework questions. The recommended and annotated links to 50+ Sites for Parents and Kids (preschool to elementary) were evaluated and chosen as the best by professional librarians using selection criteria specifically for Web sites.

1450. OH! Kids

http://www.oplin.lib.oh.us/products/oks/

From the home page of the Ohio Public Library Information Network (OPLIN), select OH! Kids. OH! Kids is a collection of educational, fun, and safe Web sites, divided by age group: WebTots (3–5), WebKids (6–9), WebKidsToo (10–13), and WebTeens (14–17). Other pages are arranged by subject. Nifty Places to Visit allows kids to explore sites on the Internet. Stuff to Do contains lots of links for recreational fun. Subjects contains links to homework help. Resources is a collection of links especially for parents, teachers, and librarians. Sites are chosen by Ohio public librarians, and selections change often. The Webmaster's address is (webmaster@ oplin.lib.oh.us).

1451. "On-Lion" for Kids

http://www.nypl.org/branch/kids/

The New York Public Library (NYPL) branch libraries have created a Web site for kids, filled with links to recommended reading, authors, and favorite characters from children's books. Other categories of links include People & Places, Science & Technology, Arts & Games, Holidays & Celebrations, Magazines, and Sports. Find out the adventures of the real Winnie-the-Pooh who "lives" at the Central Children's Room in the Donnell Library Center. Links are provided to Teen Link at the NYPL and to interesting Web sites about New York City. Parents and teachers are provided their own set of links to selected Web sites.

1452. Teen Hoopla

http://www.ala.org/teenhoopla/main.html

Teen Hoopla is an Internet guide for teens aged 12 to 18, selected by members of the Young Adult Library Services Association (YALSA) of the American Library Association. Topical categories include Life; Internet; Homework; Arts and Entertainment; Books, Comics, and Authors; Sports; Library Sites; and Activism. Teens are encouraged to submit book reviews and recommend sites to add to the Teen Hoopla links collection.

Internet Resources

Web Pages for and by School Librarians

1453. The Best Information on the Net (BIOTN)

http://www.sau.edu/CWIS/Internet/Wild/index.htm

Easy-to-access, Best Information on the Net is divided into 14 categories. Of interest are Neat New Stuff We Found This Week, Disabilities Resources, Picture Sources, and Hot Paper Topics. Information is also browseable by subject. Maintained by Marylaine Block (mblock@saunix. sau.edu), librarian at St. Ambrose University, Davenport, Iowa.

1454. Canadian Teacher-Librarians' Resource Pages

http://www3.sympatico.ca/alanbrown/resource.htm

Books, books, books! The two focuses of this Web site are children's books and reading and Canadian Internet resources of interest to elementary teacher-librarians. Look for a list of Canadian children's authors and illustrators maintained by the National Library of Canada, as well as individual Web pages of Canadian authors. Find out more about Canadian book awards, such as the Red Cedar, the Silver Birch, the Red Maple, and the Canadian Library Association Awards for Best Illustrations, Children's Book, and Young Adult Book. A link is provided to an annual listing by the National Library of Canada of all Canadian children's book award winners, as part of a national program to promote reading known as "Read Up On It." Created and updated quarterly by Alan L. Brown (alanbrown@sympatico.ca), teacher-librarian at Havenwood Public School in Mississauga, Ontario, Canada.

1455. El Dorado County Library: What's Hot on the Internet This Week

http://www.eldoradolibrary.org/thisweek.htm

Each week, the librarians at El Dorado County Library (Placerville, California) post approximately 20 to 25 recommended Web sites. There is an archive of past recommendations. Each recommendation is annotated and assigned a subject area.

1456. Kathy Schrock's Guide for Educators

http://school.discovery.com/schrockguide/index.html

Kathy Schrock's Guide for Educators is a classified list of sites on the Internet found to be useful for enhancing curriculum and teacher professional growth. Find out more about search engines, subject directories, and how to evaluate Web pages. Some of the online PowerPoint presentations include Internet for Beginners, Creating a Content-Rich Homepage for Your School, and WebQuests in Our Future—A Teacher's Role in Cyberspace. Kathy Schrock, MLS (kschrock@capecod.net), is the technology coordinator for Dennis-Yarmouth Regional School District in South Yarmouth, Massachusetts.

1457. Librarians and Library Science

http://librarians.about.com/jobs/librarians/

Updated regularly, this guide highlights Web resources related to libraries and library science. It also maintains a list of Internet links organized by categories such as academic libraries, public libraries, publications, reference, research, schools of library science, and K-12 Media Centers. The Web editor for this About.com site is Tim Wojcik (librarians.guide@about.com).

1458. Librarians' Index to the Internet

http://lii.org

The Librarians' Index to the Internet is a searchable, annotated subject directory of more than 6,000 Internet resources selected and evaluated by librarians for their usefulness to users of public libraries. The database can be searched by keywords, subjects, titles, descriptions, links, and advanced searching. The database is also browseable. Originally created by Carole Leita (leita@lii.org) at the Berkeley Public Library, Berkeley, California, and now located at Berkeley SunSITE and maintained by an indexing team of more than 95 California librarians.

1459. LION

http://www.libertynet.org/lion/

LION (Librarians Information Online Network) is sponsored by Library Services of the School District of Philadelphia as an information resource for school librarians in Philadelphia and throughout the nation. The LION webmaster is Ken Garland, catalog assistant, Library Technical Services, School District of Philadelphia, Pennsylvania.

1460. School Librarian Web Pages

http://www.cusd.chico.k12.ca.us/~pmilbury/lib.html

Peter Milbury, library media teacher at Chico High School in Chico, California, and cofounder and moderator of LM_NET, has created a Web site that features a collection of Web pages created or maintained by school librarians. Explore different categories of Web pages. Some Web pages have been designed for school libraries; others are for K-12 schools but are maintained by librarians. The Curriculum/School-Related Pages maintained by K-12 librarians and the personal Web pages of K-12 librarians all provide rich resources. This site also has links to information about creating Web sites, professional association pages, other collections of K-12 school library Web sites, and K-12 schools on the Web. School librarians with Web pages not listed are invited to add to this collection. Information on how to submit a Web site is available. Make sure your page is a registered School Librarian Web Page. Maintained by Peter Milbury (pmilbury@cusd.chico.k12.ca.us).

1461. School Library Hot Spots

http://www.assd.winnipeg.mb.ca/infozone/hotspots.html

This excellent collection of links related to school libraries is organized by topics such as instruction, reference, literature, Web awareness, materials sources and reviews, and recommended library sites. The Info Zone is a research skills site intended primarily for middle and senior high school students. Students are introduced to research as a journey of six steps:

wondering about something, seeking information, choosing information, connecting useful information, producing information, and judging the process as well as the product. The Virtual Learning Resources Center is designed for senior high school students to find academic librarian-specified sites using a HotBot search engine. Also look for a link to the Internet Library for Librarians, a comprehensive site with more than 2,300 Internet resources. Maintained by the Assiniboine South School Division, Winnipeg, Manitoba, Canada.

School Libraries on the Web

1462. A Directory of School Libraries on the Web

http://www.voicenet.com/~bertland/libs.html

K-12 school library Web pages are listed by country. School library Web pages in the United States are further sorted by state. There is also a listing of library pages maintained by school districts. There is a smaller list of state pages related to library media services. For example, the Hawaii Department of Education has a page that states the materials selection policy for school library instructional centers. A Resources for Librarians page lists Internet resources on topics of interest to librarians: acceptable use policies, Web page design and development, Web page policies, and current awareness sites. To list your own school library page, e-mail Linda Bertland (bertland@voicenet.com), librarian at Stetson Middle School, Philadelphia, Pennsylvania.

1463. Internet School Library Media Center

http://falcon.jmu.edu/~ramseyil/index.html

The Internet School Library Media Center (ISLMC) has organized information into 25 different categories. Under Selection Tools, look for reviewing sources for nonprint media and books. All curricula are represented; Language Arts resources are available for both elementary and secondary levels. Maintained by Inez Ramsey (ramseyil@jmu.edu), with the library science program at James Madison University in Harrisonburg, Virginia.

1464. Mr. Moore's Library and Information Seeking Page

http://www.hcs.K12.sc.us/high/nmbh/infolink.htm

More than 40 categories of information are alphabetically organized in an easy-to-access table format, allowing teachers and students to quickly link to more than 1,100 Internet resources selected specifically to enrich and enhance the curriculum being taught at North Myrtle Beach High School (NMBHS). These links also benefit the entire school community by providing information for parents and staff. In addition to general curriculum links, there are links to the SAT test and preparation, specific events at NMBHS such as Spirit Week, and special curriculum content links for individual classes at NMBHS (writing projects and research on multiple sclerosis, biographies, states, and nonprofit organizations). Created and maintained by Frank Moore (fmoore@sccoast.net), librarian at North Myrtle Beach High School (North Myrtle Beach, South Carolina) and KidsConnect volunteer.

Policies

Acceptable Use Governing Internet Access

1465. Acceptable Use Policies Compiled by WLMA

http://www.wlma.org/libint/aups.htm

The Washington Library Media Association (WLMA) maintains a list of links to acceptable use policies governing student Internet use. Links are provided to the Armadillo Web Server in Texas, TIES in Minnesota, the Global School Network, and the state of Indiana. See also (ftp://ftp.classroom.net/Classroom-Connect/aup-faq.txt) for FAQs on acceptable use policies in K-12 and a template to use to create one.

1466. Hot Links to Learning: Legal and Ethical Issues

http://www.ala.org/aasl/learning/hotlinks/legallinks.html

The American Association of School Librarians has created a Web site focused on acceptable use policies reflecting intellectual freedom rather than restricting student access to information. What is acceptable and unacceptable use of Internet resources? Sample acceptable use policies from schools and school districts around the United States are posted for use as models. Information is also available about the Internet Filter Assessment Project.

Copyright Laws and Issues

See also copyright as it applies to music (entry 172) and computer software (entry 210).

1467. 10 Big Myths About Copyright Explained

10 Myths:
http://www.templetons.com/brad/copymyths.html
The Quiz:
http://www.cyberbee.com/copyrtqz.html

Read 10 Big Myths About Copyright Explained, written by Brad Templeton, to find answers to some of the common myths about copyright as it applies to Internet resources. Find out why this is a myth: "If it doesn't have a copyright notice, it's not copyrighted." After reading about all 10 myths, test your copyright knowledge by taking a true/false quiz. As a self-check, answers to the quiz are provided. See also Copyright References (http://www.cyberbee.com/copyrtref.html) for a bibliography of resources on copyright and copyright issues.

1468. Copyright for Educators

http://falcon.jmu.edu/~ramseyil/copy.htm

The Internet School Library Media Center (entry 1463) provides a copyright page for educators with a list of Internet resources about copyright issues. Find out the answers to questions such as "What is fair use?" Especially helpful is the FAQs section. It answers questions such as "What is copyright?" and "Where should copyright notices be placed?" From the Library of Congress, find out What's New. The U.S. Copyright Office provides a guideline for reproduction of copyrighted books, periodicals, and music.

1469. **Fair Use Guidelines for Educational Multimedia**

http://www.libraries.psu.edu/mtss/fairuse/default.html

What is fair use as applied to educational multimedia? The nonlegislative report adopted September 27, 1996, by the Subcommittee on Courts and Intellectual Property Committee on the Judiciary, U.S. House of Representatives, is available online in its entirety. Though only the courts can authoritatively determine whether a particular use is fair use, these guidelines are designed to help clarify copyright law as it applies to students producing their own educational multimedia projects for a specific course and to educators who are incorporating portions of lawfully acquired copyrighted works when producing their own educational multimedia programs for their own teaching tools in support of curriculum-based instructional activities at educational institutions.

1470. **Tell It to the Judge: A Copyright Quiz for Educators**

http://www.news.com/Quiz/Entry/

Take this online interactive quiz to test your knowledge of basic copyright law. How would you answer these questions: "If I give credit, am I still infringing on a copyright?" "Is there anything that I can post to the Web that I did not create myself?" This copyright quiz was written by Jane Black (janeb@cnet.com) of Cnet, Inc., publishers of *News.Com* (http://www.news.com), an online tech news magazine.

Intellectual Freedom and Censorship

1471. **ALA's Banned Books Week**

http://www.ala.org/bbooks/

The American Library Association annually celebrates the freedom to read during its Banned Books Awareness Week. This site gives the background story and a list of the previous year's most challenged books.

1472. **ALA's Office for Intellectual Freedom**

http://www.ala.org/oif.html

The Office for Intellectual Freedom is charged with implementing ALA policies concerning the concept of intellectual freedom as embodied in the Library Bill of Rights, the American Library Association's basic policy on free access to libraries and library materials. The goal of the office is to educate librarians and the general public about the nature and importance of intellectual freedom in libraries. From this page you can link to the Freedom to Read Foundation, the Library Bill of Rights, and past issues of the *Intellectual Freedom Action News*, a newsletter. There is an FAQs section on Libraries and the Communications Decency Act: What You Should Know, and information about the ALA-led challenge to the Communications Decency Act.

1473. **Banned Books and Censorship Resources**

http://www.georgesuttle.com/censorship/index.shtml

Censorship resources are divided into six categories for easy access to this comprehensive collection of online resources. Book censorship, bans, and challenges are differentiated from censorship, bans, and challenges in other media, including the Internet, music and recordings, the arts, and television and radio. Links are provided to selected court decisions and organizations, such as the American Civil Liberties Union and the American Communication Association. Look for extensive information from general censorship resources, as well as resources linked to U.S. laws, specifically the First Amendment. Maintained by George Suttle (George@GeorgeSuttle.com).

1474. **Bonfire of Liberties: Censorship of the Humanities**

http://www.humanities-interactive.org/bonfireindex.html

The bonfire was a very efficient form of censorship in an age when books were handwritten and only a few copies existed. Today, censors practice other equally effective methods. This image-rich exhibition explores censorship throughout history, including a decree from Pope Justinian in A.D. 553 that forbade all Bibles except those in Latin and Greek, and a 1987 federal order by U.S. District Judge W. Brevard Hand that banned 45 texts from Alabama classrooms on the ground that they "promoted a godless humanist system of beliefs." Some of the exhibition areas visitors can link to include In Our Image, pointing out the common practice by 18th- and 19th-century curators of adding fig leaves and draperies to nude statues and paintings for modesty, and Much Ado About Drama, highlighting dramatic productions that have been censored, such as *Lysistrata* by Aristophanes, banned in A.D. 66 for antiwar sentiment, banned in the United States in 1955 for indecency, and banned in Greece in 1967 by the military dictatorship. Shakespeare is categorized as a Dangerous Writer. *Macbeth* has been censored for the opening incantation of the witches, and literature textbooks published for schools that include *Romeo and Juliet* are routinely expurgated, without any indication that lines have been omitted. The classic *Romeo and Juliet* movie directed by Franco Zeffirelli (1968) has been banned in schools because it "romanticizes teen-age suicide," "contains nudity," "has no suitable role models," and "encourages drug use." Restrictions in Wonderland contains information about censorship of children's books, including *Alice in Wonderland, Cinderella, A Wrinkle in Time,* and books written by Judy Blume. A topical outline with links provides easy navigation through the exhibition. Bonfire of Liberties is part of the Humanities Interactive series produced by the Texas Humanities Resource Center.

Materials Selection

1475. **Evaluating Web Resources**

http://www2.widener.edu/Wolfgram-Memorial-Library/webeval.htm

Why is it necessary to evaluate information on the Internet? Because anyone can and probably will put anything on a Web server. Before selecting online resource materials, students, educators, and parents need to satisfactorily answer questions such as: Who is the author? Are the facts accurate? Does the author have a bias? Is the information biased? What is the author's purpose?

The five traditional criteria for print evaluation (accuracy, authority, objectivity, currency, and coverage) can also be applied to Web pages. This Web site provides teaching materials on evaluating the information content of Web resources. It includes a PowerPoint presentation and a bibliography of teaching materials on applying critical-thinking techniques to Web resources. Creators and Webmasters are Jan Alexander (Janet.E.Alexander@widener.edu) and Marsha Tate (Marsha.A.Tate@widener.edu), reference librarians at the Wolfgram Memorial Library of Widener University (Chester, Pennsylvania).

1476. School Media Specialist Workbook for Writing Selection Policies (ALA)

gopher://riceinfo.rice.edu:1170
Path: **Main Menu/More About Armadillo and Other Gophers/Acceptable and Unacceptable Use of Net Resources (K12)/ALA Workbook for Selection Policy Writing**

The American Library Association workbook is excellent for helping to write or update a school library media center's collection development policy, including the selection policy. Every school system should have a comprehensive policy on the selection of instructional materials. It should relate to and include all materials (e.g., textbooks, library books, periodicals, films, filmstrips, videocassettes, records, audiocassettes, CDs, computer software, CD-ROMs, and Internet resources).

A comprehensive policy on the selection of instructional materials will also enable school professionals to rationally explain the school program to the community. Most importantly in a crisis, when a complaint has been made, the use of any materials being objected to can be explained by demonstrating that those materials were selected according to written policy. A good policy for the selection of instructional materials should include basic sections on objectives, responsibility, criteria, procedures for selection, reconsideration of materials, policies on controversial materials, and other special areas of concern to your school or school district.

1477. Selection Criteria for Web Pages: How to Tell if You Are Looking at a Great Web Site

http://www.ala.org/parentspage/greatsites/criteria.html

The Children and Technology Committee of the Association for Library Service to Children (ALSC), a division of the American Library Association, has prepared detailed selection criteria for Web sites. Criteria for evaluating Web sites cover four areas: authorship/sponsorship, purpose, design and stability, and content. This information is very useful for those who need to evaluate Web sites and for those who teach Web page literacy.

Technology

Staff Development and Online Tutorials

See also "Online Tutorials" (entries 239–242), "Tools, Tips, and Templates" for Web page design (entries 258–268), The WebQuest Page (entry 32), Quia! (entry 293), and Filamentality (entry 261).

1478. Acrobat Reader Tutorial

http://w3.aces.uiuc.edu/AIM/scale/tutorials/Acrobat/

There are many PDF (portable document format) documents available on the Web. PDF is a format of Web publishing that replicates an original document's exact look, which is not always possible with HTML (Hypertext Markup Language) documents. PDF documents are not viewable online; they must be downloaded by the user and require Adobe Acrobat Reader to be viewed. This Web page provides a step-by-step tutorial on how to use Acrobat Reader to view PDF documents. For those who do not have this free software, a link is provided to download Acrobat Reader.

1479. Adobe Photoshop

http://desktopPublishing.com/photoshoptips.html

A multitude of Photoshop tips and techniques are provided in the compilation of Internet links. Look for Web pages containing step-by-step procedures for creating professional-looking effects.

1480. Desktop Publishing

http://desktopPublishing.com

Desktop Publishing has reviews on the latest products, as well as tips and techniques on how to publish professional-looking documents from your desktop computer. With more than 5,800 pages on topics ranging from fonts to how to shrink GIFs, this is a comprehensive site for anyone working with desktop publishing. The Webmaster's address is (webmaster@desktopPublishing.com).

1481. Internet Explorer 4.0 Tutorial for Teachers

http://www.actden.com/ie4/index.htm

Mo'Jo invites teachers to join an online tutorial to find out how to use Internet Explorer 4.0 (IE4) in the classroom to make learning more fun and effective. Suggestions are given on how to look for Web sites and customize searches. Find out about favorites, channels, and security zones.

1482. Introduction to Communicator

http://help.netscape.com/products/client/communicator/IntroComm/Introcom.html

After installing Netscape Communicator, try this online handbook, which provides comprehensive information on how to use each of Communicator's components. Step-by-step instructions provide help for setting preferences, setting a home page, working with bookmarks, and creating Web pages using Composer. A hyperlinked table of contents and index make it easy to access specific information.

1483. Learning About Microsoft Excel

http://s9000.furman.edu/DD/labs/Excel/index.html

Microsoft Excel is a popular cross-platform spreadsheet software. Each of the lessons provided introduces a specific Excel capability. Lessons are intended to be used in sequence. Authored by Ken Abernethy (aberneth@s9000.furman.edu) and Tom Allen (allen@s9000.furman.edu).

1484. Learning About Microsoft Word

http://s9000.furman.edu/DD/labs/word/index.html

Lessons and rescues are available for Microsoft Word 6.x for Windows and Macintosh, Microsoft Word 7.x (Office97) for Windows, and Microsoft Word (Office98) for Windows and Macintosh. Lessons are for beginners, intermediate, and advanced, and links are provided to other Internet sites featuring lessons, tutorials, and tips. Authored by Ken Abernethy (aberneth@ s9000.furman.edu) and Tom Allen (allen@s9000.furman.edu).

1485. Learning About PowerPoint

http://s9000.furman.edu/DD/labs/powerpt/index.html

Microsoft PowerPoint is a popular multimedia presentation software application. Lessons have been designed to introduce specific capabilities and are intended to be used in sequence. Authored by Ken Abernethy (aberneth@s9000.furman.edu) and Tom Allen (allen@s9000. furman.edu).

1486. Microsoft Access Tutorials

http://mis.bus.sfu.ca/tutorials/MSAccess/tutorials.html

These Microsoft Access tutorials are in Adobe Acrobat PDF format. You can download them individually or as a set. Created by Michael Brydon (brydon@unixg.ubc.ca).

1487. Microsoft Training and Classroom Resources

http://www.microsoft.com/education/tutorial/

Microsoft provides a list of tutorials to choose from, depending on learning styles, to help learn how to use Microsoft's software products and to integrate their use into the classroom. Look for In and Out of the Classroom practical guides to help teachers, administrators, and students learn how to use Microsoft software. Hands On Tutorials are step-by-step tutorials. Online Tutorials are interactive tutorials.

1488. Netscape Navigator Handbook

http://home.netscape.com/eng/mozilla/3.0/handbook/

Lessons are available on the functionality of Netscape Navigator and how to author pages using Netscape Gold. Look for an in-depth explanation of each menu item and dialog box; the tools for using e-mail, newsgroups, and bookmarks; and a guide to the preference items you can set. An explanation of the elementary concepts of the Internet and an index to terms with definitions are also provided.

1489. Polaris Internet Guide

http://www.provide.net/~bfield/polaris/topframe/frametry.htm
or
http://www.provide.net/~bfield/polaris/topnoframe/contents.htm [no-frames version]

The Polaris Internet Guide is a comprehensive online tutorial covering the basics of data communications, including e-mail, the World Wide Web and Web browsers, Internet chat, file transfer protocol, Gopher, and Usenet. Information on this well-organized Web site can be used as course content for inservice professional development sessions for teachers or to help students and parents learn more about the Internet. The Webmaster is Richard Beddingfield (habedd@southeast.net).

1490. Yahoo! How-To: A Tutorial for Web Surfers

http://howto.yahoo.com

An excellent tutorial for Web surfers, Yahoo! How-To explains how to use Yahoo! (entry 1373). Designed for the novice Internet browser, this site can also be helpful for more experienced surfers. Step-by-step instructions are given on how to customize Yahoo! to retrieve only the information specified by the user. Searching rules, strategies, and tips help users find specific information using the Yahoo! directory. A glossary explains terminology such as *cookie, domain, GIF,* and *emoticons.* There are links to beginner, intermediate, and advanced Web guides. Yahoo! Internet Life Surf School is a user-friendly Web guide to navigating the Net that provides advice on plug-ins. There are also links to beginner, intermediate, and advanced HTML guides.

Technology Plans

1491. National Center for Technology Planning

http://www.nctp.com

Various examples of school technology plans are located on this National Center for Technology Planning Web page. NCTP is a clearinghouse founded in 1992 to facilitate the exchange of information related to technology planning. The goals of NCTP are to collect and disseminate information and to help school districts and other agencies with technology planning.

This NCTP site provides one-stop assistance with planning and writing school technology plans. Information is given about online workshops. More than 100 technology plans are posted at this site, and more are being added. These plans are divided into national technology plans and regional, state, district, city, building-level, and higher-education technology plans.

Available for downloading in Adobe Acrobat format is the Guidebook for Developing Effective Technology Plans, version 2.0. This site was created and is maintained by Dr. Larry S. Anderson (larry@nctp.com).

1492. Technology Planning FAQ

http://www.netc.org/tech_plans/FAQs.html

Frequently asked questions are answered in this site. Find out the answers to questions such as "What is a technology plan?" "Why have a technology plan?" "Who needs to be involved?" "What steps need to be taken?" "What makes a plan successful?" and "Where can I get help with the planning process?" Read these FAQs to find the answers to some of your questions.

1493. Technology Plans

http://www.eduplace.com/links/tech.html

A technology plan offers a vision of how the application of new technologies in a school or district can enhance curriculum, and it details the steps and budget necessary to integrate these applications in the classroom. Houghton Mifflin has compiled an excellent list of links to technology plans written by K-12 schools.

Staying Current

See also "Computer Science Journals and Magazines" (entries 275–282) and "Education Journals and Magazines" (entries 96–102).

1494. The Adventures of CyberBee Web Site

http://www.cyberbee.com

The Adventures of CyberBee is a tie-in page to a regular column in *MultiMedia Schools* magazine, and the CyberBee archives are located on this site. Featured topics include acceptable use, copyright, curriculum integration, citing Internet resources, and tips for Webmasters. This Web site was created and is maintained by Linda C. Joseph (ljoseph@freenet.columbus.oh.us), library media specialist, Columbus Public Schools.

1495. *ASCD Education Bulletin*

http://www.ascd.org/pubs/bulletin/ebullet.html

The *ASCD Education Bulletin* is a monthly publication of the Association for Supervision and Curriculum Development (http://www.ascd.org). The "Web Wonders" column features annotated Web sites of interest to educators. Back issues are available from November 27, 1995.

You may also wish to subscribe to the *ASCD Education Bulletin* as a free newsletter.

E-mail: **majordomo@odie.ascd.org**
Instructions: In the body of the message, type:
subscribe bulletin

It doesn't matter what you put on the subject line. You can drop your subscription at any time by sending the message:

unsubscribe bulletin
to the same address.

1496. Blue Web'n Learning Applications Library

http://www.kn.pacbell.com/wired/bluewebn/

The Blue Web'n Web site is a searchable database of online curriculum and resources categorized by audience, content area, and type. The Blue Web'n Update is separate and is sent to more than 6,000 subscribers. It lists the weekly additions to the Blue Web'n Learning Applications Library. Blue Web'n is a Pacific Bell educational project. To subscribe to the Blue Web'n Update:

E-mail: **majordomo@lists.sdsu.edu**
Instructions: On the first line of the body of your message, type:
subscribe bluewebn [your complete e-mail address]

1497. CyberBee

http://www.infotoday.com/MMSchools/MMStocs/MMScybertoc.html

CyberBee is a regular column in *MultiMedia Schools* (entry 1503), published bimonthly. Full-text columns with in-text links to annotated sites are available from September 1996. Past columns have focused on science fairs, reference, and cyberspace summer camps.

1498. "Internet Reviews"

http://www.bowdoin.edu/~samato/IRA/
or
http://www.ala.org/acrl/resrces.html

"Internet Reviews" is a monthly column in *College & Research Libraries News,* a publication of the Association of College & Research Libraries. Archives are from 1994 and are searchable.

1499. *Internet World*

http://www.internetworld.com

The current issue is highlighted with a full-color cover. An annotated table of contents is provided. The full text of articles from several columns, such as Ask the Net.Answer Man, The Surfboard, Internet News, Bookshelf, and Letters to the Editor, are available to read online. This is just enough to whet your appetite to purchase a subscription. Online ordering information is available. Back issues are available, and the database of back issues is searchable by cover or keyword. Articles from back issues are available in full text and contain embedded links to sites on the Internet.

1500. K12opps Mailing List Web Archive

http://archives.gsn.org/k12opps/

Educators and others announce educational Web sites and other information of interest to educators on the K12opps mailing list. The archives are searchable and browseable from January 1995.

To subscribe to the K12opps electronic mailing list:

E-mail: **majordomo@gsn.org**
Instructions: On the first line of the body of the message, type:
subscribe k12opps

K12opps is a service of the Global SchoolNet Foundation. Direct any questions or comments to Yvonne Marie Andres (yvonne@gsn.org), curriculum director.

1501. *Knowledge Quest*

http://www.ala.org/aasl/kqweb/index.html

Knowledge Quest is published five times a year by the American Association of School Librarians (AASL). Concerned with the development of programs and services at the building level, from preschool through high school, this journal publishes articles that help school library media practitioners integrate theory and practice. *Knowledge Quest* also provides information on new developments in school library media and related fields. The table of contents is listed for the current issue, as are subscription information and guidelines for authors.

1502. *Library Journal Digital*

http://www.ljdigital.com

Library Journal Digital is the companion to *Library Journal,* the oldest independent national library publication, founded in 1876. The online version has selected full-text articles that cover news, features, and commentary with analyses of public policy, technology, and management developments. Evaluative reviews are written by librarians to help readers make purchasing decisions. Reviews cover books, audio and video, CD-ROMs, Web sites, and magazines. Regular columns include "WebWatch" (*see* entry 1508), a review of Internet sites.

1503. *MultiMedia Schools*

http://www.infotoday.com/MMSchools/

MultiMedia Schools is a practical, how-to magazine that addresses multiple technologies used in K-12 schools, such as CD-ROM, multimedia, online, and the Internet. Articles, columns, news, and product reviews are contributed by practicing educators who use new technologies in the classroom and media center. This Web site has selected articles from the current and past issues. *MultiMedia Schools* features three Internet columns, CyberBee (entry 1497), The Net Works, and VOICES of the Web.

1504. *School Library Media Research*

http://www.ala.org/aasl/SLMR/

School Library Media Research is the refereed research journal of the American Association of School Librarians (AASL). The purpose of the journal is "to publish substantive, refereed articles to inform, inspire, motivate, and assist school library media practitioners in integrating theory and practice; to encourage scholarship and research in the school library media field, education, psychology, and other related disciplines." Full-text articles are online and are enhanced with in-text links. Information is provided on how to submit manuscripts for review.

1505. *SLJ Online*

http://www.slj.com

SLJ Online is the Web companion to *School Library Journal.* Each month, a selection of full-text articles are available from the current issue, as well as news and opinion pieces. Other online features include a collection of most requested articles, indexes to *School Library Journal* in print, and a calendar of upcoming events. A library Web site is featured each month as a "best of the Web."

1506. The "SurfFor" Archive

http://www.bookwire.com/slj/surf-for.articles

"SurfFor" is a monthly column in *School Library Journal,* written by Gail Junion-Metz. Each month's column presents Internet sites related to a theme. During January there were links to Black History Month and the Martin Luther King, Jr. holiday. April's theme was career resources for teens and younger kids. Other themes have focused on the planet Mars, teachers' Net skills, young surfers, and sites appropriate for elementary school students.

1507. **Surfing the Net With Kids**

http://www.surfnetkids.com

Surfing the Net With Kids is a weekly column written by syndicated newspaper columnist Barbara J. Feldman (feldman@surfnetkids.com). A Web version is available, as well as a free e-mail edition. Each week, Feldman evaluates the educational content of Web sites, and then writes about her favorite sites, organized by topic. Sites are reviewed and rated using a star system. Archives of past columns are available beginning January 30, 1996. Some examples of past topics include Microbes, Ecology Games for Earth Day, Women's Suffrage, Your Heart, History of the Calendar, and Harry Houdini.

1508. **"WebWatch" Archive**

http://www.ljdigital.com/articles/multimedia/webwatch/webwatcharchive.asp

"WebWatch" is a monthly column in *Library Journal Digital* (entry 1502). Each month Web sites are reviewed, using a theme such as Art and Art History on the Web, The History of Slavery, Sports on the Web, Photography on the Web, and Book Information Sources. Reviews are evaluative and give pros, cons, and a bottom line for each Web site. *Note:* If you are unable to access the site through the address listed here, go to *Library Journal Digital's* home page and click on WebWatch. You'll find a link to the archives at the end of the current column.

Discussion Groups

1509. **The Big6 Skills Information Problem-Solving Approach**

http://www.big6.com

Big6, developed by Michael Eisenberg and Bob Berkowitz, is a process-based, problem-solving approach to teaching library and information skills within the context of the school curriculum, rather than in isolation. This problem-solving application can be used with people of any age who need and use information.

The Big6 Skills Electronic Discussion Group is an Internet-based discussion listserv that focuses on sharing ideas, problem solving, and the theory and practice involved with Big6.

Big6

E-mail: **listserv@listserv.syr.edu**
Instructions: On the first line of the body of the message, type:
subscribe BIG6 [your first name and last name]

1510. **Library Media Specialists Network (LM_NET)**

E-mail: **listserv@listserv.syr.edu**
Instructions: On the first line of the body of the message, type:
subscribe LM_NET [your first name and last name]

LM_NET is an online discussion group focusing on topics of interest to the school library media community, including the latest on school library media services, operations, and activities. Practitioners help practitioners, share ideas, and solve problems. Volunteers offer to act as mentors in all areas of school library media technology. LM_NET disseminates invaluable information about new publications, legislation, network resources, conferences, workshops, and employment opportunities. When you subscribe, you will be asked to confirm your subscription by e-mailing back a reply with **OK** as the only letters typed in your message. If you do not confirm with OK within 48 hours of initially subscribing, your subscription to the LM_NET listserv will not be activated.

Helpful Hint: After you have successfully subscribed to LM_NET, use the digest command to set your mail from LM_NET so that you receive one message a day instead of numerous messages. The subject lines of the messages will become a table of contents for each compiled daily message. To set mail to digest format, send an e-mail message to:
listserv@listserv.syr.edu
On the first line of the body of your message, type:
set LM_NET digest

To undigest your mail and have it sent as individual messages again, send an e-mail message to:
listserv@listserv.syr.edu
On the first line of the body of your message, type:
set LM_NET nodigest

1511. **LM_NET Listserv Archives**
http://www.askeric.org/Virtual/Listserv_Archives/LM_NET.html

All messages posted to LM_NET are archived by month and year beginning January 1995. Information is accessible by browsing and by keyword-searching e-mail message subject lines using PLWeb information retrieval software, which allows for complex searching. Archived LM_Net messages can be retrieved by subject, date, author, or thread.

1512. **LM_NET On The Web**
http://ericir.syr.edu/lm_net/

From this site, you can browse or search many educational listserv archives, including the LM_NET archives. The LM_NET FAQs section is available, as are the subscription addresses to various educational listservs. The mentors' list, a two-part document, lists people from all over the United States who are willing to work as mentors in specific subject areas or areas of expertise.

Also given are useful tips for keeping your mailbox free of junk mail and a list of links of interest to school library media professionals. The LM_NET list managers are Peter Milbury (pmilbury@ericir.syr.edu) and Jim Neal (jwnlpsd@primenet.com).

1513. **Public Librarians Discussing Young Adult and Children's Literature**
E-mail: **majordomo@nysernet.org**
Instructions: On the first line of the body of the message, type:
subscribe PUBYAC [your first name and last name]

To subscribe to the digested format of PUBYAC,

E-mail: **majordomo@nysernet.org**
Instructions: On the first line of the body of the message, type:
subscribe PUBYAC-DIGEST [your first name and last name]

1514. **School Librarians, Public Librarians, and Educators Discussing Children's Literature**

E-mail: **listserv@bingvmb.cc.binghamton.edu**
Instructions: On the first line of the body of the message, type:
subscribe KIDLIT-L [your first name and last name]

1515. **Young Adult Library Services Association**

E-mail: **listproc@ala.org**
Instructions: On the first line of the body of the message, type:
subscribe YALSA-L

Site Index

Sites are indexed by entry number.

Subject Index

Sites are indexed by entry number.

Need Another Copy? Order It Now!

Order the 2001–2002 Edition Now!